D1833151

THE LALITA VISTARA, OR MEMOIRS OF THE EARLY LIFE OF SAKYA SINHA

THE LALITA VISTARA,
OR
MEMOIRS OF THE EARLY LIFE OF SAKYA SINHA

BIBLIOTHECA INDICA;
A
COLLECTION OF ORIENTAL WORKS
PUBLISHED BY THE
ASIATIC SOCIETY OF BENGAL.
OLD SERIES, NOS. 51, 73, 143, 144, 145, and 237.

EDITED BY

RAJENDRALALA MITRA, LL. D.

Honorary Member of the Royal Asiatic Society of Great Britain and Ireland, and of the Physical Class of the Imperial Academy of Sciences, Vienna; Corresponding Member of the German and of the American Oriental Societies, and of the Royal Academy of Science, Hungary; Fellow of the Royal Society of Northern Antiquaries, Copenhagen, &c., &c.

GYAN

Published by

GYAN

Gyan Publishing House
5, Ansari Road
Daryaganj, New Delhi-110002
Phone: 011-47034999, 9811692060
E-mail: books@gyanbooks.com

Distribution Network
gyanbooks.com
India, USA, Canada, UK, Australia, France

© Publisher

All rights reserved. No part of this work may be reproduced, stored, adapted, or transmitted in any form or by any means, electronic, mechanical, photocopying, micro-filming, recording or otherwise, or translated in any language, without the prior written permission of the copyright owner and the publisher.

ISBN : 978-81-212-2386-7 (PB)
First Published, 1877

2nd Impression 2021

Printed at: Gyan Press, Delhi.

The book is sold subject to the condition that it shall not, by way of trade or otherwise, be lent, resold, hired out, or otherwise circulated without the prior publisher's written consent.

The Lalita Vistara,
of
Memoirs of the Early Life of Sakya Sinha
Edited by: Rajendralala Mitra

BIBLIOTHECA INDICA;

A

COLLECTION OF ORIENTAL WORKS

PUBLISHED BY THE

ASIATIC SOCIETY OF BENGAL.

OLD SERIES, NOS. 51, 73, 143, 144, 145, and 237.

THE LALITA VISTARA,

OR

MEMOIRS OF THE EARLY LIFE OF S'ÁKYA SIÑHA.

EDITED BY

RA'JENDRALA'LA MITRA, LL. D.

Honorary Member of the Royal Asiatic Society of Great Britain and Ireland, and of the Physical Class of the Imperial Academy of Sciences, Vienna; Corresponding Member of the German and of the American Oriental Societies, and of the Royal Academy of Science, Hungary; Fellow of the Royal Society of Northern Antiquaries, Copenhagen, &c., &c.

CALCUTTA:

PRINTED BY C. B. LEWIS, BAPTIST MISSION PRESS.

1877.

INTRODUCTION.

How finally to preclude the miseries incident to mundane existence is the problem which has engrossed the attention of nearly all the philosophical writers of India. "The complete cessation of pain should be the ultimate object of man"* said Kapila, and the chief motive of Gautama is "the attainment of beatitude through the annihilation of pain."† Patanjáli, Kaṇáda and Vyása have likewise been impelled to their tenets by a similiar desire, and the sayings of Nának and Guru Govind and Chaitanya afford incontestable proofs of their intolerance of mundane suffering which led them to yearn for a peaceful hereafter at the sacrifice of the present. It was an intense feeling of a like nature that led a prince, two thousand four hundred years ago, to forego the pleasures of an oriental palace, and to betake to the privations and sufferings of the life of an anchorite. In the language of his biographers, the sights successively, during his pleasure excursions, of an old man, a sick man, a

* Sáṅkhya Sútras, Aphorism 1st.

† Nyáya Sútra, Aph. 2nd.

corpse and a recluse, the emblems of age, disease, death, and religion—of the bane and the antidote—awakened in his mind a sense of the sad realities of this life, and led him thenceforth to apply himself assiduously to the study of different systems of philosophy, and to the performance of the most rigorous austerities. Fasting by day exposed to the burning rays of the midday sun, and sleeping by night under the canopy of heaven in the heavy rains of autumn, or the piercing cold of winter, he lived but for the attainment of an unknown quantity, the *summum bonum* of existence. His penance and his studies did not, however, afford him the consolation he sought; and he was at last induced to renounce his tutors and their learning, and to proclaim himself a reformer. The tenets he promulgated attained a world-wide celebrity, and his followers now include nearly one-fifth of the human race.

But great as was the success of this renowned teacher, the history of his life is involved in mysteries which the light of modern research has yet scarcely dispelled. India never had her Xenophon or Thucydides, and her heroes and reformers, like her other great men, have to look for immortality in the ballads of her bards, or the legends of romancers. S'ákya Siñha, the reformer to whom I have above alluded, for a time had not even that advantage. He was known only through the misrepresentations of his enemies, the Bráhmans. The orientalist, however, has now no longer to complain of paucity of information regarding him. The discoveries of Hodgson in Nepal, of Upham and Turnour in Ceylon, of C'Soma de Körösi in Tibet, and of Klaporth, Remusat, Beal and others in China, have placed at his disposal a large mass of legends in Sanskrit, Páli, Tibetan and Chinese, which record with more than Boswellian zeal and assiduity, though not with like fidelity, even the most trivial circumstances connected with the life and the preachings of the great reformer. But it is an arduous task to attempt to put skin and living flesh upon the dry bones of old legends; still more so to resuscitate an authentic identity, or prove the verity of a picture founded upon such materials. Written at different times by different persons, under very dissimilar circumstances, in various climes, those legends cannot be expected to be very homogeneous in their character, or concurrent in their testimony. They abound in contradictions, fictions and fables which altogether vitiate their worth as historical records. But in a country where a few coins and inscriptions are the only representatives of her history for many hundreds of years, ballads and legends acquire an importance which in more favoured climes is seldom accorded to them. Besides, inasmuch as they are mostly based upon a substratum of truth, and the Páli, the Tibetan and the Chinese writings are avowed translations from the Sanskrit, they have certain points of correspondence and unity which cannot fail to be of interest to the scientific antiquarian.

The task is no doubt difficult to deduce the truth from the mass of fictions in which it is buried in these writings by the zeal of unscrupulous and bigoted votaries; but inasmuch as these are almost the only materials from which a knowledge of genuine Buddhism can be obtained, they have a peculiar claim to consideration from the Indian historian.

Buddhist writings, whether Indian or foreign, are divided into three classes, technically called the *Tripiṭhaka* or "the three repositories." The first of these comprises the sayings of Buddha himself (Sútra), and as such, constitutes the corner-stone of Buddhism. Upon it were founded the Buddhist systems of philosophy (Abhidharma) and ethics (Vinaya). The works included under these three heads are, however, of very unequal merit, and held in very different estimation by their followers. Nor has the principle of the triple division been very strictly adhered to, for there are now many works of such a miscellaneous character that they may be included under all the three divisions. It is evidently on this account that the Nepalese and the Tibetan Buddhists have adopted other and more comprehensive classifications.

The religious literature of the Tibetans is comprised in the great collection called the Kahgyur, and that is divided, for facility of reference, into seven classes, each of which includes a variety of works of unequal merit and extent. The first class is called Dulva or discipline; the 2nd, Sherch'hin or metaphysics; 3rd, Phalch'hin or rules of the religious community; 4th, Dhomseks, miscéllaneous doctrines; 5th, Do-de, aphorisms or sayings of Buddha; 6th, Nyangdas, or final deliverance; and 7th, Gyut, or mystical doctrine. Under the triple division, the first constitutes the Vinaya, the next three the Abhidharma, and the rest Sútras.

The Nepalese divide their books into twelve classes, and each class has a number of orders and varieties. They have, nevertheless, selected some of their most important works which they hold, without any reference to their character, to be the scriptures of their faith. These are pre-eminently their Holy Writ. They include under this head the following works: *viz.*, 1st, the Ashṭasáhasriká; 2nd, the Gaṇḍa Vyuha; 3rd, the Das'abhumís'vra; 4th, Samádhirája; 5th, the Lankávatára; 6th, the Saddharma-puṇḍarka; 7th, Tathágata Guhyaka; 8th, the Lalita Vistara; and 9th the Suvarṇa Prabhása. According to Mr. Hodgson, "Divine worship is constantly offered to these nine works * * * by the Buddhists of Nepal. The aggregation of the nine is now subservient to ritual fancies; but it was originally dictated by a just respect for the pre-eminent authority and importance of these works, which embrace, in the first, an abstract of the philosophy of Buddhism, in the seventh a treatise on the esoteric doctrines, and in the seven remaining ones, a full illustration of every point of the ordinary doctrine and discipline, taught in the easy and effective way of example and anecdote, interspersed with occasional instances of dogmatic instruction."* I have not had an opportunity of examining all these nine works; my remarks must necessarily be confined to those I have seen, and they include the 1st, 2nd, 4th, 6th, 7th, and 8th.

* Illustrations of the Literature and Religion of the Buddhists, p. 19.

The first treatise, Ashṭasáhasriká, is avowedly an abridgment of a much larger work called *Prajñá Páramitá*, or "transcendental knowledge." It is a prose work in five bulky volumes, but it is said to comprise matter enough to equal, according to the Indian mode of reckoning, a hundred and twenty-five thousand stanzas of 32 syllables each. Looking to the bulk of the work this estimate is by no means exaggerated; but some say that the numerals refer to the number of separate topics discussed in the work, and not to its extent. The same doubt exists as to the object of the numerals which make the names of other redactions of this work, which are all in prose. The specific name of this great work is Rakshyá Bhagavatí, and each volume is called a Rakshyá. "The subject of this work", says Hodgson, "is of a highly speculative character, belonging rather to philosophy than religion. The cast of thought is sceptical in the extreme, endless doubts are started, and few solutions of them attempted. S'ákya appears surrounded by his disciples, by whom the arguments on each topic are chiefly maintained, S'ákya acting generally as moderator, but sometimes as sole speaker. The topics discussed are the great first principles of Buddhism; the tenets of the four schools of Bauddha Philosophy are mentioned, but those of the Svábhávika alone, largely discussed. The object of the whole work seems rather to be proof of the practice, that doubt is the end as well as beginning of wisdom, than the establishment of any particular dogmas of philosophy or religion: and from the evidence of this great work it would appear, that the old Buddha philosophers were rather sceptics than atheists."* As a repository of metaphysical and ontological discussions the work was a valuable one, but it was too large and two rambling to be of much use, and even as early as the second century before the Christian era an attempt was made to condense it, and a redaction of "a hundred thousand" was produced (*S'atasáhasriká Prajñá Páramitá*). It retained, however, all the defects of the original, and could not therefore supersede it. A second redaction of "twenty-five thousand" (*Panchaviñs'a Sáhasriká*) followed; but it too failed. A third attempt resulted in the *Das'asáhasriká*, or "ten thousand;" but that likewise proved insufficient. The fourth redaction is the *Ashṭasáhasriká*, or "eight thousand." In Mr. Beal's Catalogue of the Chinese Tripíṭhaka the first and the fourth recensions have been named; as also an exegesis on the original text by Nargárjuna Bodhisattva, which was translated into Chinese by Kumárajíva in circa, A. D. 400. As the handiest of the five redactions, the last is the most approved, and held in the highest appreciation. Its proper name, like that of its predecessors, is *Prajṇá Páramitá*; but it is best known by the specific name of *Ashṭasáhasriká*. It is divided into 32 chapters. The salutation at its beginning is somewhat peculiar. Instead of the usual formula of salutation to the three Ratnas, or to Buddha, or to Bodhisattvas, adoration is paid to the work itself, to the renowned *Prajñá Páramitá*, and the same is then repeated in a set of

* Illustrations of the Literature, &c., of the Buddhists, p. 23.

verses which describes the work "as the source of knowledge of Tathágata." The name being in the feminine gender, the work is addressed throughout as a female. The scene is laid in a garden near the Vulture Peak (Gidhrakúṭa) at Rájagriha. When Bhagaván S'ákya was once sojourning there in the company of a large number of disciples and followers, Sáriputra opened a discourse by asking Subhuti information on various philosophical topics, relating to the fundamental principles of Buddhism, and the replies and discussions which followed form the subject of the work. The topics refer to forms and their archetypes; to the means of attaining true knowledge; to the lives of the 24 Bodhisattvas; to various forms of meditation; to *tathatá* or sameness, that is the relation of material objects to their archetypes; to Máyá-purusha or typical human beings; to explanations of various Buddhist maxims; to the means of overcoming the miseries of mundane existence; to universal knowledge, and the mode of attaining it; and to a variety of other recondite questions of speculative theology and metaphysics.

The *Gaṇḍavyuha* is a narrative work in which the disciples and followers of S'ákya, in his presence, discourse on practical Buddhism. In the first chapter Manjus'rí explains to Sudhana-kumára the cardinal principles of Buddhism. In the second and the third Sudhana and Meghas'rí discourse on the same topic, and on the descent of Bodhisattvas. The fourth is devoted to an exposition, by Supritishṭhita, a Bhikshu, of the manner in which Buddhist faith should be sought. In the fifth, the career of Buddha is expatiated upon by one Meghadraviḍa in reply to Sudhana. In the sixth, a S'reshṭhi or banker comes forward to solve the doubts and difficulties of Sudhana relating to certain points of faith. In the next, Sáradhaya expatiates on the glory of Buddha. A female mendicant of the name of A'vá next explains how a Bodhisattva should study the Bodhi religion. Another mendicant of the same sex then explains the proper course of life for Bodhisattvas. In the ninth, a Ṛishi of the name of Bhíshmottara-nirghosha, in reply to Sudhana, explains the duties of Bodhisattvas. The discussion of the subject is continued in several of the succeeding sections, the interlocutors being successively a Bráhmaṇa named Jayoshmáyatana, a maiden of the name of Maitráyáṇi, daughter of Maitráyana, one of the principal followers of S'ákya; Sudarsana a Bhikshu, Prabhútá a nun, Vidusa a householder, and others. In Section 18, Sudhana expounds the subject to Nala, a king, whose kingdom is described at some length, and who is apparently the same with the hero of the Naishadha, and king of Berar, whose story finds so prominent a place in an episode of the Mahábhárata. In the next he goes to the town of Suprabhá, and converts to his faith its king, Maháprabha. He next goes to the house of Chhalá, a nun, from whose head issues a halo of brilliant light; and then goes in quest of an itinerant hermit *(Parivrájaka)* Sarvagámina by name, with whom he discourses on the maxim, *mayánuttaráyai:* "Nothing by me of the future" &c. From Sections 22 to 30 the topic of discussion between Sudhana and different hermits is, "How should the Bodhisattva knowledge be taught by a Bodhisattva." (*Kathañ bodhisattvena bodhisattvacharyán s'ikshayitavyam.*) The subject of the 31st is an interview of Sudhana with a goddess named Vará, who shows him many jewels of rare value. In the next Vásantí, a goddess, replies to his query "Show me the way to omniscience, by which the Bodhisattvas attain their tenfold powers on earth." Other recondite questions of this character follow through twenty successive sections, in which Sudhana either instructs, or is instructed, by some monk, or nun, or god, or goddess in the mysteries of the Buddhist religion. The work is of considerable antiquity, and is, I believe, the same with the *Ghana-vyúha*, which was translated into Chinese under the name of *Ta-shing-mi-yen-king* by Amoghavajra of the Tang dynasty in 907—960 of the Christian era.

I have not seen any MS. of the 3rd work, *Da-s'abhumis'vara*. According to Hodgson it contains "an account of the ten Bhumis, or heavens, or stages of perfectibility," the names of the ten being thus given in Dr. Cowell and Professor Eggeling's Catalogue;—(1) Pramuditá, (2) Vimalá, (3) Prabhákarí, (4) Archismatí, (5) Sudurjayá, (6) Abhimukhí, (7) Durañgamá, (8) Achalá, (9) Sádhumatí, (10) Dharmamedyá. In Mr. Beal's Report on the Chinese Tripíṭhaka, this work occurs under the name of *Shi-chu-king*, which was translated from the Sanskrit by Kumárajíva and another.

The fourth is *Samádhirája*, a work of the class called Vyákaraṇa or narrative, in which various forms of meditations are described at length, and details are given of the actions by which the perfection of Buddhist wisdom is acquired. The work extends to forty chapters. As the subjects are of a peculiarly recondite character which cannot be briefly analysed in a manner to be thoroughly intelligible, I refrain from attempting to describe the work at length. It was apparently not translated into Chinese, for I do not see its name mentioned in Mr. Beal's report.

The *Lankávatára* is a moderate-sized work of 198 folia, comprising, according to the Indian mode of calculation, about 3000 s'lokas. It is written partly in prose Sanskrit, partly in Gáthá verse. It treats of a miraculous visit paid by S'ákya to the king of Lanká (Ceylon), and of his preachings in that island. It is divided into ten chapters (*parivartas*). Three different translations of it exist in the Chinese, one under the name *Ta-shing-jih-ling-kia-king*, another under *Lankia-o-po-ta-lo-pao-king*, and the third under *Jih-ling-kia-king*,—the last by Bodhíruchi of the Wei Dynasty. (Circa. 221—223.)

The *Saddharma-puṇḍarika* or "the lotus of good law," has already been translated into French by Burnouf, and calls for no remark. It was translated into Chinese by Che-yen, of the Sung dynasty, (960—1278) under the name of *Fa-hwa-san-mui-king*. An epitome of it appears among the books of the western Tsin catalogue, and a commentary of it in select explanations under the name of *Fa-hwa-in-kia*, (Beal, pp. 14 & 104).

The seventh is named *Tathágata Guhyaka*, otherwise called *Guhya-samagha* or "a collection of secrets."

Like the last, it is written partly in Gáthá verse, and partly in Sanskrit prose, and is divided into eighteen chapters. It belongs to the class Tantra, and treats of various esoteric rites and mantras, dwelling largely on the peculiar marks that are characteristic of the body of Tathágata, and on various forms of meditation.

As a Tántric composition of the esoteric kind, it has all the characteristics of the worst specimens of S'ákta works of that type. The professed object, in either case, is devotion of the highest kind—absolute and unconditional—at the sacrifice of all worldly attachments, wishes and aspirations; but in working it out theories are indulged in and practices enjoined which are at once the most revolting and horrible that human depravity could think of, and compared to which the worst specimens of Holiwell Street literature of the last century would appear absolutely pure. A shroud of mystery alone serves to prevent their true characters being seen, but divested of it works of the description would deserve to be burnt by the common hangman. Looking at them philosophically the great wonder is that even a system of religion so pure and so lofty in its aspirations as Buddhism could be made to ally itself with such pestilent dogmas and practices. The chapters of the work are, as is usually the case with the Tantras, called *Paṭalas*, and the similitude is carried out in every respect. The first chapter opens with details about various kinds of Samádhi or meditation appropriate for' the higher order of the Buddhist clergy. The second gives directions as to the mode in which Buddha is to be reflected upon. The third and the fourth describe various kinds of diagrams and mystical figures necessary to be drawn when engaged in the worship of Buddha. In the fifth are detailed the characteristics and quaḷifications necessary for a neophyte to undertake certain forms of secret worship, and among the practices enjoined which promote the attainment of perfection, debauchery of the most bestial character, not even excepting mothers, sisters and daughters, is reckoned as most essential.* These are followed by an account of how, during the height of meditation in the case of perfect devotees, the crown of the head bursts open, and rays of light issue therefrom. Certain prayers to be addressed by Bodhisattvas to Bhagaván are also given.

The sixth is devoted to secret mantras, like the Vija mantras of the Tantras, to meditation of mystic diagrams, and to training necessary for such meditation. The most appropriate food for devotees while engaged in this worship is said to be the flesh of elephants, horses and dogs,† to the exclusion of rice. The means of attaining perfection, described in the next chapter, are not to be austerity, privations and painful rigorous observances, but the enjoyment of all the pleasures of the world,‡ and the way in which some

* मातृभगिनीपुत्रीश्च कामयेद्यस्तु साधकः ।
स सिद्धिं विपुलां गच्छेन्महायानाग्रधर्मेषु ॥ fol. 15.

† हस्तिमांसं हयमांसं श्वानमांसं तथोत्तमं ।
भक्षयेदाहारकृत्यर्थं न चान्नन्तु विभक्षयेत् ॥ fol. 20.

‡ दुष्करैर्नियमैस्तीव्रैः सेव्यमानो न सिध्यति ।
सर्वकामोपभोगैस्तु सेवयंश्चाशु सिध्यति ॥ fol. 21.

of the pleasures are described are simply revolting.*

The eighth opens with a hymn, by Ratnaketu, in praise of Bhagaván, and then gives the ritual of the worship aforesaid. The ninth is devoted to the ritual of the worship of Vajradhara, the diagrams, the forms of meditation, and the secret mantras required for the same. The tenth is a dialogue between Tathágata and Vajradhara, in course of which the latter explains the details of adoration with a secret mantra called *Mahá-siddhi-pradáyaka-mantra*, or that which grants the highest transcendental powers. In the next, Tathágata explains the mystery of the sacred syllables *om*, *áh*, *hum*, and the uses thereof. This is followed, in the next chapter, by instructions as to the rituals to be observed in performing particular kinds of meditations and the rewards derivable therefrom. All castes and classes are declared to be fit for the performance of such meditations, provided they follow the rules. The subject is continued in the next in which *japa* or silent recitations of mantras of various kinds are enjoined. These recitations may be accomplished by the body (*káyajápa*), by speech (*vágjápa*), by the mind (*chittajápa*), by the passions (*rágajapa*), and by other means.

The fifteenth section is particularly disgusting in its details, as it describes the adoration of Buddha through damsels of twelve years of age, daughters of Chaṇḍálas, dancing women, and other low castes, and by observances of rituals of the most revolting kind. Daily intercourse with daughters of the Chaṇḍála caste

* भगे लिङ्गं प्रतिष्ठाप्य बुद्धबिम्बं विभावयेत् । fol. 22.

in out of the way places is deemed an essential of the highest importance,* and particular stress is laid on their personal charms.† A variety of mantras are given for the purpose of these adorations, and also incantations and charms for curing diseases, for causing hallucination or death, for acquiring superhuman powers, and for other purposes. The mantras are of the usual type, formed of the mystic syllables, *om*, *hum*, *hah*, *ah*, &c. One of these includes twenty-three such syllables.

The sixteenth is exclusively ritualistic, giving directions for various kinds of secret worship, and the most appropriate diagrams, mantras, homas, and offerings of various kinds required for them. The oblations to be offered on the homa fire include, among other things, ordure, flesh, oil, &c.‡ The ceremonials described are throughout in the highest degree mystical.

The next two sections are quite as mystical and revolting as the last, but they are not so entirely ritualistic. They are made up of a great number of dialogues between Bhagaván, Vajradhara, Vajrapáṇi, and other Bodhisattvas, in which the esoteric doctrines of the faith are discussed at length, and various duties, discipline, forms, observances, rituals and practices are inculcated. All the ritualistic forms of *dhyána*, *dháraṇá*, *mudrá*, *nyása*, *sádhana*, &c., of reflection, meditation, gesticulation, regulation of breath, and other

* द्वादशाब्दिकां कन्यां चण्डालस्य महात्मनः ।
सेवयेत् साधको नित्यं निर्जनेषु विशेषतः ॥ fol. 73.

† पद्मनेत्रां विशालाक्षीं नटीकन्यान्तु शोभनां । fol. 73.

‡ विण्मूत्रमांसतैलाद्यैराहुतिं प्रतिपादयेत् । fol. 78.

manifestations of mummery which characterize the Tántric cult of the Hindus are all faithfully reproduced, and interspersed with hymns, prayers, hallelujahs, &c. Some of these are in themselves of perfectly unexceptionable character. Others, absurd, unmeaning, or stupid as they are, are not in themselves such as to be particularly objectionable. But they are sometimes disfigured by injunctions which are highly repulsive. Not satisfied with the order given in the last chapter to make offerings of excrementitious matter on the homa fire, the author goes to the length of recommending such substance as human food,* denouncing all repugnance to such articles as sinful,† and enjoining that no food or drink should be taken by a worshipper, which has not been mixed with ordure, or urine, or flesh-meat of some kind.‡ Such injunctions would, doubtless, be best treated as the ravings of madmen. Seeing, however, that the work in which they occur is reckoned to be the sacred scripture of millions of intelligent human beings, and their counterparts exist in almost the same words in Tantras which are held equally sacred by men who are by no means wanting in intellectual faculties of a high order, we can only deplore the weakness of human understanding which yields to such delusion in the

* समयचतुष्टयं च बुद्धज्ञानोदधिप्रभोः ।
विण्मूत्रं सदा भक्ष्यमिदं गुह्यं महाद्भुतं ॥ fol. 85.

† विण्मूत्रशुक्ररक्तानां जुगुप्सां नैव कारयेत् ।
भक्षयेद्विधिना नित्यमिदं गुह्यं त्रिवज्रजम् ॥ fol. 91.

‡ भक्ष्यं वा भोज्यं वा पानं यत्किंचिद्भक्षयेद् व्रती ।
विण्मूत्रमांसयोगेन विधिवत् परिकल्पयेत् ॥ fol. 92.

name of religion, and the villainy of the priesthood which so successfully inculcates them.

The eighth is the *Lalita Vistara.* It is a work of the narrative kind, and, like the preceding seven, has the epithets *Mahávaipulya* and *Maháyána Sútra* attached to it. In extent it holds rank between the Ashṭasáhasriká and the Saddharma on the one side and the Tathágata Guhyaka and Lankávatára on the other. According to the Indian system of computation its extent is about six thousand verses of 32 syllables to the verse, divided into 27 chapters of unequal length. The chapters invariably begin in prose, but, like most of the other Mahávaipulya Sútras, have some poetry at the end, and sometimes also in the middle, which generally contains an abstract of the circumstances detailed in the prose portion, and seem to have been introduced for their corroboration. The *Rgya-tch'er-rol pa* of the Tibetans, though avowedly a close translation of this work and marked by all its peculiarities, has little of the corroborative poetry, and yet it is evident that when the translation was prepared in the sixth or the seventh century of the Christian era, the poetry was in existence; as we find the substance of it is given in Tibetan verse in such places where the Sanskrit has no counterpart in prose. The substance of the Burmese legend of Godama of which an English translation has been some time since published* by the Right Rev. Bishop Bigandet, is likewise taken from the Sanskrit original; but the Burmese author

* It first appeared in the form of an article in the Journal of the Indian Archipelago, and was subsequently collected in an octavo volume.

does not follow his text with the scrupulousness which characterises the Tibetan version, and it has beside none of the poetry. The Burmese have a shorter work on the life of their Godama. It is named the *Malalangara Wattoo*, and is likewise founded upon the Sanskrit; but it partakes not of the elaboration of the original.

In the Chinese, there are several recensions of the Lalita Vistara. One of them is named *Fang-kwang-ta-chwang-yan-king*. It was translated by the Shaman (*Sramana*) Devakara of the Tang dynasty (Circa 620—904). It is divided into four books, twelve chapters (*Kiouen*), and twenty-seven sections (*Vaggas* or *Phin*), of which the last division obtains in the Sanskrit and the Tibetan versions. From a comparison of M. Foucaux's French version of the Tibetan text with the Chinese it appears that section for section the two agree very closely, "and from a comparison of the contents of the chapters," Mr. Beal adds, "this agreement is still more evident." I am not in a position to say if the Chinese version contains any counterpart of the Gáthá portion of the Sanskrit text; probably it does not, for the value of the Gáthá, as will be shown lower down, depends upon its being the *ipsissima verba* of certain ancient records which the Sanskrit author quotes in support of the authenticity of his prose text, but which in a translated form would amount to mere repetition, of no use as corroborative proofs. It is obviously this consideration that has likewise led to the omission of the Gáthá from the Burmese and the Tibetan versions.

Another Chinese version of the Lalita Vistara is called *Pou-yaou-king.* It comprises thirty sections in eight chapters and two volumes. It was "translated from the Sanskrit by the Indian priest Dharmaraksha, during the Western Tsin period (265—313 A. D.)."* Its contents have been given in M. Senart's *Legende du Bouddha*, and judging from them the work would seem to be a loose version of the Sanskrit Text.

The following extract from the Introduction to Mr. Beal's "Romantic Legend of Sákya Buddha," supplies information regarding other Chinese versions of the Lalita Vistara.

"A very valuable date, later than which we cannot place the origin of the story, may be derived from the colophon at the end of the last chapter of the book. It is there stated that the 'Abhinishkramana Sútra' is called by the school of the Dharmaguptas *Fo-pen-hing-king ;* by the Sarvástivádas it is called *Ta-chwang-yen* (great magnificence, *i. e.*, 'Lalita Vistara'); by the Mahásanghikas it is called *Ta-sse, i. e.*, Mahavastu.

"We know from the 'Chinese Encyclopædia,' *Kai-yuen-shi-kiau-mu-lu*, that the *Fo-pen-hing* was translated into Chinese from Sanskrit, by a priest called Chu-fa-lan, so early as the eleventh year of the reign of Wing-ping *(Ming-ti)*, of the Han dynasty, *i. e.* 69 or 70 A. D. We may, therefore, safely suppose that the original work was in circulation in India for some time previous to this date.

"It must be borne in mind, however, that several translations of the 'Legend of Buddha' are quoted

* Beal's Tripiṭhaka, p. 19.

under the name *Fo-pen-hing.* The first, which we have already alluded to, the original of which was lost so early as the beginning of the Tang dynasty, was in five chapters (*kiouen*). There is allusion to another translation (*Kai-yuen-shi-kiau-mu-lu*, vol. i. chap. i, fol. $\frac{36}{2}$), bearing the same name but in *one* chapter, now lost. Again, it is stated (vol. ii, chap. xiii, fol. $\frac{20}{2}$, and vol. iii, chap. xx, fol. $\frac{32}{2}$ *op. cit.*) that a work called '*Fo-sho-hing-tsan-king-fu*,' in five chapters, composed originally by Asvagosha, and translated into Chinese by Dharmalatsin, an Indian priest of the Northern Liang dynasty (502-555 A. D.), is also called by many writers *Fo-pen-hing.* Again (vol. ii, chap. xiii, fol. $\frac{21}{1}$, *op. cit.*), it is said that a work called *Fo-pen-hing-king*, in seven chapters, was translated by a Shaman of Liang-Chau (called *Ratnamegha*, chap. xx, fol. $\frac{32}{2}$, *op. cit.*), of the Sung dynasty (420-477 A. D.). The writer then adds that this last-named translation is sometimes called *Fo-pen-hing-tsan-king.*"*

According to the classification of the Káhgyur the Lalita Vistara comes under the fifth head of *Mdo-sde*, or aphorisms (Sanskrit, Sútránta) of which it forms the second volume. The Nepalese likewise call it a Sútránta, but by the rules of their arrangement it falls under the head of Vyákaraṇa of the class called *Gáthá.* What this Gáthá is, I shall notice in the sequel.

Like the rest of the Sútra works of the Buddhists, the Lalita Vistara does not record the name of its author. It opens, according to the established canon of Sútra writings, with the phrase " thus hath it been

* Beal's Romantic Legend of Sákya Buddha, pp. V—VI.

heard by me," and continues "that on a certain occasion when S'ákya was dwelling in the grove of Jetavana in Oudh his disciples requested him to relate to them the history of his life, and in making this request they said, 'There exists, O Lord, an amplified treatise on religion, the noblest of Sútras, called the Lalita Vistara. It expounds the source of Bodhisattva blessings; discloses the light of Tushita; and dilates on the consultation, advent, career, birth-place, and the greatness of the birth-place of Buddha; it narrates the special excellencies of his boyhood, of his proficiency in all worldly occupations,—in writing and arithmetic, both plain and symbolical—in mechanical arts,—in the practice of the sword, bow and arrow, and in all sorts of gymnastics; it unfolds his conjugal enjoyments; recites the method of acquiring the final and immutable reward of all Bodhisattva discipline; displays the career of Tathágata triumphing over the legions of Mára, and his might and majesty in all their eighteen declensions; points out the heresies of the Buddha religion; and in short, constitutes the whole of what was imparted by former venerable and absolute Tathágata Buddhas. Thou O Lord, relate the same unto us.'" This, in fact, is a brief summary of the contents of the work under notice, and includes the headings of almost all its different chapters.

In conformity with his plan of giving his work the character of an autobiography, the author has very appropriately concluded it with the appearance of S'ákya as a teacher of mankind. In this respect the Buddhist author has a great superiority over his Bráhman antagonists, who sin against all consistency in their attempts to make one author speak for another. A notable instance of this may be found in the first line of the Mánava Dharma S'ástra in which Manu is made to commence his work with the words "Manu sat reclined &c."*

The language of the work is remarkable. It has been already observed that the work is written partly in prose and partly in poetry, and the two parts are written in language very dissimilar to each other. The words used in the two portions are obviously pure Sanskrit; but there are a great number of technical terms whose true import is unknown, and they offer great difficulty to the modern Indian or European reader unacquainted with the philosophical terminology of the Buddhists in understanding the text. The prose portion is in ordinary Sanskrit, and conformable generally to the canons of Pāṇini and his disciples. Instances of transgression do occasionally appear, but they are apparently the result of accident, or inattention, or slovenliness, and not by any means an inherent peculiarity. Such errors of grammar are not infrequent in the Puráṇas, though by no means to the same extent.

The style is verbose and tedious in the extreme, and in this the work fully bears out its title of "highly

* No doubt the commentators explain the inconsistency by presuming the actual composition to be that of a disciple recording the words of his teacher, but as the work is not so acknowledged, the inconsistency remains.

developed" or Mahávaipulya Sútra. Epithets by scores are attached to a single noun, and its verb is sometimes not to be met with before the end of the 2nd or the 3rd page. In the second chapter of the work, there is an instance in which the verb occurs seventy-one lines away from its nominative. In the larger *Prajṇá Páramitá*, instances of this dislocation are much more frequent. This is, however, not peculiar to the Buddhist writings; the Bráhmaṇic romances of the middle ages, particularly those of Daṇḍi and Vánabhaṭṭa, abound as much in instances of this description, as do the Vaipulya Sútras of the Buddhists. In the Vaishṇavite works of the 15th and 16th centuries, they occur with almost as great a profusion.

This peculiarity, however, is confined to the prose. The poetry of the Lalita Vistara is entirely different. Instead of laboured verbosity, it is noted for a lively eliptical terseness which at once indicates that it is not the composition of the same party who wrote the prose. Its different phraseology, its unpolished simplicity, its unconfined boldness of conception, its natural freshness and vigour, all tend to support the same opinion. Although written in a variety of metres from the facile octosyllabic anushṭup to the most complicated Sárdulavikriḍita, which includes 19 syllables to the foot, it is nowhere wanting in the simplicity of style, or the easy natural flow of its language.* Nepalese chroni-

* These remarks on the Gáthá are taken principally from an article by the editor in the Journal of the Asiatic Society, Vol. XXIII, pp. 604, et seq.

clers call this species of poetry by the generic name of Gáthá (ballad), probably from its having been principally used by the scalds and bards of mediæval India. For nearly a similar reason, the Balenese style the language of their poets the *Káwi* or 'poetical,' and the language of the Vedas is called *Chhandas* (metrical), whence by a well-known euphonic law, we have the Zend of the old Persians. M. Burnouf, the first European scholar who noticed these poetical effusions, describes their language "to be a barbarous Sanskrit in which the forms of ages, of Sanskrit, Páli, and Prákṛit, appear to be confounded."

It differs from the Sanskrit more in its neglect of the grammatical rules of the latter than from any inherent peculiarity of its own. The niceties of the Sanskrit forms of declension and conjugation find but a very indifferent attention from the Gáthá versifier; he uses or rejects the usual case-affixes according to the exigencies of his metre with as much veneration for the rules of Páṇini as the West Indian Negro has for those of Lindley Murray; indeed, the best illustration that can be given of the relation which exists between the Sanskrit, the Gáthá and the Páli, would be extracts from the literature of the Negroes. The following paragraph from a Negro version of the New Testament by some Moravian Missionaries bears exactly the same relation to the English of the *Times* newspaper, as the Páli does to the Sanskrit of the Puráṇas, and the affinity of its translation to the same standard, may be very appropriately likened to that of the Gáthá to the Bráhmanic language of the gods.

"Drie deh na bakka, dem holi wan bruiloft na Cana na Galilee, en mamma va Jesus been ce dapeh. 2. Ma dem ben kali Jesus nanga him disciple toe va kom na da bruiloft. 3. En tah wieni kaba, mamma va Jesus takki na him, dem no habi wieni morro. 4. Jesus takki na him nu mamma noe worko me habi nanga joe. Tem va mi noben kom jette."

Translation.—" Three days after back, them hold one marriage in Cana of Galilee, and mamma of Jesus been there. 2. But them been call Jesus with him disciples to come to that marriage. 3. And when wine end, mamma of Jesus talk to him: Them no have wine more. 4. Jesus talk to him me mamma how work me have with you, time of me no come yet."

The Gáthá exists only in a versified form, and is to be met with in that class of Buddhist writings called the *Mahávaipulya* or the "highly developed" Sútras. It occurs generally at the end, and not unoften in the middle, but never at the commencement, of a chapter, and contains a poetical abstract of the subject described in the prose portion of the works. Its peculiarities are those of a language in a state of transition; it professes to be Sanskrit, and yet does not faithfully conform to its rules. In it we find the old forms of the Sanskrit grammar gradually losing their expressive power, and prepositions and periphrastic expressions supplying their places, and time-hallowed verbs and conjugations juxtaposed to vulgar slangs and uncouth provincialisms. At one place, orthography is sacrificed for the sake of prosody, and a word of a single short syllable is inflated into one of three syllables, while at others the latter yields to the former, and a molossus supplies the place of a pyrrhic or a tribrach. A spirit of economy pervades the whole, and syllables and words are retrenched and modified with an unsparing hand. According to M. Burnouf, instances of these peculiarities occur in most of the works of the highly developed class, and I have noticed them in several works, but as those works have not yet been printed I shall confine my remarks to what have been met with in the Lalita Vistara. These appear generally to be referable to, (A) exigencies of metre, (B) provincialisms, and (C) errors of syntax and prosody, either accidental or current in the age when the poetry of the Gáthá was composed.

A. Of the changes which may be attributed to the exigencies of metre, (α) prolongation, (β) contraction, (γ) and elision of vowels, (δ) elisions of consonants, (ε) and the segregation of compound consonants and long vowels into their simple elements, appear to be the most frequent. I shall quote a few instances.

(α.) Of the prolongation of vowels the following may be taken as examples. They are not so frequently met with as contractions.

ना च for न च   ते for ताः
सो च for स च   स्मितामुखी for स्मितमुखी
प्रयातो for प्रयातः   छत्रापताक for छत्रपताका
रोदमान for रुदमान   करोथ for कुरुथ

(β.) Of contractions of vowels, instances occur almost in every s'loka. They are generally effected by the use of short for long vowels, and the substitution of i and u for é, ai, o and au. For example:

यामि for यामे	च्छिम for च्छिमा
धरेन्ति for धारयन्ति	भवि for भावि
द्रुमवर for द्रुमवराः	लभेन for लाभेन
माय for माया	प्रमद for प्रमदा
घट्ट for घट्टा	प्रभ for प्रभा
पुजमेतां for पूजामेतां	वश्चित परिगत for वश्चिता पारगता
यथ for यथा	लपकवधं for लपाकवधां
तथ for तथा	लस्य for लस्याः
सद for सदा	मय for मया.
मिथ्यप्रयोग for मिथ्याप्रयोग	

(γ.) Elisions of vowels and consonants are also very frequent; they are effected principally with a view to economy and euphony. Final s'es are invariably elided, and the words declined as if they had ended in vowels. This evidently bears some relation to the rule which says, " all words with s final may be used as having a final : *sarve sántáh adantásch.* In the Vedas this peculiarity is frequently noticed. Take for instance :

नभे for नभसि	मना for मनसः
अप्सराः for अप्सरसः	एन for एतेन
सदार्चिस्कन्धे for सदार्च्चिषि स्कन्धे	नृपति for नृपते
	जानमि for जानामि
इम दृष्ट वधां for इमां दृष्ट्वा अवधां	उदरि for उदरे
	सजगे for सर्व्वजगते
निश्चरी for निश्चचार	गेह्नि for गह्ने
प्रखिधेन्ति for प्रखिध्यायन्ति	सर्वं for सर्व्वं

(δ.) Of the division of long vowels and compound consonants into their short and simple elements, the following are instances of constant occurrence :

रातिये for राज्ञ्याः or राज्ञ्याम्
तुरियेभि for तुर्य्यभ्यः
गिजानेा for ज्ञानेा
इथि for स्त्री
तुरिय for तुर्य्यं
अकिचाम्तस for अक्षाम्तस
किलंश for क्लेश
सिरि for श्री
थिरी for स्त्री
देविये for देव्याः
पूजाराहम् for पूजार्हम्
पदुमानि for पद्मानि
दानचरिया for दानचर्य्या
सुपिन for स्वप्न
वियूह for व्यूह
रतन for रत्न
अखियानं for आख्यानं
भारियर for भार्य्या
वजिरिकाय for वज्रकाय
अखितं for अक्तं
सुकुल for सुक्ल
न्यसिय for न्यस्य
आभुणिय for आभुन्य
अवम्पिय for अवम्प्रः

(ɛ.) The tendency to segregation of aspirated consonants forms a principal characteristic of mediæval and modern Indian phonology. The Páli and the Prákrit owe their origin entirely to this cause; the Hindi and the Márhaṭṭi indulge in it to a large extent; and the Bengáli is not exempt from its influence. The process, however, of effecting this change is not uniform. In languages with a strong vocalic tendency, the sharpness of compound consonants is filed off by the elision of the first letter and the reduplication of the second. Thus *abja* (lotus) is converted into *ajja*; *karma* (work) to *kamma*. In compounds of a liquid and an aspirated letter, the former is invariably elided without reference to its position, and accordingly "*padma*" [lotus] is changed to *padda*, "*sadma*" [house] into *sadda*, and *haridrá* [turmeric] into *haliddá*. The Italian, which is by far the most vocalic of all European languages, has this tendency in a prominent degree. In it, the Latin *subjunctivus* passes into *sag-*

giuntivo, *perfectio* into *perfetto*, *absorbeo* into *assorbire*, &c., &c. In languages which abound in consonantal finals, compound consonants are segregated by the interposition of a vowel between them, the final vowel being occasionally elided; thus in the Hindi, the Sanskrit word "*marma*" [a joint] is, by the interposition of an *a* after the *r* and the elision of the final *a*, converted into *maram*; *dharam*, *karam* and *parab* are instances of the effect of the same rules. These rules, however, are not universal in their application, and exceptions are very frequent.

B. The provincialisms of the Gáthá include (α) neglect of gender, number and case, (β) abbreviations and omissions of declensions, (γ) corruption of pronouns, and (δ) new forms of conjugation.

α.—Of the neglect of gender, number and case, the following may be taken as examples:

विमुद्धनिर्म्मंथं for विमुद्धनिर्म्मंथानि p. 292 (singular for plural).

बुद्धक्षेत्रं for बुद्धक्षेत्राणि p. 292 (ditto).

तानपि for तावपि p. 291 (plural for dual).

आसनिना for आसनात् p. 177 (instrumental for ablative).

बोधिमण्ड for बोधिमण्डात् p. 462 (objective for ablative).

ऊर्द्धं हस्ता for ऊर्द्धौं हस्तौ p. 324 (plural for dual).

केचिद्देवपादे for केचिद्देवपादेन p. 324 (locative for instrumental).

त्रिलोकं for त्रिलोकी p. 316 (neuter for feminine).

कारखां for कारखाणि p. 325 (singular feminine for plural neuter).

मध्यमाः for मध्यमानि p. 236 (masculine for neuter).

मुक्तहारं for मुक्ताहारः p. 237 (dative for nominative).

मञ्चकं for मञ्चकः p. 237 (ditto).

β.—Under the head of abbreviations and omissions of declension, the most remarkable peculiarity appears to be the use of उ in the room of all flectional affixes. This helps in a great measure to give sweetness and variety to the style, but at the same time it contributes to render the meaning dubious, and the study of the Gáthá a matter of great difficulty to those who have nothing but their knowledge of the Sanskrit grammar to help them. In the Páli and the Prákrit, the use of this occasional substitute is confined to the first person of the nominative singular. In the Brajabhákhá, however, it has a much wider range. In the following verse, it is used both for the nominative and the dative, as well as a euphonic adjunct to verbs in the second person of the indicative:

सो ते कहा मसखरी करऊ। कुवचन बोले तुमहि मरऊ।
पीयाके मन उपजे रोष। भलो चाहत कत चावे दोष।*

The use of the *u* in Gáthá, is made with much reserve and the regular inflections of the Sanskrit prevail. The locative *i* (इ) is not subject, as in the Sanskrit, to any change of form by association with a vowel. In the vocative a long *á* (आ) is the most approved case-affix. In some cases, however, inflections are altogether dropped.

γ.—The following are the corruptions of pronouns which are frequently met with in the Lalita Vistara.

* De Tassy's Chrestomathie Hindie, p. 79.

They apparently lead the way to the formation of pronouns in the modern vernaculars.

मह्य for मम and मत्तः	मि for मह्यं and मया
तुभ्य for त्वय, त्वां and तव	ति for त्वया
अयु for एषः	तस्सा for तस्य
ते for ता	अमभिः for एभिः
कहिं for कुत्र and केन	

δ.—The new forms of conjugation observable in the Gáthá are attributable mostly to corrupt pronunciation; they follow no fixed rule, and are the results of that natural tendency to abbreviation which in English originates "won't" from "will not" and "shan't" from "shall not." The following are a few examples, in addition to what have been adduced above under other heads:

ददमि or देमि for ददामि	स्मः for अस्मः
विवरो for न्यवृणोत्	आसि for अस्ति
भोसि for भवसि	मुषि for अमुषन्
भोति for भवति	अजनेहि for माजनय
भोन्ति for भवन्ति	रमिष्यसि for रंस्यसे
भेष्यि for भविष्यामि-व-म-ति-तः अन्ति-स थ-:थ	आरुहि for अरोहत्
	अरक्षो or रक्षी for अरक्षात्
भवोति for भवति	उत्थि for उत्तिष्ठ
अभूविः for अभूः	घाणुवन्ती for घ्रायन्ति
अवभूवन् for अभूवन्	दद for ददस्व
भवि for भविष्यसि and भवानि	शुणोहि for शृणु
भविय and भविया for भवेत्	प्रेक्षेमि for पश्यामि
भेहि for भव	मुषमी for अमुष्ण
भविया and भविय for भूत्वा	परिकथ for परिकथय
अनुभवियां for अनुभूय	न्यसी for निदधुः
प्रभामि and प्रभाम for प्रभवामि and प्रभाम	शुणित्वा for श्रुत्वा

ओरुहित्वा for अवरुह्य	जनेन्ति for जनयन्ति
ग्लपयिमु for ग्लापयामः	दर्शेन्ति for दर्शयन्ति
त्यजित्वि for हित्वा	जनेहि for जनय
बुझित्व for बुद्ध्वा	मोचेहि for मोचय
एन्ति for आयान्ति	बोधेहि for बोधय
उपेन्ति for उपयन्ति	पूरेहि for पूरय

It may be remarked that the corruptions above quoted are, in many instances, the precursors of forms adopted in other affiliated dialects. In Sanskrit the third person singular of the verb *to be* is *Bhavati*, which in the Gáthá changes to *Bhoti* by the conversion of the *v* into *o* and the elision of the *a* before and after it, (*Bhonti* in the plural and *Bhosi* in the second person singular,) and thence we have *hoti*, *hosi* and *honti* in the Mágadhi; *Hae* and *Haen* in the Khariboli, and *áhe*, *ahet* and *ahes* in the Marhaṭṭi. In the Hindi, notwithstanding the re-duplication of the root in *hotáhae*, the original form is still distinctly indicated. *S'unitvá* for *s'rutvá* is the first step to the formation of *s'uniá* in Bengali, while *s'unohi* passes into *s'uno* with nothing but the elision of an inflection, which in the original Sanskrit, is oftener omitted than retained.

In connexion with this part of my subject the following remarks of Dr. John Muir will be read with interest. I quote them from the second volume of his invaluable 'Sanskrit Texts,' pp. 119 to 122.

" There are, however, some other forms discoverable in the Gáthá dialect, which have been either passed over, or but briefly noticed by Bábu Rájendralál, and which yet present some points of remarkable interest. Thus the plural instrumental in *ebhiḥ*, which is so general in the Vedás, is in constant use in the Gáthás also, as in the instances *s'ákiyebhih*, *sattvebhih*, *guṇebhih*, *simhásanebhih*, *dárakebhih*, *chetakebhiḥ*, employed instead of the form, *s'ákyaiḥ*, *sattvaiḥ*, etc., which is alone current in modern Sanskrit. It is from this older form in *ebhiḥ* that the Páli form of the same case in *ebhi*, or *ehi*, is derived, as in the word *buddhebhi*, or *buddhehi* (Clough, Páli Gram., p. 19). Again, we find in the Gáthás various other cases besides those above noticed in which the case-terminations of the declension in *a* are substituted, in the case of words ending in consonants, for those proper to the latter form of declension. Thus, for *jagataḥ* and *jagati* (the gen. and loc. of *jagat*), we have *jagasya* and *jage*; for *námná* (instr. of *náman*), we have *námena*; for *mahátmánam* we have *mahátmam*; for *anantayas'asam* we have *anantayas'am*; for *karmaṇaḥ* (gen. of *karman*) we have *karmasya*; and for *duhitaram*, accusative of the word *duhitṛi* (ending in *ṛi*), we have *duhitám*, the accusative of feminine nouns ending in *á*. This change is one to which the Páli inclines (as in the form *Brahmassa*, as one of the genitives of Brahman), and to which a still more decided tendency is observable in the Prákṛit. (See Cowell's Prákṛit Gram. Introd., pp. xxiii., xxiv.) On the other hand, we find also in the Gáthás instances of the quite different change of *e* into *i* in the locative, as *loki*, *gehi*, *udari*, for the proper form *loke*, *gehe*, *udare*. The particle *api* (*also*) is contracted to *pi*, as in Prákṛit; thus we have *ahampi* for *aham api*, *tubhyampi* for *tubhyam api*, *vayampi* for *vayam api*, *napi* for *năpi*; *tathăpi* for *tathápi*, *punopi* for *punar api*: so also *iti* is contracted to *ti*, as in *ahanti* for *aham iti* Again, we have the peculiar forms *jihmi*, *jihma*, and *jaha* for *yathá*; *yathariva* for *yathaiva* (precisely as in Páli, Clough's Gram., p. 11); *síti* for *samṛiti*; *paṭhe* for *patheshu*, and *ishṭikán* for *yashṭi-dhárakán* (macebearers).

Many of the changes in the Gáthá verbs are in part the same which we find in Páli. Thus, for the correct Sanskrit forms *chodayanti*, *tarpayishyanti*, *nivarttayati* and *dhárayanti*, we have *chodenti*, *tarpeshyati*, *nivartteti* and *dharenti*, which, in Páli, would be *chodenti*, *tappessati*, *nivatteti*, and *dharenti*. Again, for *avalambate* we have *olambate*, which would take the same form in Páli. The modifications *avachi* for *avochat*, *munchi* for *amunchat*, *gachchhi* for *agachchhat*, *dhyáyi* for *adhyáyat*, correspond in some measure to such Páli forms as *akási* for *akárshit*, *ahási* for *ahárshit*, *adási* for *adát*, *ahosi* for *abhút*, *aṭṭhási* for *asthát*, *abadhi* for *abadhít*, etc.: and *snapinsum* for *snápa-*

yámasuḥ or *asisnapan*, is nearly the same as the Páli form *apachinsu*, the third person plural of the third preterite. The Gáthá forms *dars'ishyasi* for *drakshyasi*, *suṇishyati* for *s'roshyati*, *kshipishyati* for *kshepsyati*, and *spṛis'ishyati* for *sparkshyati* or *sprakshyati*, are analogous to the Páli forms *vedissámi* for *vetsyámi*, *bhunjissámi* for *bhokshyámi*, and *dessissámi* for *dekshyámi*. The Gáthá past indeclinable particles also, such as *bhavitvá*, *ramitvá*, *hanitvá*, *labhitvá*, *stuvitvá*, *manitvá*, *vijihitvá*, *s'uṇitvá*, *spṛis'itvá* for *bhútvá*, *mantvá*, *hatvá*, *labdhvá*, *stutvá*, *matvá*, *vi+hitvá*, *s'rutvá*, and *spṛishṭvá*, are formed on the same principle as the similar Páli ones, *pavisitvá*, *jánitvá*, *bhuṇjitvá*, for *pra+veshṭvá*, *jñátvá*, and *bhuktvá*. Of the forms *karitya* and *kariyána* for *kṛitvá*, the latter coincides in its termination with such Páli forms as *sutvána* and *disvána* for *s'rutvá* and *dṛishṭvá*. Again, we have the forms *kampayantó*, *várayanto*, *vinishkramanto*, *víryavanto* (part. nom. sing.), for *kampayan*, etc., which coincides with the Páli and Prákṛit. The same may be said of *pekshasi* for *prekshase*; *táva* for *távat*; *smaráhi*, *kurvahi*, *bhaṇáhi*, *vasdhi*, for *smara*, *kuru*, *bhaṇa* and *vasa* respectively; *deviye* and *deviye for devyáḥ*; *tapasmi* for *tapasi*; *talasmin* for *tale*; *arhantebhiḥ* for *arhadbhiḥ*; *prabháyă* for *prabhăyá*, *vácháyă* for *váchá*. For *tyaktvá* I find the word *chhorayitvá*, which does not seem to be much used in Sanskrit, though Wilson, in his Dictionary, gives *chhoraṇa* in the sense of "leaving." I quote the following additional anomalous forms, viz., *pithitá* for *pishṭá*, *pithitáni* for *prathitáni*, *visnapi* for *vyasnápayan*, *snapit* for *snápayitvá*, *kshipiṇsu* for *kshipanti*, *bhaviya* for *bhavet*, *pratishṭhihitvá* for *pratishṭháya*, *datti* for *dadati*, *deti* for *dadáti*, *dásmi* for *dásyámi*, *díyatu* for *diyatám*, *darthi* for *dadataḥ*, *daditu* for *dátum*, *detí*, *dadia* and *dadiya* for *dattvá*; *kurumi* for *karomi*, *karonti* for *kurvanti*, or *karishyanti*; *karoma* for *karishyámaḥ*; *kareya* for *kuryuḥ*; *karitya*, *kariye*, and *kariyá* for *kṛitvá*; *prakarohi* for *prakuru*; *gṛihítya*, *grahiya* for *gṛihítvá*; *bhinanmi* for *bhinadmi*; *vademi* for *vadámi*; *vyusthaya* for *vyutthaya*; *sthihiya* for *sthitvá*; *utthihitvá* for *uttháya*; *áruhitya* for *áruhya*, *paráhaniya* for *paráhatya*; *utthihet* for *uttishṭhet*; *charoti* for *charati*; *miṇitvá* for *matvá*; *s'akkitam* and *s'aktitam* for *s'aktam*; *uchchhrepaya* for *utkshepaya*; *miyati* for *mriyate*; *pŭrima* for *púrva*; *vidu* for *vidván*; *vidubhiḥ* for *vidvadbhiḥ*; *lábhase* for *lábháya*; *samskṛitataḥ* for *samskritát*, or *samskṛitataḥ* ; *jánamí* for *jánámi* ; *bhási* for *bháshate* ; *vinenti* for *vineshyati* ; *janeshi* or *janaishí*, for *janayishyati* ; *adṛis'uḥ* for *adrákshuḥ* ; *pas'yeta* for *dris'yate* ; *adhyeshṭu* for *adhyetum* ; *chintayá* for *chintayitvá* ; *vademi* for *vadámi* ; *vandima* for *vandámahe* ; *atikrametum* for *atikramitum*. (In all these cases, I should observe, the Sanskrit equivalents are given according to the notes in the printed edition of the Lalita Vistara.) Nouns and participles are frequently lengthened by the addition of the syllable *ka*, as *rodantako*, *gachhamánake*, *bḥáshamáṇikáḥ*, *dadantikáḥ*, *roditavyakaḥ*, *ágatikáḥ*, *dásinikah* for *rudan* (or rather *rodanto*), *gachhamáne*, *bháshamáṇáḥ*, *dadatyaḥ*, *roditavyaḥ*, *ágktáḥ*, *dásikáḥ*. This insertion of *ka* is also to be noticed in the following verses of the Vájasaneyi sanhitá, xxiii 22, f.; where *yaká* and *asakau*, *yakaḥ* and *asakau*, stand for *yá*, *yaḥ*, and *asau*.

Very peculiar is the use of the *a* privative in *ajaneḥi* for *má janaya*, " do not cause."

The use of abbreviated, or otherwise irregular, forms, such as *labhi* for *lapsyase*, or *labdhaḥ*, *gachchi* for *agachhat*, *chali* for *chalitá*, *munchi* for *amunchat*, *avachi* for *avochat*, *nives'ayi* for *nives'itaḥ*, *chhádayi* for *chhádayati*, *prichari* for *prayacharah* and *paricháriní*, *varichari* for *varácharaṇam*, *tyaji* for *tyaktá*, *tyaktvá*, and *tyaktaván*, *smari* for *smṛitam* and *smaraṇam*, *varshi* for *varshitvá*, *vraji* for *avrajat*, *spars'i* for *sprashṭum*, *utthi* for *uttishṭha* and *uttháya*, is extremely common, and, as will be seen from the equivalents following each word, these forms are very variously interpreted by the commentator, and supposed to stand for verbs in the present, past, and future tense, and in the imperative mood, and for participles active and passive, as well as for nouns. The penultimate syllable of verbs is very often lengthened, as in the Vedic *leṭ* form, as in *mochayáti*, *dharshayáti*, *saháti*, *labhdti*, *dṛis'ási*, *vrajási*, for *mochayăti*, etc., for which the commentator generally substitutes the present tense, but sometimes the past, and sometimes the future. This form is even found with the augment in *adṛis'ási*, rendered by the commentator *pas'yati* or *adrákshit*.

C. In the collocation of words and phrases the Gáthá strictly follows the rules of Sanskrit Syntax, but in the formation of compound terms it admits of many licenses highly offensive to the canons of Páṇini and his commentators. They seem, however, to be the consequence of haste, inattention, and colloqualism, and are not referable to any dialectic peculiarity. The same may be said of the errors of Prosody which, notwithstanding the anxiety of the Gáthá versifiers to avoid false metre even at the expense of etymology, prevail to a great extent in their compositions. In this respect the Gáthá may be likened to the Kabits of the Bhâts of modern India, who in their attempt to combine freedom of elocution, harmony and grammar in their improvisations sadly offend against all three.

Of the origin of the Gáthá, nothing appears to be known for certain. M. Burnouf is inclined to attribute it to ignorance. He says :—

"This fact (the difference of language of the different parts of the Vaipulya Sútras indicates in the clearest manner that there was another digest (of the Buddhist literature prepared, besides those of the three convocations), and it agrees with the development of the poetical pieces in which these impurities occur, in shewing that those pieces do not proceed from the same hand to which the simple Sútras owe their origin. There is nothing in the books characterised by this difference of language, which throws the smallest light on its origin. Are we to look on this as the use of a popular style which may have developed itself subsequent to the preaching of Sákya, and which would thus be intermediate between the regular Sanskrit and the Páli,—a dialect entirely derived from, and manifestly posterior to, the Sanskrit? or should we rather regard it as the crude composition of writers to whom the Sanskrit was no longer familiar, and who endeavoured to write in the learned language, which they ill understood, with the freedom which is imparted by the habitual use of a popular but imperfectly-determined dialect? It will be for history to decide which of these two solutions is correct; to my mind the second appears to be the more probable one, but direct evidence being wanting, we are reduced to the inductions furnished by the very few facts as yet known. Now, these facts are not all to be found in the Nepalese collection; it is indispensably necessary in order to understand the question in all its bearings, to consult for an instant the Singalese collection and the traditions of the Buddhists of the South. What we thence learn is, that the sacred texts are there written in Páli; that is to say, in a dialect derived immediately from the learned idiom of the Bráhmans, and which differs very little from the dialect which is found on the most ancient Buddhist monuments in India. Is it in this dialect that the poetical portions of the great Sútras are composed? By no means; the style of these portions is an indescribable melange in which incorrect Sanskrit bristles with forms of which some are entirely Páli, and others popular in the most general sense of the term. There is no geographical name to bestow upon a language of this kind; but it is at the same time intelligible how such a jargon may have been produced in places where the Sanskrit was not studied systematically, and in the midst of populations which had never spoken it or had known only the dialects derived more or less remotely from the primitive source. I incline then to the belief that this part of the great Sútras must have been written out of India, or, to express myself more precisely, in countries situated on the western side of the Indus, or in Kashmir, for example; countries where the learned language of Bráhmanism and Buddhism would be cultivated with less success than in Central India. It appears to me almost impossible that the jargon of these poems, could have been produced in an epoch when Buddhism flourished in Hindustán. There, in fact, the priests had no other choice but between these two idioms; either the Sanskrit, *i. e.*, the language which prevails in the compositions collected in Nepal, or the Páli, that is the dialect which is found on the ancient Buddhist inscriptions of India, and which has been adopted by the Buddhists of Ceylon."*

This opinion, we venture to think, is founded on a mistaken estimate of Sanskrit style. The poetry of the Gáthá has much artistic elegance which at once indicates that it is not the composition of men, who were ignorant of the first principles of grammar. Its authors display a great deal of learning, and discuss the subtlest questions of logic and metaphysics with much tact and ability, and it is difficult to conceive that men who were perfectly familiar with the most intricate forms of Sanskrit logic; who expressed the most abstruse metaphysical ideas in precise and often in beautiful language; who composed with ease and elegance in *A'rya*, *Toṭaka* and other difficult

* *Histoire du Buddhisme Indien*, p. 105.

measures; were unacquainted with the rudiments of the language in which they wrote, and even unable to conjugate the verb to be, in all its forms. This difficulty is greatly enhanced, when we bear in mind that the prose portion of the Vaipulya Sútras is written in perfectly pure Sanskrit, and has no trace whatever of the provincialisms and popular forms so abundant in the poetry. If these Sútras be the productions of men beyond the Indus imperfectly acquainted with the Sanskrit, how happens one portion of them to be generally accurate in every respect, while the other is so corrupt? What could have been the object of writing the same subject twice over in the same work, once in pure prose and then in incorrect poetry?

It might be supposed—what is most likely the case—that the prose and the poetry are the productions of two different ages; but the question would then arise, how came they to be associated together? What could have induced the authors of the prose portions to insert in their works, the incorrect productions of Trans-Indus origin? Nothing but a sense of the truthfulness and authenticity of those narratives, could have led to their adoption. But how is it likely to be supposed that the most authentic account of S'ákya, within three hundred years after his death, was to be had only in countries hundreds of miles away from the place of his birth, and the field of his preachings? The great Sútras are supposed to have been compiled about the time of the third convocation (309 B. C.), when it is not at all likely that the sages of Central India would have gone to Kashmir in search of data, which could be best gathered at their own threshold.

The more reasonable conjecture appears to be that the Gáthá is the production of bards, who were contemporaries or immediate successors of S'ákya, who recounted to the devout congregations of the prophet of Magadha, the sayings and doings of their great teacher, in popular and easy flowing verses, which, in course of time, came to be regarded as the most authentic source of all information connected with the founder of Buddhism. The high estimation in which the ballads and improvisations of bards are held in India and particularly in the Buddhist writings, favours this supposition; and the circumstance that the poetical portions are generally introduced in corroboration of the narrative of the prose, with the words: तत्रेदमुच्यते, "Thereof this may be said," affords a strong presumptive evidence.

According to the *Mahawanso*, the Buddhist scriptures were chaunted chapter after chapter as they were compiled by the Theros of the first convocation. This could scarcely have been possible had not the Sútras been in verse, and that they were in verse and in the Gáthá form too, we learn in another part of the same work (Chap. 37th).*

* When Buddhoghoso offered to undertake the translation of the Cingalese version of the Pitakattayan into Páli, the priesthood of the Maháviháro at Anurádhápura, "for the purpose of testing his qualifications, gave him only two GA'THA's, saying, Hence prove thy qualification; having satisfied ourselves on this point, we will then let thee have all the books." Journal As. Soc. VI., p. 508.

The learned Professor Max Müller* and Dr. Weber† have adopted this theory of the origin of the Gáthá dialect. They have both discussed the question at some length, and come to the same conclusion. The late Professor Lassen thought otherwise.‡ He supported M. Burnouf's hypothesis, and elaborated his arguments; but as those arguments have already been met above, it is not necessary to notice them at length again. Dr. Muir delivers his opinion with some hesitation. He says, "The peculiarities of the Gáthá dialect are so anomalous that it is very difficult to explain them. In any case, it is clear that, if not a spoken language, it was at least a written language in a remote age; and it therefore exemplifies to us some portion of the process by which the Sanskrit was broken down and corrupted into the derivative dialects which sprang out of it."§

Professor Benfey, while adopting the theory put forth by me, suggests a slight modification. He says, "On the other hand, Bábu Rájendralála's views on the origin of the Gáthás have very much to recommend them: they require only a slight modification, the substitution of inspired believers,—such as most of the older Buddhists were,—sprung from the lower classes of the people,—in the place of professional bards."‖ Had the learned Professor used the word

* Chips, I. pp. 297 f.

† Indische Studien III, pp. 139, 140.

‡ Indische Alt. II, p. 9.

§ Sanskrit Texts, II, p. 126.

‖ Göttingen Gelehrte Anziegen, for 1861, p. 134.

addition, instead of "substitution," there would have been nothing to take exception to. That some of the more ardent followers of S'ákya, who succeeded to his ministry and propagated his religion after his nirvána, did record his teachings in prose or verse is but natural to suppose; and that some of the Gáthás are due to them cannot be positively denied; but from all that is known of the history of the early leaders of Buddhism it is difficult to infer that those leaders belonged to the "lower classes of the people," and were so generally ignorant as not to be able to write in tolerably correct Sanskrit. Most of them were Bráhmaṇs or Kshatriyas, and all noted for their learning, wisdom and ability. It is but natural to suppose that Buddhist writers of a subsequent age should quote from the sayings and writings of those leaders, and not from those of the lower orders of the people, who, though they formed the great bulk of the congregation, rarely took any prominent part in the teachings of the Buddhist doctrine, and their authority could not be quoted with any prospect of giving authenticity to the narratives of later writers. Though caste distinctions were abolished as far as the reception of the religion was concerned, and among the clergy, the writings of the Nepalese Buddhists leave no doubt that, as a social distinction, caste did hold its ground among them with nearly as much firmness and tenacity as among the Bráhmanists during the Hindu period; and frequent references are made to Bráhman Buddhists, who were mostly men of consequence. In our own days instances are not wanting of seceders from Hinduism calling themselves "Brahman Christians." It would not be reasonable therefore to attribute the literary deficiencies of the Gáthás to the ignorance of the lower orders. Those deficiencies, besides, are obviously not due to ignorance, but to colloquialisms, archaisms and other causes, which mark the linguistic peculiarities of the age when the Gáthás were written. The colloquial character of the language of bards, or popular rhapsodists, on the other hand, is well known both in Europe and in India. Mostly composed *extempore*, their ballads and romances could not attain much purity of diction; and in a great measure they depended on their colloquial simplicity for their success. A large audience of different classes and orders of men could not be influenced by refined diction, and high-flown language. A single slang, or homely word, in such a case was more effectual than a whole volume of the purest Johnsonèse. This is particularly well understood in India. Our Ghaṭaks or rhapsodists are not ignorant men—they can write with fair accuracy in Sanskrit; but their ballads and eulogistic verses bristle with slang and colloquial and vernacular forms of speech; and the more they do so, the more successful are they in winning the approbation of large audiences. That the ancestors of our Ghaṭaks and Bháṭs also well understood this principle and carefully followed it, there is no reason to doubt. In the writings of the Bengali Kulajñas there is ample evidence to show that such has been the case for at least a thousand years, and before that the principle of action must have been the same. So great is the attachment of the people to this popular form of diction that in the present day even the recitation of the Mahábhárata and the Rámáyaṇa cannot secure a large audience until the narrative of the original is largely intermingled with slang and local colouring. When the original texts are read and expounded in plain prose in the morning, on ceremonial occasions called *Katha-kathá*, the audience is limited to a few persons—rarely more than a dozen; but when in the afternoon the same narratives are embellished by a Kathaka with all the ingenuity of a professed wit and clever vernacularist, whole villages crowd round him, and drink with avidity every word that falls from his lips. The institution of Bháṭs is as old as Indo-Aryan civilization; there are several references to it in the Vedas; and in all religious and quasi-religious gatherings and feasts, at marriages, shráddhas and solemn assemblies, it has ever been the practice for the Bháṭs to recite long strings of verses in praise of the host, his ancestors, his caste, and his country. At convocations and religious assemblies the theme of praise is necessarily the founder of the religion and the objects of worship; but everywhere the language is as simple, slangy and homely as possible. In the present day the vernacular language of the place is what is generally preferred; but some Sanskrit verses are invariably added, and they are very much of the character of the Buddhist Gáthás. There is no reason to doubt that at the three great councils, the proceedings commenced and ended with the recitation of eulogistic verses. The Mahâwanso, as shown above, distinctly mentions the reciting of Gáthás, and the qualification of the teacher was tested by making him recite some. The same must have been the case in all the convocations and conferences, and the most reasonable conclusion on the premises appears to me, therefore, to be that the bulk of the Gáthás are, as aforesaid, due to rhapsodists, or professional bards, and probably only a few to religious teachers.

The Hon'ble Mr. Turnour is of opinion that the religion of S'ákya was originally "preached and spread among the people" in the Páli language, and yet in his edition of the Mahâwanso he has shewn that Mahindo, son of As'oka, translated the Buddhist scriptures into Cingalese from the digest prepared at the convocation held in the 27th year of his father's reign, and that from that recension the Páli version was got up in the middle of the fifth century (459 and 477 A. C.), admitting thereby that the language used at As'oka's convocation was other than Páli, for if As'oka's edition had been in that language a new edition from the Cingalese recension would have been quite uncalled for, if not useless. As a collateral evidence it may be noticed that the history of S'ákya as recorded in the Burmese "Malalangara Wottoo"* which is a paraphrase of the Páli Lalita Vistara, bears a closer approximation to the narrative of the Gáthá than to that of the prose of the great

* For a translation of this work, vide Journal, American Oriental Society, Vol. III., pp. 1 et seq.

Sútras, shewing the former to be a more authentic, at least a more generally received, version than the latter.

The language of the Gáthá is believed, by M. Burnouf, to be intermediate between the Páli and the pure Sanskrit. Now, as the Páli was the vernacular language of India from Cuttack to Kapurdagiri within three hundred years after the death of S'ákya, it would not be unreasonable to suppose that the Gáthá, which preceded it, was the dialect of the millions at the time of S'ákya's advent and for some time before it. If our conjecture in this respect be right, it would follow that the Sanskrit passed into the Gáthá six hundred years before the Christian era; that three hundred years subsequently it changed into the Páli; and that thence, in two hundred years more, preceded the Prákrit and its sister dialects, the Sauraseni, the Drávidi* and the Páñchálí, which in their turn formed the present vernacular dialects of India.

* Commenting on this word as published in my paper on the "Peculiarities of the Gáthá Dialect" in the Journal of the Asiatic Society, (XXIII. p. 614). Dr. J. Muir observes; "if by the Drávidi is meant the Telegu, or any of its cognate languages, it is a mistake to class it with the northern Prákrits." (*Sanskrit Texts* II, p. 127.) It must be obvious from the manner in which the word has been used in the text that a Prákritic dialect is intended, and not the Telegu, nor any of its cognate dialects. That a Prákritic dialect of the kind was once recognised is abundantly evident from the writings of Indian philologists and rhetoricians. It is referred to by the author of the Sáhitya Darpaṇa by the phrase, *Draviḍí Dráviḍádishu.* Ráma Tarkavágís'a reckons it among the *Vibháshás.* Jumara Nandi, in his vṛitti on Kramadís'vara, says that the Vibháshás differ but slightly from the Mahárásht̤ri. (*Kathanchidbhedá, Mahá-*

Of course these dates are mere rough estimates, designed to help enquiry, and not intended to fix the exact limits of time. Dialects take a long time in forming; their transition from one state to another is extremely irregular, at times making sudden starts and then lying dormant, quickened among some communities and under particular circumstances, and retarded among others, differing even in the case of different individuals, but on the whole spreading over long periods, which, in the present condition of the history of ancient India, it is impossible to determine with any exactitude.

From what has been stated above, it must be obvious that I hold the Gáthás to be fragments of the earliest works on the life of the founder of Buddhism. They must have been compiled immediately after his death, if not during his lifetime on particular prominent occasions of his ministry. There is no reason to doubt that they were recited at the opening of the first convocation, when a life of the founder would be the very first thing to engage the attention of, and most agreeable to, the devout fol-

ráshṭryádeh. s'akábhira-ḍraviḍoḍrávantyávantisrávanti-práchyá-saura-seni-váhliki dákshiṇátyádi bháshá bhedá náṭakádau pátrabhede cha). Márkaṇḍeya, in his *Prákrita Sarvasva*, expresses the same opinion. His words are: *S'añkarábhira-cháṇḍala-s'avara-dráviḍauḍrajáh.* It is to be regretted that there are not many Dráviḍi characters represented in the dramatic literature of the Hindus, but of the few who may be suspected to be so, nowhere has a Draviḍian dialect been put in their mouths. The language they are made to speak in is a form of Prákrit, and not a cognate of the Telegu tongue.

lowers who assembled to give shape and permanence to the doctrines of their great teacher. Whether these Gáthás were ever put together in the form of a biography or simply recited as fragments it is impossible now to determine; certain it is that no work purely in Gáthá verse has yet been met with: if it ever existed, it has not escaped the wreck of time. The earliest Chinese version is said to have been in verse, but there is nothing to show that it was taken from a versified original. The Gáthás, however, were held sacred and preserved with great care. None was deemed competent to discuss on the principles of religion who knew them not by-heart, and there is no reason to doubt that all the life of S'ákya now extant owe their origin to them.

Next to the Gáthás the most ancient and authentic text on the life of the last Buddha is the Lalita Vistara. M. Senart describes it, as far as it goes, as the "type of the most complete, the most perfect, and also the most authoritative"* of all on the subject. Unquestionably it is the source from which all the biographies now extant in Ceylon, Tibet and China have been drawn. It is of the greatest importance therefore to determine its exact date, and in this respect it is to be regretted that we have nothing more positive than inferences founded on insufficient data.

The latest date to which the work can be brought is the 6th century A. D., when the Tibetan version was

* "Le type le plus complet, le plus parfait, et aussi le plus autorisè de ouvrages qui se rapportent à cet partie de la légende." *Essai sur la Legénde du Buddha*, p. 5.

prepared. Anterior to it there is the Páli version of the 5th century. Then the Chinese versions of the 4th, 3rd, and the 1st centuries, carry the history of the work back to over eighteen hundred years. The Chinese version of the year A. D. 69-70 is particularly important. Though it is no longer extant, the fact of its having been made is not open to any doubt. The question then arises, how far further back can the Lalita Vistara be carried? M. Foucaux, in the Introduction to his translation of the Tibetan version, assumes the Sanskrit text, as we now possess it, to have been compiled at the time of the 3rd convocation. He says: "D'après ce qui précède, et puisque le Lalita vistara, dont la traduction tibétaine insérée dans le Kah-gyour est la copie fidèle, présente tous les caractères qui distinguent les Soûtras développés, il s'ensuit qu'il faut attribuer la rédaction que nous avons entre les mains au troisième concile qui eut lieu quatre cents ans environ après la mort du Bouddha, ce qui assigne à ce livre la date de deux mille ans, et cela en choisissant, comme je l'ai fait, l'époque la plus rapprochée entre celles que nous fournit la chronologie bouddhique." (p. xvi.)

The convocation here referred to is apparently that of Kanishka. If so, it was held nineteen hundred, and not two thousand, years ago. If we take it to be that of As'oka, the date would be two thousand one hundred years. To fix the date of the work at two thousand years it would be necessary to assume that it was produced, not at, nor for, a convocation, but at a time intermediate between the two convocations.

To make this clear it is necessary to enter into some details about Buddhist dates.

Now, the starting point of early Buddhist chronology is the Nirváṇa, and the most important epochs are the four subsequent convocations. The first is, by some, assumed to have happened 543 years before the commencement of the Christian era, while others bring it down to 477 before that era. The first convocation was held immediately after the death of S'ákya, and its date must be the same as that of the Nirváṇa. The second convocation, like the Nirváṇa, has two dates; one, according to a prophecy, a hundred years after the Nirváṇa, and the other, according to the Páli annals, one hundred and sixty-six years after that event. In either case the sovereign under whom it was held is said to have been Kálás'oka. The third was held in the seventeenth year of As'oka's reign, or 246 or 242 B. C.; and the last in the reign of Kanishka, a little after B. C. 33. Of these the As'oka convocation is the most authentic. Next to the date of Chandragupta no date in ancient Indian history is so well established as that of As'oka, and in all enquiries regarding Buddhist dates, it must be accepted as the starting-point. The probable time of the last convocation is also fairly well established. It is to this that the learned scholar refers in the above extract. It appears, however, too recent to be reliable. The interval between it and the time when the first Chinese version was published would be scarcely sixty years, and this appears to me to be too short for a religious work to attain sufficient sanctity in the land of its birth to be accepted as the text-book of the faith, and to travel to China. Had the text been admitted as a revelation by the founder, the case would have, of course, been different; but as the composition of an uninspired writer, it could not so readily attain that distinction, particularly when there were many works extant with much higher claims to reverence and faith. If any reliance is to be reposed on Buddhist tradition, the simple Sútras must be accepted to be the oldest records, compiled at the first convocation immediately after the death of the founder, and acknowledged to comprise the very *ipsissima verba* of the great teacher. Works on ethics and philosophy were, likewise, compiled at that time, and they got wide currency. And looking at them the last convocation cannot be accepted as the probable time of the origin of the Lalita Vistara.

The third convocation or that which was held under the presidency of As'oka, is not open to the objection above urged. It was held long before the time of the Chinese translation, and there was ample interval between the two events to give time for works compiled in India, to attain full credit as sacred scriptures, and to go out of India in that garb of sanctity. It was, besides, convened expressly for the purpose of condemning schismatic doctrines and books, and for settling which of the books then extant were so authentic as to be accepted as sacred. It is open, however, to one serious objection. It is difficult to conceive that it was then for the first time that a biography of the saint was thought of. At the time a great many of the Avadánas and Játakas were well known, and believed to be authentic. They are alleged to contain the sayings of Buddha, which bear the same relation to the Sútras and earlier works which the Hadiths do to the Qurán, and imply the existence of preceding works. All the leading facts in connexion with the life of the Reformer were then well known and accepted as unquestioned truths, and repeatedly represented in bas-reliefs at Sánchi, Baráhat and Buddha Gayá; and in the face of them it is extremely difficult to believe that there was no biography of the founder recorded at the time, and that nothing was done in that line until two centuries later. It appears to me extremely inconsistent to assume that records in stone, literal and pictorial, preceded writing in books by two centuries and more, or even that they were synchronous. Had the early Buddhists been generally unlettered people, who neglected to preserve their scriptures, the case would have been different; but seeing that the founder of the religion did not himself write any book, and that the very first thing his followers did immediately after his death was to reduce to writing the sayings of their teacher, and to classify them under different heads, it would be quite unwarrantable to suppose that a life of the saint was not thought of until several centuries afterwards.

The next date would be that of the second convocation, but it has been held by scholars who have carefully studied the subject and are well able to speak with great weight, to be apocryphal, and it opens the very large and much vexed question of the date of the Nirváṇa, which it is not my wish to discuss here. If the authenticity of the prophecy which said that a convocation would be held a hundred years after the Nirváṇa be admitted, and Kálás'oka be acknowledged to be the same with Dharma As'oka, or the As'oka of the laṭs, the son of Vindusára, the Nirváṇa would be brought to the fifth decade of the fourth century, or only a few years before the invasion of India by Alexander the Great, when, according to Greek historians, Buddhism was well established in the country. This would be quite absurd, and therefore the theory of identifying the two As'okas may at once be rejected as untenable.

The next hypothesis is to deny the identity of Kálás'oka, but to admit an interval of a hundred years from the death of Buddha to the father of the nine Nandas, and then, relying on a prophecy which says that As'oka would come a hundred years after Kálás'oka, to cast up the figures of this nameless father's reign and those of his successors to the inauguration of As'oka, and to make a total of 218 years as the interval between the Nirváṇa and As'oka. This too, however, is open to a grave objection. The As'oka Avadána gives eleven lineal descendants from Bimbisára, the contemporary of S'ákya, to As'oka, and these, within 218 years, would give an average of 19 years and 9 months to each, without reckoning the reign of Chandragupta, which is omitted in that work. The thirteen lineal descendants noticed in the Vishṇu Purâṇa would with those figures give an average of 16 years and 9 months to each reign, without making any allowance for the 100 years assigned by that work to the nine Nandas. The ten lineal descendants of the Mahâwanso, in the same way, would give 21 years and 9 months to each reign. But even the highest of these three figures would be too small for an average human generation, which is 33 years, or three generations to the century. By accepting the date of Buddha's death to have been 543 B. C., the interval between the Nirváṇa and As'oka would be raised to 297 years, and they would give an average of 23 to 29 years to each generation, or higher if the time of Bimbisára, the contemporary of S'ákya, be excluded, and this result would be very near what one would *à priori* have a right to expect. The prophecy of 100 years is not of any importance, and must go the way of all prophecies. In the As'oka Avadána, a prophecy of S'ákya is quoted, which says that Upa Gupta, the religious preceptor of As'oka, would be born a hundred years after the Nirváṇa. If this really did happen and the latest date of the Nirváṇa be accepted as the true one, the sage would have been 131 years old when he expounded the principle of Buddhism to his royal pupil. In the same way one Piṇḍola, who was according to a Páli legend, a contemporary of Buddha, must have wonderfully preserved his activity for near 250 years, to be fit for missionary duties in the time of As'oka, for he is said to have been deputed by that monarch to preach Buddhism all over India. I look upon the prophecy as a piece of pious fraud, designed to exalt the rank of the great teacher who succeeded in converting and becoming the spiritual guide of so mighty a sovereign as As'oka, and the Piṇḍola story, a case of accidental identity of names afterwards converted into a positive identity of persons. In the As'oka Avadána the name appears as Supiṇḍola Bharadvája. I would have referred both to circumstances connected with the history of Kálás'oka afterwards confounded with Dharmás'oka, but it is futile to place any reliance upon stories which deal in spans of human life over a century. At the same time I must admit that to reject the genealogy altogether would be to reject evidence better than which we do not possess, and to vitiate irremediably the authenticity of those facts on which the fictitious character of Kálásoka's convocation has been attempted to be established. If the convocation could be accepted as a historical fact, it would appear to be the most appropriate time for the Lalita Vistara. It is acknowledged by the southern Buddhists that at that meeting the text-books of the faith were to some extent revised and added to, and there is nothing to prohibit the supposition that a prose life of the founder of the religion was then got up.

The "Buddhists themselves go much higher up, and insist upon the Lalita Vistara being of the date of the first convocation. "Comme tous les ouvrages primitifs du bouddhisme," says M. Foucaux, "le Lalita Vistara passe pour avoir été rédigé par l'un des principaux disciples du Bouddha, immédiatement après la mort de ce dernier, et d'après le récit qu'il avait fait luimême des événements de sa vie."*

He very justly adds: "Il est probable, en effet, que l'un des premiers besoins des nouveaux con-

* Histoire du Buddha, p. XI.

vertis au bouddhisme fut de connaître quelle avait été la vie du fondateur de leur religion, soit pour se prévaloir de la perfection du maître, soit pour imiter ses vertus." But he assigns very good reasons to show that this belief cannot be accepted as historically correct. I have myself shown above that the Gáthás were most probably what were produced at the first convocation to give an account of the life of the saint; and if the Gáthás sufficed to meet the wants of the people at that convocation, it must follow that a prose compilation quoting those Gáthás as vouchers must come some time after that date; and what could be a better time than that of the convocation which was held to recast the scriptures? It is said many prose works were then elaborated, and it would be hard to believe that none was thought of in connexion with the life of the founder. On the contrary the most probable inference seems to be that it was one of the earliest that was thought of and taken in hand. Denying his convocation, still the time of Kálásoka, a century or a century and a half after the first poetical version, would be by no means an unreasonable date. Any how the work cannot be carried more than fifty years before that time, and that may be accepted as the *terminus à quo*, and the latest some fifty years or more before the convocation of As'oka in the year 246 B. C., whether it be called the second or the third. The sculptures of the time of As'oka preclude the possibility of bringing the work down to a later period. This argument places the work between 300 to 450 B. C., and greater certainty is at present unapproachable.

Of the contents of the Lalita Vistara, Csoma de Körös has given a fair, though brief, *resumè*, in the twentieth volume of the Asiatic Researches (pp. 285 et seq); and after the publication of M. Foucaux's elegant translation into French of the Tibetan version, Bishop Bigandet's translation into English of the Páli version, M. Beal's rendering into English of the Chinese version, M. Senart's comment on all the three, and Professor Lefmann's German translation of about one-fourth of the Sanskrit text, it would be of no use to attempt an abstract. I abstain therefore from the task. A complete translation of the whole into English is what is now required for comparison with the other texts, and I had this object in view when this edition of the text was undertaken. A translation of the first three chapters was published, and nearly three-fourths of the text was rendered into English in MS., but circumstances intervened which prevented me from carrying out my intention. The publication of the last fasciculus of the text has been hitherto delayed solely with a view to bring out the translation along with it. But so many complaints (and very justly) have been made on account of the delay, that I am obliged to issue the text apart from the translation. I entertain, however, a hope that I shall soon have an opportunity of bringing out the latter as an independent publication. For the present the published pages of the translation must remain as a specimen of the style of the text.

The life of Buddha is divisible into two parts; the first referring to his birth, infancy, boy-hood, and manhood to the time of his attaining religious perfection; and the second embracing his career as the teacher of a new faith, and the history of his death and funeral. The Lalita Vistara comprises the first part, and, as far as it goes, it is the most complete account we have on the subject. There is no single work in the Sanskrit language which gives the second in the same way. For it the Sútras and the Avadánas are our only guide; but they are fragmentary, unconnected, often unreliable, and not unoften discordant. The life in Páli, compiled by Buddhaghosha, has a great advantage in this respect, as it includes the career of the great teacher from his birth to death; but its authenticity is questionable, and it was compiled nearly a thousand years after the date of the events it describes. Nor has the time yet arrived for the completion, from the materials now accessible to oriental scholars, of such a complete biography as would meet the requirements of historical accuracy. Much has yet to be done to bring to light the salient points in the Buddhist literatures of Nepal, Tibet, China, Ceylon, and Burmah before such a work can be successfully completed.

The present is the season for collecting facts, for bringing together scattered materials, and not for working on them and drawing conclusions. And I trust, therefore, that the volume I now present to the public in a complete form, will not be an unacceptable contribution to the stock of materials already collected by European scholars. It has its defects, and no one is more painfully aware of them than I am. Two of them have been specially pointed out in a Prospectus lately published by Dr. Lefmann of Heidelberg. It has been said, "Nachdem die Calcuttaer Ausgabe sich als unkritisch und unbrauchbar erwiesen und dazu unvollständig geblieben, ist das berechtigte Verlangen nach einer correcten Ausgabe dieses wichtigen Textes oft genug gestellt worden." The "incompleteness" I am now able to remove. Such as it is, the text will now be found complete. I regret I can do nothing to mend its "uncritical" character. But in justice to myself I must add, that the edition does not pretend to any critical exposition, and nothing should be expected from it but just what it assumes to be—an eclectic text compiled from five MSS., retaining all the errors of the MSS. where no single MS. gives a correct version, and never attempting to decide which is correct and which is wrong, except in a few occasional foot-notes, which may be taken for what they are worth,—in short to give the substance of five MSS., and not to sit in judgment on them. For a first edition of a little-known and scarce work this was deemed the safest course. The Sanskrit in which the prose portion of the work is written is not pure, and it is overloaded with Buddhist technical terms which were perfectly unknown to oriental scholars, both in Europe and in India, when the sheets passed through the press, and even now is but very imperfectly understood; the construction of the sentences is involved, and frequently dubious; and the MSS. at command were all more or less corrupt; the poetical portions are written in a different dialect, and their peculiarities were, when I took them in hand, totally unknown to me, as they were to all European scholars, and the task was to deduce intelligible meaning from unintelligible jargon, in very much the same way in which an English scholar, without knowing the history and the topics of the Bible, would draw intelligible meaning from the extract printed on page 25 from the Moravian version of the Bible. Buddhist literature was little known and but imperfectly understood three and twenty years ago when the text was printed, and the apprehension of tampering with the original by hasty and unauthorised emendations beset me at every step. And under the circumstances I cannot venture to cherish the idea that I have been always successful in my attempt to interpret the Gáthás. A whole library of Buddhist books has since been published; a host of able and distinguished scholars have devoted their time and attention to the subject; and quite a mass of new light has been brought to bear upon it. It is therefore but reasonable to suppose that those who will follow me will find the task of editing the work greatly facilitated, and it will be a source of satisfaction to me to know that my labours have, to even a small extent, helped to the understanding of an old and very important work in Buddhist literature. That my notes on the Gáthás will be of some use to future enquirers, even if they serve only as beacons, I have every reason to believe.

In preparing the text of this, the first edition of the Lalita Vistara, for the press, I have had the use of the following five MSS.:

1st. A 4to. volume of yellow arsenecised paper, written in the Bengali character, originally copied for the College of Fort William, but now belonging to the Asiatic Society of Bengal. In the printed Catalogue of the Society's Sanskrit Library, it occurs under the head of Upapuráṇas, and is named "*Buddha Púrana*, by Parásara," (No. 508) having been mistaken for a Pauráṇic work of the Hindus. In the colophon of the codex the name is, however, correctly given.

2nd. Ditto ditto, belonging to the Serampur College. This and the last were copied under the superintendence of the late Dr. William Carey from the same original, and are, generally, very corrupt.

3rd. A puthi of 246 folia, written in the Newári character on yellow arsenecised paper, having from 7 to 9 lines on each page. On its cover, the name of the work is given as *Dharmarájávadána.* On the centre of the first page there is a vignette representing Buddha seated on a lotus supported by two lions, and surrounded by worshippers of various classes. The central figure has an aureole behind its body, and behind that a large tree. The sun and the moon and two snow-capped mountains are shown in the back ground. The MS. was procured for the Asiatic Society by B. H. Hodgson, Esq. According to its epigraph it was copied at a place "to the north of the great Vihára called Pas'ubandana, to the west of the great Vihára called Harṇavarṇa, sacred to S'ákya, the noblest of saints, in the city of Lalitápuri, during the reign of Rájyaprakás'amalla Deva, in the Newári year 871 = A. D. 1751, (the day of completion being) Wednesday, the 13th of the wane, in the month of A's'vina, when the moon was in the constellation Hastá, and the Yoga was Vaidhriti, for the edification of one Samantabhadra, son of Dharmarája, by Purnás'rí, and grandson of Dhanadeva and his wife Dhanavatí."*

4th. Ditto of 230 folia, written as above, and having 8 lines on each page. It bears no date, but is apparently about a hundred and fifty years old. Obtained by B. H. Hodgson, Esq. for the Library of the Asiatic Society. Very carefully copied, and apparently correct, corresponding closely with the last.

5th. Ditto of 131 folia, written in the Nágari character, and having 12 lines on each page. Copied at Káthamándu for the editor, under the superintendence of B. H. Hodgson, Esq. Generally correct, but apparently copied from an original different from the above.

In collating these MSS. and preparing the notes on the Gáthá portion of the work I had the invaluable assistance of my late respected tutor Paṇḍit Vis'vanátha S'ástrí. A profound Sanskrit scholar, thoroughly versed in the Mahábháshya and other leading

* महोत्सवः श्रीललितापुरीवरा मनोरमाः सर्व्वजगत् सुखान्विताम्। तस्यैव पुर्य्यां नृपनायको महान् गुणाकीर्णो जयते चारित्रवर्णं। सर्व्वविद्या महोत्साही श्रीश्रीराज्य-प्रकाशमल्लदेवमहीपतिः। संवत्सरे च नैपाले अग्निमुनिनागमास आश्विन वसिते तिथौ नवोद्भिदिने तारायां हस्ता योगे वैधृति वारे बुधे सम्पूर्णो जातः ग्रन्थो ललितविस्तरः। विहारस्था . धर्म्मवर्णमहाविहारस्य श्रीश्रीशाक्यमुनीन्द्रस्य पश्चिमादिग्भे श्रीपद्मचन्द्रमहाविहारे उत्तरदिग्भागे श्रीश्रीवज्राचार्य्यो महात्मा श्रीश्रीधनदेवस्य भार्य्या श्रीश्रीधनवतीनामं गुणवी श्रीदत्तास्तया आत्मजा श्रीश्रीधर्म्म-राजमहात्मा तस्य श्रीश्रीचन्द्रा गुणवती श्रीश्रीपूर्ण श्रीनामाः तया आत्मजाः श्रीश्रीसमन्त-भद्रनामाः इतीयमोक्षम . सार्थमिचार्थं लिखितं सम्पूर्णम् ॥

works of the Páṇini school, and familiar with the idiom of the dramatic Prákrits, which he had made a special subject of his study, he brought to the task a qualification which few could command. Seated at his feet, I had studied the Sanskrit language for years; and I feel profoundly grateful to him for the advice and instruction which he always placed at my service. Most of the Sanskrit works, which I have edited, have benefited very largely by his co-operation and supervision; and I deeply mourn the loss I have sustained by his untimely death. I have also to acknowledge my obligation to the distinguished scholar and orientalist, Brian Haughton Hodgson, Esq., who was the first to throw open the field of Nepalese Buddhism to European scholarship, and to write some of the most valuable papers that have yet been published on the subject, for procuring for me and for the Asiatic Society of Bengal three most valuable MSS. Without those MSS. it would have been impossible for me to carry the work through the press in a satisfactory manner.

MANIKTOLLAH,

August 30*th*, 1877.

ERRATA.

Page 5, line 12, *for* puṇḍarka *read* puṇḍarika.
„ 7, „ 19, *for* Nargárjuna *read* Nágárjuna.
„ 14, „ 1, *for* are simply *read* is simply.
„ 27, „ 26, *for* गच्छे *read* मेच्छे.
„ 30, „ 22, *for* in *read* in the.

ललितविस्तरः।

प्रथमाध्यायप्रारम्भः।

ॐ नमो दशदिगनन्तापर्य्यन्तलोकधातुप्रतिष्ठितसर्व्वबुद्धबोधिसत्त्वार्य्यश्रावकप्रत्येकबुद्धेभ्योऽतीतानागतप्रत्युत्पन्नेभ्यः॥

एवं मया श्रुतमेकस्मिन्समये भगवाञ्छ्रावस्त्यां विहरति स्म जेतवनेऽनाथपिण्डदस्यारामे महता भिक्षुसङ्घेन सार्द्धं द्वादशभिर्भिक्षुसहस्रैः। तद्यथा। आयुष्मता च ज्ञानकौण्डिन्येन। आयुष्मता चाश्वजिता। आयुष्मता च वाष्पेण। आयुष्मता च महानाम्ना। आयुष्मता च भद्रिकेण। आयुष्मता च यशोदेवेन। आयुष्मता च विमलेन। आयुष्मता च सुबाहुना। आयुष्मता च पूर्णेन। आयुष्मता च गवाम्पतिना। आयुष्मता चोरुविल्वाकाश्यपेन। आयुष्मता च नदीकाश्यपेन। आयुष्मता च गयाकाश्यपेन। आयुष्मता च शारिपुत्रेण। आयुष्मता च महामौद्गल्यायनेन। आयुष्मता च महाकाश्यपेन। आयुष्मता च महाकात्यायनेन। आयुष्मता च कफिलेन। आयुष्मता च कौण्डिन्येन। आयुष्मता च चुनन्देन। आयुष्मता च मैत्रायणीपुत्रेण। आयुष्मता चानिरुद्धेन। आयुष्मता च नन्दिकेन। आयुष्मता च कस्फिलेन। आयुष्मता च सुभूतिना। आयुष्मता च रेवतेन। आयुष्मता च खदिरवनीकेन। आयुष्मता चामोघराजेन। आयुष्मता च महापारणिकेन। आयुष्मता च कक्कुलेन। आयुष्मता च नन्देन।

आयुष्मता च राहुलेन । आयुष्मता च स्वागतेन । आयुष्मता चानन्देन । एवम्प्रमुखैर्द्वादशभिर्भिक्षुसहस्रैः सार्द्धं द्वात्रिंशता च बोधिसत्त्वसहस्रैः, सर्व्वैरेकजातिप्रतिबद्धैः सर्व्वबोधिसत्त्वपारमितानिर्ज्जातैः सर्व्वबोधिसत्त्वाभिज्ञावस्थिताविक्रीडितैः सर्व्वबोधिसत्त्वधारणीप्रतिभानप्रतिलब्धैः सर्व्वबोधिसत्त्वधारणीप्रतिलब्धैः सर्व्वबोधिसत्त्वध्यानसुपरिपूर्णैः सर्व्वबोधिसत्त्वप्रतिसम्यक्कृतिकृतैः सर्व्वबोधिसत्त्वसमाधिवशिताप्राप्तैः सर्व्वबोधिसत्त्ववशिताप्रतिलब्धैः सर्व्वबोधिसत्त्वक्षान्त्यवकीर्णैः । सर्व्वबोधिसत्त्वभूमिपरिपूर्णैः । तद्यथा । मैत्रेयेण च बोधिसत्त्वेन महासत्त्वेन धरणीश्वरराजेन च बोधिसत्त्वेन महासत्त्वेन सिंहकेतुना च बोधिसत्त्वेन महासत्त्वेन सिद्धार्थमतिना च बोधिसत्त्वेन महासत्त्वेन प्रशान्तचारित्रमतिना च बोधिसत्त्वेन महासत्त्वेन प्रतिसंवित्प्राप्तेन च बोधिसत्त्वेन महासत्त्वेन नित्यायुक्तेन च बोधिसत्त्वेन महासत्त्वेन महाकरुणाचन्द्रिणा च बोधिसत्त्वेन महासत्त्वेन एवम्प्रमुखैर्द्वात्रिंशता च बोधिसत्त्वसहस्रैः ॥

तेन खलु पुनः समयेन भगवाञ्छ्रावस्तीं महानगरीमुपनिःश्रित्य विहरति स्म । सत्कृतो गुरुकृतो मानितः पूजितश्चतसृणां परिषदां राज्ञां राजकुमाराणां राजमन्त्रिणां राजमहामात्रानां राजपादमूलिकानां क्षत्रियब्राह्मणगृहपत्यमात्यपार्षद्यानां पौरजानपदानां अन्यतीर्थिकश्रमणब्राह्मणचरकपरिव्राजकानां । लाभी च भगवान् प्रभूतानां खादनीयभोजनीयास्वादनीयाकल्पिकानां चीवरपिण्डपात्रशयनासनग्लान-

प्रत्ययभैषज्यपरिष्काराणां लाभाग्र्ययशोऽग्र्यप्राप्तश्च भगवान् सर्व्वे चाऽनुपलिप्तः पद्म इव जलेनोदारस्य भगवतः कीर्त्तिशब्दश्लोको लोकेऽभ्युद्गतः अर्हन्सम्यक्सम्बुद्धो विद्याचरणसम्पन्नः सुगतो लोकवित्परः पुरुषो दम्यसारथिः शास्ता देवानाञ्च मनुष्याणाञ्च बुद्धो भगवान्पञ्चचक्षुः समन्वागतः । स इमञ्च लोकं परञ्च लोकं सदेवकं समारकं सब्रह्मकं सश्रमणब्राह्मणीम्प्रजाम् सदेवमानुषान्स्वयं विज्ञाय साक्षात्कृत्योपसम्पद्य विहरति स्म सद्धर्मं देशयति स्म । आदौ कल्याणं मध्ये कल्याणं पर्य्यवसाने कल्याणं स्वर्थंसुव्यञ्जनं केवलं परिपूर्णं परिशुद्धं पर्य्यवदातं ब्रह्मचर्य्यं सम्प्रकाशयति स्म ॥

तेन खलु पुनः समयेन भगवान् रात्र्यां मध्यमे यामे बुद्धालङ्कारव्यूहं नाम समाधिं समापन्नोऽभूत् । समनन्तरसमापन्नस्य च भगवत इमं बुद्धालङ्कारं नाम समाधिमथ तत्क्षणमेव भगवत उपरिष्टान्मूर्द्ध्नः सदुष्णीष*विवरान्तरात्पूर्व्वबुद्धानुस्मृत्यसङ्गज्ञानालोकालङ्कारं नाम रश्मिश्चचार । सा सर्व्वा शुद्धावासान् देवभवनान्यवभास्य महेश्वरदेवपुत्रप्रमुखानप्रमेयान्देवपुत्रान्सञ्चोदयामास । ततश्च तथागतरश्मिजालाः निश्चार्य्येमां सञ्चोदना गाथा निश्चरन्ति स्म ।

ज्ञानप्रभं हततमसुप्रभाकरं शुभप्रदं शुभविमलाग्रतेजसम् ।
प्रशान्तकायं शुभशान्तमानसं मुनिं समाश्लिष्यत शाक्यसिंहम् ॥
ज्ञानोदधिं शुद्धं महानुभावं धर्म्मेश्वरं सर्व्वविदं मुनीशम् ।

* सोष्णीषेति संस्कृतं ।

देवातिदेवं नरदेवपूज्यं धर्म्मे स्वयम्भुं वशिनं श्रयध्वं ॥
यो दुर्द्दमञ्चित्तमवर्त्तयद्वशे यो मारपाशैरवमुक्तमानसः ।
यस्याप्यवध्याविह दर्शनश्रवाः स्वयान्तकः शान्तविमोक्षपारगम् ॥
आलोक्यभूतं तमतुल्यधर्म्मं तमोनुदं सत्यवेदितारम् ।
शान्तक्रियं बुद्धममेयबुद्धिं भक्त्या समस्ता उपसङ्क्रमध्वम् ॥
स वैद्यराजोऽमृतभेषजप्रदः स वादिशूरः कुगणिप्रतापकः ।
सद्धर्म्मबन्धुः परमार्थकोविदः स नायकोऽनुत्तरमार्गदेशक इति ॥

समनन्तरस्पृष्टाश्च खलु पुनस्ते शुद्धावासकायिका देवपुत्राः तया बुद्धानुस्मृत्यसङ्गज्ञानालोकया रश्म्या* आभिश्चैवंरूपाभिर्गाथाभिः सञ्चोदिताः समनन्ततः† प्रशान्ताः समाधेर्व्युत्थाय‡ तान् बुद्धानुभावेनाप्रमेयासङ्ख्येयागणनासमतिक्रान्तकल्पातिक्रान्तान् बुद्धान् भगवतोऽनुस्मरन्ति स्म । तेषाञ्च बुद्धानां भगवतां यानि बुद्धक्षेत्रगुणव्यूहपर्षन्मण्डलानि याश्च धर्म्मदेशनास्ता आसन् । ताः सर्व्वा अनुस्मरन्ति स्म । अथ खलु तस्यां रात्रौ प्रशान्तायामीश्वरश्च नाम शुद्धावासकायिका देवपुत्रा महेश्वरो नाम नन्दश्च सुनन्दश्च मन्दितश्च प्रशान्तश्च प्रशान्तविनीतेश्वरश्चैते चान्ये च सम्बहुलाः शुद्धावासकायिका देवपुत्रा अतिक्रान्ताऽतिक्रान्तैर्व्वर्णैः सर्व्वावन्तं जेतवनं दिव्येनावभासेनावभास्य येन भगवांस्तेनोपसङ्क्रामन्नुपसङ्क्रम्य भगवतः पादौ शिरसाऽभिवन्द्यैकान्ते तस्थुः । एकान्ते स्थिताश्च ते शुद्धावासकायिका देवपुत्रा भगवन्तमेतदवोचन् । अस्ति भगवंल्ललितविस्तरो नाम धर्म्मपर्य्यायः। सूत्रान्तो

* रश्मिः स्त्रीलिङ्गेऽप्येव बहुतरप्रयोगात् । † समन्तत इति बोध्यं । ‡व्युत्थायेति संस्कृतं ।

महावैपुल्यनिचयो बोधिसत्त्वकुशलमूलसमुद्भावनस्तुषितवरभवनविकिरणसञ्चिन्त्यावक्रमणविक्रीडनगर्भस्थानविशेषसन्दर्शनोऽभिजातजन्मभूमिप्रभावसन्दर्शनः सर्व्वाबालचर्य्यागुणविशेषसमतिक्रमसार्व्वलौकिकशिल्पस्थानकर्म्मस्थानलिपिसङ्ख्यामुद्रागणनाऽसिधनुःकलापयुद्धमालम्भसर्व्वसत्त्वप्रतिविशिष्टसन्दर्शनान्तःपुरविषयोपभोगसन्दर्शनः सर्व्वबोधिसत्त्वचरितनिष्यन्दनिष्पत्तिफलाधिगमपरिकीर्त्तनो बोधिसत्त्वविक्रीडितः सर्व्वमारमण्डलविध्वंसनस्तथागतः बलवैशारद्याष्टादशावेनिकसमुच्चयोऽप्रमाणबुद्धधर्म्मनिर्द्देशः पूर्व्वकैरपि तथागतैर्भाषितं पूर्व्वं। तद्यथा भगवता पद्मोत्तरेण च धर्म्मकेतुना दीपङ्करेण च गुणकेतुना महाकरेण च ऋषिदेवेन श्रीतेजसा च सत्यकेतुना च वज्रसंहतेन च सर्व्वाभिभुवा च हेमवर्णेन च अत्युच्चगामिना च प्रवातसारेण च पुष्पकेतुना च वररूपेण च सुलोचनेन च ऋषिगुप्तेन च जिनवक्त्रेण च उन्नतेन च पुष्पितेन च ऊर्णातेजसा च पुष्करेण च सुरश्मिना च मङ्गलेन च सुदर्शनेन च महासिंहतेजसा च स्थितबुद्धिदत्तेन च वसन्तगन्धिना च सत्यधर्म्मविपुलकीर्त्तिना च तिष्येण च पुष्येण च लोकसुन्दरेण च विस्तीर्णभेदेन च रत्नकीर्त्तिना च उग्रतेजसा च ब्रह्मतेजसा च सुघोषेण च सुपुष्पेण च सुमनोज्ञघोषेण च सुचेष्टरूपेण च प्रहसितनेत्रेण च गुणराशिना च मेघस्वरेण च सुन्दरवर्णेन च आयुस्तेजसा च सलीलगजगामिना च लोकाभिलाषितेन च जितशत्रुणा च सम्पूजितेन च विपश्यिता च शिखिना च विश्वभुवा च क्रकुच्छन्देन च

कनकमुनिना च काश्यपेन च तथागतेनार्हता सम्यक्सम्बुद्धेन भाषितपूर्व्वस्तं भगवानप्येतर्हि सम्प्रकाशयेत् ॥ बहुजनहिताय बहुजनसुखाय लोकानुकम्पायै महतो जनकायस्यार्थाय सुखाय देवानाञ्च मनुष्याणाञ्च अस्य च महायानोद्भावनार्थं सर्व्वपरप्रवादिनाञ्च निग्रहार्थं सर्व्वबोधिसत्त्वानाञ्चोद्भावनार्थं सर्व्वमाराणाञ्चाभिभवनार्थं सर्व्वबोधिसत्त्वयानिकानाञ्च पुद्गलानां वीर्य्यारम्भसंजननार्थं सद्धर्म्मस्य चानुपरिग्रहार्थं त्रिरत्नवंशस्यानुपरिग्रहार्थं त्रिरत्नवंशस्यानुपच्छेदनार्थं बुद्धकार्य्यस्य च परिसन्दर्शनार्थमित्यधिवासयति स्म भगवांस्तेषां देवपुत्राणां तूष्णीभावेन सदेवकस्य लोकस्यानुकम्पामुपादाय ॥ अथ खलु देवपुत्रा भगवतस्तूष्णीभावेनाधिवासनां विदित्वा तुष्टा उदग्रा आत्तमनसः प्रमुदिताः प्रीतिसौमनस्यजाता भगवतः पादौ शिरसाऽभिवन्द्य भगवन्तं त्रिःप्रदक्षिणीकृत्य दिव्यैश्चन्दनचूर्णैरगुरुचूर्णैर्मान्दारपुष्पैश्चाभ्यवकीर्य्य तत्रैवान्तर्दधुः । अथ खलु भगवांस्तस्यामेव रात्र्यामत्ययेन कारीरो मण्डलमाचव्यूहस्तेनोपसङ्क्रामदुपसङ्क्रम्य भगवान्प्रज्ञप्त एवाऽऽसनेन्यषीदद्बोधिसत्त्वगणपुरस्कृतः श्रावकसङ्घैः पुरस्कृतो निषद्य भगवान्भिक्षूनामन्त्रयति स्म । इति हि भिक्षवो रात्रौ प्रशान्तायामीश्वरो नाम शुद्धावासकायिको देवपुत्रो महेश्वरश्च नाम नन्दश्च आनन्दश्च सुनन्दश्च चन्दनश्च महितश्च प्रशान्तश्च विनीतेश्वरश्चैते चान्ये च सम्बहुलाः शुद्धावासकायिका देवपुत्राः पूर्व्ववद्यावत्तत्रैवान्तर्दधुः । अथ खलु ते बोधिसत्त्वास्ते च महाश्रावका येन भगवांस्ते-

नाञ्जलिं प्रणम्य भगवन्तमेतदवोचन्। तत्साधु भगवंस्तं ललित-
विस्तरं नाम धर्म्मपर्यायं देशयतु। तद्भविष्यति बहुजनहिताय
बहुजनसुखाय लोकानुकम्पायै महतो जनकार्य्यस्यार्थाय हिताय
सुखाय देवानाञ्च मनुष्याणाञ्च। एतर्हि चागतानाञ्च बोधि-
सत्त्वानां महासत्त्वानामधिवासयति स्म भगवांस्तेषां बोधि-
सत्त्वानां महासत्त्वानां तेषाञ्च महाश्रावकाणां तूष्णीभावेन
सदेवमानुषासुरस्य लोकानुकम्पामुपादाय। तत्रेदमुच्यते।

रात्र्यामिहास्यां मम भिक्षवोऽद्य सुखोपविष्टस्य निरङ्गणस्य*।
प्रविष्टमानस्य शुभैर्व्विहारैरेकाग्रचित्तस्य समाहितस्य॥
अथागमन्देवसुता महर्षयः प्रतीतवर्णविमलश्रियोज्ज्वलाः।
श्रियाऽवभास्येह च जेतसाह्वयं वनं मुदा मेऽन्तिकमभ्युपागताः॥
महेश्वरश्चन्दन ईशनन्दो प्रशान्तचित्तो महितः सुनन्दः।
शान्ताह्वयश्चाप्युतदेवपुत्रस्तास्ताश्च बह्व्योऽथ च देवकोट्यः॥
प्रणम्य पादौ प्रतिदक्षिणञ्च कृत्वैव मान्तस्थुरिहागता मे।
प्रगृह्य चैवाञ्जलिमङ्गुलीभिः सगौरवा मामिह ते ययाचुः॥
इदं मुनेरागनिसूदनाख्यं वैपुल्यसूत्रं हि महानिदानम्।
यद्भाषितं सर्व्वतथागतैः प्राग्लोकस्य सर्व्वस्य हितार्थमेतत्॥
तस्मादिदानीमपि भाषितो मुनिः स बोधिसत्त्वौघपरिग्रहेच्छया।
परं महायानमिदं प्रभाषयन्परं प्रवादांश्च मुषिश्च धर्षयन्॥
अध्येषणां देवगणस्य तूष्णीमस्थाद्देवमधिवासनञ्च।
सर्व्वे च तुष्टा मुदिता उदग्रा पुष्पाणि चिक्षेपु† रवाप्रहर्षम्॥

---

* वक्रचेत्यत्रद्व्यनकारे स्वर्यः।   † चिक्षिपुरिति सं।

तद्भिक्षवो मे शृणुतेह सर्व्वे वैपुल्यसूत्रं हि महानिदानम्।
यद्भाषितं सर्व्वतथागतैः प्राग्लोकस्य सर्व्वस्य हितार्थमेवेति॥

इति ललितविस्तरे निदानपरिवर्त्तो नाम प्रथमः॥

अथ द्वितीयाध्यायप्रारम्भः।

तत्र भिक्षवः कतमस्सु ललितविस्तरो नाम धर्म्मपर्यायः सूत्रान्तो महावैपुल्य इह भिक्षवो बोधिसत्त्वस्य तुषितवरभवनावस्थितस्य पूज्योपपूजितस्याभिषेकप्राप्तस्य देवशतसहस्रस्तुतस्तोमितवर्णितप्रशंसितस्य लब्धाभिषेकस्य प्रणिधानसमुद्गतस्य सर्व्वबुद्धधर्म्मसमुदागतबुद्धस्सुविपुलपरिशुद्धज्ञाननयनस्य स्मृतिमतिगतिधृत्युत्तप्तविपुलबुद्धेः दानशीलक्षान्तिवीर्य्यध्यानप्रज्ञामहोपायकौशल्यपरमपारमिताप्राप्तस्य महामैत्रीकरुणामुदितोपेक्षाब्रह्मपथकोविदस्य महाभिज्ञासङ्गावरणज्ञानसन्दर्शनाभिमुखीभूतस्य स्मृत्युपस्थानसम्यक्प्रहाणर्द्धिपादेन्द्रियबलबोध्यङ्गमार्गसर्व्वबोधिपक्षधर्म्मसुपरिपूर्णकोटिप्राप्तस्य अपरिमितपुण्यसम्भारलक्षणानुव्यञ्जनसमलङ्कृतकायस्य दीर्घानुपरिवर्त्तिनो यथावादितथाकार्य्यवितथवाक्कर्म्मसमुदाहारकस्य* ऋज्वकुटिलावङ्काप्रतिहतमानसस्य सर्व्वमानमदद्दर्पभयविषादापगतस्य सर्व्वसत्त्वसमचित्तस्य अपरिमितबुद्धकोटिनियुतशतसहस्रपर्य्युपासितस्य बहुबोधिसत्त्वकोटिनियुतशतसहस्रावलोकितवदनस्य शक्रब्रह्ममहेश्वरलोकपालदेवनागयक्षगन्धर्व्वासुरगरुडकिन्नरम-

* यथासमर्थसमासो बोध्यः।

होरगराक्षसगणैरभिनन्दितयशसः सर्व्वपदप्रभेदनिर्देशासङ्ग-
प्रतिसंविदवतारज्ञानकुशलस्य सर्व्वबुद्धभाषिताधारणस्मृतिभा-
जनाभिक्षेपानन्तापर्य्यन्तधारणीप्रतिलब्धस्य महाधर्म्मनौस्मृत्यु-
पस्थानसम्यक्प्रहाणर्द्धिपादेन्द्रियबलबोध्यङ्गमार्गपारमितोपाय-
कौशल्यधर्म्मरत्नपुण्यसमुदानीतमहासार्थवाहस्य चतुरोघपा-
रगमनाभिप्रायस्य निहतमानप्रत्यर्थिकस्य सर्व्वपरप्रवादि-
सुनिगृहीतस्य सङ्ग्रामशीर्षसुप्रतिष्ठितस्य क्लेशरिपुगणनिसूद-
नस्य ज्ञानवरवज्रदृढप्रहरणस्य बोधिचित्तमूलमहाकरुणा-
दण्डाध्याशयोद्गतस्य गम्भीरवीर्य्यसलिलाभिषिक्तस्य उपाय-
कौशलकर्णिकस्य बोध्यङ्गध्यानकुशलस्य समाधिकिञ्जल्कस्य
गुणगणविमलसरसिसुजातस्य विगतमदमानपरिदाहशशि-
विमलविस्तीर्णपत्रस्य शीलश्रुतप्रसाददशदिगप्रतिहतगन्धिनो
लोके ज्ञानवृद्धस्याष्टाभिर्लोकधर्म्मैरनुपलिप्तस्य महापुरुषपद्मस्य
पुण्यज्ञानसम्भारविसृतसुरभिगन्धिनः प्रज्ञाज्ञानदिनकरकिर-
णैर्व्विकसितसुविशुद्धशतपत्रपद्मतापनस्य चतुर्ऋद्धिपादपरम-
जवजवितस्य चतुरार्य्यसत्यसुतीक्ष्णनखदंष्ट्रस्य चतुर्ब्रह्मविहार-
निःसृतदर्शनस्य चतुःसङ्ग्रहवस्तुसङ्गृहीतशिरसः द्वादशाङ्ग-
प्रतीत्यसमुत्पादानुबोधानुपूर्व्वसमुद्गतकायस्य सप्तत्रिंशद्बोधिपक्ष-
धर्म्मसम्प्रतिपूर्णस्य विजातनानाविद्याज्ञानकेशरिणस्त्रिविमोक्षमु-
खविजृम्भकस्य समर्थविदर्शनासुविशुद्धनयनस्य ध्यानविमोक्ष-
समाधिसमापत्तिगिरिदरीगुहानिवसितस्य चतुरीर्य्यापथ-
विनयनोपवनसुवर्द्धिततरोर्दशबलवैशारद्याभ्यासीभावितबलस्य

विगतभवविभवभयलोमहर्षणस्यासङ्कुचितपराक्रमस्य तीर्थ्यशश-
मृगगणसङ्घप्रमथनस्य नैरात्म्यघोषोदाहारमहासिंहनादना-
दिनः पुरुषसिंहस्य विमुक्तिध्यानमण्डलप्रशप्रभ* रश्मितीर्थि-
कखद्योतगणनिःप्रभङ्करस्य अविद्यातमोन्धकारतमःपटलवि-
तिमिरकरणस्योत्तप्तबलवीर्य्यस्य देवमनुष्येषु पुण्यतेजस्तेजितस्य
महापुरुषदिनकरस्य कृष्णपक्षापगतस्य शुक्लपक्षप्रतिपूर्णस्य
मनाग† प्रियदर्शनस्य अप्रतिहतचक्षुरिन्द्रियस्य देवशतसहस्र-
ज्योतिर्गणप्रतिमण्डितस्य ध्यानविमोक्षज्ञानमण्डलस्य बोध्यङ्ग-
सुखरश्मिशशिकिरणस्य बुद्धविबुद्धमनुजकुमुदविबोधकस्य महा-
पुरुषचन्द्रस्य समचतुष्पर्षद्द्वीपानुपरीतस्य सप्तबोध्यङ्गरत्नसमन्वा-
गतस्य सर्व्वसत्त्वसमचित्तप्रयोगस्याप्रतिहतबुद्धेर्दशकुशलकर्म्मप-
थशततपसः सुसमृद्धप्रतिपूर्णविशेषगमनाभिप्रायस्याप्रतिहत-
धर्म्मराजवरप्रवरधर्म्मरत्नचक्रप्रवर्त्तकस्य चक्रवर्त्तिवंशकुलकुलो-
दितस्य गम्भीरदुरवगाहप्रतीत्यसमुत्पादसर्व्वधर्म्मरत्नप्रतिपूर्ण-
स्याट्तश्रुतविपुलविस्तीर्णारम्भज्ञानशीलवेलानतिक्रमणस्य महा-
पद्मगर्भचरणस्य सागरवरधरविपुलबुद्धेः पृथिव्यप्तेजोवायुसमचि-
त्तस्य मेरुकल्पदृढबलाप्रकम्पमानस्यानुनयप्रतिघापगतस्य गगन-
तलविमलविपुलासङ्गविस्तीर्णबुद्धेरध्याशयसुप्रतिशुद्धस्य सुदत्त-
दानस्य सुकृतपूर्व्वयोगस्य सुकृताधिकारस्य दत्तसत्यङ्कारस्य पर्य्ये-
षितस्य सर्व्वकुशलमूलस्य वासितवासनस्य निर्य्याणमिव सर्व्वकुश-
लमूलस्य सप्तसङ्ख्येयेषु कल्पेषु समुदानीतसर्व्वकुशलमूलस्य दत्तस-

---

* प्रशाप्रभा । † ममनाम ।

शविधदानस्य पञ्चविधपुण्यक्रियावस्तूपसेवितवतस्त्रिविधं कायि-
केन चतुर्विधं वाचा त्रिविधं मनसा सुचरितवतः दशकुशलकर्म्म
पथाद्यासेवितवतश्चत्वारिंशदङ्गसमन्वागतसम्यक्प्रयोगसमासेवित-
वतः चत्वारिंशदङ्गसमन्वागतसम्यक्प्रणिधानं प्रणिहितवतः चत्वा-
रिंशदङ्गसमन्वागतसम्यगध्याशयप्रतिपन्नवतः चत्वारिंशदङ्गसम-
न्वागतसम्यग्विमोक्षपरिपूरितवतः चत्वारिंशदङ्गसमन्वागतसम्य-
गधिमुक्तिस्वीकृतवतः चत्वारिंशत्सु बुद्धकोटिनियुतशतस-
हस्रेष्वनुप्रव्रजितवतः पञ्चपञ्चाशत्सु बुद्धकोटिनियुतशतसहस्रेषु
दानानि दत्तवतः अर्धचतुर्थेषु प्रत्येकबुद्धकोटिशतेषु कृताधि-
कारवतः अप्रमेयासंख्येयान् सत्त्वान्स्वर्गमोक्षमार्गप्रतिपादितवतः
अनुत्तरं सम्यक्सम्बोधिमभिसम्बोद्धुकामस्यैकजातिप्रतिबद्धस्य
इतश्च्युत्वा तुषितवरभवने स्थितस्य श्वेतकेतुनाम्नो देवपुत्रोत्त-
मस्य सर्व्वदेवसङ्घैः सम्पूज्यमानस्यायमितश्च्युतोमर्त्त्यस्य लोको-
त्पन्नो न चिरादनुत्तरं सम्यग्सम्बोधिमभिसम्भोत्स्यतीति ।
तस्मिन्महाविमाने सुखोपविष्टस्य द्वात्रिंशद्भूमिसहस्रप्रतिसंस्थिते
वितर्द्दिनिर्य्यूहतोरणगवाक्षहर्म्यकूटागारप्रासादसमलङ्कृते उ-
च्छ्रितछत्रध्वजपताकारत्नकिङ्किणीजालवितानवितते * मान्दा-
रवमहामान्दारवपुष्पसंस्तरणसंस्तृते अप्सरसः कोटिनियुत-
शतसहस्रसङ्गीतिप्रचरिते अतिमुक्तकचम्पकपाटलकोविदार-
मुचिरिन्द † महामुचिरिन्दाशोकन्यग्रोधकिन्दुक ‡ शणकर्णि-
कारकेशररसालरत्नवृक्षोपशोभिते हेमजालसञ्छन्ने महता

* मान्दारवेत्यत्र मान्दारक इति ख ॥ † मुचुकुन्दः । ‡ कुन्दक इति ख ॥

पूर्णकुम्भोपशोभिते * समन्तव्यूहोपशोभिते ज्योतिर्मालिकासुमनोवाते देवकोटिनियुतशतसहस्राभिमुखनयनावलोकितेऽलोके महाविपुलधर्म्मसङ्गीतिसर्व्वकामरतिवेगक्लेशच्छेदने व्युपगताखिलक्रोधप्रतिघमानमददर्पापनयने प्रीतिप्रासादप्रामोद्योत्तमविपुलस्मृतिसञ्जनने सुखोपविष्टस्य तस्मिन्महाधर्म्मसाङ्कथ्ये प्रवृत्ते तेभ्यस्तुरशीतिभ्यस्तूर्य्यसङ्गीतिसहस्रनिर्नादितेभ्यो बोधिसत्त्वस्य पूर्व्वशुभकर्म्मोपचयेनेमाः सञ्चोदना गाथा निश्चरन्ति स्म ॥

स्मर विपुलपुण्यनिचयं स्मृतिमतिगतिमनन्तप्रज्ञाप्रभाकरम् ।
अतुलबलविपुलविक्रमव्याकरणं दीपङ्करस्यापि ॥
स्मर विपुलनिर्म्मलमनस्त्रिमलमलप्रहीणशान्तमददोषम् ।
शुभविमलशुद्धचित्ता दानचरीया† स्मृत्वाऽतिपुरे ॥
स्मर कुलकुलीनाः शमथशीलव्रतं क्षमादमश्चैव ।
वीर्य्यबलध्यानप्रज्ञानिषेविताकल्पकोटिनियुतानि ॥
स्मर स्मर अनन्तकीर्त्ते सम्पूजिता ये‡ऽतिबुद्धकोटिनियुतानि ।
सर्व्वाङ्करुणायमानः कालोऽयमा उपेचस्व ॥
च्यव च्यव § हि च्युतिर्विधिज्ञा जरामरणक्लेशसूदना विरजा ।
समुदीक्षन्ते बहवो देवासुरनागयक्षगन्धर्वाः ॥
कल्पसहस्रं रमित्वा ‖ तृप्ता नाभवन्नभसीव ¶ समुद्रे ।

* पूर्णकुम्भेत्युचितं। † चर्य्या। ‡ तानि यानि। § चव तु या साचाद्दिद्देश्यते सा तु द्रुततरोच्चरिततया न परिस्फुटसौया। अद दोला वि चवलो सङ्कीरा पदर वीर सो विसड। चलो विजुरिव पडिवो दोलिण वि एक जासेव इति पिङ्गलसत्रात्। एवमन्यचाप्यूह्यं। ‖ रन्त्वा। ¶ चच्चलीव चच्चांशीवेति शुद्धम्।

साधु भव प्रज्ञाढ्य तर्पय जनतां चिरतृषार्त्ताम् ॥
किञ्चाप्यनिन्दितयशस्त्वं धर्म्मरतिरतो न चासि कामरतः ।
अथ च पुनरमलनयनामनुकम्पां सदेवकं लोकं ॥
किञ्चापि देवनयुताः श्रुत्वा धर्म्मं न ते वितृप्यन्ते ।
अथ च पुनारक्षणगतामपायसंस्थानवेक्षस्व ॥
किञ्चाविमलचक्षुः पश्यसि बुद्धान्दशदिशि लोके ।
धर्म्मं शृणोषि च ततस्त्वं धर्म्मवरं विभज लोके ॥
किञ्चापि तुषितभवनं तव पुण्यश्रियाऽभिशोभते श्रीमन् ।
अथ च पुनः करुणमानस प्रवर्ष जम्बुध्वजे वर्षम् ॥
समतीत्य कामधातुदेवान् ये रूपधातुकाऽनेके* ।
सर्व्वेत्यभिनन्दन्ते स्पृशेयं षिद्धुशतं बोधिं ॥
निहताभिमारकर्म्मन् जितास्त्वयान्ये कुतीर्थिका नाथ ।
केन † सकलजगतक्षिबोधे अयं स कालो मा उपेक्षस्व ॥
क्लेशाग्निना प्रदीप्ते लोके त्वं वीर मेघवद्व्याप्य ।
अभिवर्षामृतवर्षं शमय क्लेशाग्नरमरूणाम् ॥
त्वं वैद्यधातुकुशलश्चिरातुरान् सत्यवैद्यः सत्यवान् ।
त्रिविमोक्षगदयोगैर्निर्वाणसुखे स्थापय शीघ्रम् ॥
अश्रुत्वा सिंहनादं क्रोष्टुकगणा नदन्त्य नुचष्टाः ‡ ।
नद बुद्धसिंहनादं त्रासय परतीर्थिकशृगालान् ।
प्रज्ञाप्रदीपहस्तो बलवीर्य्यबलो जिनो धरणीमण्डे § ।

---

* इहशब्दाकेसन्धिरार्षो ज्ञातव्यः । † येन । ‡ अनुचष्टा इतिपाठः । § मण्डले ॥

करतलवरेण धरणीपरो हनित्वा* जिनं हि मारम् ॥
समुदीक्ष्यन्ते पालास्त्वतुरो † ये तुभ्यं दास्यन्ते पात्रम् ।
शक्राश्च ब्रह्मणा युता ये जातं त्वा ग्रहिष्यन्ति ॥
व्यवलोकयाभिर्व्यग्रःकुशलरत्नकुलोदितान् कुलकुलीनान् ।
यत्र स्थित्वा सुमते दर्शिष्यसि ‡ बोधिसत्त्वचरितम् ॥
यत्रैव भाजनेस्मिन्मणिरत्नं तिष्ठते भवति श्रीमन् ।
मणिरत्नं विमलबुद्धे प्रवर्षं जम्बुध्वजे वर्षम् ॥
एवं बहुप्रकाराः सङ्गीतिरवानुनिस्सरा गाथाः ।
चोदेन्ति § करुणामनसमयं स कालो मा उपेक्षस्वेति ॥
इति श्रीललितविस्तरे समुत्साहनपरिवर्त्तो नाम द्वितीयः ॥२॥

अथ तृतीयाध्यायप्रारम्भः ॥

इति हि भिक्षवो बोधिसत्त्व एवं धर्म्मकालसञ्चोदितः सन् ततो महाविमानान्निष्क्रम्य धर्म्मोच्चयो नाम महाप्रासादो यत्र निषद्य बोधिसत्त्वस्तुषितेभ्यो देवेभ्यो धर्म्मन्देशयति स्म । तं बोधिसत्त्वोऽभिरोहति स्म अभिरुह्य च सुधर्म्मे सिंहासने निषीदति स्म ॥ अथ ये देवपुत्रा बोधिसत्त्वस्य सभागाः समयानसम्प्रस्थितास्तेऽपि तमेव प्रासादमभिरोहन्ति स्म । ये च दशदिक्सन्निपतिता बोधिसत्त्वाः सभागचरिता बोधिसत्त्वस्य देवपुत्राश्च तेऽपि तं प्रासादमभिरुह्य यथा प्रत्यर्हेषु सिंहासनेषु स्वकस्वकेषु निषी-

* हत्वा † चत्वारः ॥ ‡ द्रक्ष्यसि इति पं ॥ § चोदयन्ति इति पं ॥

इन्ति स्म। अपगताप्सरोगणा अपगतप्राकृतदेवपुत्राः समा-
गाध्याग्रयपरिवारा अष्टषष्ठिकोटिसहस्रपरिवारा इति हि
भिक्षवो द्वादशभिर्वर्षैर्बोधिसत्त्वो मातुः कुक्षिमवक्रमिष्यतीति॥

अथ शुद्धावासकायिका देवपुत्रा जम्बुद्वीपमागत्य दिव्यं वर्ष-
मन्तर्द्धाय ब्राह्मणवेषेण ब्राह्मणान्वेदानध्यापयन्ति स्म। यस्यैवं-
रूपा गर्भावक्रान्तिर्भवति स द्वात्रिंशता महापुरुषलक्षणैः समन्वा-
गतो भवति। यैः समन्वागतस्य द्वे गती भवतो न तृतीया स
चेदगारमध्यावसति राजा भवति चक्रवर्त्ती चतुरङ्गो विजि-
तवान्धार्म्मिको धर्म्मराजः सप्तरत्नसमन्वागतः तस्येमानि
सप्तरत्नानि भवन्ति। तद्यथा चक्ररत्नं हस्तिरत्नं अश्वरत्नं
स्त्रीरत्नं मणिरत्नं गृहपतिरत्नं परिणायकरत्नमेव सप्तमं॥

कथं रूपेण राजा चक्रवर्त्ती चक्ररत्नेन समन्वागतो भवति।
इह राज्ञः क्षत्रियस्य मूर्द्धाभिषिक्तस्य तदेव पोषधेयं पञ्चदश्यां
शिरःस्नातस्योपवासोषितस्योपरिप्रासादतलगतस्य स्त्यागारपरि-
वृतस्य पूर्व्वस्यां दिशि दिव्यं चक्ररत्नं प्रादुर्भवति। सहस्रारं सने-
मिकं सनाभिकं सुवर्णवर्णैः कर्म्मालङ्कृतं* सप्ततालमुच्चैः समन्ता
दृष्टाऽन्तःपुरं राज्ञः क्षत्रियस्य मूर्द्धाभिषिक्तस्य तद्दिव्यं चक्ररत्न-
मेवं भवति॥ श्रुतं खलु मया यस्य किल राज्ञः क्षत्रियस्य मूर्द्धा-
भिषिक्तस्य तदेव पोषधेयं पञ्चदश्यां शिरः स्नातस्योपवासोषि-
तस्योपरिप्रासादतलगतस्य स्त्र्यागारपरिवृतस्य पूर्व्वस्यां दिशि
दिव्यं चक्ररत्नं प्रादुर्भवति स भवति राजा चक्रवर्त्ती (अभूवमहं

---

* सुवर्णवर्णकर्म्मालङ्कृतमिति पाठः॥

राजा चक्रवर्त्ती यो न्वहं * दिव्यं चक्ररत्नं मीमांसयेयम्) अथ राजा क्षत्रियो मूर्द्धाभिषिक्त एकांसमुत्तरासङ्गं कृत्वा दक्षिणं जानुमण्डलं पृथिव्यां प्रतिष्ठाप्य दक्षिणेन पाणिना तद्दिव्यं चक्ररत्नं प्रार्थयेदेवं चावेदयेत्। प्रवर्त्तयस्व भर्त्तर्दिव्यं चक्ररत्नरत्नं धर्म्मेण माऽधर्म्मेण ॥ अथ तद्दिव्यं चक्ररत्नं राज्ञा क्षत्रियेण मूर्द्धाऽभिषेकेन प्रवर्त्तितं सम्यगेव खड्गी विहायसा पूर्व्वेण व्रजति अन्वेति राजा चक्रवर्त्ती सार्द्धं चतुरङ्गेण बलकायेन। यत्र पृथिवीप्रदेशे तद्दिव्यं चक्ररत्नं सन्तिष्ठते तत्र राजा क्षत्रियो मूर्द्धाभिषिक्तो वासङ्कल्पयति सार्द्धं चतुरङ्गेण बलकायेन । अथ ये ये भवन्ति पूर्व्वस्यान्दिशि राजानो मण्डलिनस्ते रूप्य-पात्रीं सुवर्णचूर्णपरिपूर्णामादाय स्वर्णपात्रीं वा रूप्यचूर्णपरि-पूर्णामादाय राजानं चक्रवर्त्तिनं प्रत्युत्तिष्ठन्ति । एहि देव स्वागतं देवायेदं देवस्य राज्यमृद्धञ्च स्फीतञ्च क्षेमञ्च सुभिक्षञ्च रमणीयञ्चाकीर्णबहुजनमनुष्यञ्च अध्यावसतु देव स्वकं विजित-मनुप्राप्तम्। एवमुक्ते राजा क्षत्रियो मूर्द्धाभिषिक्तस्तान् राज्ञो-मण्डलिन एतदवोचत् । कारयन्तु भवन्तः स्वकानि राज्यानि धर्म्मेण हन्त भवन्तो मा प्राणिनंघातयिष्यथ मा दत्तादास्यथ †-मा कामेषु मिथ्याचरिष्यथ मा मृषां वचथ यावमाने विजिते अधर्म्ममुत्पद्यते माऽधर्म्मचारिणो रोचथ । एवं खलु राजा क्षत्रियो मूर्द्धाभिषिक्तः पूर्व्वान्दिशं विजित्य पूर्व्वसमुद्रमव-गाह्य पूर्व्वसमुद्रमवतरति । पूर्व्वसमुद्रमवतीर्य्य सम्यगेव खड्गा

---

* यतोऽहमिति युक्तम् ॥ † दत्तमादास्यथ इत्युचितम् ॥

विहायसा दक्षिणेन व्रजति अन्वेति राजा चक्रवर्त्ती सार्द्धं-चतुरङ्गेण बलकायेन पूर्व्ववदेवं दक्षिणान्दिशं विजयति। यथा दक्षिणामिव पश्चिमामुत्तरां दिशं विजयति। उत्तरां दिशं विजित्य उत्तरसमुद्रमवगाहते। अवगाह्योत्तरात्समुद्रा-त्प्रत्युत्तरति। प्रत्युत्तीर्य्य सम्यगेव चक्रा विहायसा राजधानी-मागत्योपरि अन्तःपुरद्वारेऽन्तमेवास्थात्। एवंरूपेण राजा क्षत्रियो मूर्द्धाभिषिक्तश्चक्ररत्नेन समन्वागतो भवति॥

कथंरूपेण राजा चक्रवर्त्ती हस्तिरत्नेन समन्वागतो भवति। इह राज्ञः क्षत्रियस्य मूर्द्धाभिषिक्तस्य पूर्व्ववद्धस्तिरत्न-मुत्पद्यते। सर्व्वं श्वेतं सप्ताङ्गं सुप्रतिष्ठितं स्वर्णपृष्ठकं स्वर्णध्वजं स्वर्णालङ्कारहेमजालप्रतिच्छन्नं ऋद्धिमन्तं विहायसा गामिनं विकुर्व्वाणधर्म्मिणं यदुत बोधिर्नाम नागराजो। यदा च राजा क्षत्रियो मूर्द्धाभिषिक्तस्तद्धस्तिरत्नं मीमांसितुकामो भवति। अथ सूर्य्यस्यात्युद्गमनवेलायान्तद्धस्तिरत्नमभिरुह्य इमामेव महापृथिवीं समुद्रपरिखां समुद्रपर्य्यन्तां समन्ततोऽन्वाहिण्ड्य स्वराजधानीमागत्य प्रग्रासनरतिः प्रत्यनुभवति। एवंरूपेण राजा चक्रवर्त्ती हस्तिरत्नेन समन्वागतो भवति॥

कथंरूपेण राजा चक्रवर्त्ती अश्वरत्नेन समन्वागतो भवति। अथ राज्ञः क्षत्रियस्य मूर्द्धाभिषिक्तस्य पूर्व्ववद-श्वरत्नमुत्पद्यते। सर्व्वं नीलकृष्णशिरसं मुञ्जकेशमश्मादृतवदनं स्वर्णध्वजं स्वर्णालङ्कारहेमजालप्रतिच्छन्नमृद्धिमन्तं विहाय-सागामिनं विकुर्व्वाणधर्म्मिणं यदुत वालाहकं नामाश्वराजम्।

यदा राजा क्षत्रियो मूर्द्धाभिषिक्तोऽश्वरत्नं मीमांसितुकामो भवति अथ सूर्य्यस्याभ्युद्गमनवेलायामश्वरत्नमभिरुह्य इमामेव महापृथिवीं समुद्रपरिखां समुद्रपर्य्यन्तां समन्ततोऽन्वाहिण्ड्य राजधानीमागत्य प्रत्याशनरतिः प्रत्यनुभवति । एवंरूपेण राजा चक्रवर्त्ती अश्वरत्नेन समन्वागतो भवति ॥

कथंरूपेण राजा चक्रवर्त्ती मणिरत्नेन समन्वागतो भवति । इह राज्ञः क्षत्रियस्य मूर्द्धाभिषिक्तस्य पूर्व्ववन्मणिरत्नमुत्पद्यते । शुद्धनीलवैदूर्य्यमष्टांशं सुपरिकर्म्मकृतं तस्य खलु पुनर्मणिरत्नस्याभया सर्व्वमन्तःपुरमवभासेन स्फुटं भवति । यदा च राजा क्षत्रियो मूर्द्धाभिषिक्तस्तन्मणिरत्नं मीमांसितुकामो भवति अथ रात्र्यामर्द्धरात्रसमयेऽन्धकारतमिस्रायां तन्मणिरत्नं ध्वजाग्रे उत्थापयित्वा उद्यानभूमिं निर्याति सुभूमिदर्शनाय तस्य तस्य खलु पुनर्मणिरत्नस्याभया सर्व्वावन्तश्चतुरङ्गबलकायमवभासेन स्फुटीभवति सामन्तेन योजनं ये खलु तस्य मणिरत्नस्य सामन्तके मनुष्याः प्रतिवसन्ति ते तेनावभासेनाऽऽस्फुटं भासमाना अन्योऽन्यं सञ्जानन्त्यन्योऽन्यं पश्यन्त्यन्योऽन्यमाहुः । उत्तिष्ठत भद्रमुखाः कर्म्मान्तानि कारयत आपणानि प्रसारयत दिवा मन्यामहे सूर्य्यमभ्युद्गतमेवं राजा क्षत्रियो मूर्द्धाभिषिक्तो मणिरत्नेन समन्वागतो भवति ॥

कथंरूपेण राजा चक्रवर्त्ती स्त्रीरत्नेन समन्वागतो भवति । इह राज्ञः क्षत्रियस्य मूर्द्धाभिषिक्तस्य पूर्व्ववत्स्त्रीरत्नमुत्पद्यते । सदृशी क्षत्रिया नातिदीर्घा नातिह्रस्वा नातिस्थूला नातिकृशा

नातिगौरी नातिकृष्णा अभिरूपा प्रासादिका दर्शनीया। तस्याः सर्व्वरोमकूपेभ्यश्चन्दनगन्धः प्रवाति। मुखाच्चोत्पलगन्धः प्रवाति। काचिलिन्दिकसुखसंस्पर्शा। शीतलकाले चास्या उष्णानि संस्पर्शानि गात्राणि भवन्ति। उष्णकाले च शीतसंस्पर्शानि। सा राजानं चक्रवर्त्तिनं मुक्त्वा नान्यस्मिन्मनसाऽपि रागं करोति किं पुनः कायेन। एवंरूपेण राजा चक्रवर्त्ती स्त्रीरत्नेन समन्वागतो भवति॥

कथंरूपेण राजा चक्रवर्त्ती गृहपतिरत्नेन समन्वागतो भवति। इह राज्ञः क्षत्रियस्य मूर्द्धाभिषिक्तस्य पूर्व्ववद्गृहपतिरत्नमुत्पद्यते। पण्डितो व्यक्तो मेधावी दिव्यचक्षुः स तेन दिव्यचक्षुषा सामन्तेन योजनं सस्वामिकानि निधानानि पश्यति सस्वामिकानि भवन्ति अस्वामिकानि तैः राज्ञश्चक्रवर्त्तिनो धनेन करणीयं करोति॥ एवंरूपेण राजा चक्रवर्त्ती गृहपतिरत्नेन समन्वागतो भवति॥

कथंरूपेण राजा चक्रवर्त्ती परिणायकरत्नेन समन्वागतो भवति। इह राज्ञः क्षत्रियस्य मूर्द्धाभिषिक्तस्य पूर्व्ववत्परिणायकरत्नमुत्पद्यते। व्यक्तो मेधावी राज्ञश्चक्रवर्त्तिनश्चिन्तितमात्रेणोद्योजयितव्यां सेनामुद्योजयति स्म। एवंरूपेण राजा चक्रवर्त्ती परिणायकरत्नेन समन्वागतो भवति। एभिः सप्तभी रत्नैः समन्वागतो भविष्यति चास्य पुत्रसहस्रं शूराणां वीराणां वराङ्गरूपिणां परसैन्यप्रमर्द्दकानां स इमां महापृथ्वीं ससागरपर्य्यन्तामखिलामकण्टकामदण्डेनाशस्त्रेणाभिनि-

र्जित्याभ्यासयति ॥ स चेदगारादनगारिकां प्रव्रजिष्यति वान्तछन्दरागो नेता अनन्यदेवः शास्ता देवानाञ्च मनुष्याणाञ्चेति । अथान्येऽपि देवपुत्रा जम्बुद्वीपमागत्य प्रत्येकबुद्धेभ्य आरोचयन्ति स्म। रिञ्चतमार्षाबुद्धक्षेत्र इतो द्वादशवर्षात्यये बोधिसत्त्वो मातुः कुक्षिमवक्रमिष्यति । तेन खलु पुनर्भिक्षवः समयेन राजगृहे महानगरे गोलाङ्गुलपरिवर्त्तने पर्व्वते मातङ्गो नाम प्रत्येकबुद्धो विहरति स्म। स तं शब्दं श्रुत्वा कर्दम इव शिलायां प्रास्थाय विहायसा सप्ततालमात्रमत्युद्गम्य च तेजोधातुं समापद्योल्केव परिनिर्वाति स्म॥ तस्य पित्तश्लेष्मस्नाय्वस्थिमांसरुधिरञ्चासीत्तत्सर्व्वं तेजसा पर्य्यवदानमगच्छच्छुद्धशरीराण्येव भूमौ प्रापतन्नद्यापि च तानि ऋषिपदान्येव सञ्ज्ञायन्ते ॥

तेन खलु पुनर्भिक्षवः समयेन वाराणस्यां ऋषिपत्तने मृगदावे पञ्च प्रत्येकबुद्धशतानि विहरन्ति स्म। तेऽपि तं शब्दं श्रुत्वा विहायसा सप्ततालमात्रमत्युद्गम्य तेजोधातुं समापद्योल्केव परिनिर्व्वान्ति स्म । यत्तेषां पित्तश्लेष्ममांसास्थिस्नायुरुधिरञ्चाभूत् तत्सर्व्वं तेजसा पर्य्यवदानमगच्छच्छुद्धबुद्धशरीराण्येव भूमौ प्रापतन्नस्मिन्नृषयः पतिता इति तस्मात्प्रभृति ऋषिपत्तनसञ्ज्ञोत्पादिता*अभयदत्ताश्च तस्मिन्मृगाः प्रतिवसन्ति इति तदग्रेण मृगदावस्य मृगदावो मृगदाव इति सञ्ज्ञोदपादि ॥

इति हि भिक्षवो बोधिसत्त्वस्तुषितवरभवनस्थितश्चत्वारि महाविलोकितानि विलोकयन्ति स्म ॥ कतमानि चत्वारि ।

* उत्पन्ना इति धं ।

तद्यथा । कालविलोकितं द्वीपविलोकितं देशविलोकितं कुलविलोकितञ्च । किं कारणं हि भिक्षवो बोधिसत्त्वः कालविलोकितं विलोकयति स्म । बोधिसत्त्व आदिप्रवृत्ते लोके सत्त्वसम्वर्त्तनीकालसमये मातुः कुक्षिमवक्रामति अथ तर्हि यदा व्यक्तो लोकः सुस्थितो भवति जातिः प्रज्ञायते जरा प्रज्ञायते व्याधिः प्रज्ञायते मरणं प्रज्ञायते तदा बोधिसत्त्वो मातुः कुक्षिमवक्रामति ॥ किं कारणं बोधिसत्त्वो द्वीपविलोकितं विलोकयति स्म । न बोधिसत्त्वाः प्रत्यन्तद्वीपेषूपपद्यन्ते न पूर्व्वविदेहे नापरगोदानीये न चोत्तरकुरौ अथ तर्हि जम्बुद्वीप एवोपपद्यन्ते ॥

किं कारणं भिक्षवो बोधिसत्त्वो देशविलोकितं विलोकयति स्म । न बोधिसत्त्वाः प्रत्यन्तजनपदेषु । मनुष्यान्धजात्या जडा एडमूकजातीया अभव्याः सुभाषितदुर्भाषितानामर्थं ज्ञातुम् । अथ तर्हि बोधिसत्त्वा मध्यमेष्वेव जनपदेषूपपद्यन्ते ॥ किं कारणं हि भिक्षवो बोधिसत्त्वः कुलविलोकितं विलोकयति स्म । न बोधिसत्त्वा हीनकुलेषूपपद्यन्ते । चण्डालकुलेषु वा वेणुकारकुलेषु वा रथकारकुलेषु वा पुक्कसकुलेषु वा । अथ तर्हि कुलद्वये एवोपपद्यन्ते । ब्राह्मणकुले क्षत्रियकुले च । तत्र यदा ब्राह्मणगुरुको लोको भवति तदा ब्राह्मणकुलेषूपपद्यन्ते । यदा क्षत्रियगुरुको लोको भवति तदा क्षत्रियकुले उपपद्यन्ते ॥ एतर्हि भिक्षवः क्षत्रियगुरुको लोकस्तस्माद्बोधिसत्त्वाः क्षत्रियकुले उपपद्यन्ते । तमर्थं च सम्प्रतीत्य

बोधिसत्त्वस्तुषितवरभवनस्थश्चत्वारि महाविलोकितानि विलोकयति स्म ।

एवञ्चावलोक्य तूष्णीमभूदिति हि भिक्षवस्ते देवपुत्रा बोधिसत्त्वस्या*न्योन्यं परिपृच्छन्ति स्म । कतमस्मिन्कुलरत्ने कियद्रूपायां जनन्यां बोधिसत्त्वः †प्रतिष्ठतेति । तत्र केचिदाहुः । इदं वैदेहीकुलं मगधेषु जनपदेषु ऋद्धञ्च स्फीतक्षेमसुभिक्षञ्चेदं प्रतिरूपमस्य बोधिसत्त्वस्य गर्भस्थानम् । अपरे त्वाहुः । न तत्प्रतिरूपं । तत्कस्मात् । तथा हि । तत्र मातृशुद्धं पितृशुद्धमपुष्टं चञ्चलमनवस्थितं परिप्लुत्यल्पपुण्यकं पुण्याभिष्यन्दितं न विपुलपुण्याभिषिक्तं सत्कुलप्रदेशोपचारं नोद्याननगरखण्डागाकीर्णं कर्पटमिव प्रत्यन्तवासं तेन न तत्प्रतिरूपं ॥

अपरेऽप्याहुः । इदं पुनः कौशलकुलं महावाहनञ्च महापरिवारञ्च महाधनञ्च तत्प्रतिरूपमस्य बोधिसत्त्वस्य गर्भप्रतिसंक्रामणायेति । अपरे त्वाहुः । तदप्यप्रतिरूपं । तत्कस्माद्धेतोः । तथा हि । कौशलकुलं मातङ्गच्युत्युपपन्नं न मातृपितृशुद्धं हीनाधिमुक्तिकं न कुलोदितं न चापरिमितधनरत्ननिधिसमुत्थितं तेन न तत्प्रतिरूपम् ।

अपरेप्याहुः । इदं वंशराजकुलं ऋद्धञ्च स्फीतञ्च क्षेमञ्च सुभिक्षञ्चेदं प्रतिरूपमस्य बोधिसत्त्वस्य गर्भस्थानायेति । अपर एवमाहुः । इदमप्यप्रतिरूपं । किं कारणम् । तथाहि ।

---

* अत्र द्वितीयार्थे षष्ठी । † अत्र स्थिरार्थः ।

वंशराजकुलं प्राकृतञ्च चण्डञ्च न चोज्ज्वलिततेजसं परपुरुषजन्मानिवृत्तश्च न मातृपितृस्वतेजःकर्माभिनिर्वृत्तश्चोच्छेदवादी च तत्र राजा। तेन तदप्यप्रतिरूपम् ॥

अपरे त्वाहुः। इयं वैशाली महानगरी ऋद्धा च स्फीता च क्षेमा च सुभिक्षा च रमणीया चाकीर्णबहुजनमनुष्या च वितर्दिनिर्यूहतोरणगवाक्षहर्म्यकूटागारप्रासादतलसमलङ्कृता च पुष्पवाटिका वनराजिसङ्कुसुमिता च अमरभवनपुरप्राकाश्या सा प्रतिरूपाऽस्य बोधिसत्त्वस्य गर्भप्रतिसंस्थानायेति। अपरे प्राहुः। साऽप्यप्रतिरूपा। किं कारणं। तथा हि। तेषां नास्ति परस्परन्यायवादिता नास्ति धर्माचरणं नोत्तममध्यवृद्धज्येष्ठानुपालिता एकैक एव मन्यते अहं राजा अहं राजेति न च कस्यचिच्छिष्यत्वमभ्युपगच्छति न धर्मत्वं। तेन साप्यप्रतिरूपा।

अपरे त्वेवमाहुः। इदं प्रद्योतनकुलं महाबलञ्च महावाहनञ्च परचमूभिरपि विजयलब्धञ्च तत्प्रतिरूपमस्य बोधिसत्त्वस्य गर्भप्रतिसंस्थानायेति। अपरे त्वेवमाहुः। तदप्यप्रतिरूपं ॥ किं कारणं। तथा हि। ते चण्डाश्चपलाश्च रौद्राश्च परुषाश्च साहसिकाश्च न च कर्मादर्शिनः। तेन तदप्यप्रतिरूपमस्य बोधिसत्त्वस्य गर्भप्रतिसंस्थानायेति ॥

अपर एवमाहुः। इयं मथुरा नगरी ऋद्धा च स्फीता च क्षेमा च सुभिक्षा चाकीर्णबहुजनमनुष्या च राज्ञः सुबाहोः शूरकंसकुलस्य राजधानिः सा प्रतिरूपास्य बोधिसत्त्वस्य गर्भप्रतिसंस्थानायेति। अपरे त्वाहुः। साप्यप्रतिरूपा

किं कारणं। तथाहि॥ स राजा मिथ्यादृष्टिकुलवंशप्रसूतो दस्यूराजा न युज्यते चरमभविकस्य बोधिसत्त्वस्य मिथ्यादृष्टिकुले उपपत्तुं। तेन साप्यप्रतिरूपा।

पुनरन्येऽप्याहुः। अयं हस्तिनापुरे महानगरे राजा पाण्डवकुलप्रसूतः शूरो वीर्य्यवान्वराङ्गरूपसम्पन्नः परसैन्यप्रमर्द्दकानां तत्कुलं प्रतिरूपमस्य बोधिसत्त्वस्य गर्भप्रतिसंस्थानायेति। अपरेऽप्याहुः। तदप्यप्रतिरूपं॥ किं कारणं। तथा हि। पाण्डवकुलप्रसूतैः कौरववंशोऽतिव्याकुलीकृतो युधिष्ठिरो धर्म्मस्य पुत्र इति कथयति भीमसेनो वायोरर्ज्जुन इन्द्रस्य नकुलसहदेवावश्विनोरिति। तेन तदपि कुलमप्रतिरूपमस्य बोधिसत्त्वस्य गर्भसंस्थानायेति।

अपर आहुः। इयं मिथिला नगरी अतीव रमणीया मैथिलस्य राज्ञः सुमित्रस्य निवासभूमिः। स राजा प्रभूतहस्त्यश्वरथपदातिबलकायसमन्वितः प्रभूतहिरण्यसुवर्णमणिमुक्तावैदूर्य्यशङ्खशिलाप्रवालजातरूपरजत वित्तोपकरणः सर्व्वसामन्तराजाऽभीतबलपराक्रमो मित्रवान्धर्म्मवत्सलस्तत्कुलं प्रतिरूपमस्य बोधिसत्त्वस्य गर्भप्रतिसंस्थानायेति। अन्य ऊचुः। तदप्यप्रतिरूपमस्ति। असौ राजा सुमित्र एवंगुणयुक्तः किन्त्वतिवृद्धो न समर्थः प्रजाः सन्तानयितुमतिबहुपुत्रश्च। तस्मात्तदपि कुलमप्रतिरूपमस्य बोधिसत्त्वस्य गर्भप्रतिसंस्थानायेति।

एवं भिक्षवस्ते बोधिसत्त्वा देवपुत्राश्च सर्व्वस्मिञ्जम्बुदीपे षोडशजानपदेषु यानि कानिचिदुच्चोच्चानि राजकुलानि तानि

व्यवलोकयन्तस्तानि सर्व्वाणि सदोषाण्यद्राक्षुः । तेषां चिन्तामनस्कारप्रयुक्तानां ज्ञानकेतुध्वजो नाम देवपुत्रोऽवैवर्त्तिको बोधाय कृतनिश्चयः । अस्मिन्महायाने स तां महतीं बोधिसत्त्वदेव पर्षदमेतदवोचत् । एतन्मार्षा एतमेव बोधिसत्त्वमुपसङ्क्रम्य परिप्रच्छामः । कीदृग्गुणसम्पन्ने कुले चरमभविको बोधिसत्त्वः प्रत्याजायत इति ॥ साध्विति ते सर्व्वे कृताञ्जलिपुटा बोधिसत्त्वमुपसङ्क्रम्य पर्य्यप्राक्षुः । कीदृग्गुणसम्पन्ने सत्पुरुषकुञ्जरके चरमभविको बोधिसत्त्वः प्रत्याजायत इति ॥ ततो बोधिसत्त्वस्तं महान्तं बोधिसत्त्वगणं देवगणञ्च व्यवलोक्य एतदवोचत् । चतुःषष्ट्याकारैर्मार्षैः सम्पन्नं कुलं भवति यत्र चरमभविको बोधिसत्त्वः प्रत्याजायते । कतमैश्चतुःषष्ट्याकारैः । तद्यथा । अतिज्ञातञ्च तत्कुलं भवति । अक्षुद्रानुपघाति च तत्कुलं भवति । जातिसम्पन्नञ्च तत्कुलं भवति । पुरुषयुगसम्पन्नञ्च तत्कुलं भवति । अदीनञ्च तत्कुलं भवति । पूर्व्वपुरुषयुगसम्पन्नञ्च तत्कुलं भवति । अभिजातपुरुषयुगसम्पन्नञ्च तत्कुलं भवति । अभिलक्षितपुरुषयुगसम्पन्नञ्च तत्कुलं भवति । महेशाख्यपुरुषयुगसम्पन्नञ्च तत्कुलं भवति । बहुस्त्रीकञ्च तत्कुलं भवति । बहुपुरुषञ्च तत्कुलं भवति । अभीतञ्च तत्कुलं भवति । अदीनालीनञ्च तत्कुलं भवति । अलुब्धञ्च तत्कुलं भवति । शीलवच्च तत्कुलं भवति । प्रज्ञवच्च तत्कुलं भवति । अमान्यानवेक्षितञ्च तत्कुलं भवति । अवन्ध्यविर्य्यनिवेशितञ्च तत्कुलं भवति । भोगांश्च परिभुनक्ति । दृढमित्रञ्च तत्कुलं भवति । तिर्य्यग्योनिगत-

प्राणानुपरोधकरञ्च तत्कुलं भवति । कृतज्ञञ्च तत्कुलं भवति । स्वच्छन्दगामि च तत्कुलं भवति । अदोषगामि च तत्कुलं भवति । अमोहगामि च तत्कुलं भवति । अभयगामि च तत्कुलं भवति । अनवद्याभीरु च तत्कुलं भवति । अमोघविहारि च तत्कुलं भवति । स्थूलभिक्षु च तत्कुलं भवति । क्रियाधिमुक्तञ्च तत्कुलं भवति । त्यागाधिमुक्तञ्च तत्कुलं भवति । दानाधिमुक्तञ्च तत्कुलं भवति । पुरुषकारमति च तत्कुलं भवति । दृढविक्रमञ्च तत्कुलं भवति । बलविक्रमञ्च तत्कुलं भवति । श्रेष्ठविक्रमञ्च तत्कुलं भवति । ऋषिपूजकञ्च तत्कुलं भवति । देवतापूजकञ्च तत्कुलं भवति । चैत्यपूजकञ्च तत्कुलं भवति । पूर्व्वप्रेतपूजकञ्च तत्कुलं भवति । अप्रतिबद्धवैरञ्च तत्कुलं भवति । दशदिग्विघुष्टशब्दञ्च तत्कुलं भवति । महापरिवारञ्च तत्कुलं भवति । अभेद्यपरिवारञ्च तत्कुलं भवति । अनुत्तरपरिवारञ्च १ तत्कुलं भवति । कुलज्येष्ठञ्च तत्कुलं भवति । कुलश्रेष्ठञ्च तत्कुलं भवति । कुलवशिताप्राप्तञ्च तत्कुलं भवति । महेशाख्यञ्च तत्कुलं भवति । मातृज्ञञ्च तत्कुलं भवति । पितृज्ञञ्च तत्कुलं भवति । श्रामणि च तत्कुलं भवति । ब्राह्मण्यञ्च तत्कुलं भवति । प्रभूतधनधान्यकोषागारञ्च तत्कुलं भवति । प्रभूतहिरण्यसुवर्णमणिमुक्ताजातरूपरजतवित्तोपकरणञ्च तत्कुलं भवति । प्रभूतहस्त्यश्वोष्ट्रगवेडकञ्च तत्कुलं भवति । प्रभूतदासीदासकर्म्मकर-

---

१ अनन्तपरिवारञ्चेत्यपि ।

पौरुषेयश्च तत्कुलं भवति। दुःप्रधर्षश्च तत्कुलं भवति। सर्व्वार्थसिद्धश्च तत्कुलं भवति। चक्रवर्त्तिकुलश्च तत्कुलं भवति। पूर्व्वकुशलमूलसहायोपचितश्च तत्कुलं भवति। बोधिसत्त्वकुलकुलोदितश्च तत्कुलं भवति। अनवद्यश्च तत्कुलं भवति सर्व्वजातिवाददोषैः। सदेवके लोके समारके सब्रह्मके सश्रमणब्राह्मणिकायां प्रजायां एभिर्मार्षैश्चतुःषष्ठ्याकारैः समन्वागतश्च तत्कुलं भवति॥

यस्याश्चरमभविको बोधिसत्त्व उत्पद्यते द्वात्रिंशता मार्षा गुणाकारैः समन्वागता सा स्त्री भवति यस्याः स्त्रियाश्चरमभविको बोधिसत्त्वः कुक्षाववक्रामति॥ कतमैर्द्वात्रिंशता। यदुताभिज्ञातायाः स्त्रियाः कुक्षौ चरमभविको बोधिसत्त्वोऽवक्रामति॥ अभिलपिताया अच्छिद्रोपचाराया जातिसम्पन्नायाः कुलसम्पन्नाया रूपसम्पन्नाया नामसम्पन्नाया आरोहपरिणाहसम्पन्नाया अप्रसूतायाः शीलसम्पन्नायाः त्यागसम्पन्नायाः स्मितमुख्याः प्रदक्षिणग्राहिण्या व्यक्ताया विनीताया विशारदाया बहुश्रुतायाः पण्डिताया अशठाया अमायाविन्या अक्रोधनाया अपगतेर्ष्याया अमत्सराया अचञ्चलाया अचपलाया अमुखराया क्षान्तिसौरभ्यसम्पन्नाया अपत्रपसम्पन्नाया मन्दरागद्वेषमोहाया अपगतमातृग्रामदोषायाः पतिव्रतायाः सर्व्वाकारगुणसम्पन्नायाः १ स्त्रियाः कुक्षौ चरमभविको बोधिसत्त्वोऽवक्रामति॥ एभिर्मार्षा द्वात्रिंशताकारैः समन्वागता सा स्त्री यस्याः स्त्रियाः कुक्षौ चरमभविको बोधिसत्त्वोऽवक्रा-

---

१ पञ्चस्वपि ग्रन्थेषु गणनया एकत्रिंशद्गुणा एव लभ्यन्ते न तु द्वात्रिंशत्तमः॥

मति॥ न खलु पुनर्भिक्षवः कृष्णपक्षे बोधिसत्त्वो मातुः कुक्षावक्रामति अपि तु शुक्लपक्षे एवं पञ्चदश्यां पूर्णायां पूर्णिमायां पुष्यनक्षत्रयोगे पोषधपरिगृहीताया मातुः कुक्षौ चरमभविको बोधिसत्त्वोऽवक्रामति॥

अथ खलु ते बोधिसत्त्वास्ते देवपुत्रा बोधिसत्त्वस्यान्तिकादिमामेवंरूपां कुलपरिशुद्धिं मातृपरिशुद्धिं श्रुत्वा चिन्तामनस्कारा अभूवन्। कतमं केवलं एवं गुणसमन्वागतं भवेद्यावद्विधमनेन सत्पुरुषेण निर्दिष्टमेतेषां चिन्तामनस्कारप्रयुक्तानामेतदभूत्। इदं खल्वपि शाक्यकुलमृद्धञ्च स्फीतञ्च क्षेमञ्च सुभिक्षञ्च रमणीयञ्चाकीर्णबहुजनमनुष्यञ्च राजा शुद्धोदनो मातृशुद्धः पितृशुद्धः पत्नीशुद्धः परिक्षयमलसम्पन्नः स्वाकारः सुविज्ञापकः पुण्यतेजस्तेजितो महासम्मतकुले प्रसूतश्चक्रवर्त्तिवंशकुलकुलोदितोऽपरिमितधननिधिरत्नसमन्वागतः कर्म्मदृक्च विगतपापदृष्टिकश्च सर्व्वशाक्यविषये चैको राजा पूजितो मानितः श्रेष्ठी गृहपत्यमात्यपारिषद्यानां प्रासादिको दर्शनीयो नातिवृद्धो नातितरुणोऽतिरूपः सर्व्वगुणोपेतः शिल्पज्ञः कालज्ञ आत्मज्ञो धर्म्मज्ञः सत्त्वज्ञो लोकज्ञो लक्षणज्ञो धर्म्मराजो धर्म्मानुशास्ता अवरोपितकुशलमूलानाञ्च सत्त्वानां कपिलवस्तुमहानगरनिलयः। येऽपि तत्रोपपन्नास्तेऽपि तत्स्वभावा एव राज्ञश्च शुद्धोदनस्य मायादेवी सुप्रबुद्धस्य शाक्याधिपतेर्दुहिता नवतरुणी रूपयौवनसम्पन्ना अप्रसूता अपगतपुत्रदुहितृका सुरूपा सलेख्यविचित्रेव दर्शनीया देवकन्येव सर्व्वाल-

शृङ्गारभूषिता अपगतमद्यपानदोषा सत्यवादिन्यकर्कशा अप-
रुषा अचपलाऽनवद्या कोकिलस्वरा अप्रलापिनी मधुरप्रिय-
वादिनी व्यपगताखिलक्रोधमदमानदर्पप्रतिघा अनीर्षुका
कालवादिनी त्यागसम्पन्ना शीलवती पतिसन्तुष्टा पतिव्रता
परपुरुषचिन्तामनस्कारापगता समसंहतशिरःकर्णनासा भ्रम-
रवरसदृशकेशी सुललाटी सुभ्रूर्व्यपगतभ्रुकुटिका स्मितमुखी
पूर्व्वाभिलाषिणी श्लक्ष्णमधुरवचना प्रदक्षिणग्राहिणी ऋज्वी
अकुटिला अशठाऽमायाविन्यपुण्यार्थसम्पन्नाऽचपलाऽचप-
लाऽमुखरा अविकीर्णवचना मन्दरागद्वेषमोहक्षान्तिसौर-
भ्यसम्पन्ना करचरणनयनस्वारचितशुद्धि १ मृदुतरुणहस्तपादा
काकचिह्निकसुखसंस्पर्शा नवनलिनेन्दीवरपत्रसुविशुद्धनयना
रक्तोत्तुङ्गनासा सुप्रतिष्ठिताङ्गी सेन्द्रायुधमिव यष्टिः सुविनीता
सुविभक्तान्तप्रत्यङ्गाऽनिन्दिताङ्गी बिम्बोष्ठी चारुदर्शना अनु-
पूर्व्वग्रीवा स्वलङ्कृता सुमना वार्षिकी सुविशुद्धदर्शना सुविनी-
तांशा अनुपूर्व्वसुजातबाहुसमापोदरी अनुपहतपार्श्वा गम्भीर-
नाभिमण्डला वृत्तसुविस्तीर्णश्लक्ष्णकठिनकटिर्वज्रसंहननकल्प-
वृत्तभगाचा गजभुजसमसमाचितवृत्तोरू ऐणेयमृगसदृश-
पाणिपादा अगति नयनातिरम्या अप्रतिहतचक्षुरिन्द्रिया
मनापप्रियदर्शना २ क्षीरजरूपप्रतिविशिष्टा मायानिर्मितमिव
बिम्बं मायानामसङ्कथिता कलाविचक्षणा नन्दन इवापरः

---

१ स्वचितहस्तिरित्यन्योपा। २ मनसा आप्यते प्राप्यत इति मनापं मनोज्ञमित्यर्थः।
शान्तस्याद्वन्द्वाश्रयणात् सन्धिः छिन्नाति बहुतरैतादृशप्रयोगदर्शनादित्यनुमीयते।
इदमपचे यच्छोधितं तदनेन प्रत्याख्यातम्।

प्रकाशा शुद्धोदनस्य महाराजस्यान्तःपुरमध्यगता सा प्रतिरूपा बोधिसत्त्वस्य जननी। या सेयं कुलपरिशुद्धिर्बोधिसत्त्वेनोदाहृता सा शाक्यकुल एव दृश्यते। तत्रेदमुच्यते॥

प्रासादिधर्म्मोच्चयशुद्धसत्त्वः सुधर्म्मसिंहासनसन्निषण्णः।
सभागदेवैः परिवारितो ऋषिः सम्बोधिसत्त्वेभि १ र्महायशोभिः॥
तत्रोपविष्टस्य अभूद्धि चिन्ता कतमत्कुलं शुद्धसुसत्त्वजाकं।
यद्बोधिसत्त्वप्रतिरूपजन्म माता पिता कुत्र च शुद्धभावा॥
व्यवलोकयन्तः खलु जम्बुषाण्डं यः क्षत्रियो राजकुले महात्मा।
सर्व्वान् सदोषाननुचिन्तयन्तः शाक्यं कुलञ्चाद्दृशु २ र्वीतदोषं॥
शुद्धोदनो राजकुले कुलीनो नरेन्द्रवंशः सुविशुद्धगात्रः।
ऋद्धश्च स्फीतश्च निराकुलश्च सगौरवं सज्जनधार्म्मिकश्च॥
अन्येऽपि सत्त्वाः कपिलाह्वये पुरे सर्व्वे सुशुद्धाशयधर्म्मयुक्ताः।
उद्यानआरामविहारमण्डिता ३ कपिलाह्वये शोभति ४ जन्मभूमिः॥
सर्व्वे महानग्नबलैरुपेता विस्तीर्णहस्ता नवरत्नवन्तः।
इष्वस्त्रविद्यासु च पारगामिनो न चापरं हंसि ५ स्वजीवितार्थम्॥
शुद्धोदनस्य प्रमदा प्रधाना नारीसहस्रेषु हि साग्रप्राप्ता।
मनोरमा मायकृतेव ६ बिम्बं नामेन ७ सा उच्यति ८ मायादेवी॥
सुरूपरूपा अथ देवकन्या सुविभक्तगात्रा शुभनिर्मलाङ्गी।
नसोऽस्ति देवो न च मानुषो वा यो माय ९ दृष्ट्वाथ लभेत तृप्तिम्॥
न रागरक्ता न च दोषदुष्टा श्लक्ष्णा मृदू सा ऋजुस्निग्धवाक्या।

१ अत्र तृतीयाबहुवचने एकारस्तु वैदिकरीत्या। २ अद्राक्षुरिति सं। ३ अथा-सन्धिरार्षः। ४ शोभते इति सं। ५ घ्नन्तीति सं। ६ मायाजालमिव इति सं। ७ मालेति सं। ८ उच्यते इति सं। ९ मायां दृष्ट्वा इति सं।

अकर्कशा चापलता च सौम्या स्मितामुखा१ सा भ्रुकुटीप्रहीणा ॥
ह्रीशा व्यपत्रापिणी धर्म्मचारिणी निर्माणमानाश्च २ अचञ्चला च।
अनीर्षुका चाप्यशठा अमाया त्यागानुरक्ता सदमैत्रचित्ता ॥
कर्म्मेषु च मिथ्यप्रयोगहीना ३ सत्ये स्थिता कायमनःसुसंवृता।
स्त्रीदोषजालं भुवि यत्प्रभूतं सर्व्वं ततोऽस्याः ४ खलु नैव विद्यते ॥
न विद्यते कन्या मनुष्यलोके गन्धर्वलोकेऽथ च देवलोके।
मायायदेवीये समाज्ञतावरी प्रतिरूप ५ सा वै जननी महर्षेः ॥
जातीशतां पञ्च मनूनकारि सा बोधिसत्त्वस्य बभूव माता।
पिता च शुद्धोदन तत्र तत्र६ प्रतिरूप७ तस्याज्जननी गुणान्विता ॥
व्रते स्थिता तिष्ठति तापसीव व्रतानुचारी ८ सह धर्मचारिणी।
राज्ञाभ्यनुज्ञातवरप्रलब्धा द्वात्रिंश मासा ९ न काम सेवति१०॥
यत्र प्रदेशेऽस्थिहते निषीदते शय्यागता चङ्क्रमणस्य तस्याः।
आभाषितो भाति सदेवभासो आभाये ११ तस्याः
शुभकर्म्मनिष्ठया: १२ ॥
न सोऽस्ति देवासुरमानुषो वा यो रागचित्तेन समर्थ१३ प्रेक्षितुम्।
पश्यन्ति माता दुहिताश्च १४ सर्व्वे दृव्यांपयेष्वार्य्यगुणोपपेता: ॥
मायायदेव्या: १५ शुभकर्म्महेतुना विवर्द्धते राजकुलं विशालम्।
प्रदेशराज्ञामपि चापचारो विवर्द्धते कीर्त्तियशस्य पार्थिवे ॥

---

१ स्मितमुखी इति पं। २ निर्मांना चञ्चला इति पं। ३ मिथ्याप्रयोगहीनेति पं।
४ तस्मान्नमस्या इति युक्तम्। ५ मायाख्यदेव्या समोन्नतावरा प्रतिरूपा इति पं।
६ शुद्धोदनश्चेति पं। ७ प्रतिरूपा इति पं। ८ व्रतानुचारिणी। ९ द्वात्रिंश-न्मासान्। १० कामं सेवते। ११ चाभयेति पं। १२ शुभकर्मनिष्ठायाः। १३ समर्थः।
१४ दुहितरश्चेति पं। १५ मायाख्यदेव्याः।

यथा च मायाप्रतिरूपभाजनं यथार्थवस्त्र: परमं विराजते।
पश्येत १ एका अधिकं गुणान्विता ह्यान्विता सा
जननी च माया॥
जम्बुध्वजेऽन्या न हि सास्ति नारी या स्यात् समर्था
धरितुं २ नरोत्तमं।
अन्यत्र देव्याऽतिगुणान्वितायाः ह्यनागबलप्रबलं हि यस्याः॥
एवं हि ते देवसुता महात्मा ३ सम्बोधिसत्त्वाश्च विशालप्रज्ञाः।
वर्णन्ति ४ मायां जननीं गुणान्वितां प्रतिरूप-
५ शाक्यकुलनन्दनस्येति॥
इति श्रीललितविस्तरे कुलपरिशुद्धिपरिवर्त्तो नाम तृतीयः
सर्गः॥

चतुर्थसर्गप्रारम्भः।

इति हि भिक्षवो बोधिसत्त्वो जम्बुकुलं व्यवलोक्य उच्चध्वजं नाम तुषितालये महाविमानं चतुःषष्टियोजनायामविस्तारेण यस्मिन्बोधिसत्त्वः संनिषद्य तुषितेभ्यो देवेभ्यो धर्मं देशयति स्म तं महाविमानं बोधिसत्त्वोऽभिरोहति स्म। अभिरुह्य सर्व्वान्भूषितकायिकान्देवपुत्रानामन्त्रयते स्म। सन्निपतन्तु भवन्तश्च्युत्याकारप्रयोगं नाम धर्म्मानुस्मृतेर्व्वानुशासनं पश्चिमबोधिसत्त्वस्यान्तिकाद्धर्म्मश्रवणं श्रोष्यथेतीदं खल्वपि वचनं श्रुत्वा सर्व्वे भूषितकायिका देवपुत्राः साप्सरोगणास्तस्मिन्

१ दृश्यते। २ धारयितुमिति सं। ३ महाबलाः। ४ वर्णयन्तीति सं। ५ प्रतिरूपेति सं।
६ सगणपरिवारसमेति।

विमाने सन्निपतन्ति स्म । तत्र बोधिसत्त्वश्चतुर्महाद्वीपके लोकधातुविस्तरप्रमाणो मण्डलमात्राधिष्ठितोऽभूत् । तावच्चित्रस्तावद्दर्शनीयस्तावत्स्वलङ्कृतस्तावत्सुरुचिरो यावत्सर्व्वे कामावचरा देवा रूपावचराश्च देवपुत्राः स्वेषु स्वेषु भवनव्यूहेषु श्मशानसञ्ज्ञामुत्पादयामासुः । तत्र बोधिसत्त्वः स्वपुण्यविपाकनिष्यन्दपरिमण्डिते सिंहासने निषीदति स्म । अनेकमणिरत्नपादप्रत्युप्ते अनेकपुष्पसंस्तरसंस्तृते अनेकदिव्यगन्धवासोपवासिते अनेकसारवरगन्धनिर्धूपिते अनेकवर्णदिव्यपुष्पगन्धसंस्तरसंस्तृते अनेकमणिरत्नशतसहस्रप्रभोज्ज्वलिततेजसि अनेकमणिरत्नजालसञ्छन्ने अनेककिङ्किणीजालसमीरिताभिनादिते अनेकरत्नघण्टाशतसहस्ररणितनिर्घोषे अनेकरत्नजालशतसहस्रपरिस्फुटे अनेकरत्नगणशतसहस्रसञ्छादिते अनेकपट्टशतसहस्रातिप्रलम्बिते अनेकपट्टदामशतसहस्रसमलङ्कृते अनेकाप्सरःशतसहस्रनृत्यगीतवादित्रपरिगीते अनेकगुणशतसहस्रवर्णिते अनेकलोकपालशतसहस्रानुपालिते अनेकशतसहस्रनमस्कृते अनेकब्रह्मशतसहस्रप्रणते अनेकबोधिसत्त्वशतसहस्रपरिगृहीते दशदिगनेकबुद्धकोटीनियुतशतसहस्रसमन्वाहृते अपरिमितकल्पकोटीनियुतशतसहस्रपारमितासम्भारपुण्यविपाकनिष्यन्दसमुद्गते ॥ इति हि भिक्षव एवङ्गुणसमन्वागते सिंहासने निषद्य बोधिसत्त्वस्तां महतीं देवपर्षदमामन्त्रयते स्म । व्यवलोकयत मार्षा बोधिसत्त्वस्य कायं शतपुण्यलक्षणसमलङ्कृतं । व्यवलोकयत पूर्व्वदक्षिणपश्चिमोत्तरास्वध ऊर्द्धं समन्ताद्दशदिक्षु अप्रमे-

यासङ्ख्यागणनासमतिक्रान्तान् बोधिसत्त्वान् ये तुषितवरभवनस्थाः सर्व्वे चरमभवाभिमुखा देवगणपरिवृताः च्यवनकालं देवतासंहर्षणं धर्म्मालोकमुखं सम्प्रकाशयतोऽद्राक्षुः। सा सर्व्वा देवपर्षद् बोधिसत्त्वाधिष्ठानेन तान् बोधिसत्त्वान् दृष्ट्वा पुनर्येन बोधिसत्त्वस्तेनाञ्जलिं प्रणम्य पञ्चमण्डलैर्नमस्यन्ति स्म। एवं चोदानमुदानयन्ति स्म ॥ साध्वचिन्त्यमिदं बोधिसत्त्वाधिष्ठानं यत्र हि नाम वयं व्यवलोकितमात्रेणैतो बोधिसत्त्वान् पश्याम इति ॥

अथ बोधिसत्त्वः पुनरपि तावत्तीन्देवपर्षदमामन्त्र्यैवमाह। तेन हि मार्षाः शृणुत च्युत्याकारं देवतासंहर्षणं धर्म्मालोकमुखं यदेते बोधिसत्त्वा एभ्यो देवपुत्रेभ्यो भाषन्ते अष्टोत्तरमिदं मार्षा धर्म्मा लोकमुखं शतं। यदवश्यं बोधिसत्त्वेन च्यवनकालसमये देवपर्षदि सम्प्रकाशितम् ॥ कतमत्तदष्टोत्तरशतं। यदुत श्रद्धा मार्षा धर्म्मालोकमुखमभेद्याशयतायै संवर्त्तते। प्रसादो धर्म्मालोकमुखमाविलचित्तप्रसादनतायै संवर्त्तते। प्रामोद्यं धर्म्मालोकमुखं प्रश्रब्धै संवर्त्तते। प्रीतिधर्म्मालोकमुखं चित्तविशुद्धै संवर्त्तते। कायसंवरो धर्म्मालोकमुखं त्रिकायपरिशुद्धै संवर्त्तते। वाक्संवरो धर्म्मालोकमुखं चतुर्व्वाग्दोषपरिवर्जनतायै संवर्त्तते। मनःसंवरो धर्म्मालोकमुखमभिघातव्यापादमिथ्यादृष्टिप्रहाणाय संवर्त्तते। बुद्धानुस्मृतिधर्म्मालोकमुखं दर्शनविशुद्धै संवर्त्तते। धर्म्मानुस्मृतिधर्म्मालोकमुखं धर्म्मदेशनाविशुद्धै संवर्त्तते। सङ्घानुस्मृतिधर्म्मा-

लोकमुखं न्यायावक्रमणतायै संवर्त्तते। त्यागानुस्मृतिधर्म्मालोक-
मुखं सर्व्वोपाधिप्रतिनिःसर्गायै संवर्त्तते। शीलानुस्मृतिधर्म्मालो-
कमुखं प्रणिधानपरिपूर्य्यै संवर्त्तते। देवतानुस्मृतिधर्म्मालोक-
मुखमुदारचित्ततायै संवर्त्तते। मैत्रीधर्म्मालोकमुखं सर्व्वोपा-
धिकपुण्यक्रियावस्त्वभिभावनतायै संवर्त्तते। करुणा धर्म्मालोकमु-
खमविहिंसायै संवर्त्तते। मुदिताधर्म्मालोकमुखं सर्व्वारत्यपकर्षणतायै
संवर्त्तते। उपेक्षाधर्म्मालोकमुखं कामजुगुप्सनतायै संवर्त्तते। अनि-
त्यप्रत्यवेक्षाधर्म्मालोकमुखं कामरूप्यारूप्यरागसमतिक्रमाय संव-
र्त्तते। दुःखप्रत्यवेक्षाधर्म्मालोकमुखं प्रणिधानसमुच्छेदनाय संव-
र्त्तते। अनात्मप्रत्यवेक्षा धर्म्मालोकमुखमात्माऽनभिनिवेशनतायै
संवर्त्तते। शान्तप्रत्यवेक्षा धर्म्मालोकमुखमनुनयासनूक्षणतायै संव-
र्त्तते। ह्रीधर्म्मालोकमुखमध्यात्मोपशमाय संवर्त्तते। अपत्राप्य-
धर्म्मालोकमुखं वहिःप्रशमाय संवर्त्तते। सत्यं धर्म्मालोकमुखं देव-
मनुष्याविसंवादनतायै संवर्त्तते। भूतं धर्म्मालोकमुखमात्मावि-
संवादनतायै संवर्त्तते। धर्म्मचरणं धर्म्मालोकमुखं धर्म्मप्रतिशरण-
तायै संवर्त्तते। त्रिशरणगमनं धर्म्मालोकमुखं त्र्यपायसमतिक्रमाय
संवर्त्तते। कृतज्ञता धर्म्मालोकमुखं कृतकुशलमूलाविप्रणाशाय
संवर्त्तते। कृतवेदिता धर्म्मालोकमुखं पराभिमन्यतायै संवर्त्तते।
आत्मज्ञता धर्म्मालोकमुखमात्मानुकर्षणतायै संवर्त्तते। सत्त्व-
ज्ञानता धर्म्मालोकमुखं परापत्समतायै संवर्त्तते। धर्म्मज्ञता
धर्म्मालोकमुखं धर्म्मानुधर्म्मप्रतिपत्त्यै संवर्त्तते। कालज्ञता धर्म्मा-
लोकमुखममोघदर्शनतायै संवर्त्तते। निहतमानता धर्म्मालोकमुखं

ज्ञागताप्रतिपूर्य्यै संवर्त्तते । अप्रतिहतचित्तता धर्म्मालोकमुख-
मात्मपरानुरक्षणतायै संवर्त्तते। अनुपनाहो धर्म्मालोकमुखम-
कौकृत्याय संवर्त्तते। अधिमुक्तिर्धर्म्मालोकमुखमविचिकित्सापरमतायै
संवर्त्तते । अशुभप्रत्यवेक्षा धर्म्मालोकमुखं कामवितर्कप्रहाणाय
संवर्त्तते । अव्यापादो धर्म्मालोकमुखं व्यापादवितर्कप्रहाणाय
संवर्त्तते। अमोहो धर्म्मालोकमुखं सर्व्वाज्ञानविधमनतायै संव-
र्त्तते। धर्म्मार्थिकता धर्म्मालोकमुखमर्थप्रतिशरणतायै संवर्त्तते।
धर्म्मकामता धर्म्मालोकमुखं लोकप्रतिलम्भाय संवर्त्तते । श्रुतपर्य्ये-
ष्टिधर्म्मालोकमुखं योनिशोधनधर्म्मप्रत्यवेक्षणतायै संवर्त्तते । सम्य-
क्प्रयोगो धर्म्मालोकमुखं सम्यक्प्रतिपत्त्यै संवर्त्तते। नामरूपपरि
ज्ञानं धर्म्मालोकमुखं सर्व्वसङ्गसमतिक्रमाय संवर्त्तते। हेतुदृष्टिस-
मुद्घाटो धर्म्मालोकमुखं विद्याधिमुक्तिप्रतिलम्भाय संवर्त्तते। अनु-
नयप्रतिघप्रहाणं धर्म्मालोकमुखमनुत्पन्नतानामनवतायै संवर्त्तते।
स्कन्धकौशल्यं धर्म्मालोकमुखं दुःखपरिज्ञानतायै संवर्त्तते। धातु-
समता धर्म्मालोकमुखसमुदयप्रहाणाय संवर्त्तते। आयतनापकर्ष-
णधर्म्मालोकमुखं मार्गभावनतायै संवर्त्तते । अनुत्पादक्षान्तिध-
र्म्मालोकमुखं निरोधसाक्षात्क्रियायै संवर्त्तते । कायगतस्मृति-
धर्म्मालोकमुखं साक्षात्क्रियायै संवर्त्तते । कायगतस्मृतिधर्म्मा-
लोकमुखं कायविवेकतायै संवर्त्तते । वेदनागतानुस्मृतिधर्म्मा-
लोकमुखं सर्व्ववेदितप्रतिप्रश्रब्ध्यै संवर्त्तते। चित्तगतानुस्मृतिधर्म्मा-
लोकमुखं मायोपचितप्रत्यवेक्षणतायै संवर्त्तते । धर्म्मागतानु-
स्मृतिधर्म्मालोकमुखं वितिमिरज्ञानतायै संवर्त्तते। चत्वारि सम्य-

क्प्रहाणानि धर्म्मालोकमुखं सर्व्वाकुशलधर्म्मप्रहाणाय सर्व्वकुशल-
प्रतिपूर्त्यै संवर्त्तते। चत्वारो ऋद्धिपादा धर्म्मालोकमुखं काय-
चित्तलघुत्वाय संवर्त्तते। श्रद्धेन्द्रियधर्म्मालोकमुखमपरप्रणेयतायै
संवर्त्तते। वीर्य्येन्द्रियधर्म्मालोकमुखं सुविचिन्तितज्ञानतायै
संवर्त्तते। स्मृतीन्द्रियं धर्म्मालोकमुखं सुकृतकर्म्मतायै संवर्त्तते।
समाधीन्द्रियं धर्म्मालोकमुखं चित्तविमुक्त्यै संवर्त्तते। प्रज्ञेन्द्रियं
धर्म्मालोकमुखं प्रत्यवेक्षणज्ञानतायै संवर्त्तते। श्रद्धाबलं धर्म्मा-
लोकमुखं मारबलसमतिक्रमाय संवर्त्तते। वीर्य्यबलं धर्म्मालोक-
मुखमवैवर्त्तिकतायै संवर्त्तते। स्मृतिबलं धर्म्मालोकमुखं असं-
हार्य्यतायै संवर्त्तते। समाधिबलं धर्म्मालोकमुखं सर्व्ववितर्क-
प्रहाणाय संवर्त्तते। प्रज्ञाबलं धर्म्मालोकमुखमनवमृद्यतायै
संवर्त्तते। स्मृतिसम्बोध्यङ्गं धर्म्मालोकमुखं यथावद्धर्म्मप्रजानतायै
* संवर्त्तते। धर्म्मप्रविचयसम्बोध्यङ्गं धर्म्मालोकमुखं सर्व्वधर्म्मप्रति-
पूर्त्यै संवर्त्तते। वीर्य्यसम्बोध्यङ्गं धर्म्मालोकमुखं सुविचितबुद्धि-
तायै संवर्त्तते। प्रीतिसम्बोध्यङ्गं धर्म्मालोकमुखं समाध्यायिकतायै
संवर्त्तते। प्रश्रब्धिसम्बोध्यङ्गं धर्म्मालोकमुखं कृतकरणीयतायै
संवर्त्तते। समाधिसम्बोध्यङ्गं धर्म्मालोकमुखं समतानुरोधाय
संवर्त्तते। उपेक्षासम्बोध्यङ्गं धर्म्मालोकमुखं सर्व्वोपपत्तिजुगुप्स-
नतायै संवर्त्तते। सम्यग्दृष्टिधर्म्मालोकमुखं न्यायावक्रमणतायै
संवर्त्तते। सम्यक्सङ्कल्पो धर्म्मालोकमुखं सर्व्वकल्पविकल्पपरि-
कल्पप्रहाणाय † संवर्त्तते। सम्यग्वाग्धर्म्मालोकमुखं सर्व्वाक्षर-

---

* प्रज्ञानतायै इत्यर्थः। † अत्र परिकल्परहितोऽपि पाठः।

रुतघोषवाक्पथप्रतिश्रुतसमतानुबोधनतायै संवर्त्तते। सम्यक्क-र्म्मान्तो धर्म्मालोकमुखं स्वकर्म्मविपाकतायै संवर्त्तते। सम्यगाजीवो धर्म्मालोकमुखं सर्व्वैषणाप्रतिप्रश्रब्ध्यै संवर्त्तते। सम्यग्व्यायामो धर्म्मालोकमुखं परतीरगमनाय संवर्त्तते। सम्यक्स्मृतिधर्म्मा-लोकमुखमस्मृत्यमानसिकतायै संवर्त्तते। सम्यक्सम-माधिधर्म्मालोकमुखमकोप्यचेतःसमाधिप्रतिलम्भाय संवर्त्तते। बोधिचित्तधर्म्मालोकमुखं त्रिवंशानुपच्छेदाय संवर्त्तते। आशयो धर्म्मालोकमुखं हीनयानास्पृहणतायै संवर्त्तते। अध्याशयोग धर्म्मालोकमुखमुदारबुद्धधर्म्मावलम्बनतायै संवर्त्तते। प्रयोगो धर्म्मालोकमुखं सर्व्वकुशलधर्म्मपरिपूर्य्यै संवर्त्तते। दानपारमिता-धर्म्मालोकमुखं लक्षणानुव्यञ्जनबुद्धक्षेत्रपरिशुद्ध्यै मत्सरिसत्त्व-परिपाचनतायै संवर्त्तते। शीलपारमिता धर्म्मालोकमुखं सर्व्वा-क्षणापायसमतिक्रमाय दुःशीलसत्त्वपरिपाचनतायै संवर्त्तते। क्षान्तिपारमिताधर्म्मालोकमुखं सर्व्वव्यापादखिलदोषमानम-दर्पप्रहाणाय व्यापन्नचित्तसत्त्वपरिपाचनतायै संवर्त्तते। वीर्य्य-पारमिता धर्म्मालोकमुखं सर्व्वकुशलमूलधर्म्मालोकमुखोत्तार-णाय कुशीदसत्त्वपरिपाचनतायै संवर्त्तते। ध्यानपारमिताधर्म्मा-लोकमुखं सर्व्वज्ञानाभिज्ञोत्पादाय विक्षिप्तचित्तसत्त्वपरिपाच-नतायै संवर्त्तते। प्रज्ञापारमिता धर्म्मालोकमुखमविद्यामोह-तमोऽन्धकारोपलम्भदृष्टिप्रहाणाय दुष्प्रज्ञसत्त्वपरिपाचनतायै संवर्त्तते। उपायकौशलं धर्म्मालोकमुखं यथाधिमुक्तसत्त्वोपायपथ-सन्दर्शनाय सर्व्वबुद्धधर्म्माविधमनतायै संवर्त्तते। चत्वारि सङ्ग्रह-

वस्तूनि धर्म्मालोकमुखं सत्त्वसङ्ग्रहाय सम्बोधिप्राप्तस्य धर्म्मसम्प्रत्य-
वेक्षणतायै संवर्त्तते। सत्त्वपरिपाको धर्म्मालोकमुखमनात्मसुखा-
नध्यवसानाय परिखेदतायै संवर्त्तते। सद्धर्म्मपरिग्रहो धर्म्मालो-
कमुखं सर्व्वसत्त्वसङ्क्लेशप्रहाणाय संवर्त्तते। पुण्यसम्भारो धर्म्मा-
लोकमुखं सर्व्वसत्त्वोपजीव्यतायै संवर्त्तते। ज्ञानसम्भारो धर्म्मा-
लोकमुखं दशबलप्रतिपूर्य्यै संवर्त्तते। शमथसम्भारो धर्म्मालोकमुखं
तथागतसमाधिप्रतिलम्भाय संवर्त्तते। विदर्शनासम्भारो धर्म्मा-
लोकमुखं प्रज्ञाचक्षुःप्रतिलम्भाय संवर्त्तते। प्रतिसंविदवतारो
धर्म्मालोकमुखं धर्म्मचक्षुःप्रतिलम्भाय संवर्त्तते। प्रतिशरणाव-
तारो धर्म्मालोकमुखं बुद्धचक्षुःपरिशुद्ध्यै संवर्त्तते। धारणी-
प्रतिलम्भो धर्म्मालोकमुखं सर्व्वबुद्धभाषिताधारणतायै संवर्त्तते।
प्रतिभानप्रतिलम्भो धर्म्मालोकमुखं सर्व्वसत्त्वसुभाषितसन्तोषणायै
संवर्त्तते। आनुलोमिकधर्म्मक्षान्तिधर्म्मालोकमुखं सर्व्वबुद्ध-
धर्म्मानुलोमनतायै संवर्त्तते। अनुत्पत्तिकधर्म्मक्षान्तिधर्म्मालोक-
मुखं व्याकरणप्रतिलम्भाय संवर्त्तते। अवैवर्त्तिकधर्म्मालोकमुखं
सर्व्वबुद्धधर्म्मप्रतिपूर्य्यै संवर्त्तते। भूमेर्भूमिसङ्क्रान्तिज्ञानं धर्म्मा-
लोकमुखं धर्म्मज्ञानाभिषेकतायै संवर्त्तते। अभिषेकभूमिधर्म्मा-
लोकमुखमवक्रमणजन्माभिनिष्क्रमणदुष्करचर्य्याबोधिमण्डलो-
पसङ्क्रमणमारध्वंसनबोधिविबोधनधर्म्मचक्रप्रवर्त्तनमहापरिनि-
र्व्वाणसन्दर्शनतायै संवर्त्तते। इदं तन्मार्षा अष्टोत्तरं धर्म्मालोक-
मुखं शतं यदवश्यं बोधिसत्त्वेन च्यवनकालसमये देवपर्षदि
सम्प्रकाशितम्॥

अस्मिन् खलु पुनर्भिक्षवो धर्म्मालोकमुखपरिवर्त्ते बोधिसत्त्वेन निर्द्दिश्यमाने तस्यां देवपर्षदि चतुरशीतिदेवपुत्रसहस्राणामनुत्तरायां सम्यक्सम्बोधौ चित्तान्युत्पन्नान्ते स्म ॥

द्वात्रिंशतश्च देवपुत्रसहस्राणां पूर्व्वपरिकर्म्मकृतानामनुत्पत्तिकेषु धर्म्मेषु क्षान्तिप्रतिलम्भोऽभूत् षट्त्रिंशतश्च देवपुत्राणां देवनयुतानां विरजो विगतमलं धर्म्मेषु धर्म्मचक्षुर्विशुद्धं सर्व्वञ्च तुषितवरभवनं जानुमात्रं दिव्यैः पुष्पैः सञ्छादितमभूत् ॥

इति हि भिक्षवो बोधिसत्त्वः तस्या देवपर्षदो भूयस्या मात्रया संहर्षणार्थं तस्यां वेलायामिमां गाथामभाषत ॥

तुषितवरभवननिलयाद्यदा च्यवति नायकः पुरुषसिंहः ।
आमन्त्रयते देवान् प्रमादमखिलं विसर्जयत ॥
या काचिद्रतिर्य्युष्मा * दिव्या मनसा विचिन्तिता श्रीमन् ।
सर्व्वशुभकर्म्महेतोः फलमिदं शृणुतास्य कर्म्मस्य † ॥
तस्माद् भवत कृतज्ञा अपूर्व्वशुभसञ्चयं चपिलेह ।
मा गच्छत पुनरपायामसाध्यासुखवेदना यत्र ॥
धर्म्मश्च यःश्रुतोऽयं ममान्तिके गौरवमुपजनित्वा ।
तत्र प्रतिपद्य प्राप्स्यथ नियतं सुखमनन्तम् ॥
सर्व्वे अनित्या अकामा अध्रुवा न च शाश्वताऽपि न कल्पाः
मायामरीचिसदृशाः विद्युत्फेनोपमाश्चपलाः ॥
न च कामगुणरतिभिस्तृप्तिर्लवणोदकं यथा पीत्वा ॥

---

* रतिर्युष्माकमिति शुद्धं ॥ † कर्मण इत्यर्थः ॥

ते हन्तयेष (१) प्रज्ञा आर्य्या लोकोत्तरा विरजा ।
न तरन्तुतुल्यकल्पा सप्रीतिस्थापरेभिः संवासः ॥
अन्योन्यगमनयुक्तो यथैव सामायिकामस्य ।
न च लभते सहाया न मित्रज्ञातिजनो नपरिवाराः ॥
अन्यच कर्म्म (२) सुकृतादनुबध्नाति पृष्ठतो याति ।
तस्मात्सहित (३) समग्रा अन्योन्यं मैत्रचित्तहितचित्ताः ॥
धर्म्माचरणं चरेथाः (४) सुचरितचरणा (५) न तप्यन्ते हि ।
बुद्धमनुस्मरेथा (६) धर्म्मसङ्घं तथाऽप्रमादं च ॥
श्रुतशीलदाननिरता चान्त्या सौरभ्यसम्पन्नाः (७) ।
दुःखमनित्यमनात्म निरीक्षथ (८) येऽभिन्नो (९) इमं धर्म्मं ॥
हेतुप्रत्ययप्रयुक्तं वर्त्तन्तेऽस्वामिका जडसुखा ।
यां काञ्चिदृद्धिं मह्यं (१०) पश्यत प्रभाश्च ज्ञानगुणताश्च ॥
सर्व्वां शुभकर्म्महेतोः शीलेन श्रुतेन चाप्रमादेन ।
अनुशिक्ष्यध्वं मह्यं (११) शीले श्रुतेन चाप्रमादेन ॥
दानयमसंयमेन सत्त्वार्थं हितार्थं मित्रार्थं (१२) ।
न च वाक्यरुतरवेण शक्याः सम्पादितुं कुशलधर्म्माः ॥
प्रतिपत्तिमारभेथा यथा च वदथा तथाकरोथा (१३) ।
मा खलु परावकाशं स्वयं यतध्वं सदा प्रयत्नेन ॥
न च कश्चिद्दत्ता ददते (१४) न चाप्यदत्ता भवति सिद्धिः ।

---

१ हस्तये एषा इत्यर्थः सन्धिरार्षः। २ कर्म्मण इत्यर्थः। ३ सहिता इत्यर्थः। ४ चरतेत्यर्थः। ५ सुचरिताचरणा इत्यर्थः। ६ अनुस्मरतेत्यर्थः। ७ क्षान्तिसौरभ्यसम्पन्ना इत्यर्थः। ८ निरीक्षतेत्यर्थः। ९ यमभिज्ञमित्यर्थः। १० ऋद्धिं ममेत्यर्थः ११ अनुशिक्षध्वं मामित्यर्थः। १२ सत्त्वार्थं हितार्थं मित्रार्थमित्यर्थः। १३ आरभत वदत कुरुतेत्यर्थः। १४ ददातीत्यर्थः।

G

समनुस्मरथा (१) पूर्व्वं यद्दुःखं संसारे चिरमनुभूतम् ॥
न च निर्वृतिर्विरागो समनुगतो मिथ्या नियतमेव ।
तस्मात्क्षणं लभित्वा (२) मित्रप्रतिरूपदेशवासञ्च ॥
श्रेष्ठञ्च धर्मश्रवणं शमेथ (३) रागादिकान् क्लेशान् ।
मानमददर्पविगताः सदार्जवाऽमन्दवाचश्च ॥
अशठाश्च निर्व्वाणगतिपरायणा युञ्जत मार्गाभिसमयाय ।
मोहकलुषान्धकारं प्रज्ञाप्रदीपेन विधमथा (४) सर्व्वम् ॥
मानुशयदोषजालं विदारयत ज्ञानवज्रेण ।
किमति सुबहु वदेयं धर्म्मं (५) युष्माकमर्थयुक्तम् ॥
न च तत्रावतिष्ठेथा यत्र धर्म्मस्यापराधः ।
बोधिर्यथा प्राप्यः स्याद्धर्म्मश्च प्रवर्षयताम्लतगामि (६) ॥
पुनरपि विशुद्धचित्ता उपसेवत वरधर्म्मश्रवणायेति ।
इति श्री ललितविस्तरे धर्म्मालोकमुखपरिवर्त्तो नाम चतुर्थः ॥

पञ्चमाध्यायप्रारम्भः ॥

इति हि भिक्षवो बोधिसत्त्वस्तां महतीन्देवपर्षदमनया धर्म्यया गाथया सन्दर्श्य समादाप्य समुत्तेज्य सम्प्रहर्ष्य क्षमापयित्वा मङ्गल्यान्देवपर्षदमामन्त्रयते स्म ॥ गमिष्यामहं मार्षा जम्बुद्वीपं । मया पूर्व्वं बोधिसत्त्वचर्य्यां चरता सत्त्वाश्चतुर्भिः सङ्ग्रहवस्तुभिर्निमन्त्रिताः । दानेन प्रियवचनेनार्थक्रियया

१ समनुस्मरतेत्यर्थः । २ लब्ध्वा इत्यर्थः । ३ शमयतेत्यर्थः । ४ विधमतेत्यर्थः । ५ धर्म्ममित्यर्थः ।
६ मृतगामिनमित्यर्थः ।

समानार्थतया च। तदयुक्तमेतन्मार्षा मम भवेदकृतज्ञता च यदहमनुत्तरायां सम्यक्सम्बोधौ नाभिसम्बुद्धेयम्॥

अथ ते तुषितकायिका देवपुत्रा रुदन्तो बोधिसत्त्वस्य चरणौ परिगृह्यैवमाहुः। इदं खलु सत्पुरुषतुषितवरभवनं त्वया विहीनं न भ्राजिष्यते। अथ बोधिसत्त्वस्तां महतीं देवपर्षदमेवमाह। अयं मैत्रेयो बोधिसत्त्वो युष्माकं धर्मं देशयिष्यति। अथ बोधिसत्त्वो मैत्रेयं बोधिसत्त्वं यौवराज्ये प्रतिष्ठाप्य स्वकाच्छिरसः पट्टमौलं चावतार्य्य मैत्रेयस्य बोधिसत्त्वस्य शिरसि प्रतिष्ठापयामास॥ एवं चात्रोचत्। समानन्तरेण त्वं सत्पुरुषानुत्तरां सम्यक् सम्बोधिमभिसम्भोत्स्यसे।

अथ बोधिसत्त्वो मैत्रेयं बोधिसत्त्वं तुषितभवनेऽभिनिषद्य पुनरपि तां महतीं देवपर्षदमामन्त्रयति स्म॥ कीदृशेनाहं मार्षा रूपेण मातुःकुक्षाववक्रामेयं। तत्र केचिदाहुर्मार्षा मानवरूपेण। केचिदाहुः शक्ररूपेण। केचिदाहुर्ब्रह्मरूपेण। केचिदाहुर्महाराजिकरूपेण। केचिदाहुर्वैश्रवणरूपेण। केचिदाहुर्गन्धर्व्वरूपेण। केचिदाहुः किन्नररूपेण। केचिदाहुर्महोरगरूपेण। केचिदाहुर्महेश्वररूपेण। केचिदाहुश्चन्द्ररूपेण। केचिदाहुः सूर्य्यरूपेण। केचिदाहुर्गरुडरूपेण॥ तत्रोग्रतेजा नाम ब्रह्मकायिको देवपुत्रः पूर्व्वर्षिजन्मच्युतोऽवैवर्त्तिकोऽनुत्तरायाः सम्यक् सम्बोधेः स एवमाह। यथा ब्राह्मणानां मन्त्रवेदशास्त्रपाठेष्वागच्छति तादृशेनैव रूपेण बोधिसत्त्व मातुः कुक्षावक्रामितव्यम्। तत्पुनः कीदृशः। गजवरमहाप्रमाणः षड्-

हस्तो हेमजालसञ्छन्नः सुरुचिरः सुरक्तशीर्षः स्फुटितगलित-
रूपवान् श्रीमान् । एतच्छ्रुत्वा रूपं ब्राह्मणवेदशास्त्रतत्त्वज्ञो
व्याकर्षितस्ताय भाविद्वात्रिंशल्लक्षणोपेतः ॥

इति हि भिक्षवो बोधिसत्त्वो जन्मकालमवलोक्य तुषितवरभवनस्थः एवं राज्ञः शुद्धोदनस्य गृहवरेऽष्टौ पूर्व्वनिमित्तान्युपदर्शयति स्म। कतमान्यष्टौ। तद्यथा। व्यपगततृणखरेणुकण्टकशर्कराकाठिन्यं निर्म्मलं सुसिक्तं सुशोभित(१)मनाकुलवातं तमोरजोविगतं दंशमशकमक्षिकापतङ्गसरीसृपापगतमवकीर्णकुसुमं समं पाणितलजातं तद्गृहं संस्थितमभूदिदं प्रथमं पूर्व्वनिमित्तं प्रादुरभूत् ॥

ये च हिमवत्पर्व्वतराजनिवासिनः पत्रगुप्तशुकशारिकाकोकिलहंसक्रौञ्चमयूरचक्रवाककुणालकलविङ्कजीवञ्जीवकादयो विचित्ररुचिरपक्षा मनोज्ञप्रियभाषिणः शकुनिगणास्ते आगत्य राज्ञः शुद्धोदनस्य गृहवरे वितर्द्दिनिर्य्यूहतोरणगवाक्षहर्म्यकूटागारप्रासादतलेषु स्थित्वा प्रमुदिताः प्रीतिसौमनस्यजाताः स्वकस्वकानि रुतान्युदाहरन्ति स्म। इति द्वितीयं पूर्व्वनिमित्तं प्रादुरभूत् ॥

ये च राज्ञः शुद्धोदनस्यारामरमणीयेषु चोद्यानरमणीयेषु नानापुष्पफलवृक्षा नानर्तुकालिकास्ते सर्व्वे पुष्पिताः सङ्कुसुमिता अभूवन्निदं तृतीयं पूर्व्वनिमित्तं प्रादुरभूत् ॥

याश्च राज्ञः शुद्धोदनस्य पुष्करिण्यो जलपरिभोग्य-

---

१ सुशोधितमिति वा।

जाताः सर्व्वाः शकटचक्रप्रमाणैरनेककोटीनियुतशतसहस्रपत्रैः
पद्मैः सञ्छादिता अभूवन्निदं चतुर्थं पूर्व्वनिमित्तं प्रादुरभूत् ॥

ये च राज्ञः शुद्धोदनस्य गृहवरे भोजनविषयाः सर्पिस्तैल-
मधुफाणितशर्कराद्या नाना ते परिभुज्यमानाः क्षयं न
गच्छन्ति स्म परिपूर्णा एव सन्दृश्यन्ते स्म । इदं पञ्चमं पूर्व्वनि-
मित्तं प्रादुरभूत् ॥

ये च राज्ञः शुद्धोदनस्य गृहवरप्रधाने महत्यन्तःपुरे
भेरीमृदङ्गपणवतुणववीणावेणुवल्लकीसम्पताडप्रभृतयस्तूर्य्यभा-
ण्डास्ते सर्व्वे स्वयमेवाघट्टिता एव मनोज्ञशब्दं प्रमुञ्चन्ति स्म ।
इदं षष्ठं पूर्व्वनिमित्तं प्रादुरभूत् ॥

यानि च राज्ञः शुद्धोदनस्य गृहवरप्रधाने सुवर्णरूप्यमणि-
मुक्तावैदूर्य्यशङ्खशिलाप्रवालादीनां रत्नानां भाजनानि तानि
सर्व्वाणि निरवशेषं विवृतविमलविशुद्धप्रतिपूर्णान्येवं विरोचन्ते
स्म । इदं सप्तमं पूर्व्वनिमित्तं प्रादुरभूत् ॥

विमलविशुद्धया चन्द्रसूर्य्यजिह्मीकरणया प्रभया काय-
चित्तोद्बिल्यसञ्जनन्या तद्गृहं समन्तादवभासितमभूदिदमष्टमं
पूर्व्वनिमित्तं प्रादुरभूत् ॥

मायादेवी स्नाताऽनुलिप्तगात्रा विविधाभरणविष्कम्भितभुजा
सुश्लक्ष्णसुनीलवस्त्रवरधारिणी प्रीतिप्रामोद्यप्रसादप्रतिलब्धा
सार्द्धं दशभिः स्त्रीसहस्रैः परिवृता पुरस्कृता राज्ञः शुद्धोदनस्य
सङ्गीतिप्रासादे सुखोपविष्टस्यान्तिकमुपसङ्क्रम्य दक्षिणे पार्श्वे
रत्नजालप्रत्युप्ते भद्रासने निषद्य स्मितमुखी व्यपगतभृकुटिका

प्रहसितवदना राजानं शुद्धोदनमाभिर्गाथाभिरभाषत ॥

साधो शृणुष्व मम पार्थिव धर्म्मपाल याचामि (१) ते (२) नृपतेऽद्य वरं प्रयच्छ ।

अभिप्रायमप्यथ चित्तमनःप्रहर्षं तन्मे शृणुष्व भव प्रीतमना उदग्रः ॥

गृह्णामि देवव्रतशीलवरोपवासमष्टाङ्गपोषधमहं जगति मैत्र-चित्ता ।

प्राणेषु हिंसविरता (३) सदा शुद्धभावा प्रेमं (४) यथात्मनि परेषु तथा करोमि ॥

स्तैण्या विवर्जितमनाः मदलोभहीना कामेषु मिथ्या नृपते न समाचरिष्ये ।

सत्ये स्थिता अपिशुना परुषप्रहीणा सम्भिप्रलापमशुभं न समाचरिष्ये ॥

व्यापाददोषखिलमोहमदप्रहीणा सर्व्वा अविद्यविगता (५) स्वधनेन तुष्टा ।

सम्यक्प्रयुक्ता अकुशानिलया अनीर्ष्या कर्म्म यथा दश इमे कुशला (६) चरिष्ये ॥

मा त्वं नरेन्द्र मयि कामरुषां (७) कुरुष्व शीलव्रतेष्वभिरता यशः संवृता च ।

---

१ याचे इति शुद्धम् । २ तंत्वत इत्यर्थः पञ्चम्यर्थे षष्ठी बोध्या । ३ प्राणिषु हिंसाविरता इति शु० । ४ प्रेम इति शु० । ५ सर्व्वाविद्याविगतेति शु० । ६ कर्म्माणि यथा दश इमानि कुशलमेति शु० । ७ कामरूपामिति शु० ।

मा ते अपुण्य (१) नृपते भवि(२)दीर्घरात्रमनुमोदय हि मम शीलव्रतोपवासम् ॥

छन्दो ममैष नृपते प्रविशाद्य शीघ्रं प्रासादहर्म्यशिखरे स्थित-धार्त्तराष्ट्रे ।

सखीभिः सदा परिवृता सुखं मोदयेयं पुष्पाभिकीर्णशयने मृदुके सुगन्धे ॥

न च काञ्चुकीयपुरुषा न विदारकाश्च न च प्राकृततमाः पुरतोऽस्ति (३) देयाः ।

नो वाऽमनाप मम रूप (४) न शब्दगन्धाश्चान्यत्र दृष्टमधुरा-च्छृणुयां सुशब्दान् ॥

ये रोधबन्धनगताः परिमुञ्च सर्व्वान् द्रविणाम्बरांश्च पुरुषान्ध-निनः कुरुष्व ।

वस्त्रान्नपान रथयुग्म (५) तथाश्वयानं दद सप्तरात्रिकमिदं जगतः सुखार्थम् ॥

नो चेद्विवादकलहा न च रोषवाक्याश्चान्योन्यमैत्रमनसो हित-सौम्यचित्ताः ॥

अस्मिन् पुरे पुरुषेष्टिकदारकाश्च देवाश्च नन्दनगताः सहिता रमन्ताम् ।

न च राजदण्डभटा न तथा कुदण्डा नोत्पीडना नापि च तर्जनताडना वा ॥

---

१ अपुण्यमिति पा०। २ भावीति पा०। ३ सन्तीति पा०। ४अमनापं अमरूपमिति पा०। ५ वस्त्रान्नपानं रथयुग्ममित्यर्थः ।

सर्व्वान् प्रसन्नमनसो हितमैत्रचित्तान् वीतस्य इव जगतां यथ एक पुत्रम् (१) ।

श्रुत्वैव राजवचनं परमं उदग्रं प्राहास्तु सर्व्वमिदमेव (२) यथा तवेच्छा ॥

अभियाच (३) तुभ्यं (४) अनुचिन्तितानि यथा याचसे तव वरं तदहं ददामि ।

आज्ञाप्य पार्थिववरः स्वकपारिषद्यान् प्रासादश्रेष्ठशिखरे प्रकरोथ (५) ऋद्धिम् ॥

पुष्पाभिकीर्णरुचिरां वरधूपगन्धां छत्रापताक (६) समलङ्कृत तालपङ्क्तिम् ।

विंशत्सहस्ररणशौण्ड विचित्रवर्म्मा (७) नाराचशूलशरशक्तिगृहीतखड्गाः ॥

परिवारयाथ (८) धृतराष्ट्रमनोज्ञघोषं देव्या भयार्थं (९) करुणाश्रित (१०) रक्षमाणाः ।

स्त्रीभिस्तु सा परिवृता यथ (११) देवकन्या स्नातानुलिप्तप्रवराम्बरभूषिताङ्गी ॥

तूर्य्यैः सहस्रसमनुगीतमनोज्ञघोषैरारुह्य देव्युपविशेष मरुत्स्तुतेव ।

दिव्यैर्महार्घसुविचित्रितरत्नपादे आस्तीर्ण (१२) पुष्पविविधैः शयने मनोज्ञे ॥

---

१ यथा एकपुत्रमिति पा०। २ सर्व्वमिदमेवमिति पा०। ३अभियाचस्वेति पा०। ४तुभ्यमिति तवेति षष्ठ्यर्थे चतुर्थीयत्नेन सर्व्वत्र। ५ प्राकरोदथेति पा०। ६ छत्रपताका इति पा०। ७ रणशौण्डा विचित्रवर्म्माण इति पा०। ८परिवारयतेति पा०। ९ देव्याः अभयार्थमिति पा० अभिप्रायः। १०करुणामाश्रिता इत्यर्थः।११यथा इति पा०। १२आस्तीर्णे इति पा०।

शयने स्थिता विगलिता मणिरत्नचूडा यथ मिश्रकावन-
गता (१) खलु देवकन्या ।

अथ खलु भिचवश्चत्वारो महाराजानः शक्रश्च देवानामिन्द्रः सुयामश्च देवपुत्रः सन्तुषितश्च सुनिर्म्मितश्च परनिर्म्मितवशवर्त्ती च सार्थवाहश्च मारपुत्रो ब्रह्मा च सहपतिर्ब्रह्मोत्तरश्च पुरोहितः सुब्रह्मा च पुरोहितः प्रभाव्यूहाभास्वरश्च महेश्वरश्च शुद्धावासकायिका निष्ठागताश्चैकनिष्ठश्च एतानि चान्यानि चानेकानि देवशतसहस्राणि सन्निपत्याऽन्योन्यमेवमाहुः । अशुक्रमेतन्मार्षा अस्माकं स्यादकृतज्ञता चादयमेकाकिनमद्वितीयं बोधिसत्त्वमुत्सृजेम । कोऽस्माकं मार्षा उत्सहते बोधिसत्त्वं सततशमितमनुबद्धुमवक्रमणगर्भस्थानजन्मयौवनभूमिदारकक्रीडान्तःपुरनाटकसन्दर्शनाभिनिष्क्रमणदुष्करचर्य्याबोधिमण्डलोपसङ्क्रमणमारधर्षणबोध्यभिसम्बोधनधर्म्मचक्रप्रवर्त्तनं । यावन्महापरिनिर्वाणाद्धितचित्ततया स्निग्धचित्ततया प्रियचित्ततया मैत्रचित्ततया सौम्यचित्ततया तस्यां वेलायामिमां गाथामभाषन्त ॥

को वोत्सहेत वररूपधरं अनुबन्धयितुं सततं प्रीतिमनाः ।
कः पुण्यतेज(२)यशसा वचसा स्वयमात्मनेच्छति विवर्द्धयितुं(३ ॥
यस्येप्सितं त्रिदशदेवपुरे दिव्यैः सुखैर्हि रमितुं (४) सततं ।
परमाप्सरोभिरिह कामगुणैरनुवर्द्धितुं (५) विमलचन्द्रमुखं ॥

---

१ यथा मिश्रकवनगता इत्यर्थः । २ पुण्यतेजसमिति बोध्यं । ३ विवर्द्धुमिति बोध्यं । ४ रन्तुमिति सर्व्वत्र बोध्यं । ५ अनुवर्द्धुमिति बोध्यं ।

H

तच(१) मिश्रके वनवरे रुचिरे दिव्याकरे रमितुं (२) देवपुरे ।
पुष्पोत्करे कनकचूर्णनिभे अनुबन्धत विमलतेजधरं (३) ॥
यथेप्सितं रमितुं चित्ररथे तच (४) नन्दने सुरवधूसहितः ।
मान्दारवैः (५) कुसुमपचचिते अनुबन्धतामिमं महापुरुषं ॥
याम्याधिपत्यमथ वा तुषितैरथ वाऽपि प्रार्थयत चेश्वरतां ।
पूजा रहो भवितुं (६) सर्व्वजगे (७) अनुबन्धत इममनन्तयशं (८)॥
यो इच्छति (९) निर्म्मितपुरे रुचिरे वशवर्त्तिदेवभवने रमितुं ।
मनसैव सर्व्वमनुभूतक्रियमनुबन्धतु इमं गुणाग्रधरं ॥
महेश्वरो न च प्रदुष्टमनाः सर्व्वविद्याश्रुतिपारगतः ।
कामेश्वरो वशितपारगतो (१०) गच्छत्यसौ हितकरेण सह ॥
तच(११)कामधातु(१२)समतिक्रमितुं मतिर्य्यस्य ब्रह्मपुरमावसितुं।
चतुरप्रमाणतेजधरः (१३) सोऽद्यानुबद्धयितुं (१४) महापुरुषः॥
अथवाऽपि यस्य मनुजेषु मतिर्वरचक्रवर्त्तिविषये विपुले ।
रत्नाकरमभयसौख्यप्रदमनुबन्धत विपुलपुण्यधरं ॥
पृथिवीश्वरस्तथापि श्रेष्ठसुतो आढ्यो महाधनमहानिचयः ।
परिवारवान्निहतप्रचुगणो गच्छत्यसौ हितकरेण सह॥
रूपञ्च भोग अपि(१५)चेश्वरता कीर्त्तिर्यशश्च बलवता गुणवता(१६)।
आदेयवाक्यैर्भुवि याच्यरतं ब्रह्मेश्वरं समुपयात विदुम् (१७) ॥

---

१ तथा इति मु०। २ रन्तुमिति मु०। ३ विमलतेजोधरमिति मु०। ४ तथा इति मु०। ५ मान्दारकैरित्यनुमीयते। ६ रहसिपूजाभवनार्थमित्यर्थः। ७ सर्व्वजगति इत्यर्थः। ८ चनन्तयशसमितिबोध्यं। ९ य इच्छति इत्यर्थः। १० वशितापारगत इत्यर्थः। ११ तथा इत्यर्थः। १२ कामधातुमित्यर्थः। १३ चतुःप्रमाणतेजोधरमित्यर्थः। १४ चनुबद्धुं योग्य इत्यर्थः। १५ भोगोऽपि। १६ बलवता गुणवतेत्यर्थः। १७ याच्यं रतमित्यर्थः।

ये दिव्यकाम तथ (१) मानुषकीय इच्छति (२) त्रिभुवि
सर्व्वसुखं ।

ध्याने सुखस्य प्रविवेकसुखं धर्म्मेश्वरं समनुबन्धयतां (३) ॥

रागप्रहाण तथ दोषमपि यो इच्छते तथ क्लिशेब्रजहं (४) ।

शान्तं प्रशान्तमुपशान्तमनघं दान्तचित्तमनुयातु लघुम् ॥

शिक्षाय शिक्ष तथ (५) प्रत्येकजिनान् सर्व्वज्ञज्ञानमनुपूरयितुं ।

दशभिर्बलैर्गदितुं सिंह इव गुणसागरं समनुयाचत विदुं ॥

प्रथितुं अपायपथं (६) यथामतिर्विंष्टतुस्य पञ्चतिपथं स्मृतं ।

अष्टाङ्गमार्गगमनेन गतिं अनुबन्धत गतिपथान्तकरम् ॥

यो (७) इच्छति सुगत (८) पूजयितुं धर्म्मस्य तेषु श्रुति
कारुणिके (९) ।

प्राप्तुञ्चुणानपि च सङ्गतान् गुणसागरं समनुयातु इमं ॥

जातिजरामरणदुःखक्षयं संसारबन्धनं विमोक्षयितुं ।

चरितुं विशुद्धगगनान्तसमं तं शुद्धसत्त्वमनुबन्धयत ॥

इतो मनापप्रिय सर्व्वजगे (१०) वरलक्षणगुणोपचितं ।

आत्मा(११)परस्य तथ (१२) मोचयितुं प्रियदर्शनं समुपयात
विदुं ॥

शीलसमाधि तथ प्रज्ञमयं (१३) गम्भीरदुर्दर्शदुरुपगमं ।

---

१ दिव्यंकामं तथा इत्यर्थः । २ मानुषीयमिच्छन्तीत्यर्थः । ३ समनुबध्नयतामित्यर्थः ।
४ रागप्रहाणं तथा दोषप्रहाणं य इच्छति तथाक्लेशजयमित्यर्थः । ५ शिक्षितुं तथा
इत्यर्थः । ६ अपायपथमित्यर्थः । ७ य इत्यर्थः । ८ सुगतमित्यर्थः । ९ तस्य श्रुति
कारुणिकमिल्येवमुचितमितिभाति । १० मनापप्रियं सर्व्वजगतीत्यर्थः । ११ आत्मा-
नमित्यर्थः १२ तथा इत्यर्थः । १३ शीलसमाधिमयं तथा प्रज्ञामयमित्यर्थः ।

यो इच्छते(१)विदु विमुक्तिलभे(२)सो(३)वैद्यराजमनुयातु लघुं ॥
एते च अन्य गुण(४)नैकविधा उपपत्तिसौख्य तथ(५)निर्वृतये ।
सर्व्वैर्गुणेभिः प्रतिपूर्ण (६) सिद्धये शुद्धसत्वं समनुयात विदुमिति॥

इदं खलु वचनं श्रुत्वा चतुरशीतिसहस्राणि चातुर्महाराजिकानां देवानां शतसहस्रत्रयस्त्रिंशानां शतसहस्रं यामानां शतसहस्रं तुषितानां शतसहस्रं निर्म्माणरतानां शतसहस्रं परनिर्म्मितवशवर्त्तिनां देवानां षष्टिसहस्राणि मारकायिकानां पूर्व्वशुभकर्म्मनिर्य्यातानां अष्टषष्टिसहस्राणि ब्रह्मकायिकानां बहूनि शतसहस्राणि यावदकनिष्ठानां देवानां सन्निपतितान्यभूवन् । अन्ये च भूयः पूर्व्वदक्षिणपश्चिमोत्तराभ्यो दिग्भ्यो बहूनि देवशतसहस्राणि सन्निपतितान्यभूवन् । तेभ्यो ये उदारतमा देवपुत्रास्तेतामहतीं देवपर्षदङ्गाथाभिरभ्यभाषन्त ॥

हन्त शृणोथ (७) वचनं अमरेश्वराहो (८) अस्मिन् द्विधा अपि च याद्दृशसत्वभूताः ।
त्यक्त्वार्थकामरति ध्यानसुखं प्रणीतं (९) अनुबन्धयाम इममुत्तम (१०) शुद्धसत्वम् ॥
आक्रान्तपाद (११) तथ गर्भस्थितं महात्मं पूजारथं अतियशमभिपूजयाम ।

---

१ य इच्छति । २ विमुक्तिलाभायेत्यर्थः । ३ स इत्यर्थः । ४ अन्ये गुणा इत्यर्थः । ५ उपपत्तिसौख्याय तथा इत्यर्थः । ६ गुणैः परिपूर्णमित्यर्थः । ७ शृणुतेत्यर्थः । ८ अमरेश्वरा अहो इत्यर्थः सम्बोधनार्थः । ९ अर्थकामरतिं ध्यानसुखं प्रणीयेत्युचितम् । १० उत्तममित्यर्थः । ११ आक्रान्तपादं तथा महात्मानं पूजार्हं अतियशसमित्यर्थः ।

पुष्पैः सुरचितमृषिं परिरक्षयन्तं यस्यावतारलभेन (१) न मनः प्रहर्षं ॥

सङ्गीतितूर्य्यरचितैश्च सुवाद्यैश्च वर्णान् गुणान् कथयतो (२) गुणसागरस्य ।

कुर्व्वाम देवमनुजान् प्रहर्षणीयान् यच्छ्रुत्वा बोधिवरचित्ते न जनेष्वनेर्ष्या ॥

पुष्पाभिकीर्ण (३) नृपतेश्च करोम (४) गेहं कालागुरूत्तमसुधूपितसौम्यगन्धं ।

यं घ्रात्वा देवमनुजाश्च भवन्त्युदग्रा (५) विगतज्वराश्च सुखिनश्च भवन्त्यरोगाः (६) ॥

मान्दारवै(७)श्च कुसुमैस्तथ पारिजातैश्चन्द्रैः सुचन्द्रतथ (८) स्फारविरोचमानैः ।

पुष्पाभिकीर्ण (९) कपिलाह्वयं करोम (१०) पूजार्थं पूर्व्वशुभकर्म्मसमुद्गतस्य ॥

यावच्च गर्भ(११)वसते विमलैरलिप्तो यावज्जरामरण(१२)चान्तकरः प्रसूतः (१३) ।

तावत्प्रसन्नमनसो अनुबन्धयाम एषा मतिर्मतिधरस्य करोम (१४) पूजां ।

---

१ लाभेनेत्यर्थः । २ कथयन्त इत्यर्थः । ३ पुष्पाभिकीर्णमित्यर्थः । ४ करिष्याम इत्यर्थः । ५ भविष्यन्तीत्यर्थः । ६ भविष्यन्तीत्यर्थः । ७ मान्दारवैरित्यनुमीयते । ८ सुचन्द्रैस्तथा इत्यर्थः । ९ पुष्पैरभिकीर्णमित्युचितं । १० करिष्याम इत्यर्थः । ११ गर्भे इत्यर्थः । १२ जरामरणस्येत्यर्थः । १३ प्रसविष्यति इत्यर्थः । १४ करिष्याम इत्यर्थः ।

लाभाः सुलब्धविपुलाः सुरमानुषाणां द्रक्ष्यन्ति ये इमु (१)
सप्तपदाक्रमन्तम् ।
ब्रह्मैश्च शक्रनिकरैः परिगृह्यमाणं गन्धोदकैः स्नपयमान (२)
सुशुद्धसत्त्वं ॥
यावच्च लोक अनुवर्त्तनतां करोति अन्तःपुरे वसति कामक्लिशे-
प्रघाती (३) ।
यावच्च निष्क्रमति राज्यमपास्य सर्व्वं तावत्प्रसन्नमनसो अनु-
बन्धयाम ॥
यावदुपैति महिमण्डि(४)ह्रयं गृहीत्वा यावच्च बोधिं स्पृशते
विनिहत्य मारं ।
अध्येष्टु ब्राह्मणयुतेभि (५) प्रवर्त्ति चक्रं तावत्करोम (६) विपुलां
सुगतस्य पूजां ॥
यो बुद्धकार्य्यकृते नेष्यति चित्रहस्तसत्त्वान् कोटीनियुतानस्तेते
विनीतान् ।
निर्वाणमार्गमुपयास्यति शान्तिभावं तावन्महाशयचरितं न
जहाम सर्व्वे इति ॥

अथ भिक्षवः कामधात्वीश्वरीणां देवकन्यानां बोधिसत्त्वस्य रूपकायपरिनिष्पत्तिं दृष्ट्वा एतदभवत् । कीदृशी त्वेषा कन्या भविष्यति या इमं वरप्रवरशुद्धसत्त्वं धारयिष्यति । ताः कौतूहलजाता वरप्रवरपुष्पधूपदीपगन्धमाल्यविलेपनचूर्णचीवरपरि-

१ इममित्यर्थः । २ स्नापयमानमित्यर्थः । ३ कामक्लेशघाती इत्यर्थः । ४ मण्डो-
मण्डले इत्यर्थः । ५ अध्येष्टुं ब्राह्मणयुतैः प्रवर्त्तते इत्यर्थः । ६ करिष्याम इत्यर्थः
एवमन्यत्र वर्त्तमानप्रयोगे भविष्यत् प्रयोगः ।

गृहीता दिव्यमनोमयात्मभावप्रतिलब्धाः पुण्यविपाकाधिष्ठाना-धिष्ठितास्तस्मिन् क्षणेऽमरपुरभवनादन्तर्हिताः कपिलाह्वये महापुरवर उद्यानशतसहस्रप्रतिमण्डिते राज्ञः शुद्धोदनस्य गृहे धृतराष्ट्रे महाप्रासादे अमलप्रतिभवनप्रकाशे विगलिताम्बर-धारिण्यः शुभविमलतेजःप्रतिमण्डिता दिव्याभरणस्तम्भितभुजाः शयनवरगतां मायादेवीमेकाङ्गुलिकयोपदर्शयन्त्यो गगनतल-गताः परस्परं गाथाभिरभ्यभाषन्त ॥

अमर पुरगतान (१) अप्सराणां (२) रूपमनोरम (३) दृष्ट्वा बोधिसत्त्वे।

मतिरियमभवत् तदा हि तासां प्रमद(४)नु कीदृश(५) बोधि-सत्त्वमाता ॥

ताश्च सहितपुष्पमाल्यहस्ता (६) उपगमि(७)वेश्म (८) नृपस्य जातकाङ्क्षाः।

पुष्पं तथ(९)विलेपनं गृहीला दशनखकाञ्जलिभिर्नमस्यमानाः॥

विगलितवसनाः सलीलरूपाः करतल (१०) दक्षिण अङ्गु-लिम्प्रणाम्य (११)।

शयनगत विदर्श (१२) मायादेवीं साधु निरीक्षय रूपमा-नुषीणां (१३) ॥

---

१ अमरपुरगतानामित्यर्थः। २ अप्सरसामित्यर्थः। ३ रूपमनोरमं मनो-रमरूपमिति यावत् आहितादित्वात् पूर्व्वनिपातः एवं सर्व्वत्रैताहशस्थले बोध्यम्। ४ प्रमदा इत्यर्थः। ५ कीदृशी इत्यर्थः। ६ सपुष्पमाल्यहस्ता इत्यर्थः। ७ उपा-गमन्नित्यर्थः। ८ वेश्मनि इत्यर्थः। ९ तथा इत्यर्थः। १० करतलेनेत्यर्थः। ११ प्रणम्येत्यर्थः। १२ शयनगतां विदर्शेत्यर्थः। १३ निरीक्षत रूपं मानुषं इत्यर्थः।

वयमिह अभिमन्यथा (१) आत्मा परममनोरमस्वरूपमप्स-
राणां (२) ।
इमां नृपतिवधूं निरीक्षमाणा जिह्मि विपश्यत (३) दिव्यआत्म-
भावान् ॥
रतिरिव सदृशी गुणान्विता च जननिरियं प्रवराग्रपुङ्गलस्य ।
मणिरतन (४) यथा सुभाजनस्थं तथ (५) इव भाजन (६)
देवदेवदेवे (७) ॥
करचरणतलेभि (८) यावदूर्द्धं अङ्गमनोरमदिव्यअतिरेकं ।
प्रेक्षितु(९)नयनान्न चास्ति तृप्ति भूयःप्रहर्षति चित्तमानसस्य ॥
शशिरिव गगने विराजतेऽस्या वदनवरस्य विराजति गात्र-
भासा (१०) ।
रविरिव विमला शशीव दीप्ता तथ प्रभनिश्चरतेस्य (११) आत्म-
भावात् ।
कनकमिव सुधातु जात रूपो वर्ण विरोचति देवियै तथैव(१२)॥
भ्रमरवरनिकाशकुन्तलानि मृदुकसुगन्धअवास्यमूर्द्धजानि ।
कमलदलनिभे तथास्य नेत्रे दशनविशुद्धनभेव ज्योतिषा (१३) ॥
चाप इव तनूदरी विशाला पार्श्वसमुद्गता नास्ति (१४) सन्धिः ।

---

१ अभिमन्यामहे इत्यर्थः । २ आत्मनपरममनोरमरूपमप्सरसामित्यर्थः । ३ यथा विपश्यन्ति तथा पश्यन्तित्यर्थः । ४ मणिरत्नमित्यर्थः । ५ तथा इत्यर्थः । ६ भाजन-मित्यर्थः । ७ स्थबे इति शेषमापूर्य्य देवदेवगेष इत्युचितं स्तृतीयदेवशब्दस्तु छन्दोऽनु-रोधेन इति बोध्यं । ८ करचरणतलादारभ्येत्यर्थः । ९ दृष्ट्वा नयनानां न चास्ति तृप्तिरित्यर्थः । १० विराजते इत्यर्थः । ११ तथा प्रभा निश्चरतेऽस्या इत्यर्थः । १२ जातरूपवर्णं विरोचति देव्यास्तथैवेत्यर्थः । १३ तथास्या नेत्रे दशनानि विशुद्ध-नभ इव ज्योतींषि इत्यर्थः । १४ पार्श्वसमुद्गतसन्धीत्यर्थः ।

गजभुजगद्रुमोरुजङ्घा सुजान्वनुपूर्व्वसमुद्गताङ्गाः ॥

करतलचरणं समं सुरक्तं व्यक्तमिदं खलु देवकन्या गान्या ।

एवं बहुविधं निरीक्ष्य देवीं कुसुमं क्षिप्त (१) प्रदक्षिणञ्च कृत्वा ॥

सुप्रियवसतिं जिनस्य माता पुनरपि देवपुरं गता क्षणेन ।

अथ चतुरि (२) चतुर्दिशासु पालाः शक्र सुयाम (३) तथैव निर्म्मितिः ॥

देवगणाः कुम्भाण्डराक्षसासुरमहोरगकिन्नराश्च अवोचन् ॥

गच्छत पुरतो नरोत्तमस्य पुरुषवरस्य करोथ (४) रक्षगुप्तिं ।

मा कुरुत जगे(५)मनःप्रदोषं मा च करोथ विहेठ(६)मानुषाणां ॥

यत्र गृहवरेऽस्ति मायादेवी तत्र समय सपारिषद्य (७) सर्व्वे ।

असिधनुःशरशक्तिखड्गहस्ता गगनतलस्थिता निरीक्षयत ॥

श्रुत्व च्यवनकाल देवपुत्रा उपगमि मायसकाश (८) हृष्टचित्ताः ।

पुष्प तथ (९) विलेपनं गृहीत्वा दशनखमञ्जलिभि (१०) र्नमस्यमानाः ॥

च्यव च्यव हि नरेन्द्र शुद्धसत्त्व अयं समयो भवनोऽद्य वादिसिंह ।

कृप करुण जनित्व (११) सर्व्वलोके अस्मिन्नध्येष धर्म्मदानहेतो रिति ॥

अथ खलु भिक्षवो बोधिसत्त्वस्य च्यवनकालसमये पूर्व्वस्यां

---

१ क्षिप्त्वेत्यर्थः । २ चत्वार इत्यर्थः । ३ शक्रः सुयमा इत्यर्थः । ४ सर्व्वदा च करोथेत्यस्य स्थाने कुरुतेति बोध्यम् । ५ जगतीति सप्तम्यर्थः । ६ विहेठामित्यर्थः । ७ समयाः सपारिषद्या इत्यर्थः । ८ श्रुत्वा च्यवनकालमुपागमन्मायासकाशमित्यर्थः । ९ पुष्पन्तथा इत्यर्थः । १० दशनखकाञ्जलिभिरित्यर्थः । ११ कृपां करुणां जनित्वा चाध्येषेत्यर्थः ।

दिशि बहूनि बोधिसत्त्वशतसहस्राणि सर्व्वे एकजातिप्रतिबद्धाः तुषितपुरवरभवनवासिनो येन बोधिसत्त्वस्तेनोपासङ्क्रामन्तो बोधिसत्त्वस्य पूजाकर्म्मणे चातुर्महाराजकायिकेभ्यो देवेभ्यश्चतुरशीतिसहस्राप्सरःशतसहस्राण्येवं त्रयस्त्रिंशद्यमेभ्यः तुषितेभ्यो निर्म्माणरतिभ्यः परनिर्म्मितवशवर्त्तिभ्यो देवेभ्यश्चतुरशीत्यप्सरःशतसहस्राणि नानातुर्य्यसङ्गीतिवादितेन येन बोधिसत्त्वस्तेनोपासङ्क्रामन् ॥

अथ खलु बोधिसत्त्वः श्रीगर्भे सिंहासने सर्व्वपुण्यसमुद्गते सर्व्वदेवनागसन्दर्शने महाकूटागारे निषद्य सार्द्धन्तैर्बोधिसत्त्वैर्देवनागयक्षकोटीनियुतशतसहस्रैः परिवृतः पुरस्कृतस्तुषितवरभवनात् प्रचलति स्म। प्रचलता च भिक्षवो बोधिसत्त्वेन तथारूपा कायात् प्रभा प्रमुक्ताऽभूत्। यया प्रभयाऽयं त्रिसाहस्रमहासाहस्रो लोकधातुरेवं विपुलविस्तीर्णेन महोदारेण सुप्रचलितपूर्व्वेण दिव्यप्रभा समतिक्रान्ता तेनावभासेन परिस्फुटोऽभूत् ॥ या अपि लोकान्तरिका आघा स्फुटान्धकारा तमिस्रा यत्रेमौ चन्द्रसूर्य्यावेवं महानुभावावेवं महर्द्धिकावेवं महेशाख्यौ आभया आभां वर्णेन वर्णं तेजसा तेजो नातितपतो नाभि विलोकतः। तत्र ये सत्त्वा उपपन्नास्ते स्वकानपि बाहुप्रसारितान्न पश्यन्ति। तत्रापि तस्मिन् समये महत उदारस्यावभासस्य प्रादुर्भावोऽभूत्। ये च तत्र सत्त्वा उपपन्नास्ते तेनैवावभासेन स्फुटाः समाना अन्योन्यं सम्यक् पश्यन्ति स्म अन्योन्यं सञ्जानन्ते स्म। एवञ्चाहुः। अन्येऽपि किल भोः सत्त्वा इहोपपन्नाः किल भो इति।

अयञ्च त्रिसाहस्रमहासाहस्रो लोकधातुरयं षड्विकारमष्टादशमहानिमित्तमभूत्। अकम्पत प्राकम्पत सम्प्राकम्पत। अवेधत प्रावेधत सम्प्रावेधत। अचलत् प्राचलत् सम्प्राचलत्। अक्षुभ्यत प्राक्षुभ्यत सम्प्राक्षुभ्यत। अरणत् प्रारणत् सम्प्रारणत्। अगर्जत् प्रागर्जत् सम्प्रागर्जत्। अन्तेऽवनमति स्म। मध्ये उन्नमति स्म। मध्येऽवनमति स्म। अन्ते उन्नमति स्म। पूर्व्वस्यां दिश्यवनमति स्म। पश्चिमायां दिश्यवनमति स्म। पूर्व्वस्यां दिश्युन्नमति स्म। पश्चिमायां दिश्युन्नमति स्म। दक्षिणस्यां दिश्यवनमति स्म। उत्तरस्यां दिश्युन्नमति स्म। उत्तरस्यां दिश्यवनमति स्म। दक्षिणस्यां दिश्युन्नमति स्म। तस्मिन् समये हर्षणीयास्तोषणीयाः प्रेमणीयाः प्रसादनीया अवलोकनीयाः प्रह्लादनीया निर्वर्णनीया असेचनीया अप्रतिकूला अनुत्रासकराः शब्दाः श्रूयन्ते स्म। न च कस्यचित् सत्त्वस्य तस्मिन् क्षणे विहेठा वा त्रासो वा भयं वा स्तम्भितत्वं वाऽभूत्॥ न च भूयः सूर्य्याचन्द्रमसोर्न्न ब्रह्मशक्रलोकपालानां तस्मिन् क्षणे प्रभा प्रज्ञायते स्म। सर्व्वे नरकतिर्य्यग्योनियमलोकोपपन्नाश्च सत्त्वास्तस्मिन् क्षणे विगतदुःखा अभूवन् सर्व्वसुखसमर्पिताः। न कश्चित्सत्त्वस्य रोगो बाधते स्म द्वेषश्च मोहश्च ईर्ष्या वा मात्सर्य्यं वा मानो वा म्रक्षो वा मदो वा क्रोधो वा व्यापादो वा परिदाहो वा सर्व्वसत्त्वास्तस्मिन् क्षणे मैत्रचित्ता हितचित्ताः परस्परं मातापितृसञ्ज्ञिनोऽभूवन्। अघट्टितानि च दिव्यमानुष्यकाणि तूर्य्यकोटिनियुतशतसहस्राणि मनोज्ञघोषमुत्सृजन्ति

स्म ॥ देवकोटीनियुतशतसहस्राणि पाणिभिरंसैः शिरोभिश्च महाविमानं वहन्ति स्म ॥ तानि चाप्सरःशतसहस्राणि स्वां स्वां सङ्गीतिं सम्प्रयुज्य पुरतः पृष्ठतो वामदक्षिणे च स्थित्वा बोधिसत्त्वं सङ्गीतिरुतस्वरेणाभिस्तुवन्ति स्म ॥

पूर्व्वकर्म्मशुभसञ्चितस्य ते दीर्घरात्रकुशलोदितस्य ते ।
सत्यधर्म्मनयशोधितस्य ते पूजा अद्य विपुला प्रवर्त्तते ॥
पूर्व्वि तुभ्य बहुकल्पकोटियो दानदत्तप्रियपुत्त्रस्त्रीधराः ।
तस्य दानचरितस्य तत् फलं येन दिव्यकुसुमाः (१) प्रवर्षिताः ॥
आत्ममांस (२) तुलयित्व ते विभो क्षुत्पिपासुप्रियपक्षिकारणात् ।
तस्य दानचरितस्य तत् फलं प्रेतलोकि लभि (३) पानभोजनं ॥
पूर्व्वि तुभ्य बहुकल्पकोटियो शीलरक्षितमखण्डनव्रतं ।
तस्य शीलचरितस्य तत् फलं येन अक्षण अपाय (४) शोधिताः ॥
पूर्व्वि तुभ्य बहुकल्पकोटियो क्षान्ति भावित निदानबोधय(५) ।
तस्य क्षान्तिचरितस्य तत् फलं मैत्रचित्तभूतदेवमानुषाः (६) ॥
पूर्व्वि तुभ्य बहुकल्पकोटियो वीर्य्य(७)भावितमलीनमुत्तमं ।
तस्य वीर्य्यचरितस्य तत्फलं येन काय (८) यथ मेरु शोभते ॥
पूर्व्वि तुभ्य बहुकल्पकोटियो ध्यान ध्यापित किलेशध्यासनात्(९) ।
तस्य ध्यानचरितस्य तत्फलं येन क्लेश (१०) जगतो न बाधते ॥

---

१ पुंस्त्वमार्षत्वात् । २ आत्ममांसं तोलयित्वा इत्यर्थः । ३ प्रेतलोके लभिष्यतीत्यर्थः । ४ अक्षणा अपाया इत्यर्थः । ५ क्षान्तिर्भाविता निदानबोधायेत्यर्थः । ६ मैत्रचित्तीभूतदेवमानवा इत्यर्थः । ७ वीर्य्यमित्यर्थः । ८ कायं यथा मेरुरित्यर्थः । ९ ध्यानध्यापित क्लेशध्वंसनादित्यर्थः । १० क्लेश इत्यर्थः । ११ पूर्व्वं त्वया बहुकल्पकोटिपर्य्यन्तं ध्यानं ध्यातं क्लेशाध्यासात् तुभ्यमिति तु कृचित्त्वेत्यस्यार्थेऽपि अयद्युतमथ उभयमपि सङ्गतं भाति अर्थस्य ज्ञतेः ।

पूर्व्वि तुभ्य बहुकल्पकोटीयो प्रज्ञ भावित (१) किलेशच्छेदनी।
तस्य प्रज्ञचरितस्य (२) तत्फलं येन लाभ (३) परमा वि-
रोचते॥
मैत्रधर्म्मिककिलेशसूदना सर्व्वसत्त्वकरुणाय उद्गता (४)।
मोदप्राप्त परमा उपेक्षका ब्रह्मभूत सुगता नमोऽस्तु ते॥
प्रज्ञउल्कप्रभतेजसोद्गता (५) सर्व्वदोषतममोहशोधका (६)।
चक्षुभूत (७) त्रिसहस्रनायका मार्गदेशिक मुने नमोऽस्तु ते॥
ऋद्धिपादवरभिज्ञ कोविदा सत्यदर्शि परमार्थनिश्चित: (८)।
तीर्ण (९) तारयसि अन्यप्राणिनो दासभूत सुगता नमोऽस्तु ते॥
सर्व्वोपायवरभिज्ञ कोविदा (१०) दर्शयसि च्युतिमच्युतच्युतिं।
लोकधर्म्मभवनानुवर्त्तसे नैव लोकि (११) क्वचिदेव लिप्यसे॥
लोभदोषपरमं विचिन्तिया येषु दर्शन अवन्ध्य दृश्यते (१२)।
किं पुन: शृणुय यातिधर्म्मतां अद्य प्रीति विपुला जनिष्यति (१३)॥
जिह्म सर्व्वतुषितालये भुतो जम्बुद्वीपि पुरि यो उदागत: (१४)।
प्राणिकोटिनियुता विचिन्तिया बोधयिष्यति प्रसुप्त क्लेशता॥
चन्द्र स्फीत पुरमद्य भेष्यते (१५) देवकोटिनियुतै: समाकुलं।

---

१ प्रज्ञाभावितेत्यर्थः। २ प्रज्ञाचरितस्येत्यर्थः। ३ लाभा इत्यर्थः। ४ सर्व्वसत्त्वकरुणायै उद्गतेत्यर्थः अत्र सर्व्वत्र पादान्ते आकारः स्वल्पनर्थकः केवलं छन्दोऽनुरोधादेव दत्त एवं क्वचिदेकारैकारौ इत्यनुमीयते। ५ प्रज्ञोल्काप्रभातेजसोद्गतेत्यर्थः। ६ सर्व्वदोषतमोमोहशोधकेत्यर्थः। ७ चक्षुर्भूतेत्यर्थः। ८ ऋद्धिपादवराभिज्ञ कोविद सत्यदर्शिन्नित्यर्थः। ९ तीर्णः पूर्व्वं यथाऽन्यान् दासभूतानित्यर्थः। १० सर्व्वोपायवराभिज्ञकोविदेत्यर्थः। ११ लोकधर्म्मभवनायामनुवर्त्तसे नैव लोके इत्यर्थः। १२ लोभं दोषं विचिन्तयित्वा यस्य दर्शनं अवन्ध्येत्यर्थः। १३ शृणुयात यतिधर्म्मान् अद्य प्रीतिर्विपुला इत्यर्थः। १४ यथा भूतो जम्बुद्वीपे पुरि इत्यर्थः। १२ प्राणिकोटिनियुतान्विचिन्तयित्वा प्रसुप्तान् क्लिष्टानित्यर्थः। १५ चन्द्रं स्फीतं भविष्यते इत्यर्थः।

अप्सरोभि तुरियैर्निर्नादितं राजगेहि मधुरं शृणिष्यति (१) ॥
पुण्यतेज भरिता शुभकर्म्मा नारि सा परमरूप उपेता (२) ।
यस्य पुत्र अयमेव समृद्धिस्त्रिसहस्रलोक अभिभाति श्रियेये(३) ॥
नो भूयो पुरवरेऽस्मिन्देहिनां लोभदोषकलहा विवादता ।
सर्व्व (४) मैत्रमनसः सगौरवा भाविनो नरवरस्य तेजसा ॥
राजवंश नृपतेः प्रवर्द्धते (५) चक्रवर्त्तिकुलराजसम्भवः ।
भेष्यते कपिलाह्वयं पुरं रत्नकोष भरितं (६) सुसमृद्धं ॥
यक्षराक्षसकुम्भाण्डगुह्यका देवदानवगणाः सइन्द्रकाः (७) ।
ये स्थिता नरवरस्य रक्षकास्तेषु मोक्ष न चिरेण भेष्यति (८) ॥
पुण्युपार्जितु स्तुविन्न नायकं प्रेमगौरवमुपस्थपिस्य नः (९) ।
सर्व्वबोधि परिणामयामहे चिप्र भो यथ त्वं नरोत्तम ॥
इति श्रीललितविस्तरे प्रचलपरिवर्त्तो नाम पञ्चमः ॥

षष्ठसर्गप्रारम्भः ॥

इति हि भिक्षवः शिशिरकाले निर्गते वैशाखमासे विशाखानक्षत्रानुगते ऋतुप्रवरे वसन्तकालसमये तरुवरपत्राकीर्णे वरप्रवरपुष्पसङ्कुसुमिते शीतोष्णतमोरजोविगते मृदुशाद्वलधरणीतले सुसंस्थिते त्रिभुवनज्येष्ठो लोकमहितो

---

१ अप्सरोभिस्तुर्य्यै राजगेहे श्रोष्यतीत्यर्थः । २ पुण्यतेजसा (भरिता) परिपूर्णा शुभकर्म्मणा नारी परमरूपोपेता इत्यर्थः । ३ यस्याः श्रिये इत्यर्थः । ४ सर्व्वे इत्यर्थः । राजवंशः प्रवर्द्धिष्यते इत्यर्थः । ६ भविष्यते रत्नकोषपरिपूर्णमित्यर्थः । ७ सेन्द्रका इत्यर्थः । ८ तेषां मोक्षो भविष्यतीत्यर्थः । ९ पुण्यमुपार्जितुं स्तुत्वा उपस्थापयस्व सर्व्वबोधीम् परिणमामः क्षिप्रं यथा इत्यर्थः ।

व्यवलोक्य वसन्तकालसमये पञ्चदश्यां पूर्णिमायां पोषधपरिगृहीताया मातुः पुष्यनक्षत्रयोगे बोधिसत्त्वस्तुषितवरभवनाच्च्युत्वा स्मृतः सम्प्रजानन् पाण्डुरगजरूपो भूत्वा षड्दन्त इन्द्रगोपकशिराः सुवर्णराजीदन्तः सर्व्वाङ्गप्रत्यङ्गहीनेन्द्रियो जनन्या दक्षिणायां कुक्षाववक्रामत ॥ अवक्रान्तस्सन् दक्षिणावचरो ऽभून्न जातु वामावचरः मायादेवी सुखशयने संसुप्ता इमं स्वप्नमपश्यत् ।

हिमरजतनिभश्च षड्विषाणः सुचरण (१) चारुभुजः सुरक्तशीर्षा ।
उदरमुपगतो गजप्रधानो ललितगतिर्दृढवज्रगात्रसन्धिः ॥
न च मम सुख जातु एव रूपं (२) दृष्टमपि श्रुतं नापि चानुभूतं ।
कायसुखचित्तसौख्यभावा यथरिव (३) ध्यानसमाहिता अभूवं ॥

अथ खलु मायादेवी आभरणविगलितवसना प्रह्लादितकायचित्तप्रीतिप्रामोद्यप्रसादप्रतिलब्धा शयनवरतलादुत्थाय नारीगणपरिवृता पुरस्कृता प्रासादवरशिखरादवतीर्य्य येनाशोकवनिका तेनोपजगाम । साऽशोकवनिकायां सुखोपविष्टा राज्ञः शुद्धोदनस्य दूतं प्रेषयति स्म । आगच्छतु देवो देवी ते द्रष्टुकामेति ॥ अथ स राजा शुद्धोदनः तद्वचनं श्रुत्वा प्रहर्षितमनाः कम्पितशरीरो भद्रासनादुत्थायामात्यनैगमपारिषद्यबन्धुजनपरिवृतो येनाशोकवनिका तेनोपसङ्क्रामदुपस-

---

१ सुचरणः इति साधुः । २ सुखं जातु एव रूपमित्यर्थः । यथैवेत्यर्थः । ३ उपसङ्क्रमितुमिति योग्यम् ।

क्रान्तस्य (३) न शक्नोति स्म । अशोकवनिकायां प्रवेष्टुं गुरुतरमिवात्मानं मन्यते स्म । अशोकवनिकाद्वारस्थितो मुहूर्त्तं सञ्चिन्त्य तस्यां वेलायामिमां गाथामभाषत ॥

न स्मरि (१) रणशौण्डिमूर्द्ध्नि संस्थस्य मह्यं (२) एवं गुरु शरीरं मन्यते यादृशोऽद्य (३) ।

स्वकुलगृहमिदमद्य न प्रभामि (४) प्रवेष्टुं किमिह मम भवेद्धोः कन्नु पृच्छेय (५) वाहमिति ॥

अथ खलु शुद्धावासकायिका देवा गगनतलगता अर्द्धकायमभिनिर्म्माय राजानं शुद्धोदनं गाथयाध्यभाषत ॥

शततपगुणयुक्तस्त्रिसाहस्रलोकेषु पूज्यो मैत्रकरुणालाभी पुण्यज्ञानाभिषिक्तः ।

तुषितपुरि (६) च्यवित्वा बोधिसत्त्वो महात्मा नृपति तव सुतत्वं मायकुक्षोपपन्नः (७) ॥

दशनखतदञ्जलीनत्वा (८) स्वं शिरः कम्पयन्तो (९) नृपतिरनुप्रविष्टश्चित्रकारानुयुक्तः ।

माय तदगिरीक्ष्यमाण (१०) दर्पोपनीतां वदति कुरुमि (११) किं ते प्रिये शोभमानि ॥

देव्याह । हिमरजतनिकाशश्चन्द्रसूर्य्यातिरेकः सुचरण सुविभक्तः षड्विषाणो महात्मा ।

---

१ स्मरामीत्यर्थः । २ ममेत्यर्थः । ३ यादृशमद्येत्यर्थः । ४ प्रभवामीत्यर्थः । ५ पृच्छेयमित्यर्थः । ६ तुषितपुरादित्यर्थः । ७ नृपते तव सुतत्वं प्राप्य मायाकुक्षावुपपन्न इत्यर्थः । ८ दशनखकाञ्जलिमञ्जलमेत्यर्थः । ९ कम्पयन्नित्यर्थः । १० मायाम्तामनिरीक्षमाण इत्यर्थः । ११ करोमि इत्यर्थः ।

गजवरदृढसन्धिर्वज्रकल्पः सुरूप उदरि (१) मम प्रविष्टस्तस्य हेतुं शृणुष्व ॥

वितिमिरचिरसहस्रं पश्यमि भ्राजमानं देवनयुत देवीयस्तुवन्तो (२) प्रयानं ।

न च मम खिलदोषा (३) नैव रोषो न मोहो ध्यानसुखमहं वै (४) जानमी शान्तचित्ता ॥

साधु नृपति (५) शीघ्रं ब्राह्मणानानयास्मिन् वेदउपनिपाठाये गृहे सुविधिज्ञान् (६) ।

सुपिन मम हि येमं व्याकरी तत्त्वयुक्तं किमिद मम भवेया श्रेय (७) पापं कुलस्य ॥

वचनमिम शृणित्वा (८) पार्थिवस्तत्क्षणेन ब्राह्मण कृतवेदाना- नयच्छास्त्रपाठा (९) ।

माय पुरत स्थिता ब्राह्मणानामवोचत् सुपिन मय य दृष्टस्तस्य हेतुं शृणोथ (१०) ॥

ब्राह्मणा श्राहुः॥ ब्रूहि देवि कीदृशस्त्वया स्वप्नो दृष्टः श्रुत्वा ज्ञास्यामः ॥

देवी प्राह॥ हिमरजतनिकाशश्चन्द्रसूर्यातिरेकः सुचरण (११) सुविभक्तः षड्विषाणो महात्मा ।

---

१ उदरे इत्यर्थः। २ पश्यामि देवनयुता देव्यस्तुवन्तीत्यर्थः। ३ ममाखिलदोषा इत्यर्थः। ४ जानामीत्यर्थः। ५ नृपते इत्यर्थः। ६ वेदोपनिषत्पाठाय सुविधिज्ञानि- त्यर्थः। ७ स्वप्नं मम हि इमं व्याकुरु तत्त्वयुक्तं किमिदं मम भवेत् श्रेय इत्यर्थः। ८ वचनमिदं श्रुत्वेत्यर्थः। ९ ब्राह्मणान् शास्त्रपाठिन इत्यर्थः। १० माया पुरतः स्थित्वा मया यो दृष्टः शृणुतेत्यर्थः। ११ सुचरणः इत्यर्थः।

गजवरहृद्धसन्निभिर्वेश्मकल्पः कुक्षि उदरि (१) मम प्रविष्टस्तस्य हेतुं भणध्वं ॥

वचनमिम श्रुणित्वा ब्राह्मणा एवमाहुः प्रीति विपुल विन्दा (२) नास्ति पापं कुलस्य ।

पुत्र तव जनेषी लक्षणैर्भूषिताङ्गं राजकुलकुलीनं चक्रवर्त्तिं महात्मं (३) ॥

स च पुन विजहित्वा कामराज्यं च गेहं प्रव्रजित (४) निरपेक्षः सर्व्वलोकानुकम्पी ।

बुद्धो भवति एषो दक्षिणीयस्त्रिलोके अमृतरसवरेण तर्प्पयेत् (५) सर्व्वलोकं ॥

व्याकरित्व गिरं सौम्यां भुक्त्वा पार्थिवभोजनं ।

आच्छादनानि चोक्षृत्य प्रक्रान्ता ब्राह्मणाः पुनः (६) ॥

इति हि भिक्षवो राजा शुद्धोदनो ब्राह्मणेभ्यो लक्षणनिमित्तज्ञेभ्यः पञ्चकेभ्यः स्वप्नाध्यायीपाठकेभ्यः प्रतिश्रुत्य हृष्टतुष्टोदयात्मा प्रमुदितः प्रीतिसौमनस्यजातः तान् ब्राह्मणान् प्रभूतेन प्रणीतेन खादनीयभोजनीयास्वादनीयेन सन्तर्प्य सम्प्रवार्य्याऽऽच्छादनानि च दत्त्वा विसर्जयति स्म ॥ तस्याञ्च वेलायां कपिलवस्तुनि महानगरे चतुर्षु महानगरद्वारेषु

---

१ उदरे इत्यर्थः । २ वचनमिदं श्रुत्वा प्रीतिं विपुलां विन्देत्यर्थः । ३ पुत्रं त्वं जनिष्यसि चक्रवर्त्तिनं महात्मानमित्यर्थः । ४ पुनर्विहाय प्रव्रजिता इत्यर्थः । ५ बुद्धो भविष्यति इति बोध्यम् वर्त्तमानसामीप्ये वर्त्तमानवद्वा पाणिनीये ३ । ३ । १३१ । इति वर्त्तमानसमीपे भविष्यति वर्त्तमानवत् प्रयोगत्वात् । तर्पयेत् तर्पयिष्यतीत्यर्थः च्व लोडर्थलक्षणे च (३ । ३ । ८) इत्यनेन कर्द्ध्मौहूर्त्तिके भविष्यति लिङ् प्रयोगत्वात् । अनेन वोऽधिसर्वोऽपरेषैमामतरिष्यतीति ध्वनितम । ६ आक्रान्ता प्रयाता इत्यर्थः ।

सर्व्वनगरचत्वरशृङ्गाटकेषु च दानञ्च दापयति स्म । अन्न-मन्नार्थिभ्यः पानं पानार्थिकेभ्यो वस्त्राणि वस्त्रार्थिकेभ्यो यानानि यानार्थिकेभ्य एवं गन्धमाल्यविलेपनचूर्णशय्योपाश्रयं प्राजीविकं प्राजीवकार्थिभ्यो यावदेव बोधिसत्त्वस्य पूजाकरणे ॥

अथ खलु भिक्षवो राज्ञः शुद्धोदनस्यैतदभवत् । कतमस्मिन् गृहे मायादेवी सुखमनुपक्लिष्टा विहरेदिति ॥ अथ तत्क्षणमेव चत्वारो महाराजानो राजानं शुद्धोदनमुपसङ्क्रम्यैवमाहुः । अल्पोत्सुक्यं देव तव सुखं तिष्ठ उपेक्षक वयं हि बोधिसत्त्वस्य वेश्म वै मापयामहे ॥ अथ खलु शक्रो देवानामिन्द्रो राजानं शुद्धोदनमुपसङ्क्रम्यैवमाह ।

हीन विमानपालानां त्रयस्त्रिंशानामुत्तमं ।
वैजयन्तसमं वेश्म बोधिसत्त्वस्य दास्यहं (१) ॥

अथ खलु सुयामो देवपुत्रो राजानं शुद्धोदनमुपसङ्क्रम्यैवमाह ।

मदीयं भवनं दृष्ट्वा विस्मिताः शक्रकोटियः (२) ।
सुयामभवनं श्रीमद्बोधिसत्त्वस्य दास्यहं ॥

अथ खलु तुषितो देवपुत्रो राजानं शुद्धोदनमुपसङ्क्रम्यैवमाह ॥

यत्रैव उषितः पूर्व्वं तुषितेषु महायशाः ।
तदेव भवनं रम्यं बोधिसत्त्वस्य दास्यहं ॥

---

१ अहमेव बोधिसत्त्वाय दास्याम्यहमित्यर्थः एवं परत्र सर्व्वत्र बोध्यं । २ शक्रकोट्य इत्यस्य स्थाने कोटिय इति प्रयुक्तं तत्तु छन्दोनुरोधात् छन्दोनुरोधाद्वर्णमात्रादि वृद्धिह्रासे न दोषः छन्दोऽनुरोधस्य प्राधान्यत्वात् ध्वनितञ्चेदं पिङ्गलेन यद् दोषो विषमस्य इत्यनेन यथा परिगणित। वर्णमात्राधिक्ये हित्यादीनामप्येकता तथा वर्णादीनां न्यूनपूरणेऽपि न दोष इति फलितं । छन्दोभङ्गस्यादोषे ज्ञेम ए घघर अयवतुष्ठा इति पिङ्गलसूत्रस्य छन्दोभङ्गदूषणविधायकस्याप्यारम्भो वृथा स्यात् फलाभावात् अतः ममागतं छन्दोभङ्गस्तु न कर्त्तव्य एवेति पिङ्गलमतं एवं सर्व्वत्र बोध्यम् ।

अथ खलु सुनिर्म्मितो देवपुत्रो राजानं शुद्धोदनमुपसङ्क्रम्यैवमाह ।

मनोमयमहं श्रीमद्वेश्म नानारत्नमयं ।
बोधिसत्त्वस्य पूजार्थमुपनेष्यामि पार्थिव ॥

अथ खलु परनिर्म्मितवशवर्त्ती देवपुत्रो राजानं शुद्धोदनमुपसङ्क्रम्यैवमाह ॥

यावन्तः कामधातुस्थाः विमानाः शोभनाः क्वचित् ।
तानि ते मद्विमानस्य (१) भवन्त्यभिहतप्रभाः ॥
तत् प्रयच्छाम्यहं श्रीमद् वेश्म रत्नमयं शुभं ।
बोधिसत्त्वस्य पूजार्थमानयिष्यामि पार्थिव ॥
दिव्यैः पुष्पैः समाकीर्णं दिव्यगन्धोपवासितं ।
उपनामयिष्ये (२) विपुलं यत्र देवी वसिष्यति ॥

इति हि भिक्षवः सर्व्वैः कामावचरैर्द्देवेश्वरैर्बोधिसत्त्वस्य पूजार्थं कपिलाह्वये पुरवरे स्वकस्वकानि गृहाणि मापितान्यभूवन् । राज्ञाऽपि शुद्धोदनेन मनुष्यातिक्रान्तं देव्याः सम्प्राप्तं गृहं संस्कारितमभूत् । तत्र बोधिसत्त्वो महाव्यूहस्य समाधेरनुभावेन सर्व्वेषु तेषु गृहेषु मायादेवीमुपदर्शयति स्म । अभ्यन्तरगतश्च बोधिसत्त्वो मायादेव्याः कुक्षौ दक्षिणे पार्श्वे पर्य्यङ्कमाभुज्य निषण्णोऽभूत् । सर्व्वे ते देवेश्वराः एकैक एवं सञ्जानते स्म । ममैव गृहे बोधिसत्त्वस्य माता प्रतिवसति नान्यत्रेति ॥ तत्रेदमुच्यते ।

महाव्यूहोपस्थितं समाधिं च चिन्तयित्वा निर्म्मितम्मिणित्वा (३) ।
सर्व्वे च देवा अभिप्रायपूरिता नृपस्य पूर्णश्च तदा मनोरथः ॥

---

१ येन ते मद्विमानेनात्युचितं । २ उपानयिष्ये इत्यर्थः । ३ समाधिञ्च चिन्तयित्वा निर्म्मितं मत्वा इत्यर्थः ।

अथ खलु तस्यां देवपर्षदि केषांश्चिद्देवपुत्राणामेतदभवत्। येऽपि तावच्चातुर्महाराजकायिका देवपुत्रास्तेऽपि तावन्मनुष्याश्रये दुर्गन्धे निर्विद्यापक्रामन्ति। कः पुनर्वादो ये तदन्ये उदारतमा देवास्त्रयस्त्रिंशा वा यामा वा तुषिता वा तत्कथं हि नाम सर्व्वलोकाभ्युद्गतो बोधिसत्त्वः शुचिर्निरामगन्धः सत्त्वरत्नः सन्तुषिताद्देवनिकायाच्च्युत्वा दुर्गन्धे मनुष्याश्रये दशमासान्मातुः कुक्षौ स्थित इति ॥ अथ खल्वायुष्मानानन्दो बुद्धानुभावेन भगवन्तमेतदवोचत्। आश्चर्यं भगवन् यावज्जुगुप्सनीयश्च मातृग्रामस्तथागतेनोक्तो यावद्रागचरितश्च। इदं तु भगवन्नाश्चर्य्यतरं कथं हि नाम सर्व्वलोकाभ्युद्गतो भगवान् पूर्व्वं बोधिसत्त्वभूत एवं तुषिताद्देवनिकायाच्च्युत्वा मनुष्याश्रये दुर्गन्धे मातुर्दक्षिणे पार्श्वे कुक्षावुपपद्य स्थित इति। नाहं भगवन्निदमुत्सहे एवं वक्तुं यथैव पूर्व्वं भगवता व्याकृतमिति। भगवानाह। इच्छसि त्वमानन्द रत्नव्यूहं बोधिसत्त्वपरिभोगं द्रष्टुं यो मातुः कुक्षिगतस्य बोधिसत्त्वस्य परिभोगोऽभूत् ॥ आह ॥ अयमस्य भगवन्कालः अयं सुगत समयस्तथागत तं बोधिसत्त्वपरिभोगमुपदर्शय यं दृष्ट्वा प्रीतिं वेत्स्यामः ॥

अथ खलु भगवांस्तथारूपनिमित्तमकरोत्। यद्ब्रह्मा सहाम्पतिः सार्द्धमष्टषष्टिब्रह्मशतसहस्रैर्ब्रह्मलोकादन्तर्हितो भगवतः पुरतः प्रत्यस्थात्। स भगवतः पादौ शिरसाभिवन्द्य भगवन्तं त्रिःप्रदक्षिणीकृत्यैकान्तेऽस्थात् प्राञ्जलिकृतो भगवन्तं नमस्यन्। तत्र खलु भगवाञ्जानन्नेव ब्रह्माणं सहाम्पतिमामन्त्रयते स्म॥

गृहीतस्तथा ब्रह्मन् स बोधिसत्त्वपरिभोगो दशमासिको यो मम बोधिसत्त्वभूतस्य मातुः कुक्षिगतस्याऽभूत् ॥ आह । एवमेतत् भगवन्नेवमेतत् सुगत ॥ भगवानाह । क्व स इदानीं ब्रह्मन्नुपदर्शय तं ॥ आह । ब्रह्मलोके स भगवन् ॥ भगवानाह । तेन हि त्वं ब्रह्मन्नुपदर्शय तं दशमासिकं बोधिसत्त्वपरिभोगं ज्ञास्यन्ति कियत्संस्कृतमिति ॥

अथ खलु ब्रह्मा सहाम्पतिस्तान् ब्राह्मणानेतदवोचत् । तिष्ठन्तु भवन्तो तावद्बोधिसत्त्वपरिभोगमानयामि ॥ अथ खलु ब्रह्मा सहाम्पतिर्भगवतः पादौ शिरसाभिवन्द्य भगवतः पुरतोऽन्तर्हितस्तत्क्षणमेव ब्रह्मलोके प्रत्यष्ठात् ॥

अथ खलु ब्रह्मा सहाम्पतिः सुब्रह्माणं देवपुत्रमेतदवोचत् । गच्छ त्वं मार्षा इतो ब्रह्मलोकमुपादाय यावत् त्रयस्त्रिंशद्भवनं शब्दमुदीरयद्घोषमनुश्रावय रत्नव्यूहं बोधिसत्त्वपरिभोगं वयं तथागतस्यान्तिकमुपनामयिष्यामः॥ यो युष्माकं द्रष्टुकामः स शीघ्रमागच्छत्विति॥ अथ खलु ब्रह्मा सहाम्पतिश्चतुरशीत्या देवकोटीनियुतशतसहस्रैः सार्द्धन्तं रत्नव्यूहं बोधिसत्त्वपरिभोगं परिगृह्य महति ब्राह्मे विमाने त्रियोजनशतके प्रतिष्ठाप्यानेकैर्देवकोटीनियुतशतसहस्रैः समन्ततोऽनुपरिवार्य्य जम्बुद्वीपमवतारयति स्म॥

तेन खलु पुनः समयेन कामावचराणां देवानां महासन्निपातोऽभूत् भगवत्सकाशे गन्तुं ॥ स खलु पुनः रत्नव्यूहो बोधिसत्त्वपरिभोगो दिव्यैर्वस्त्रै दिव्यैर्माल्यैर्दिव्यैर्गन्धैर्दिव्यैश्च पुष्पैर्दिव्यैर्वाद्यैर्दिव्यैश्च परिभोगैरभिसंस्कृतोऽभूत् । तावन्महेशाख्यैश्च देवैः

परिस्रुतोऽभूत् । यः शक्रो देवानामिन्द्रो महासुमेरौ समुद्रे स्थित्वा दूरत एव मुखे तालच्छत्रकं दत्त्वा शीर्षंव्यवलोकनेनानुव्यवलोकयति स्म । उन्मेषाध्यायिकया वा न च शक्नोति स्म द्रष्टुं तत्कस्मान्महेशाख्या हि देवा (१) ब्राह्मणाः इतरास्त्रयस्त्रिंशा यामास्तुषिता अभिनिर्म्माणरतयः परनिर्म्मितवशवर्त्तिनः कः पुनर्वादः शक्रो देवानामिन्द्रो मोहं ते वै यान्ति स्म ॥ अथ खलु भगवांस्तं दिव्यं वाद्यनिर्घोषमन्तर्धापयति स्म ॥ तत्कस्मात् शब्दश्रवणादेव जाम्बुद्वीपिका मनुष्या उन्मादमापत्स्यन्त इति ॥

अथ खलु चत्वारो महाराजानः (२) शक्रं देवानामिन्द्रमुपसङ्क्रम्यैवमाहुः ॥ कथं देवानामिन्द्र करिष्यामो न लभामहे रत्नव्यूहं बोधिसत्त्वपरिभोगं द्रष्टुं ॥ स तानवोचत् ॥ किमहं मार्षाः करिष्याम्यहमपि न लभे द्रष्टुं । अपि तु खलु पुनर्मार्षा भगवतः समीपमुपनीतं द्रक्ष्यामः । त आहुः ॥ तेन हि देवानामिन्द्र तथा कुरु यथाऽस्य क्षिप्रं दर्शनं भवेत् । शक्र आह ॥ आगच्छत मार्षा मुहूर्त्तं यावदतिक्रान्तातिक्रान्ततमा देवपुत्रा भगवन्तं प्रतिसम्मोदयन्ते। तदेकान्ते स्थित्वा शीर्षोन्मिजितकया (३) भगवन्तमनुविलोकयन्ति स्म॥ अथ खलु ब्रह्मा सहाम्पतिः सार्द्धं तैश्चतुरशीत्या देवकोटीनियुतशतसहस्रैस्तं रत्नव्यूहं बोधिसत्त्वपरिभोगं गृहीत्वा येन तथागतस्तेनोपसङ्क्रामति स्म॥ स खलु पुना रत्नव्यूहो बोधिसत्त्वपरिभोगोऽभिरूपः प्रासादिको दर्शनीयश्चतुरस्रश्चतु.

---

१ गन्धर्वमहोरगा इतरा इति वा पाठः। २ महाराजाः इत्युचितं छान्दसत्वात् एवमन्यत्रापि। ३ शीर्षोन्मीलितकयेत्यर्थः।

कोणः उपरि च कूटागारसमलङ्कृत एवं प्रमाणस्तद्यथापि नाम षण्मासजातो दारकः उच्चैस्त्वेन। तस्य खलु पुनः कूटागारस्य मध्ये पर्य्यङ्कः प्रज्ञप्तस्तद्यथाऽपि नाम षण्मासजातस्य दारकस्य भित्तिफलकः। स खलु पुनः रत्नव्यूहो बोधिसत्त्वपरिभोग एवं वर्णसंस्थानो यस्य न कश्चित् सदेवके लोके समारके सब्रह्मके सदृशोऽस्ति। आकृत्या वा वर्णेन वा देवाः खल्वपि तं दृष्ट्वा आश्चर्य्यप्राप्ता अभूवन्। चक्षूंषि तेषां विभ्रमन्ति स्म। स च तथागतस्याक्षिकमुपनीतोऽतीवभासते तपति विरोचते स्म। तद्यथाऽपि नाम विभान्तं सुवर्णकुशलेन कर्म्मकारकेण सुपरिनिष्ठितमपगतकाचदोषमेवन्तस्मिन् समये कूटागारो* विराजते स्म॥ तस्मिंश्च खलु पुनर्भिक्षवो बोधिसत्त्वपरिभोगे पर्य्यङ्कः प्रज्ञप्तो यस्य सदेवके लोके नास्ति कश्चित् सदृशो वर्णेन वा संस्थानेन वाऽन्यत्र कम्बुग्रीवाया बोधिसत्त्वस्य। यत् खलु पुनर्महाब्राह्मणचीवरं प्रावृतमभूत् तत्तस्य बोधिसत्त्वपर्य्यङ्कस्याग्रतो न भासते स्म। तद्यथाऽपि नाम वातवृष्ट्याभिहतः कृष्णकम्बलः। स खलु पुनः तस्मिन् प्रथमे कूटागाराभ्यन्तरे तादृशरत्नकूटागार उरगसारचन्दनमयो यस्यैकसुवर्णधरणीसाहस्रं लोकधातुमूल्यं क्षमते तथाविधेनोरगसारचन्दनेन स कूटागारः समन्तादनुलिप्तः तादृश एव च तदाभ्यं द्वितीयोऽपि कूटागारः कृतः। कूटागाराभ्यन्तरतः असक्तो बद्धः स्थितः। तदाभ्यं तादृश एव तृतीयोऽपि कूटागारः। सपर्य्यङ्के तस्मिन् गन्धमये तृतीये कूटा-

---

* अत्र सर्व्वत्र पुंस्त्वमार्षत्वात्।

गारे व्यवस्थापितः सम्प्रतिष्ठन्नसाख खलु पुन उरगसार चन्दनस्यैवंरूपो वर्णस्तद्यथाऽपि नामाभिजातस्य वैदूर्य्यस्य। तस्य खलु पुनर्गन्धः कूटागारस्योपरि सामन्ताद्यावन्ति कानिचिद्दिव्यातिक्रान्तानि पुष्पाणि सन्ति सर्व्वाणि तस्मिन् कूटागारे बोधिसत्त्वस्य पूर्व्वकुशलमूलविपाकेनानुलिप्तान्येव जायन्ते स्म॥

स खलु पुना रत्नव्यूहो बोधिसत्त्वपरिभोगो दृढसारोऽभेद्यो वज्रोपमः स्पर्शने च काचिलिन्दिकसुखसंस्पर्शः (१)। तस्मिन् खलु पुना रत्नव्यूहे बोधिसत्त्वपरिभोगे ये केचित् कामावचराणां देवानां भवनव्यूहास्ते सर्व्वे तस्मिन् सन्दृश्यन्ते स्म।

(यामेव च रात्रिं बोधिसत्त्वो मातुः कुक्षिमवक्रान्तस्तामेव रात्रिमध आपःस्कन्धमुपादाय (२) अष्टषष्टियोजनशतसहस्राणि महापृथिवीं भित्त्वा यावद्ब्रह्मलोकं पद्ममभ्युद्गतमभूत्। न च कश्चित्तं पद्मं पश्यति स्म॥ अन्यत्र सारथिनरोत्तमाद्ब्रह्मणश्च सहम्पतेर्महाब्रह्मणः। ये चेह त्रिसाहस्रमहासाहस्रलोकधातवो ते ओजोमण्डलो वा रसो वा तत् सर्व्वं तस्मिन् महापद्मे मधुविन्दुः सम्प्रतिष्ठते स्म) (३)॥

तमेनं महाब्रह्मा शुभवैदूर्य्यभाजने प्रक्षिप्य बोधिसत्त्वस्योपनामयति (४) स्म। तं बोधिसत्त्वः परिगृह्य परिभुङ्क्ते स्म

---

१ काचिलिन्दिक इत्यनुमीयते। २ यथा स्कन्धमुपादायेति बोध्यं। ३ द्वितीयसङ्ख्यके पुस्तके "बोधिसत्त्वपरिभोगमुपदर्श्य यं दृष्ट्वा प्रीतिं वेत्स्याम" एतद्वाक्यानन्तरं (८८ पत्रे १६ पङ्क्तेः परं) "अथ खलु आनन्द पूर्व्वमहं बोधिसत्त्वचर्य्यां चरामीति" वाक्यपूर्व्वकं () एतच्चिह्नाभ्यन्तरः पठितो यः पाठः प्रायो वर्त्तते अत्रापि सुसंस्कृत एतदपरपुस्तकेष्वप्येवैषः पाठः। ४ उपानयति स्मेति मन्तव्यं।

महाब्रह्मणोऽनुकम्पामुपादाय। नास्ति स कश्चित् सत्त्वः सत्त्वनि-काये यस्य(१)स ओजोविन्दुः परिभुक्तः सम्यक् सुखेन परिणमेद-न्यत्र चरमभविकाद्बोधिसत्त्वात् सर्व्वबोधिसत्त्वभूमिपरिपूर्णात् ॥

कस्य च कर्म्मणो विपाकेन स ओजोविन्दुः बोधिसत्त्वस्योपतिष्ठते स्म। दीर्घरात्रं खल्वपि बोधिसत्त्वेन पूर्व्वं बोधिसत्त्वचर्य्यां चरता ग्लानेभ्यः सत्त्वेभ्यो भैषज्यं दत्तमाशापराणां सत्त्वानामाशा परिपूरिता शरणागताश्च न परित्यक्ता नित्यञ्चाग्रपुष्पमग्रफ-लमग्ररसं तथागतेभ्यश्चैत्येभ्यस्तथागतश्रावकसङ्घेभ्यो मातापितृ-भ्यश्च दत्त्वा पश्चादात्मना परिभुक्तं तस्य कर्म्मणो विपाकेन महाब्रह्मा बोधिसत्त्वस्य तं मधुविन्दुमुपनामयति (२) स्म ॥

तस्मिन् खलु पुनः कूटागारे यानि कानिचित् सत्त्वातिक्रा-न्तातिक्रान्तानि मायागुणरतिक्रीडासमवसृतस्थानानि तानि सर्व्वाणि तस्मिन् प्रादुर्भूतानि सन्दृश्यन्ते स्म ॥ बोधिसत्त्वस्य पूर्व्वकर्म्मविपाकेन तस्मिन् खलु पुना रत्नव्यूहे बोधिसत्त्वपरिभोगे शतसहस्रव्यूहं नाम वासोयुगं प्रादुर्भूतं। न स कश्चित् सत्त्वः सत्त्व-निकाये संविद्यते यस्य तत्प्रादुर्भवेदन्यत्र चरमभविकाद्बोधि-सत्त्वात्। न च ते के चन उदारोदाररूपशब्दगन्धरसस्पर्शा ये तस्मिन् कूटागारे न सन्दृश्यन्ते स्म ॥ स च कूटागारपरि-भोग एवं सुपरिभोग एवं सुपरिनिष्पन्नः स्वान्तर्व्वहिरेवं सुपरिनिष्ठितः एवं मृदुकश्च तद्यथाऽपि नाम काचिलिन्दिक-सुखसंस्पर्शो निदर्शनमात्रेण न तु तस्योपमा संविद्यते ॥ धर्म्मता

१ पेयेत्यर्थः। २ उपानयति।

खल्वेषा बोधिसत्त्वस्य पूर्व्वकेण प्रणिधानेन इयं चेतना अभूत्स्य । बोधिसत्त्वेन मनुष्यलोके उपपत्तव्यमिति निष्क्रम्य चानुत्तरां सम्यक्सम्बोधिमभिसम्बुद्ध्य धर्म्मचक्रं प्रवर्त्तयितव्यं ॥ यस्याश्च मातुः कुक्षावुपपत्तिर्भवति तस्या दक्षिणे कुक्षावुदित एव रत्नव्यूहः कूटागारोऽभिनिवर्त्तते ॥ पश्चाद्बोधिसत्त्वस्तुषितेभ्यश्च्युत्वा तस्मिन् कूटागारे पर्य्यङ्के निषण्णः सम्भवति न हि चरमभविकस्य बोधिसत्त्वस्य कललार्बुदघनपेशीभावः कायः सन्तिष्ठते । अथ तर्हि सर्व्वाङ्गप्रत्यङ्गलक्षणसम्पन्नः सन्निषण्ण एवं प्रादुर्भवति । स्वप्नान्तरगता च बोधिसत्त्वमाता मायादेवी महानागं कुञ्जरमवक्रान्तं सञ्जानीते स्म ॥

तस्य खलु पुनस्तथा निषण्णस्य शक्रो देवानामिन्द्रश्चत्वारश्च महाराजानोऽष्टाविंशतिभिश्च यक्षसेनापतयो गुह्यकाधिपतिश्च नाम यक्षकुलं यतो वज्रपाणेरुत्पत्तिस्ते बोधिसत्त्वं मातुः कुक्षिगतं विदित्वा सततसमितमनुबद्धा भवन्ति स्म ॥ सन्ति खलु पुनश्चतस्रो बोधिसत्त्वपरिचारिका देवता उत्खली च नाम उत्खली च नाम ध्वजवती च नाम प्रभावती च नाम ता अपि बोधिसत्त्वं मातुः कुक्षिगतं ज्ञात्वा सततं समितं रक्षन्ति स्म । शक्रोऽपि देवानामिन्द्रः सार्द्धं पञ्चमात्रैर्देवपुत्रशतैस्तैर्बोधिसत्त्वं मातुः कुक्षिगतं ज्ञात्वा सततं समितमनुबध्नाति स्म ॥

बोधिसत्त्वस्य खलु मातुः कुक्षिगतस्य कायस्तथाविधोऽभूत्तद्यथाऽपि नाम पर्व्वतमूर्द्ध्नि रात्र्यामन्धकारतमिस्रायां महानग्निस्कन्धो योजनादपि दृश्यते यावत् पञ्चभ्योऽपि योज-

तेभ्यो दृश्यते। एवमेव बोधिसत्त्वस्य मातुः कुक्षिगतस्यात्म-भावोऽभिनिर्वृत्तोऽभूत् । प्रभास्वरोऽभिरूपः प्रासादिको दर्शनीयः स तस्मिन् कूटागारे पर्य्यङ्के निषण्णोऽतीव शोभते स्म वैदूर्य्यप्रत्युप्तमिवाभिजातं जातरूपं । बोधिसत्त्वमाता च निधाय स्थिता पश्यति स्म कुक्षिगतं बोधिसत्त्वं। तद्यथाऽपि नाम महतोऽभ्रकूटाद्विद्युतो निःसृत्य महान्तमवभासं जनयन्त्येवमेव बोधिसत्त्वो मातुः कुक्षिगतः श्रिया तेजसा वर्णेन च तं प्रथमं सर्व्वरत्नकूटागारमवभासयति स्म । अवभास्य द्वितीयं गन्धरत्नकूटागारमवभासयति स्म । तमवभास्य तृतीयं गन्धरत्नकूटागारमवभासयति स्म । तमवभास्य सर्व्वावन्तं मातुरात्मभावमवभासयति स्म। तमवभास्य यत्र चासने निषण्णो भवति स्म तदवभासयति स्म । तदवभास्य सर्व्वगृहमवभासयति स्म । सर्व्वगृहमवभास्य गृहस्योपरिष्टान्निःसृत्य पूर्व्वां दिशमवभासयति स्म॥ एवं दक्षिणां पश्चिमां उत्तरामध ऊर्द्धं समन्ताद्दशदिशः क्रोशमात्रमेकैकस्यां दिशि मातुः कुक्षिगतो बोधिसत्त्वः श्रिया तेजसा वर्णेन चावभासयति स्म ॥

आगच्छन्ति स्म खलु भिक्षवश्चत्वारो महाराजानोऽष्टाविंशतिश्च महायक्षसेनापतयः सार्द्धं पञ्चमात्रैर्यक्षशतैः पूर्व्वाह्णकालसमये बोधिसत्त्वस्य दर्शनाय वन्दनाय पर्य्युपासनाय च धर्म्मश्रवणाय तदा बोधिसत्त्वस्तानागतान् विदित्वा दक्षिणपाणिमभ्युत्क्षिप्य एकाङ्गुलिकया आसनमुपदर्शयति स्म। निषीदन्ति स्म ते लोकपालादयो यथा प्रज्ञप्तेष्वासनेषु। पश्यन्ति स्म बोधि-

सत्त्वं मातुः कुक्षिगतं जातरूपमिव विग्रहं दक्षं चालयन्तं विचारयन्तं प्रतिष्ठापयन्तं। तेऽपि प्रीतिप्रामोद्यप्रासादप्रतिलब्धाः। बोधिसत्त्वस्तेषां चेदमेव चित्तं विज्ञाय दक्षिणपाणिमुत्क्षिप्य सञ्चारयति स्म सञ्चार्य्य विचारयति स्म ॥ मातरञ्च नमस्करोति स्म। निषण्णांश्च तान् विदित्वा बोधिसत्त्वो धर्म्यया कथया सन्दर्शयति स्म। समुत्तेजयति स्म। समादापयति स्म। सम्प्रहर्षयति स्म। यदा च ते प्रक्रमितुकामा भवन्ति तदा बाधते स्म। तदा तेषां चतुर्णां महाराजानामेवं भवति स्म। विसर्जिताश्च वयं बोधिसत्त्वेनेति बोधिसत्त्वं बोधिसत्त्वमातरञ्च त्रिःप्रदक्षिणीकृत्य प्रक्रामन्ति स्म। अयं हेतुरयं प्रत्ययो यद्बोधिसत्त्वो रात्र्यां प्रशान्तायां दक्षिणपाणिं सञ्चार्य्य विचारयति स्म। विचार्य्य पुनरपि स्मृतः सम्प्रजानंस्तं पाणिं प्रतिष्ठापयति स्म ॥ पुनरपरे यदा बोधिसत्त्वस्य केचिद्दर्शनायागच्छन्ति स्म स्त्रियो वा पुरुषो वा दारको वा दारिका वा तान् बोधिसत्त्वः पूर्व्वतरमेव प्रतिसम्मोदयते स्म पश्चाद्बोधिसत्त्वमाता ॥

इति हि भिक्षवो बोधिसत्त्वो मातुः कुक्षिगतः सन् सत्त्वप्रतिसम्मोदनकुशलो भवति स्मेति न कश्चिद्देवो वा नागो वा यक्षो वा मनुष्यो वाऽमनुष्यो वा यः शक्नोति स्म बोधिसत्त्वं पूर्व्वतरं प्रति सम्मोदयितुं। अथ तर्हि बोधिसत्त्व एव तावत् पूर्व्वतरं प्रति सम्मोदयते स्म पश्चाद्बोधिसत्त्वमाता ।

निर्गते खलु पुनः पूर्व्वाह्णकालसमये मध्याह्नकालसमये प्रत्युत्थिते अथ खलु शक्रो देवानामिन्द्रोऽतिक्रान्ताऽतिक्रान्ताश्च

त्रयस्त्रिंशद्देवपुत्रा बोधिसत्त्वस्य दर्शनाय वन्दनाय पर्य्युपासनाय च धर्म्मश्रवणाय चागच्छन्ति स्म । तांश्च बोधिसत्त्वो दूरत एवागच्छतो दृष्ट्वा दक्षिणं सुवर्णवर्णं बाहुं प्रसार्य्य शक्रं देवानामिन्द्रं देवांश्च त्रयस्त्रिंशान् प्रति सम्मोदयते स्म ॥ एकाङ्गुलिकया चासनान्युपदर्शयति स्म । न च शक्नोति स्म भिक्षवः शक्रो देवानामिन्द्रो बोधिसत्त्वस्याज्ञां प्रतिरोद्धुं । निषीदति स्म शक्रो देवानामिन्द्रस्तदन्ये च देवपुत्रा यथा प्रज्ञप्तेष्वासनेषु । बोधिसत्त्वो निषण्णान् विदित्वा धर्म्म्यया कथया सन्दर्शयति स्म । समादापयति स्म समुत्तेजयति स्म सम्प्रहर्षयति स्म । येन च बोधिसत्त्वः पाणिं सञ्चारयति स्म तन्मुखा बोधिसत्त्वमाता भवति स्म । ततस्तेषामेवं भवति स्म । अस्माभिः सार्द्धं बोधिसत्त्वो सम्मोदयते स्म एकैकश्चैवं सञ्जानीते स्म । मयैव सार्द्धं बोधिसत्त्वः संलपति मयैव सम्मोदत इति ॥

तस्मिन् खलु पुनः कूटागारे शक्रस्य देवानामिन्द्रस्य त्रयस्त्रिंशानां देवानाञ्च प्रतिभासः सन्दृश्यन्ते स्म । न खलु पुनरन्यत्रैवं परिशुद्धो बोधिसत्त्वपरिभोगो भवति यथा मातुः कुक्षिगतस्य बोधिसत्त्वस्य । यदा च भिक्षवः शक्रो देवानामिन्द्रस्तदन्ये च देवपुत्राः प्रक्रमितुकामा भवन्ति स्म । तदा बोधिसत्त्वस्तेषां चैतमेव चेतःपरिवितर्कमाज्ञाय दक्षिणपाणिमुत्क्षिप्य सञ्चारयति स्म सञ्चार्य्य विचार्य्य पुनरपि स्मृतः सम्प्रजानन् प्रतिष्ठापयति स्म । मातरञ्च न बाधते स्म । तदा शक्रस्य देवानामिन्द्रस्यान्येषां च त्रयस्त्रिंशानां देवानामेवं

भवति स्म। विसर्जिता वयं बोधिसत्त्वेनेति ते बोधिसत्त्वं बोधिसत्त्वमातरं च त्रिःप्रदक्षिणीकृत्य प्रक्रामन्ति स्म॥

निर्गते च खलु पुनर्भिक्षवो मध्याह्नकालसमये प्रत्युपस्थिते सायाह्नकालसमये अथ खलु ब्रह्मा सहाम्पतिरनेकैर्ब्रह्मकायिकैर्देवपुत्रैः शतसहस्रैः परिवृतः पुरस्कृतस्तं दिव्यमोजोबिन्दुमादाय येन बोधिसत्त्वस्तेनोपसङ्क्रामति स्म। बोधिसत्त्वं द्रष्टुं वन्दितुं पर्य्युपासितुं धर्म्मञ्च श्रोतुं समन्वाहरति स्म॥ भिक्षवो बोधिसत्त्वो ब्रह्माणं सहाम्पतिमागच्छन्तं सपरिवारं विदित्वा पुनरेव च बोधिसत्त्वो दक्षिणं सुवर्णवर्णपाणिमुत्क्षिप्य ब्रह्माणं सहाम्पतिं ब्रह्मकायिकांश्च देवपुत्रान्प्रतिसम्मोदयते स्म॥ एकाङ्गुलिकया चासनान्युपदर्शयति स्म। न च शक्तिरस्ति भिक्षवो ब्रह्मणः सहाम्पतेर्बोधिसत्त्वस्याज्ञां प्रतिरोद्धुं। निषीदति स्म भिक्षवो ब्रह्मा सहाम्पतिस्तदन्ये च ब्रह्मकायिका देवपुत्रा यथाप्रज्ञप्तेष्वासनेषु। बोधिसत्त्वो निषण्णान् विदित्वा धर्म्यया कथया सन्दर्शयति स्म समादापयति स्म समुत्तेजयति स्म सम्प्रहर्षयति स्म। येन बोधिसत्त्वः पाणिं सञ्चारयति स्म तन्मुखा च मायादेवी भवति स्म। ततस्तेषामेकैकस्य एवं भवति स्म। मया सार्द्धं बोधिसत्त्वः संलपति मामेव प्रतिसम्बोधयत इति॥

यदा च ब्रह्मा सहाम्पतिस्तदन्ये च ब्रह्मकायिका देवपुत्रा गन्तुकामा भवन्ति स्म। तदा बोधिसत्त्वस्तेषां चेतसैव चेतःपरिवितर्कमाज्ञाय दक्षिणं सुवर्णवर्णं बाहुं उत्क्षिप्य सञ्चारयति स्म। सञ्चार्य्य विचारयति स्म। सञ्चार्य्य विचार्य्याविसर्जनाकारेण पाणिं

सञ्चारयति स्म । मातरं न बाधते स्म । ततो ब्रह्मणः सहाम्पते-स्तदन्येषाञ्च ब्रह्मकायिकानां देवपुत्राणामेवं भवति स्म । विस-र्जिता वयं बोधिसत्त्वेनेति । ते बोधिसत्त्वं बोधिसत्त्वमातरञ्च त्रिःप्रदक्षिणीकृत्य प्रक्रामन्ति स्म । बोधिसत्त्वः स्मृतः सम्प्रजानन् पाणिं प्रतिष्ठापयति स्म ॥

आगच्छन्ति स्म खलु पुनर्भिक्षवः पुनः पूर्व्वदक्षिणपश्चि-मोत्तराभ्यो दिग्भ्योऽधस्तादुपरिष्टात् समन्ताद्दशभ्यो दिग्भ्यो बहूनि बोधिसत्त्वशतसहस्राणि बोधिसत्त्वस्य दर्शनाय वन्द-नाय पर्य्युपासनाय धर्म्मश्रवणाय धर्मसङ्गीतिसङ्गायनाय च । तेषामागतानां बोधिसत्त्वः कायात् प्रभामुत्सृज्य महाव्यू-हानि सिंहासनान्यभिनिर्म्मिमीते स्म । अभिनिर्माय तान् बोधिसत्त्वांस्तेष्वासनेषु निषीदयति स्म। निषण्णांस्तैनान् विदित्वा परिपृच्छति स्म । परिप्रश्नयति स्म । यदुतास्यैव बोधिस-त्त्वस्य महायानस्य विस्तरं विभागतामुपादाय । न च तं कश्चिदन्यः पश्यति स्म । अन्यत्र सभागेभ्यो देवपुत्रेभ्यः । अयं भिक्षवो हेतुरयं प्रत्ययो येन बोधिसत्त्वः प्रक्रान्तायां रात्र्यां कायात् प्रभामुत्सृजति स्म । न खलु पुनर्भिक्षवो मायादेवी बोधिसत्त्वे कुक्षिगते गुरुकायतां सञ्जानीते स्म अन्यत्र लघुता-मेव मृदुतामेव सौख्यतामेव । नवोदरगतानि दुःखानि प्रत्यनु-भवति स्म ॥ न च रागपरिदाहेन वा द्वेषपरिदाहेन वा मोह-परिदाहेन वा परिदह्यते स्म ॥ न च कामवितर्कां वा व्यापा-दवितर्कां वा विहिंसावितर्कां वा वितर्कयति स्म ॥ न च शीतं

न चोष्णं जिघत्सां वा पिपासां वा तमो वा रजो वा क्लेशं वा सञ्जानीते स्म पश्यति वा। न चास्या अमनापा रूपशब्दगन्धरसस्पर्शा वा आभासमागच्छन्ति स्म। न च पापकान् स्वप्नान् पश्यति स्म। न चास्याः स्त्रीमाया न शाठ्यं नेर्ष्या न स्त्रीक्लेशा बाधन्ते स्म। पञ्चशिक्षापदसमादात्ता खलु पुनः शीलवती दशकुशलकर्म्मपथे प्रतिष्ठिता तस्मिन् समये बोधिसत्त्वमाता भवति स्म। न च बोधिसत्त्वमातुः कश्चित्पुरुषे रागचित्तमुत्पद्यते स्म। नापि कस्य चित्पुरुषस्य बोधिसत्त्वमातुरन्तिके॥ ये च केचित् कपिलाह्वये पुरवरे अन्येषु वा जनपदेषु देवनागयक्षगन्धर्व्वासुरगरुडभूताविष्टाः स्त्रीपुरुषदारकदारिका वा ते सर्व्वे बोधिसत्त्वमातुः सह दर्शनादेव स्वस्थाः स्मृतिप्रतिलब्धा भवन्ति स्म। ते चामनुष्याः क्षिप्रमेव प्रक्रमन्ति स्म॥ ये च केचिन्नानारोगस्पृष्टाः सत्त्वा भवन्ति स्म। वातपित्तश्लेष्मसन्निपातकैः रोगैः पीड्यन्ते स्म। चक्षुरोगेण वा श्रोतोरोगेण वा घ्राणरोगेण वा जिह्वारोगेण वा ओष्ठरोगेण वा दन्तरोगेण वा कण्ठरोगेण वा गलगण्डरोगेण वा उरोगण्डकुष्ठक्षयशोषोन्मादापस्मारज्वरकुक्षिरोगैः पिटकविसर्पिविचर्च्चिकाद्यै रोगैः सम्पीड्यन्ते स्म तेषां बोधिसत्त्वमाता दक्षिणपाणिं मूर्द्ध्नि प्रतिष्ठापयति स्म। ते सह प्रतिष्ठापिते पाणौ विगतव्याधयो भूत्वा स्वकस्वकानि गृहाणि गच्छन्ति स्म॥ अन्ततो मायादेवी तृणगुल्मकमपि धरणितलादभ्युत्क्षिप्य ग्लानेभ्यो सत्त्वेभ्योऽनुप्रयच्छति स्म। ते सह प्रतिलम्भादरोगनिर्व्विकारा भवन्ति स्म। यदा च मायादेवी स्व

दक्षिणपार्श्वं प्रत्यवेक्षते स्म तदा पश्यति स्म बोधिसत्त्वं कुक्षिगतं। तद्यथाऽपि नाम सुपरिशुद्धे आदर्शमण्डले मुखमण्डलं दृश्यते। दृष्ट्वा च पुनस्तुष्टा उदग्रा आत्तमना प्रमुदिता प्रीतिसौमनस्य-जाता भवति स्म॥

बोधिसत्त्वस्य खलु पुनर्भिक्षवो मातुः कुक्षिगतस्याधिष्ठितं सततं समितं रात्रिन्दिवं दिव्यानि तूर्य्याणि अभिनिर्म्मीय प्रवा-द्यन्ति स्म। दिव्यानि च पुष्पाणि अभिप्रवर्षन्ति स्म। कालेन देवाः प्रवर्षन्ति स्म। काले वायवो वान्ति स्म। कालेन ऋतवो नक्षत्राणि परिवर्त्तन्ते स्म। क्षेमञ्च राज्यं सुभिक्षञ्च समनाकु-लमनुभवति स्म। सर्व्वे च कपिलाह्वये महापुरे शाक्या अन्ये च सत्त्वाः खादन्ति स्म पिबन्ति स्म रमन्ते स्म क्रीडन्ति स्म प्रवि-चारयन्ति स्म दानानि च ददति स्म पुण्यानि च कुर्व्वन्ति स्म कौमदीवियथातुर्म्मासामेकान्ते क्रीडासुखविहारैर्विहरन्ति स्म। राजाऽपि शुद्धोदनः समागतब्रह्मचर्य्योऽपगतकार्य्यो नार्य्यपि सुपरिशुद्धा तपोवनगत इव धर्म्ममेवानुवर्त्तते स्म॥

एवं रूपेण भिक्षवो ऋद्धिप्रातिहार्य्येण समन्वागतो बोधि-सत्त्वो मातुः कुक्षिगतोऽस्थात्। तत्र खलु भगवानायुष्मन्तमा-नन्दमामन्त्रयते स्म। द्रक्ष्यसि त्वमानन्द रत्नव्यूहं बोधिसत्त्वप-रिभोगं यत्र बोधिसत्त्वो मातुः कुक्षिगतो व्याहार्षीत्। आह। पश्येयं भगवन् पश्येयं(१) सुगत॥ तं दर्शयति स्म तथागतः। आयु-ष्मत आनन्दस्य(२) शक्रस्य देवानामिन्द्रस्य चतुर्णां लोकपालानां

---

१ अत्र तदर्थे विधिलिङ्। २ आनन्दस्य शक्रस्येत्यादौ कर्म्मणि षष्ठी बोध्या।

च तदन्येषां च देवमनुष्याणां । दृष्ट्वा च ते तुष्टा उदग्रा आत्तम-
नसः प्रमुदिताः प्रीतिसौमनस्यजाता अभूवन् । स च ब्रह्मा सहा-
म्पतिः पुनरेव च ब्रह्मलोके समारोप्य प्रतिष्ठापयति स्म चैत्यार्थं॥

तत्र खलु भगवान् पुनरपि भिक्षूनामन्त्रयते स्म ॥

इति हि भिक्षवो बोधिसत्त्वेन दशमासकुक्षिगतेन षट्‌त्रिंश-
न्नयुतानि देवमनुष्याणां त्रिषु यानेषु परिपाचितान्यभूवन् ॥
तत्रेदमुच्यते ।

बोधिसत्त्व अग्रसत्त्वो मातुः कुक्षिसंस्थितः ।
प्रकम्पिता च षड्विकार (१) मेदिनी सकानना ॥
सुवर्णवर्ण आभ मुक्ता सर्व्वापाय (२) शोधिताः ।
प्रहर्षितास्र देवसङ्घा धर्म्मराजु भेष्यते (३) ॥
सुसंस्थितो महाविमान नेकरत्नचित्रिते (४) ।
यत्र वीर आरुहित्व (५) तिष्ठते विनायकः ॥
गन्धोत्तमचन्दनेन पूरितो विरोचते ।
यस्य भूमिरस्य त्रिसहस्रमूल्यरत्नपूरिता ॥
महासाहस्रलोकधातु गृह्य॑भिनयित्व(६)ना ।
उद्गतो गुणाकरस्य पद्म ओजविन्दुको (७) ॥
सो सप्तरात्र पुण्यतेजा ब्रह्मलोकस्य उद्गतः ।
यतो गृहीत्व ब्रह्म ओजो बोधिसत्त्वोपनामयी (८)॥
नास्ति सर्व्वसत्त्वकायि भुक्त यो जरेय तं ।

---

१ षड्विकारा इत्यर्थः। २ सुवर्णवर्णा आभा सर्व्वापाया इत्यर्थः। ३ राज्यं भोक्ष्यते इत्यर्थः।
४ महाविमानेऽनेकेत्यादीनि सुगमम्। ५ आरुह्येत्यर्थः। ६ महासाहस्रलोकधातुं भित्त्वेत्यर्थः।
७ ओजोबिन्दुक। ८ स सप्तरात्रं यं गृहीत्वा ब्रह्मा बोधिसत्त्वायोपानयत् इति सुगमम्।

अन्यत्र सुचरित्व बोधिसत्त्व ब्रह्मकल्पसन्निभे (१) ॥
अनेककल्प पुण्यतेज ओजबिन्दु संस्थितो ।
यं भुञ्जित्व सत्त्वकाय चित्तग्रामबुद्धु गच्छिषु (२) ॥
शक्रब्रह्मलोकपाला: पूजनाय नायकं ।
त्रीणि काल आगमित्व बोधिसत्त्वअन्तिकं (३) ॥
वन्दयित्व पूजयित्व धर्म्मांश्च शृणुते वरं ।
प्रदक्षिणं करित्व सर्व्वं गच्छन्ति यथागता: (४) ॥
बोधिसत्त्व धर्म्मकाम एन्ति लोकधातुषु ।
प्रभाविव्यूह आश्रमेषु निषण्ण स्वर्णदृष्टिषु (५) ॥
परस्परं च श्रुत्व धर्म्मं यानश्रेष्ठमुत्तमं ।
प्रयान्ति सर्व्वि हृष्टचित्ता वर्णमाल भाषतो (६) ॥
ये च इस्त्रि दारिका दुःखिता च तदाऽभवन् ।
भूतस्पृष्टा क्षिप्तचित्ता: नग्ना: पांशुरूषिता: (७) ॥
तेऽपि सर्व्वे दृष्ट माया (८) भान्ति लब्धचेतना: ।
स्मृतीमतीगतीउपेत गेह गेह गच्छिषु (९) ॥
वाततो वा पित्ततो वा श्लेष्मसान्निपातकै: ।
ये च चक्षुरोगा: श्रोतरोगा: कायचित्त पीडिता: (१०) ॥

---

१ सर्व्वसत्त्वनिकाये भुक्त्वा धारयेत् सुचरिताद्बोधिसत्त्वाद्ब्रह्मकल्पसन्निभादित्यर्थः । २ अनेककल्पं पुण्यतेजा ओजोबिन्दुः संस्थितः भुक्त्वा सत्त्वनिकायचित्तग्रामबुद्धिं गत इत्यर्थः । ३ त्रिकालमागत्य बोधिसत्त्वान्तिकमित्यर्थः । ४ वन्दित्वा पूजयित्वा शृण्वन्ति त्वा सर्व्वे इत्यर्थः । ५ बोधिसत्त्वा धर्म्मकामा आयान्ति प्रभाव्यूहेषु निषण्णा स्वर्णदृष्टेषु इत्यर्थः । ६ श्रुत्वा सर्व्वे वर्णमालां भाषन्त इत्यर्थः । ७ या च स्त्री इत्यर्थः । ८ दृष्ट्वा मायामित्यर्थः । ९ स्मृतिमतिमत्युपेता गेहे गेहेऽगच्छन्नित्यर्थः । १० वातेन पित्तेन चक्षूरोगिणः श्रोत्ररोगिणः कायचित्ते इत्यर्थः ।

नैकरूपनैकजातिव्याधिभिश्च ये हताः ।
स्नापिते स्म माय मूर्ध्नि पाणि भान्ति निर्जराः (१) ॥
अथापि वा वृक्षस्य मूलिं भूमितो गृहील सा ।
ददाति माय आतुराण सर्व्व भान्ति निर्जराः ॥
सौख्यप्राप्ता निर्व्विकारा गेहि गेहि गच्छिषु (२) ।
भैषज्यभूति वैद्यराजि कुक्षि सम्प्रतिष्ठिते (३) ॥
यस्मि कालि मायदेवी स्वतनु निरीक्षते ।
अद्दृशाति बोधिसत्त्व कुक्षिये प्रतिष्ठितं (४) ॥
यथैव चन्द्रमन्तरीक्ष तारकैश्च परिवृतं ।
तथैव माय बोधिसत्त्व लक्षणैः समलङ्कृतं (५) ॥
नो च तस्य रागदोष नैव मोह बाधते ।
कामच्छनैवन्द तस्य इर्षि नैव हिंसता (६) ॥
तुष्टचित्त हृष्टचित्त प्रीतिसौमनःस्थितः ।
क्षुधा पिपासा शीतोष्ण नैव तस्य बाधते (७) ॥
अघट्टिताश्च नित्यकाल दिव्यतूर्य्य वादिषुः ।
प्रवर्षन्ति दिव्यपुष्पं गन्धाग्रश्रेष्ठ शोभनं (८) ॥
देवपश्चिमानुषाणाञ्चामानुषाणां ।
विहठ नो विहिंसिता तच ते परस्परं (९) ॥

---

१ स्नापयति माया पाणिं । २ गृहीत्वा माया आतुरेभ्यः सर्व्वे गेहे गेहेऽगच्छन्नित्यर्थः । ३ भैषज्यभूते वैद्यराजे कुक्षावित्यर्थः । ४ यस्मिन् काले मायादेवी पश्यति बोधिसत्त्वं कुक्षावित्यर्थः । ५ मायां बोधिसत्त्वं अन्तरिक्षे इत्यर्थः । ६ न च तं रागद्वेषौ मोहो कामेच्छा ईर्षा तं हिंसात्वमित्यर्थः । ७ तुष्टचित्तो हृष्टचित्तो प्रीति सौमनस्यस्थितः क्षुत्पिपासा शीतोष्ण तमित्यर्थः । ८ अघट्टितानि नित्यकाल दिव्यतूर्य्याणि अवादिषुः दिव्यपुष्पाणि श्रेष्ठाग्रगन्धानि शोभनानि इत्यर्थः ॥ ९ देवपश्चिमानुषामानुषाणां विहेठा विहिंसात्वमित्यर्थः ।

रमन्ति सर्व्वे क्रीडयन्ति अन्नपानं ददन्ति च ।
आनन्दशब्दं घोषयन्ति हृष्टतुष्टमानसाः (१) ॥
क्षमाराज्याकुलं सर्व्वं काले देवो हि वर्षते ।
तृणाश्च पुष्प ओषधीयस्तस्मि कालि रोहिषुः (२) ॥
राजगेहि सप्तरात्र रत्नवर्ष वर्षितः ।
यतो दरिद्रसत्त्व गृह्णाति ददन्ति भुञ्जते (३) ॥
नास्ति सत्त्व यो दरिद्र यो च आसि दुःखितो ।
मेरुमूर्ध्नि नन्दनवन इव सत्त्वनन्दिताः (४) ॥
सो च राजु शोकियान पोषधी उपोषितो ।
राज्यकार्य्यु नो करोति धर्म्ममेव गोचरी (५) ॥
तपोवनञ्च सो प्रविष्ट मायदेवीं पृच्छति ।
कीदृशन्ते कायसौख्यमयसत्त्वधारिणीति (६) ॥
इति श्रीललितविस्तरे गर्भावक्रान्तिपरिवर्त्तो नाम षष्ठः ॥ ६ ॥

सप्तमाध्यायप्रारम्भः ॥

इति हि भिक्षवो दशमासेषु निर्गतेषु बोधिसत्त्वस्य जन्मकालसमये प्रत्युपस्थिते राज्ञः शुद्धोदनस्य गृहोद्याने द्वात्रिंशत्पूर्व्वनिमित्तानि प्रादुरभूवन् ॥ कतमानि द्वात्रिंशत् । सर्व्वपुष्पाणि सङ्कोभूतानि न पुष्पन्ति स्म ॥ पुष्करिणीषु चोत्पल-

---

१ क्रीडन्ति ददतीत्यर्थः । २ वर्षति तृणानि पुष्पौषध्यस्तस्मिन् काले रोहन्ति । ३ राजगेहे सप्तरात्रं रत्नवर्षो हष्टो यं दरिद्रसत्त्वो गृह्णाति खादन् भुङ्क्ते इत्यर्थः । ४ सत्त्वो दरिद्रो यथासि दुःखितः सत्त्व आनन्दस्य इत्यर्थः । ५ स शोचमानः पोषधिमुपोषितो राज्यकार्य्यं धर्म्मगोचरमेवेत्यर्थः । ६ स प्रविष्ट इत्यर्थः ।

पद्मकुमुदपुण्डरीकाण्यभ्युद्गतानि कुड्मलीभूतानि न पुष्पन्ति स्म। तदा च पुष्पफलवृक्षा धरणीतलादभ्युद्गम्य क्षारकजाता न फलन्ति स्म। अष्टौ च वृक्षाः प्रादुरभवन् विंशतिश्च रत्ननिधानशतसहस्राणि चोत्सृत्य व्यवस्थितानि दृश्यन्ते स्म। अन्तःपुरे च रत्नाङ्कुराः प्रादुरभूवन्। सुगन्धितैलपूरिताः परिवासिताश्च गन्धोदकाः शीतोष्णाः (१) प्रस्रवन्ति स्म। हिमवत्पर्व्वतपार्श्वाच्च सिंहपोतका आगत्याभिनन्दन्तः कपिलाह्वयं पुरवरं प्रदक्षिणीकृत्य द्वारमूलेष्ववतिष्ठन्ते स्म। नच कञ्चित् सत्त्वं विहेठयन्ति स्म। पञ्चशतानि पाण्डुराणां हस्तिशावकानां आगत्य राज्ञः शुद्धोदनस्याग्रकरैश्चरणानभिलिखन्ति स्म। मेखलावद्धकाश्च देवदारका राज्ञः शुद्धोदनस्यान्तःपुरे उत्सङ्गेनोत्सङ्गं परिवर्त्तमानाः सन्दृश्यन्ते स्म। गगनतलगतार्द्धकायिका नागकन्या नानापूजोपकरणपरिगृहीता अध्यालम्बमानाः सन्दृश्यन्ते स्म। दश च नागकन्या सहस्राणि मयूराङ्गहस्तकपरिगृहीता गगनतलेऽवस्थिताः सन्दृश्यन्ते स्म। दश च पूर्णकुम्भसहस्राणि कपिलवस्तुमहानगरं प्रदक्षिणीकुर्व्वन्तः सन्दृश्यन्ते स्म। दश च देवकन्यासहस्राणि गन्धोदकभृङ्गारपरिगृहीता मूर्द्ध्नि धारयन्त्योऽवस्थिताः सन्दृश्यन्ते स्म। दश च देवकन्यासहस्राणि छत्रध्वजपताकापरिगृहीता अवस्थिताः सन्दृश्यन्ते स्म। बहूनि चाप्सरःशतसहस्राणि शङ्खभेरीमृदङ्गपणवैः घण्टावसक्तैः प्रतीक्षमाणानि व्यवस्थितानि सन्दृश्यन्ते स्म। सर्व्वे वायवश्चावस्थिता

१ अत्र चतुःस्थानेषु नपुंसकप्रयोग उचितः सुगन्धितैलपूरितानीत्यादिवत्।

न वान्ति स्म । सर्व्वनदीनां प्रस्रवणानि न वहन्ति स्म । चन्द्रसूर्य्यवि-
मानानि नक्षत्रज्योतिर्गणाश्च न वहन्ति स्म। पुष्यनक्षत्रयुक्तमभूत्।
रत्नजातपरिस्फुटं च राज्ञः शुद्धोदनस्य गृहं संस्थितमभूत् ।
वैश्वानरश्च न ज्वलति स्म । कूटागारप्रासादतोरणशालक
तलेषु च मणिरत्नान्यभिप्रलम्बमानानि च सन्दृश्यन्ते स्म । दूष्य-
गन्धाश्च विविधरत्नगन्धाश्च प्रावृतः सन्दृश्यते स्म । काकोलूकगृध्र
वृकशृगालशब्दाश्चान्तर्हिता अभूवन् । सुजातजातशब्दाश्च
श्रूयन्ते स्म । सर्वजनपदकर्म्मान्ताश्च समुच्छिन्ना अभूवन् । उत्-
कूलनिकूलाश्च पृथिवीप्रदेशाः समाः समवस्थिताः सर्व्ववीथी-
चत्वरशृङ्गाटकरथ्यान्तरापणमुखानि च पाणितलप्रष्ठानीव
पुष्पाभिकीर्णानि विरोचन्ते स्म । सर्व्वाश्च गुर्व्विण्यः सम्यक्
सुखेन प्रसूयन्ते स्म। सर्व्वे शालवनदेवदेवताश्च पत्रेष्वर्द्धकाया-
नभिनिर्म्माय नमस्यन्तः स्थिताः सन्दृश्यन्ते स्म । इमानि
द्वात्रिंशत्पूर्व्वनिमित्तानि प्रादुरभूवन् ॥

अथ खलु मायादेवी बोधिसत्त्वस्य जन्मकालसमयं ज्ञात्वा
बोधिसत्त्वस्यैव तेजोनुभावेन रात्र्यां प्रथमे यामे राजानमुप-
सङ्क्रम्य गाथाभिरध्यभाषत ॥

देव शृणु हि मह्यं (१) भाषतो जन्मतव्ये
अचिरचिरचिरेण जात उद्यानबुद्धिः ।
यदि च तव न रोषो नैव दोषो न मोहः

---

१ "मह्यं" मम। अचिरचिरचिरेण चिरकालादपि जाता उद्यानगमने बुद्धिः शाकपार्थिवादित्वात् गमनशब्दलोपः चिप्रमद्य गच्छेयं क्रीडोद्यानभूमिं चयनिरार्थः ।

चिरप्रभव प्रजेया क्रीडउद्यानभूमिं ॥
त्वमिह तपसि खिन्नो धर्म्मचित्तप्रयुक्तो
अहञ्च चिरप्रविष्टा युद्धसत्त्वं धरेन्ती (१)।
द्रुमवर प्रतिबुद्धाः फुल्लिताः शालवृक्षाः
युक्त भविय देवा गन्तुमुद्यानभूमिं (२) ॥
ऋतुप्रवर वसन्तो योषितां मण्डनीयो
भ्रमरवरविघुष्टाः कोकिलाबर्हिगीताः।
सुचिर चिरविचित्रा भ्राम्यते पुष्परेणुः
साधु ददहि आज्ञां गच्छामो मा विलम्बं (३) ॥
वचनमिमु श्रुणित्वा देविये पार्थिवेन्द्र-
स्तुष्टो मुदितचित्तः पारिषद्यानवोचत्।
हयगजरथपङ्क्त्या वाहनान् योजयध्वं
प्रवरगुणसमृद्धां लुम्बिनीं मण्डयध्वं (४) ॥
नीलगिरिनिकाशान् मेघवर्णानुबद्धान्
विंशतिश्च सहस्रान्योजयध्वं गजानां।
मणिकनकविचित्रान्हेमजालोपगूढान्
घण्टरुचिरपार्श्वान् षड्विषाणान् गजेन्द्रान् (५) ॥
हिमरजतनिकाशान्मुञ्जकेशान्सुकेशान्
विंशति च सहस्रान्योजयध्वं हयानां।

---

१ प्रयुक्तधर्म्मचित्ते। धारयन्तीत्यर्थः। २ द्रुमवरा युक्तं भवेत् इत्यर्थः। ३ ऋतुप्रवरो वसन्तः कोकिलबर्हिभिर्गीता यत्र पुंस्त्वमार्गत्वात् सुचिरं भ्राम्यते पुष्परेणवो देवि गच्छाम इति वक्ष्यमाणवचनस्य सम्बन्धाभिप्रायेणेत्यर्थः। ४ इदं श्रुत्वा देवा इत्यर्थः। ५ विंशतिसहस्राम् षड्भावचिरपार्श्वान्।

कनकरचितपार्श्वान् किङ्किणीजालनद्धान्
पवनजवितवेगान् वाहनान् पार्थिवस्य (१) ॥
नरगण रणशौण्डान् शूर सङ्ग्रामकामान्
असिधनुशरशक्तिपाशखड्गाग्रहस्तान् ।
विंशति च सहस्राण्योजयध्वं सुशीघ्रं
माय सपरिवारां रक्षथा अप्रमत्ताः (२) ॥
मणिकनकनिषिक्तां लुम्बिनीं मण्डयध्वं
विविधवसनरत्नैः सर्व्ववृक्षा प्रवेथा ।
विविधकुसुमचित्रं नन्दनं वा सुराणां
वद तथ मम शीघ्रं सर्व्वमेतद्विधाय (३) ॥
वचनमिमु निशम्य पारिषद्यैः क्षणेन
वाहन कृतसज्जा लुम्बिनी मण्डिता सा ।
पारिषद्य आह ॥
जय जय हि नरेन्द्र आयुःपाले हि दीर्घं
सर्व्वं कृतु यथोक्तान्ते कालु देव प्रतीक्ष (४) ॥
सो च नरवरेन्द्रो हृष्टचित्तो भवित्वा
गृहवरतनु प्रविष्टो इस्त्रिकानेवमाह ।
यस्य अह मनापो या च मे प्रीतिकामा

१ विंशतिसहस्राणीत्यर्थः सर्व्वत्रास पुंस्त्वमार्षत्वात्। २ नरगणान् शूरान् असिधनुः-शरेत्यादिहस्तान् विंशतिसहस्रान् मायां रक्षतेति। ३ सर्व्ववृक्षान् प्रवेशयत वदत तथा कृत्यमिदं ममेति कर्म्मणि षष्ठी मामित्यर्थः। ४वचनमिदं वाहनानि कृतसज्जानि कृतानीति शेषः अथ आयुःपालोऽपि दीर्घमित्यस्य दीर्घमायुः पालय त्वं दीर्घायुर्भवेति यावत् अथवा हे आयुःपाल त्वमेव दीर्घकालं कृतं कालं प्रतीक्षामहे।

या मि कुरुत आशां मण्डयित्वात्मभावं (१) ॥
वरसुरभिसुगन्धां भावरक्तां विचित्रां
वसन मृदु मनोज्ञा प्रावृणोथा उदारा: ।
उरसि विगलितानां मुक्तहारा भवेथा:
आभरणविभूषां दर्शयेथाऽद्य सर्वा: (२) ॥
तूर्यपणवमृदङ्गां वीणवेणुमुकुन्दां
तूर्यशतसहस्रान्योजयध्वं मनोज्ञं ।
भूयःकुरुत हर्षं देवकन्यान यूयं
शृणु मधुरघोषं देवताऽपि स्पृहेयु: (३) ॥
एक रथवरेऽस्मिं तिष्ठतां मायदेवी
मा च पुरुष स्त्री अन्य तत्रारुहेया ।
नारि विविधवर्णास्तं रथं वाहयन्तां
मा च कश्चित् प्रतिकूलं माऽमनापं शृणेया (४) ॥
हयगजरथपत्ती सैन्यश्रीमद्विचित्रा
द्वारि स्थित नृपस्य श्रूयते उग्रघोष: ।
क्षुभितजलनिधेर्वा श्रूयते एव शब्दो
माय यद्गृहातो निर्गता द्वारमूलं (५) ॥

---

१ स च भूत्वा प्रवरमं "इष्टिकाम्" वहिधारकाम् चरं यथमे प्रीतिकामः स मे करोत् चन यस्य मनसि चरं मनापः सुरूपवानिति बुद्धिरितिस्पष्टार्थः । २ वरसुरभिगन्धानि भावरक्तानि विचित्राणि वसनानि मृदूनि मनोज्ञानि प्रावृणुत उरसि विगलित मुक्ताहारा भवत दर्शयताद्य सर्वं इति प्राकृतपर्य्यायाः । ३ तूर्यपणवमृदङ्गान्वीणावेणुमुकुन्दान्देवकन्यानां शृणुत "देवताऽपि" चाप स्पृहेरार्थः । ४ एकस्मिन्नस्मिन् माया देवी पुरुषो मा को चान्यस्तत्रारुहेत् नार्य्यो वाहयत नाययत इति । ५ हयगजरथपत्तीनां श्रीमद्विचित्रसैन्यानां स्थितानां माया यद्गृहात इति ।

अष्ट शतसहस्रा नादिता मञ्जुवाद्यैं
सो च रथविचित्रो मण्डितः पार्थिवेन ।
अपि चमरसहस्रैः दिव्यसिंहासनेभि- (१)
श्चतुरि रतनवृक्षाः पत्रपुष्पोपपेताः ॥

अभिनन्दितमनोज्ञा हंसक्रौञ्चाम्मयूराण्
ध्वजपताकासोत्थिता वैजयन्त्यः ।
किङ्किणिवरजालैर्नादिते दिव्यवस्त्रैः
सुरवधु गगनेऽस्मिं तं रथं प्रेषयन्ते (२) ॥

दिव्यमधुरघोषं श्रावयन्त्यस्तुवन्ति
उपविशति यदा सा माय सिंहासनाये ।
प्रचलित चिसहस्रा मेदिनी षड्विकारा
पुष्पवर क्षिपिंसु अम्बरा भ्रामयीषु (३) ॥

अथ जगति श्रेष्ठो जायते लुम्बिनीये
चतुरि जगतिपालास्तं रथं वाहयन्ते ।
त्रिदशपतिरपीन्द्रो मार्गशुद्धिं करोति
ब्रह्म पुरत गच्छी दुर्जनां वारयन्तो (४) ॥

अमरशतसहस्राः प्राञ्जलीका नमन्ते
नृपति मुदितचित्तो वीक्षते तां वि ूहां ।

---

१ अष्टाः शत सहस्राणि च च चामरसहस्रैर्दिव्यसिंहासनैरिति । २ (अथ ये इत्युक्त) ये चत्वारो रत्नदृक्षा हंसक्रौञ्चमयूराणां अभिनन्दितमनोज्ञास्तेष्वांच ध्वजपताका वैजयन्त्यश्चाभिश्च दिव्यवस्त्रैश्च मण्डित इति पूर्वेणान्वयः किङ्किणीवरजालैः सुरवध्वोऽस्मिन् प्रचलने इति । ३ उपविष्टा माया प्रचलिता पुष्पवराम् क्षिपन्तो अम्बरे भ्रामयिता । ४ जनियति चत्वारो जगतीपाला वहन्ति ब्रह्मा पुरतो गच्छति दुर्जनां-मान्वारयन् ।

तस्य भवति एवं व्यक्तोऽयं देवदेवो
यस्य चतुरि पाला शक्र सेन्द्राश्च देवाः (१) ॥
कुरुत विपुलपूजां व्यक्तयं शुद्ध भावी
नास्ति त्रिभुवि सत्त्वो यः सहे पूजमेतां ।
देव अथ च नागाः शक्र ब्रह्मा च पालाः
मूर्द्धं तदफलेर्ष्या जीवितं चास्य गच्छेत् (२) ॥
अयु पुनरतिदेवः सर्व्वपूजां सहाति (३) ।

अथ खलु भिक्षवो मायादेवी च चतुरशीत्या हयरथसहस्रैः सर्व्वालङ्कारभूषितैः परिवृता चतुरशीत्या गजरथसहस्रैः सर्व्वालङ्कारविभूषितैः चतुरशीत्या चमूपत्तिसहस्रैः शूरैर्वीरैर्वराङ्गरूपिभिः सुसन्नद्धदृढवर्म्मकवचितैरनुपरिगृहीता षष्ट्या च शाक्यकन्यासहस्रैः पुरस्कृता चत्वारिंशता च सहस्रैः राज्ञः शुद्धोदनस्य ज्ञातिकुलप्रसूतैः शाक्यैः वृद्धदहरमध्यमैः संरक्षिता षष्ट्या च सहस्रैः राज्ञः शुद्धोदनस्यान्तःपुरेण गीतवाद्यसमन्यक्तुर्य्यताडावचरसङ्गीतिसम्प्रवादितेन परिवृता चतुरशीत्या च देवकन्यासहस्रैः परिवृता चतुरशीत्या च नागकन्यासहस्रैश्चतुरशीत्या च गन्धर्व्वकन्यासहस्रैश्च चतुरशीत्या च किन्नरकन्यासहस्रैश्चतुरशीत्या चासुरकन्यासहस्रै-

---

१ चमरव्रतधरत्वादि प्रांशुलिकानि चव पुंस्त्वमार्षत्वात् नृपतिर्मुदितचित्तो वीक्षते तं सूनुं चत्वारः शक्रा । २ कुर्व्वते व्यक्तोऽयं शुद्धोभावीति यदेत् पूजामेतां देवोऽथ शक्रो ब्रह्मा "तदफलेर्ष्या" यदि यः कोऽपि एतेषु मध्ये इमां पूजां सहतोयात्तस्य मूर्द्धाप्रस्फुटेत् इत्यर्थोयमता व्याख्या । ३ अयंपुनः चातिदेवः सहति ।

नानाव्यूहालङ्कारालङ्कृताभिर्नानागीतवाद्यवर्णभाषिणीभिरनु-
गम्यमाना निर्य्याति स्म। सर्व्वं च लुम्बिनीवनं गन्धोदक-
सिक्तं दिव्यपुष्पाभिकीर्णमिवतमभूत्। सर्व्ववृक्षाश्च तस्मिन्वन-
वरे अकाले पत्रपुष्पफलानि ददति स्म। देवैश्च तथा तद्वनं सम-
लङ्कृतमभूत्। तद्यथाऽपि नाम मिश्रकावनं देवानां समलङ्कृतं ॥

अथ खलु मायादेवी लुम्बिनीवनमनुप्रविश्य तस्माद्रथव-
रादवतीर्य्य नरमरुत्कन्यापरिवृता वृक्षेण वृक्षं पर्य्यटन्ती
वनाद्वनं चङ्क्रम्यमाणा द्रुमाद्द्रुमं निरीक्षमाणा अनुपूर्व्वेण ये-
नासौ प्लक्षो महाद्रुमरत्नवरप्रवरः सुविभक्तशाखः सुपत्र-
मञ्जरीधरो दिव्यमानुष्यकनानापुष्पसम्पुष्पितो वरप्रवर
सुरभिगन्धी नानारङ्गवस्त्राभिप्रलम्बितो विविधमणिविचित्र-
प्रभोज्ज्वलितः सर्व्वरत्नमूलदण्डशाखापत्रसमलङ्कृतः सुविभक्त-
विस्तीर्णशाखः करतलनिभभूमिभागे सुविभक्तविस्तीर्णनील-
तृणे मयूरग्रीवासन्निभे काचिलिन्दिकसुखसंस्पर्शे धरणीतले
संस्थितः पूर्व्वजिनजनित्रीप्रतिनिवासितः देवसङ्गीत्यनुगीतः
शुभविमलविशुद्धः शुद्धावासदेवशतसहस्रैः प्रशान्तचित्तैरभि-
नतः जटामुकुटावलम्बिताऽवनतमूर्द्धभिरभिनन्द्यमानस्तं प्लक्ष
वृक्षमुपजगाम ॥

अथ स प्लक्षो वृक्षो बोधिसत्त्वस्य तेजोऽनुभावेनाऽवनम्य
प्रणमति स्म॥ अथ मायादेवी गगनतलगतेव विद्युद्दृष्टिं दक्षि-
णबाहुं प्रसार्य्य प्लक्षशाखां गृहीत्वा सलीलं गगनतलं प्रेक्ष-
माणा विजृम्भमाणा स्थिताऽभूत्॥ अथ तस्मिन् समये

षष्ट्यप्सरःशतसहस्राणि कामावचरदेवेभ्य उपसङ्क्रम्य माया-
देव्या उपस्थाने परिचर्य्यां कुर्व्वन्ति स्म ॥

एवं रूपेण खलु पुनर्ऋद्धिप्रातिहार्य्येण समन्वागतो बोधिसत्त्वो मातुः कुक्षिगतोऽस्थात्। स परिपूर्णानां दशानां मासानामत्ययेन मातुर्दक्षिणपार्श्वान्निष्क्रमति स्म। स्मृतः सम्प्रजानन्ननुपलिप्तो गर्भमलैर्य्यथा नान्यः कश्चिदुच्यतेऽन्येषां गर्भमल इति ॥

तस्मिन् खलु पुनर्भिक्षवः समये शक्रो देवानामिन्द्रो ब्रह्मा च सहाम्पतिः पुरतः स्थितावभूतां। यौ बोधिसत्त्वं परमगौरवजातौ दिव्यकौशिकवस्त्रान्तरितं सर्व्वाङ्गप्रत्यङ्गैः स्मृतौ सम्प्रज्ञौ प्रतिगृह्णीतः स्म ॥

यस्मिंश्च कूटागारे बोधिसत्त्वो मातुः कुक्षिगतोऽस्थात् तं ब्रह्मा सहाम्पतिर्ब्रह्मकायिकाश्च देवपुत्रा अभ्युत्क्षिप्य ब्रह्मलोकञ्चैत्यार्थं पूजार्थं चोपनामयामासुः (१)। अपरिगृहीतः खलु पुनर्बोधिसत्त्वः केनचिन्मनुष्यभूतेन ॥ अथ तर्हि बोधिसत्त्वं देवताः प्रथमतरं प्रतिगृह्णन्ति स्म। अथ बोधिसत्त्वो जातमात्रः पृथिव्यामवतरति स्म। समनन्तरावतीर्णस्य च बोधिसत्त्वस्य च महासत्त्वस्य महापृथिवीं भित्त्वा महापद्मं प्रादुरभूत्। नन्दोपनन्दौ च नागराजानौ (२)। गगनतलेऽर्द्धकायौ स्थित्वा शीतोष्णे द्वे वारिधारेऽभिनिर्म्माय बोधिसत्त्वं स्नापयतः स्म। शक्रब्रह्मलोकपालाः पूर्व्वङ्गमाश्चान्ये

---

१ उपानयामासुरिति। २ नागराजौ इति।

च बहवो देवपुत्राः शतसहस्रा ये बोधिसत्त्वं जातमात्रं नाना-गन्धोदकमुक्तकुसुमैः स्नापयन्तोऽभ्यवकिरन्ति स्म । अन्त-रिक्षे च द्वे चामरे रत्नच्छत्रं च प्रादुरभूत् ॥ स तस्मिन् महापद्मे स्थित्वा चतुर्दिशमवलोकयति स्म ॥ चतुर्दिशमवलोक्य सिंहा-वलोकितं महापुरुषावलोकितं व्यवलोकयति स्म ॥

तस्मिन् खलु पुनः समये बोधिसत्त्वस्य पूर्व्वकुशलमूलविपा-कजन्मप्रतिष्ठितेन दिव्यचक्षुः प्रादुरभूत् । येन दिव्येन चक्षुषा सर्व्वावन्तं त्रिसाहस्रं महासाहस्रं लोकधातुं सनगरनिगमग्राम-जनपदराष्ट्रराजधानिं सदेवमानुषं पश्यति स्म । सर्व्वसत्त्वानाञ्च चित्तचरितञ्च प्रजानाति स्म । ज्ञात्वा च व्यवलोकयति स्म । अस्ति त्वन्यो कश्चित् सत्त्वो यो मया सदृशः शीलेन च समा-धिना वा प्रज्ञया वा कुशलमूलचर्य्यया वा । यदा च बोधि-सत्त्वः त्रिसाहस्रमहासाहस्रलोकधातौ न कश्चित् सत्त्वमा-त्मतुल्यं पश्यति स्म ॥

अथ तस्मिन् समये बोधिसत्त्वः सिंह इव विगतभयभैर-वोऽसन्त्रस्तोऽस्तम्भितः सुचिन्तितं स्मृत्वा चिन्तयित्वा सर्व्वसत्त्वानां चित्तचरितानि ज्ञात्वा सुपरिस्फुटीतो बोधिसत्त्वः पूर्व्वां दिश-मभिमुखः सप्तपदानि प्रक्रान्तः पूर्व्वङ्गमो भविष्यामि सर्व्वेषां कुशलमूलानां धर्म्माणां । तस्य प्रक्रमत उपर्य्यन्तरीक्षेऽपरिगृहीतं दिव्यश्वेतं विपुलं छत्रं चामरशुभे गच्छन्तमनुगच्छन्ति स्म ॥ यत्र यत्र च बोधिसत्त्वः पदमुत्क्षिपति स्म । तत्र तत्र पद्मानि प्रादुर्भवन्ति स्म । एवं दक्षिणां दिशमभिमुखः सप्तपदानि

प्रक्रान्तः । दक्षिणीयो भविष्यामि देवमनुष्याणां ॥ पश्चिमां दिशमभिमुखः सप्तपदानि प्रक्रान्तः सप्तमे पदे स्थित्वा सिंहवत् नादनात्मिकां वाचं भाषते स्म । अहं लोके ज्येष्ठोऽहं लोके श्रेष्ठ इयं मे पश्चिमा जातिः करिष्यामि जातिजरामरण-दुःखस्यान्तं ॥ उत्तरां दिशमभिमुखः सप्तपदानि प्रक्रान्तः । अनुत्तरो भविष्यामि सर्व्वसत्त्वानां ॥ अधोदिशमभिमुखः सप्तपदानि प्रक्रान्तः । निहनिष्यामि मारं च मारसेनाञ्च । सर्व्वनैरयिकाणाञ्च निरयाग्निप्रतिघाताय महाधर्म्ममेघवृष्टिं वर्षिष्यामि (१) । येन ते सुखसमर्पिता भविष्यन्ति । उल्लोकनीयो भविष्यामि सर्व्वसत्त्वानां ॥ समनन्तरभाषिता चेयं वाग् बोधिसत्त्वेन ॥

अथ तस्मिन् समये अयं त्रिसाहस्रमहासाहस्रलोकधातुः स्वरेणाऽभिविज्ञप्तोऽभूदियं बोधिसत्त्वकर्म्मविपाकजा अभिज्ञाधर्म्मता ॥ यदा बोधिसत्त्वश्चरमभविको जायते यदा चानुत्तरां सम्यक्सम्बोधिमभिसम्बुध्यते तदाऽस्येमान्येवंरूपाणि ऋद्धिप्रातिहार्य्याणि भवन्ति ॥ तस्मिन् खलु पुनर्भिक्षवः समये संहर्षितरोमकूपजाताः सर्व्वसत्त्वा अभूवन् ॥ महतश्च पृथिवीचालस्य लोके प्रादुर्भावोऽभूत् भैरवस्य रोमहर्षणस्य । अघट्टितानि च दिव्यमानुष्यकाणि तूर्य्याणि सम्प्रवादितानि । सर्व्वर्त्तुकालिकाश्च वृक्षास्तस्मिन् त्रिसाहस्रमहासाहस्रलोकधातौ सकुसुमिताः फलिताश्च ॥ विशुद्धाच्च गगनतलान् मेघशब्दाः श्रूयन्ते स्म ॥ अपगतमेघाच्च गगनाच्छनैः सूक्ष्मः सूक्ष्मो देवो

१ वर्षयिष्यामि ।

वर्षन्ति स्म ॥ नानादिव्यकुसुमवस्त्राभरणगन्धचूर्णव्यामिश्राः परमसुखसंस्पर्शाश्च सौम्याश्च सुगन्धवाताः प्रवान्ति स्म ॥ व्यपगततमोरजोधूमनीहाराश्च सर्व्वा दिशः सुप्रसन्ना विराजन्ते स्म ॥ उपरिष्टाच्चान्तरिक्षाददृश्या गम्भीरा महाब्रह्मघोषाः संश्रूयन्ते स्म ॥ सर्वचन्द्रसूर्य्यशक्रब्रह्मलोकपालप्रभाश्चाभिभूता अभूवन् ॥ परमसुखसंस्पर्शया च सर्व्वसत्त्वकायचित्तसुखसञ्जनन्या लोकोत्तरयाऽनेकशतसहस्रवर्णप्रभया सर्व्वस्त्रिसाहस्रलोकधातुः परिस्फुटोऽभूत् ॥ समनन्तरजातस्य खलु पुनर्बोधिसत्त्वस्यैकान्तसुखसमर्पिताः सर्व्वसत्त्वा अभूवुः । सर्व्वे रागद्वेषमोहदर्पारतिविषादभयलोभेर्ष्यामात्सर्य्यविगताः । सर्व्वे अकुशलक्रियाप्रतिविरताः ॥ व्याधितानां सत्त्वानां व्याधय उपशान्ताः ॥ क्षुत्पिपासितानां सत्त्वानां क्षुत्पिपासा प्रस्रब्धाऽभूत् । मद्यमदमत्तानां च सत्त्वानां मदापगमः संवृत्तः ॥ उन्मत्तैश्च स्मृतिः प्रतिलब्धा ॥ चक्षुर्विकलैश्च सत्त्वैश्चक्षुः प्रतिलब्धं । श्रोत्रविकलैश्च सत्त्वैः श्रोत्रं ॥ मुखप्रत्यङ्गविकलेन्द्रियाश्चाविकलेन्द्रियाः संवृत्ताः ॥ दरिद्रैश्च धनानि प्रतिलब्धानि ॥ बन्धनबद्धाश्च बन्धनेभ्यो विमुक्ताः ॥ आवीचिमादिं कृत्वा सर्व्वनैरयिकाणां सत्त्वानां सर्व्वकारणादुःखं तस्मिन् समये प्रस्रब्धं ॥ तिर्य्यग्योनिगतानामन्योऽन्यं भक्षणादिदुःखं यमलोकिकानां सत्त्वानां क्षुत्पिपासादिदुःखं व्युपशान्तमभूत् । यदा च बोधिसत्त्वो जातमात्रः सप्तपदानि प्रक्रान्तोऽभूत् ॥ असङ्ख्यकल्पकोटिनियुतशतसहस्रैः सुचरितचरणैर्महावीर्य्यमहाभ्यासधर्म्मताप्रतिल-

येन तस्मिन् समये दशदिग्लोकधातुस्थिता बुद्धा भगवन्तस्तं पृथिवीप्रदेशं वज्रमयमधितिष्ठन्ति स्म॥ येन महापृथिवी तस्मिन् प्रदेशेऽवतीर्य्य तावन् महाबलवेगसमन्वागतो हि भिक्षवो जातमात्रो बोधिसत्त्वः सप्तपदानि प्रक्रान्तोऽभूत्॥ सर्व्वलोकान्तराणि च तस्मिन् समये महताऽवभासेन स्फुटान्यभूवन्॥ महांश्च तस्मिन् समये गीतशब्दोऽभून्नृत्यशब्दः॥ अप्रमेयाश्च तस्मिन् समये पुष्पचूर्णगन्धमाल्यरत्नाभरणवस्त्रमेघा अभिप्रवर्षन्ति स्म॥ परमसुखसमर्पिताश्च सर्व्वसत्त्वा अभूवन्॥ सङ्क्षेपादचिन्त्या सा क्रियाऽभूत्। यदा बोधिसत्त्वो लोके प्रादुरभूत् सर्व्वलोकाभ्युद्गतः॥

अथ खल्वायुष्मानानन्द उत्थायासनादेकांसमुत्तरासङ्गं कृत्वा दक्षिणं जानुमण्डलं पृथिव्यां प्रतिष्ठाप्य येन भगवांस्तेनाञ्जलिं प्रणम्य भगवन्तमेतदवोचत्। सर्व्वसत्त्वानां भगवंस्तथागत आश्चर्य्यभूतोऽभूत्॥ बोधिसत्त्व एवाऽभूत् धर्म्मसमन्वागतस्तेकः पुनर्वाद एवं अनुत्तरां सम्यक्सम्बोधिमभिसम्बुद्धः॥ एषोऽहं भगवंस्तत्प्रथमकृत्त्वोऽपि यावत् पश्चाच्छतकृत्त्वोऽपि यावदनेकशतसहस्रशोऽप्यहं भगवन् बुद्धं भगवन्तं शरणं गच्छामि॥ एवमुक्ते भगवानायुष्मन्तमानन्दमेतदवोचत्॥ भविष्यन्ति खलु पुनरानन्दाऽनागतेऽध्वन्यनेके भिक्षवः अभावितकाया अभावितचित्ता अभावितशीला अभावितप्रज्ञा बाला अपण्डिता अधिमानिका उद्धता उन्नता असदृप्ता विक्षिप्तचित्ताः काङ्क्षापरीता विचिकित्साबहुला अश्रद्धा श्रवणचलाः श्रवणप्रति-

रूपकास्ते न श्रद्धास्यन्ति इमामेवं रूपां बोधिसत्त्वस्य गर्भावक्रान्तिपरिशुद्धिं ॥ तेऽन्योन्यमेकान्ते सन्निपत्यैवं वक्ष्यन्ति । पश्यत यूयमेतदयोग्यतमं बोधिसत्त्वस्य किल मातुः कुक्षिगतस्योच्चारप्रस्रावमण्डलपरिमिश्रस्य ईदृशी विभूतिरासीत् । स च किलाभिनिष्क्रामन् मातुर्दक्षिणाया कुक्षेरनुपलिप्तो गर्भमलेनाभूदिति । कथमेतद्युज्यते ॥ न पुनस्ते मोहपुरुषा एवं ज्ञास्यन्ति । न सुकृतकर्म्मणां सत्त्वानामुच्चारप्रस्रावमण्डले कायः सम्भवतीति ॥ भद्रिका खल्वपि तथारूपाणां गर्भावक्रान्तिर्भवति । गर्भावस्थितस्य सत्त्वानुकम्पया हि बोधिसत्त्वो मनुष्यलोके उपपद्यते । न देवभूत एवं धर्म्मचक्रं प्रवर्त्तयति ॥ तत् कस्मान्मा खल्वानन्द सत्त्वाः कौषीद्यमापत्स्यन्ते । भगवान् तथागतोऽर्हन् सम्यक्सम्बुद्धो वयं तु मनुष्यमात्रा न वयं समर्थास्तत्स्थानं परिपूरयितुमिति कौषीद्यमापद्येरन् ॥ न खलु पुनस्तेषां मोहपुरुषाणां धर्म्मस्तैन्यकानामेवं भविष्यति । अचिन्त्यो हि स सत्त्वानां नासावस्माभिरप्रामाणिकः कर्त्तव्य इति ॥ अपि तु खल्वानन्द बुद्धर्द्धिप्रातिहार्य्यमपि ते तस्मिन् काले नाऽवकल्पयिष्यन्ति । किमङ्ग पुनर्बोधिसत्त्वभूतस्य तथागतस्य बोधिसत्त्वस्य प्रातिहार्य्याणि ॥ ये चानन्द (१) कियन्तस्ते मोहपुरुषा बहुपुण्याभिसंस्कारमभिसंस्करिष्यन्ति । ये बुद्धधर्म्मान् प्रतिक्षेप्स्यन्ति लाभसत्कारश्लोकाऽभिभूता उच्चारलग्ना लाभसत्काराऽभिभूता इतरजातीयाः ॥

---

१ पश्यानन्देति वा पाठः ।

आनन्द आह । एवंरूपा भगवन् अनागतेऽध्वनि भिक्षवो भविष्यन्ति । य इमामेवं भद्रिकां सूत्रान्तां प्रतिक्षेप्स्यन्ति । प्रतिपक्षं वक्ष्यन्ति च ॥

भगवानाह । एवंरूपाश्च ते आनन्द सूत्रान्तां प्रपिक्षेप्स्यन्ति प्रतिवक्ष्यन्ति चानेकप्रकारान् चान्योन्यप्रकारानभिसंस्कारानभिसंस्करिष्यन्ति । अनर्थिकाश्च ते श्रामण्ये न भविष्यन्ति ॥

आनन्द आह । का पुनर्भगवंस्तथारूपाणामसत्पुरुषाणां गतिर्भविष्यति कोऽभिसम्परायः ॥

भगवानाह । यां गतिं बुद्धबोधिमन्तर्धाप्याऽतीतानागतप्रत्युत्पन्नानां च बुद्धा भगवन्तो व्याख्यायन्ते ते तां गतिं गमिष्यन्ति॥

अथ खल्वायुष्मानानन्दः संहर्षितो रोमकूपजातो नमो बुद्धाय इत्युक्त्वा भगवन्तमेतदवोचत् । मूर्च्छा मे भगवन् कायस्याऽभूदिमं तेषामसत्पुरुषाणां समुदाचारं श्रुत्वा ॥

भगवानाह । न तेषामानन्द समाचारा विषमसमुदाचाराः । खलु पुनस्ते सत्त्वा भविष्यन्ति । ते तेन विषमेन समुदाचारेणावीचौ महानरके प्रपतिष्यन्ति ॥

तत् कस्य हेतोः ॥

ये केचिदानन्द भिक्षवो वा भिक्षुक्यो वा उपासको वा उपासिका वा इमामेवं रूपां सूत्रान्तां तावच्छ्रुत्वा नाऽधिमोक्ष्यन्ति न श्रद्धास्यन्ति न प्रतिवेत्स्यन्ति ते च्युताः समाना आवीचौ महानरके प्रपतिष्यन्ति ॥ माऽऽनन्द तथागता अप्रामाणिकं अकार्षुः ॥

तत् कस्माद्धेतोः ॥

अप्रमेयो ह्यानन्द तथागतो गम्भीरो विपुलो दुरवगाहः। येषां केषांचिदानन्द इमामेवंरूपां सूत्रान्तान्तावकुलोपपत्तिं श्रुत्वा ते प्रीतिप्रामोद्यप्रसादलाभास्तैः सत्त्वैः सुलब्धाः ॥ अमोघं च तेषां मानुष्यजीवितं च सुचरितचरणाश्च ते दत्तश्च तैः सारं मुक्ताश्च ते त्रिभ्योऽपायेभ्यो भविष्यन्ति च ते पुत्रास्तथागतस्य परिप्राप्तश्च तैः सर्व्वकार्य्यं अमोघश्च तेषां श्रद्धाप्रतिलम्भः सुविभक्तश्च तै राष्ट्रपिण्डः प्रसन्नाश्च तेऽग्रसत्त्वाः सञ्छिन्नास्तैर्मारपापीयसः। निस्तीर्णश्च तैः संसाराटवीकान्तारः। समुद्धृतश्च तैः शोकशल्यः। प्राप्तं च तैः प्रामोद्यवस्तु। सुपरिगृहीतानि च तैः शरणगमनानि ॥ दक्षिणीयाश्च ते। पूजार्हा दुर्लभप्रादुर्भावाश्च ते लोके धारयितव्याः ॥

तत्कस्य हेतोः ॥

तथा हि ते सर्व्वलोके इममेवं सर्व्वलोकविप्रतिपत्त्यनीकं तथागतधर्मं श्रद्दधन्ति। न ते आनन्द सत्त्वा अवरकेण कुशलमूलेन समन्वागता भविष्यन्ति। तथानन्द सत्त्वा ममैक जातिप्रतिबद्धानि मित्राणि भविष्यन्ति ॥

तत्कस्माद्धेतोः ॥

कश्चिदानन्द श्रवणादेव प्रियो भवति मनापश्च। कश्चिदानन्द दर्शनेनाऽपि प्रियो भवति मनापश्च न तु खलु पुनः श्रवणेन ॥ कश्चिदानन्द दर्शनेन श्रवणेनाऽपि प्रियो भवति मनापश्च। तेषां केषांचिदानन्दोऽहं दर्शनेन वा श्रवणेन वा प्रियो

मनापो भवेयं मित्रात्वं तत्र गच्छन् । न तानि मनैकजातिबद्धानि मित्राणीति दृष्टास्ते तथागतेन मोचयितव्यास्ते तथागतशरणागताः । ते तथागतगुणप्रत्यंशाः । ते तथागतेन कर्त्तव्या उपासकाः । ते ममान्तिकात् खल्वप्यानन्द पूर्व्वं बोधिसत्त्वचर्य्यामेव तावच्चरतो ये केचिद्भयार्द्दिताः सत्त्वा आगत्याऽभयं प्रतियाचन्ते स्म । तेभ्योऽहं सत्त्वेभ्योऽभयं दत्तवान् ॥ किमङ्ग पुनरेतर्ह्यनुत्तरां सम्यक्सम्बोधिमभिसम्बुद्ध श्रद्धयाऽऽनन्द योगः करणीय इदं तथागतो विज्ञापयति । यदानन्द तथागतेन युष्माकं करणीयं कृतं तत्तथागतेन शोधितो यानशब्दः श्रवणेनाप्यानन्द मित्रस्य । ननु योजनशतान्तरमपि गच्छन्ति गत्वा च संमुखिता भवन्त्यदृष्टा पूर्व्वमित्रं । दृष्टा कः पुनर्वादो य इमानि निसृष्टकुशलमूलान्यवलोकयन्ति । शास्तन्यानन्द तथागता अर्हन्तः सम्यक्सम्बुद्धाः पूर्व्वमित्राण्येते सत्त्वास्तथागतानामस्माकमप्येते मित्राणि भवन्तीति ॥

तत्कस्मात् ॥

खलु पुनरानन्द मित्रस्य प्रियं मनापश्च भवति । तस्यापि मित्रस्य यत्प्रियं मित्रं तदपि प्रियमेव भवति मनापं च । तस्मात्तर्ह्यानन्दारोचयामि वः प्रतिवेदयामि वः । श्रद्धामात्रकमुत्पादयत अनुपरिनन्दिष्यामो वयं तान् अनागतानां तथागतानामर्हतां सम्यक्सम्बुद्धानामन्तिकेऽस्माकमपि मित्राणीति विदित्वा यथाऽभिप्रायं परिपूरयिष्यन्ति ॥ तद्यथाऽपि आनन्द कस्य चिदेव पुरुषस्यैकः पुत्रको भवेत् । सुवचाः

प्रदक्षिणग्राही स च पुरुषो वल्गुमित्रो भवेत्। स च तस्मिन् पितरि कालगते न हि विहन्यते पितृमित्रसुपरिगृहीतः। एवमेवानन्द ये केचिन्मम श्रद्धास्यन्ति तानहमुपाददामि मित्राणीव मम तानि ते मम शरणङ्गताः॥ वल्गुमित्रस्य तथागतस्यानि च तथागतस्य मित्राणि भूतवादीनि न मृषावादीन्यनुपरिवदाम्यहं॥ भूतवादीनि यानि तथागतस्य मित्राण्यनागतार्हन्तः सम्यक्सम्बुद्धाः। श्रद्धया आनन्द योगः करणीयः तत्राऽहं युष्मान् विज्ञापयामीति॥

इति हि जाते बोधिसत्त्वे गगनतलगतान्यप्सरःकोटीनियुतशतसहस्राणि दिव्यैः पुष्पधूपगन्धमाल्यविलेपनवस्त्राभरणैर्मायादेवीमभ्यवकिरन्ति स्म॥ तत्रेदमुच्यते॥

शुभविमलविशुद्धहेमप्रभाश्चन्द्रसूर्य्यप्रभाः
षष्टिदशशतसहस्रदेवाप्सरा मञ्जुघोषस्वराः।
तस्मिन् क्षणे उपेत्य तां लुम्बिनीं मायादेव्यब्रुवन्
मा खलु जनि विषादं तुष्टास्तव प्रस्थापिता वयं (१)॥
भण हि किङ्करणीयं किं कुर्व्वामहे किन्नु कार्य्यञ्च ते
वयं तव सुखस्थ्युपस्थापिकाः प्रेमभावस्थिताः।
अपि च भव उदग्र हर्षान्विता मा च खेदं जनेहि
जरामरणविघातिं वैद्योत्तमं अद्य देवी जनेषी लघुं (२)॥
अथ (३) द्रुम परिफुल्ल सम्पुष्पिताः शालवृक्षा इमे

---

१ षष्टिदशशतसहस्रदेवाऽप्सरसो मायादेवीमब्रुवन् जनयेति। २ उद्‌भ्रमा कुरुष्व जरामरणविघातकं जनयिष्यति इति। ३ वर्षेति वा पाठः।

यत्र चमरशतसहस्र पार्श्वे स्थिता भ्रामयन्तो भुजान् ।
यत्र च चलित ससागरा मेदिनी षड्विकारा इयं
दिवि भुवि च विघुष्ट लोकोत्तमं त्वं जनेषी सुतं (१) ॥
यत्र च प्रभ विशुद्धा विभ्राजते स्वर्णवर्ण शुभा
तूर्य्यशत मनोज्ञा वादिता घुष्यन्तेऽम्बरे ।
यत्र च शतसहस्रशुद्धावासाः शुभा वीतरागाः सुरा
नमिषु मुदितचित्ता यद्य जनेषी सर्व्वलोकहितं (२) ॥
शक्रमपि ब्रह्म पालाऽपि चान्ये च देवताः
तुष्ट मुदितचित्ताः पार्श्वे स्थिता नामयन्तो भुजां ।
सो च पुरुषसिंह शुद्धव्रतो भित्वा कुक्षिं विनिर्गर्भोषितः
कनकगिरिनिकाश शुद्धव्रतो निष्क्रमी नायकः (३) ॥
शक्रमपि च ब्रह्म तो पाणिभिः सम्प्रतीच्छा मुनिं
क्षेत्र शतसहस्र कम्पिता आभ मुक्ता शुभा ।
अपि च त्रिषु अपायि सत्त्वाः सुखी नास्ति दुःखं
पुन अमरशतसहस्रा पुष्पा क्षिपी भ्रामयन्त्यम्बरात् (४) ॥
वीर्य्यबलउपेत वज्रात्मिका मेदिनी संस्थिताऽभूत्तदा
पद्म रुचिरचित्र अभ्युद्गतो यत्र चक्राङ्कचित्रेभिः
पद्भ्यां स्थितो विनायकः ।

---

१ द्रुमाः परिफुल्लिता यथा चामरशतसहस्राणि । चत्र भ्रमा भ्रामयन्तीति शेषः । यथा चलिता विघुष्टं जनयिष्यसि । २ यथा प्रभा स्वर्णवर्णा तूर्य्यशतानि मनोज्ञानि वादितानि घुष्यन्ते यथा च नमन्ति जनयिष्यसि । ३ शक्रोऽपि ब्रह्मा पाला अपि चान्या तुष्टा भुजाम् स च पुरुषसिंहः कनकगिरिनिकाशो निरक्रामीत् । ४ शक्रोऽपि ब्रह्मा सम्प्रत्यच्छादयतां क्षेत्रं शतसहस्रं कम्पितमाभा अपायेषु सुखिनः पुनरमरशतसहस्राणि पुष्पाणि क्षिपन्ति ।

सप्तपदा क्रमित्वा ब्रह्मस्वरो मुञ्चि घोषोत्तमं
जरामरणविघाती वैद्योत्तमो भैष्यिसर्व्वोत्तमः (१) ॥
गगनतले हि स्थित्वा ब्रह्मोत्तमः शक्र देवोत्तमः
सुचिरुचिरप्रसन्नगन्धोदकैर्विस्नपी विनायकं ।
अपि च उरगराजा शीतोष्णे दे वारिधारे
शुभेऽप्यमुञ्चतान्तरिचे स्थितो
अमरशतसहस्रं गन्धोदकैर्विस्नपी विनायकं (२) ॥
लोकपालाश्च सम्भ्रान्ताः सन्धारयन्ति करैः शोभनैः ।
त्रिसहस्रा इयं भूमिः कम्पते सचराचरा (३) ॥
प्रभा च रुचिरा मुक्ता अपायाश्च विशोधिताः ।
क्लेशदुःखाश्च ते (४) शान्ता जाते लोके विनायके ॥
क्षिपन्ति मरुतः पुष्पी जातेऽस्मिन्नरनायके ।
क्रम सप्तपदां वीरः क्रमते बलवीर्य्यवान् (५) ॥
पादौ निक्षिपते यत्र भूमौ पद्मवराः शुभाः ।
अभ्युद्गच्छन्ततो मह्यां सर्व्वरत्नविभूषितां (६) ॥
यदा सप्तपदां गत्वा ब्रह्मस्वरमुदाहरिं (७) ।
जरामरणविघाती भिषग्वर इवोद्गतः ॥
व्यवलोकयित्वा च विशारदो दिशस्ततो गिरमुञ्चति (८) अर्थयुक्तां ।

---

१ वीर्य्यबलोपेता पद्मानि रुचिरचित्राणि चाभ्युद्गतानि चक्राङ्कचिताभ्यामिति सप्तपदानि चमुचद् भैषज्यसर्व्वोत्तमः। भैषज्यसर्व्वोत्तम इत्यस्य भैषज्यदाने सर्व्वोत्तम इत्यभिप्रायः। २ शक्रो देवोत्तमो व्यस्नापयत् उरगराजोऽमुञ्चद्व्यस्नापयत्। ३ चकम्पत त्रिसहस्रा इयमवनिः सचराचरा। ४ च पुंस्त्वमार्जवात्। ५ पुष्पाणि क्रमान्सप्तपदानि इति। ६ चाभ्युद्गच्छन्ति तत्र सर्व्वरत्नविभूषितायामिति। ७ उदाहरदिति। ८ चामुञ्चदिति।

ज्येष्ठोऽहं सर्व्वलोकस्य श्रेष्ठो लोके विनायकः ॥

इयं च जातिर्मम पश्चिमा इति हास्यं च मुक्तं नरनायकेन ।

स लोकपालैर्मरुद्भिश्च (१) सेन्द्रैः प्रसन्नचित्तैर्वरगन्धवारिभिः ॥

संस्कारितो लोकहितार्थकारी अपि चोरगेन्द्रैः सहितैः समन्तैः ।

गन्धोदधाराविसरे स्नपिंसु अन्येऽपि देवनियुताः स्थित

अन्तरीक्षे (२) ॥

स्नपित् सुगन्धोऽयजिनं स्वयम्भु श्वेतं च विपुलं छत्रं चामारांश्च

शुभाम्बरां (३) ।

अंतरीक्षे गता देवाः स्नापयन्ति नरर्षभं ॥

वृद्धि विपुल जाता देव सुतो भूषितो लक्षणै-

र्महाकुलरतनस्य वृद्धिश्च भूता व्यक्तोऽसौ चक्रवर्त्तीश्वरः ।

एष विप्रतिश्चतुर्जम्बुध्वज एकछत्रोभवेत् कोष्टराजस्तथा

नृप क्रमतः प्रादुर्भूतः साधु किं करवाम देवि (४) ॥

इत्युक्त्वाऽप्सरोगणस्तूष्णीमभूत् ॥ कपिलवस्तुमहानगरा-

त्पुरुषा आगत्य राजानं शुद्धोदनमाश्लिष्य क्रमात् ॥

पुरुष पुरतु गत्वा शुद्धोदनमब्रवीत्तं हर्षितो

वृद्धि विपुल देव जाता नृपेशाकियानां कुले ।

पञ्चविंशतिसहस्र जाताः सुताः शाकियानां गृहे

---

१ मरुद्भिश्चेति । २ गन्धोदधाराविसरणेन स्नापयामासुरन्यान्यपि देवनियुतानि स्थितानि । ३ स्नापयित्वा सुगन्धोदकैः । चच दत्तवानिति अध्यं कृत्वा छत्रं चाम-राणि शुभाम्बराणि च दत्तवानित्यर्थः । ४ वृद्धिर्विपुला जाता महाकुलरतस्य इति ।

सर्व्वे बलउपेत नग्नाः समा दुष्प्रधर्षाः परैः (१) ॥

अपरपुरुषा आहुः ॥

देव शृणु आनन्दशब्दं समाश्छन्दकप्रमुखानि चेटीसुता अष्टौशता

अपि च दशसहस्रा जाता नराः कण्ठकप्रमुखाः ।

तुरगवर प्रधान हेमप्रभा मुञ्जकेशावरा

विंशतिश्च सहस्रपर्य्यन्तकाः कोट्टराजास्तथा (२) ॥

नृपति श्रमत लेभि विक्रमी साधु देव जय

आज्ञा खलु ददाहि गच्छामो किन्ना करोमो नृप ।

त्वमिह वर्धितुप्राप्तु भृत्या वयं भद्रदेव जय

विंशतिश्च सहस्र नागोत्तमा हेमजालोज्ज्वलाः (३) ॥

त्वरितमुपगमित्तु राज्ञो गृहं गर्ज्जमानास्ते

छन्दकबलप्रभृगोपामुखा जात षष्टिशता ।

इयमपि प्रसूति देवदेवोत्तमे वृद्धि राज्ञां गृहे

अपि च नृपति गच्छ प्रेक्ष स्वयं सर्व्वमेव प्रभो (४) ॥

पुष्पतेजःप्रभे नरमरुतसहस्रये हर्षिता दृष्टिजाते

गुणाक्षोधिवर अशोक सम्प्रस्थिताः क्षिप्र भीमाः जिनाः (५) ।

इति हि भिक्षवो जाते बोधिसत्त्वे तत्क्षणं दानविसर्गः पुन-

---

१ पुरुषः पुरतो हस्तिर्विपुला अपश्याम्यानां पञ्चविंशतिसहस्रं बलोपेता इति । २ शृणु आनन्दशब्दं छन्दकप्रमुखा अष्टशतं दशसहस्रं तुरगवराः प्रधाना वरमुञ्जकेशा विंशतिसहस्रपर्य्यन्तका कोट्टराजान इति । ३ नृपते श्रमतो शृणु विक्रमिन् आज्ञां खलु देहि गच्छाम करवाम वर्द्धिताप्राप्तो विंशतिसहस्रमिति । ४ त्वरितमुपागमन् छन्दकबलप्रभृगोपप्रमुखा जाता षष्टिशतं प्रसूतिर्देवदेवोत्तमे अत्र हस्तिशब्दस्य हस्तिदायिकेत्यर्थः । ५ नरमरुतसहस्राणि हर्षितानि अशोके क्षिप्रमिति । अशोकनराद्धं गमिष्यति पञ्चसपि पुस्तकेषु पूर्व्वार्द्धपर्य्यन्तमेव ।

द्युत्तरं प्रवर्त्तंति स्म । पञ्च च कुलिकाशतानि प्रसूयन्ते स्म । दश च कन्यासहस्राणि यशोवतीप्रमुखानि अष्टौदासीशतानिच्छन्दकप्रमुखानि दश वडवासहस्राणि दश किशोरसहस्राणि कण्टकप्रमुखानि पञ्च करेणुसहस्राणि पञ्च कपिलासहस्राणि तानि सर्व्वाणि राज्ञः पुस्तकावरोपितानि कुमारस्य क्रीडार्थं दत्तान्यभूवन् ॥ चतुर्णां च द्वीपकोटीशतसहस्राणां मध्ये पृथिवीप्रदेशे अश्वत्थयष्टिः प्रादुरभूत् । अन्तर्द्वीपे च चन्दनवनं प्रादुर्बभूव । बोधिसत्त्वस्य परिभोगार्थं बोधिसत्त्वस्यैवानुभावेन । पञ्चोद्यानशतानि समन्तान्नगरस्य प्रादुर्बभूवुर्बोधिसत्त्वस्य परिभोगाय ॥ पञ्च च निधानसहस्राणि धरणीतलादुत्प्लुत्य मुखं दर्शयन्तिस्म ॥ इति हि ये केचिद्राज्ञः शुद्धोदनस्यार्थाभिप्रेता अभूवन् । ते सर्व्वे समृद्धाः संसिद्धाभिप्रेता अभूवन् ॥

ततो राज्ञः शुद्धोदनस्यैतदभूत् । किमहं कुमारस्य नामधेयं करिष्यामीति ॥ ततोऽस्यैतदभूत् । अस्य हि जातमात्रेण मम सर्व्वार्थसमृद्धाः संसिद्धाः ॥ यन्त्वहमस्य सर्व्वार्थसिद्ध इति नाम कुर्य्यां ॥ ततो राजा बोधिसत्त्वं महता सत्कारेण सत्कृत्य सर्व्वार्थसिद्धोऽयं कुमारो नाम्ना भवतु इति नामास्याकार्षीत् ॥

इति हि भिक्षवो जाते बोधिसत्त्वे मातुः कुक्षिपार्श्वमक्षतमनुपहतमभवद्यथा पूर्व्वन्तथा पश्चात् ॥ त्रिभविष्यदम्बुकूपाः प्रादुरभूवन् । अपि च सुगन्धतैलपुष्करिण्यः ॥ पञ्चाप्सरःसहस्राणि दिव्यगन्धपरिवासिततैलपरिगृहीतानि बोधिसत्त्वमात-

रमुपसङ्क्रम्य सुजातजाततामक्लान्तकायताञ्च परिपृच्छन्ति स्म ॥ पञ्च चाप्सरःसहस्राणि दिव्यानुलेपनपरिगृहीतानि बोधिसत्त्वमातरमुपसङ्क्रम्य सुजातजाततामक्लान्तकायताञ्च परिपृच्छन्ति स्म ॥ पञ्च चाप्सरःसहस्राणि दिव्यगन्धोदकपरिपूर्णघटपरिगृहीतानि बोधिसत्त्वमातरमुपसङ्क्रम्य सुजातजाततामक्लान्तकायतां परिपृच्छन्ति स्म ॥ पञ्च चाप्सरःसहस्राणि दिव्यदारकचीवरपरिगृहीतानि बोधिसत्त्वमातरमुपसङ्क्रम्य सुजातजाततामक्लान्तकायताञ्च परिपृच्छन्ति स्म ॥ पञ्चाप्सरःसहस्राणि दारकाभरणपरिगृहीतानि बोधिसत्त्वमातरमुपसङ्क्रम्य सुजातजाततामक्लान्तकायतां च परिपृच्छन्ति स्म ॥ पञ्चाप्सरःसहस्राणि दिव्यतूर्य्यसङ्गीतिसम्प्रभणितेन बोधिसत्त्वमातरमुपसङ्क्रम्य सुजातजाततामक्लान्तकायताञ्च परिपृच्छन्तिस्म ॥ यावन्तश्चेह जम्बुद्वीपे बाह्याः पञ्चाभिज्ञा ऋषयस्ते सर्व्वे गगनतलेनागत्य राज्ञः शुद्धोदनस्य पुरतः स्थित्वा जयवृद्धिशब्दमनुश्रावयन्ति स्म ॥

इति हि भिक्षवो जातमात्रो बोधिसत्त्वः सप्तरात्रं लुम्बिनीवने दिव्यमानुष्यकैस्तूर्य्यताडावचरैः सत्क्रियते स्म । गुरुक्रियते स्म । मान्यते स्म । पूज्यते स्म । खाद्यभोज्यस्वादनीयानि यानि विश्राण्यन्ते स्म । सर्व्वशाक्यगणाश्च सन्निपत्यानन्दशब्दमुदीरयन्ति स्म । दानानि च ददति स्म । पुण्यानि च कुर्व्वन्ति स्म । द्वात्रिंशच्च ब्राह्मणशतसहस्राणि दिने दिने सन्तर्प्यन्ते स्म । येषाञ्च योऽर्थस्तैस्तद्गृहीयते स्म । शक्रश्च

देवानामिन्द्रो ब्रह्मा च तस्यां ब्राह्मणपर्षदि माणवकरूपमभि-
निर्म्मायायासने निषद्येमां मङ्गल्यां गाथामध्यभाषेतां ॥

आपायाश्च यथा शान्ताः सुखि सर्व्वं यथा जगत् ।
ध्रुवं सुखावहो जातः सुखे स्थापयिता जगत् ॥
यथा वितिमिरा चाभा रविचन्द्रसुरप्रभाः ।
अभिभूता न भासन्ते ध्रुवं पुण्यप्रभोद्भवः ॥
पश्यन्त्यनयना यच्च श्रोचहीनाः (१) शृण्वन्ति च ।
उन्मत्तकाः स्मृतिवन्तो भविता (२) लोके चेति ये ॥
न बाधन्ते यथा क्लेशा जातं मैत्रं जनं जगत् ।
निःसंशयं ब्रह्मकोटीनां भविता पूजनार्ह ते (३) ॥
यथा सुपुष्पिताः शाला मेदिनी च समास्थिता ।
ध्रुवं सर्व्वजगत्पूज्यः सर्व्वज्ञोऽयं भविष्यति ॥
यथा निराकुलो लोको महापद्मो यथोद्भवः (४) ।
निःसंशयं महातेजा लोकनाथो भविष्यति ॥
यथा च मृदुका वाता दिव्यगन्धोपवासिताः ।
शाम्यन्ति व्याधिं सत्त्वानां वैद्यराजो भविष्यति (५) ॥
वीतरागा येमे रूपधातौ मरुच्छताः ।
कृताञ्जलि नमस्यन्ति दक्षिणीयो भविष्यति (६) ॥
यथा च मनुजा देवान्देवाः पश्यन्ति मानुषान् ।

---

१ यश्चश्रोत्रहीना इति वा पाठः । २ भविता इत्यस्य जाता इति तात्पर्य्यार्थः ।
३ पूजनार्हश्चे इति । न संशयं ब्रह्मलोके सत्त्वानां भविता शिवमिति वा पाठः ।
४ महापद्मोद्भवो यथा इत्युचितम् । ५ शमयन्तीति । ६ मरुच्छतानि कृताञ्ज-
लीनि इति ।

विहरेऽस्मिन् यथाऽस्योऽयं सार्थवाहो भविष्यति ॥
यथा च ज्वलनः शान्तः सर्वा नद्यः स्ववस्थिताः ।
सूक्ष्मश्च कम्पते भूमिः भविता तत्त्वदर्शक इति ॥

इति हि भिक्षवः सप्तरात्रजातस्य बोधिसत्त्वस्य माता मायादेवी कालमकरोत् ॥ सा कालगता त्रयस्त्रिंशद्देवेषूपपन्ना स्यात् ॥ खलु पुनर्भिक्षवो युष्माकमेवं बोधिसत्त्वापराधेन मायादेवी कालगतेति । न खल्वेवं द्रष्टव्यं ॥

तत्कस्माद्धेतोः ॥

एतत् परमं हि तस्यायुः प्रमाणमभूत् । अतीतानामपि बोधिसत्त्वानां सप्तरात्रजातानां जनयित्र्यः कालमकुर्वन् ॥

तत्कस्माद्धेतोः ॥

विवृद्धस्य हि बोधिसत्त्वस्य परिपूर्णेन्द्रियस्याभिनिष्क्रामतो मातुर्हृदयमस्फुटत् ॥

इति भिक्षवः सप्तमे दिवसे यादृशेन व्यूहेन मायादेवी कपिलवस्तुनो महानगरवरादुद्यानभूमिमभिनिष्क्रान्ताऽभूत् । ततः कोटीशतसहस्रगुणोत्तरेण महाव्यूहेन बोधिसत्त्वः कपिलवस्तुमहानगरं प्राविशत् ॥ तस्य च प्रविशतः पञ्च पूर्णकुम्भसहस्राणि गन्धोदकपरिपूर्णानि पुरतो नीयन्ते स्म ॥ एवं पञ्च कन्यासहस्राणि मयूरहस्तकपरिगृहीतानि पुरतो गच्छन्ति स्म ॥ पञ्च कन्यासहस्राणि तालवृन्तकपरिगृहीतानि पुरतो गच्छन्ति स्म ॥ पञ्च कन्यासहस्राणि गन्धोदकभृङ्गारपरिगृहीतानि पुरतो गच्छन्ति स्म । मार्गमवसिञ्चन्ति स्म ॥ पञ्च कन्यासहस्राणि

विचित्रपटोत्क्षेपपरिगृहीतानि पुरतो गच्छन्ति स्म ॥ पञ्च च
कन्यासहस्राणि नवविचित्रप्रलम्बनमालापरिगृहीतानि पुरतो
गच्छन्ति स्म ॥ पञ्च कन्यासहस्राणि स्वस्तिभद्रालङ्कारपरि-
गृहीतानि पुरतो गच्छन्ति स्म मार्गं शोधयन्त्यः ॥ पञ्च कन्या-
सहस्राणि भद्रासनपरिगृहीतानि पुरतो गच्छन्ति स्म ॥ पञ्च च
शङ्खशतसहस्राणि घण्टापरिगृहीतानि माङ्गल्यशब्दं श्रावयन्ति
पुरतो गच्छन्ति स्म ॥ विंशति नागसहस्राणि सर्व्वालङ्कारभूषि-
तानि पुरतो गच्छन्ति स्म॥ विंशति हयसहस्राणि सुवर्णालङ्कार-
सञ्छन्नानि सर्व्वालङ्कारभूषितानि पुरतो गच्छन्ति स्म ॥
अशीतिरथसहस्राणि श्वेतछत्रध्वजपताकाकिङ्किणीजालसमल-
ङ्कृतानि बोधिसत्त्वस्य पृष्ठतोऽनुगच्छन्ति स्म ॥ चत्वारिंश-
त्पदातिसहस्राणि शूराणां वीराणां वराङ्गरूपिणां सन्नद्ध-
दृढवर्म्मकवचानां बोधिसत्त्वं गच्छन्तमनुगच्छन्ति स्म ॥
गगनतलगतानि चाप्रमेयासङ्ख्येयान्यभिज्ञातानि कामावचर-
देवपुत्राः कोटीनियुतशतसहस्राणि नानाप्रकारमनेकव्यूहैर्बो-
धिसत्त्वस्य पूजां कुर्व्वन्तोऽनुगच्छन्ति स्म ॥ यस्मिंश्च वरप्रवर-
रथे बोधिसत्त्वः समधिरूढोऽभूत् स च कामावचरैर्देवैरनेकै-
र्मणिव्यूहैः समलङ्कृतोऽभूत् ॥ विंशति च देवकन्यासहस्राणि
सर्व्वालङ्कारविभूषितानि रत्नसूत्रपरिगृहीतानि तं रथं वहन्ति
स्म ॥ द्वयोश्चाप्सरसोर्मध्ये एका मानुषी कन्या द्वयोर्मानुषीक-
न्ययोर्मध्ये एकाप्सरा न चाप्सरसो मानुषीणामामगन्धं जिघ्रन्ति

स्म ॥ न च मानुष्योऽप्सरसां रूपं दृष्ट्वा प्रमादमापद्यन्ते स्म यदिदं बोधिसत्त्वस्य तेजोऽनुभावेन ॥

इति हि भिक्षवः कपिलाह्वये पुरवरे सर्व्वार्थसिद्धैः पञ्चमात्रैः शाक्यशतैः पञ्च गृहशतानि निर्म्मापितान्यभूवन् बोधिसत्त्वमुद्दिश्य ॥ ते बोधिसत्त्वं नगरं प्रविशन्तं स्वस्वगृहद्वारमूले स्थित्वा कृताञ्जलिपुटा अभिनतकायाः सगौरवमाहुः । इह भोः सर्व्वार्थसिद्ध प्रविशेह । देवादिदेव प्रविशेह । भोः शुद्धसत्त्व प्रविशेह । भोः प्रीतिप्रामोद्यकर प्रविशेह । भो अनिन्दितयशः प्रविशेह । भोः समन्तचक्षुः प्रविशेह । भो असमसम प्रविशेह । भोः बहुगुणतेजोधर लक्षणानुव्यञ्जन स्वलङ्कृतकाय प्रविशेति ॥ ततस्तोपादाय कुमारस्यैव सर्व्वार्थसिद्धः सर्व्वार्थसिद्ध इति संज्ञाऽगमत् ॥

तत्र राजा शुद्धोदनस्तेषां सर्व्वेषामनुवर्त्तनार्थं बोधिसत्त्वं सर्व्वगृहेषु प्रवेश्य चतुर्णां मासानामत्ययाद्बोधिसत्त्वं स्वगृहे प्रवेशयति स्म ॥ तत्र च मायारत्नव्यूहो नाम प्रासादस्तं बोधिसत्त्वः समारूढोऽभूत् ॥ तत्र ते वृद्धवृद्धाः शाक्याः सन्निपत्यैवं मतं धारयन्ति स्म । के नु खलु समर्था बोधिसत्त्वं पोषयितुं वर्द्धयितुं संस्थापयितुं हितचित्ततया मैत्रचित्ततया गुणचित्ततया सौम्यचित्ततया चेति ॥ तत्र पञ्च मात्राणि शाक्यवधूशतान्येकैका एवमाहुः । अहं कुमारमुपस्थास्य इति ॥

तत्र महल्लकमहल्लिकाः शाक्या एवमाहुः । सर्व्वा एता वधूका नवा दहरास्तरुण्यो रूपयौवनमदमत्ता नैताः समर्था

बोधिसत्त्वं कालेन कालमुपस्थातुं॥ अथ च पुनरियं महाप्रजावती गौतमी कुमारस्य मातृष्वसा एषा समर्था कुमारं सम्यक्सुखेन संवर्द्धयितुं। राजानं च शुद्धोदनमभिधारयितुं॥ इति हि ते सर्व्वे समग्रा भूत्वा महाप्रजावतीं गौतमीमुत्साहयन्ति स्म॥ इति हि महाप्रजावती गौतमी कुमारं संवर्द्धयति स्म॥ तत्र बोधिसत्त्वस्यार्थे द्वात्रिंशद्धात्र्यः संस्थापिता अभूवन्॥ अष्टावङ्कधात्र्यः। अष्टौ क्षीरधात्र्यः। अष्टौ मलधात्र्यः। अष्टौ क्रीडाधात्र्यः॥

ततो राजा शुद्धोदनः सर्व्वं शाक्यगणं सन्निपात्यैवं मीमांसते स्म॥ किन्नु खल्वयं कुमारो राजा भविष्यति चक्रवर्त्ती आहोस्विदभिनिष्क्रमिष्यति प्रव्रज्यायै॥ तेन च समयेन हिमवतः पर्व्वतराजस्य पार्श्वे असितो नाम महर्षिः प्रतिवसति स्म। पञ्चाभिज्ञः सार्द्धं नरदत्तेन भागिनेयेन॥ स बोधिसत्त्वस्य जातमात्रस्य बहून्याश्चर्य्याद्भुतप्रातिहार्य्याण्यद्राक्षीत्। गगनतलगतांश्च देवपुत्रान् बुद्धशब्दमनुश्रावयतोऽम्बराणि च भ्रामयत इतस्ततः प्रमुदितान् परिभ्रमतोऽद्राक्षीत्॥ तस्यैतदभूत्। यन्न्वहं अवलोकयेयमिति॥ स दिव्येन चक्षुषा सर्व्वं जम्बुद्वीपमनुविलोकयन्नद्राक्षीत्। कपिलाह्वये महापुरे राज्ञः शुद्धोदनस्य गृहे कुमारं जातं शतपुण्यतेजस्तेजितं सर्व्वलोकमहितं द्वात्रिंशन्महापुरुषलक्षणैः समलङ्कृतगात्रं। दृष्ट्वा च पुनर्नरदत्तं माणवकमामन्त्रयते स्म। यत् खलु माणवक जानीहि जम्बुद्वीपे महारत्नमुत्पन्नं। कपिलवस्तुनि महानगरे राज्ञः शुद्धोदनस्य गृहे कुमारो

जातः शतपुण्यतेजस्तेजितः सर्व्वलोकमहितो द्वात्रिंशन्महापुरुषलक्षणैः समन्वागतः ॥ स चेदगारमध्यावसिष्यति राजा भविष्यति चतुरङ्गबलश्चक्रवर्त्ती विजितवान् धार्म्मिको धर्म्मराजो जनपदस्थो महावीर्य्यप्राप्तः सप्तरत्नसमन्वागतः ॥ तस्येमानि सप्त रत्नानि भवन्ति । तद्यथा । चक्ररत्नं हस्तिरत्नमश्वरत्नं मणिरत्नं स्त्रीरत्नं गृहपतिरत्नं परिणायकरत्नमेवं सप्तरत्नसमन्वागतश्च ॥ अस्य पुत्रसहस्रं भविष्यति । शूराणां वीराणां वराङ्गरूपिणां परसैन्यप्रमर्द्दकानां ॥ स इमं महापृथिवीमण्डलं समुद्रपरिखमदण्डेनाशस्त्रेण स्वेन धर्म्मेण बलेनाभिभूयाभिनिर्जित्य राज्यं करिष्यत्यैश्वर्य्याधिपत्येन ॥ स चेत्पुनरगारादनगारिकां प्रव्रजिष्यति तथागतो भविष्यति । अर्हन् सम्यक्सम्बुद्धो नेता अनन्यनेयः शास्ता लोके सम्बुद्धः । तदेतस्योप सङ्क्रमिष्यामि च तद्द्रष्टुमिति ॥

अथ खल्वसितो महर्षिः सार्द्धं नरदत्तेन भागिनेयेन राजहंस इव गगनतलादभ्युद्गम्य समुत्प्लुत्य येन कपिलवस्तु महानगरं तेनोपसङ्क्रामदुपसङ्क्रम्य ऋद्धिं प्रतिसंहृत्य पद्भ्यामेव कपिलवस्तु महानगरं प्रविश्य येन राज्ञः शुद्धोदनस्य निवेशनं तेनोपसङ्क्रामदुपसङ्क्रम्य राज्ञः शुद्धोदनस्य गृहद्वारेऽस्थात् ॥

इति हि भिक्षवोऽसितो देवर्षिः पश्यति स्म राज्ञः शुद्धोदनस्य गृहद्वारेऽनेकानि प्राणिशतसहस्राणि सन्निपतितानि ॥ अथ खल्वसितो महर्षिर्दौवारिकमुपसङ्क्रम्यैवमाह । गच्छ त्वं भोः पुरुष राज्ञः शुद्धोदनस्य निवेदय द्वारे ऋषिर्व्यवस्थित इति ॥

परमिति दौवारिकोऽसितस्य महर्षेः प्रतिश्रुत्य येन राजा शुद्धोदनस्तेनोपसङ्क्रामदुपसङ्क्रम्य कृताञ्जलिपुटो राजानं शुद्धोदनमेवमाह। यत् खलु देव जानीहि ऋषिर्जीर्णो वृद्धो महल्लको द्वारे स्थितः। एवञ्च वदति राजानमहं द्रष्टुकाम इति॥ अथ राजा शुद्धोदनोऽसितस्य महर्षेरासनं प्रज्ञाप्य तत्पुरुषमेवमाह। प्रविशतु ऋषिरिति॥

अथ स पुरुषो राजकुलान्निष्क्रम्यासितं महर्षिमेवमाह। प्रविशेति॥

अथ खल्वसितो महर्षिर्येन राजा शुद्धोदनस्तेनोपसङ्क्रामदुपसङ्क्रम्य पुरतः स्थित्वा राजानं शुद्धोदनमेवमाह। जय जय महाराज चिरमायुः पालय धर्मेण राज्यं कारयेति॥

अथ स राजा शुद्धोदनोऽसितस्य महर्षेरर्घ्यपाद्याभ्यर्चनं कृत्वा साधु सुष्ठु च परिगृह्यासनेनोपनिमन्त्रयते स्म॥ सुखोपविष्टञ्चैनं ज्ञात्वा सगौरवः सप्रतीतिरेवमाह। न स्मराम्यहमृषे दर्शनं तत्केनार्थेनेहाभ्यागतोऽसि किं प्रयोजनं॥

एवमुक्तेऽसितो महर्षिः राजानं शुद्धोदनमेतदवोचत्। पुत्रस्ते महाराज जातस्तमहं द्रष्टुकाम इहागत इति॥

राजा आह। स्वपिति कुमारो महर्षे मुहूर्त्तमागमय यावदुत्थास्यतीति॥

ऋषिरवोचत्। न महाराज तादृशा महापुरुषाश्चिरं स्वपन्ति जागरशीलास्तादृशाः सत्पुरुषा भवन्ति॥

इति हि भिक्षवो बोधिसत्त्वोऽसितस्य महर्षेरनुकम्पया जागरणनिमित्तमकरोत् ॥

अथ खलु राजा शुद्धोदनः सर्वार्थसिद्धं कुमारमुभाभ्यां पाणिभ्यां साधु च सुष्ठु चानुपरिगृह्यासितस्य महर्षेरन्तिकमुपानयति स्म ॥ इति दर्शितो महर्षिर्बोधिसत्त्वमवलोक्य द्वात्रिंशन्महापुरुषलक्षणैः समन्वागतमशीत्यनुव्यञ्जनसुविचित्रगात्रं शक्रब्रह्मलोकपालातिरेकवपुषं शतसहस्रातिरेकतेजसं सर्वाङ्गसुन्दरं दृष्ट्वा चोदानमुदानयति स्म । आश्चर्यपुद्गलो बतायं लोके प्रादुर्भूत इत्युत्थायासनात्कृताञ्जलिपुटो बोधिसत्त्वस्य चरणयोः प्रणिपत्य प्रदक्षिणीकृत्य च बोधिसत्त्वं परिगृह्य निध्यायन्नवस्थितोऽभूत् ॥ सोऽद्राक्षीत् बोधिसत्त्वस्य द्वात्रिंशन्महापुरुषलक्षणानि यैः समन्वागतस्य पुरुषपुङ्गवस्य द्वे गती भवतो नान्या ॥ स चेदगारमध्यावसति राजा भवति । चतुरङ्गश्चक्रवर्ती पूर्ववद्यावदैश्वर्याधिपत्येन ॥ स चेत्पुनरगारादनगारिकां प्रव्रजति तथागतो भविष्यति विघुष्टशब्दः सम्यक्सम्बुद्धः ॥ स तं दृष्ट्वा प्रारोदीत् । अश्रूणि च प्रवर्त्तयति गभीरञ्च निश्वसति स्म ॥

अद्राक्षीद् राजा शुद्धोदनोऽसितं महर्षिं रुदन्तमश्रूणि च प्रवर्त्तयमानं गम्भीरञ्च निश्वसन्तं ॥ दृष्ट्वा च स हर्षितरोमकूपजातस्त्वरितं दीनमना असितं महर्षिमेतदवोचत् । किमिदन्त्वं रोदिषि अश्रूणि च प्रवर्त्तयसि गम्भीरञ्च निश्वसिषि । मा खलु कुमारस्य काचिद्विप्रतिपत्तिः ॥

एवमुक्तेऽसितो महर्षी राजानं शुद्धोदनमेवमाह। नाहं महाराज कुमारस्यार्थेन रोदिमि नाप्यस्य काचिद्विप्रतिपत्तिः किन्त्वात्मानमहं रोदिमि॥

तत्कस्माद्धेतोः॥

अहमस्मि महाराज जीर्णो वृद्धो महल्लकोऽयञ्च सर्व्वार्थसिद्धः कुमारोऽवश्यमनुत्तरां सम्यक्सम्बोधिमभिसम्भोत्स्यति। सम्बुध्य चानुत्तरं धर्म्मचक्रं प्रवर्त्तयिष्यति। अप्रवर्त्तितं श्रमणेन वा ब्राह्मणेन वा देवेन वा मारेण वा अन्येन वा पुनः केनचिल्लोके सह धर्म्मेण॥ सदेवकस्य लोकस्य हिताय सुखाय धर्म्मं देशयिष्यति। आदौ कल्याणं मध्ये कल्याणं पर्य्यवसाने कल्याणं स्वर्थं सुव्यञ्जनं केवलं परिपूर्णं परिशुद्धं पर्य्यवदातं ब्रह्मचर्य्यं पर्य्यवसाने धर्म्मं सम्प्रकाशयिष्यति॥ अस्माकं धर्म्मं श्रुत्वा जातिधर्म्मिणः सत्त्वा जात्या परिमोक्ष्यन्ते। एवं जराव्याधिमरणशोकपरिदेवदुःखदौर्म्मनस्योपायासेभ्यः परिमोक्ष्यन्ते॥ रागद्वेषमोहाग्निसन्तप्तानां सत्त्वानां सद्धर्म्मजलवर्षेण प्रह्लादनं करिष्यति। नानाकुदृष्टिगहनप्रस्कन्नानां सत्त्वानां कुपथप्रयातानामृजुमार्गेण निर्व्वाणपथमुपनेष्यति। संसारपञ्जरचारकावरुद्धानां क्लेशबन्धनबद्धानां सत्त्वानां बन्धननिर्मोक्षं करिष्यति। अज्ञानतमस्तिमिरपटलपर्य्यवनद्धनयनानां प्रज्ञाचक्षुरुत्पादयिष्यति। क्लेशशल्यविद्धानां शल्योद्धरणं करिष्यति॥ तद्यथा। महाराज औदुम्बरपुष्पं कदाचित् कर्हिचिल्लोके उत्पद्यते॥ एवमेव महाराज कदाचित्कर्हिचिद्बहुभिः

कल्पकोटिनियुतैर्बुद्धा भगवन्तो लोक उत्पद्यन्ते ॥ सोऽयं कुमारोऽवश्यमनुत्तरां सम्यक्सम्बोधिमभिसम्भोत्स्यते । अभिसम्बोध्य च सत्त्वकोटिनियुतशतसहस्राणि संसारसागरात् पारमुत्तारयिष्यति । अमृते च प्रतिष्ठापयिष्यति ॥ वयञ्च तं बुद्धरत्नं न द्रक्ष्याम इत्येवमहं महाराज रोदिमि परिदीनमना दीर्घञ्च निश्वसामि । यदहमिमन्नाराधयामि ॥ यथाऽस्माकं महाराज मन्त्रवेदशास्त्रेष्वागच्छति । नार्हति सर्व्वार्थसिद्धः कुमारोऽगारमध्यावसितुं ॥

तत्कस्य हेतोः ॥

तथा हि महाराज सर्व्वार्थसिद्धः कुमारो द्वात्रिंशन्महापुरुषलक्षणैः समन्वागतः ॥

कतमैर्द्वात्रिंशता ॥

तद्यथा । उष्णीषशीर्षो महाराज सर्व्वार्थसिद्धः कुमारः । अनेन महाराज प्रथमेन महापुरुषलक्षणेन समन्वागतः सर्व्वार्थसिद्धः कुमारः । अभिन्नाञ्जनमयूरकलापाभिनीलवेल्लितप्रदक्षिणावर्त्तकेशः । समविपुलललाटः । ऊर्णा महाराज सर्व्वार्थसिद्धस्य भ्रुवोर्मध्ये जाता हिमरजतप्रकाशा । गोपक्ष्मनेत्राभिनीलनेत्रः । समचत्वारिंशद्दन्तः । अविरलदन्तः । शुक्लदन्तः । ब्रह्मस्वरो महाराज सर्व्वार्थसिद्धः कुमारः । रसरसाग्रवान् । प्रभूततनुजिह्वः । सिंहहनुः । सुसंवृत्तस्कन्धः । सप्तच्छदोच्छ्रितांसः । सूक्ष्मसुवर्णवर्णच्छविः । स्थितः । अनवनतप्रलम्बबाहुः । सिंहपूर्व्वार्द्धकायः । न्यग्रोधपरिमण्डलो महा-

राज सर्व्वार्थसिद्धः कुमारः। एकैकरोम ऊर्द्ध्वाग्र प्रदक्षिणं।
कोशोपगतवस्तिगुह्यः। सुविवर्त्तितोरुः। ऐणेयमृगराजजङ्घः।
दीर्घाङ्गुलिः। आयतपार्ष्णिपादः। मृदुतरुणहस्तपादः।
आङ्गुलिकहस्तपादः। दीर्घाङ्गुलिधरः। पादतलयोर्महाराज
सर्व्वार्थसिद्धस्य कुमारस्य चक्रे जाते चित्रेऽर्च्चिष्मती प्रभास्वरे
सिते सहस्रारनेमिके सनाभिके। सुप्रतिष्ठितसमपादो महा-
राज सर्व्वार्थसिद्धः कुमारः। अनेन महाराज द्वात्रिंश-
न्महापुरुषलक्षणेन समन्वागतः सर्व्वार्थसिद्धः कुमारः*। न च
महाराज चक्रवर्त्तिनामेवंविधानि लक्षणानि भवन्ति। बोधि-
सत्त्वानाञ्च तादृशानि लक्षणानि भवन्ति॥ संविद्यन्ते खलु पुन-
र्महाराज सर्व्वार्थसिद्धस्य कुमारस्य कायेऽशीत्यनुव्यञ्जनानि।
यैः समन्वागतः सर्व्वार्थसिद्धः कुमारो नार्हत्यागारमध्यावसि-
तुमवश्यमभिनिष्क्रमिष्यति प्रव्रज्यायै॥

कतमानि च तानि महाराजाशीत्यनुव्यञ्जनानि॥

तद्यथा। तुङ्गनखश्च महाराज सर्व्वार्थसिद्धः कुमारः।
ताम्रनखश्च स्निग्धनखश्च वृत्ताङ्गुलिश्च अनुपूर्व्वचित्राङ्गुलिश्च
गूढशिरश्च गूढगुल्फश्च घनसन्धिश्च अविषमसमपादश्चायतपा-
दपार्ष्णिश्च महाराज सर्व्वार्थसिद्धः कुमारः। स्निग्धपाणिलेखश्च
तुल्यपाणिलेखश्च गम्भीरपाणिलेखश्चाजिह्मपाणिलेखश्चानुपूर्व्व-
पाणिलेखश्च बिम्बोष्ठश्चानुच्चशब्दवचनश्च मृदुतरुणताम्रजिह्वश्च
गजगर्ज्जिताभिस्तनितमेघस्वरमधुरमञ्जुघोषश्च परिपूर्णव्यञ्जनश्च

* अत्र सकलया चिन्तयुक्ता एव भवन्ति अतस्तु द्वात्रिंशत् पाठोऽप्येवमेव सकलपुस्तकेषु।

महाराज सर्व्वार्थसिद्धः कुमारः। प्रलम्बबाहुश्च शुचिगात्रवस्तुसम्पन्नश्च मृदुगात्रश्च विशालगात्रश्चादीनगात्रश्चापूर्व्वगात्रश्च सुसमाहितगात्रश्च सुविभक्तगात्रश्च पृथुविपुलसुपरिपूर्णजानुमण्डलश्च वृत्तगात्रश्च महाराज सर्व्वार्थसिद्धः कुमारः। सुपरिमृष्टगात्रश्चाजिह्मगात्रश्चानुपूर्व्वगात्रश्च गम्भीरनाभिश्चाजिह्मनाभिश्चानुपूर्व्वनाभिश्च शुच्याचारश्च ऋषभवत् समन्तप्रासादिकश्च परमसुविशुद्धवितिमिरालोकसमप्रभश्च नागविलम्बितगतिश्च महाराज सर्व्वार्थसिद्धः कुमारः। सिंहविक्रान्तगतिश्च ऋषभविक्रान्तगतिश्च हंसविक्रान्तगतिश्चाभिप्रदक्षिणावर्त्तगतिश्च वृत्तकुक्षिश्चाजिह्मकुक्षिश्च चापोदरश्च व्यपगतच्छिद्रदोषनीलकाद्यशरीरश्च वृत्तदंष्ट्रश्च महाराज सर्व्वार्थसिद्धः कुमारः। तीक्ष्णदन्तश्चानुपूर्व्वदंष्ट्रश्च तुङ्गनासश्च शुचिनयनश्च विमलनयनश्च प्रहसितनयनश्चायतनयनश्च विशालनयनश्च नीलकुवलयदलसदृशनयनश्च सहितभ्रूश्च महाराज सर्व्वार्थसिद्धः कुमारः। चित्रभ्रूश्च सङ्गतभ्रूश्चानुपूर्व्वभ्रूश्चासितभ्रूश्च पीनगण्डश्चाविषमगण्डश्च व्यपगतगण्डदोषश्चानुपहतकूर्षश्च सुविदितेन्द्रियश्च सुपरिपूर्णेन्द्रियश्च महाराज सर्व्वार्थसिद्धः कुमारः। सङ्गतमुखललाटश्च परिपूर्णोत्तमाङ्गश्चासितकेशश्च सहितकेशश्च सुसङ्गतकेशश्च सुरभिकेशश्चापरुषकेशश्च अनाकुलकेशश्चानुपूर्व्वकेशश्च सुकुञ्चितकेशश्च श्रीवत्सस्वस्तिकनन्द्यावर्त्तवर्द्धमानसंस्थानकेशश्च महाराज सर्व्वार्थसिद्धः कुमारः। इमानि तानि महाराज सर्व्वार्थसिद्धस्य कुमारस्याशीत्यनुव्यञ्जनानि। यैः

समन्वागतः सर्व्वार्थसिद्धः कुमारो नार्हत्यागारमध्यावसितु-मवश्यमभिनिष्क्रमिष्यति प्रव्रज्यायै ॥

अथ खलु राजा शुद्धोदनोऽसितस्य महर्षेः सकाशात् कुमारस्येदं व्याकरणं श्रुत्वा तुष्ट उदग्र आत्तमना प्रीतिप्रमुदितः सौमनस्यजात उत्थायासनाद्बोधिसत्त्वस्य चरणयोः प्रणिपत्येमां गाथामभाषत ।

वन्दितस्त्वं सुरैः सेन्द्रैः ऋषिभिश्चापि पूजितः ।
वैद्यो सर्व्वस्य लोकस्य वन्देऽहमपि त्वां विभो ॥

इति हि भिक्षवो राजा शुद्धोदनोऽसितं महर्षिं सार्द्धं नरदत्तेन भागिनेयेनानुरूपेण भक्तेन सन्तर्प्पयति स्म । वस्त्राभिच्छाद्य प्रदक्षिणमकरोत् ॥ अथ खल्वसितो महर्षिस्तत एवर्द्धा विहायसा प्राक्रमत् । येन स्वाश्रमस्तेनोपासङ्क्रामत् ॥

अथ तत्र खल्वसितो महर्षिर्नरदत्तं माणवकमेतदवोचत् । यदा त्वं नरदत्त शृणुया बुद्धो लोक उत्पन्न इति तदा त्वं गत्वा तस्य शासने प्रव्रजेः । तत्ते भविष्यति दीर्घरात्रमर्थाय हिताय सुखायेति । तत्रेदमुच्यते ।

दृष्ट्वा देवगणाननन्तजगतां बुद्धप्रबोद्गारिणः
ह्यसितो देवर्षिर्हिमाचलगतः प्रीतिं परां प्राप्तवान् ।
बुद्धो नाम पदं * किमेतदिह भो हर्षावहं प्राणिनां
प्राह्लादं मम काय एति सुखितां शान्तश्च चित्तम्परं ॥
किं देवश्चासुरोऽथवाऽपि स भवेद्गरुडोऽथवा किन्नरो

* बुद्धेति नामपदमिति ।

बुद्धो नाम (१) किमेतदद्भुतपदं प्रीतिकरं मोहनं ।
दिव्याचक्षुष प्रेक्षते दश दिशः शैलामहीसागरां
रूपं पश्यति चाद्भुतं बहुविधं भूमौ गिरौ सागरे (२) ॥
आभेयं प्रविराजते सुरुचिरा प्रह्लादयन्ती तनुं
जाताश्चैव यथा हि शैलशिखरे स्निग्धाः प्रवालाङ्कुराः ।
वृक्षाश्चैव यथा सुपुष्पभरिता नानाफलैर्मण्डिताः (३)
सुव्यक्तं चिभवे भविष्यति यथाद्य लोकोद्भवः शोभनः ॥
भूमिर्भाति यथा च पाणिसदृशा सर्वा समा निर्मला
देवाश्चैव यथा प्रहृष्टमनसः खे भ्रामयन्त्यम्बरान् ।
यद्वत् सागरनागराजनिलये रत्नाः स्रवन्तोऽद्भुताः
सुव्यक्तं जिनरत्न अभ्युनिलये धर्माकरस्योद्भवः (४) ॥
यद्वच्छान्त अपाय दुःखविगताः सत्त्वाश्च सौख्यान्विता
यद्वद्देवगणा नभस्तलगता गच्छन्ति हर्षान्विताः ।
यथा च स्निग्धरवं मनोज्ञ शृणुयां दिव्यामुषप्रीतिनां
रत्नस्येह प्रादुर्भाव चिभवे यस्य निमित्ता इमे (५) ॥
असितः प्रेक्षति अभ्युदाश्चर्यमिदं दिव्येन वै चक्षुषा
सोऽद्राक्षीत् कपिलाह्वये पुरवरे शुद्धोदनस्यालये ।
जातं लक्षणपुण्यतेजभरितं नारायणस्थामवत्
दृष्ट्वा चात्तमना उदग्रमनसः स्थामाश्च संवर्द्धितं (६) ॥

---

१ बुद्धनामेति। २ दिव्यचक्षुषा प्रेक्षत शैलमहीसागरान् पश्यन्निति। ३ सुपुष्पपूर्णा इत्यर्थः। ४ रत्नानि बहुलानि जिनरत्नस्येति स्रवन्ते इत्यस्य अभिप्रायेणान्वय इत्यर्थः। ५ यद्वच्छान्तोऽपायो मनोज्ञं शृणोति रत्नस्य प्रादुर्भावो निमित्तानामिति। ६ प्रेक्षत् लक्षणपुण्यतेजोभिर्भरितं परिपूर्णं नारायणवत् "स्थामवन्तं" परात्क्रमवन्तमिति।

उत्पुष्पचरितोऽतिविस्मितमना चासौ स्वशिष्यान्वित
आगत्या कपिलाह्वयं पुरवरं द्वारि स्थितो भूपतेः ।
अनुबद्धा बहुप्राणिकोटिनियुता दृष्ट्वा ऋषिर्जीर्णको
अवची सारथि राज्ञ वेदय लघु द्वारे ऋषिस्तिष्ठति (१) ॥
श्रुत्वा चाभ्यु प्रविश्य राजभवनं राज्ञे तथाख्यातवान्
द्वारे देव तपस्वि तिष्ठति महाजीर्णो ऋषिर्जर्जरः ।
सो चापि अभिनन्दते ऋषिवरः प्रावेष्टु राज्ञो गृह-
माज्ञा दीयतु ताव पार्थिववरा देमि प्रवेशं तथा (२) ॥
स्थाप्या चासनमस्य चाह नृपतिर्गच्छ प्रवेशं दद
अषितः सारथिवाक्य श्रुत्व मुदितः प्रीत्या सुखेनान्वितः ।
शीतं वारि यथाभिकाङ्क्षि तृषितो भुक्त्वार्दितो चासनं
तद्वत् सौख्यभिनन्दते ऋषिवरस्तं द्रष्टु सत्त्वोत्तमं (३) ॥
जय भोः पार्थिव इत्युवाच मुदितश्चायुश्चिरं पालय
दृष्टुं स्थित्व निषद्य दान्तमनस शान्तेन्द्रियः स्वरतः ।
राजा वै अभिवाद्य तं मुनिवरं प्रोवाच किं कारणं
आगामस्त्व पार्थिवेन्द्रनिलये यद्ब्रूहि शीघ्रं मुने (४) ॥
पुत्रस्ते वररूप पारमिगतो जातो महातेजवान् (५)
द्वात्रिंशद्वरलक्षणैः कवचितो नारायणस्थामवान् ।
तं द्रष्टुं हि ममेप्सितं नरपते सर्व्वार्थसिद्धं सुत-

---

१ आगत्य अनुबद्धानि बहुप्राणिकोटिनियुतानि अवोचत् सारथो राज्ञ इति । २ तपस्वी स च प्रवेष्टुं ईप्सति तावत्पार्थिववर ददामि प्रवेशं तस्य । ३ स्थाप्य चासनमेवं देहि सारथिवाक्यं श्रुत्वा यथाभिकाङ्क्ष्य भुक्त्वाऽर्दितः शीतं (प्राप्नोति शेषः) अभिनन्दते द्रष्टुं । ४ स्थित्वा निषद्योदान्तमनाः स्वरत आसनमिति । ५ वररूपः पारमितागतस्तेजस्वीति ।

मित्यर्थी समुपागतोऽस्मि नृपते मा त्वन्नकार्षी मम ॥
साधु स्वागतु याचसे किम इतः प्रीतोऽस्मि ते दर्शना-
द्देवोऽसौ प्रथितः कुमार वरदो द्रष्टुं न शक्योऽधुना ।
साधुस्ताव मुहूर्त्तमागम इतो यद्रक्ष्यसे निर्मलं
चन्द्रं वा यथ पूर्णमासि विमलं तारागणैर्मण्डितं (१) ॥
यदाऽसौ प्रतिबुद्ध सारथिवरः प्रतिपूर्णचन्द्रप्रभ-
स्तं राजा प्रतिस्पृश्य वज्रिवपुषं सूर्य्यातिरेकप्रभं ।
दत्त्वा पश्य स्वयं नृदेवमहितं हेमाभबिम्बोपम-
मसितो दृष्ट्व च तस्य तौ सुचरणौ चक्राङ्कितौ शोभनौ (२) ॥
प्रत्युत्थाय ततः कृताञ्जलिपुटश्चरणानि सो वन्दते
चक्रे स्तम्भ महात्ममाप्तकुशलो निध्यायतः प्रेक्षते ।
सोऽपश्यद्वरलक्षणैः कवचितं नारायणस्थामवान्
शीर्षं कल्प्य स वेदशास्त्रकुशलो द्वे तस्य पश्ये गती (३) ॥
राजा वा भुवि चक्रवर्त्ति बलवान्बुद्धस्य लोकोत्तमः
चास्यं त्यक्त्वा सुदीनकायमनसो गम्भीर निश्वस्य च ।
उद्विग्नश्च बभूव पार्थिववरः किं ब्राह्मणो रोदिति
मा विघ्नं खलु पश्यतेऽयमसितः सर्व्वार्थसिद्धस्य मे (४) ॥
भूतं व्याहर किन्नु रोदिषि स्वयं श्रेयोऽथ किं पापकं
पापं नास्ति न चान्तरायमिह भोः सर्व्वार्थसिद्धस्य ते ।

---

१ स्वागतं कुमारः साधु तावन्मुहूर्त्तमागमनयोग्य द्रक्ष्यसि यथा पूर्णचन्द्रमिति । २ प्रतिबुद्धः सारथिवरो यत्न दृष्टा । ३ सोऽवन्दत परिष्वज्य निध्यायन् प्रैक्षत नारायणस्थामवन्तं प्रव्रज्या यास्यतीति । ४ चक्रवर्त्ती त्यक्त्वा सुदीनकायमना गभीर निश्वसन्नसित इति ।

ज्ञात्वान यथ शोचमी नरपते जीर्णोऽस्मि यज्जर्ज्जरो
यद्वं भेष्यति बुद्धु लोकमहितो धर्म्मं यदा वक्ष्यते (१) ॥
न द्रक्ष्ये यथ लब्धप्रीतिमनसं इत्यर्थं रोदाम्यहं
यस्या काचि भवन्ति लक्षणवरा द्वात्रिंशतो निर्म्मला: ।
द्वे तस्या गतयो न अन्य इतियो आगमिष्ट एवं नृप
राजा वा भवि चक्रवर्त्ति बलवान् बुद्धोऽथ लोकोत्तम: (२) ॥
नास्य कामगुणेभिरर्थिक पुनर्बुद्धो भवभेष्यति
श्रुत्वा व्याकरणं ऋषे: स नृपति: प्रीती सुखे लब्धवान् ।
प्रत्युत्थाय तत: कृताञ्जलिपुटश्चरणावृषी वन्दते
देवैश्च अभिपूजित: सुवचनानृषिभिश्च संवर्णित: (३) ॥
वन्दे त्वा वरसार्थवाह त्रिभवे सर्व्वजगत्पूजित-
मथित: प्राह च आगमेय मुदित: संश्रूयतां भाषितं ।
बुद्धो बोधि यदा स्पृशोषि अमते वर्त्तेति चक्रे शुभं
शीघ्रं प्रव्रज शासनेऽस्य मुनये त्वं प्राप्स्यसे निर्वृतिं (४) ॥
वन्दित्वा चरणौ ऋषी मुनिवर: कृत्वा च प्रादक्षिणं
लाभास्ते नृपते सुलब्ध विपुला यस्यादृशस्ते सुत: ।
एषो लोक सदेवकं समनुजं धर्म्मेण तर्प्येष्यति
निष्क्रामं कपिलाह्वयादृषिवरोऽरण्येस्थित: स्वाश्रम इति (५) ॥

इति हि भिक्षवो जातमात्रस्य महेश्वरो देवपुत्र: शुद्धा-

---

१ यथराज: शोचामि भविष्यामि वृद्धे। वक्ष्यति इति । २ पश्यामि यथं इत्यर्थं रोदिष्यामि यस्य काये तस्य गती चान्या कदापि नास्ति भविष्यति चक्रवर्त्ती इति । ३ न अनुनाथार्थिक: पुनर्भविष्यति प्रीतिसुखे वचनमेतेति। ४ वरसार्थवाहं सर्व्वजगत्पूजितं आगमेयं बोधिर्यदा अमति वर्तते मुने: प्राप्स्यसि इति । ५ प्रदक्षिणं कृत्वा लोकं तर्प्पयिष्यति निरक्रामदिति।

वासकायिकान्देवपुत्रानामन्त्र्यैवमाह । योऽसौ मार्षाः अप्रमेय-
कल्पकोटिनियुतशतसहस्रकृतकर्म्मदानशीलक्षान्तिवीर्य्यध्यान-
प्रज्ञोपायश्रुतचरणव्रततपःसुचरितचरणो महामैत्रीमहाकरु-
णामहामुदितासमन्वागत उपेक्षासमुद्गतबुद्धिः सर्व्वसत्त्वहित-
सुखोद्यतो दृढवीर्य्यकवचसुसन्नाहसन्नद्धः पूर्व्वजिनकृतकुशल-
मूलोदितः शतपुण्यलक्षणसमलङ्कृतः सुकृतनिश्चयपराक्रमः
परपक्षप्रमथनः सुविमलशुद्धाशयसम्पन्नः सुचरितचरणो महा-
ज्ञानकेतुध्वजो मारबलान्तकरस्त्रिसाहस्रमहासाहस्रसार्थ-
वाहो देवमनुष्यपूजितो महायष्टयज्ञः सुसमृद्धपुण्यनिचय-
स्मरणाभिप्रायो जातिजरामरणान्तकरः सुजातजात इक्ष्वा-
कुराजकुलसम्भूतो जगद्विबोधयिता बोधिसत्त्वो महासत्त्वो
मनुष्यलोके उत्पन्नो न चिरादसावनुत्तरां सम्यक्सम्बोधिमभि-
सम्भोत्स्यते । तत्र गच्छामस्तमभिवन्दितुं मानयितुं पूजयितु-
मभिष्टोतुमन्येषाञ्च मानाभिभूतानां देवपुत्राणां मानमदद्दर्प-
च्छेदनार्थं तेऽस्मानभिवन्दमानान्दृष्ट्वा तेऽपि बोधिसत्त्वं वन्दि-
ष्यन्ति मानयिष्यन्ति पूजयिष्यन्ति च तत्तेषां भविष्यति दीर्घ-
रात्रमर्थाय हिताय सुखाय यावदमृताधिगमाय । राज्ञश्च
शुद्धोदनस्य जयवृद्धी अनुश्रावितारो भविष्यन्ति तत्त्वव्याकर-
णेन च बोधिसत्त्वं व्याहृत्य पुनरप्यागमिष्यामः ॥

अथ खलु महेश्वरो देवपुत्रो द्वादशभिर्देवपुत्रसहस्रैः परि-
वृतः पुरस्कृतः सर्व्वकपिलवस्तुमहानगरमवभासेन स्फुटयित्वा
येन राज्ञः शुद्धोदनस्य निवेशनं तेनोपसङ्क्रामदुपसङ्क्रम्य दौवा-

रिकेराज्ञातो निवेद्य राज्ञाभ्यनुज्ञातो राजकुलं प्रविश्य बोधिसत्त्वस्य पादौ शिरसाभिवन्द्यैकांसमुत्तरासङ्गङ्कृत्वानेकशतसहस्रं कृत्वा प्रदक्षिणं निपद्य बोधिसत्त्वमङ्के समारोप्य राजानं शुद्धोदनमाश्वासयति स्म। तुष्टो महाराज भव परमप्रीतश्च।

तत्कस्माद्धेतोः ।

यथा महाराज बोधिसत्त्वस्य लक्षणैरनुव्यञ्जनैश्च कायः समलङ्कृतो यथा च कुमारोऽभिभवति सदेवमानुषासुरलोकं वर्णेन तेजसा लक्ष्म्या च निःसंशयं महाराज बोधिसत्त्वोऽनुत्तरां सम्यक्सम्बोधिमभिसम्भोत्स्यते ॥

इति हि भिक्षवो महेश्वरो देवपुत्रः सार्द्धं शुद्धावासकायिकैर्देवपुत्रैर्बोधिसत्त्वस्य महापूजोपस्थानं कृत्वा बोधिसत्त्वं तथ्यव्याकरणेन व्याकृत्य पुनरपि स्वभवनं प्राक्रमत्। तत्रेदमुच्यते ॥

जातस्य तस्य गुणसागरसागरस्य
ज्ञात्वा सुरेश्वरमरुत् भुव ते उदग्राः ।
यस्या सुदुर्लभभवो बहुकल्पकोट्यां
एन्तोऽथ तं श्रमण पूजयितुं मुनीन्द्रं (१) ॥
परिपूर्णद्वादशसहस्र मरुद्भिरिष्टा
मणिरत्नचूडसमलङ्कृत ईर्य्यवन्तः ।
कपिलाह्वयं पुरवरं समुपेत्य शीघ्रं
द्वारि स्थिता नरपतेः सुविलम्बचूडाः (२) ॥

---

१ सुरेश्वरमरुतो भुवं यस्य रूपाय श्रजेम जातस्येत्यादि पिण्डार्थं कर्त्तव्यं बोध्या । २ परिपूर्णद्वादशसहस्रं मरुतो विशिष्टा मणिरत्नचूडाःसमलङ्कृता ईर्य्यावन्तः।

R

ते द्वारपालमवदन् सुमनोज्ञघोषाः
प्रतिवेदयस्व नृपतेर्भवनं प्रविश्य।
दौवारिको वचन श्रुत्य गृहं प्रविष्टः
प्रकृताञ्जलिपुटो नृपतिं बभाषे (१)॥
जय देव नित्यमनुपालय दीर्घमायुः
द्वारे स्थिता विपुलपुण्यविशुद्धभासः।
मणिरत्नचूडसुविभूषित ईर्य्यवन्तः
परिपूर्णचन्द्रवदनाः शशिनिर्मलाभाः (२)॥
छायां न तेष नृपते कश्चिदप्यपश्यत्
शब्दं न चैव चरणोत्क्षिपणे शृणोमि।
न च मेदिनीं विचरतो रजमुत्क्षिपन्ति
दृष्टिं न यान्ति च जनाः समुदीक्षतो वै (३)॥
कायप्रभा सुविपुला च विभाति तेषां
वाचा मनोज्ञ यथ नास्तीह मानुषाणां।
गम्भीरश्लक्ष्णसुश्लिलास्य सुखाकराश्च
शङ्का हि मे सुरगणा न हि ते मनुष्याः (४)॥
वरपुष्पमाल्यमनुलेपनपट्टदामां
पाणी गृहीत्व उदीक्षिषु गौरवेण।
निःसंशयं नृपति द्रष्टु कुमारमेते

---

१ प्रतिवेदय वचनं श्रुत्वा। नृपतेरिति द्वितीयार्थे षष्ठी। २ मणिरत्नचूडासुविभूषिता ईर्य्यावन्तः। ३ तेषां पश्यामि चरणोत्क्षेपणे विचरन्तो रज उत्क्षिपन्ति समुदीक्षन्तः। ४ मनोज्ञा यथा न वर्त्तीव गम्भीरश्लक्ष्णसुश्लोकाः साकारा इति।

देवाधिदेव महतागत पूजनार्थं (१) ॥
राजा निशम्य वचनं परमं उदग्रो
गच्छा भणा हि प्रविशन्तु गृहं भवन्तः ।
न हि मानुषाण इयमीदृश ऋद्धि काचित्
यथ भाषसे च गुण तेष यथा च ऋद्धी (२) ॥
दौवारिकः कृताञ्जलिपुटो महतैवमाह
प्रविशी भवन्त अनुज्ञातु नराधिपेन ।
ते हृष्टतुष्टमनसो वरमाल्यगन्धं
गेहं प्रविष्ट नृपतेरमरालयं वा (३) ॥
दृष्ट्वा च तां सुरवरां प्रविशन्त गेहं
प्रत्युत्थितो नृपतिरञ्जलि सम्प्रगृह्य ।
संविद्यन्त इम आसन रत्नपादा
अत्रा निषीदत भवन्तनुकम्प्य बुद्धा (४) ॥
ते मानदर्पविगताः स्थित आसनेषु
यज्ञार्थि आगत इह नृपते शृणुष्व ।
पुत्रस्तवातिपृथुपुण्यविशुद्धकायो
जातः सुजातचरणं वय द्रष्टुकामाः (५) ॥
अस्मो विधिज्ञ वरलक्षणलक्षणज्ञा

---

१ अनुलेपनपट्टदामानि पाणौ गृहीत्वा उदीक्षन्ते नृपते द्रष्टुं देवाधिदेवं महत आगता इति। २ गच्छ भण मानुषाणामीदृशी ऋद्धिर्यथा गुणाश्चैषां। ३ महत एवमाह प्रविशन्तु भवन्तोऽनुज्ञातं वरमाल्यगन्धं गृहीत्वा प्रविष्टा अमरालयं वा इत्यत्र वाशब्द इवार्थे तेनामरालयमिवेत्यर्थः। ४ ताम् सुरवराम् प्रविशतो गेहमञ्जलिं संविशन्त इमानि आसनानि रत्नपादानि अत्र निषीदन्तु भवन्तोऽनुकम्प्य बुद्धमिति। ५ स्थिता यज्ञार्थं आगता इह वयं। अत्र तमित्यूह्य समन्वयः कार्य्यः।

येषां यथा भवति या गति यः प्रयोगः ।
तत्साधु पार्थिववर प्रजहस्व खेदं
पश्याम लक्षणविचित्रितभूषिताङ्गं (१) ॥
स स्त्रीगणैः परिवृतो नृपतिः प्रहृष्टो
गृह्य कुमारमसमज्वलनार्चिवर्णं ।
उपनामयत् सुरवराणविलम्बचूडां
द्वारान्त निष्क्रमतु कम्पितचित्तहृस्तः (२) ॥
दृष्ट्वैव ते सुरवराः क्रम नायकस्य
तावानखा विमलपत्रविशुद्धतेजाः ।
ते उत्थितास्त्वरितमुपविलम्बचूडा
मूर्ध्नाभिवन्दिषु क्रमं विमलप्रभस्य (३) ॥
यथ लक्षणा यथ च दर्शित लक्षिता च
यथ पुण्यतेज शिरमूर्द्धविलोकितस्य ।
यथ ईर्ष्य नेत्र विमलाप्रभ ऊर्णकेशा
निःसंशयं स्पृशति बोधि विजित्य मारं (४) ॥
ते तं स्तुवन्ति गुणभूत यथार्थदर्शी
ध्यायी गुणां विगतक्लेशतमोनुदस्य ।
सुचिरेण सत्त्वरतनस्य हि प्रादुर्भावो

---

१ अयं स्त्री विचित्राः प्रजहीहि पश्यामो विचित्रलक्षणभूषिताङ्गमिति । २ अशोकम् असमज्वलनार्चिर्वर्णमुपानीयाविलम्बितचूडाम् द्वारान्ते निरक्रमत् । अत्र सुरवराणविलम्बितचूडामित्यस्य सुरवराणामविलम्बितचूडानां निकटे इत्यर्थः । ३ क्रमं तावनखा विमलपत्रविशुद्धतेजस उपविलम्बितचूडा मूर्ध्नाऽभ्यवन्दिषुः । ते उत्थिता इत्यन्वितार्थः । ४ यथा लक्षणानि यथादर्शिता लक्षणता पुण्यतेजः शिरऊर्द्धविलोकितञ्च यथेर्ष्या नेत्रविमलप्रभा ऊर्णाकेशा बोधिर्विजित्येति ।

जातीजरामरणक्लेशरणञ्जहस्य (१) ॥
आदीप्त सर्व्व त्रिभवं त्रिभिरग्नि तप्तं
सङ्कल्परागविषयारणिउत्थितेन ।
त्वं धर्म्ममेघ त्रिसहस्र स्फुटिल धीर
अमृतोदकेन प्रशमिष्यति क्लेशतापं (२) ॥
त्वं मैत्रवाक्य करुणान्वित ब्रह्मवाक्यो
प्रशस्तरारचितघोषमनोज्ञवाणिं
त्रिसहस्र आज्ञापरिविज्ञापन जगस्य
क्षिप्रं प्रमुञ्च भगवन्नमृतबुद्धघोषं (३) ॥
भग्नाः कुतीर्थिकगणा विपरीतदृष्टी
भवरागबन्धमनिमग्न स्थिता भवाये ।
हेतुप्रतीत्य तव शून्य शृणित्य धर्म्मा
सिंहस्य क्रोष्टुकगणेव पलायितास्ते (४) ॥
भित्त्वा अविद्यपटलं महक्लेशधूमं
पर्य्यस्थिता जनताये नियतप्रकाशे ।
ज्ञानार्चिं प्रज्ञप्रभविद्यविलोकितेन
सर्व्वं जगे विधमये महदन्धकारं (५) ॥

---

१ गुणभूतं यथार्थदर्शिनं त्वां ज्ञात्वा गुणाम् सत्यरत्नस्य जातिजरामरणक्लेशरणञ्जह-क्लेति । २ आदीप्तं सर्व्वं त्रिभिरग्निभिस्तप्तं धर्म्ममेघेन त्रिसहस्रं लोकधातुं स्फुटयित्वा । अत्र स्वामहृदयेऽप्यन्विरार्थः । ३ मैत्रवाक्यः करुणान्वितत्रिसहस्रजगदाज्ञापरिविज्ञापनं जगतो महाबुद्धघोषमिति । ४ विपरीतदृष्टयो भवरागबन्धनिमग्ना हेतुप्रतीताम् । शून्याम् श्रुत्वा धर्म्माम् क्रोष्टुकगणा इवेति । ५ अविद्यापटलं महाक्लेशधूमं पर्य्यव-स्थितायां जनतायां नियतप्रकाशकेन ज्ञानार्चिःप्रज्ञाप्रभाविद्याविलोकितेन जगति विध्वंसयेति ।

लाभाः सुलब्ध विपुला मरुमानुषाणां
यत्रोद्भवोऽद्भुत इहेदृशि शुद्धसत्त्वे ।
पिथिता अपायपथ स्फीत मरुत्पथानि
भेष्यन्ति सत्त्वरतनेन विशोधकेन (१) ॥
वर्षित्व दिव्यकुसुमां कपिलाह्वयेऽस्मिन्
कृत्वा प्रदक्षिण स्तुविल च गौरवेण ।
बुद्धः सुबुद्ध इति वाक्यमुदीरयन्तः
प्रक्रामन्ते सुरगणा गगने सलीला (२) इति ॥

इति जन्मपरिवर्त्तो नाम सप्तमः ॥ ७ ॥

अष्टमाध्यायप्रारम्भः ॥

इति हि भिक्षवो यामेव रात्रिं बोधिसत्त्वो जातस्तस्यामेव रात्र्यां विंशति कन्यासहस्राणि नैगमक्षत्रियब्राह्मणगृहपति महाशाक्यकुलेषु जातानि । तास्च सर्व्वा मातापितृभिर्बोधिसत्त्वाय दत्ता उपस्थापनपरिचर्य्यार्थे ॥ विंशति कन्यासहस्राणि राज्ञा शुद्धोदनेन दत्तानि बोधिसत्त्वस्योपस्थानपरिचर्य्यार्थे ॥ विंशति कन्यासहस्राणि मित्रामात्यात्मज्ञातिसालोहितैर्द्दत्तानि बोधिसत्त्वस्योपस्थानपरिचर्य्यार्थे ॥ विंशति कन्यासहस्राणि अमात्यपार्षद्यैर्द्दत्तानि बोधिसत्त्वस्योपस्थानपरिचर्य्यार्थे ॥ तदा

१ सुलब्धा मरुमानुषाणामिति कर्त्तरिषष्ठी मरुमानुषैरित्यर्थः इहमस्य शुद्धसत्त्वस्य पिहिता अपायपथा स्फीता मरुत्पथा भविष्यन्ति सत्त्वरत्नेन । २ इहा दिव्यकुसुमानि प्रदक्षिणं स्तुत्वा प्राक्रमन्निति ।

च भिक्षवो महल्लकमहल्लिकाश्चाः शाक्याः सन्निपत्य राजानं शुद्धोदनमुपसंक्रम्यैवमाहुः । तत्खलु देव जानीयाः देवकुले कुमार उपनीयतामिति ॥

राजाऽऽह । साधूपनीयतां कुमारस्तेन हि पश्यतां नगरमुपशोभ्यन्तां वीथीचत्वरशृङ्गाटकाऽऽपणरथ्यामुखानि । अपनीयन्ताममङ्गल्याः काणकुब्जबधिरान्धकसंस्थितविरूपरूपाः । अपरिपूर्णेन्द्रिया अपनीयन्तां । मङ्गलानि च घुष्यन्तां पुण्यभेर्यस्ताड्यन्तां माङ्गल्यघण्टाः । समलङ्क्रियन्तां पुरवरद्वाराणि । वाद्यन्तां सुमनोज्ञतूर्यताडावचराणि । सन्निपात्यन्तां सर्व्वकोट्टराजानः । एकीभवन्तु श्रेष्ठिगृहपत्यमात्यदौवारिकपारिषद्याः । युज्यन्तां कन्यारथाः । उपानीयन्तां पूर्णकुम्भाः । सन्निपात्यन्तामधीयाना ब्राह्मणाः । अलङ्क्रियन्तां देवकुलानि ॥ इति हि भिक्षवो यथोक्तं पूर्व्वं सर्व्वङ्कृतमभूत् ॥

ततो राजा शुद्धोदनः स्वगृहं प्रविश्य महाप्रजावतीं गौतमीमामन्त्र्यैवमाह । अलङ्क्रियतां कुमारो देवकुलमुपनेष्यते ॥

इति हि साध्विति प्रतिश्रुत्य महाप्रजावती गौतमी कुमारं मण्डयति स्म ॥ ततः कुमारो मण्ड्यमानः प्रहसितवदनो व्यपगतभ्रूकुटिकः परमया मधुरया वाचा मातृस्वसारमेवमाह । अम्ब कुत्राहमुपनेष्यतेति ॥ आह । देवकुलं पुत्र ॥ ततः कुमारः स्मितमुपदर्शयन् प्रहसितवदनो मातृस्वसारं गाथाभिरध्यभाषत ॥

जातस्य मम इय कम्पित त्रिसहस्रः

शक्रश्च ब्रह्मा सुराश्च महोरगाश्च ।
चन्द्रश्च सूर्य्यं तथ वै श्रवणः कुमारो
मूर्द्धाक्रमेषु निपतित्व नमस्ययन्ते (१) ॥
कतमोऽन्य देव मम उत्तरियो विशिष्टो
यस्मिन् मम प्रणयसे त्वमिहाद्य अम्ब ।
देवातिदेव अहु उत्तम सर्व्वदेवैः
देवो न मेऽस्ति सदृशः कुत उत्तरी वा (२) ॥
लोकानुवर्त्तन प्रतीत इति अम्ब यास्ये
दृष्ट्वा विकुर्वित ममा जनता उदग्रा ।
अधिमात्र गौरव करिष्यति चित्रकारो
ज्ञास्यन्ति देवमनुजाः स्वयमेव देवः (३) ॥

इति हि भिक्षवः सर्व्वैः स्तुतिभिर्मङ्गलैः प्रत्युपस्थितैरपरिमितालङ्कारालङ्कृतेषु वीथीचत्वरशृङ्गाटकान्तरापणमुखेष्वन्तःपुरेऽस्य कुमारस्य रथमलङ्कृत्य राजा शुद्धोदनो ब्राह्मणनैगमश्रेष्ठिगृहपत्यमात्यकोट्टराजदौवारिकपारिषद्यमित्रज्ञातिपरिवृतः पुरस्कृतो धूपेन धूपितेन मुक्तपुष्पाभिकीर्णेन हयगजरथपत्तिकलिलेनोच्छ्रितच्छत्रध्वजपताकावैजयन्तीनानातुर्य्यसम्प्रवादितेन मार्गेण कुमारं गृहीत्वा गच्छति स्म ॥ देवताशतसहस्राणि च बोधिसत्त्वस्य रथं वहन्ति स्म ॥ अनेकानि च

---

१ मम प्रभावादित्युक्तं इयं भूमिः कम्पिता त्रिसहस्रो लोकधातुश्च कम्पितः सूर्य्यंस्तथा मूर्द्ध्ना क्रमेण निपत्य नमस्यन्ति. २ कतमोऽन्यो देवो मम उत्तरो यं मां देवातिदेवोऽत्युत्तमः सर्व्वदेवेषु उत्तरो भावी कश्चिदित्यर्थः । ३ लोकानुवर्त्तनप्रतीत्यै विकुर्वितमिति विशेषेण कृतमनुष्ठितमिति यावत् मम अतिमात्रं गौरवं चित्रकार इति ।

देवपुत्राप्सरःकोटीनियुतशतसहस्राणि गगनतलगतानि पुष्पवर्षाण्यभिप्रवर्षन्ति तूर्य्याणि च प्रवादयन्ति स्म ॥ इति हि राजा शुद्धोदनो महता राजव्यूहेन महत्या राजर्द्ध्या महता राजानुभावेन कुमारं गृहीत्वा देवकुलं प्रवेशयति स्म ॥ समनन्तरं प्रतिष्ठापितश्च बोधिसत्त्वेन दक्षिणश्चरणः क्रमतलस्तस्मिन् देवकुलेऽथ ता अचेतन्या देवप्रतिमाः (तद्यथा । शिवस्कन्दनारायणकुवेरचन्द्रसूर्य्यवैश्रवणशक्रब्रह्मलोकपालप्रभृतयः प्रतिमाः) सर्व्वाः स्वेभ्यः स्वेभ्यः स्थानेभ्यो व्युत्थाय बोधिसत्त्वस्य क्रमतलयोर्निपतन्ति (१) स्म ॥ तत्र देवमनुष्याः शतसहस्राणि हीहीकारकिलकिलाप्रमुखप्रक्ष्वेडितशतसहस्राणि प्रामुञ्चंश्चैलविक्षेपणानि चाकार्षुः ॥ सर्व्वञ्च कपिलवस्तुमहानगरं षड्विकारं प्राकम्पितं । दिव्यानि च पुष्पाणि च प्रावर्षन् ॥ तूर्य्यशतसहस्राणि चाप्रवादितानि प्रणेदुः ॥ याश्च देवताप्रतिमास्ताः सर्व्वाः स्वकस्वकमुपदर्श्येमा गाथा अभाषन्त ।

नेरु मेरुर्गिरिराज पर्व्वतवरो जातु नमेत्सर्षपं
नो वा सागर नागराजनिलयो जातु नमेद्गोष्पदं ।
चन्द्रादित्य प्रभङ्करा प्रभकरा खद्योतकं नो नमेत्
प्रज्ञापुण्यकुलोदितो गुणधरः कस्मान्नमेद्देवताः (२) ॥
यद्वत् सर्षप गोष्पदे च सलिलं खद्योतका वा भवे-
देवश्च त्रिसहस्रदेवमनुजा ये केचि मानाश्रिताः ।

---

१ [illegible] । २ गिरिराजः पर्व्वतवरो जातु [illegible] जातु चन्द्रादित्यौ प्रभाकरौ प्रभाकरमिति ।

मेरुसागरचन्द्रसूर्य्यसदृशो लोके स्वयम्भूत्तमो
यं लोको ह्यभिवन्द्य लाभ लभते स्वर्गंस्तथा निर्वृतिं (१) ॥

अस्मिन् खलु पुनर्भिक्षवो बोधिसत्त्वेन देवकुले प्रविश्य सन्दर्श्यमाने (२) द्वात्रिंशतां देवपुत्रशतसहस्राणामनुत्तरायां सम्यक्सम्बोधौ चित्तान्युदपद्यन्त ॥ अयं हि भिक्षवो हेतुरयं प्रत्ययो येनोपेक्षको बोधिसत्त्वो भवति स्म ॥ देवकुलमुपनीयमान इति ॥ * ॥

इति देवकुलोपनयनपरिवर्त्तो नामाष्टमः ॥ ८ ॥

नवमाध्यायप्रारम्भः ॥

अथ खलु भिक्षव उदायनो नाम ब्राह्मणो राज्ञः पुरोहित उदायिनः पिता स पञ्चमात्रैर्ब्राह्मणशतैश्च परिवृतो हस्तोत्तरे चित्रानक्षत्रे राजानं शुद्धोदनमुपसङ्क्रम्यैवमाह। यत्खलु देव जानीया आभरणानि कुमारस्य क्रियतामिति ॥ राजा तमाह। बाढं गाढं क्रियतामिति। तत्र राज्ञा शुद्धोदनेन पञ्चमात्रैश्च शाक्यशतैः पञ्चमात्राण्याभरणशतानि कारितान्यभूवन्। तद्यथा। हस्ताभरणानि पादाभरणानि मूर्द्धाभरणानि कण्ठाभरणानि मुद्रिकाभरणानि कर्णिकाः केयूराणि मेखलाः सुवर्णसूत्राणि किङ्किणीजालानि रत्नजालानि मणिप्रत्युप्ताः पादुका नानारत्नसमलङ्कृता हाराः कटका हर्षा मुकुटानि कार-

---

१ सर्वेषां भवन्ति येकेचित्सत्त्वास्तेषु तत्रा मेरुसागरचन्द्रसूर्य्यसदृशो स्वामिमिति। चित्तप्रसन्नेन चित्तवचसोरत्यानुवचते। २ सन्दृश्ये इत्युचितमिति।

स्थिता च पुष्यनक्षत्रयोगमनुयुक्तेन ते शाक्यराजानं शुद्धोदनमनुपश्यन्त्येवमाहुः। इच्छदेव मण्ड्यतां कुमार इति॥

राजा आह। अलमलङ्कृतश्च पूजितो भवद्भिः कुमारः। मयाऽपि कुमारस्य सर्वाभरणानि कारितानि॥

तेऽवोचन्। सप्तसप्तरात्रिन्दिवमस्माकमाभरणानि कुमारः काये आबध्नातु ततोऽस्माकममोघो व्यायामो भविष्यतीति॥

तत्र रात्रौ विनिर्गतायामादित्य उदिते विमलव्यूहनामोद्यानं तत्र बोधिसत्त्वो विनिर्गतोऽभूत्। तत्र महाप्रजावत्या गौतम्या बोधिसत्त्वोऽङ्के गृहीतोऽभूत्॥ अशीतिश्च स्त्रीसहस्राणि प्रत्युद्गम्य बोधिसत्त्वस्य वदनं प्रेक्षन्ते स्म॥ दश च कन्यासहस्राणि प्रत्युद्गम्य बोधिसत्त्वस्य वदनं प्रेक्षन्ते स्म॥ पञ्च ब्राह्मणसहस्राणि प्रत्युद्गम्य बोधिसत्त्वस्य वदनं प्रेक्षन्ते स्म॥ तत्र यानि भद्रिकेण शाक्यराजेनाभरणानि कारितान्यभूवन्। तानि बोधिसत्त्वस्य काये आबध्यन्ते स्म। तानि समनन्तरं बद्धानि बोधिसत्त्वकायप्रभया जिह्मीकृतान्यभूवन्। न भासन्ते न तपन्ति स्म न विरोचन्ते स्म॥ तद्यथापि नाम जाम्बूनदस्य सुवर्णस्य पुरतो मषीपिण्ड उपनिक्षिप्तो न भासते न तपति न विरोचते। एवमेव तान्याभरणानि बोधिसत्त्वस्य कायप्रभया स्पृष्टानि न भासन्ते न विरोचन्ते न तपन्ति स्म॥ एवं यान्याभरणानि बोधिसत्त्वस्य काये आबध्यन्ते स्म तानि जिह्मीभवन्ति स्म। तद्यथापि नाम मषीपिण्डः॥ तत्र विमला नामोद्यानदेवता सा औदारिकमात्मभावमभिसंदर्श्य पुरतः स्थित्वा राजानं

शुद्धोदनस्य महान्तं शाक्यगणं गाथाभिरध्यभाषत च।

सर्व्वेयं क्षितिरत्नमेदिनी सनगरनिगमा पूर्णा काञ्चन-
सिञ्चिता यदि भवेत्सुरुचिर विमला एकाकिनी।
जम्बूकाञ्चनेन भवति उपगता न भासी इतरः सकाञ्चनप्रभः
श्रिरिरहिता जाम्बुकाञ्चनसन्निभा पुनर्भवेत् सकल इयं मही(१)॥
रोमे श्याभ प्रमुक्त नायके श्रिरिश्रिरिभरिते ना भासी न तपी
न शोभते
न च प्रभवति श्याभार्थैः सुगतस्य काचि ना भवति यथा मषिः
स्वतेजेन।
अयं स्वलङ्कृतो गुणशतभरितो नो तस्याभरणानि विरोचिषु
सुविमलवपुषचन्द्रसूर्य्यप्रभास्य ज्योतिषा तथ मणिज्वलना: (२)॥
शक्रब्रह्मप्रभा न भासते पुरतः श्रिरिघने यस्य लक्षण काय
चिचितः परमशुभफलैः किं तस्य भरणेभिरितरैः परकृत-
करणैः।
अपनेथा भरणा मा हेठता अबुध बुधकरो नायकुर्विभ-
भूषणार्थिकः
परममतिकरखेटस्याभरणानि दर्थि एष सुरुचिर विम-
लाम् (३)॥

---

१ सुरुचिरा जाम्बूनदकाञ्चनेन नभासते नीरचिता जाम्बूनदकाञ्चनसन्निभ सकला इति। २ रोमश्यामाभा प्रमुक्ता नायकेन श्रीभिर्भरिता श्रीभी-परिपूर्णा न भासते तपति शोभते चाभया चन्द्र कार्ये "न भवति" न शोभते इत्यु-चितम् स्वतेजसा गुणशतपरिपूर्णस्याभरणानि विरोचयन्ति सुविमलवपुषं ज्योति-षच तथा मणिज्वलना इति। ३ शोभने यस्य लक्षणैः कायस्याभरणैरपनयता-भरणानि हेठयत चेटीश्च आभरणानि ददत एतानि सुरुचिरविमलानि।

यज्जातो वसुभूमिच्छन्दको नृपतिकुल शुभे
तुष्टाः शाकिय विस्मिताश्च अभवन्प्रमुदितमनसो ।
वृद्धिः शाक्य कुलनन्दनस्य योत्तमा भविष्यति विपुला (१) ।

इत्युक्त्वाऽसौ देवता बोधिसत्त्वं दिव्यैः पुष्पैरभ्यवकीर्य्य तत्रैवान्तर्दधे ॥ * ॥

इति आभरणपरिवर्त्तो नाम नवमः ॥ ९ ॥ * ॥

दशमाध्यायप्रारम्भः ।

इति हि भिक्षवः संवृद्धः सन् कुमारः । तदा माङ्गल्यशतसहस्रैः लिपिशालामुपनीयते स्म ॥ दशभिर्दारकसहस्रैः परिवृतः पुरस्कृतः दशभिश्च रथसहस्रैः खादनीयभोजनीयास्वादनीयपरिपूर्णैर्हिरण्यसुवर्णपरिपूर्णैश्च ॥ येन कपिलवस्तुनि महानगरे वीथीचत्वररथ्यान्तरापणमुखेष्वभ्यवकीर्य्यतेऽस्माभिर्विश्राम्यते चष्टाभिश्च तूर्य्यशतसहस्रैः प्रघोष्यमाणैः। महता च पुष्पवर्षेणाभिप्रवर्षता (२) वितर्दिनिर्य्यूहतोरणगवाक्षहर्म्यकूटागारप्रासादतलेषु कन्याशतसहस्राणि स्थितान्यभूवन् । विगलितालङ्काराभरणालङ्कृतानि रत्नभद्रं करेण गृहीतानि मार्गंशोधयन्त्यो बोधिसत्त्वस्य पुरतो गच्छन्ति स्म । अष्टौ च मरुत्कन्यासहस्राणि बोधिसत्त्वं प्रेक्षमाणाः कुसुमानि च क्षिपन्ति स्म ॥ देवनागयक्षगन्धर्व्वासुरगरुडकिन्नरमहोरगाश्चार्द्धकायिका गगनतलात्पुष्पपट्ट-

---

१ यो भूमवै सञ्छन्दको नृपतिकुले शाक्याः शाक्यकुलनन्दनस्येति । २ उपलक्षितामोत्सूत्रम् ।

दारकाभ्यभिप्रक्रमयन्ति स्म ॥ सर्व्वे च शाक्यगणाः शुद्धोदनं राजानं पुरस्कृत्य बोधिसत्त्वस्य पुरतो गच्छन्ति स्म ॥ अनेनैवं-रूपेण व्यूहेन बोधिसत्त्वो लिपिशालामुपनीयते स्म ॥ समनन्तरं प्रवेशितश्च बोधिसत्त्वो लिपिशालां ॥ अथ विश्वामित्रो नाम दारकाचार्य्यो बोधिसत्त्वस्य श्रियञ्च तेजश्च असहमानो धरणितलेऽधोमुखः प्रपतति स्म ॥ तं तथा पतितं दृष्ट्वा शुभाङ्गो नाम तुषितकायिको देवपुत्रो दक्षिणेन करतलेन परिगृह्योत्थापयामास । उत्थाप्य च गगनतलस्थो राजानं शुद्धोदनं तञ्च महान्तं जनकायं गाथाभिरध्यभाषत ।

शास्त्राणि यानि प्रचरन्ति च देवलोके
सङ्ख्या लिपिश्च गणनाऽपि च धातुतन्त्रं ।
ये शिल्पयोग पृथु लौकिक अप्रमेया-
स्तेष्वेषु शिक्षितु पुरा बहुकल्पकोट्यः (१) ॥
किन्तू जनस्य अनुवर्त्तनतां करोति
लिपिशालमागतु सुशिक्षितशिक्षणार्थं ।
परिपाचनार्थम्बहुदारक अग्रयाने
अन्यांश्च सत्त्वनियुतानमृते विनेतुं (२) ॥
लोकोत्तरेषु चतुःसत्यपथे विधिज्ञो
हेतुप्रतीत्यकुशलो यथ सम्भवति ।

---

१ ये शिल्पयोगा पृथवो लौकिका शिक्षितः पुरा बहुकल्पकोटिपर्य्यन्तमिति ।

२ किन्तु "जनस्यानुवर्त्तनतां" लोकानुसारतां लिपिशालायां गच्छतु "परिपाचनार्थं" परिपक्वकरणार्थं बहुदारकाम् "अग्रयाने" श्रेष्ठयानमार्गधर्म्मे अन्यानि च सत्त्वनियुतानि इति ।

यच वाग्निरोधक्षयुसंज्ञतुसीतिभाव-
व्यक्तिम्विधिज्ञः किमथो लिपिशास्त्रमात्रे (१) ॥
नैतस्य आचरितु उत्तरि वा त्रिलोके
सर्व्वेषु देवमनुजेष्वयमेव ज्येष्ठः ।
नामानि तेष लिपिनां न हि वेत्थ यूयं
यत्रैष शिक्षितु पुरा बहुकल्पकोट्यः (२) ॥
चित्तनधार जगतो विविधां विचित्रा-
मेकक्षणेन अयु जानति शुद्धसत्त्वः ।
अदृश्यरूपरहितस्य गतिञ्च वेत्ति
किं वा पुनोऽथ लिपिमक्षर दृश्यरूपां (३) ॥

इत्युक्त्वा स देवपुत्रो बोधिसत्त्वं दिव्यैः कुसुमैरभ्यर्च्य तत्रैवान्तर्दधे ॥ तत्र धात्र्यश्च चेटीवर्गाश्च स्थापिता अभूवन् । परिशेषाः शाक्याः शुद्धोदनप्रमुखाः प्राक्रामन्त ॥

अथ बोधिसत्त्व उरगसारचन्दनमयं लिपिफलकमादाय दिव्यवर्षकं सुवर्णतिलकं समन्तान्मणिरत्नप्रत्युप्तं विश्वामित्रमाचार्य्यमेवमाह । कतमां भो उपाध्याय लिपिं मे शिक्षयिष्यसि । ब्राह्मीं खरोष्टीं पुष्करसारीं अङ्गलिपिं वङ्गलिपिं मगधलिपिं माङ्गल्यलिपिं मनुष्यलिपिं अङ्गुलीयलिपिं शकारिलिपिं ब्रह्मवल्लीलिपिं द्राविडलिपिं किनारिलिपिं दक्षिणलिपिं उग्रलिपिं संख्यालिपिं अनुलोमलिपिं अर्द्धधनुर्लिपिं दरदलिपिं खास्य-

---

१ यस्तु चत्यपर्येषु चेतुप्रतीतिकुशलो यथा निरोधक्षयसंज्ञतत्पतिभाव इति । २ यत्र-रक्षमित्यूह्य आचरणमाचरितुमुत्तीर्णत्वापां लिपीनां वेद शिक्षितः पुरा बहुकल्प-कोटिपर्य्यन्तमिति । ३ चित्तधरो जगतोऽयं जानाति पुनरत्र लिपिमक्षरस्येति ।

लिपिं चीनलिपिं हूणलिपिं मध्याक्षरविस्तरलिपिं पुष्पलिपिं देवलिपिं नागलिपिं यक्षलिपिं गन्धर्व्वलिपिं किन्नरलिपिं महोरगलिपिं असुरलिपिं गरुडलिपिं मृगचक्रलिपिं चक्रलिपिं वायुमरुल्लिपिं भौमदेवलिपिं अन्तरीक्षदेवलिपिं उत्तरकुरुद्वीपलिपिं अपरगोडानिलिपिं पूर्व्वविदेहलिपिं उत्क्षेपलिपिं निक्षेपलिपिं विक्षेपलिपिं प्रक्षेपलिपिं सागरलिपिं वज्रलिपिं लेखप्रतिलेखलिपिं अनुद्रुतलिपिं शास्त्रावर्त्तालिपिं गणनावर्त्तलिपिं उत्क्षेपावर्त्तलिपिं निक्षेपावर्त्तलिपिं पादलिखितलिपिं द्विरुत्तरपदसन्धिलिपिं यावद्दशोत्तरपदसन्धिलिपिं मध्याहारिणिलिपिं सर्व्वरुतसङ्ग्रहणिलिपिं विद्यानुलोमालिपिं विमिश्रितलिपिं ऋषितपस्तप्तां रोचमानां धरणीप्रेक्षणलिपिं सर्व्वौषधिनिष्यन्दां सर्व्वसारसङ्ग्रहणीं सर्व्वभूतरुतग्रहणीमासां भो उपाध्याय चतुःषष्टिलिपीनां कतमां लिपिं मां त्वं शिष्ययिष्यसि ॥

अथ विश्वामित्रो दारकाचार्य्यो विस्मितः प्रहसितवदनो हतमदद्र्प इमां गाथामभाषत।

आश्चर्यं शुद्धसत्त्वस्य लोके लोकानुवर्त्तिनः
शिक्षितः सर्व्वशास्त्रेषु लिपिशालामुपागतः ॥
येषामहं नामधेयं लिपीनां न प्रजानामि।
तत्रैष शिक्षितः सन्तो लिपिशालामुपागतः ॥
वक्त्रं चास्य न पश्यामि मूर्द्धानं तस्य नैव च।
शिक्षयिष्ये कथं ह्येनं लिपिप्रज्ञापारगतं ॥
देवातिदेवो ह्यतिदेवः सर्व्वदेवोत्तमो विभुः ।

अचमस्तु विशिष्टश्च लोकेष्वप्रतिपुद्गलः ॥
अस्यैव तनुभावेन प्रज्ञोपायं विशेषतः ।
शिक्षितं शिक्षयिष्यामि सर्व्वलोकपरायणं ॥

इति हि भिक्षवो दश दारकसहस्राणि बोधिसत्त्वेन सार्द्धं लिपिं शिक्षन्ते स्म ॥ तत्र बोधिसत्त्वाधिष्ठानेन तेषां दारकाणां मातृका वाचयतां । यदा अ-कारं परिकीर्त्तयन्ति स्म । तदा अनित्यः सर्व्वसंस्कारशब्दो निश्चरति स्म । आ-कारे परिकीर्त्त्यमाने आत्मपरहितशब्दो निश्चरति स्म । इ-कारे इन्द्रियवैपुल्यशब्दः । ई-कारे ईतिबहुलं जगदिति । उ-कारे उपद्रवबहुलं जगदिति । ऊ-कारे ऊनसत्त्वं जगदिति । ए-कारे एषणासमुत्थानदोषशब्दः । ऐ-कार ऐर्यापथः श्रेयानिति । ओ-कारे ओघोत्तरशब्दः । औ-कारे औपपादुकशब्दः । अं-कारे अमोघोत्पत्तिशब्दः । अः-कारे अस्तंगमनशब्दो निश्चरति स्म ॥ क-कारे कर्म्मविपाकावतारणशब्दः । ख-कारे खसमसर्व्वधर्म्मशब्दः । ग-कारे गम्भीरधर्म्मप्रतीत्यसमुत्पादावतारणशब्दः । घ-कारे घनपटलाविद्यामोहान्धकारविधमनशब्दः । ङ-कारेऽङ्गविशुद्धिशब्दः । च-कारे चतुरार्य्यसत्यपथशब्दः । छ-कारे छन्दरागप्रहाणशब्दः । ज-कारे जरामरणसमतिक्रमणशब्दः । झ-कारे झषध्वजबलनिग्रहणशब्दः । ञ-कारे ज्ञापनशब्दः । ट-कारे पटोपच्छेदनशब्दः । ठ-कारे ठपनीयप्रश्नशब्दः । ड-कारे डमरमारनिग्रहणशब्दः । ढ-कारे मीढविषया इति । ण-कारे रेणुक्लेशा इति । त-कारे तथातासम्भेदशब्दः । थ-कारे

थामबलवेगवैशारद्यशब्दः । द-कारे दानदमसंयमसौरभ्य-शब्दः । ध-कारे धनमार्य्याणां सप्तविधमिति । न-कारे नाम-रूपपरिज्ञानशब्दः । प-कारे परमार्थशब्दः । फ-कारे फलप्राप्ति-साक्षात्क्रियाशब्दः । ब-कारे बन्धनमोक्षशब्दः । भ-कारे भवति भवशब्दः । म-कारे मदमानोपशमनशब्दः । य-कारे यथावद्धर्म्मप्रतिवेधशब्दः । र-कारे रत्यरतिपरमार्थरतिशब्दः । व-कारे वरयानशब्दः । श-कारे शमथविपश्यनाशब्दः । ष-कारे षडायतननिग्रहषडभिज्ञज्ञानावाप्तिशब्दः । स-कारे सर्व्वज्ञ-ज्ञानाभिसम्बोधनशब्दः । ह-कारे हतक्लेशविरागशब्दः । क्ष-कारे परिकीर्त्यमानक्षणपर्य्यन्ताभिलापसर्व्वधर्म्मशब्दो निश्चरति स्म ॥

इति हि भिक्षवस्तेषां दारकाणां मातृकां वाचयतां बोधि-सत्त्वानुभावेनैव प्रमुखान्यसङ्ख्येयानि धर्म्ममुखसहस्राणि निश्च-रन्ति स्म ॥ तदाऽनुपूर्व्वेण बोधिसत्त्वेन लिपिशालास्थितेन द्वात्रिंशद्दारकसहस्राणि परिपाचितान्यभूवन्। अनुत्तरायां सम्यक्सम्बोधौ चित्तान्युत्पादितानि द्वात्रिंशद्दारकसहस्राणां । अयं हेतुरयं प्रत्ययो यच्छिक्षितोऽपि बोधिसत्त्वो लिपिशाला-मुपागच्छति स्म ॥

इति लिपिशालासन्दर्शनपरिवर्त्तो नाम दशमः ॥

एकादशाध्यायप्रारम्भः ॥

इति हि भिक्षवो यावद्विवृद्धः कुमारः । अथापरेण सम-येन कुमारस्सदृशैः कुमारैरमात्यपुत्रैः सार्द्धं कृषिग्राममवलो-

कथितुं गच्छति स्म। अवलोक्य च कृषिकर्मान्तमन्यतमामुद्यान-भूमिं प्रविशति स्म॥ तत्र बोधिसत्त्व एकाकी अद्वितीयो अनुचङ्क्रममाणोऽनुविचरञ् जम्बुवृक्षमपश्यत् प्रासादिकं दर्शनीयं। तत्र बोधिसत्त्वश्छायायां पर्य्यङ्केन निषीदति स्म॥ निषद्य च स बोधिसत्त्वश्चित्तैकाग्रतामासादयति स्म। आसाद्य च विविक्तं कामैर्विविक्तं पापकैरकुशलैर्धर्मैः सवितर्कं सविचारं विवेकजं प्रीतिसुखं प्रथमं ध्यानमुपसम्पद्य विहरति स्म॥ सवितर्कविचाराणां व्युपशमादध्यात्मसम्प्रसादाच्चेतस एकोतिभावादवितर्कमविचारं प्रीतिसुखं द्वितीयं ध्यानमुपसम्पद्य विहरति स्म॥ स प्रीतेर्विरागादुपेक्षको विहरति स्म। स्मृतिमान् सम्प्रजानन्सुखञ्च कायेन प्रतिसंवेदयति स्म॥ यत्तदार्य्या आचक्षन्ते उपेक्षकः स्मृतिमान् सुखविहारी निष्प्रीतिकं तृतीयकं ध्यानमुपसम्पद्य विहरति स्म॥ स सुखस्य च प्रहाणाद्दुःखस्य च प्रहाणात् पूर्व्वमेव च सौमनस्यदौर्मनस्ययोरस्तङ्गमादुःखसुखोपेक्षास्मृतिपरिशुद्धं चतुर्थं ध्यानमुपसम्पद्य विहरति स्म॥ तेन च समयेन पञ्च ऋषयो बाह्याः पञ्चाभिज्ञाः ऋद्धिमन्तो विहायसङ्गमा दक्षिणाया दिश उत्तरां दिशं गच्छन्ति स्म॥ ते तस्य वनषण्डस्योपरि गच्छन्तः प्रत्याहता इव न शक्नुवन्ति स्म गन्तुं। ते संविग्नरोमकूपजाता इमां गाथामभाषन्त।

वयमिह मणिवज्रकूटं गिरिं मेरुमभ्युद्गतं तिर्य्यगत्यर्थविस्तारिकं।

गज इव सहकारशाखाकुलां इच्छन्दां प्रदारित निर्धाविताऽनेकशः (१) ॥

वयमिह मरुणां पुरे चाऽपि ब्रजा गता यक्षगन्धर्ववेश्मानि चोर्ध्वं नभे निश्रिताः ।

इमं पुनर्वनषण्डमासाद्य सीदाम भोः कस्य लक्ष्मीर्निवर्त्तेति ऋद्धेर्बलं (२) ॥

अथ तत्र या वनषण्डदेवता सा तानृषीन् गाथयाऽध्यभाषत ।

नृपतिपतिकुलोदितः शाक्यराजात्मजो बालसूर्य्यप्रकाशप्रभः ।

स्फुटितकमलगर्भवर्णप्रभश्चारुचन्द्राननो लोकज्येष्ठो विदुः ॥

अयमिह वनमाश्रितो ध्यानचिन्तापरो देवगन्धर्व्वनागेन्द्रयक्षार्चितः ।

भवशतगुणकोटीसंवर्द्धितस्तस्य लक्ष्मीर्निवर्त्तेति ऋद्धेर्बलं (३) ॥

ततस्तेऽधस्तादवलोकयन्तोऽद्राक्षुः कुमारं श्रिया तेजसा च आज्वल्यमानं॥ तेषामेतदभूत् । कोन्वयं निषण्णः। वैश्रवणो धनाधिपतिर्भवेत् । आहोस्विन्मारः कामाधिपतिः । अथ महोरगेन्द्रः । अथेन्द्रो वज्रधरः । अथ रुद्रः कुम्भाण्डाधिपतिः । अथ कृष्णो महोत्साहः। उत चन्द्रो देवपुत्रः। उत सूर्य्यः सहस्ररश्मिः । उत राजा चक्रवर्त्ती भविष्यति । तस्याञ्च वेलायामिमां गाथामभाषन्त ।

---

१ तिर्य्यंगत्यर्थंविचारं सहकारशाखाकुलाम् इच्छन्दान् प्रदार्य्य "निर्धाविता" निर्धावमाना बभूविमेत्यर्थः । २ भवतां गम्यं यक्षगन्धर्व्ववेश्मनि नभसि "निश्रिताः" चाश्रिताः सीदामो निवर्त्तयति ऋद्धेर्बलमित्यकाकस्य देवेबलमित्यर्थः । ३ निवर्त्तयतीति ।

रूपं वैश्रवणातिरेकसदृशं यद्वा कुबेरो ह्ययं
आहो वज्रधरस्य वैष प्रतिमा चन्द्रोऽथ सूर्यो ह्ययं ।
कामोऽङ्गाधिपतिस्तु वा प्रतिकृती रुद्रस्य कृष्णस्य वा
श्रीमान् लक्षणविचिताङ्ग अनघो बुद्धोऽथ वा स्यादयं (१) ॥

ततः सा वनदेवता तानृषीन् गाथया प्रत्यभाषत ।

या श्रीर्वैश्रवणे च वै निवसते या वा सहस्रेक्षणे
लोकानां परिपालकेषु चतुर्षु या वा सुरेन्द्रश्रियां ।
ब्रह्मे या च सहाम्पतौ निवसते या च ग्रहेषु श्रियः
सा श्रीः प्राप्य इमं हि शाक्यतनयं नोपैति कान्तिं किल (२) ॥

अथ ते ऋषयस्तस्या देवताया वचनमुपश्रुत्य धरणितले प्रतिष्ठन्तः पश्यन्ति स्म बोधिसत्त्वं ध्यायन्तं मण्ड्यमानेन कायेन तेजोराशिमिव ज्वलन्तं ॥ ते बोधिसत्त्वमुपनिध्याय गाथाभिरभितुष्टुवुः ॥ तत्रैक आह ।

लोके क्लेशाग्निसन्तप्ते प्रादुर्भूतो ह्ययं ह्रदः ।
अयं तं प्राप्स्यते धर्मं यज्जगन् मोचयिष्यति ॥

अपरोप्याह ।

अज्ञानतिमिरे लोके प्रादुर्भूतः प्रदीपकः ।
अयं तं प्राप्स्यते धर्मं यज्जगद्भासयिष्यति ॥

अपरोऽप्याह ।

शोकसागरकान्तारे यानश्रेष्ठमुपस्थितं ।

---

१ आहोस्वित् वैषा लक्षणविचित्रिताङ्गोऽनघोऽर्हन्नित्युचितम् । २ ब्रह्मादि यक्षेषु श्रीः प्राप्येममित्युचितम् ।

अयं तं प्राप्स्यते धर्म्मं यज्जगत्तारयिष्यति ॥

अपरोऽप्याह ।

क्लेशबन्धनबद्धानां प्रादुर्भूतः प्रमोचकः ।
अयं तं प्राप्स्यते धर्म्मं यज्जगन्मोचयिष्यति ।

अपरोऽप्याह ।

जराव्याधिकिलिष्टानां प्रादुर्भूतो भिषग्वरः ।
अयं तं प्राप्स्यते धर्म्मं जातिमृत्युप्रमोचकं ॥

अथ खलु ते ऋषयो बोधिसत्त्वमाभिर्गाथाभिस्तुत्वा त्रिःप्रदक्षिणीकृत्य विहायसा प्राक्रामन् ॥ राजाऽपि शुद्धोदनो बोधिसत्त्वमपश्यन् बोधिसत्त्वेन विना न रमते स्म ॥ सोऽवोचत् । कुमारः क्व गतो नैनं पश्यामीति ॥ तत्र महान् जनकायो निर्धावितोऽभूत् कुमारं परिगवेषमाणः ॥ ततोऽन्यतम अमात्यो बोधिसत्त्वं पश्यति स्म जम्बुच्छायायां पर्य्यङ्कनिषण्णं ध्यायन्तं ॥ सा च वृक्षाणां तस्मिन् समये छाया परिवृत्ताऽभूत् । जम्बुच्छाया च बोधिसत्त्वस्य कायं न विजहाति स्म ॥ स तं दृष्ट्वा आश्चर्य्यप्राप्तः तुष्ट उदग्रमनाः प्रमुदितः प्रीतिसौमनस्यजातः शीघ्रं शीघ्रं त्वरमाणरूपो राजानं शुद्धोदनमुपसङ्क्रम्य गाथाभिरध्यभाषत ।

पश्य देवकुमारोऽयं जम्बुच्छायां हि ध्यायति ।
यथा शक्रोऽथवा ब्रह्मा श्रिया तेजेन शोभते (१) ॥
यस्य वृक्षस्य छायायां निषण्णोवरलक्षणः ।
सैनं न जहते छाया ध्यायन्तं पुरुषोत्तमं (२) ॥

---

१ जम्बुच्छायायां तेजसेति । २ न जहातीति ।

अथ राजा शुद्धोदनो येन सजम्बुवृक्षस्तेनोपसङ्क्रामन् सोऽद्राक्षीत् बोधिसत्त्वं श्रिया तेजसा च ज्वलन्तं दृष्ट्वा चेमां गाथामभाषत ।

हुताशनो वा गिरिमूर्ध्नि संस्थितः शशीव नक्षत्रगणावकीर्णः ।
वेधन्ति गात्राणि मि पश्यतो इमं ध्यायन्तु तेजेन प्रदीपकल्पं(१)॥

स बोधिसत्त्वस्य पादावभिवन्द्येमां गाथामभाषत ।

यदा चासि मुने जातो यदा ध्यायसि वार्चिष्मन् ।
एकद्विरपि ते नाथ पादौ वन्दे विनायक (२)॥

तत्र तिलवाहका दारकाः शब्दं कुर्वन्ति स्म । तानमात्या एवमाहुः । मा शब्दं कार्यमिति ॥

तेऽवोचन् । किमेतदिति ॥ अमात्या आहुः ।

व्यावृत्ते तिमिरनुदस्य मण्डलेऽपि व्योमाभं शुभवरलक्षणाग्रधारिं (३) ।
ध्यायन्तं गिरिमिव निश्चलं नरेन्द्रपुत्रं सिद्धार्थं न जहाति सैव वृक्षच्छाया ॥

तत्रेदमुच्यते ।

ग्रीष्मे वसन्त समुदागत ज्येष्ठमासे
सम्पुष्पिते कुसुमपल्लवसम्प्रकीर्णे ।
क्रौञ्चामयूरशुकशारिकसम्प्रघुष्टे
भूयिष्ठ शाकियसुता अभिनिष्क्रमन्ति (४)॥

---

१ वेधन्ति गात्राणि मे पश्यत इमं ध्यायन्तं तेजसेति । २ एवं प्रथमं द्वितीयमपि ते पादमित्युषितम् । ३ शुभवराग्रलक्षणधरं । ४ वसन्ते समुदागते क्रौञ्चमयूरशुकशारिकासम्प्रघुष्टे भूयिष्ठाः शाक्यसुता अभिनिष्क्रमन्ति क्वेति ।

छन्दकेत्युवाच परिवारितु दारकेभिः
हन्ता कुमार विनिगच्छम लोचनार्थं।
किं वो गृहे निवसतां हि यथा द्विजस्य
हन्त व्रजाम वय चोदनकारियन्तं (१) ॥
मध्याह्नकालसमये सुविशुद्धसत्त्वः
पञ्चाशतैः परिवृतः सह चेटकेभिः।
न च मातु नैव च पितुः प्रतिवेदयित्वा
सो बुद्ध निष्क्रमिति गच्छि कृषाणग्रामं (२) ॥
तस्मिंश्च पार्थिववरस्य कृषाणग्रामे
जम्बुद्रुमोऽभवदनेकविशालशाखः।
दृष्ट्वा कुमार प्रतिबुद्ध दुःखेन चार्तो
धिक् संस्कृतेति बहुदुःखकृपिं करोति (३) ॥
सो जम्बुच्छायमुपगम्य विनीतचित्त-
स्तृणकानि गृह्य स्वय संस्तर संस्तरित्वा।
पर्य्यङ्कमाभुजिय ऋज्जु करित्व कायं
चत्वारि ध्यान शुभ ध्यायि स बोधिसत्त्वः (४) ॥
पञ्च ऋषि खपथेन हि गच्छमाना
जम्बूयमूर्ध्नि न प्रभोन्ति पराक्रमेतुं।

---

१ छन्दक इत्युवाच परिवारितो दारकैर्हन्त हे कुमारा विनिर्गच्छाम आलोकनार्थं वयमिति चोदनादिवक्तृमित्यनुमीयते। २ पञ्चाशद्भिश्चेटकैर्मातरं पितरं प्रतिवेद्य च बुद्धो निष्क्रम्यागच्छत्। ३ कुमारः प्रतिबुद्धः संज्ञातमिति। ४ स जम्बुच्छायामुपगम्य तृणानि गृहीत्वा आस्तरणमास्तृत्य पर्य्यङ्कमाभुज्य ऋजुं कृत्वा ध्यानानि शुभानि व्यध्यायत्।

ते विस्मिता निहतमानमदाश्च भूत्वा
सर्व्वे समग्र सहिताः समुदीक्षयन्ते (१) ॥
वय मेरु पर्व्वतवरं तथ चक्रवालं
निर्भिद्य गच्छम जवेन असज्जमानाः ।
ते जम्बुवृक्ष न प्रभाम अतिक्रमेतुं
को न्वत्र हेतुरयमद्य भविष्यतीह (२) ॥
अवतीर्य्य मेदिनितले च प्रतिष्ठिहित्वा
पश्यन्ति शाक्यतनयं तहि जम्बुमूले ।
जाम्बूनदार्चिसदृशप्रभ तेजरश्मिं
पर्य्यङ्क बन्धुत ध्यायतु बोधिसत्त्वं (३) ॥
ते विस्मिता दृशनखाः करियान मूर्द्धा
प्रणताः कृताञ्जलिपुटा न्यपतन् क्रमेषु ।
साधोः सुजातसुमुखे करुणाश्रयस्य
क्षिप्रं विबोध अमृतेन विनष्टसत्त्वान् (४) ॥
परिवृत्त सूर्य्य न जही सुगतस्य छाया
ओलम्बते द्रुमवरं यथ पद्मपत्रं ।
देवाः सहस्र बहवः स्थित अञ्जलीभि-
र्वन्दन्ति तस्य चरणौ कृतनिश्चयस्य (५) ॥

---

१ पञ्चर्षयो गच्छन्तो जम्बुमूर्द्धानं प्रभवन्ति स्म पराक्रमितुं समग्राः समुदीक्षन्ते स्म । २ वयं मेरुं तथा चक्रमाम जम्बुवृक्षं प्रभवामोऽतिक्रमितुं । ३ मेदिनीतले प्रतिष्ठाय पश्यन्ति स्म तज्जम्बुमूले जाम्बूनदार्चिःसदृशप्रभं तेजोरश्मिं पर्य्यङ्कं बद्ध्वा ध्यायन्तमिति । ४ दृशनखान् कृत्वा "क्रमेषु" पादेषु सुजातसुमुखस्य विबोधकस्य । ५ परिवृत्ते सूर्य्ये अजहाति सुगतं अवलम्बते यथा सहस्रं स्थिता वन्दन्ते स्म इति ।

शुद्धोदनस्य स्वगृहे परिमार्गमाणः
सम्पृच्छते क नु गतः स हि मे कुमारः ।
मातृस्वसा अवचि मार्गित नो लभामि
सम्पृच्छ्यतां नरपते क गतः कुमारः (१) ॥
शुद्धोदनस्त्वरितु पृच्छति काञ्चुकीयं
दौवारिकं तथपि चान्तर्जन समन्तात् ।
दृष्टः कुमार मम केन विनिष्क्रमन्तो
श्रृणुते च रूपगतु देव क्षपाण्ययामं (२) ॥
सो शीघ्रमेव त्वरितं सह शाकियेभि-
र्निष्क्रान्तु प्रेक्षि ऋषियामगिरिं प्रविष्टं ।
यथ सूर्य्यकोटिनियुतानि समुद्गतानि
तथ प्रेक्षते हितकरं शिरिया ज्वलन्तं (३) ॥
मुकुटञ्च खड्ग तथ पादुक छोरयित्वा
कृत्वा दशाङ्गुलि शिरी अभिवन्दिते तं ।
साधू सुभूतवचना ऋषयो महात्मा
व्यक्तं कुमार अभिनिष्क्रमि बोधिहेतोः (४) ॥
परिपूर्णद्वादशशताः सुप्रसन्नदेवाः
पञ्चशता उपगता तथ शाकियानां ।
दृष्ट्वा च ऋद्धि सुगते गुणसागरस्य

---

१ सम्पृच्छते क्व चावोचत् मार्गितो नो लभामि इति । २ त्वरितं पृच्छति क्व तथापि विनिष्क्रमन् शृणुते च उपगतो देवेति । ३ स शाक्यैर्निष्क्रान्तः प्रेक्षितुं यथा तथा प्रेक्षते च श्रिया इति । ४ खड्गं तथा पादुके "छोरयित्वा" त्यक्त्वा "दशाङ्गुलिं कृत्वा" बद्धाञ्जलिर्भूत्वा शिरसा अभिवन्दते च साधु महात्मानः कुमारोऽभिनिष्क्रान्तो बोधिहेतवे इत्यवोचन् इत्यूचम् ।

सम्बोधि चित्त अनयं दृढआशयेन (१) ॥
सो कम्पयित्व निखिल इमामेव भूमिं
स्मृतु सम्प्रजानु प्रतिबुद्ध ततः समाधेः ।
ब्रह्मस्वरः पितरमालपते सुधीमा-
नुत्सृज्य तात कृषिका पुरतो भवेषां (२) ॥
यदि स्वर्णकार्य्य अहु स्वर्ण प्रवर्षयिष्ये
यदि वस्त्रकार्य्यं अहमेव प्रदास्य वस्त्रां ।
अथवान्यकार्य्य अहमेव प्रवर्षयिष्ये
सम्यक्प्रयुक्त भव सर्व्वजने नरेन्द्र (३) ॥
अनुश्रावयित्व पितरञ्जन पारिषद्यां-
स्तस्मिन् क्षणे पुरवरं पुन सो प्रवेक्षी ।
अनुवर्त्तमान जगतोऽस्मिहते पुरेऽस्मि
नैष्कर्म्ययुक्तमनसः सुविशुद्धसत्त्व (४) इति ॥

इति कृषिग्रामपरिवर्त्तो नाम एकादशः ॥ ११ ॥

द्वादशाध्यायप्रारम्भः ॥

इति हि भिक्षवः संवृद्धे कुमारे राजा शुद्धोदनोऽपरेण समयेन शाक्यगणेन सार्द्धं संस्थागारे निषण्णोऽभूत् ॥ तत्र ते

---

१ परिपूर्णद्वादशशतं यत्शतं तथा शाक्यानां षष्टिं पश्यतश्च सम्बोधौ चित्तम-नयत् दृढाशयेन इति । २ स कम्पयित्वा निखिलामिमां भूमिं स्मृतः सम्प्रजानन् प्रतिबुद्धवान् आलपति स्म उत्सृज्य कृषिं "भवेषां" चिन्तास्वरूपामित्यर्थः । ३ स्वर्ण-कार्य्यं अहं स्वर्णं वस्त्रकार्य्यं प्रदास्ये वस्त्राणि अन्यकार्य्यं सम्यक्प्रयुक्तो भव सर्व्व-जनति इति । ४ अनुश्रावयित्वा जनान् पुनः स प्रविवेश अनुवर्त्तमानो जगत इहा-स्मिन् नैष्कर्म्ययुक्तमना इति ।

महल्लक महल्लिकाश्चाः शाक्या राजानं शुद्धोदनमेवमाहुः । यत् खलु देव जानीया अयं सर्व्वार्थसिद्धः कुमारो नैमित्तिकैर्ब्राह्मणैः कृतनिश्चयैश्च दैवतैश्च एव निर्दिष्टः । यदि कुमारोऽभिनिष्क्रमिष्यति तथागतो भविष्यति । अर्हन् सम्यक्सम्बुद्धः ॥ उत नाभिनिष्क्रमिष्यति राजा भविष्यति । चक्रवर्त्ती च विजितवान् धार्म्मिको धर्म्मराजः सप्तरत्नसमन्वागतस्तस्येमानि सप्तरत्नानि भविष्यन्ति । तद्यथा । चक्ररत्नं हस्तिरत्नं अश्वरत्नं मणिरत्नं स्त्रीरत्नं गृहपतिरत्नं परिणायकरत्नमेवं सप्तरत्नं ॥ पूर्णञ्चास्य पुत्रसहस्रं शूराणां वीराणां वराङ्गरूपिणां परसैन्यप्रमर्द्दकानां ॥ स इमं पृथिवीमण्डलमदण्डेनाशस्त्रेणाभिनिर्जित्याध्यावसिष्यति सह धर्म्मेणेति । तस्मान्निवेशनं कुमारस्य क्रियतामिति ॥ तत्र स्त्रीगणपरिवृतो रतिं वेत्स्यति नाभिनिष्क्रमिष्यति एवमस्माकं चक्रवर्त्तिवंशस्य चानुपच्छेदो भविष्यति । मानिताश्च भविष्यामो ऽनवद्यास्च सर्व्वकोट्टराजैः ॥

ततो राजा शुद्धोदन एवमाह । यद्येवं तेन हि व्यवलोकयत कतमा कन्या कुमारस्यानुरूपा स्यात् ॥ तत्र पञ्चमात्राणि शाक्यशतानि एकैकमेवमाहुः । मम दुहिताऽनुरूपा स्यात् कुमारस्य सुरूपा मम दुहितेति ॥

राजा आह । दुरासदः कुमारः तत् प्रतिवेदयिष्यामः । तावत् कुमारस्य कतमा ते कन्या रोचत इति ॥ ततस्ते सर्व्वे सन्निपत्य कुमारस्यैनां प्रकृतिमारोचयन्ति स्म ॥

कुमार उवाच । सप्तमे दिवसे प्रतिवचनं श्रोष्यथेति ॥ ततो

बोधिसत्त्वस्यैतदभवत्। विदितं मयानन्तकामदोषाः सरण-सर्व्वराशशोकदुःखमूला भयङ्करविषपत्रसन्निकाशा ज्वलननिभा असिधारातुल्यरूपाः कामगुणे न मेऽस्ति च्छन्दं रागो न चाहं शोभे स्त्र्यागारमध्ये यो न्वहमुपवने वसेयं तूष्णीं ध्यानसमाधि-सुखेन शान्तचित्त इति॥ स पुनरपि मीमांसोपायकौशल्य-मामुखीकृत्य सत्त्वपरिपाकमेव वक्ष्यमाणो महाकरुणां सञ्ज-नय्य तस्यां वेलायामिमां गाथामभाषत।

सङ्कीर्ण पङ्कि पदुमानि विरूढिमेन्ति
आकीर्ण राजु जलमध्य लभाति पूजां।
यदि बोधिसत्त्व परिवारबलं लभन्ते
तद सत्त्वकोटिनियुतान्यमृते विमेन्ति (१)॥

येषापि पूर्व्वक अभूद्विदुबोधिसत्त्वाः
सर्व्वेभि भार्य्यसुत दर्शित इस्त्रिगाराः।
न च रागरक्त न च ध्यानसुखेभि भ्रष्टा
हन्तानुशिक्षयि अहंपि गुणेषु तेषां (२)॥

न च प्राकृता मम वधूरनुरूप या
स्याद्यस्या न ईर्ष्यदिगुणाः सद सत्यवाक्या।
या मह्य चित्तमभिराधयतेऽप्रमत्ता
रूपेण जन्मकुलगोत्रतथा सुशुद्धा (३)॥

---

१ सङ्कीर्णानि पङ्कैः पद्मानि विरूढिमायान्ति आकीर्णानि राजन्ति जलमध्ये लभन्ते बोधिसत्त्वो लप्स्यते तदा विमोक्ष्यति। २ पूर्व्वका अभूवन् सर्व्वैर्भार्यासुता दर्शिताः स्त्र्यागाराणि रागरक्ता ध्यानसुखैरनुशिक्षिष्येऽहमपि गुणान् इति। ३ वधूरनुरूपा ईर्ष्यादिगुणाः सदा मां चित्ते अभ्याराधयत्यप्रमत्ता जन्मकुलगोत्रैरिति।

सा गाथलेखलिखिते गुणअर्थयुक्ता
या कन्य ईदृश भवेन्मम तां वरेथाः ।
न ममार्थ प्राकृतजनेन असंस्तुतेन
यस्या गुणा कथयमी मम तां वरेथाः (१) ॥
या रूप यौवन वरा न च रूपमत्ता
माता स्वसा वै यथ वर्त्तति मैत्रचित्ता ।
त्यागे रता श्रमणब्राह्मणदानशीला
तां तादृशी मम वधूं वरयस्व तात (२) ॥
यस्यावमानु रखिला न च दोषमस्ति
न च शाठ्य ईर्ष्य न च माय न च ऋजु भ्रष्टा ।
स्वप्नान्तरेऽपि पुरुषेषु परेभि रक्ता
तुष्टा स्वकेन पतिना सद संयत अप्रमत्ता (३) ॥
न च गर्विता न अपि उद्धत न प्रगल्भा
निर्मान मानविगताऽपि च न चेटिभूता ।
न च पान गृद्धु न रसेषु न शब्दगन्धे
निर्लोभ भिध्यविगता स्वधनेन तुष्टा (४) ॥
सत्ये स्थिता नपि च चञ्चल नैव भ्रान्ता
न च उद्धता न च स्थिता ह्रिरिवस्त्रछन्ना ।
न च दृष्टिमङ्गलरता सद धर्मयुक्ता

---

१ गाथालेखलिखिते गुणार्थयुक्ता कन्या ईदृशी यां तां वरय। ममार्थे गुणान् कथयामि तां मां वरय इति। २ रूपेण यौवनेन यथा वर्त्तते तां वरय इति। ३ यस्या अवमानं अखिला दोषाः सन्ति शाठ्यमीर्ष्या माया परेषु अभिरक्ता सदा संयता इति। ४ नापि उद्धता निर्माणा चेटीभूता। पाने गर्धिनी निर्लोभा निध्याविगतेति।

कायेन वाच मनसा सद शुद्धभावा (१) ॥

न च स्यान निर्लज्जा न च मानमूढा

मीमांसयुक्त सुलता सद धर्म्मचारी ।

श्वश्रू च तस्य श्वशुरे यथशास्त्रप्रेमा

दासीकलत्रजनि यादृशमात्मप्रेम (२) ॥

शास्त्रे विधिज्ञ कुशला गणिका यथैव

पश्चात् स्वपेत् प्रथममुत्थितते च शय्यात् ।

मैत्रानुवर्त्ति अकुहापि च मातृभूता

एतादृशीमपि नृपते वधुकां वृणीष्व (३) ॥

अथ खलु भिक्षवो राजा शुद्धोदन इमां गाथां वाचयित्वा पुरोहितमामन्त्रयते स्म ॥ गच्छ त्वं महाब्राह्मण कपिलवस्तुनि महानगरे सर्व्वगृहाण्यनुप्रविश्य कन्या व्यवलोकय । यस्या एते गुणाः संविद्यन्ते क्षत्रियकन्याया वा ब्राह्मणकन्याया वा वैश्यकन्याया वा शूद्रकन्याया वा । तां कन्यामस्माकं प्रतिवेदय ॥ तत्कस्माद्धेतोः । न हि कुमारः कुलार्थिको न गोत्रार्थिको गुणार्थिक एव कुमारः । तस्यां च वेलायामिमां गाथामभाषत ।

ब्राह्मणीं क्षत्रियां कन्यां वैश्यां शूद्रीं तथैव च ।

यस्या एते गुणाः सन्ति तां मे कन्यां प्रवेदय ॥

---

१ नापि चपला स्थिरा "स्थिरवचना" शोभनवचना सत्यामत्युपयुक्तवचनाच्छादितेति यावत् । सदा भावा सदा इति । २ स्यात् न अविमलज्जा नामोक्ता मीमांसायुक्ता सदा धर्म्मचारिणी श्वश्रूणां तस्य यथाशास्त्रप्रेमा दासीकलत्रजनेषु यादृशमात्मनि प्रेम तादृशं प्रेम एतेष्वपि यस्या इति भाव इति । ३ विधिज्ञा स्वपिति उत्तिष्ठते शय्यातो मैत्रानुवर्त्तिनी अकुहका एतादृशीमपि वधूकांवृणीष्वेति ।

न कुलेन न गोत्रेण कुमारो मम विस्मितः (१) ।
गुणे सत्ये च धर्मे च तत्रास्य रमते मनः ॥

अथ खलु भिक्षवः स पुरोहितस्तं गाथालेखं गृहीत्वा कपिलवस्तुनि महानगरे गृहाद्गृहं व्यवलोकयन् गत्वा हिण्डन् कन्यां पर्य्येषते स्म (२) ॥ एवङ्गुणयुक्तामपश्यन् (न चैव गुणयुक्तां कन्यां) सोऽनुपूर्व्वेण विचरन्नेव दण्डपाणेः शाक्यस्य निवेशनं तेनोपसङ्क्रामन् स तं निवेशनं प्रविष्टोऽद्राक्षीत्। कन्यामभिरूपां प्रासादिकां दर्शनीयां परमया शुभवर्णपुष्कलतया समन्वागतां नातिदीर्घां नातिह्रस्वां नातिस्थूलां नातिकृशां नातिगौरीं नातिकृष्णां प्रथमयौवनावस्थितां स्त्रीरत्नमिवाख्यायमानां नोपमां (३) ॥

अथ सा दारिका पुरोहितस्य चरणौ गृहीत्वा एवमाह ।
किंन ते महाब्राह्मण कार्य्यं ॥

पुरोहित आह ।

शुद्धोदनस्य तनयः परमाभिरूपो
द्वात्रिंशलक्षणधरो गुणतेजयुक्तः ।
तेनेतिगाथ लिखिता गुणये वधूनां
यस्या गुणास्ति हि इमे स हि तस्य पत्नी (४) ॥

स तस्यास्तं गाथालेखमुपनामयति स्म (५) ॥ अथ सा दारिका तं गाथालेखं वाचयित्वा स्मितमुपदर्श्य तं पुरोहितं गाथयाऽध्यभाषत ।

---

१ "विस्मितः" हर्षित इति निष्कृष्टार्थः । २ परीक्षाति स्म अन्वेषणं करोति स्म । ३ अनुपमामित्युचितम् । ४ गुणतेजोयुक्त इतिगाथा "गुणये" गुणाय गुणानुसन्धाना-येति यावत् । गुणाः सन्ति या चेति । ५ उपानयति स्मेति ।

यस्येति ब्राह्मण गुणा अनुरूप सर्व्वे
सो मे पतिर्भवतु सौम्य सुरूपरूपः ।
भण हि कुमार यदि कार्य्य मा विलम्बं
मा हीनप्राकृतजनेन भवेय वासः (१) ॥

अथ खलु स पुरोहितो राजानमुपसंक्रम्यैव तमर्थमारोचयति स्म । दृष्टा मया देव कन्या कुमारस्यानुरूपा स्यात् ॥

आह । कस्यासौ ॥

आह । दण्डपाणेर्देव शाक्यस्य दुहिता ॥

अथ राज्ञः शुद्धोदनस्यैतदभवत् । दुरासदः कुमारः शुभाधिमुक्तश्च प्रायेण च मातृग्रामो संविद्यमानगुणोऽपि गुणानात्मनि प्रतिजानीते । यन्न्वहमशोकभाण्डानि कारयेयं यानि कुमारः सर्व्वदारिकाभ्योऽनुप्रयच्छेत् । तत्र यस्यां दारिकायां कुमारस्य चक्षुरभिनिवेक्ष्यति तां कुमारस्य वरयिष्यामीति ॥

अथ खलु राजा शुद्धोदनोऽशोकभाण्डानि कारयति स्म सुवर्णमयानि रूप्यमयानि वैदूर्य्यमयानि नानारत्नमयानि ॥ कारयित्वा च कपिलवस्तुनि महानगरवरे घण्टाघोषणां कारयामास । सप्तमे दिवसे कुमारो दर्शनं दास्यत्यशोकभाण्डकानि च दारिकाभ्यो विश्राणयिष्यति ॥ तत्र सर्व्वदारिकाभिः संस्थागारे सन्निपतितव्यम् ॥

इति हि भिक्षवः सप्तमे दिवसे बोधिसत्त्वः संस्थागारमुपसंक्रम्य भद्रासने न्यषीदत् ॥ राजाऽपि शुद्धोदनश्छन्नान् पुरु-

१ "यस्येति" "यस्यैते" "अनुरूप" अनुरूपाः "सो" स "सौम्य" सौम्यः "कुमार" कुमारं "कार्य्यं" कार्य्यं विलम्बं मा कुरु इत्यर्थः । "भवेय" भवतु ।

याम् ज्ञापयति स्म । यस्यां दारिकायां कुमारस्य चक्षुः सन्नि-विशेत्तां ममारोचयध्वं ॥

इति हि भिक्षवो यावन्त्यः कपिलवस्तुनि महानगरे दारिकास्ताः सर्वा येन संस्थागारो येन बोधिसत्त्वस्तेनोपासङ्क्रामन् । बोधिसत्त्वस्य दर्शनाय अशोकभाण्डानि च ग्रहीतुं ॥

इति हि भिक्षवो बोधिसत्त्वो यथागताभ्यस्ताभ्यो दारिकाभ्योऽशोकभाण्डान्यनुप्रयच्छति स्म ॥ ताश्च दारिका न शक्नुवन्ति स्म बोधिसत्त्वस्य श्रियं तेजश्च सोढुं । ता अशोकभाण्डानि गृहीत्वा शीघ्रमेव प्रक्रामन्ति स्म ॥ अथ दण्डपाणेः शाक्यस्य दुहिता गोपा नाम शाक्यकन्या सा दासीगणपरिवृता पुरस्कृता येन संस्थागारो येन च बोधिसत्त्वस्तेनोपसङ्क्रामदुपसङ्क्रम्यैकान्तेऽस्थात् बोधिसत्त्वमनिमिषाभ्यां नयनाभ्यां प्रेक्षमाणा । तद्यथा । बोधिसत्त्वेन सर्वाण्यशोकभाण्डानि दत्तानि ॥ तदा सा बोधिसत्त्वमुपसङ्क्रम्य प्रहसितवदना बोधिसत्त्वमेवमाह । कुमार किन्ते मयापनीतं यस्त्वं मां विमानयसि ॥

आह । नाहं त्वां विमानयाम्यपितु खलु पुनस्त्वमसि पश्चादागता इति ॥ स तस्यै अनेकशतसहस्रमूल्यमङ्गुलीयकं निर्मुच्य प्रादात् ॥

सा प्राह । कुमारेदमहन्तवान्तिकादर्हामि ॥

आह । इमानि मदीयाभरणानि गृह्यन्तां ॥

सा आह । न वयकुमारं व्यलङ्करिष्यामोऽलङ्करिष्यामो वयं मारं ॥ इत्युक्त्वा सा कन्या प्राक्रामत् ॥

ततस्तैर्गुप्तपुरुषैः राजानं शुद्धोदनमुपसंक्रम्यैष वृत्तान्तो निवेदितोऽभूत् । देव दण्डपाणेः शाक्यस्य दुहिता गोपा नाम शाक्यकन्या तस्यां कुमारस्य चक्षुर्निविष्टं मुहूर्त्तञ्च तयोः संलापोऽभूत् ॥ इत्येतत् खलु वचनं श्रुत्वा राजा शुद्धोदनो दण्डपाणेः शाक्यस्य पुरोहितं दौत्येन प्रेषयति स्म । या ते दुहिता सा मम कुमाराय प्रदीयतामिति ॥

दण्डपाणिराह । आर्य्य कुमारो गृहे सुखं संवृद्धः । अस्माकं चायं कुलधर्म्मः शिल्पज्ञस्य कन्या दातव्या नाशिल्पज्ञस्येति ॥ कुमारस्य न शिल्पज्ञो नासिधनुष्कलापयुद्धसालम्भविधिज्ञः । तत्कथमशिल्पज्ञायाहं दुहितरं दास्यामि ॥ इत्येतच्च राज्ञः प्रतिवेदितं ॥

ततो राज्ञ एतदभवत् । द्विरपितदहं सह धर्म्मेण चोदितः । यदाऽपि मयोक्तं कस्माच्छाक्यकुमाराः कुमारस्योपस्थानाय नागच्छन्तीति । तदाऽप्यहमभिहितः । किं वयमस्योपस्थानं करिष्याम इति । एतच्चुपेतमिति प्रध्यायन्निषण्णोऽभूत् ॥ बोधिसत्त्वश्चैनं वृत्तान्तमश्रौषीत् । श्रुत्वा च येन राजा शुद्धोदनस्तेनोपसंक्रामदुपसंक्रम्यैवमाह । देव किमिदन्दीनमनाश्चिष्ठसि ॥

राजा आह । अलं ते कुमाराऽनेन ॥

कुमार आह । देव सर्व्वथा तावदवश्यमेवमाख्यातव्यं ॥ यावत्त्रिरपि बोधिसत्त्वो राजानं शुद्धोदनं परिपृच्छति स्म ॥

ततो राजा शुद्धोदनो बोधिसत्त्वाय तां प्रकृतिमारोचयति स्म ॥ तां श्रुत्वा बोधिसत्त्व आह । देव अस्ति पुनरिह नगरे कश्चिद् यो मया सार्द्धं समर्थः शिल्पेन शिल्पमुपदर्शयितुं ॥ ततो

राजा शुद्धोदनः प्रहसितवदनो बोधिसत्त्वमेवमाह । शक्ष्यसि पुनस्त्वं पुत्र शिल्पमुपदर्शयितुं ॥

आह । वाढं शक्ष्यामि देव तेन हि सन्निपात्यन्तां सर्व्वशिल्पज्ञाः । येषां पुरतः स्वं शिल्पमुपदर्शयिष्यामि ॥ ततो राजा शुद्धोदनः कपिलवस्तुनि महानगरवरे घण्टाघोषणां कारयति स्म । सप्तमे दिवसे कुमारः स्वं शिल्पमुपदर्शयिष्यति । तत्र सर्व्वशिल्पज्ञैः सन्निपतितव्यं ॥

तत्र सप्तमे दिवसे पञ्चमात्राणि शाक्यकुमारशतानि सन्निपतितान्यभवन् । दण्डपाणेश्च शाक्यस्य दुहिता गोपा नाम शाक्यकन्या तत्र जयपताका स्थापिताऽभूत् । यो वाऽत्रासिधनुष्कलापयुद्धशास्त्रेषु जेष्यति तस्यैषा भविष्यतीति ॥ तत्र सर्व्वपुरतो देवदत्तः कुमारो नगरादभिनिष्क्रामति स्म ॥ श्वेतश्च हस्ती महाप्रमाणो बोधिसत्त्वस्यार्थे नगरं प्रवेश्यते स्म ॥ तत्र देवदत्तः कुमार ईर्ष्यया च शाक्यबलमदेन च मत्तः स तं हस्तिनं वामेन पाणिना शुण्डायां गृहीत्वा दक्षिणेन पाणिना चपेटया एकप्रहारेणैव हतोऽभूत् (१) ॥ तस्यानन्तरं सुन्दरनन्दः कुमारोऽभिनिष्क्रामति स्म । सोऽद्राक्षीत्तं हस्तिनं नगरद्वारे । हतं दृष्ट्वा च पर्य्यपृच्छत् । केनायं हत इति ॥

तत्र महाजनकायाः आहुः । देवदत्तेनेति ॥

स आह । सुशोभनमिदं देवदत्तस्य ॥ स तं हस्तिनं लाङ्गूलेन गृहीत्वा नगरद्वारादपकर्षयति स्म । तदनन्तरं बोधिसत्त्वो

१ "हतोऽभूद्" इत्यत्र जघान इत्युचितम् ।

रथाभिरूढोऽभिनिष्क्रामति स्म । अद्राक्षीद्देवदत्तस्तं हस्तिनं ।
हतं दृष्ट्वा च पर्य्यपृच्छत् । केनायं हत इति ॥

आहुः । देवदत्तेनेति ॥

आह । अशोभनं देवदत्तस्य । केन पुनरस्मान्नगरद्वारा-
दपकर्षितः ॥

आहुः । सुन्दरनन्देनेति ॥

आह । शोभनमिदं सुन्दरनन्दस्य किन्तु महाकायोऽयं
सत्त्वः सोऽयं क्लिन्नः सर्व्वनगरं दौर्गन्ध्येन स्फुरयिष्यतीति ॥ ततः
कुमारो रथस्थ एवैकपादं भूमौ प्रसार्य्य पादाङ्गुष्ठेन तं हस्तिनं
लाङ्गूलेन गृहीत्वा सप्तप्राकारांस्सप्त च परिखा अतिक्रम्य वहिर्न-
गरस्य क्रोशमात्रे क्षिपति स्म ॥ यत्र च प्रदेशे स हस्ती पतित-
स्तस्मिन् प्रदेशे महद्बिलं संवृत्तं । यत्साम्प्रतं हस्तिगर्त्तेत्यभि-
धीयते ॥ तत्र देवमनुष्याः शतसहस्राणि हाहा-कारकिलि-
किलाप्रक्ष्वेडितशतसहस्राणि प्रामुञ्चन्चैलविक्षेपांश्चाकार्षुः ॥
गगनतलगताश्च देवपुत्रा इमे गाथेऽभाषन्त ।

यथ मत्तगजेन्द्रगतीनां पादाङ्गुष्ठतलेन गृहीत्व गजेन्द्रं ।
सप्त पुरा परिखा अतिक्रम्य क्षिप्त वहिस्त्वपुरात्तु अयं हि (१)॥
निःसंशयमेष सुमेधा मानबलेन समुच्छ्रितकायां ।
संसारपुरात्तु वहिर्धा एष क्षिपिष्यति प्रज्ञाबलेन (२)॥

इति हि पञ्चमात्राणि शाक्यकुमारशतानि नगरान्निष्क्रम्य

---

१ "यथ" यथा "मत्तगजेन्द्रगतीनां" मत्तगजेन्द्रगतिं "गृहीत्व" गृहीत्वा "पुरा" पुरस्य "क्षिप्त" क्षिप्तवान् इति । २ "समुच्छ्रितकायां" समुच्छ्रितकायान् "वहिर्धा" वहिः "क्षिपिष्यति" क्षेप्स्यति इति ।

येनान्यतमः पृथिवीप्रदेशो यत्र शाक्यकुमाराः शिल्पमुपदर्शयन्ति स्म तेनोपासङ्क्रामत् ॥ राजाऽपि शुद्धोदनो महल्लकमहल्लिकाश्चास्य शाक्या महांश्च जननिकायो येनासौ पृथिवीप्रदेशस्तेनोपासङ्क्रामत् ॥ बोधिसत्त्वस्य चान्येषाञ्च शाक्यकुमाराणां शिल्पविशेषं द्रष्टुकामाः ॥ तत्रादित एव ये शाक्यकुमारा लिपिविधिज्ञास्तेन सार्द्धं लिपिं विशेषयन्ति स्म ॥ तत्र तैः शाक्यैर्विश्वामित्र आचार्य्यः साक्षी स्थापितोऽभूत् । स त्वं व्यवलोकय कतमोऽत्र कुमारो लिपिज्ञाने विशिष्यते यदि वा लेख्यतो यदि वा बहुलिपिनिर्द्देशतः ॥ अथ विश्वामित्रो दारकाचार्य्यः प्रत्यक्षो बोधिसत्त्वस्य लिपिज्ञाने स्मितमुपदर्शयन्निमे गाथेऽभाषत ।

मनुष्यलोकेऽथ देवलोके गन्धर्व्वलोकेऽप्यसुरेन्द्रलोके ।
यावन्ति केचिल्लिपि सर्व्वलोके तत्रैष पारङ्गतु शुद्धसत्त्वः (१) ॥
नामापि यूयञ्च अहञ्च तासां लिपिं न जानामि न चाक्षराणां ।
यान्येष जानाति मनुष्यचन्द्रो अहमत्र प्रत्यक्ष विजेष्यतेऽयं (२) ॥

शाक्या आहुः । विशिष्यतां तावत् कुमारो लिपिज्ञाने सङ्ख्याज्ञाने कुमारो विशेषयितव्यो जिज्ञास्यस्य ॥ तत्रार्ज्जुनो नाम शाक्यगणको महामात्रः सङ्ख्यागणनासु पारङ्गतः स साक्षी स्थापितोऽभूत् । स त्वं व्यवलोकय कतमोऽत्र कुमारो विशिष्यते सङ्ख्याज्ञानत इति ॥ तत्र बोधिसत्त्वस्योद्दिशति

---

१ "यावन्ति" यावत्यः "लिपि" लिपयः "पारङ्गतु" पारङ्गत इति । २ "यान्येष" या एव "प्रत्यक्ष" प्रत्यक्षमिति ।

स्म । एकश्च शाक्यकुमारो निक्षिपति स्म न च परिप्रापयति स्म ॥ ततो बोधिसत्त्व आह । उद्दिशत यूयमहं निक्षेप्स्यामीति ॥ तत्रैकः शाक्यकुमारो बोधिसत्त्वस्योद्दिशति स्म । न च परिप्रापयति स्म ॥ द्वावपि त्रयोऽपि पञ्चापि दशापि विंशत्यपि त्रिंशदपि चत्वारिंशदपि पञ्चाशदपि शतमपि यावत् पञ्चाऽपि शाक्यकुमारशतानि युगपदुद्दिशन्ति स्म । न च परिप्रापयन्ति स्म बोधिसत्त्वस्य निक्षिपतः ॥

बोधिसत्त्व आह । अलमलमनेन विवादेन सर्व्वे इदानीमेकीभूत्वा ममोद्दिशताहं निक्षेप्स्यामीति ॥

तत्र पञ्चमात्राणि शाक्यकुमारशतान्येकवचनोदाहारेण पूर्व्वचरितं समुद्दिशन्ति स्म ॥ बोधिसत्त्वश्चासम्मूढो निक्षिपति स्म ॥ एवमपर्य्यन्ताः सर्व्वशाक्यकुमाराः पर्य्यन्तश्च बोधिसत्त्वः ॥ ततोऽर्ज्जुनो गणको महामात्र आश्चर्य्यप्राप्त इमे गाथेऽभाषत ।

ज्ञानस्य शीघ्रतां साधु बुद्धेः सुपरिगच्छतां ।
पञ्चमात्रशतान्येतेऽधिष्ठितो गणनापथे (१) ॥
ईदृशी च इयं प्रज्ञा बुद्धिर्ज्ञानं स्मृतिर्मतिः (२) ।
अद्यापि शिक्षते चायं गणितं ज्ञानसागरः ॥

ततः सर्व्वशाक्यगण आश्चर्य्यप्राप्तः परमविस्मयमापन्नोऽभूत् । एककण्ठश्चेमां वाचमभाषत । जयति जयति भोः सर्व्वार्थसिद्धः कुमारः ॥ सर्व्वे चासनेभ्य उत्थाय कृताञ्जलिपुटा भूत्वा

१ सुपरिगच्छतामित्यनुमीयते "पञ्चमात्रशतान्यते" पञ्चमात्रशत एतस्मिन्नित्यर्थः ।
२ बुद्ध्यादि बोधिसत्त्वस्यास्तीति शेषः ।

बोधिसत्त्वं नमस्कृत्य राजानं शुद्धोदनमेतदवोचत् । लाभास्ते महाराज परमाः सुलब्धाः । यस्य ते पुत्र एवं शीघ्रो लघुचपलः परिपृच्छाप्रतिभान इति ॥

अथ स राजा शुद्धोदनो बोधिसत्त्वमेवमाह । शक्यसि पुत्रार्जुनेन गणकेन महामात्रेण सार्धं संख्यागणनकौशल्यगणनागतिमनुप्रवेष्टुं ॥

आह । तेन हि गण्यतां ॥

अथार्जुनो गणको महामात्रो बोधिसत्त्वमेवमाह । जानीषे त्वं कुमार कोटिशतोत्तरां नाम गणनागतिं ॥

आह । जानाम्यहं ॥

आह । कथं पुनः कोटिशतोत्तरा गणनागतिरनुप्रवेष्टव्या ॥

बोधिसत्त्व आह । शतं कोटीनामयुतं नामोच्यते । शतमयुतानां नियुतं नामोच्यते । शतं नियुतानां कङ्करं नामोच्यते । शतं कङ्कराणां विवरं नामोच्यते । शतं विवराणामक्षोभ्यं नामोच्यते । शतमक्षोभ्याणां विवाहं नामोच्यते । शतं विवाहानामुत्सङ्गं नामोच्यते । शतमुत्सङ्गानां बहुलं नामोच्यते । शतं बहुलानां नागबलं नामोच्यते । शतं नागबलानां तिटिलम्भं नामोच्यते । शतं तिटिलम्भानां व्यवस्थानप्रज्ञप्तिर्नामोच्यते । शतं व्यवस्थानप्रज्ञप्तीनां हेतुहिलं नामोच्यते । शतं हेतुहिलानां करहुर्नामोच्यते । शतं करहूणां हेत्विन्द्रियं नामोच्यते । शतं हेत्विन्द्रियाणां समाप्तलम्भं नामोच्यते । शतं समाप्तलम्भानां गणनागतिर्नामोच्यते ।

शतं गमनागतीनां निरवद्यं नामोच्यते। शतं निरवद्यानां मुद्राबलं नामोच्यते। शतं मुद्राबलानां सर्व्वबलं नामोच्यते। शतं सर्व्वबलानां विसंज्ञागतिर्नामोच्यते। शतं विसंज्ञागतीनां सर्व्वसंज्ञा नामोच्यते। शतं सर्व्वसंज्ञानां विभूतङ्गमा नामोच्यते। शतं विभूतङ्गमानां तल्लक्षणं नामोच्यते। इति हि तल्लक्षणगणनया सुमेरुः पर्व्वतराजो लक्षनिक्षेपक्रियया परिक्षयं गच्छेत्॥ अतोऽप्युत्तरं ध्वजाग्रवती नाम गणना। यस्यां गणनायां गङ्गानदीवालुकाः समा लक्षनिक्षेपक्रियया परिक्षयं गच्छेयुः॥ अतोऽप्युत्तरं ध्वजाग्रनिशामणिर्नाम गणना। अतोऽप्युत्तरं वाहनप्रज्ञप्तिर्नाम। अतोऽप्युत्तरं कुरुता नाम। अतोऽप्युत्तरं सर्व्वनिक्षेपा नाम गणना। यस्यां गणनायां दश गङ्गानदीवालुकाः समा लक्षनिक्षेपक्रियया परिक्षयं गच्छेयुः॥ अतोऽप्युत्तरं अग्रसारा नाम गणना। यत्र कोटीशतं गङ्गानदीवालुकाः समा लक्षनिक्षेपक्रियया परिक्षयं गच्छेयुः॥ अतोऽप्युत्तरं परमाणुरजःप्रवेशानुगता नाम गणना। यत्र तथागतं स्थापयित्वा बोधिमण्डवराग्रगतश्च सर्व्वधर्म्माभिषेकाभिमुखं बोधिसत्त्वं। नान्यः कश्चित्सत्त्वः सत्त्वनिकाये संविद्यते यत्र एषा गणनाऽनुप्रवेष्टव्या॥

अर्ज्जुनोऽवोचत्। कथं कुमार परमाणुरजःप्रवेशगणना ऽनुप्रवेष्टव्या॥

बोधिसत्त्व आह। सप्तपरमाणुरजांसि रेणुः। सप्तरेणवस्त्रुटिः। सप्त त्रुटिरेकं वातायनरजः। सप्त वातायनरजांस्येकं शशरजः।

सप्त शशरजांस्येकमेडकरजः। सप्तैडकरजांस्येकं गोरजः। सप्तगो-रजांस्येकं लिक्षारजः। सप्तलिक्षाः सर्षपः। सप्त सर्षपा यवः। सप्त यवा अङ्गुलीपर्व्व। द्वादशाङ्गुलीपर्व्वाणि वितस्तिः। द्वे वितस्ती हस्तः। चत्वारो हस्ता धनुः। धनुःसहस्रं मागधक्रोशः। चत्वारः क्रोशा योजनं॥ तत्र को युष्माकं योजनपिण्डं प्रजानाति। कियन्ति तानि परमाणुरजांसि भवन्ति॥

अर्ज्जुनोऽवोचत्। अहमेव तावत्कुमार सम्मोहमापन्नः। किमङ्ग पुनर्ये चान्येऽल्पबुद्धयः॥ निर्दिशतु कुमारो योजन-पिण्डं कियन्ति तानि परमाणुरजांसि भवन्तीति॥

बोधिसत्त्वोऽवोचत्। तत्र योजनपिण्डः परमाणुरजसां परि-पूर्णमक्षोभ्यं नियुतमेकं त्रिंशच्च कोटिनियुतं शतसहस्राणि षष्टिश्च कोटिशतानि द्वाविंशतिश्च कोट्यः पञ्च च दशशतसहस्राणि द्वा-दश च सहस्राणि एतावान्योजनपिण्डः परमाणुरजोनिक्षेपश्च। अनेन प्रवेशेनायं जम्बुद्वीपः सप्तयोजनसहस्राणि। गोदानीयो ऽष्टौ योजनसहस्राणि। पूर्व्वविदेहो नव योजनसहस्राणि। उत्तरः कुरुद्वीपो दशयोजनसहस्राणि। अनेन प्रवेशेनेमञ्चातुर्द्वीपकं लोकधातुं प्रमुखं कृत्वा परिपूर्णकोटिशतं। चातुर्द्वीपकानां लोकधातूनां यच्च कोटिशतं महासमुद्राणां। कोटिशतं चक्रवा-लमहाचक्रवालानां। कोटिशतं चातुर्महाराजिकानां देवानां। कोटिशतं त्रयस्त्रिंशानां। कोटिशतं यामानां। कोटिशतं तुषि-तानां। कोटिशतं निर्म्माणरतीनां। कोटिशतं परनिर्म्मित-वशवर्त्तिनां। कोटिशतं ब्रह्मकायिकानां। कोटिशतं ब्रह्म-

पुरोहितानां । कोटिशतं ब्रह्मपार्षद्यानां । कोटिशतं महाब्रह्मणां । कोटिशतं परीत्ताभानां (१) । कोटिशतं अप्रमाणाभानां । कोटिशतं आभास्वराणां । कोटिशतं परीत्तशुभानां (२) । कोटिशतं अप्रमाणशुभानां । कोटिशतं शुभकृत्स्नानां । कोटिशतं अनभ्रकाणां । कोटिशतं पुण्यप्रसवानां । कोटिशतं वृहत्फलानां । कोटिशतं असञ्ज्ञिसत्त्वानां । कोटिशतं अवृहाणां । कोटिशतं सुदृशां । कोटिशतं सुदर्शनानां । कोटिशतं अकनिष्ठानां देवानां ॥

अयमुच्यते । त्रिसाहस्रमहासाहस्रलोकधातुर्विपुलश्च विस्तीर्णश्च । यावन्ति योजनशतानि परमाणुरजांसि त्रिसाहस्रमहासाहस्रलोकधातौ यावन्ति योजनसहस्राणि यावन्ति योजनकोट्यो यावन्ति योजननियुतानि यावद्यावन्त्यो योजनायसारा गणनाः कियन्ति तानि परमाणुरजांसि इत्याह ॥ सङ्ख्यागणना । व्यतिवृत्ता ह्येषा गणना तदुच्यते असङ्ख्येयमिति ॥

अतः असङ्ख्येयतमानि परमाणुरजांसि यानि त्रिसाहस्रमहासाहस्रलोकधातौ भवन्ति । अस्मिन् खलु पुनर्गणनापरिवर्त्ते बोधिसत्त्वेन निर्द्दिश्यमाने अर्ज्जुनो गणको महामात्रः सर्व्वश्च शाक्यगणस्तुष्ट उदग्र आत्तमनाः प्रमुदित आश्चर्याद्भुतप्राप्तोऽभूत् ॥ ते सर्व्वे एकैकैर्वस्त्रैः स्थिता अभूवन् । परिशिष्टैर्वस्त्राभरणैर्बोधिसत्त्वमभिच्छादयन्ति स्म ॥ अथ खल्वर्ज्जुनो गणको महामात्र इमे गाथे अभाषत ।

---

१ प्रेताभानामित्यनुमियते । २ लोकविशेष इति विलमजेन ।

कोटीशतश्च अयुता नियुतास्तथैव नियुतानि कङ्करगती तथ विम्बरांश्च ।

अक्षोभ्यो परम ज्ञानु न मेऽभ्यतोऽर्थे महोत्तरेगणनाप्रतिम-मस्य ज्ञानं (१) ॥

अपि च भोः शाक्याधिपाह्वरजांसिचयन्तथा द्रुमवरि श्रोष-धियो जलस्य विन्दून् ।

उद्धारेण न्यसेय एकिमेषो को पुनि विस्मयः पञ्चभिः शतेभिः (२) ॥

तत्र देवमनुजाः शतसहस्राणि हाहाकारकिलकिलाप्रक्ष्वे-डितशतसहस्राणि प्रामुञ्चन् ॥ गगनतलगताश्च देवपुत्रा इमां गाथामभाषन्त ।

यावन्ति सत्त्व निखिले चित्तध्वयुक्ताश्चिन्तानि चेतसिकसम्भित वितर्कितानि ।

हीनाः प्रणीत तथ सङ्क्षिपविक्षिपा ये एकक्षिं चित्तं परिवर्त्ति प्रजानि सर्व्वान् (३) ॥

---

१ “अयुताः” अयुतानि “नियुताः” नियुतानि “कंक-रगती तथ” कङ्कर-गतिस्तथा “अक्षोभ्यो” अक्षोभ्यीयं “परम” परमं “ज्ञानु” ज्ञानं “अतोर्थे” अभिज्ञार्थे “महोत्तरे गणनाप्रतिमस्य” मम उत्तरोत्तरगणनायामप्रतिमस्य ।
२ “शिखावचरजांसियं” शिखावचरलोकधातुरजांसि इत्यर्थः । “द्रुमवरिश्रोष-धियो” द्रुमवरौषधयः “न्यसेय” न्यसामि “एकिमेषो” एकोन्मेषः “को पुनि विस्मयः” कः पुनर्विस्मयः “शतेभिः” शतैः । पञ्चशतादीनां न्यासे तु को विस्मय इत्याशयः ।
३ “यावन्ति” यावन्तः “सत्त्व” सत्त्वाः “निखिले” सर्व्वजगतीत्यर्थः “चित्तध्व-युक्ताः” अध्वयुक्ताः “चेतसिकसम्भितवितर्कितानि” चेतसिकसम्भावितवितर्कितानि “प्रणीत तथ” प्रणीतास्तथा “सङ्क्षिपविक्षिपाः” सङ्क्षेपविक्षेपाः “एकक्षिं चित्त” एकस्मिंश्चित्ते “परिवर्त्ति” परिवर्त्तते “प्रजानि” प्रजानाति ।

इति हि भिक्षवोऽभिभूताः सर्व्वे शाक्यकुमारा अभूवन्। बोधिसत्त्व एव विशिष्यते स्म। तदनन्तरं लङ्घिते प्लविते जविते सर्व्वत्र बोधिसत्त्व एव विशिष्यते स्म ॥ गगनतलगताश्च देवपुत्रा इमा गाथा अभाषन्त।

व्रततपगुणेन संयमेन शमदममैत्रबलेन कल्पकोट्यः।
तस्य लघुलघुकायचित्ते नेता तस्य जनस्य विशेष्यतां प्रहृष्टो-
याः (१) ॥

इह गृहगत युष्मे पश्यथा सत्त्वसारं अपि च द्रुमह हित्वा
गच्छतेऽयं वनेन।
अपरिमितजिनानां पूजनामेव कुर्व्वन् मणिकनकविचित्रैर्लोक-
धातुष्वनन्ता (२) ॥

न च पुन गति आगतिश्च अस्य यूयं प्रजानथ तावद्वृद्धि-
प्राप्तः।
कोऽत्र जगति विस्मयं जनेया अचकृत्र एव करोथ गौरवोऽ
स्मिन् (३) ॥

एवं खलु बोधिसत्त्व एव विशिष्यते स्म॥ तत्र शाक्या आहुः। युद्धेषु तावत्कुमारो विशेषयितव्यो जिज्ञासितव्य ॥ तत्र बोधिसत्त्व

---

१ "व्रततपगुणेन" व्रततपश्चागुणेन "शमदममैत्रबलेन" शमादममैत्रबलेन "कल्पकोट्यः" कल्पकोटिपर्य्यन्तमित्यर्थः "तस्य" तथा "लघुलघुकायचित्त" लघुलघुकायचित्तः "प्रहृष्टायाः" प्रहृष्टत। २ "गृहगत" गृहगतं "युष्मे" यूयं "पश्यथाः" पश्यत "गच्छतेऽयं" गच्छत्ययं "पूजनामेव" पूजनमेव "लोकधातु-ष्वनन्ता" लोकधातुषु अनन्तेषु। ३ "पुन गति आगतिश्च" पुनर्गतिमागतिश्च "प्रजानथ" प्रजानीथ "तावद्वृद्धिप्राप्तः" तावद्यद्वृद्धिप्राप्तः "जनेया" जनयेत् "करोथ गौरवोऽस्मिन्" करोति गौरवमस्मिन् गौरवजनकं कार्य्यं करोतीत्यर्थः।

एकान्ते स्थितोऽभूत् तानि च पञ्चमात्राणि शाक्यकुमारशतानि युगपद्युध्यन्ति स्म ॥ इति हि द्वात्रिंशच्छाक्यकुमाराः शालम्भाय स्थिताः। तदा नन्दश्चानन्दश्च बोधिसत्त्वमभिगतौ शालम्भाय तौ समनन्तरं स्पृष्टावेव बोधिसत्त्वेन पाणिना तौ बोधिसत्त्वस्य वर्णं तेजश्चासहमानौ धरणीतले प्रपतितावभूतां ॥ तदनन्तरं देवदत्तः कुमारो गर्व्वितश्च मानी च बलवानेव स्तब्धः शाक्यमानेन च बोधिसत्त्वेन सार्द्धं विस्पर्द्धमानः सर्व्वावन्तं गगनमण्डलं वा प्रदक्षिणीकृत्य विक्रीडमानो बोधिसत्त्वमभिपतति स्म ॥ अथ बोधिसत्त्वोऽसम्भ्रान्त एवात्वरमाणो दक्षिणेन पाणिना सलीलं देवदत्तं कुमारं गृहीत्वा त्रिर्गगनतले परिवर्त्त्यमानं निग्रहार्थमविहिंसाबुद्ध्या मैत्रेण चित्तेन धरणीतले निक्षिपति स्म यथास्य कायं नाबाधते स्म ॥

ततो बोधिसत्त्वोऽप्याह । अलमलमनेन विवादेन सर्व्वं एकीभूत्वा इदानीं शालम्भायागच्छतेति ॥

अथ ते सर्व्वे एकीभूत्वा बोधिसत्त्वमभिनिपतिताः। ते समनन्तरं स्पृष्टा बोधिसत्त्वेन बोधिसत्त्वस्य श्रियं तेजश्च कायबलं स्थाम चासहमानाः स्पृष्टमात्रा एव बोधिसत्त्वेन धरणितले प्रापतन्॥ तत्र मरुन्मनुजशतसहस्राणि हीहीकार किलकिलाप्रक्ष्वेडित शतसहस्राणि अकार्षुः ॥ गगनतलगताश्च देवपुत्रा महान्तं पुष्पवर्षमभिप्रवर्ष्यैकस्वरेणेमा गाथा अभाषन्त ।

यावन्त सत्त्वा दशसु दिशासु ते दुष्टमल्ल महनग्नसमा
भवेयुः ।

एकक्षणेन निपतेयु नरर्षभस्य संचूर्णमान निपतेयु क्षितीतले-
ऽस्मिं (१) ॥

मेरुः सुमेरु तथ वज्रकचक्रवालौ ये चान्य पर्व्वत कचिद्सन्ति
हिमाद्य ।
पाणिभ्य दृष्ट्वा मषिचूर्णनिभां प्रकुर्य्यात् को विस्मयो मनुज-
चाम्रयके कुमारे (२) ॥

एषो द्रुमेन्द्रप्रवरे महदुष्टमनं मारं ससैन्य सबलं सरथं ध्वजाये ।
मैत्रीबलेन विनिहत्य हि कृष्णबन्धुं यावत् स्पृशिष्यति अनुत्तर-
बोधि शान्तं (३) ॥

एवं कृत्वा बोधिसत्त्व एव विशिष्यते स्म ॥ अथ दण्डपाणिः शाक्यकुमारानेतदवोचत् । विज्ञापितमिदं दृष्टञ्च हन्तेदानीमिषुक्षेपमुपदर्शयत ॥ तत्रानन्दस्य द्वयोः क्रोशयोरयस्मयी भेरी लक्ष्यं स्थापिताऽभूत् ॥ तस्यानन्तरं देवदत्तस्य चतुर्षु क्रोशेषु अयस्मयी भेरी स्थापिताऽभूत् ॥ सुन्दरनन्दस्य षट्सु क्रोशेष्वयस्मयी भेरी स्थापिताऽभूत् ॥ दण्डपाणेर्योजनद्वयेऽयस्मयी भेरी स्थापिताऽभूत् ॥ बोधिसत्त्वस्य दशसु क्रोशेषु अयस्मयी भेरी स्थापिताऽभूत् ॥ तस्यानन्तरं सप्त ताला अय-

१ "यावन्त" यावन्तः "कुडमल" कुडमलाः "मत्तगजसमाः" मत्तागजरत्नसमाः "निपतेयु नरर्षभस्य" निपतेयुर्नरर्षभेण "संचूर्णमान" संचूर्णमानं "क्षितीतलेऽस्मिन्" क्षितितलेऽस्मिन्नपि निपतेयुरित्यस्य द्विरावृत्तिर्व्यर्था ॥ २ "सुमेरु तथ" सुमेरुस्तथा "येचान्ये पर्व्वत कचिदसन्त" येचान्ये पर्व्वताः कचिदसन्त "पाणिभ्य दृष्ट्वा मषिचूर्णनिभां" पाणिभ्यां दृष्ट्वा मषीचूर्णनिभाम् "मनुज चाम्रयके" मनुजाम्रयके । ३ "एषो द्रुमेन्द्रप्रवरे" एष द्रुमेन्द्रप्रवरतुल्यमित्यर्थः "महदुष्टमनं" महादुष्टमनस्कमित्यर्थः "ससैन्य" ससैन्यं "स्पृशिष्यति" स्प्रक्ष्यति "अनुत्तर-बोधि" अनुत्तरबोधौ ।

अयो वराहप्रतिमा यन्त्रयुक्ता स्थापिताऽभूत् ॥ तत्रानन्देन द्वाभ्यां क्रोशाभ्यां भेर्य्याहताऽभूत्। तत उत्तरं न शक्नोति स्म ॥ देवदत्तेन चतुःक्रोशस्था भेर्य्याहताऽभूत्। नोत्तरं शक्नोति स्म ॥ सुन्दरनन्देन षट्क्रोशस्था भेर्य्याहताऽभूत्। नोत्तरं शक्नोति स्म ॥ दण्डपाणिना द्वियोजनस्था भेर्य्याहताऽभूत्। निविद्धा च नोत्तरं शक्नोतिस्म ॥ तत्र बोधिसत्त्वेन यद्यदेव धनुरुपनाम्यते स्म। तत्तदेवाच्छिद्यते स्म ॥

ततो बोधिसत्त्व आह। अस्तीह नगरे किञ्चिदन्यद् धनुर्यन्ममारोपणं सहेत कायबलं स्थाम च ॥

राजा आह। अस्ति पुत्र ॥

कुमार आह। क्व तद्देव ॥

राजा आह। तव पुत्र पितामहः सिंहहनुर्नामाऽभूत्। तस्य यद्धनुस्तदेतर्हि देवकुले गन्धमाल्यैर्महीयते न पुनः कश्चिच्छक्नोति स्म तद्धनुरारोपयितुं प्रागेव पूरयितुं ॥

बोधिसत्त्व आह। आनीयतां देव तद्धनुर्जिज्ञासिष्यामः ॥

तावत्तावद्धनुरुपनामितमभूत् (१) ॥ तत्र सर्व्वे शाक्यकुमाराः परमेणापि प्रयत्नेन व्यायच्छमाना न शक्नुवन्ति स्म तद्धनुरारोपयितुं प्रागेव पूरयितुं ॥ ततस्तद्धनुर्दण्डपाणेः शाक्यस्योपनामितमभूत् ॥ अथ दण्डपाणिः शाक्यः सर्व्वकायबलस्थाम सञ्जनय्य तद्धनुरारोपयितुमारब्धोऽभून्न (२) शक्नोति स्म ॥ याव-

१ "उपनामितमभूत्" उपानीतमभूत् एवमग्र सर्व्वत्रायम्। २ "आरब्धोऽभूत्" आरब्धवानित्युचितम्।

बोधिसत्त्वस्योपनामितमभूत्। तद्बोधिसत्त्वो गृहीत्वा आसनाद्-गुत्थितमेवार्द्धपर्य्यङ्कं कृत्वा वामेन पाणिना गृहीत्वा दक्षिणेन पाणिना एकाङ्गुल्यग्रेणारोपितमभूत् (१) ॥ तस्य धनुष आरोप्यमाणस्य सर्व्वं कपिलवस्तु महानगरं शब्देनाभिविज्ञप्तमभूत् ॥ सर्व्वनगरजनस्य विक्लवीभूतोऽन्योन्यमपृच्छत्। कस्यायमेवंविधः शब्द इति ॥ एतदवोचत्। सिद्धार्थेन कुमारेण पैतामहधनुरारोपितं तस्यायं शब्द इति ॥ तत्र देवमनुजशतसहस्राणि हाहाकारकिलकिलाप्रक्ष्वेडितशतसहस्राणि प्रामुञ्चन् ॥ गगनतलगताश्च देवपुत्रा राजानं शुद्धोदनं तञ्च महान्तं जनमिकायं गाथयाऽध्यभाषन्त।

यथ पूरित एष धनुर्मुनिना
न च उत्थितु आसनिना च भुमी।
निःसंशयं पूर्णमभिप्रायु मुनि-
संघु भेष्यति जित्व च मारचमूं (२) ॥

इति हि भिक्षवो बोधिसत्त्वस्तद्धनुः पूरयित्वेषुं गृहीत्वा तादृशेन बलस्थाम्ना तमिषुं क्षिपति स्म ॥ येन च या आनन्दस्य भेरी यावद्देवदत्तस्य यावत् सुन्दरनन्दस्य यावद्दण्डपाणेस्ताः सर्व्वा अभिनिर्भिद्य ताश्च दशक्रोशस्थां स्वकामयस्मयीं भेरीं सप्ततालान् यन्त्रयुक्तां वराहप्रतिमामभिनिर्भिद्य स इषुर्धरणीतलं प्रविश्य अदर्शनाभासोऽभूत् ॥ यत्र च प्रदेशे स इषु-

१ "आरोपितमभूत्" आरोपितमकरोदित्युचितम् ॥ २ "यथ" यथा "पूरित एष" पूरितमेतत् "उत्थितु" उत्थितः "आसनिना" आसनात् "भुमी" भूम्याः "पूर्णमभिप्रायु" पूर्णोऽभिप्रायः "भेष्यति" भेत्स्यति "जित्व" जित्वा।

भूमितलं भित्त्वा प्रविष्टस्तस्मिन्प्रदेशे कूपः संवृत्तः। यदद्यापि शरकूप इत्यभिधीयते॥ तत्र देवमनुष्यशतसहस्राणि हाहा-कारकिलकिलाप्रक्ष्वेडितशतसहस्राणि प्रामुञ्चन्। सर्व्वश्च शाक्य-गणो विस्मितोऽभूत् आश्चर्य्यप्राप्तः॥ आश्चर्य्यं भो न च नाम अनेन योग्यता कृता इदञ्च ईदृशं शिल्पकौशलं॥ गगनतल-गताश्च देवपुत्रा राजानं शुद्धोदनं तञ्च महान्तं जनकाय-मेवमाहुः। कोऽत्र विस्मयः तत्कस्मात्।

एष धरणिमण्डे पूर्व्वबुद्धासनस्थः
समर्थ धनुर्गृहीत्वा शून्यनैरात्मबाणैः।
क्लेशरिपुं निहत्वा दृष्टिजालञ्च भित्त्वा
शिव विरज मशोकां प्राप्स्यते बोधिमग्र्यां (१)॥

एवमुक्त्वा देवपुत्रा बोधिसत्त्वं दिव्यैः पुष्पैरभ्यवकीर्य्य प्राक्रामन्॥ एवं लङ्घिते प्राक्ष्वसिते लिपिमुद्रागणनासंख्या-सालम्भधनुर्व्वेदे जविते प्लविते तरणे इष्वस्त्रे हस्तिग्रीवा-यामश्वपृष्ठे रथे धनुष्कलापे स्थैर्य्ये स्थाम्नि सुशौर्य्ये बाहुव्यायामे-ऽङ्कुशग्रहपाशग्रहे उद्यानिर्याणे अवयाने मुष्टिबन्धे शिखाबन्धे छेद्ये भेद्ये तरणे स्फालने अक्षुण्णवेधित्वे मर्म्मवेधित्वे शब्दवेधित्वे दृढप्रहारित्वेऽक्षक्रीडायां काव्यव्याकरणे ग्रन्थरचिते रूपे रूप-कर्म्मणि अधीतेऽग्निकर्म्मणि वीणायां वाद्यनृत्ये गीतपठिते आख्याते हास्ये लास्ये नाट्ये विडम्बिते माल्यग्रन्थने संवाहिते

---

१ "धरणिमण्डे" धरणीमण्डले। "समर्थ" समर्थः "निहत्वा" निहत्य "शिव विरजमशोकां" शिवां विरजस्कामशोकां "बोधिमग्र्यां" बोधिप्राप्त्यमग्र्यां गति-मित्यर्थः।

मणिरागे वस्त्ररागे मायाकृते स्वप्नाध्याये शकुनिरुते स्त्रीलक्षणे पुरुषलक्षणे अश्वलक्षणे हस्तिलक्षणे गोलक्षणे अजलक्षणे मिश्रितलक्षणे कैटभेश्वरलक्षणे निर्घण्टौ निगमे पुराणे इतिहासे वेदे व्याकरणे निरुक्ते शिक्षायां छन्दसि यज्ञकल्पे ज्योतिषि साङ्ख्ये योगे क्रियाकल्पे वैशेषिके वेशिके अर्थविद्यायां बार्हस्पत्ये आश्चर्य्ये आसुरे मृगपक्षिरुते हेतुविद्यायां जतुयन्त्रे मधूच्छिष्टकृते सूचीकर्म्मणि विदलकर्म्मणि पत्रच्छेद्ये गन्धयुक्तौ इत्येवमाद्यासु सर्व्वकर्म्मकलासु लौकिकादिषु दिव्यमानुष्यकातिक्रान्तासु सर्व्वत्र बोधिसत्त्व एव विशिष्यते स्म ॥

अथ खलु पुनस्तेन समयेन दण्डपाणिः शाक्यः स्वां दुहितरं गोपां शाक्यकन्यां बोधिसत्त्वाय प्रादात्। सा च राज्ञा शुद्धोदनेनानुपूर्व्वेण बोधिसत्त्वाय वृताऽभूत् ॥ तत्र सत्यपि बोधिसत्त्वश्चतुरशीतिस्त्रीसहस्राणां मध्ये प्राप्तो लोकानुभवेन तथा च समागं क्रीडन्तं परिचारयन्तमात्मानमुपदर्शयति स्म ॥ तेषां चतुरशीतिस्त्रीसहस्राणां गोपा शाक्यकन्या सर्व्वासामग्रमहिष्यभिषिक्ताऽभूत् ॥ तत्र खल्वपि गोपा शाक्यकन्या न कञ्चिद्दृष्ट्वा वदनं छादयति स्म श्वश्रूं वा श्वशुरं वाऽन्तर्जनं वा ॥ ते तामुपध्यायन्ति स्म विचारयन्ति स्म। नववधूका हि नामाप्रतिलीना तिष्ठते। या पुनर्विवृत्तैव सदा ॥ ततो गोपा शाक्यकन्या एतां प्रकृतिं श्रुत्वा सर्व्वस्यान्तर्जनस्य पुरतः स्थित्वा इमा गाथा अभाषत।

विवृत्तः शोभते आर्य्य आसनस्थानचङ्क्रमे।

मणिरत्नं ध्वजाग्रे वा भासमानं प्रभास्वरं ॥
गच्छंस्तु शोभते आर्य्य आगच्छन्नपि शोभते ।
स्थितो वाथ निषस्रो वा आर्य्यः सर्व्वच शोभते ॥
कथयञ्छोभते आर्य्यस्तूष्णीभूतोऽपि शोभते ।
कलविङ्को यथा पक्षी दर्शनेन स्वरेण वा ॥
कुशचीरी निर्वस्त्रो वा मन्दचैलः कृशतनुः ।
शोभतेऽसौ स्वतेजेन (१) गुणवान् गुणभूषितः ॥
सर्व्वेण शोभते आर्य्यो यस्य पापं न विद्यते ।
किंयद्विभूषितो बालः पापकारी न शोभते ॥
ये किल्बिषांश्च हृदये मधुराः सुवाचः
कुम्भो विषस्य परिषिक्त यथाऽमृतेन ।
दुःस्पर्शशैलशिलवत् कठिनान्तरात्मा
सर्व्वस्य वा चिरमदर्शन तादृशानां (२) ॥
सर्व्वेऽपि ते न शिष्टा सर्व्वमुपेन्ति सौम्याः
सर्व्वेषु तीर्थ इव सर्व्वजगोपजीव्याः ।
दधिक्षीरपूर्णघटतुल्य सदैव आर्य्याः
श्रेष्ठं सुदर्शन सुमङ्गल तादृशानां (३) ॥

---

१ "स्वतेजेन" स्वतेजसा । २ "किल्बिषांश्च" किल्बिषाणि च ये किल्बिषादीन्धारयन्तीति शेषः । "परिषिक्त यथा" परिषिक्तो यथा "दुःस्पर्शशैलशिलवत्" दुःस्पर्शशैलशिलावत् "सर्व्वस्य" सर्व्वेषां तादृशानां चिरमदर्शनं योग्यमित्यर्थः । ३ "शिष्ट सर्व्वमुपेन्ति" शिष्टानां सर्व्वस्य निकटे उपयन्ति प्राप्नुवन्ति लोकुर्व्वन्तीति यावत् "सर्व्वजगोपजीव्याः" सर्व्वजगत उपजीवकाः "दधिक्षीरपरिपूर्णघटतुल्य" दधिक्षीरपरिपूर्णघटतुल्याः "सुदर्शन सुमङ्गल" सुदर्शनं सुमङ्गलं ।

ये पापमित्र परिवर्जित दीर्घरात्रं
कल्याणमित्ररतनैश्च परिगृहीताः ।
पापं विवर्जयि निवेशयि शुक्लधर्मे
सफलं सुमङ्गल सुदर्शन तादृशानां (१) ॥
ये कायसंवृत सुसंयतकायदोषा
ये वाचसंवृत सदा अवकीर्णवाचः ।
गुप्तेन्द्रियाः सुनिभृताश्च मनःप्रसन्नाः
किंनादृशान वदनप्रतिच्छादयित्वा (२) ॥
वस्त्रासहस्र यदि च्छादयि आत्मभावं
चित्तश्च येष विवृतं न हिरी न लज्जा ।
न च येष ईदृश गुणा नपि सत्यवाक्यं
नग्ना विनग्नरतने विचरन्ति लोके (३) ॥
याश्चित्तगुप्त सततेन्द्रियसंयताश्च
न च अन्यसत्त्वमनसा स्वपतीन तुष्टाः ।
आदित्यचन्द्रसदृशी विवृतप्रकाशा

---

१ "पापमित्र" पापमित्रैः "परिवर्जित" परिवर्जिता "कल्याणमित्ररतनैश्च" कल्याणमित्ररत्नैश्च "पापं विवर्जयि" पापविवर्जिताः "निवेशयि" निविष्टाः "सुमङ्गलसुदर्शन" सुमङ्गलं सुदर्शनम् । २ "कायसंवृत" संवृतकायाः "वाचसंवृत" संवृतवाचः "सुनिभृताश्च" सुनिभृताश्च "किंनादृशान" किंनादृशानां "वदनप्रतिच्छादयित्वा" वदनप्रतिच्छादनेन इति । ३ "वस्त्रासहस्र" वस्त्रसहस्रं "छादयि" छादयति "येषविवृतं" येषां विवृतं "न हिरी" न ह्री "येष ईदृश" येषामीदृशाः "नपि" नापि "विनग्नरतने" विनग्नरत्नाः । वस्त्रसहस्रं यदि छादयति] तर्हि येषां चित्तनिभृतलौकिकलज्जानिवृत्तिसत्यवाक्यादिगुणा न सन्ति तानेव छादयति । [ये तु] चित्तनिभृतादिगुणवन्तस्ते तु नग्ना भूत्वा लोके विचरन्तीत्यर्थः ।

किं तादृशीन वदनप्रतिच्छादयित्वा (१) ॥ अपि च ।

जानन्ति आशय मम ऋषयो महात्मा
परचित्तबुद्धिकुशलास्तथ देवसङ्घाः ।
यथ मम शील गुण सम्वर अप्रमादो
वदनावगुण्ठनमतः प्रकरोमि किं मे (२) ॥

अश्रौषीच्छ्रियवो राजा शुद्धोदनो गोपाया शाक्यकन्याया एवंरूपसर्व्वगाथाप्रतिभाननिर्देशं । श्रुत्वा च पुनस्तुष्ट उदग्र आत्तमनाः प्रमुदितः प्रीतिसौमनस्यजातोऽनेकरत्नप्रत्युप्तेन पुष्पयुक्तेन कोटीशतसहस्रमूल्येन च मुक्ताहारेणाभिजातलोहितमुक्ताप्रत्युप्तया च सुवर्णमालया गोपां शाक्यकन्यामभिच्छाद्येदमुदानमुदानयति स्म ।

यथा च पुत्रो मम भूषितो गुणै-
स्तथा च कन्या स्वगुणैः प्रभासते ।
विशुद्धसत्त्वौ तदुभौ समागतौ
समेति सर्पिर्यथ सर्पिमण्ड (३) इति ॥

अनुपूर्व्वेण यथा पूर्व्ववत् बोधिसत्त्वप्रमुखाः स्वपुरं प्राक्रामन् ॥

इति शिल्पसन्दर्शनपरिवर्त्तो नाम द्वादशः ॥

---

१ "चित्तगुप्ता" गुप्तचित्ताः "सततेन्द्रियसंयताश्च" सततं संयतेन्द्रियाश्च "चन्द्र-वज्जनमना" चन्द्रवज्जनमनस्विन्यः "तपतीव" तपतिवत् "आदित्यचन्द्रसदृशी" आदित्यचन्द्रसदृशाः "किन्तादृशीन" किन्तादृशेनां "वदनप्रतिच्छादयित्वा" वदनप्रतिच्छादनेन । २ "आशय" आशयं "महात्मा" महात्मानः "पर-चित्तबुद्धिकुशलाश्च" परचित्तज्ञानकुशलाश्च इत्यर्थः "यथ मम शीलगुण-सम्वर" यथा मम शीलं गुणाः सम्वरः । ३ "सर्पिर्यथ" सर्पिर्यथा "सर्पिमण्डः" सर्पिःमण्डः । यथा सर्पिः सर्पिःमण्डतां प्राप्य स्वादुतरं भवति तथैव गोपाऽपि बोधिसत्त्वं प्राप्य अतितरां शुशुभे इति भावः ॥

त्रयोदशाध्यायप्रारम्भः॥

इति हि भिक्षव आत्महितहर्षमुदीरयन्त आगता आसन्। बोधिसत्त्वस्यान्तःपुरमध्यगतस्यानेकदेवनागयक्षगन्धर्व्वासुरगरुडकिन्नरमहोरगशक्रब्रह्मलोकपालाः॥ ये बोधिसत्त्वस्य पूजाकर्म्मणि औत्सुक्यमापद्यन्ते स्म॥ तत्र भिक्षवोऽपरेण समयेन सम्बहुलानां देवनागयक्षगन्धर्व्वासुरगरुडकिन्नरमहोरगशक्रब्रह्मलोकपालानामेतदभवत्। अति चिरं बतायं सत्पुरुषोऽन्तःपुरे विलम्बते। ये चास्येमे दीर्घरात्रं परिपाचिताः सत्त्वाश्चतुर्भिः सङ्ग्रहवस्तुभिर्दानेन प्रियवाक्येन अर्थक्रियया समानार्थतया यस्य बोधिसत्त्वस्य धर्म्मदेशितमाज्ञास्यन्ति तत्रैव च तानि धर्म्मभाजनानि सर्व्वाण्यन्तर्हितानि भविष्यन्ति। बोधिसत्त्वस्य पश्चादभिनिष्क्रम्यानुत्तरां सम्यक्सम्बोधिमभिसम्भोत्स्यते॥ ततस्ते सगौरवाः सप्रतीताः (१) प्राञ्जलीभूता बोधिसत्त्वं नमस्यन्ति स्म॥ एवमभिप्रायाश्चोदीक्षमाणाःस्थिता अभूवन्। कदा च नाम तद्भविष्यति। यदयं वरप्रवरं शुद्धसत्त्वमभिनिष्क्रामन्तं पश्यामोऽभिनिष्क्रम्य च तस्मिं महाद्रुमराजमूलेऽभिनिषद्य सबलं मारं धर्षयित्वानुत्तरां सम्यक्सम्बोधिमभिसम्बुद्धं (२) दशभिस्तथागतबलैः समन्वागतं चतुर्भिश्च तथागतवैशारद्यैः समन्वागतमष्टादशभिश्चावेणिकैर्बुद्धधर्म्मैः समन्वागतं त्रिपरिवर्त्तं द्वादशाकारमनुत्तरं धर्म्मचक्रं प्रवर्त्तयन्तं महता बुद्धविक्रीडितेन

---

१ सप्रश्रयाः। २ सम्यक्सम्बोधिमभिसम्बोधयन्तमित्यनुमीयते।

सदेवमानुषासुरलोकं यथाधिमुक्त्या सुभाषितेन सन्तोषयन्तं ॥

तत्र भिक्षवो बोधिसत्त्वो दीर्घरात्रमसङ्क्षेयां कल्पामुपादाय सततं समितं परप्रणेयोऽभूत् । सार्व्वलौकिकलोकोत्तरेषु धर्म्मेषु स्वयमेवाचार्य्यः सर्व्वकुशलमूलधर्म्मचर्य्यासु दीर्घकालं च कालज्ञो वेलाज्ञः समयज्ञोऽभूत् । अच्युतोऽभिज्ञः पञ्चाभिज्ञाभिः समन्वागतोऽभूत् ॥ ऋद्धिपादविक्रीडितः सर्व्वेन्द्रियकुशलः कालाकालज्ञः कालवेदी महासागर इव प्राप्तां वेलां नातिक्रामति स्म ॥ सोऽभिज्ञज्ञानबलेन समन्वागतः स्वयमेव सर्व्वं जानाति स्म । अयं कालः प्रग्रहस्यायं कालो निग्रहस्यायं कालः सङ्ग्रहस्यायं कालोऽनुग्रहस्यायं काल उपेक्षाया अयं कालो भाषितस्यायं कालः तूष्णीम्भावस्यायं कालो निष्क्रमस्यायं कालः प्रव्रज्याया अयं कालः स्वाध्यायस्यायं कालः मौमनस्यस्यायं कालः प्रविवेकस्यायं कालः क्षत्रियपर्षदमुपसङ्क्रमितुं यावदयं कालो ब्राह्मणगृहपतिपर्षदमुपसङ्क्रमितुमयं कालो देवनागयक्षगन्धर्व्वासुरगरुडकिन्नरमहोरगशक्रब्रह्मलोकपालभिक्षुभिक्षुण्युपासकोपासिकापर्षदमुपसङ्क्रमितुमयं कालो धर्म्मदेशनाया अयं कालः प्रतिसंलीनस्य सर्व्वत्र बोधिसत्त्वो नित्यकालं कालज्ञो भवति स्म कालवेदी ॥

अथ च पुनर्भिक्षवो धर्म्मताप्रतिलम्भ एष चरमभाविनां बोधिसत्त्वानां । यदवश्यं दशदिग्लोकधातुस्थितैः बुद्धैर्भगवद्भिरन्तःपुरमध्यगताः सङ्गीतितूर्य्यनिर्नादितैरेभिरेवंरूपैर्धर्म्ममुखैः सञ्चोदितव्या भवन्ति ॥ तत्रेदमुच्यते ।

ये सत्त्वाया दशदिशि लोके तेषु विशेषास्तव रतितुष्टैः ।
गाथा गीता इम रतिमधुराः सञ्चोदेन्ति नरवरप्रवरं (१) ॥
पूर्वी तुभ्यं अयु कृतु प्रणिधी दृष्ट्वा सत्त्वान्दुःखशतभरितां ।
तेन त्रायं जगति च शरणे भेष्ये नाथो हितकर परम (२) ॥
साधो वीरा स्मर वरि पुरीमां या ते आसीज्जगहित प्रणिधिः ।
कालो वेला अयु तव समयो निष्क्रम्याहि ऋषिवरप्रवर (३) ॥
यस्यार्थे ते धनवर विविधास्त्यक्ताः पूर्वे शिरकरचरणा ।
भेष्ये बुद्धो नरमरुदमको लोकज्येष्ठो गुणशतनिचितः (४) ॥
त्वं शीलेन व्रततपचरितस्त्वं क्षान्तीये जगहितकरणः ।
त्वं वीर्येण शुभगुणनिचितो ध्याने प्रज्ञे न तु समु विभवे (५) ॥
क्रोधाविष्टाखिलमल बहवस्ते मैत्रीये त्वयि स्फुट सुगता ।
कारुण्यान्ते बहुविध सुबुधे मिथ्यात्वे आशुभगुणरहिते (६) ॥
पुण्यज्ञाने शुभनिचितात्मा ध्यानाभिज्ञो व्रततपविरजो ।

---

१ "इम रतिमधुराः" इमा रतिमधुराः । "सञ्चोदेन्ति" सञ्चोदयन्ति । २ "पूर्वी तुभ्यं" पूर्वं त्वया "अयु कृतु प्रणिधी" इदं कृतं प्रणिधानं "सत्त्वान्दुःखशतभरितां" सत्त्वान्दुःखशतपरिपूर्णानित्यर्थः "शरणे" शरणागतानामित्यर्थः "भेष्ये" भविष्यसि "नाथो" नाथेति । ३ "वीरा" वीर "वरि पुरीमां" वरां पुरीमिमां "या ते आसीज्जगहित प्रणिधिः" यस्ते आसीज्जगतो हिताय प्रणिधिः प्रणिधानमित्यर्थः "अयु" अयं "निष्क्रम्याहि" निष्क्रम्य एहि । ४ "धनवर" धनवराः "पूर्वे" पूर्वं "शिरकरचरण" शिरःकरचरणानि "भेष्ये" भविष्यसि "नरमरुदमकः" नरमरुद्दमकः । ५ "व्रततपचरितः" आचरितव्रततपाः "क्षान्तीये" क्षान्त्या "जगहितकरणः" जगद्धितकरणः "ध्याने प्रज्ञे न तु समु" ध्यानेन प्रज्ञया न तु समः । ६ "क्रोधाविष्टाखिलमल" क्रोधावेशा अखिलमलाः "मैत्रीये" मैत्र्या "स्फुट" स्फुटं "सुगता" हे सुगत "बहुविध" बहुविधं "मिथ्यात्वे आशुभगुणरहिते" मिथ्यात्वेन अशुभगुणेन रहिते इत्यर्थः ।

आभासेथी इम इम दिशतो मेघामुक्तः शशिरिव विमलः (१) ॥
एते चान्ये बहुविध रुचिरास्तूर्य्यघोषा जिनरुतरचिताः ।
ये चोदेन्ति सुरनरमहितं निष्क्रम्याही अयु तव समयु (२) इति ॥

बोधिसत्त्वस्य खलु पुनर्भिक्षवस्तस्मिन्गृहवरप्रधाने सर्व्वोपकरणसमृद्धिसमुदिते यथाभिप्रायसुखविहारानुकूलेऽमरपुरभवनप्रकाशे वितर्द्दिनिर्य्यूहतोरणगवाक्षहर्म्यकूटागारप्रासादवरप्रवरे सर्व्वरत्नविचित्रालङ्कारविविधभक्तिसुविभक्ते उच्छ्रितच्छत्रध्वजपताकानेकरत्नकिङ्किणीजालसमलङ्कृतेऽनेकपट्टदामशतसहस्राभिप्रलम्बिते नानारत्नप्रत्युप्ते मुक्ताहाराभिप्रलम्बिते विचित्रपट्टरत्नसङ्क्रमोपशोभिते अवसक्तपट्टमाल्यदामकलापे गन्धघटिकानिर्धूपितेऽवश्यायपट्टविततविताने सर्व्वर्त्तुकपुष्पपरमसुगन्धिसुरुचिराभिप्रकीर्णपुष्करिणीपुण्डरीकनवनलिनीजालसंस्थानपरिभोगबहुले पत्रगुप्तशुकशारिकाकोकिलाहंसमयूरचक्रवाककुणालकलविङ्कजीवञ्जीवकादिनानाविधद्विजगणमधुरस्वरनिकूजिते नीलवैदूर्य्यमये धरणीतले संस्थानपरिभोगे सर्व्वरूपप्रतिभाससन्दर्शने अह्लादनयनाभिरम्ये परमप्रीतिप्रामोद्यसञ्जनने तस्मिन्गृहवरप्रधानेऽध्यावसतो बोधिसत्त्वस्योदारवरशरणभवननिवासिनोऽमलविमलनिर्म्मलाङ्गस्याऽमुक्तमाल्याभरणस्य प्रवरसुरभिगन्धानुलेपनानुपलिप्तगात्रस्य शुक्लशुभविमलविशु-

---

१ "पुण्यशाने" पुण्यशानेन "शततपविरक्तः" शततपोविरक्ताः "आभासेथी" आभासथे "इम इम दिशतः" इमस्तासु दिक्षु "शशिरिव" शशीव । २ "बहुविध" बहुविधाः "चोदेन्ति" चोदयन्ति "निष्क्रम्याही" निष्क्रम्येति "अयु तव समयु" अयमत्र समय इति ।

दूष्यनिर्मलवस्त्रप्रावृतशरीरस्यानेकदिव्यपुष्पगुच्छसुविन्यस्तमृदुकाचिलिन्दिकसुखसंस्पर्शवराङ्गरचितशयनवरतलाभिरूढस्यामरवधूभिरिव सर्व्वतोऽनवद्याप्रतिकूलदर्शनशुभोपचारचरितस्याभिरूपान्तःपुरमध्यगतस्य शङ्खभेरीमृदङ्गपणवतुणववीणावल्लकीसम्यताडावचरसुघोषकमधुरवेणुनिर्नादितघोषरुतनानातूर्य्यसङ्गीतिसम्प्रयोगप्रतिबोधितस्य ये च नारीगणाः स्निग्धसुरुचिरैर्मधुरमनोज्ञस्वरवेणुनिर्नादितनिर्घोषरुतै र्बोधिसत्त्वं प्रतिसम्बोधयन्ति स्म ॥ तेषां दशदिगवस्थितानां बुद्धानां भगवतामधिष्ठानेन तेभ्यस्तूर्य्यनिर्नादनिर्घोषरुतेभ्य इमा बोधिसत्त्वस्य सञ्चोदना गाथा निश्चरन्ति स्म ।

या नार्य्यः प्रमुदितमनाः प्रसन्नचित्ता
वेणुभ्यो मधुरमनोरमं रणन्ते ।
आवेशाद्दशदिग्गतां जिनोत्तमानां
गाथेमा विविध विचित्ररूपाः (१) ॥

पूर्व्वन्ते वयु व्रतु प्रणिधी अभूषि वीरा
दृष्ट्वेमां जनत सदा अनाथभूतां ।
मोचिष्ये जरमरणात्तथाऽन्यदुःखान्
बुद्धित्वा पदमजरं परमशोकं (२) ॥

---

१ "प्रमुदितमनाः" प्रमुदितमनस्काः "वेणुभ्यः" वेणुभिः "रणन्ते" रणन्ति "दशदिग्गतां" दशदिग्गतानां "गाथेमाः" गाथा इमाः "विविध" विविधाः।
२ "वयु व्रतु प्रणिधी" इदं व्रतं प्रणिधानं "अभूषि वीरा" अभूद्वीर "जनत" जनतां "अनाथभूतां" अनाथीभूतां "मोचिष्ये" मोचयिता "जरमरणं" जरामरणं "अन्यदुःखान्" अन्यदुःखानि "बुद्धित्वा" बद्धा ।

सन्नाहो पुरवरत इत: शीघ्रं निष्क्रम्या परमऋषिभिश्च चीर्णं ।
आक्रम्य धरणितलप्रदेशं सम्बुद्ध्या अनुत्तरजिनज्ञानं (१) ॥
पूर्व्वे ते धनरतन विविधा त्यक्ताभूत् करचरणप्रियात्मा ।
एषोऽयं तव समयो महर्षे धर्म्मौघं जगि विभज अनन्तं (२) ॥
शीलन्ते शुभ विमलमखण्डं पूर्व्वन्ते वरव्रतसमभावी ।
शीलेनागतिसदृश महर्षे मोचेशी जगु विविधक्लेशै: (३) ॥
क्षान्तीये भव व्रतचरितस्त्वं क्षान्त्यास्ते जगि विविध दुरुक्ता: ।
क्षान्तीये शमदम निरतात्मा नैष्क्रम्ये मति कुरु द्विपदेन्द्र (४) ॥
वीर्य्यन्तेऽतुलमचलमकम्पं पूर्व्वन्ते पृथु सुगत अभूवन् ।
धर्षित्वा नमुचिमतं ससैन्यं शोषिष्ये चय सकलअपायां (५) ॥
यस्यार्थे व्रततप चरितस्त्वं ध्यायित्वा कलिकलुषक्लेशां ।
त्वं वर्षा अमृतजलममोघं तर्पेही चिरक्षुषितानभावां (६) ॥
तां पूर्व्वां गिर वरमनुचिन्त्या निष्क्रम्या पुरवरत इत: शीघ्रं ।

---

१ "निष्क्रम्या" निष्क्रम्य "परम ऋषिभिश्च" परमर्षिभिश्च "सम्बुद्ध्या" सम्बुद्ध्य किन्तु सम्बोधय इत्युचितं । २ "पूर्व्वे ते धनरतन विविधा त्यक्ताभूत्" पूर्व्वं ते धनरत्नानि विविधानि त्यक्तान्यभूवन् "करचरणप्रियात्मा" करचरणयुक्तप्रियशरीरमित्यर्थः "जगि" जगति । ३ "शुभ" शुभं "वरव्रतसमभावी" वरव्रतं भावितं "शीलेनागतिसदृश" शीलेनागतदृशेत्यर्थः "मोचेशी" मोचय "जगु" जगत् "विविधक्लेशैः" विविधक्लेशैः । ४ "क्षान्तीये" क्षान्त्या "व्रतचरितः" व्रताचरितः क्षान्त्याचरणव्रतयुक्तस्त्वमसीत्यर्थः "जगि विविध" जगति विविधाः "दुरुक्ताः" उपायाः कथिता इत्यर्थः "क्षान्तीये शमदमनिरतात्मा" क्षान्त्या शमादमाभ्यां निरतात्मन्नित्यर्थः "नैष्क्रम्ये" निष्क्रमणे "मति" मतिं । ५ "अभूवन्" अभूत् "धर्षित्वा" धर्षयित्वा "शोषिष्ये" शोषयिष्यसि "चय" चीन् "सकल अपायां" सकलापायान् चय वीर्य्यन्ते पूर्व्वन्ते इत्यत्र ते शब्दस्य पुनरुक्तिरेवैव । ६ "व्रततपचरितस्त्वं" व्रततपश्चाचरितवांस्त्वं "ध्यायित्वा" ध्यात्वा "कलिकलुषक्लेशां" कलिकलुषक्लेशान् "त्वं वर्षा" त्वं वर्षय "तर्पेही" तर्पय "चिरक्षुषितानभावां" चिरक्षुषितानभावान् ।

बुद्धित्वा पदमच्युतमशोकं तर्पिष्ये अमृतरसेन क्षुधार्त्तान् (१) ॥
प्रज्ञा या परिचरि कुशलं ज्ञानं ते शृणु विपुलमनन्तं।
मूढानां विमतिपथस्थितानां प्रज्ञाभां प्रभंकररुचिरां कुरु त्वं (२) ॥
मैत्रायां भव व्रतचरितस्त्वं कारुण्यवरमुदित उपेक्षये।
यामेवाचरितस्त्वं तामेवा वरचरि विभज जगस्य (३) ॥
एतानी दशदिशि जिनतेजैर्गाथा निगुणकुसुमविचित्राः।
तूर्य्येभ्यो विविधमनोरमं रणन्ते चोदेन्ती शयनगतं कुमारं (४) ॥
यदि पुन प्रमुदित रतिकर प्रमदाः
सुरुचिर सुमधुर प्रभणिषु तुरियैः।
अथ जिन दशदिशि सुरनरदमका
गिरिवरमनु रचितु रवि तुरियैः (५) ॥
इत त्वयि हितकर बहुगुण जनता
निजिनितु जिनगुण विचरथि गतिषु।
स्मर स्मर पुरिमक व्रततपचरणा

---

१ "गिरि वरमनुचिन्त्या" गिरिं वरामनुचिन्त्य "निष्क्रम्या" निष्क्रम्य "बुद्धित्वा" बुद्ध्वा "तर्पिष्ये" तर्पयिष्यसि इति। २ "परिचरि" परिचारिणी "कुशलं" कुशलता कौशल्यमिति यावत् "विमतिपथस्थितानां" कुमतिपथस्थितानामित्यर्थः। ३ "मैत्रायां" मैत्रीं "व्रतचरितस्त्वं" व्रताचरितोऽसि त्वं "उपेक्षये" मा उपेक्षय "यामेवाचरितस्त्वं" यदेवाचरितवांस्त्वं "तामेवा वरचरि" तदेव वराचरणं "जगस्य" जगतोऽर्थे। ४ "एतानी" एताः "जिनतेजैः" जिनतेजोभिः "तूर्य्येभ्यो" निःसृत्येति शेषः "रणन्ते" रणन्ति "चोदेन्ती" चोदयन्ति। ५ "यदि पुन" यदि पुनः "प्रमुदित रतिकर" प्रमुदिता रतिकराः "सुरुचिर सुमधुर" सुरुचिरं सुमधुरं "प्रभणिषु तुरियैः" प्राभाणिषुस्तूर्यैः "जिन" जिनाः "गिरिवरमनुरचितु" गिरिवरमनुरचितवन्तः "रवि तुरियैः" रवं तूर्य्यैः।

लघु व्रज द्रुमवरु स्पृशय पदमच्युतं (१) ॥
सुद्धपित नरमरु जिनगुणरहिता
त्वयि मतिप्रतिबलश्च्युततरसददा ।
दशबलगुणधर बुधजनमहिते
लघु त्वयि नरपति विभजति च्युतं (२) ॥
त्यजि त्वयि पुरि भवे धनमणिकनकाः
सखिप्रियसुत महि सनगरनिगमा ।
शिरमपि त्यजि स्वकुल करचरणनयना
जगतिय हितकरु जिनगुणनिरता (३) ॥
पुरि तुम नरवर सुत नृपु यदभू-
र्नरु तव अभिमुख इम गिरमवची ।
दद मम इम महि सनगरनिगमां
त्यजि तद प्रमुदितु न च मनु क्षुभितो (४) ॥

---

१ "कृत त्वयि" कृता त्वया "बहुगुण" बहुगुणा "निजिनितु" निर्जित्य "जिनगुण" जिनगुणान् "पुरिमक" पुरोभिमां "व्रततपचरणा" व्रततप आचारणानि च "द्रुमवरु" द्रुमवरं "स्पृशय" स्पर्शय । २ "सुद्धपित नरमरु" सुद्धपितान् नरमरुतः "जिनगुणरहिता" जिनगुणरहितान् "मतिप्रतिबलश्च्युततरसददा" मतिप्रीतिबलाच्युतरसदे "दशबलगुणधर" दशबलगुणधरे "नरपति विभजति च्युतं" नरपतिर्विभजत्यच्युतं । ३ "त्यजित्वयि" त्यक्ता त्वया "पुरि" पुरा "धनमणिकनकाः" धनमणिकनकानि "सखिप्रियसुत" सखिप्रियसुताः "महि" मही "शिरमपि त्यजि" शिरोऽपि त्यक्तं "स्वकुल" स्वकुलं "करचरणनयना" करचरणनयनानि "जगतिय हितकरु" जगतो हितकर "जिनगुणनिरता" जिनगुणनिरत । ४ "पुरि तुम" पुरा त्वं "सुत नृपु यदभूः" सुतो नृपलोके यदा बभूः "नरु तव" नरस्तव "इमगिरमवची" इमां गिरमवोचत् "दद" देहि "इम महि" इमां महीं "त्यजि तद प्रमुदितु" त्यक्ता तदा त्वं प्रमुदितः बभूरिति शेषः "मनु क्षुभितो" मनः क्षुब्धं ।

पुरि तुम नरपति स्वकुल द्विज यदभू-
र्गुरुजन परिचरि न च ऋुचि परतो ।
स्थापयसि द्विजवर बहुजन कुशले
च्युत ततु भवगतु गतु पुन निलयं (१) ॥
पुरि तुम नृपसुत ऋषिवर यदभू-
श्छिनि तव तनुरुह कलि नृप रुषितो ।
हत त्वयि कुलक्रिये न च मनु क्षुभितो
अयु तव यह अवि तद करणचरणैः (२) ॥
पुर पुन ऋषिसुत त्वयि पुर यदभू-
र्गतरतु गुरुभर गिरिवरनिलये ।
हत भव नृपति न विपक्षत रुषुणा
छप तव तहिं नृप न च मनु क्षुभितो (३) ॥
पुरि तुम गुणधर मृगपति यदभू-
र्गिरि नदि बहुजलि हृदय मनु पुरुषो ।

---

१ "पुरि तुम" पुरा त्वं "नरपति स्वकुल" नरपते स्वकुले "द्विज यदभूः" द्विजो यदा बभूः "गुरुजन परिचरि" गुरुजनानाम् पर्य्यचरः "ऋुचि परतो" चक्रुचः पराम् "स्थापयसि द्विजवर बहुजन कुशले" चस्थापयः हे द्विजवर बहुजनान् कुशले "च्युत ततु भव गतु" च्युत्वा ततो भवगतः "गतु पुन निलयं" गतः पुनर्निलयं । २ "पुरि तुम" पुरा त्वं "ऋषिवर यदभूश्छिनि तव" ऋषिवरो यदा बभूः छिन्नस्त्वया "तनुरुह कलि" तनुरुहः कलिः "नृप रुषितो" रुष्ट नृपाच्च छिन्ना इत्यर्थः "हत त्वयि कुलक्रिय न च मनु क्षुभितो" हतास्त्वया कुल-क्रिया न च मनः क्षुब्धं "अयु तव यह अवि तद" अयन्तवायहः सुत सदा । ३ "पुन ऋषिसुत" पुनर्ऋषिसुतः "त्वयि पुरि यदभूः" त्वं पुरा यदा बभूः "ग्रतरतु गुरुभर" गतरतः गुरुभरः "हत भव" हतो भवः "नृपति" "हे नृपते" "विपक्षत रुषुणा" विपक्षेषुणा "छप तव तहिं" छपा तव तत्र "मनु क्षुभितो" मनः क्षुब्धं ।

स्थित तव त्वयि महस्थलपति स्थापिते
उपनयि तव पुरि न च मनु क्षुभितो (१) ॥
पुरि तुम मरुवर त्यजितु तु यदभू-
र्मणि तव प्रपतितु जलधरि विपुले ।
र्व्यवसिय चपयतु स्वय महउदधिं
लभि तद मणि पुन दृढबल वृषभी (२) ॥
पुरि तुम सुपुरुष ऋषिवर यदभू-
र्द्विज तव उपगतु भव मम शरणं ।
भणि ऋषि द्विजवर नररिपुउपने
त्यजि स्वय स्वकि तनु न च द्विज त्यजसे (३) ॥
स्मर ऋषि उपगतु पुरि द्रुमनिलये
दृषि भणि तरुरुह कति द्रुम गणये ।
सुविदित सुगणित यथ तहि किमला

---

१ "पुरि तुम" पुरा त्वं "गणपति यदभूः" गणपतिर्यदा बभूः "गिरि नदिषडर्णवि" गिरेः नद्याः षडर्णवायाः "हृदयमनु" हृदयमनुप्रवेशः "स्थित तव" स्थिताव तवाभूत् । "महस्थलपतिः" महस्थलपतौ त्वयि च स्थलचारिणि कस्मिंश्चिदपि "स्थापिते" उपस्थापिते "उपनयि" समीपे इत्यर्थः "पुरि" पुरा "मनु क्षुभितो" मनः क्षुब्धं । २ "पुरि तुम" पुरा त्वं "मरुवर त्यजितु तु यदभूः" हे मरुवर त्यागेच्छुस्तु यदा बभूः "मणि तव प्रपतितु जलधरि विपुले" मणिस्तव प्रपतितो जलधरे विपुले "व्यवसिय चपयतु" निश्चित्य उत्क्षिप्य "स्वय महउदधिं" स्वयं महोदधिं "लभि तद मणि पुन" लब्धस्तदा मणिः पुनः "दृढबल वृषभो" हे वृषभसमदृढबलेत्यर्थः । ३ "पुरि तुम" पुरा त्वं "ऋषिवर यदभूः" ऋषिवरो यदा बभूः "द्विज तव उपगतु" द्विजस्तवसमीपे उपगतः "भणि ऋषि" उक्ता ऋषे "द्विजवर नररिपुउपने" द्विजवरो नररिपूपवने "त्यजि स्वय स्वकिततु" त्यक्तवान् स्वयं स्वकां तनुं "न च द्विज त्यजसे" न च द्विजमत्यजः ।

तव तव अवितथ समगिर रचिता (१) ॥
हे शुक्लगुणधर पुरि द्रुम वसता
चयमतु न च त्यजि क्षतु क्षरि पुरिमां ।
महपति प्रमुदितु तव गुण क्षरते
श्रियकरि द्रुमवरं यथ श्रिव पुरिमां (२) ॥
इति तव असदृश व्रततपचरणा
बहुगुण गुणधर गुणपथि चरतः ।
त्यजि महि सनगरि अथु तव समयो
लघु अगु क्षपय हि जिनगुणचरणे (३) ॥
यद प्रमदरतन शुभवस्त्रभूषितगात्रा
वरप्रवहतुरियमनोज्ञाः सम्प्रभणिषु ।
अथ दशदिशतो जिनतेजैर्गाथ विचित्रा

---

१ "अपि उपगतु" अपि उपगतः "पुरि" पुरा "वचि भणि" वचिता भणितं उक्तमिति यावत् "नवचय कति द्रुम मध्ये" नवचयानि कति द्रुमाणि मध्ये "सुविदित सुगणित" सुविदितानि सुगणितानि "यथ नदि किसला" यथा नव किसलयानि "तव तव अवितथ" तथा तव अवितथाः "समगिर रचिता" समगिरो रचितानि कार्य्याणीति शेषः ।

२ "शुक्लगुणधर" शुक्लगुणधर "पुरि द्रुम वसता" पुरा द्रुमे वसता "चयमतु" चयमतोऽपि स द्रुम इति शेषार्थः "न च त्यजि" न च त्यक्तः "क्षतु क्षरि" तस्य क्षरणं क्षतं "पुरिमां" पुरीमिमामपि क्षरेत्यर्थः "महपति प्रमुदितु तव गुण क्षरते" महत्पतिः प्रमुदितस्तव गुणान् क्षरति "श्रिय करि द्रुमवरि" श्रीकरं द्रुमवरं "यथ श्रिव पुरिमां" यथा श्रियं पुरीमिमां ।

३ "असदृश" असदृशानि "व्रततपचरणा" व्रततपचरणानि "गुणपथि" गुणपथे "त्यजिमहि सनगरि" त्यक्त्वा महीं सनगरीं "अथुतव" अथ तव "लघु क्षपय हि जिनगुणचरणे" लघु क्षपय हि जिनगुणाचरणे ।

इति रवि सुमधुराहतघोषास्तूर्य्यस्वरेभ्यः (१) ॥
तव प्रणिधी पुरीमे बहुकल्पां लोकप्रदीपा
जरमरणग्रसिते बहु लोकेऽत्रानुभविष्ये ।
स्मर पुरिम प्रणिधी नरसिंहपते अभू-
दयु समयो त्वमिता द्विपदेन्द्रा निष्क्रमणाय (२) ॥
भवनसुत त्वमिहा बहुदानं दत्तमनेकं
धनकनकरतनशुभवस्त्रा रत्न विचित्रा ।
करचरणनयन प्रियपुत्रा राज्य समृद्धं
त्वयि त्यजितं न च तेऽखिलदोषा या च नरकेषु (३) ॥
शिवनृपति त्वमिह ब्रह्मकेतो आसि सुदंष्ट्र
रूपकरुणामनसो मणिचूडो चन्द्रप्रदीपः ।
इतिप्रमुखा करिया दृढ शूरो राजसुनेत्रो

---

१ "वद प्रमदरतन" वदा प्रमदारत्नानि "शुभवचनभूषितगाथा" शुभवचनभूषितगाथाश्च रतैः "वरप्रवचतुरियमनोज्ञाः" वरप्रवरतूर्य्यमनोज्ञाः "सन्त्रभणिषु" सन्त्राभाषिषुः "दशदिशतो" दशदिक्षु "जिनतेजैः" जिनतेजोभिरुपलक्षिता इत्यर्थः "गाथ" गाथाः "रवि" रवेषु तूर्य्यस्वरेभ्य उत्पन्ना इति शेषः ।

२ "प्रणिधी पुरीमे बहुकल्पां" प्रणिधिः पुराऽयं बहुकल्पकोटिपर्य्यन्तं "लोकप्रदीपा" हे लोकप्रदीप "जरमरणग्रसिते" जरामरणग्रस्ते "बहु लोकेऽत्रानुभविष्ये" बहुं लोके अत्र अनुभविष्यामि "पुरिम प्रणिधी" पूर्व्वमिमं प्रणिधिं "अभूदयु" अभूदयं भूतोऽयमित्यर्थः "समयो त्वमिता द्विपदेन्द्रा निष्क्रमणाय" समयस्तवेह द्विपदेन्द्र निष्क्रमणस्य ।

३ "त्वमिह" त्वयेह "धनकनकरतनशुभवस्त्रा" धनकनकरत्नशुभवस्त्राणि "रत्न विचित्रा" रत्नानि विचित्राणि "करचरणनयन" करचरणनयनानि "राज्य" राज्यं "त्वयि त्यजितं" त्वया त्यक्तं "या च नरकेषु" ये च नारकिषु ।

बङ्गनृपतिनयता रतिदाने त्वं सर्व्वं कुर्व्वन् (१) ॥

तव सुगत चरिता बङ्गकल्पां शीलचर्य्यंथे

मणिरत्नविमलसदृशा शीलविशुद्धिः ।

त्वयि चरिता चमरी यथ बालं रक्षितु

शीलं छतु त्वमिह जगति विपुलार्थः (२) ॥

शीलरतेन गजवर त्वमिहा रिपु क्षुब्धो विद्ध दशुणा

क्षपकदृणा जनिया अतिरौद्रे छादितु शोभे ।

परित्यजित रुचिराः शुभदन्ता न च

त्यजि शीलमितिप्रमुखा करिया बङ्ग तुभ्यं (३) ॥

शीलविकुर्व्वि त्वयि सहितजगतोऽहितनेका

दुःखसहस्रा बङ्गकटुका बधनबधबन्धाः चान्तिरतेन ।

परिवारित पुरिम नरपते सर्व्वसुखेन

---

१ "शिवन्नपति" हे शिवन्नपते "चासितदंष्ट्र" चास्ये सुदंष्ट्रवन् "क्षपकबलाम-नषो" क्षपाकबलाघुक्तमनः "मणिचूडो चन्द्रप्रदीपः" मणिचूड चन्द्रप्रदोप्त "इति प्रमुखा करिया" इति प्रमुखं कृत्वा "प्रूरो राजसुमेधो" प्रूर राजसुमेध "बङ्ग-नृपतिनयता" बङ्गनृपतिमेतः "सर्व्वं कुर्व्वन्" सर्व्वमकरोः। रतिदानादिकं सर्व्व-मकरोरित्यर्थः ;

२ "तव सुगत चरिता" त्वया सुगत चाचरिता "बङ्गकल्पां शीलचर्य्यंथे" बङ्गकल्पपर्यन्तं शीलचर्य्या "मणिरत्नविमलसदृशा" विमलमणिरत्नसदृशो "त्वयि चरिता चमरी यथ बालं" तव चरित्वाहि चमर्य्या यथा बालानि "रक्षितु शीलं" रक्षितं शीलं "छतु त्वमिह" छतस्त्वयेह ।

३ "गजवर" हे गजवर "त्वमिहा" त्वमेव "रिपु क्षुब्धो" क्षोभाक्षो रिपु-रित्यर्थः "क्षप कदृणा जनिया" क्षपां कदृणां जनिता "छादितु शोभे" चाच्छादिता शोभा "परित्यजित" परित्यक्ता "त्यजि" त्यक्तं "इति प्रमुखा करिया बङ्ग तुभ्यं" इति प्रमुखं कृतं बङ्ग त्वया ।

पुनर्वधकास्तव तेऽबभूवन्तस्य विज्ञात्वं (१) ॥
गिरिप्रवरनिलये तुम नाथा
यच्च यदासीद्धिमकिरणैर्मलिनं भयभीतं ।
त्वनर दृष्ट्व परिचरसि विविध फलमूलैः
सर्व्वसुखेना लघु वधकाम तवापनेती तस्य तितिचान्तं (२) ॥
दृढसंस्थितमचलमकम्प्यं वीर्य्य तवासीत्
व्रततपसविविधगुणग्रामगवेषत बोधिं ।
ज्ञातप्रवलोकन शुची वशवर्त्ती वीर्य्यबलेन
अयु समयो ललिता नरसिंहा निष्क्रमणाय (३) ॥
हयप्रवर ललिता पुरि आसीद्धेमसुवर्णा
लघु गगने व्रजसे उपजातो राजसदीपं ।
व्यसनव्रत मनुजात्मद दृष्ट्वा चमे लपेषी

---

१ "द्रोह विकुर्व्वि त्वयि" द्रोहं विकुर्व्वाणेन त्वया। "चरितनेका" चरितान्यनेकानि "दुःखशतशा" दुःखशतशानि "परिचारित पुरिम" परिचारितानि पुरा इमानि "वधकास्तव तेऽभूवन्तस्य विज्ञात्वं" ये वधका अभूवंस्ते तव निवार्य्यास्त्वया विज्ञात्वा इत्यर्थः।

२ "तुम नाथा" त्वं नाथ "यच्च यदा" यच्चो यदा "त्वं नर दृष्ट्व" त्वं नरं दृष्ट्वा "परिचरसि विविध" पर्य्यचरः विविधैः "सर्व्वसुखेना" सर्व्वसुखपूर्व्वकम् "वधकाम" वधार्थः "नवापनेती" नवापनीतः "तस्य तितिचान्तं" स च तितिचान्तं।

३ "वीर्य्य" वीर्य्यं "व्रततपसविविधगुणग्रामं" व्रततपसांविविधगुणग्रामं "एषत बोधिं" बोधं एषित प्राप्तेत्यनुमीयते "ज्ञातवलोकन" ज्ञातावलोकन "शुची वशवर्त्ती" शुचे वशवर्त्तिन् "अयु समयो ललिता" अयं समयस्तेऽद्य "नरसिंहा निष्क्रमणाय" नरसिंह निष्क्रमणस्य।

इति प्रमुखा करिया वद तुभ्यं वीर्य्यं विकुर्व्वा (१) ॥

शमदमनियमप्रसृतक्लेशा ध्यायिन अग्र्या

लघु चपलं विषयैरतिलोलं चित्त दमित्वा ।

ततु स्वगुणा त्वमिदा जगतोऽर्थे ध्यानरतेना-

मु त्वमिदानीं सत्त्वा ध्यानविकुर्व्वा (२) ॥

त्वं पुरिमे अपि सुखितु आसीद्ध्यानरतीये

नृपरचित मनुजा लघु स्थाप्य राज्याभिषिक्ती ।

दशकुशली जनिताः स्थापिता ते ब्रह्मपथेषु

च्युत मनुजा प्रविष्ट दश सर्व्वे ब्रह्मनिकेतं (३) ॥

दिशिविदिशिविविधगतिज्ञाने त्वं सुविधिज्ञो

परचरितजगतिरतज्ञाने इन्द्रियज्ञाने ।

नयविनयविविधमतिधारे पारगतस्त्वं

---

१ "जयप्रवर त्वमिदा पुरि" जयप्रवरस्त्वमिह पुरा "अजसे रूपजाते।" अजस्रोत्पन्नरूपः "अक्षणमत्तमनुजामन्दहृष्टा" अक्षणमत्तक्षिप्रान्मनुजान्मन्दा अनुदृष्टा "चले स्थापेसी" चेमे मोक्षमार्गे अस्थापयः "इति प्रमुखा करिया" इति प्रमुखं कृत्वा "वद तुभ्यं वीर्य्यं विकुर्व्वा" वद यथा कार्य्यं कृतं वीर्य्यं विकुर्व्वाणेनेत्यर्थः ।

२ "शमदमनियमप्रसृतक्लेशा" शमदमनियमप्रसृतक्लेश "ध्यायिन अग्र्या" ध्यायिनां ध्यानकारिणां मध्ये अग्र्यः श्रेष्ठः तत्सम्बुद्धौ हे ध्यायिनामग्र्य "विषयैरतिलोलं चित्त" विषयेषु अतिलोलं चित्तं "ततु स्वगुणा त्वमिदा" ततः स्वगुणास्त्वयैव "ध्यानरतेनामु" ध्यानरतेन इमान् गुणानित्यर्थः "सत्त्वा" हे सत्त्व "ध्यानविकुर्व्वा" ध्यानं विकुर्व्वाण ।

३ "पुरिमे" पुरा "सुखितु आसीद्ध्यानरतीये" सुखित आसीर्ध्यानरत्या ध्याननिरतो भूत्वेति स्पष्टार्थः "नृपरचितमनुजा लघु स्थाप्य" नृपत्वरचिता अप्राप्तनृपपदवीका इति यावत् मनुजास्तथा स्थापिता "राज्याभिषिक्ती" राज्येऽभिषिक्ताः "दशकुशली" दशकुशलधर्म्माः "स्थापिता ते ब्रह्मपथेषु" स्थापितास्ते ब्रह्मपथेषु "च्युतमनुजा" च्युता मनुजाः "प्रविष्ट" प्राविक्षन् "दश सर्व्वे" ईदृशाः सर्व्वे तुषितवरभवनाच्च्युता मनुजा ये भूतास्ते दशकुशलधर्म्मापरत्वेन ब्रह्मनिकेतनं गता इति भावः ।

अयु समयो नृपसूनो निष्क्रमणाय (१) ॥

त्वयि पुरिम जनता इम दृष्ट्वा दृष्टिविपन्नां
जरमरणविविधबहुदुःखैः कष्टगतां हि ।
भवति तव करुणा ऋजुमार्गे त्वामनुबन्धा
शततमख त्वमिह हितु लोकेऽर्थे महन्तो (२) ॥

इति विविधरुचिरगुणयुक्ता गाथ विचित्रा-
स्तु रविषु तुरियेभी जिनतेजा चोदयि वीरं ।
दुःखभरित जगत इह दृष्ट्वा मा त्वमुपेक्षा
अयु समयो त्वमिहा वरबुद्ध निष्क्रमणाय (३) ॥

विविधवस्त्ररत्नहारगन्धमाल्यभूषिताः
प्रसन्नचित्त प्रेमजात नारिया प्रहर्षिताः ।
प्रबोधयन्ति येऽप्सरत्वं तूर्य्यसम्प्रवादिते-
र्जिनानुभावि एवरूप गाथ तुर्य्य निश्चरी (४) ॥

---

१ "दिग्विदिग्मेघविघनतिभ्राने" दिग्विदिग्विविधमतिभ्राने "परचरितज्ञमतिपलभ्राने" पराचरितज्ञमतिभ्रान्ते "नयविनयविविधमतिधारे" नयविनयविविधमतिधारके "अयुसमयो" अयं समयः ।

२ "त्वयि पुरिम जनता इम" त्वं पुरा जनतामिमां "दृष्टिविपन्नां" दृष्टिरहितामित्यर्थः "जरमरणविविधबहुदुःखैः" जरामरणविविधबहुदुःखैः "भवति" भवति स्म "त्वामनुबन्धा" त्वामनुबन्धा "शततमख" हे शततमख "हितु लोकेऽर्थे महान्तो" हितयाम् लोकार्थे महती ।

३ "गाथ" गाथाः "रविषु" रवेषु "तुरियेभी" तूर्य्यैः तूर्य्याणां रवेषु जायमाना इत्यर्थः "जिनतेजा" जिनतेजसं "चोदयि" चोदयन्ति "दुःखभरित जगत" दुःखपरिपूर्णां जगतीं "मा त्वमुपेक्षा" मा त्वमुपेक्षस्व "अयु समयो त्वमिहा" अयं समयस्तवेह ।

४ "प्रसन्नचित्त" प्रसन्नचित्ताः "प्रेमजात" जातप्रेमाणः "नारिया" नार्य्यः "येऽप्सरत्वं" याभिरप्सरत्वं "जिनानुभावि" जिनानुभावनिश्रिताः "एवरूप" एवंरूपाः "गाथ तुर्य्य निश्चरी" गाथास्तूर्य्येभ्यो निश्चेरुः ।

यस्यार्थि तुभ्य कल्पनेक त्यक्तु त्यागदुस्त्यजा
सुघोर्ष शीलक्षान्तिवीर्य्य ध्यान प्रज्ञव्रत भाविता।
जगद्धितार्थ सोऽतिकालु साम्प्रतमुपस्थितो
नैष्क्राम्य बुद्धि चिन्तयाशु मा विलम्ब नायक (१)॥
त्यक्तु पूर्व्वि रत्नकोषस्वर्णरूप्यभूषणा
यष्टातियज्ञ नैकरूप तासु तासु जातिषु।
त्यक्तातिभार्य्यापुत्राधीतकायुराज्यजीवितं
बोधिहेतुरप्रमेयं त्यक्तु दुस्त्यजा त्वया (२)॥
अभूषीस्त्वमदीनपुण्य राजविश्रुतश्रिया
निमिन्धरो निमिश्च कृष्णबन्धु ब्रह्मदत्त केशरी।
सहस्रयज्ञ धर्म्म चिन्ति अर्चिमान्दृढधनो
सुचिन्तितार्थ दीनसत्त्वाय त्यक्त दुस्त्यजाः सुताः (३)॥
सोमदीप्त वीर्य्यपुण्यरश्मि यो सो भूम्यह-
त्यागवन्तु क्षामवन्तु यः कृतज्ञत्वमभूत्।

---

१ "यस्यार्थि तुभ्य" यस्यार्थं त्वया "कल्पनेक" अनेककल्पपर्य्यन्तं "त्यक्तु त्यागदुस्त्यजा" त्यक्तानि त्यागे दुस्त्यजानि वस्तूनि इत्यर्थः "सुघोर्ष" सुघोर्षानि "शीलक्षान्तिवीर्य्य" शीलक्षान्तिवीर्य्योपि "ध्यान" ध्यानं सुघोर्षमित्यर्थः "प्रज्ञव्रत भाविता" प्रज्ञाव्रतं भावितं प्राप्तमित्यर्थः "जगद्धितार्थ" जगद्धितार्थं "सोऽतिकालु" सोऽयं कालः "नैष्क्राम्यबुद्धि" निष्क्रमणबुद्धिं।

२ "त्यक्तु पूर्व्वि" त्यक्तानि पूर्व्वं "रत्नकोषस्वर्णरूप्यभूषणा।" रत्नकोषस्वर्णरूप्यभूषणानि "यष्टातियज्ञ" यष्टातियज्ञं "नैकरूप" अनेकरूपमित्यर्थः त्यक्तातिभार्य्यपुत्रधीतकायुराज्यजीवितं" त्यक्तानि भार्य्यापुत्राधीतकायराज्यजीवितानि "बोधिहेतुरप्रमेयं" बोधि हेतवेऽप्रमेयानि "त्यक्तुदुस्त्यजा" त्यक्तानि दुस्त्यजानि।

३ "कृष्णबन्धु ब्रह्मदत्त" कृष्णबन्धुर्ब्रह्मदत्तः "सहस्रयज्ञ" सहस्रयज्ञं कृत्वेति शेषः "धर्म्मं चिन्ति" धर्म्मं चिन्तयित्वा "अर्चिमान् दृढधनो" अर्चितवान् दृढधनः "सुचिन्तितार्थ" सुचिन्तिता अर्थाः "त्यक्त दुस्त्यजाः" त्यक्ता दुस्त्यजाः।

राजर्षि च चन्द्ररूपवन्तु शूर सत्यवर्द्धनो
सुभावितं गवेषितं राजि आसि सुमतिस्च स्तरतो (१) ॥
चन्द्रप्रभाविशेषगामि रेणु भूद्दिशाम्प्रति
प्रदानशूर काशिराज रत्नचूडसन्नतः ।
एभि चान्य पार्थिवेन्द्रेभिस्त्यक्त दुस्त्यजा
यथातिदृष्ट त्यागदृष्टि एष धर्मं वर्ष हि (२) ॥
दृष्टानि पूर्व्वि सत्त्वसार गङ्गवालुकोपमाः
कृतानि तेषु बुद्ध पूज अप्रमेय चिन्तिया ।
वराग्र बोधि एष मानसत्त्वमोचकारणा-
दयं स कालु प्राप्तु सुनिष्क्रमो पुरोत्तमान् (३) ॥
प्रथमेन ऽमोघदर्शि शालपुष्प पूजितो
वैरोचनः प्रसन्नचित्त प्रेषि तत्क्षणान्तरं ।

---

१ "सोमदीप्त वीर्य्य पुण्यरश्मियो" सोमदीप्तो वीर्य्यपुण्यरश्मियः "सो भूश्च त्यागवन्तु" सो भूश्च त्यागवान् "स्थामवन्तु" स्थामवान् "कृतज्ञत्वमभूत्" कृतज्ञोऽभूत् "राजर्षि च" राजर्षिश्च "चन्द्ररूपवन्तु शूर सत्यवर्द्धनो" चन्द्ररूपवान् शूरः सत्यवर्द्धनः "सुभावितं गवेषितं" सुभाषितवान् गवेषितवान् "राजि आसि" राजा आसीत् "स्तरतो" सुरतः ।

२ "चन्द्रप्रभाविशेषगामि" चन्द्रप्रभाविशेषं गताश्चन्द्रप्रभासदृशाः "रेणु भूद्दिशाम्प्रति" रेणव अभूवन्दिशं प्रति प्रतिदिशमित्यर्थः "प्रदानशूर काशिराज रत्नचूडसन्नतः" प्रदानशूरः काशिराजो रत्नचूडासन्नतः "एभि चान्यपार्थिवेन्द्रेभि त्यक्त" एभिश्चान्यैः पार्थिवेन्द्रैस्त्यक्ताः "यथातिदृष्ट त्यागदृष्टि" यथातिदृष्टा त्यागदृष्टिः "एष धर्मं वर्ष" एतद्धर्मं वर्षय ।

३ दृष्टानि पूर्व्वि सत्त्वसार" दृष्टाः पूर्व्वं सत्त्वसाराः "गङ्गवालुकोपमाः" गङ्गावालुकोपमाः "कृतानि तेषु बुद्धपूज अप्रमेयचिन्तयित्वा" कृता हि तेषु बुद्धपूजा अप्रमेयं चिन्तयित्वा "वराग्र बोधि" वराग्र्यं बोधिं "एषमानसत्त्वमोचकारणादयं" एषमानसत्त्वमोचकारणादयं "स कालु प्राप्तु सुनिष्क्रमो पुरोत्तमात्" स कालः प्राप्तः सुनिष्क्रम पुरोत्तमात् ।

हरीतकी च एक दत्त दुन्दुभिः स्वरायते
तृणोल्क गृह्य धारिता दृष्ट चन्दनगृहे (१) ॥
पुरप्रवेशि रेणु दृष्ट क्षिप्तु सुवर्णचूर्णमुष्टिका
धर्म्मेश्वराय साधका वदन्तु धर्म्म भाषते ।
नमो नमः समन्तदर्शि दृष्ट्व वाच भाषिता
महार्चिषि स्कन्धि स्वर्णमाल क्षिप्त हर्षितेन ते (२) ॥
धर्म्मध्वजो दशप्रदा निरोधु मुक्त मुष्टिना
अशोकपुष्पि ज्ञानकेतु योगयानसारथिः ।
रत्नशिखी च दीपदानि पद्मयोनि ओषधी
सर्व्वाभिभूस्य मुक्तहारि पद्मदानि सागरो (३) ॥
वितानदानि पद्मगर्भ सींहवर्ष संस्तरे
शालेन्द्रराज सर्व्वदानि क्षीरत्यागि पुष्पितो ।
यशोदत्त कुरण्टपुष्प सत्यदर्शी भाजने

---

१ प्रथमेनऽमोघदर्शि" प्रथमममोघदर्शिना "शालपुष्पपूजितो" शालपुष्पैः पूजितः "प्रशान्तचित्त प्रेषि तत्क्षणान्तरं" प्रशान्तचित्तः प्रेषितवान् तत्क्षणान्तरे "एक दत्त" एका दत्ता "दुन्दुभिः स्वरायते" दुन्दुभिः स्वरितो ध्वनित इति यावत् "तृणोल्क गृह्य धारिता दृष्ट" तृणोल्कां गृहीत्वा धारितवान् योजितवान् दृष्ट्वा ।

२ "पुरप्रवेशि रेणु दृष्ट" पुरप्रवेशसमये रेणुं दृष्ट्वा "क्षिप्तु सुवर्णचूर्णमुष्टिका" क्षिप्ता सुवर्णचूर्णमुष्टिका "साधका" साधकाय "वदन्तु धर्म्मभाषते" वदते कान्तरायेति भावः "धर्म्म" धर्म्मं "समन्तदर्शि" समन्तदर्शिने "दृष्ट्व वाच भाषिता" दृष्ट्वा वाचो भाषिताः "महार्चिषि स्कन्धि" महार्चिषि स्कन्धे "स्वर्णमाल क्षिप्त" स्वर्णमाला क्षिप्ता ।

३ "दशप्रदा निरोधुमुक्त" दशप्रदो निरोधमुक्तं "अशोकपुष्पि" अशोकपुष्पदाने ज्ञानकेतुर्नियुक्तोऽभूदित्यर्थः "ज्ञानकेतुयोगयानसारथिः" ज्ञानकेतुर्योगयानसारथिः "रत्नशिखी च दीपदानि" रत्नशिखी च दीपदाने "पद्मयोनि ओषधी" पद्मयोनिरोषधीदाने "मुक्तहारि" मुक्ताहारदाने "पद्मदानि" पद्मदाने "सागरो" सागरः ।

काशु प्रणामि ग्रामसेष नागदत्तु चीवरे (१) ॥
अत्युच्चगामी चन्दनार्धिविधुभान मुष्टिना
महाविघूष पद्मदानि रश्मिराज रत्नभिः ।
शाक्यमुनिस्य सुवर्णमुष्टि इन्द्रकेतु संस्तुतो
सूर्याननोऽवतंसके हि स्वर्णमुष्टि पङ्कि सुमती (२) ॥
नागाभिभूर्मणिप्रदानि पुष्पदूष्यसंस्तरे
भैषज्यराज रत्नच्छवि सिंहकेतु आसने ।
गुणाग्रधारि रत्नजालि सर्व्ववादि काश्यपो
गन्धाग्रिचूर्ण मुक्त अर्चि केतुपुष्प चैत्यके (३) ॥
अर्चोश्वराज कूटागारि माल्य लोक पूजितो
नगरशिखिस्य राजत्यागि सर्व्वगन्धि दुर्जये ।
महाप्रदीप आत्मत्यागी भूषणे पद्मोत्तरे

---

१ "वितानदानि" वितानदाने "पद्मगर्भ सौंश्रवर्णसंस्तरे" पद्मगर्भः सिंह-वर्णः संस्तरदाने "शारेन्द्रराज सर्पदानि" शारेन्द्रराजः सर्पदाने "चीरन्यागि पुष्पितो" चीरत्यागे पुष्पितः "यशोदत्त कुवलपुष्प" यशोदत्तः कुवलपुष्पदाने "भाजने" भाजनदाने "काशु प्रणामि ग्रामसेष नागदत्त चीवरे" कायेन प्रणामे ग्रामसेषनागदत्तचीवरदाने।

२ "चन्दनार्मिविधुभान" चन्दनाभ्यस्य विधोभवे "महाव्यूह पद्मदानि" महा-व्यूहः पद्मदाने "रश्मिराज रत्नभिः" रश्मिराजो रत्नदाने इत्युचितं "सुवर्णमुष्टि इन्द्रकेतु संस्तुतो" सुवर्णं मुष्टौ कृत्वा इन्द्रकेतुः संस्तुतो "सूर्याननोऽवतंसके" सूर्याननोऽवतंसदाने "स्वर्णमुष्टि पङ्कि सुमती" स्वर्णं मुष्टौ कृत्वा पठने सुमतिः।

३ "मणिप्रदानि" मणिप्रदाने "पुष्पदूष्यसंस्तरो" दूष्यपुष्पसंस्तरे "भैषज्यराज रत्नछवि" भैषज्यराजो रत्नछत्रदाने "सिंहकेतु आसने" सिंहकेतुरासनदाने "गुणाग्रधारि" गुणाग्रधारो "रत्नजालि" रत्नजालादिदाने "गन्धाग्रचूर्णमुक्त अर्चि" गन्धाग्रचूर्णं मुक्त्वा अर्चितः "केतुपुष्प" केतुपुष्पैः ।

विचित्रपुष्पि धर्म्मकेतु दीप कारि उत्पलैः (१) ॥
एति चान्य सत्त्वसार येभि पूर्व्व पूजितो
नानारूपविचित्र अन्य कुर्व्वता ।
आराधि ते अतीतबुद्ध नाथ पूजयास्तुना
अनाथसत्त्व शोकपूर्ण मा उपेक्षि निष्क्रम पुरोत्तमात् (२) ॥
दीपङ्करेति दृष्टमात्रि लब्ध क्षान्ति उत्तमा
अभिज्ञा पञ्च अच्युताति लब्ध आनुलोमिका ।
ततोन्तरेणैकमेक बुद्ध पूज चिन्तिया
प्रवर्त्तिता अनेककल्पसर्व्वलोकधातुषु (३) ॥
क्षीणातिकल्प अप्रमेय ते च बुद्ध निर्वृता-
स्त्वयापि सर्व्वआत्मभाव ते च नाम क्व गताः ।
क्षयान्तधर्म्मि सर्वि भावु नास्ति नित्य संस्कृते

---

१ "यशोभिराज कूटागारि" यशोभिराजेन कूटागारे "माल्य लोकपूजितो" माल्यैर्लोके पूजितः "नगरश्रियेव राजत्यागि" नगरश्रिया च राज्यत्यागिना "सर्व्वमन्त्रि दुर्जये" सर्व्वमन्त्रैर्दुर्जयेन "महाप्रदीप आत्मत्यागी" महाप्रदीपेन आत्मत्यागिना "भूपते पद्मोत्तरे" भूपतेः पद्मोत्तरेण "विचित्रपुष्पि धर्म्मकेतु दीप-कारि उत्पलैः" विचित्रपुष्पैर्धर्म्मकेतुना दीपाः कृता उत्पलैः ।

२ "एति चान्य" एते चान्ये "सत्त्वसार" सत्त्वसाराः "येभि पूर्व्व पूजितो" यैः पूर्व्वं पूजितः "नानारूपविचित्र अन्यकुर्व्वता" नानारूपविचित्राणि अन्यानि कार्य्याणि कुर्व्वद्भिः "आराधि ते अतीतबुद्ध नाथ पूजयास्तुना" आर तानतीतान् बुद्धान् नाथ पूजयासनां "अनाथसत्त्व शोकपूर्ण" अनाथसत्त्वान् शोकपूर्णान् "मा उपेक्षि" मा उपेक्षस्व ।

३ दीपङ्करेति दृष्टमात्रि" दीपङ्करेणेति दृष्टमात्रं "लब्ध क्षान्ति उत्तमा" लब्धा क्षान्तिरुत्तमा "अभिज्ञा पञ्च" अभिज्ञाः पञ्च "अच्युतातिलब्ध आनुलोमिका" अच्युता लब्धा आनुलोमिकाः "ततोन्तरेणैकमेकबुद्धपूज चिन्तिया प्रवर्त्तिता" तत अन्तरमेकमेकं बुद्धं चिन्तयित्वा पूजा प्रवर्त्तिता इत्यन्वयः ।

अनित्य कामराज्यभोग निष्क्रमा पुरोत्तमात् (१) ॥
जरारुजाव्याधिमृत्यु एन्ति दारुणा महाभया
हुताशनो व उग्रतेज भीम कल्पसंक्षये ।
क्षयान्तधर्मि सर्वि भावु नास्ति नित्यसंस्कृते
मुञ्च्छप्राप्तसत्त्व निष्क्रमा गुणधर (२) ॥

तद नारिगणस्तुणवेणुरवैर्विविधैस्तुरियैः प्रतिबोधयिषुः ।
सुखशयनगतं मनुजाधिपतिं तद तूर्यरवो अयु निश्चरतो (३) ॥
ज्वलितं त्रिभवं जरव्याधिदुःखैर्मरणाग्निप्रदीप्तमनाथमिदं ।
न च निःसरणे सद मूढ जगद् भ्रमति भ्रमरो यथ कुम्भगतो (४) ॥
अध्रुवं त्रिभवं शरदभ्रनिभं नटरङ्गसमा जगि जन्मि च्युति ।
गिरिनद्यसमं लघुशीघ्रजवं व्रजतायु जगे यथ विद्यु नभे (५) ॥
भुवि देवपुरे त्रिअपाय पथे भवतृष्णअविद्यवशा जनता ।

---

१ "औपम्यातिकल्प अप्रमेय ते" बोधातिकल्पा अप्रमेयास्ते "बुद्धनिर्देता" बुद्धनिर्देताः "सर्व्वधात्मभाव ते" सर्व्वात्मभावास्ते "क्षयान्तधर्म्मि सर्व्वि भावु" क्षयान्तधर्म्मिणः सर्व्वे भावाः "नित्यसंस्कृते" नित्यसंस्काराः "अनित्यकामराज्यभोग" अनित्याः कामराज्यभोगाः "निष्क्रमा" निष्क्रम ।

२ "जरारुजाव्याधिमृत्यु" जरारुग्व्याधिमृत्यवः "एन्ति" आयान्ति "हुताशनो व उग्रतेज" हुताशनवोग्रतेजाः "भीम कल्पसंक्षये" भीमः कल्पसंक्षये "क्षयान्तधर्मि सर्व्वि भावु" क्षयान्तधर्मिणः सर्व्वे भावाः "नास्ति नित्यसंस्कृते" न सन्ति नित्यसंस्काराः न सन्ति नित्या इत्यर्थः "निष्क्रमा गुणधर" निष्क्रम गुणधर ।

३ "तद नारिगणस्तुणवेणुरवैर्विविधैस्तुरियैः" यदा नारीगणस्तुणवेणुरवैर्विविधैस्तूर्यैः "तद तूर्यरवो अयु निश्चरतो" तदा तूर्यरवोऽयं निश्चचार ।

४ "जरव्याधिदुःखैः" जराव्याधिदुःखैः "न च निःसरणे" न च निःसरति "सद मूढ जगत्" सदा मूढं जगत् "यथ कुम्भगतो" यथा कुम्भगतः ।

५ "अध्रुव त्रिभवं शरदभ्रनिभं" अध्रुवस्त्रिभवः शरदभ्रनिभः "नटरङ्गसमा जगि जन्मिच्युति" नटरङ्गसमं जगति जन्म च्युतिश्च "गिरिनद्यसमं" गिरिनदीसमं "व्रजतायु जगे यथ विद्यु नभे" व्रजति आयुर्जगति यथा विद्युन्नभसि ।

परिवर्त्तिषु पञ्चगतिष्वबुधाः यथ कुम्भकरस्य हि चक्र भ्रमी(१) ॥
प्रियरूपवरैः सद स्निग्धरुतैः शुभगन्धरसैर्वरस्पर्शसुखैः ।
परिषिक्तमिदं कलिपाश जगत् मृग लुब्धकपाशि
यथैव हि बद्धकमपि (२) ॥
सभया मरणाः सद वैरकरा बहुशोकउपद्रवकामगुणाः ।
असिधारसमा विषपत्रनिभा त्यज हितार्यजनैर्यथ मीढघटः(३)॥
स्मृतिशोककरास्तमसीकरणा भयहेतुकरा दुःखमूल सदा ।
भवतृष्णलताय विवृद्धिकराः सभयाः मरणाः सदकामगुणाः (४)॥
यथ अग्निखदा ज्वलिताः सभयाः तथ काम इमे विदितार्यजनैः ।
महपङ्कसमा असिसिन्धुसमा मधुदिग्ध इव क्षुरधार यथा (५) ॥
यथ सर्पशिरो यथ मीढघटास्तथ काम इमे विदिता विदुषां ।

---

१ "विषपायपथे" विषपायपथेषु "भवतृष्णअविद्यवशा" भवतृष्णाऽविद्यावशा "परिवर्त्तिषु" परिवर्त्तन्ते "यथ कुम्भकरस्य हि चक्रभमी" यथा कुम्भकारस्य हि चक्रं भ्रमति ।

२ "सद" सदा "कलिपाश जगत्" कलिपाशभूतं जगत् "मृग लुब्धकपाशि यथैव हि बद्धकमपि" मृगलुब्धकपाशो यथैव हि बद्धकं बन्धनरज्जुवद्बद्धादित्यर्थः।

३ "सभया मरणाः" सभयानि मरणानि "सद वैरकरा" सदा वैरकराः "बहुशोकउपद्रव कामगुणाः" बहुशोकोपद्रवदायका कामगुणा इत्यर्थः "त्यज हितार्यजनैर्यथ" त्यज्यते हितैरार्य्यजनैर्य्यथा।

४ "तमसीकरणाः" तमः करणा अज्ञानकरा इत्यर्थः "दुःखमूल" दुःखमूलाः "भवतृष्णलताय" भवतृष्णालतायाः "सभयाः मरणाः" सभयानि मरणानि स्तवा-नीत्यर्थः "सद" सदा ।

५ "यथ अग्निखदा" यथा अग्निखदा इत्युन्नीयते "तथ काम इमे विदितार्य-जनैः" तथा कामा इमे विदिता आर्य्यजनैः "महपङ्कसमाः" महापङ्कसमाः "क्षुरधार यथा" क्षुरधारो यथा ।

तथ शूलसमा द्विजपेशिसमा यथ खानकरं किमवैर तथा (१) ॥
उदकचन्द्रसमा इमि कामगुणाः प्रतिबिम्ब इवा गिरिघोष यथा ।
प्रतिभाससमा नटरङ्गसमास्तथ स्वप्नसमा विदितार्यजनैः (२) ॥
क्षणिकावशिका इमि कामगुणास्तु इमे तथ मायमरीचिसमा ।
उदकबुद्बुदफेनसमा वितथापरिकल्पसमुत्थित बुद्ध बुधैः (३)।
प्रथमे वयसे वररूपधरः प्रिय इष्ट मतो इय बालचरी ।
जरव्याधिदुःखैर्हत वपुं विजहन्ति मृगा इव शुष्कनदी (४) ॥
धनधान्यवरो बहुद्रव्यधरो प्रिय इष्ट मतो इय बालचरी ।
परिहीनधनं पुन कृच्छ्रगतं विजहन्ति नरा इव शून्याऽटवी (५) ॥
यथ पुष्पद्रुमो सफलेव द्रुमो नर दानरतस्तथ प्रीतिकरो ।
धनहीन जरार्तितु याचनको भवते तद अप्रियु गृध्रसमः (६) ॥

---

१ "यथ सर्पिसरः" यथा सर्पिःसरांसि "तथ काम इमे विदिता विदुषां" तथा कामा इमे विदिता विद्वद्भिः "तथ" तथा "द्विजपेशिसमाः" द्विजपेशीसमाः "यथ खानकरं किमवैर तथा" यथा खानकरं कीमवैरं तथा ।

२ "इमि कामगुणाः" इमे कामगुणाः "प्रतिबिम्ब इवा" प्रतिबिम्बा इव "गिरिघोष यथा" गिरिघोषा यथा "तथ" तथा "विदितार्यजनैः" विदिता आर्यजनैः ।

३ "क्षणिकावशिका इमि" क्षणिकावशा इमे "तथ मायमरीचिसमा" तथा मायामरीचिसमाः "वितथापरिकल्पसमुत्थित" वितथापरिकल्पनसमुत्थिताः "बुद्ध" बुद्धाः ।

४ "प्रिय इष्ट मतो इय बालचरी" प्रिय इष्टश्च भवति यतःपरमियं बालचर्य्या ततः "जराव्याधिदुःखैर्हत वपुं" जराव्याधिदुःखैर्हतं वपुः "विजहन्ति" विजहति "शुष्कनदी" शुष्कनदीं ।

५ "इष्टमतो इय बालचरी" इष्टमत इयं बालचर्य्या "विजहन्ति" विजहति "शून्याऽटवी" शून्याटवीं ।

६ "यथ पुष्पद्रुमो सफलेवद्रुमो" यथा पुष्पद्रुमः सफल इव द्रुमः "नर दानरतस्तथ प्रीतिकरो" नरो दानरतस्तथा प्रीतिकरः "धनहीनजरार्तितु" धनहीनो जरार्तस्तु "याचनको भवते" याचको भवति "तद अप्रियु गृध्रसमः" तदा अप्रियो गृध्रसमः।

प्रभु द्रव्यबली वररूपधरः प्रियसङ्ग मनेन्द्रियप्रीतिकरो ।
जरव्याधिदुःखार्त्तितु क्षीणधनो भवते तद अप्रिय मृत्युसमः (१) ॥
जरया जरितः समतीतवयो द्रुम विद्युतहत यथा भवति ।
जरजीर्ण अगार यथा सभयो जरनिःसरणं लघु ब्रूहि मुने (२) ॥
जर शोषयते नरनारिगणं यथ मालुलता घनसालवनं ।
जर वीर्य्यपराक्रमवेगहरी जरपङ्कनिमग्न यथा पुरुषो (३) ।
जर रूपसुरूपविरूपकरी जर तेजहरी सद शौख्यहरी ।
परिभावकरी जर मृत्युकरी जर ओजहरी बलस्थामहरी (४) ॥
बहुरोगशतैर्घनव्याधिदुःखैरुपसृष्ट जगत् ज्वलतेव मृगाः ।
जरव्याधिगतं प्रशमीक्ष्य जगद्दुःखनिःसरणं लघु देशय हि (५) ॥
शिशिरे हि यथा हिमधातु महांस्तृणगुल्मवनौषधि ओजहरो ।
तथ ओजहरी बहुव्याधि जरा परिहीयति इन्द्रियरूपबलं (६) ॥

---

१ "प्रभु द्रव्यबली वररूपधरः" प्रभुर्द्रव्यबलवान् वररूपधरः "प्रियसङ्गमनेन्द्रियप्रीतिकरो" प्रियसङ्गो मनइन्द्रियप्रीतिकरः "जरव्याधिदुःखार्त्तितु" जराव्याधिदुःखार्त्तस्तु "भवते तद अप्रिय मृत्युसमः" भवति तदा अप्रियो मृत्युसमः ।

२ "जरितः" जीर्णः "द्रुम विद्युहतः" द्रुमो विद्युद्धतः "जरजीर्ण अगारयथासभयः" जराजीर्णश्च अगारमावसितुं यथा सभयः "जरनिःसरणं" जरानिःसरणं ।

३ "जरशोषयते नरनारिगणं" जरा शोषयति नरनारीगणं "जरवीर्यपराक्रमवेगहरी" जरा वीर्य्यपराक्रमवेगहारिणी "जरपङ्कनिमग्न यथा पुरुषो" जरापङ्कनिमग्नो यथा पुरुषः ।

४ "जर" जरा "जर तेजहरी" जरा तेजोहारिणी "सद" सदा "जर" जरा "जरओजहरी" जरा ओजोहारिणी "बलस्थामहरी" बलस्थामहारिणी ।

५ "उपसृष्ट" उपसृष्टं "ज्वलतेव मृगाः" ज्वलति मृग इवेत्यर्थः "जरव्याधिगतं" जराव्याधिगतं ।

६ "हिमधातु महांस्तृणगुल्मवनौषधिओजहरो" हिमधातुर्महांस्तृणगुल्मवनौषधिओजोहरः "तथ" तथा "बहुव्याधिजरा" बहुव्याधिर्जरा "परिहीयति" परिहीयते ।

धनधान्यमहार्थचयान्तकरः परितापकरः सह व्याधि जरा।
प्रतिघातकरः प्रियदुःखकरः परिदाहकरो यथ सूर्य्य नभे (१)॥
मरणं च्यवनं च्युतिकालक्रियाः प्रियद्रव्यजनेन वियोगु सदा।
अपुनागमनश्च असङ्गमनं द्रुमपत्रफला नदिस्रोत यथा (२)॥
मरणं वशिता न वशीकुरुते मरणं हरते नदि दारु यथा।
असहायु नरो व्रजते द्वितीयं स्वककर्म्मफलानुगतो विवशः (३)॥
मरणं ग्रसते बहुप्राणिशतं मकरेव जलाहरि भूतगणं।
गरुडो उरगं मृगराज गजं ज्वलनेव तृणौषधिभूतगणं (४)॥
इम ईदृशकैर्बहुदोषशतैर्जगु मोचयितुं कृत या प्रणिधिः।
सर तां पुरिमां प्रणिधानचरीमनु काल तव अभिनिष्क्रमितुं (५)॥
यद नारिगणः प्रहर्षितो बोधयतिं तुरियैर्महामुनिं।
तद गाथ विचित्र निश्चरी तूर्य्यशब्दात् सुगतानुभावतः (६)॥
लघु तद्व्रजति सर्व्वसंस्कृतमचिरस्थायि नभेव विद्युतः।

---

१ "सह व्याधिजरा" सहा व्याधिर्जरा "यथ सूर्य नभे" यथा सूर्यो नभसि।

२ "वियोगु सदा" वियोगः सदा "अपुनागमनश्च" अपुनरागमनश्च "द्रुमपत्रफला नदिस्रोत यथा" द्रुमपत्रफलानि नदीस्रोतसि यथा।

३ "हरते नदि दारुयथा" हरति नदी दारु यथा "असहायु नरो" असहायो नरः "व्रजते" व्रजति।

४ "मकरेव जलाहरि" मकर इव जलाहारी "गरुडो उरगं" गरुड उरगं "मृगराज गजं" मृगराजो गजं "ज्वलनेव" ज्वलन इव।

५ "इम" इभिः "जगु" जगत् "कृत या प्रणिधिः" कृतो यः प्रणिधिः "सर तां" स्मरतं "पुरिमां" पुरीमिमां "प्रणिधानचरीमनु" प्रणिधानचरीमनु "कालतव अभिनिष्क्रमितुं" कालस्तवाभिनिष्क्रमाय।

६ "यद नारिगणः" यदा नारीगणः "तुरियैर्महामुनिं" तूर्यैर्महामुनिं "तद गाथ विचित्र निश्चरी" तदा गाथा विचित्रा निश्चेरुः।

अथु काल तवा उपस्थितः समयो निष्क्रमाय सुव्रत (१) ॥
संस्कार अनित्य अध्रुवा आमकुम्भोपम भेदनात्मकाः ।
परकेलिकयाचितोपमाः पांशुनगरोपमास्तावकालिकाः (२) ॥
संस्कार प्रलोपधर्मि मेघ वर्षकालि चलितञ्च लेपनं ।
नदिकूल इवा सवालुकं प्रत्ययाधीनस्वभावदुर्ब्बलाः (३) ॥
संस्कार प्रदीपअर्चिवत्क्षिप्रउत्पत्तिनिरोधधर्म्मकाः ।
अनवस्थितमारुतोपमाः फेनपिण्डेव असार दुर्ब्बलाः (४) ॥
संस्कार निरीह शून्यकाः कदलीस्कन्धसमा निरीक्षत ।
मायोपम चित्तमोहना बालउल्लापनउल्कमुष्टिवत् (५) ॥
हेतुभि च प्रत्ययेभि वा सर्व्वसंस्कारगतं प्रवर्त्तते ।
अन्योन्यप्रतीत्यहेतुतस्तदिदं बालजनो न बुध्यते (६) ॥
यथ मुञ्जप्रतीत्यबल्वजो रज्जुर्व्यायामबलेन वर्त्तिता ।

---

१ "अचिरस्थायि समेव" अचिरस्थायिन्यो समसीव "अथु काल तवा उपस्थितः" अयं कालस्तवोपस्थितः ।

२ "संस्कार अनित्य अध्रुवाः" संस्कारा अनित्या अध्रुवाः "आमकुम्भोपम" आमकुम्भोपमाः "तावकालिकाः" ते च कालिकाः ।

३ "संस्कार प्रलोपधर्मि मेघ" संस्काराःप्रलोपधर्मिणो मेघाः "वर्षकालि" वर्षाकाले "नदिकूल इवा" नदीकूलानीव "सवालुकं" सवालुकानि ।

४ "संस्कार प्रदीपअर्चिवत्क्षिप्रउत्पत्तिनिरोधधर्म्मकाः" संस्काराः प्रदीपार्चिर्वत् क्षिप्रोत्पत्तिनिरोधधर्म्मकाः "फेनपिण्डेव असार" फेनपिण्डा इव असाराः ।

५ "संस्कार निरीह शून्यकाः" संस्कारा निरीहाः शून्यकाः कदलीस्कन्धसमास्तान्निरीक्षतेत्यर्थः "मायोपम" मायोपमाः "बालउल्लापनउल्कमुष्टिवत्" बालोल्लापनोल्कामुष्टिवत् बालानामुल्लापनं काकुवाक्यमुल्कामुष्टिश्च ज्वलितशरयष्टिः तद्वदित्यर्थः ।

६ "हेतुभि च" हेतुभिश्च "प्रत्ययेभि वा" प्रत्ययैर्वा "सर्वसंस्कारगतं" सर्वसंस्कारजातमित्यर्थः "अन्योन्यप्रतीत्यहेतुतः" अन्योन्यप्रतीतिहेतुतः ।

घटियन्त्र सचक्र वर्त्तते एष एकैक स नास्ति वर्त्तना (१) ॥
तथ सर्व्वभवाङ्ग वर्त्तिनी अन्यमन्योपचयेन निःसृता ।
एकैक स तेषु वर्त्तिनी पूर्व्वापरान्तं नोपलभ्यते (२) ॥
बीजस्य सतो यथाङ्कुरो न च यो बीज स चैवाङ्कुरो ।
न च ततो न चैव एवमनुच्छेदअशाश्वतधर्म्मता (३) ॥
संस्कारअविद्यप्रत्ययास्ते संस्कारे न सन्ति तत्त्वतः ।
संस्कार अविद्य चैव हि शून्य एते प्रकृति निरीहका (४) ॥
मुद्रात्प्रतिमुद्र दृश्यते मुद्रसङ्क्रान्ति न चोपलभ्यते ।
न च तत्र न चैव शाश्वता एवं संस्कारानुच्छेद शाश्वताः (५) ॥
चक्षुश्च प्रतीत्यरूपतश्चक्षुर्विज्ञानमिहोपजायते ।
न चक्षुषि रूप निःसृतं रूपसङ्क्रान्ति न चैव चक्षुषि (६) ॥
नैरात्म्यशुभाश्च धर्म्मि ये न पुनरात्मेति शुभाश्च कल्पिताः ।
विपरीतमसद्विकल्पितं चक्षुर्विज्ञान ततोपजायते (७) ॥

---

१ "यथ" यथा "वर्त्तिता" वर्त्तितः "घटियन्त्र" घटीयन्त्रं "सचक्र वर्त्तते" सचक्रं वर्त्तते "एष एकैक स नास्ति वर्त्तना" एष एकैका सा नास्ति वर्त्तना ।

२ "तथ सर्व्वभवाङ्ग वर्त्तिनी" तथा सर्व्वभवगा वर्त्तिनी मार्ग इत्यर्थः "अन्यमन्योपचयेन" अन्योन्योपचयेन "एकैक स तेषु वर्त्तिनी" एकैका सा तेषु वर्त्तिनी ।

३ "बीज स चैवाङ्कुरो" बीजः स चैवाङ्कुरः "एवमनुच्छेदअशाश्वतधर्म्मता" एवमनुच्छेदाशाश्वतधर्म्मता अनुच्छिन्नधर्म्मता अशाश्वतधर्म्मतेत्यर्थः ।

४ "संस्कारअविद्यप्रत्ययास्ते" संस्कारा अविद्याप्रत्ययास्ते "संस्कारअविद्य चैव" संस्कारोऽविद्या चैव "शून्य एते प्रकृतिनिरीहका" शून्या एते प्रकृतिनिरीहका ।

५ "मुद्रात्प्रतिमुद्र" मुद्रायाः प्रतिमुद्रा "मुद्रसङ्क्रान्ति" मुद्रासङ्क्रान्तिर्न "संस्कारानुच्छेद" संस्कारानुच्छेदादयः ।

६ "चक्षुश्च प्रतीत्यरूपतः" चक्षुःप्रतीतरूपतः "न चक्षुषि रूप" न चक्षुषो रूपं "रूपसङ्क्रान्ति" रूपसङ्क्रान्तिर्न ।

७ "धर्म्मि ये" धर्म्मा ये "चक्षुर्विज्ञान" चक्षुर्विज्ञानं "ततोपजायते" तत उपजायते ।

विज्ञान निरोधसम्भवं विज्ञानोत्पादव्ययं विपश्यति ।
अकहिञ्च गतं अनागतं शून्य मायोपम योगी विपश्यति (१) ॥
अरणिं यथ चोत्तरारणि हस्तव्यायामत्रयेभि सङ्गति ।
इति प्रत्ययतोऽग्नि जायते जातु कृतु कार्य्य लघु निरुध्यते (२) ॥
अथ पण्डित कश्चि मार्गते कुतयं आगतु कुत्र याति वा ।
विदिशो दिशि सर्व्वे मार्गतो नागतिरस्य गतिश्च लभ्यते (३) ॥
स्कन्धधात्वायतनानि धातवस्तृष्ण अविद्या इति कर्म्मप्रत्ययाः ।
सामग्रि तु सत्त्वसूचना सा च परमार्था तु नोपलभ्यते (४) ॥
कण्ठोष्ठप्रतीत्यतालुकं जिह्वा परिवर्त्ति अक्षरा ।
न कण्ठकगता न तालुके अक्षरैकैकस्तु नोपलभ्यते (५) ॥
सामग्रीप्रतीतस्य सा वाच मनबुद्धिवशेन निश्चरी ।
मनु वाच अदृश्यरूपिणी वाह्यतोऽभ्यन्तर नोपलभ्यते (६) ॥
उत्पादव्ययं विपश्यतो वाच रुतघोषस्वरस्य पण्डितः ।

---

१ "विज्ञान" विज्ञानं "अकहिञ्च" अकथितञ्च "शून्यमायोपम" शून्यं मायोपमं ।

२ "यथ चोत्तरारणि हस्तव्यायामत्रयेभि" यथा चोत्तरारणिर्हस्तव्यायामत्रयैः "सङ्गति" सङ्गच्छति "अग्नि जायते" अग्निर्जायते "कृतु कार्य्य" कृतं कार्य्यं ।

३ "पण्डित कश्चि मार्गते" पण्डितः कश्चिन्मार्गति "कुतयं आगतु" कुतोऽयमागतः "विदिशो" विदिशि "मार्गतो" मार्गन्ति ।

४ "तृष्ण अविद्या" तृष्णा अविद्या "सामग्रितु" सामग्रिस्तु ।

५ "कण्ठोष्ठप्रतीत्यतालुकं" कण्ठोष्ठप्रतीततालुकं "परिवर्त्ति अक्षरा" परिवर्त्तयति अक्षराम् "अक्षरैकैकस्तु" एकैकाक्षरोऽपीत्यर्थः ।

६ "सामग्रीप्रतीतस्य" सामग्रीप्रतीतायाः "सा वाच" सा वाक् "मनबुद्धिवशेन निश्चरी" मनोबुद्धिवशेन निःसृता "मनु वाच" मनोवाक् "वाह्यतोऽभ्यन्तर" वाह्याभ्यन्तरयोः ।

क्षणिकां वशिकां तदीदृशीं सर्व्ववाच: प्रतिश्रुतकोपमां (१) ॥
यथ तन्त्रप्रतीत्य दारु च हस्तव्यायामचयेभि सङ्गति।
तुणवीणसुघोषकादिभि: शब्दो निश्चरते तदुद्भव: (२) ॥
अथ पण्डितु कश्चि मार्गते कुतोऽयमागतु कुत्र याति वा।
विदिशो दिशि सर्व्वि मार्गत: शब्दगमनागमनं न लभ्यते (३) ॥
तथ हेतुभि: प्रत्ययेभिश्च सर्व्वसंस्कारगतं प्रवर्त्तते।
योगी पुनर्भूतदर्शनाच्छून्य संस्कार निरीह पश्यति (४) ॥
स्कन्धायतनानि धातव: शून्यअध्यात्मिक शून्यबाह्यका:।
सत्त्वा विविक्तमनालया धर्म्माकाशस्वभावलक्षणा (५) ॥
इय ईदृश धर्म्मलक्षणा बुद्ध दीपङ्करदर्शने त्वया।
अनुबुद्ध स्वयं यथाऽऽत्मना तथ बोधेहि सदेवमानुषां (६) ॥
विपरीतअभूतकल्पितै रागद्वेषै: परिदह्यते जगत्।

---

१ "उत्पादव्ययं विपश्यतो" उत्पत्तिव्ययं विपश्यति "वाचयतघोषस्वरस्य" वाचो यतघोषस्वरस्य "वशिकां" अवशस्थितिमित्यर्थः "प्रतिश्रुतकोपमां" प्रतिश्रुतिकोपमां प्रतिध्वनिरूपामित्यर्थः।

२ "यथ तन्त्रप्रतीत्यदारु" यथा तन्त्रप्रतीतं दारु "हस्तव्यायामचयेभि सङ्गति" हस्तव्यायामचयैः सङ्गच्छति "तुणवीणसुघोषकादिभिः" तुणववीणासुघोषकादिभिः "निश्चरते" निश्चरति।

३ "पण्डितु कश्चिमार्गतो" पण्डितः कश्चिन्मार्गति "कुतोऽयमागतु कुत्र याति वा" कुतोऽयमागतः कुत्र यास्यति वा "विदिशोदिशिसर्व्वि मार्गतः" विदिग्दिक्षु सर्वे मार्गन्ति।

४ "तथ" तथा "प्रत्ययेभिश्च" प्रत्ययैः "शून्य संस्कार निरीह पश्यति" शून्यं संस्कारं निरीहः पश्यति।

५ "शून्य अध्यात्मिक" शून्याध्यात्मिकाः "विविक्तमनालया" विविक्तमनसो विविक्तालया इत्यर्थः।

६ "इय ईदृश धर्मलक्षणा" इयमीदृशी धर्मलक्षणा "बुद्ध" बोधिता "अनुबुद्ध" अनुबुद्धा "तथ" तथा "बोधेहि" बोधय "सदेवमानुषां" सदेवमानुषाम्।

रूपमेघसमाम्बुनीतलां मुञ्च धारामम्तस्य नायका (१) ॥
त्वयि यस्य कृतेन पश्चिता दत्तु दान बहुकल्पकोटिषु ।
सम्प्राप्य हि बोधिमुत्तमामार्य्य धनसङ्गृहं करिष्ये प्राणिनां (२)॥
तां पूर्व्वचरीमनुस्मरां नार्य्य धनहीन दरिद्र दुःखितां ।
मा उपेक्षहि सत्त्वसारथे आर्य्य धनसङ्गृहि तेषु कुर्व्वहि (३) ॥
त्वयि शील सदा सुरक्षितं पिठनार्थाय अपायभूमिनां ।
स्वर्गाम्तद्वारमुत्तमं दर्शयिष्ये बहुसत्त्वकोटिनां (४) ॥
तां पूर्व्वचरीमनुस्मरां बध्वा द्वार निरयावभूमिनां ।
स्वर्गाम्तद्वार मुञ्च हि चर्द्धि हि शीलवतो चिन्तितं (५) ॥
त्वयि क्षान्ति सदा सुरक्षिता प्रतिघक्रोधशमार्थ देहिनां ।
भवार्णव सत्त्व तारिया स्थापयिष्य शिवि क्षेममज्वले (६) ॥
तां पूर्व्वचरीमनुस्मरां वैरव्यापादविहिंसाकुला ।

---

१ "विपरीतअभूतकल्पितै" विपरीताभूतकल्पितैः "रूपमेघसमाम्बुनीतलां" रूपामेघसमाम्बुनीतलां "नायका" हे नायक ।

२ "त्वयियस्य कृतेन" तव यस्य कृते "पश्चिता दत्तुदान बहुकल्प कोटिषु" पश्चितैः दत्तं दानं बहुकल्पकोटिपर्य्यन्तमित्यर्थः "करिष्ये" करिष्यसि "प्राणिनां" प्राणिनामुपकारायेत्यर्थः ।

३ "तां पूर्व्वचरीमनुस्मरां" तां पूर्व्वचरीमनुस्मर "नार्य्य धनहीन दरिद्र दुःखितां" नार्योधनहीना दरिद्रा दुःखिताः "उपेक्षहि" उपेक्षस्व "धनसङ्गृहि तेषु" धनसङ्गृहं तासु "कुर्व्वहि" कुरु ।

४ "शील" शीलं "पिठनार्थाय" अनुशासनायेति निष्कृष्टार्थः "अपायभूमिनां" अपायभूमीनां "दर्शयिष्ये बहुसत्त्वकोटिनां" दर्शयिष्यसि बहुसत्त्वकोटीनां ।

५ "तां पूर्व्वचरीमनुस्मरां" तां पूर्व्वचरीमनुस्मर पूर्व्वाचरणमनुस्मरेत्यर्थः "द्वार निरयावभूमिनां" द्वारं निरयावभूमीनां "स्वर्गाम्तद्वारमुञ्चहि" स्वर्गाम्तद्वारं मुञ्च "चर्द्धि हि शीलवतो चिन्तितं" चर्द्धिं हि शीलवतश्चिन्तयेत्यर्थः ।

६ "क्षान्ति सदा" क्षान्तिः सदा "प्रतिघक्रोधशमार्थं" प्रतिघाक्रोधशमार्थं "भवार्णव सत्त्व तारिया" भवार्णवात् सत्त्वांस्तारयित्वा "स्थापयिष्य शिवि क्षेमम-ज्वले" स्थापयिष्यसि शिवे क्षेमे अम्बरे ।

मा उपेक्ष विहिंसचारिणः शान्तिभूमिषे स्थपे इयं जगत् (१) ॥
त्वयु वीर्य्य यदर्थ सेवितं धर्म्मनावं समुदानयित्व ना।
उत्तार्य्य जगत् सर्व्वार्णवां स्थापयिष्यसि विपच्चनिर्ज्वले (२) ॥
तां पूर्व्वचरीमनुस्मरा चतुरोघैरिव मुह्यते जगत्।
लघुवीर्य्यबलं पराक्रमाः सत्त्व सन्तारय हे नायका (३) ॥
त्वयु ध्यानकिलेशध्येषणा भविता यस्य कृते न सूरता।
भ्रान्तेन्द्रिय प्राकृतेन्द्रिया क्वापि विचार्थपथे स्थपेष्यहं (४) ॥
तां पूर्व्वचरीमनुस्मर क्लेशजालैरिदमाकुलं जगत्।
मा उपेक्षहि क्लेशपद्रुतां ध्यानैकापि स्थपेहीमां प्रजां (५) ॥
त्वयि प्रज्ञा पुरा सुभाविता मोहविद्यान्धतमाहते जगे।
बऊधर्म्मप्रताभिलोकने दास्ये चक्षुषि तनुदर्शनं (६) ॥
तां पूर्व्वचरीमनुस्मरा मोहविद्यान्धतमाहते जगे।

---

१ "तां पूर्व्वचरीमनुस्मरा" तां पूर्व्वचरीमनुस्मर "उपेक्ष" उपेक्षस्व "विहिंसचारिणः" विहिंसाचारिणः "शान्तिभूमिये स्थपे इयं" शान्तिभूमौ स्थापय इदं।

२ "त्वयु वीर्य्य यदर्थं" त्वया वीर्य्यं यदर्थं "समुदानयित्व" समुदानीय "सर्व्वार्णवां" सर्व्वार्णवेभ्यः "विपच्चनिर्ज्वले" विपच्चनिर्ज्वरे विपच्चरहिते समापरहित इत्यर्थः।

३ "पूर्व्वचरीमनुस्मरा" पूर्व्वचरीमनुस्मर "लघुवीर्य्यबलं पराक्रमाः सत्त्व" लघुवीर्य्यबलपराक्रमाम् सत्त्वान् "नायका" नायक।

४ "त्वयु ध्यानकिलेशध्येषणा" तव ध्यानक्लेशाध्येषणाः "भविता यस्य कृते न सूरत" भवितारः येषां कृते न सुरत "भ्रान्तेन्द्रिय प्राकृतेन्द्रिया क्वापि विचार्थपथे स्थपेष्यहं" भ्रान्तेन्द्रियान् प्राकृतेन्द्रियान् क्वापि विचिचार्थपथे स्थापयिष्येऽहं।

५ "मा उपेक्षस्वहि" मा उपेक्षस्व "क्लेशपद्रुतां" क्लेशापद्रुतां "ध्यानैकापि स्थपेहीमां प्रजां" एकाग्रध्याने स्थापय इमां प्रजां।

६ "त्वयि" त्वया "मोहविद्यान्धतमाहते जगे" मोहाविद्यान्धतमसाहते जगति "दास्ये चक्षुषि तनुदर्शनं" दास्यसि चक्षुषी तनुदर्शने।

ददही वरप्रज्ञा सुप्रभा धर्म्मचक्षु विमलं निरञ्जण (१) ॥

इयमीदृश गाथ गिरवरी तूर्य्यसङ्गीतिरवात्तु नारीणां ।

यं श्रुत्व मिदं विवर्जिया चित्त प्रेमेति वराग्र्यबोधयेति (२) ॥

इति हि भिक्षवोऽन्तःपुरमध्यगतो बोधिसत्त्वो विरहितोऽभूत्। धर्म्मश्रवणाविरहितोऽभूत्। धर्म्ममनसिकारेण। तत्कस्माद्धेतोः ॥

तथा हि भिक्षवो बोधिसत्त्वो दीर्घरात्रं सगौरवोऽभूत् । धर्म्मेषु धर्म्मभानकेषु चाध्याशयेन धर्म्मार्थिको धर्म्मकामो धर्म्मरतिरतोऽभूत् । धर्म्मपर्य्येष्टक्लान्तो (३) यथाश्रुतधर्म्मसम्प्रकाशकोऽनुत्तरो महाधर्म्मदानपतिर्निरामिषधर्म्मदेशको धर्म्मदानेनामत्सर आचार्य्यमुष्टिविगतो धर्म्मानुधर्म्मप्रतिपन्नो धर्म्मप्रतिपत्तिशूरोऽधर्म्मलयनो धर्म्मत्राणो धर्म्मशरणो धर्म्मप्रतिशरणो धर्म्मपरायणो धर्म्मनिध्याप्तिः क्षान्तिनिर्यातः प्रज्ञापारमिताचरित उपायकौशल्यगतिङ्गतः ॥

तत्र भिक्षवो बोधिसत्त्वो महोपायकौशल्येन विक्रीडितेन सर्व्वान्तःपुरस्य यथा विमुत्या ईर्य्यापथमुपदर्श्य पौर्विकाणाञ्च बोधिसत्त्वानां लोकविषयसमतिक्रान्तानां लोकानुवर्त्तनक्रिया-

१ "पूर्व्वंचरीमनुस्मरा" पूर्व्वंचरीमनुस्मर "मोहविद्यान्धतमावृते जगे" मोहाविद्यान्धतमसावृते जगति "ददहि वरप्रज्ञा सुप्रभा धर्म्मचक्षु विमलं निरञ्जण" देहि वरप्रज्ञां सुप्रभां धर्म्मचक्षुर्व्विमलं निरञ्जनं ।

२ "इयमीदृश गाथ गिरवरी" इयमीदृशी गाथा गिरोवरः "यं श्रुत्वमिदं विवर्जिया" याः श्रुत्वा इदं जगत् विवर्ज्य "चित्त प्रेमेति" चित्तं प्रेमान्वितं प्रेमयुक्तं भवति इति भावः ।

३ "धर्म्मपर्य्येष्टक्लान्तः" धर्म्मपर्य्येषणात्क्लान्त इत्यर्थः ।

धर्म्मतामनुवर्त्त्य दीर्घरात्रं सुविदितकामदोषः सत्त्वपरिपाकवशादकामोपभोगं सन्दर्श्यापरिमितकुशलमूलोपचयपुण्यसम्भारबलविशेषणासदृशीं लोकाधिपत्यतां सन्दर्श्य देवमनुष्यातिक्रान्तं सारोदारविविधविचित्ररूपशब्दगन्धरसस्पर्शपरमरतिरमणीयं कामरतिसौख्यमुपदर्श्य सर्व्वकामरतिस्वविषयेष्वपर्य्यन्तत्वात् स्वचित्तवशवर्त्तितां सन्दर्श्य पूर्व्वप्रणिधानबलकषायकुशलमूलोपचितान्सत्त्वान्समानसंवासतया परिपाच्य सर्व्वलोकसत्कृतसत्त्वर्लक्षितचित्ततयान्तःपुरमध्यगतो यथाभिमतस्य सत्त्वधातोः परिपाककालमवेक्षमाणो भूयस्या मात्रया बोधिसत्त्वस्तस्मिन् समये पूर्व्वप्रतिज्ञामनुस्मरति स्म । बुद्धधर्म्मांश्चामुखीकरोति स्म। प्रणिधानबलञ्चाभिनिर्हरति स्म। सत्त्वेषु च महाकरुणामवक्रामति स्म । सत्त्वप्रमोक्षञ्च चिन्तयति स्म । सर्व्वसम्पदो विपत्तिपर्य्यवसाना इति प्रत्यवेक्षते स्म । अनेकोपद्रवभयबहुलञ्च संसारमुपपरीक्षते स्म । मारकलिपाशांश्च सञ्छिनत्ति स्म। संसारप्रबन्धाच्चात्मानमुच्चालयति स्म। निर्व्वाणे च चित्तं सम्प्रेषयति स्म ॥

तत्र भिक्षवो बोधिसत्त्वः पूर्व्वाह्नत एव सुविदितसंसारदोषः संस्कृतेनाध्याशयेनानर्थिकः सर्व्वोपादानपरिग्रहैरनर्थिको बुद्धधर्म्मनिर्व्वाणाभिमुखः संसारपराङ्मुखस्तथागतगोचराभिरतो मारविषये गोचरासंसृष्ट आदीप्तभवदोषदर्शी त्रैधातुकान्निःसरणाभिप्रायः संसारदोषादेरवनिःसरणकुशलः प्रव्रज्याभिलाषी निष्क्रमणाभिप्रायो विवेकनिम्नो विवेकप्रचरणो विवे-

कप्राग्भार आरब्धप्रारब्धाभिमुखः प्रविवेकप्रशमाभिकाङ्क्षी आत्मपरहितप्रतिपन्नोऽनुत्तरप्रतिपत्तिशूरो लोकस्यार्थकामो हितकामः सुखकामो योगक्षेमकामो लोकानुकम्पको हितैषी मैत्रीविहारी महाकारुणिकः सङ्ग्रहवस्तुकुशलः सततसमितोऽपरिच्छिन्नमानसः सत्त्वपरिपाकविनयकुशलः सर्व्वसत्त्वेष्वेकपुत्रकप्रेमानुगतमनसिकारः सर्व्ववस्तुनिरपेक्षपरित्यागी दाने संविभागरतः प्रततपाणिस्त्यागशूरो यष्टयज्ञः सुसमृद्धपुण्यः सुसङ्गृहीतपुण्यः परिष्कारर्विगतमदमात्सर्य्यसुनिगृहीतचित्तोऽनुत्तरो महादानपतिर्दत्वा च विपाकाप्रतिकाङ्क्षी प्रदानशूर तृष्णामर्षेर्ष्यालोभदोषमदमानमोहमात्सर्य्यप्रमुखसर्व्वारिक्लेशगणप्रत्यर्थिकनिग्रहायाभ्युत्थितः सर्व्वज्ञताचित्तोत्पादप्रबन्धाचरितो महात्यागचित्तः सन्नाहसुसन्नद्धो लोकानुकम्पको हितैषी वर्मितकवचितः सत्त्वप्रमोक्षारम्भणमहाकरुणाबलविक्रमोऽवैवर्त्तिकसर्व्वसत्त्वसमचित्तत्यागप्रहरणो यथाभिप्रायसत्त्वाशयसन्तोषणो बोधिभाजनीभूतः कालाकुशलधर्म्मवेधी बोधिपरिणामप्रणिधिरवनामितध्वजच्छिन्नमण्डलपरिबोधनदानपरित्यागी ज्ञानवरवज्रदृढप्रहरणः सुनिगृहीतक्लेशप्रत्यर्थिकः शीलगुणचरित्रप्रतिपन्नः सुरक्षितकायवाङ्मनस्कर्म्मान्तोऽणुमात्रावद्यभयदर्शी शुद्धसुपरिशीलोऽमलविमलनिर्म्मलचित्तः सर्व्वदुरुक्तदुरागतवचनसर्व्वाक्रोशपरिभाषणकुत्सनताडनतर्जनवधबन्धनावरोधनपरिक्लेशाक्षुलितचित्तोऽक्षुभितचित्तः क्षान्तिसौरभ्यसम्पन्नोऽक्षतोऽनुपहतोऽव्यापन्नचित्तः सर्व्वसत्त्वहितार्थायोत्तप्तवीर्य्यालम्बी

दृढसमादानसर्व्वकुशलमूलो धर्म्मसमुदानयताप्रत्युदावर्त्त्यस्मृति-
मान् सुसम्प्रज्ञः सुसमाहितोऽविक्षिप्तचित्तो ध्यानैकाग्रमनसि-
कारो धर्म्मप्रविचयकुशलो लब्धालोको विगततमोऽन्धकारो
ऽनित्यदुःखात्मा शुभाकारपरिभावितचेताः स्मृत्युपस्थानसम्यक्-
प्रहाणर्द्धिपादेन्द्रियबलबोध्यङ्गमार्गार्य्यसत्यसर्व्वबोधिपक्षधर्म्मसुप-
रिकर्म्मकृतमनसिकारः समथविपश्यनासुपर्य्यवदातबुद्धिः प्रती-
त्यसमुत्पादसत्यदर्शी सत्यानुबोधादपरः प्रत्ययस्त्रिविमोक्षमुख-
विक्रीडितो मायामरीचिस्वप्नोदकचन्द्रप्रतिश्रुत्काप्रतिभासोपम-
सर्व्वधर्म्मनयावतीर्णः॥

इति हि भिक्षवो बोधिसत्त्वस्यैवं भवति प्रतिकृतिरेवं धर्म्म-
विहार्य्येवं गुणमाहात्म्यविहार्य्येवं सत्त्वार्थाभियुक्तविहार्य्यभूत्॥
भूयस्या मात्रया आभिर्दशदिग्बुद्धाधिष्ठानतूर्य्यसङ्गीतिविनिः-
सृताभिः सञ्चोदितः स तस्यां वेलायां पूर्व्वकाश्च बोधिसत्त्वानां
चरमभवोपगतानामन्तःपुरपरिपाचितानि चत्वारि धर्म्ममुखा-
न्यामुखीकरोति स्म। कतमानि चत्वारि। यदिदं दानं प्रिय-
वचनमर्थक्रिया समानार्थता च॥ चतुःसङ्ग्रहवस्तुप्रयोगनिर्हा-
रविशुद्धिञ्च नाम धर्म्ममुखमामुखीकरोति स्म॥ त्रिरत्नवंशस्य
धारणाभिप्रायो विप्रणाशसर्व्वज्ञताचित्तप्रणिधानबलाधानावै-
वर्त्तविषयञ्च नाम धर्म्ममुखमामुखीकरोति स्म॥ सर्व्वसत्त्वाप-
रित्यागाध्याशमहाकरुणावतारणाञ्च नाम धर्म्ममुखमामुखी-
करोति स्म॥ सर्व्वबोधिपक्षधर्म्मपदे प्रभेदार्थातिनिश्चयज्ञानसं-
चारबलविशेषसमुदानयमहाव्यूहञ्च नाम धर्म्ममुखमामुखीक-

रोति स्म ॥ इमानि चत्वारि धर्म्ममुखान्यामुखीकृत्य बोधिसत्त्वः सर्व्वस्यान्तःपुरस्य परिपाचनार्थं तस्यां वेलायां तथारूपमृद्ध्यभिसंस्कारमभिसंस्करोति स्म ॥ यथारूपेण ऋद्ध्यभिसंस्कारेणाभिसंस्कृतेन तेभ्यः सङ्गीतिरुतेभ्यो बोधिसत्त्वानुभावेनेमान्येवंरूपाणि धर्म्ममुखशतसहस्राणि निश्चरन्ति स्म ।

तद्यथा ।

उदारच्छन्देन चाशयेनाध्याशयेन करुणा य प्राणिषूत्पाद्यते ।
चित्तवराग्रबोधाय शब्दे च रूपस्तुरियेभि निश्चरी (१) ॥
श्रद्धा प्रसादोऽधिमुक्ति गौरवं निर्म्मानता ओनमना गुरूणां ।
परिपृच्छता किं कुशलं गवेषणा अनुस्मृती भावनु शब्द निश्चरी (२)॥
दानेदमेसंयमशीलशब्दः क्षान्त्यास्य शब्दस्तथ वीर्य्यशब्दो ।
ध्यानाभिनिर्हारसमाधिशब्दः प्रज्ञाउपायस्य च शब्द निश्चरी (३)॥
मैत्राय शब्दः करुणाय शब्दो मुदिताउपेक्षाय अभिज्ञशब्दः ।
चतुःसङ्ग्रहवस्तुविनिश्चयेन सत्त्वानुपरिपाचनशब्द निश्चरी (४) ॥

---

१ "उदारच्छन्देन चाशयेनाध्याशयेन" उदारच्छन्देन उदाराशये उदाराध्याशयेनेत्यर्थः "करुणा य" करुणा या "शब्दे च" शब्दश्च "रूपस्तुरियेभि निश्चरी" रूपस्तुर्यैर्निश्चचार ।

२ "प्रसादोऽधिमुक्तिगौरवं" प्रसादोऽधिमुक्तिर्गौरवं "निर्मानता ओनमना" निर्मानता आनमनं "परिपृच्छता किं" परिपृच्छालं किं वा "अनुस्मृती भावनु शब्द निश्चरी" अनुस्मृतिर्भावना शब्दा निश्चेरु एते शब्दा निश्चेरुरित्यर्थः ।

३ "दानेदमेसंयमशीलशब्दः" दानदमसंयमशीलशब्दः "शब्दस्तथ वीर्य्यशब्दो" शब्दस्तथा वीर्य्यशब्दः एते शब्दा निश्चेरुरित्यर्थः "प्रज्ञाउपायस्य" प्रज्ञोपायस्य "शब्द निश्चरी" शब्दो निश्चचार ।

४ "मैत्राय शब्दः" मैत्र्याः शब्दः "करुणाय शब्दः" करुणायाः शब्दः "मुदिताउपेक्षाय अभिज्ञशब्दः" मुदितोपेक्षयोरभिज्ञाशब्दः "सत्त्वानुपरिपाचनशब्द निश्चरी" सत्त्वानुपरिपाचनशब्दो निश्चचार ।

स्मृत्युपस्थानप्रभेदशब्दः सम्यक्प्रहाणास्तथ ऋद्धिपादाः ।
पञ्चेन्द्रिया पञ्च बलप्रभेदा बोध्यङ्गशब्दस्तुरियेभि निश्चरी (१) ॥
अष्टाङ्गिकमार्गबलप्रभेद च शमथस्य शब्दोऽथ विपश्यनायाः ।
अनित्यदुःखार्त्तिअनात्मशब्दो अशुभार्त्तिशब्दो तुरियेभि नि-
श्चरी (२) ॥
विरागशब्दश्च विवेकशब्दः क्षयज्ञानशब्दोऽनुत्पादशब्दः ।
अनिरोधशब्दश्च अनालयश्च निर्वाणशब्दस्तुरियेभि निश्चरी(३)॥
इम एवरूपास्तुरियेभि शब्दाः सम्बोधिशब्दरनुभाव निश्चरी ।
यां श्रुत्व सर्व्वाः प्रमदानुशिक्षिता वरायसत्त्वं प्रणिधेन्ति बोधये(४)॥

इति हि भिक्षवोऽन्तःपुरमध्यगतेन बोधिसत्त्वेन तानि चतुरशीतिस्त्रीसहस्राणि परिपाचितान्यभूवन् । अनुत्तरायां सम्यक्सम्बोधौ बहूनि च देवशतसहस्राणि च ये च तत्र सम्प्राप्ता अभूवन् ॥ तत्राभिनिष्क्रमणकालसमये बोधिसत्त्वस्य ह्रीदेवो नाम तुषितकायिको देवपुत्रोऽनुत्तरायाः सम्यक्सम्बोधेः । स रात्रौ प्रशान्तायां द्वात्रिंशता देवपुत्रसहस्रैः परिवृतः पुरस्कृतो येन बोधिसत्त्वस्योपस्थानप्रासादस्तेनोपसङ्क्र-

---

१ "तथ ऋद्धिपादाः" तथर्द्धिपादाः "पञ्चेन्द्रिया पञ्चबलप्रभेदाः" पञ्चेन्द्रियाणि पञ्च बलप्रभेदाः "तुरियेभि निश्चरी" तूर्य्येभ्यो निश्चेरुः ।

२ "अष्टाङ्गिकमार्गबलप्रभेद च" अष्टाङ्गमार्गबलप्रभेदश्च "अनित्यदुःखार्त्ति अनात्मशब्दो" अनित्यदुःखार्त्त्यनात्मशब्दो "तुरियेभि निश्चरी" तूर्य्येभ्यो निश्चचार ।

३ "अनालयश्च" अनालयस्य च शब्द इत्यर्थः "तुरियेभिनिश्चरी" तूर्य्येभ्यो निश्चचार ।

४ "इम एवरूपास्तुरियेभि" इमे एवंरूपास्तूर्य्येभ्यो "सम्बोधिशब्दरनुभाव निश्चरी" सम्बोधिशब्दानुभावेन निश्चेरुः "यां श्रुत्व" यान् श्रुत्वा "प्रमदानुशिक्षिताः" प्रमदा अनुशिक्षिताः "प्रणिधेन्ति बोधये" प्रणिधापयन्ति स्म बोधाय ।

तदुपसंक्रम्य गगनतलगत एव बोधिसत्त्वं गाथाभिरध्यभाषत ।

च्युति दर्शिता अतियशा जन्म च सन्दर्शितं पुरुषसिंह ।
अन्तःपुरं विदर्शयितुं कृतानुवृत्तिस्त्वया लोके (१) ॥
परिपाचितातिबहवो मनुजलोके धर्ममनुप्राप्य ।
अयमद्य काल समयो निष्क्रम्येति मति चिन्तेहि (२) ॥
न हि बद्ध मोचयाती नयान्धपुरुषो दर्शयति मार्गं ।
मुक्तस्तु मोचयाती सचक्षुरन्धान् दर्शयति मार्गं (३) ॥
ये सत्त्व कामदासा गृहधनपुत्रभार्यपरिरक्ताः ।
ते तुभ्य शिक्षमाणा नैष्क्रम्यमती स्पृहां कुर्युः (४) ॥
ऐश्वर्य कामक्रीडा चतुर्द्वीपा सप्तरत्न विजहित्वा ।
निष्क्रान्तं त्वां विदित्वा स्पृहयेत् स नरामरो लोकः (५) ॥
किञ्चापि ध्यानसौख्यैर्विहरसि धर्मेण चासि कामरतः ।
अथ पुनश्चिरप्रसुप्तां बोधय मरुमानुषशतानि (६) ॥
अतिपतति यौवनमिदं गिरिनदी यथ चञ्चलप्रबलवेगा ।
गतयौवनस्य भवतो नैष्क्रम्यमतिर्न शोभते (७) ॥

---

१ "च्युति दर्शिता अतियशा" च्युतिर्दर्शिता अतियशस्विनो ।

२ "परिपाचितातिबहवः" परिपाचितानि अतिबहूनि: "काल समयः" कालः समयः "निष्क्रम्येतिमति चिन्तेहि" निष्क्रमणे इति मतिं चिन्तय ।

३ "बद्ध मोचयाती" बद्धो मोचयति "मोचयाती" मोचयति ।

४ "सत्त्व" सत्त्वाः "गृहधनपुत्रभार्यपरिरक्ताः" गृहधनपुत्रभार्यापरिरक्षिता इत्यनुमीयते "तुभ्य" त्वया "नैष्क्रम्यमती" निष्क्रमणमतौ ।

५ "ऐश्वर्य कामक्रीडा" ऐश्वर्यं कामक्रीडां "चतुर्द्वीपा" चतुर्द्वीपाम् "सप्तरत्न विजहित्वा" सप्तरत्नानि विजह्य ।

६ "चिरप्रसुप्तां" चिरप्रसुप्तानि "मरुमानुषशतानि" मरुन्मानुषशतानि ।

७ "अतिपतति" अतिपतितं "यथ" यथा "नैष्क्रम्यमतिर्न" निष्क्रमणमतिर्न "शोभते" शोभिष्यते इत्यर्थः ।

तस्माधुरूप प्रथमेव वरयौवनेऽभिनिष्क्रम्य ।
उच्चारय प्रतिज्ञां कुरुष्व चार्थं सुरगणानां (१) ॥
न च कामगुणरतीभिस्तृप्तिर्लवणोदधेर्यथाम्भोभिः ।
ते तृप्त एव प्रज्ञा आर्या लोकोत्तरा विरजा (२) ॥
त्वमिह प्रिय मनापो राज्ञः शुद्धोदनस्य राष्ट्रस्य ।
शतपत्त्रसदृशवदना नैष्क्रम्यमतिं विचिन्तेहि (३) ॥
आदीप्तां क्लेशतापैरनिःशरणैर्गाढबन्धनैः ।
बद्धानां शीघ्रं मोक्षमार्गे स्थापय शान्तेऽसज्जि वीरा (४) ॥
त्वं वैद्यधातुकुशलश्चिरातुरां सत्त्व रोगसंस्पृष्टां ।
भैषज्यधर्मयोगैर्निर्वाणसुखे स्थापय शीघ्रं (५) ॥
अन्धतमा अनयना मोहाकुलदृष्टिजालबद्धाः ।
प्रज्ञाप्रदीपचक्षुः शोधय शीघ्रं नरमरूणां (६) ॥
समुदीक्षन्ते बहवो देवासुरनागयक्षगन्धर्वाः ।
द्रक्ष्याम बोधि प्राप्तं निरुत्तरं धर्म श्रोष्याम (७) ॥
द्रक्ष्यति वै भुजगराजो भवनमवभासितं तव श्रिरीये ।

---

१ "प्रथमेव" प्रथमसेव ।

२ "कामगुणरतीभिः" कामगुणरतिभिः "तृप्त एव" तृप्ता एषा "आर्या लोकोत्तरा विरजा" चे आर्यं लोकोत्तर विरजः ।

३ "प्रिय मनापो" प्रियो मनापः "शतपत्त्रसदृशवदना" चे शतपत्त्रसदृशवदन "नैष्क्रम्यमतिं" निष्क्रमणमतिं "विचिन्तेहि" विचिन्तय ।

४ "आदीप्तां" आदीप्तान् "बद्धानां" बद्धान् "असज्जि वीरा" असङ्गे चे वीर ।

५ "चिरातुरां सत्त्व रोगसंस्पृष्टां" चिरातुरान् सत्त्वान् रोगसंस्पृष्टान् ।

६ "ये अन्धतमा अनयना मोहाकुलदृष्टिजालबद्धास्तेषामित्यर्थः "नरमरूणां" नरमरुतां ।

७ "द्रक्ष्याम बोधि प्राप्तं" द्रक्ष्यामो बोधिं प्राप्तं "धर्म" धर्मं ।

करिष्यति अनन्त पूजां पूरेहि व्रताशयस्तस्य (१) ॥
चत्वारि लोकपाला: ससैन्यकास्ते तव प्रतीच्छन्ते ।
दास्याम चतुरि पात्रां बोधिध्वजि पूर्वमनसस्य (२) ॥
ब्रह्मा प्रशान्तचारी उदीक्षते मैत्रवाक्करुणालाभी ।
अध्येषिष्ये नरेन्द्रं वर्त्तेन्ति निरुत्तरं चक्रं (३) ॥
बोधि परिपाचिकापि च देवता अभिष्टुव बोधिमण्डेऽस्मिन् ।
उत्पत्स्ययं परिद्रक्ष्याम्यभिबुध्यतो बोधिं (४) ॥
सत्त्वाऽपि बोधिसत्त्वानन्तःपुरि ये क्रिया विदर्शेन्ति ।
पूर्व्वङ्गमो भव त्वं मा भविष्यति पश्चिमस्तेषां (५) ॥
मञ्जुरुत मञ्जुघोषा स्मराहि दीपङ्करस्य ।
व्याकरणभूतं तथा अवितथाजिनघोषरुतं उदीरेहि (६) ॥

इति सञ्चोदनापरिवर्त्तो नाम त्रयोदशोऽध्यायः ॥ १३ ॥

---

१ "तव श्रिरीये" तव श्रिया "अनन्त पूजां" अनन्तः पूजां "पूरेहि" पूरय "व्रताशयस्तस्य" व्रतमाशयश्च तस्य स्थित इत्यर्थः ।

२ "चत्वारि लोकपालाः" चत्वारो लोकपालाः "तव प्रतीच्छन्ते" त्वां प्रतीच्छन्ते "दास्याम चतुरिपात्रां" दास्यामश्चत्वारि पात्राणि इत्येतदर्थं प्रतीच्छन्ते इत्यर्थः "बोधिध्वजि" बोधिध्वजे बोधिवर्षे इति यावत् "पूर्वमनसस्य" पूर्वमनसे पूर्वमानसायतुभ्यमित्यर्थः ।

३ बोधिःप्रशान्तचारीति वा पाठः "अध्येष्यिष्ये" अध्यापयिष्ये "वर्त्तेन्ति" वर्त्तयिष्यति ।

४ "बोधिपरिपाचिकापि" बोधिपरिपाचिका अपि "बोधिमण्डेऽस्मिन्" बोधिमण्डेऽस्मिन् "उत्पत्स्ययं" उत्पत्स्यत्ययं "अभिबुध्यतो" अभिबोधयन्तं ।

५ "सत्त्वाऽपि" सत्त्वा अपि "बोधिसत्त्वान्" बोधिसत्त्वेभ्य इत्यर्थः । "अन्तःपुरिये क्रिया विदर्शेन्ति" अन्तःपुरे याः क्रिया विदर्शयन्ति "मा भविष्यसि" मा भव ।

६ "मञ्जुरुत मञ्जुघोषा" मञ्जुरुतानि हे मञ्जुघोष "स्मराहि" स्मर "उदीरहि" उदीरय ।

चतुर्द्दशाध्यायप्रारम्भः ॥

इति हि भिक्षवो बोधिसत्त्वः सञ्चोदितः सन् तेन देवपुत्रेण राज्ञः शुद्धोदनस्येमं स्वप्नमुपदर्शयति स्म । यद्राजा शुद्धोदनः सुप्तः स्वप्नान्तरगतोऽद्राक्षीत् बोधिसत्त्वं रात्रौ प्रशान्तायामभिनिष्क्रमन्तं देवगणपरिवृतमभिनिष्क्रम्य प्रव्रजितं चाद्राक्षीत् काषायवस्त्रप्रावृतं ॥ स प्रतिविबुद्धस्त्वरितं काञ्चुकीयं परिपृच्छति स्म । अस्ति मे कुमारोऽन्तःपुरे इति ॥

सोऽवोचदस्ति देवेति ॥

ततो राज्ञः शुद्धोदनस्यान्तःपुरे शोकशल्यो हृदयेऽनुप्रविष्टोऽभूत् । अभिनिष्क्रमिष्यति अवश्यं कुमारोऽयस्येमानि पूर्व्वनिमित्तानि सन्दृश्यन्ते स्म ॥

तस्यैतदभवत् । न खल्वधुनेन कुमारेण कदाचिदुद्यानभूमिरभिनिर्गन्तव्या । स्त्रीगणमध्येऽभिरत इहैव रमतु नाभिनिष्क्रमिष्यतीति ॥

ततो राज्ञा शुद्धोदनेन कुमारस्य परिभोगार्थं त्रयो यथर्तुकाः प्रासादाः कारिता अभूवन् । ग्रैष्मिको वार्षिको हैमन्तिकश्च ॥ तत्र यो ग्रैष्मिकः स एकान्तशीतलः । यो वार्षिकः स साधारणः । यो हैमन्तिकः स स्वभावोष्णः । एकैकस्य च प्रासादस्य सोपानानि पञ्चपञ्चपुरुषशतान्युत्क्षिपन्ति स्म निक्षिपन्ति स्म । तेषां तथोत्क्षिप्यमाणानां निक्षिप्यमाणानाञ्च शब्दोऽर्द्धयोजने श्रूयते स्म ॥ मा खलु कुमारोऽभिज्ञात एवाभिनिष्क्रमत्विति । नैमित्तिकैर्वैपञ्चमिकैश्च व्याहृतमभूत् । मङ्गलद्वारेण कुमा

रोऽभिनिष्क्रमिष्यतीति ॥ ततो राजा मङ्गलद्वारस्य महान्ति कपाटानि कारयति स्म ॥ एकैकस्य कपाटं पञ्चपञ्चपुरुषशता-न्युद्घाटयन्ति अपघाटयन्ति च। तेषाञ्चार्द्धयोजनं शब्दो गच्छति स्म ॥ पञ्च चास्य कामगुणानवकृष्यानुपसंहरति स्म ॥ गीतवा-दित्रनृत्यैश्चैनं सदैव युवतय उपतस्थुः ॥

अथ भिक्षवो बोधिसत्त्वः सारथिं प्राह। गोष्ठं सारथे रथं योजयोद्यानभूमिं गमिष्यामीति ॥

ततः सारथी राजानं शुद्धोदनमुपसङ्क्रम्यैवमाह। देव कुमार उद्यानभूमिमभिनिर्यास्यतीति ॥

अथ राज्ञः शुद्धोदनस्यैतदभवत्। न कदाचिन्मया कुमार उद्यानभूमिमभिनिष्क्रामितः सुभूमिदर्शनाय। योन्वहं कुमार-मुद्यानभूमिमभिनिष्क्रामयेयं ततः कुमारो स्त्रीगणपरिवृतो रतिं वेत्स्यते नाभिनिष्क्रमिष्यतीति ॥

ततो राजा शुद्धोदनः स्नेहबहुमानाभ्यां बोधिसत्त्वस्य नगरे घण्टावघोषणां कारयति स्म। सप्तमे दिवसे कुमार उद्यानभूमिं निष्क्रमिष्यतीति सुभूमिदर्शनाय ॥ तत्र भवद्भिः सर्व्वामनापानि चापनयितव्यानि। मा कुमारः प्रतिकूलं पश्येत्। सर्व्वमनापानि चोपसंहर्त्तव्यानि विषयाभिरम्याणि ॥

ततः सप्तमे दिवसे सर्व्वं नगरमलङ्कृतमभूत्। उद्यानभूमि-रुपशोभिता नानारक्तपुष्पवितानीकृता छत्रध्वजपताकासमल-ङ्कृता ॥ ये न च मार्गेण बोधिसत्त्वोऽभिनिर्गच्छति स्म स मार्गः सिक्तः संसृष्टो गन्धोदकपरिषिक्तो मुक्तकुसुमावकीर्णो

नानागन्धघटिकानिर्धूपितः पूर्णकुम्भोपशोभितः कदलीतोरणो- च्छ्रितो नानाविचित्रपटवितानविततो रत्नकिङ्किणीजालहारा- र्द्धहाराभिप्रलम्बितोऽभूत् ॥ चतुरङ्गसैन्यव्यूहितः परिवारश्चो- द्युक्तोऽभूत् कुमारस्यान्तःपुरम्प्रतिमण्डयितुं । तत्र बोधिसत्त्वस्य पूर्व्वेण नगरद्वारेणोद्यानभूमिमभिनिष्क्रमतो महता व्यूहेन । अथ बोधिसत्त्वस्यैवानुभावेन शुद्धावासकायिकैर्द्देवपुत्रैस्तस्मिन् मार्गे पुरुषो जीर्णो वृद्धो महल्लको धमनीसन्ततगात्रः खण्डदन्तो वलीनिचितकायः पलितकेशः कुब्जो गोपानसीवक्रो विभग्नो दण्डपरायण आतुरो गतयौवनः खुरखुरावसक्तकण्ठः पुरतः प्राग्भारेण कायेन दण्डमवष्टभ्य प्रवेधयमानः सर्व्वाङ्गप्रत्यङ्गैः पुरतो मार्गस्योपदर्शितोऽभूत् ॥

अथ बोधिसत्त्वो जानन्नेव सारथिमेतदवोचत् ।

किं सारथे पुरुष दुर्ब्बल अल्पस्थाम
उच्छुष्कमांसरुधिरत्वचस्नायुनद्धः ।
श्वेतशिरो विरलदन्त कृशाङ्गरूप
आलम्ब्य दण्ड व्रजतेऽसुखं स्खलन्त (१) ॥

सारथिराह ।

एषो हि देवपुरुषो जरयाऽभिभूतः
क्षीणेन्द्रियः सुदुःखितो बलवीर्य्यहीनो ।

---

१ "पुरुषदुर्ब्बल अल्पस्थाम" पुरुषो दुर्ब्बलोऽल्पस्थामा "उच्छुष्कमांसरुधिर- त्वचस्नायुनद्धः" उच्छुष्कमांसरुधिरत्वक्स्नायुनद्धः "श्वेतशिरो विरलदन्त" श्वेत- शिरा विरलदन्तः "दण्ड व्रजते" दण्डं व्रजति "स्खलन्त" स्खलन् ।

बन्धुजनेन परिभूत अनाथभूतः
कार्य्यासमर्थ अपविद्धु वनेव दारु (१) ॥

बोधिसत्त्व आह ।

कुलधर्म्म एष अयमस्य हितं भणाहि
अथवाऽपि सर्व्वजगतोऽस्य इयं ह्यवस्था ।
शीघ्रं भणाहि वचनं यथभूतमेत-
च्छ्रुत्वा तथार्थमिह योनि सञ्चिन्तयिष्ये (२) ॥

सारथिराह ।

नैतस्य देव कुलधर्म्म न राष्ट्रधर्म्मः
सर्व्वे जगस्य जर यौवन धर्षयाति ।
तुभ्यंपि मातृपितृबान्धवज्ञातिसङ्घो
जरया अमुक्त न हि अन्य गतिर्जनस्य (३) ॥

बोधिसत्त्व आह ।

धिक् सारथे अबुधबालजनस्य बुद्धि-
र्यद्यौवनेन मदमत्त जरां न पश्यी ।
आवर्त्तयाश्विह रथं पुनरहं प्रवेक्ष्ये

---

१ "बलवीर्य्यहीनो" बलवीर्य्यहीनः "परिभूत अनाथभूतः" परिभूतोऽनाथभूतः "कार्य्यासमर्थं अपविद्ध वनेव" कार्य्यासमर्थोऽपविद्धो वने इव ।

२ "अयमस्य" इदमस्य "भणाहि" भण "भणाहि" भण "यथभूतमेतत्" यथा भूतमेतत् "योनि" योनिं ।

३ "कुलधर्म्म न" कुलधर्म्मो न "सर्व्वे जगस्य जरयौवन धर्षयाति" सर्व्वस्य जगतो जरा यौवनं धर्षयति "तुभ्यंपि" त्वमपि "अमुक्त न" अमुक्तो न "अन्य गतिः" अन्या गतिः ।

किं मह्य क्रीडरतिभिर्जरयाश्रितस्य (१) ॥

अथ बोधिसत्त्वः प्रतिनिवर्त्त्य रथवरं पुनरपि प्रविवेश ॥

इति हि भिक्षवो बोधिसत्त्वोऽपरेण कालसमयेन दक्षिणेन नगरद्वारेणोद्यानभूमिमभिनिष्क्रमन् महता व्यूहेन सोऽद्राक्षीन् मार्गे पुरुषं व्याधिस्पृष्टं दग्धं ज्वराभिभूतं दुर्ब्बलकायं स्वके मूत्रपुरीषे निमग्नमत्राणमप्रतिशरणं कृच्छ्रेणोच्छ्वसन्तं दृष्ट्वा च पुनर्बोधिसत्त्वो जानन्नेव सारथिमिदमवोचत् ।

किं सारथे पुरुष रूपविवर्णगात्रः
सर्व्वेन्द्रियेभि विकलो गुरु प्रश्वसन्तः ।
सर्व्वाङ्गशुष्क उदराकुल प्राप्तकृच्छ्रा
मूत्रे पुरीष स्वकि तिष्ठति कुत्सनीये (२) ॥

सारथिराह ।

एषो हि देवपुरुषः परमं गिलानो
व्याधीभयं उपगतो मरणान्तप्राप्तः ।
आरोग्यतेजरहितो बलविप्रहीणो
अत्राणद्वीपशरणो ह्यपरायणश्च (३) ॥

बोधिसत्त्व आह ।

---

१ "अनुवबालजनस्य बुद्धिः" अनुवबालजनबुद्धे "गदमन जरा" गदमना जरा "न पश्यो" न पश्यसि "मह्य" मम "क्रीडरतिभिः" क्रीडारतिभिः ।

२ "पुरुषरूपविवर्णगात्र" पुरुषो रूपविवर्णगात्रः "सर्व्वेन्द्रियेभि विकलः" सर्व्वेन्द्रियैर्विकलः "गुरु प्रश्वसन्तः" गुरु यथा तथा प्रश्वसन् "उदराकुल प्राप्तकृच्छ्रा" उदराकुलः प्राप्तकृच्छ्रः "पुरीष" पुरीषे "स्वकि" स्वके ।

३ "गिलानः" ग्लानः "व्याधीभयं उपगतः" व्याधिभयमुपगतः "आरोग्यतेजरहितः" आरोग्यतेजो रहितः "अत्राणद्वीपशरणो" अत्राणद्वीपशरणो ।

आरोग्यता च भवते यथ स्वप्नक्रीडा
व्याधिर्भयश्च इम ईदृश घोररूपं ।
को नाम विज्ञपुरुषो इम दृष्ट्व वस्थां
क्रीडारतिञ्च जनयेच्छुभसञ्ज्ञितां वा (१) ॥

अथ खलु भिक्षवो बोधिसत्त्वः प्रतिनिवर्त्य रथवरं पुनरपि पुरवरे प्राविशत् ।

इति हि भिक्षवो बोधिसत्त्वोऽपरेण कालसमयेन पश्चिमेन नगरद्वारेणोद्यानभूमिमभिनिष्क्रमन्नद्राक्षीत् व्यूहेन सोऽद्राक्षीत् पुरुषं मृतं कालगतं मञ्चे समारोपितं चेलवितानीकृतं ज्ञातिसङ्घपरिवृतं सर्वै रुदद्भिः क्रन्दद्भिः परिदेवमानैः प्रकीर्णकेशैः पांश्ववकीर्णशिरोभिरुरांसि ताडयद्भिरुत्क्रोशद्भिः पृष्ठतोऽनुगच्छद्भिः। दृष्ट्वा च पुनर्बोधिसत्त्वो जानन्नेव सारथिमिदमवोचत् ।

किं सारथे पुरुष मञ्चोपरिगृहीतो
उद्धूत केशनख पांशु शिरे क्षिपन्ति ।
परिचारयित्व विहरन्त्यु रस्ताडयन्तो
नानाविलापवचनानि उदीरयन्तः (२) ॥

सारथिराह ।

एषो हि देवपुरुषो मृतु जम्बुद्वीपे
न हि भूय मातृपितृ द्रक्ष्यति पुत्रदारां ।

---

१ "भवते यथ" भवति यथा "ईदृश घोररूपं" ईदृशा घोररूपाः "विज्ञपुरुषो इम दृष्ट्ववस्थां" विज्ञपुरुष इमां दृष्ट्वा अवस्थां ।

२ "पुरुष मञ्चोपरि गृहीतः" पुरुषो मञ्चोपरि गृहीतः "उद्धूतकेशनख" उद्धूतकेशनखाः "पांशुशिरे" पांशून् शिरसि "परिचारयित्व" परिचारयित्वा ।

अपहाय भोगगृहमातृपितृमित्रज्ञातिवर्गं
परलोक प्राप्तु न हि दृक्ष्यति भूय ज्ञातिं (१) ॥

बोधिसत्त्व आह ।

धिग्यौवनेन जरया समभिद्रुतेन
आरोग्य धिग्विविधव्याधिपराहतेन ।
धिग्जीवितेन पुरुषो नचिरस्थितेन
धिक्पण्डितस्य पुरुषस्य रतिप्रसङ्गैः (२) ॥

यदि जर न भवेया नैव व्याधिर्न मृत्यु-
स्तथपि च महदुःखं पञ्चस्कन्धं धरन्तो ।
किं पुन जरव्याधिर्मृत्यु नित्यानुबद्धाः
साधु प्रतिनिवर्त्यं चिन्तयिष्ये प्रमोक्षं (३) ॥

अथ खलु भिक्षवो बोधिसत्त्वः प्रतिनिवर्त्य तं रथवरं पुनरपि पुरं प्राविशत् ॥ इति हि भिक्षवो बोधिसत्त्वस्यापरेण कालसमयेनोत्तरेण नगरद्वारेणोद्यानभूमिमभिनिष्क्रामतस्तैरेव देवपुत्रैर्बोधिसत्त्वस्यानुभावेनैव तस्मिन् मार्गे भिक्षुरभिनिर्मितोऽभूत् ॥ अद्राक्षीद्बोधिसत्त्वस्तं भिक्षुं शान्तं दान्तं संयतं ब्रह्मचारिणमविक्षिप्तचक्षुर्युगमात्रप्रेक्षिणं प्रासादिकेनेर्यापथेन

---

१ "मृतु जम्बुद्वीपे" मृतो जम्बुद्वीपे "भूय मातृपितृ" भूयो मातापितरौ "पुत्रदारां" पुत्रदारान् "परलोकप्राप्तु" परलोकं प्राप्तः "भूय ज्ञातिं" भूयो ज्ञातिं ।

२ "आरोग्य" आरोग्येण "पुरुषो" पुरुषस्य "न चिरस्थितेन" अचिरस्थायिनेत्यर्थः ।

३ "जर न भवेया" जरा न भवेत् "तथपि च" तथापि च "महदुःखं" महादुःखं "पञ्च स्कन्धं धरन्तो" पञ्च स्कन्धान्धारयतः पञ्चेन्द्रियाणि धारयतः "पुन जरव्याधिमृत्यु" पुनर्जराव्याधिमृत्यवः "प्रतिनिवर्त्यं" प्रतिनिवर्त्यैव ।

सम्यक् प्रासादिकेनाभिक्रमप्रतिक्रमेण सम्यक् प्रासादिकेनालोकितव्यवलोकितेन प्रासादिकेन सङ्घाटीपिण्डपात्रचीवरधारणेन मार्गे स्थितं। दृष्ट्वा च पुनर्बोधिसत्त्वो जानन्नेव सारथिमिदमवोचत्।

किं सारथे पुरुष शान्त प्रशान्तचित्तो
नोत्क्षिप्तचक्षु व्रजते युगमात्रदर्शी।
काषायवस्त्रवसनो सुप्रशान्तचारी
पात्रं गृहीत न च उद्धत उन्नतो वा (१)॥

सारथिराह।

एषो हि देवपुरुष इति भिक्षुनामा
अपहाय कामरतयः सुविनीतचारी।
प्रव्रज्यप्राप्तः शममात्मन एषमाणो
संरागद्वेषविगतो तिष्ठति पिण्डचर्या (२)॥

बोधिसत्त्व आह।

साधु सुभाषितमिदं मम रोचते च
प्रव्रज्य नाम विदुभिः सततं प्रशस्ता।
हितमात्मनश्च परसत्त्वहितश्च यत्र
सुखजीवितं सुमधुरममृतं फलञ्च (३)॥

---

१ "पुरुष" पुरुषः "नोत्क्षिप्तचक्षु व्रजत" चानुत्क्षिप्तचक्षुर्व्रजति "वसन। सुप्रशान्त" वसनः सुप्रशान्त "गृहील" गृहीत्वा।

२ "कामरतयः" कामरतीः "प्रव्रज्यप्राप्तः" प्रव्रज्यां प्राप्तः "एषमाणो" एषमाणः "संरागद्वेषविगतो तिष्ठति" संरागद्वेषविगत आतिष्ठति "पिण्डचर्या" पिण्डचर्यां।

३ "प्रव्रज्य नाम विदुभिः" प्रव्रज्या नाम विद्वद्भिः।

अथ खलु भिक्षवो बोधिसत्त्वः प्रतिनिवर्त्त्य तं रथवरं पुनरपि पुरवरं प्राविशत् ॥ इति हि भिक्षवो राजा शुद्धोदनो बोधिसत्त्वस्येमामेवंरूपां सञ्चोदनां दृष्ट्वा च भूयस्या मात्रया बोधिसत्त्वस्य परिरक्षणार्थं प्राकारान् मापयते स्म । परिखाः खानयति स्म । द्वाराणि च गाढानि कारयति स्म । आरक्षान् स्थापयति स्म । शूरांश्चोदयति स्म । वाहनानि योजयति स्म । वर्म्माणि ग्राहयति स्म । चतुर्षु नगरद्वारेषु शृङ्गाटकेषु चतुरो महासेनाव्यूहान् स्थापयति स्म बोधिसत्त्वस्य परिरक्षणार्थं । य एनं रात्रिंदिवं रक्षन्ति स्म मा बोधिसत्त्वोऽभिनिष्क्रमिष्यतीति (१) ॥ अन्तःपुरे आज्ञान्ददाति स्म । मा स्म कदाचिच्च सङ्गीतिं विच्छेत्स्यथ । सर्व्वरतिक्रीडाश्चोपसंहर्त्तव्याः स्त्रीमायाश्चोपदर्शयत निर्ब्बध्नीत कुमारं यथानुरक्तचित्तो न निर्गच्छेत् प्रव्रज्यायै ॥

तत्रेदमुच्यते ।

द्वारे स्थापित युद्धशौण्ड पुरुषाः खड्गायुधापाणयो
हस्तीअश्वरथाश्च वर्म्मित वरा आरूढ नागावली ।
परिखा खाटक तोरणाश्च महता प्राकार उत्थापिता
द्वारा बद्ध सुगाढबन्धनकृता क्रोशस्वरानुश्रवणाः (१) ॥

---

१ अभिनिष्क्रमतीति ।

२ “ स्थापित युद्धशौण्ड ” स्थापिता युद्धशौण्डाः “ खड्गायुधापाणयः ” खड्गायुधपाणयः “ हस्तीअश्वरथाश्च वर्म्मित ” हस्त्यश्वरथाश्च वर्म्मिताः “ आरूढ नागावली ” आरूढा नागावलिं “ परिखाः खाटक ” परिखा खातकाः “ महता ” महति “ द्वाराबद्ध ” द्वाराण्याबद्धानि “ सुगाढबन्धनकृता ” सुगाढबन्धनैः “ क्रोशस्वरानुश्रवणाः ” क्रोशमात्रस्वरश्रावणानि ।

सर्व्वे शाक्यगणा विघ्नमनसो रक्षन्ति रात्रिंदिवं
निर्घोषस्य बलस्य तस्य महतः शब्दो महाञ्छ्रूयते ।
नगरं व्याकुल भीतविघ्नमनसो मास्माह् व्रजेत् सूरतो
माभूच्छाक्यकुलोदितस्य गमनं छिद्येत वंशो ह्ययं (१) ॥
आज्ञप्तो युवतीजनस्य सततं सङ्गीति मा छेत्स्यथाऽ-
वस्थानं प्रकरोथ क्रीडरतिभिर्निर्बन्ध्यथा मानसं ।
ये वा इङ्गितयमाय नेक विविधा दर्शेथ चेष्टां बहु
आरक्षां प्रकरोथ विघ्न कुरुथा मा सुव्रजेत् सूरतः (२) ॥
तस्या निष्क्रमिकालि सारथिवरे पूर्व्वे निमित्ता इमे
हंसक्रौञ्चमयूरशारिकशुका नो ते रवं मुञ्चिषुः ।
प्रासादेषु गवाक्षतोरणवरेष्वाताशमञ्चेषु च
जिह्माजिह्मसुदुर्मनाः सुदुःखिता ध्यायन्त्यधोमूर्द्धकाः (३) ॥
पुष्किनीपुष्करिणीषु पद्म हरिताऽम्लानानि म्लायन्ति च
वृक्षाः शुष्कपलाशपुष्परहिताः पुष्पन्ति भूयो न च ।
वीणावल्लकिवंशतन्त्रिरचितास्छिद्यन्ति कस्मात्तदा

---

१ "नगरं" अत्र नगर शब्देन नगरवासिजना लक्ष्यन्ते "व्याकुल भीतविघ्नमनसो" व्याकुलं भीतविघ्नमनः "सूरतो" सुरतो ।

२ "सङ्गीति माछेत्स्यथा" सङ्गीतिं मा छिन्त "प्रकरोथ" प्रकुरुत "क्रीडरतिभिर्निर्बन्ध्यथा" क्रीडारतिभिर्निर्बध्नीत "ये वा इङ्गियमाय नेक" या वा कौमाया अनेकाः "दर्शेथ चेष्टां बहु" दर्शयत चेष्टा बह्वीः "प्रकरोथ" प्रकुरुत "विघ्न कुरुथा" विघ्नं कुरुत "सूरतः" सुरतः ।

३ "तस्या निष्क्रमिकालि" तस्य निष्क्रमकाले "सारथिवरे" हे सारथिवर "पूर्व्वे निमित्ता इमे" पूर्व्वाणि निमित्तानि इमानि "शारिकशुकाः" शारिकाशुकाः "मुञ्चिषु" मुञ्चन्ति "जिह्माजिह्मसुदुर्मना" जिह्माजिह्मसुदुर्मनसः ।

भेरीश्चैव मृदङ्ग पाणिभिहतो भिद्यन्ति नो वादिषु (१) ॥
सर्वं व्याकुलमासीत्तच नगरं निद्राभिभूतं भृशं
नो नृत्ये न च गायने न रमिते भूयो मनः कस्यचित् ।
राजाऽपि परमं सुदीनमनसश्चिन्तापरो ध्यायते
हा धिक् शाक्यकुलस्य ऋद्धि विपुलामाहैव सन्त्यक्ष्यते (२) ॥
एकस्मिञ्छयने स्थितमभूद्गोपा तथा पार्थिवो
गोपा रात्रिय अर्द्धकालसमये स्वप्नानिमां पश्यति ।
सर्वेयं पृथिवी प्रकम्पितमभूच्छैलाश्चकूटावती
वृक्षा मारुतईरिताः क्षितिपति उत्पाट्य मूलोद्धृताः (३) ।
चन्द्रादित्य न भातु भूमिपतितौ सज्योतिषां खचितौ
केशानद्राक्षि लून दक्षिणभुजे मुकुटश्च विध्वंसितं ।
हस्तौ छिन्न तथैव छिन्न चरणौ नग्नाद्रशी आत्मनं
मुक्ताहार तथैव मेखलमपी छिन्नाद्रशी आत्मनः (४) ॥

---

१ "पणव वधिराऽवाद्यानि" पणवानि वधिराणि वाद्यानि "वीणावल्लकिवंश-तन्त्रिरचिताः" वीणावल्लकीवंशतन्त्रीरचिताः "भेरीश्चैव" भेर्यश्चैव "मृदङ्ग" मृदङ्गाः "भिद्यन्ति" वादने न भिन्ना भवन्ति इत्यर्थः "वादिषु" वाद्येषु ।

२ "सुदीनमनसः" सुदीनमनाः "ऋद्धिविपुलामाहैव सन्त्यक्ष्यते" ऋद्धिर्विपुला चाहैवं सन्त्यक्षति ।

३ "स्थितमभूद्गोपा" स्थिताऽभूद्गोपा "रात्रिय" रात्र्याः "स्वप्नानिमां पश्यति" स्वप्नानिमानपश्यत् "प्रकम्पितमभूत्" प्रकम्पिताऽभूत् "शैलाश्चकूटावती" सकूट-शैलवती "मारुत ईरिता" मारुतेरिताः "क्षितिपति" क्षितिं प्रति पतिता इत्यर्थः ।

४ "चन्द्रादित्य न भातु" चन्द्रसूर्यौ न भातः "केशानद्राक्षि लून" केशानद्राक्षी-लूनान् "दक्षिणभुजे" दक्षिणभुजेन "छिन्न तथैव छिन्न" छिन्नौ तथैव छिन्नौ "नग्ना द्रशी आत्मनं" नग्नामद्राक्षीदात्मानं "मुक्ताहारतथैव" मुक्ताहारैस्तथैव "द्रशी-आत्मनः" अद्राक्षीत् आत्मनःपदमैरित्यर्थः ।

अथन स्माद्रक्षि छिन्न पाद चतुरो धरणीतलस्मिं स्वपी
छत्रे दण्ड सुचित्र श्रीमरुचिरं छिन्ना द्रक्षी पार्थिवे ।
सर्व्वे आभरणा विकीर्णि पतिता मुह्यन्ति ते वारिणा
भर्त्तुश्चाभरणा सवस्त्रमुकुटां शय्यागता व्याकुला (१) ॥
उल्कां पश्यति निष्क्रमन्ति नगरात्तमसाभिभूतं पुरं
छिन्नाञ्जालिकमद्रक्षि सुपिने रत्नामिकां शोभनां ।
मुक्ताहार प्रलम्बमान पतिताः क्षुभितो महासागरो
मेरुं पर्व्वतराजमद्रक्षि तदा स्थानात्तु सङ्कम्पितं (२) ॥
एतानीदृश शाक्यकन्य सुपिनां सुपिनान्तरे अद्रक्षी
बुद्धा सा प्रतिबुद्ध अश्रुनयना स्वं स्वामिनमब्रवीत् ।
देवा किं म भविष्यते वद भणा सुपिनान्तराणीदृशां
भ्रान्ता मे स्मृति नो च पश्यमि पुनः शोकार्दितं मे मनः (३) ॥
श्रुत्वाऽसौ कलविङ्कदुन्दुभिरुतो ब्रह्मस्वरः सुस्वरो

---

१ "अथनस्माद्रक्षि छिन्न पाद" अथ स्माद्राक्षीच्छिन्नान् पादान् "धरणीतलस्मिं स्वपी" धरणीतले स्थापितान् "छत्रे दण्ड सुचित्र" छत्रं दण्डं सुचित्रं "श्रीमरुचिरं" श्रीमद्रुचिरं "छिन्ना द्रक्षी पार्थिवे" छिन्नमद्राक्षीत्पार्थिवस्य "सर्व्वे आभरणा विकीर्णि पतिता" सर्व्वाणि आभरणानि विकीर्णानि पतितानि "भर्त्तुश्चाभरणा सवस्त्रमुकुटां" भर्त्तुश्चाभरणानि सवस्त्रमुकुटानि ।

२ "पश्यति निष्क्रमन्ति" पश्यतोऽभिनिष्क्रमन्तीं "छिन्नाञ्जालिकमद्रक्षि सुपिने" छिन्नाम् जालिकामद्राक्षीत् स्वप्ने "रत्नामिकां शोभनां" रत्नात्मिकाम् शोभनाम् "मुक्ताहार प्रलम्बमान पतिताः क्षुभितो महासागरः" मुक्ताहारान् प्रलम्बमानान् पतितान् क्षुभितं महासागरं "पर्व्वतराजमद्रक्षि" पर्व्वतराजमद्राक्षीत् ।

३ "एतानीदृश शाक्यकन्य" एतानीदृशान् शाक्यकन्या "सुपिनां सुपिनान्तरे अद्रक्षी" स्वप्नान् स्वप्नान्तरे स्वप्नदशायां अद्राक्षीत् "प्रतिबुद्ध" प्रतिबुद्धा "देवा किं म भविष्यते" देव किं मे भविष्यति "भणा सुपिनान्तराणीदृशां" भण स्वप्नान्तराणि दृष्टानि मया दृष्टानीति शेषः "स्मृतिनो" स्मृतिर्नो "पश्यमि" पश्यामि ।

गोपामाखपते भव प्रमुदिता पापं न ते विद्यते।
ये सत्त्वाः कृतपुण्यपूर्व्वचरिता द्रक्ष्यन्ति स्वप्ना इमे
कोऽन्यः पश्यत्यनेकदुःखविहितः स्वप्नान्तराणीदृशां (१)।

यत्ते दृष्टा मेदिनी कम्पमाना
कूटाशैला मेदिनीये पतन्ता।
देवा नागा राक्षसा भूतसङ्घाः
सर्व्वे तुभ्यं पूज्यश्रेष्ठां करोन्ति (२)॥
यत्ते दृष्टा वृक्षमूलोद्धृतानि
केशा लूनां दक्षिणेना हृताषि।
क्षिप्रं गोपे क्लेशजालं छिनित्वा
दृष्टीजालं उद्धरी संस्कृततः (३)॥
यत्ते दृष्टौ चन्द्रसूर्य्यौ पतन्तौ
दृष्टा नक्षत्रा ज्योतिषाणी पतन्तः।
क्षिप्रं गोपे क्लेशप्रचूर्णि हत्वा
पूज्या लोके भाविनी त्वं प्रशंस्या (४)॥

---

१ "द्रक्ष्यन्ति स्वप्ना इमे" पश्यन्ति स्वप्नानिमान् "स्वप्नान्तराणीदृशां" स्वप्नान्तराणीदृशानि।

२ "कूटाशैला मेदिनीये पतन्ता" कूटशैला मेदिन्यां पतन्तः "तुभ्यं" त्वां "करोन्ति" करिष्यन्ति।

३ "दृष्टा वृक्षमूलोद्धृतानि" दृष्टानि वृक्षमूलानि उद्धृतानि "केशा लूनां दक्षिणेनाहृताषि" केशान् लूनान् दक्षिणेनाहस्तेनः "छिनित्वा" छित्वा "दृष्टीजालं" दृष्टिजालं "उद्धरी संस्कृततः" उद्धरिष्यसि संस्कृततः संस्कारत इत्यर्थः।

४ "दृष्टा नक्षत्रा ज्योतिषाणी पतन्तः" दृष्टानि नक्षत्राणि ज्योतींषि पतन्ति "क्लेशप्रचूर्णि" क्लेशप्रचुरम्।

यत्ते दृष्टो मुक्तहारं विशीर्णं
नग्नं सर्व्वं कायमीदृग्दृशासि ।
क्षिप्रं गोपे स्त्रीकायं जहित्वा
पुरुषत्वं वै भेष्यसे नाचिरेण (१) ॥
यत्ते दृष्टं मञ्चकं छिन्नपादं
छत्रे दण्डे रत्नचित्रं प्रभग्नं ।
क्षिप्रं गोपे ओघ चत्वारि तीर्णा
मां द्रक्ष्यसि एकच्छत्रं त्रिलोके (२) ॥
यत्ते दृष्टा भूषणा उह्यमाना
चूडा वक्त्रा मह्यमह्ये दृशासि ।
क्षिप्रं गोपे लक्षणैर्भूषिताङ्गं
मां सम्पश्यी सर्व्वलोकैः स्तुवन्तं (३) ॥
यत्ते दृष्टा दीपकोटीशतानि
नगराभिनिष्क्रान्तं तत्पुरञ्चान्धकारं ।
क्षिप्रं गोपे मोहविद्यान्धकारे
प्रज्ञालोकं कुर्व्वमी सर्व्वलोके (४) ॥

---

१ "यत्ते" यच्चयेति सम्बन्धावबोध्यं "मुक्तहारं विशीर्णं" मुक्ताहारो विशीर्णः "कायमीदृग्दृशासि" कायमीदृशमद्राक्षीः "स्त्रीकायं जहित्वा" स्त्रीकायं त्यक्त्वा "भेष्यसे नाचिरेण" भविष्यसि अचिरेण ।

२ "दृष्टं मञ्चकं छिन्नपादं" दृष्टो मञ्चकश्छिन्नपादः "छत्रे दण्डे रत्नचित्रं प्रभग्नं" छत्रं दण्डो रत्नचित्रः प्रभग्नः "ओघ चत्वारि तीर्णा" ओघांश्चतुरस्तीर्णा ।

३ "दृष्टा भूषणा उह्यमाना" दृष्टानि भूषणानि उह्यमानानि "चूडा वक्त्रा मह्य-मह्ये दृशासि" चूडां वक्त्राणि मम मध्ये चाद्राक्षीः "सम्पश्यी" सन्द्रक्ष्यसि ।

४ "दृष्टा दीपकोटीशतानि" दृष्टानि दीपकोटिशतानि "नगराभिनिष्क्रान्तं" नगरा-भिनिष्क्रान्तानि "तत्पुरञ्चान्धकारं" तत्पुरी चान्धकारा "मोहविद्यान्धकारे" मोहविद्यान्धकारे "कुर्व्वमी" करिष्यामि ।

यत्ते दृष्टं मुक्तहारं प्रभग्नं
छिन्नञ्चैव स्वर्णसूत्रं विचित्रं ।
क्षिप्रं गोपे क्लेशजालं छिनित्वा
सञ्ज्ञासूत्रमुद्धरी संस्कृतात्तः (१) ॥
यत्ते गोपे चित्रकारं करोषि
नित्यं पूजां गौरवेणोत्तमेन ।
नास्ती तुभ्यं दुर्गतिर्नैव शोकः
क्षिप्रम्भाषी प्रीतिप्रामोद्यलाभाः (२) ॥
पूर्व्वे मह्यं दान दत्तं प्रणीतं
शीलं चीर्णं भाविता नित्य क्षान्तिः ।
तस्मान्मह्यं ये प्रसादं लभन्ते
सर्व्वे भान्ति प्रीतिप्रामोद्यलाभाः (३) ॥
कल्पाकोटी संस्कृता मे अनन्ता
बोधेर्मार्गो शोधितो मे प्रणीतः ।
तस्मान्मह्यं ये प्रसादं करोन्ति
सर्व्वे छिन्नास्तेषु त्रीण्यपायाः (४) ॥

---

१ "दृष्टं मुक्तहारं प्रभग्नं" दृष्टो मुक्ताहारः प्रभग्नः "छिनित्वा" छित्त्वा "सञ्ज्ञासूत्रमुद्धरी संस्कृतात्तः" सञ्ज्ञासूत्रमुद्धरिष्यामि संस्कृततः ।

२ "यत्ते" यत्त्वं "चित्रकारं" चित्रं करोति शेषः "करोषि" अकरोः "नास्ती तुभ्यं" नास्ति तव "क्षिप्रं भाषी" क्षिप्रं भविष्यन्ति ।

३ "पूर्व्वे मह्यं दान" पूर्व्वं मया दानं "नित्य" नित्यं "तस्मान्मह्यं" तस्मान्मम "लभन्ते" लप्स्यन्ते "सर्व्वे भान्ति" सर्व्वेषां तेषां भविष्यन्ति इत्यर्थः ।

४ "कल्पाकोटीसंस्कृताः" कल्पकोटिसंस्काराः "बोधेर्मार्गो शोधितो" बोधिमार्गः शोधितः "तस्मान्मह्यं" तस्मान्मम "करोन्ति" करिष्यन्ति "छिन्नास्तेषु" छिन्नास्तेषां "त्रीण्यपायाः" त्रयोऽप्यपायाः ।

हर्षं विन्दा मा च खेदं जनेहि
तुष्टिं विन्दा सञ्जनेही च प्रीतिं ।
क्षिप्रभेष्ये प्रीतिप्रामोद्यलाभी
मेहि गोपे भद्रकाते निमित्ताः (१) ॥

सो पुण्यतेजभरितो शिरितेजगर्भो
पूर्वं निमित्त सुपिने इमि अद्राक्षीति ।
ये भोन्ति पूर्वशुभकर्मसमुच्चयानां
निष्क्रम्यकालसमये नरपुङ्गवानां (२) ॥
सो अद्राक्षीति च करां चरणा विशालं
महसागरेभि चतुभिर्जल लोडयन्ता ।
सर्वामिमां वसुमतीं शयनं विशिष्टं
मेरुञ्च पर्वतवरं शिरसोपधानं (३) ॥
आभा प्रमुक्त सुपिने तद अद्राक्षीति
लोके विलोकितु महान्तमसान्धकारं ।
छत्रोद्गतं धरणितो स्फुरते त्रिलोकं

---

१ "विन्दा" विन्द "जनेहि" जनय "विन्दा" विन्द "सञ्जनेही" सञ्जनय "क्षिप्रम् भेष्ये प्रीतिप्रामोद्यलाभी मेहि" क्षिप्रं भविष्यसि प्रीतिप्रामोद्यलाभा एवि "भद्रकाते" भद्रकाणि तानि "निमित्ताः" निमित्तानि ।

२ "सो पुण्यतेजभरितो शिरितेजगर्भो" स पुण्यतेजोभरितः श्रीतेजोगर्भः "पूर्वं निमित्त सुपिने इमि अद्राक्षीति" पूर्वनिमित्तानि स्वप्ने इमानि अद्राक्षीत् "निष्क्रम्यकालसमये" निष्क्रमणकालसमये ।

३ "सो अद्राक्षीति च" सोऽद्राक्षीच "करां चरणा विशालं" करान् चरणानि विशालानि "महसागरेभि चतुर्भिर्जल" महासागरैश्चतुर्भिर्जले "लोडयन्ता" लोडयमानाम् "शिरसोपधानं" शिरउपधानं ।

आभा यस्य स्पृष्ट विनिपातदुःखा प्रशान्ताः (१) ॥
छन्नाः प्रभावचतुरि पाशिकपादलेखा
चतुर्वर्ण एकशकुनाकुल एकवर्णः ।
मीढगिरी परमहीन जुगुप्सनीयो
अभिभूय चङ्क्रमति तत्र च नोपलिप्तो (२) ॥
भूयोऽद्राक्षी सुपिनि नद्य जलप्रपूर्णाः
बहुसत्त्वकोटिनियुतानि च उह्यमानाः ।
सो नाव कृत्व प्रतरित्व पारं प्रतार्य
स्थापेति सो स्थलवरे अभये अशोके (३) ॥
भूयोऽद्राक्षि बहुआतुर रोगस्पृष्टा
आरोग्यतेजरहिता बलविप्रहीनां ।
सो वैद्यभूत बहु औषध सम्प्रयच्छा
मोचेति सत्त्वनियुतां बहुरोगस्पृष्टां (४) ॥

---

१ "आभाप्रमुक्त सुपिने तदद्राक्षीति" आभां प्रमुक्तां स्वप्ने तदा अद्राक्षीत् "त्रिलोकितु महान्तमसान्धकारं" त्रिलोक्यां महातमसोऽन्धकारं "हयोद्गतं चरणि स्फुरते त्रिलोक" हयमुद्गतं चरण्यां स्फुरति त्रिलोक्यां "यस्य स्पृष्ट" येन स्पृष्टा तस्य "विनिपातदुःखाः" विनिपातदुःखानि "प्रशान्ताः" प्रशान्तानि ।

२ "चतुरिपाशिकपादलेखाः" चतस्रः पाशिपादलेखाः "एकशकुनाकुल" एकशकुनोऽकुलः "मीढगिरी परमहीनजुगुप्सनीयो" मीढगिरिः परमहीनो जुगुप्सनीयः "नोपलिप्तो" अनुपलिप्तः ।

३ "भूयो दृष्टी सुपिनि नद्य जलप्रपूर्णा" भूयोऽद्राक्षील्स्वप्नेनदीर्जलप्रपूर्णाः "उह्यमानाः" उह्यमानानि "सो नावकृत्व प्रतरित्व" सनावं कृत्वा प्रतीर्य "स्थापेति सो स्थलवरे" अस्थापयत् स स्थलवरे ।

४ "भूयोऽद्राक्षि" भूयोऽद्राक्षीत् "बहुआतुर" बह्वातुराम् "आरोग्यतेजरहितां बलविप्रहीनां" आरोग्यतेजोरहिताम् बलविप्रहीनाम् "सो वैद्यभूत बहु औषध" स वैद्यभूतो बहूनि औषधानि "सम्प्रयच्छा" सम्प्रदाय "मोचेति सत्त्वनियुतां बहुरोगस्पृष्टां" मोचयत् सत्त्वनियुतानि बहुरोगस्पृष्टानि ।

सिंहासने च त्वि निषद्य सुमेरुपृष्ठे
शिष्यां कृताञ्जलिपुटा नमरोनमन्तां ।
चन्द्राननश्च यथु पश्यसि आत्मनश्च
आनन्दप्रश्रब्धमनरीं गगने सुवक्तः (१) ॥
एवंविधा सुपिनि पश्यसि बोधिसत्त्वो
मञ्जुक्षोभनरतस्य च यानि पुरि ।
यां श्रुत्व देवमनुजा अभवन् प्रहृष्टा
न चिराद्भविष्यति अयं नरदेवदेव (२) इति ॥

इति स्वप्नपरिवर्त्तो नाम चतुर्दशोऽध्यायः ॥ १४ ॥

पञ्चदशोऽध्यायः ॥

अथ खलु भिक्षवो बोधिसत्त्वस्यैतदभूत्। अयुक्तमेतन्मम स्याद-
कृतज्ञता च यदहमप्रतिवेद्य महाराज्ञः शुद्धोदनस्यानुज्ञा-
तस्य पित्रा निष्क्रमेयं ॥ स रात्रौ प्रशान्तायां स्वकादुपस्थान-
प्रासादादवतीर्य्य राज्ञः शुद्धोदनस्य प्रासादतले प्रतिष्ठितोऽभूत्॥

प्रतिष्ठितमात्रस्य च पुनर्बोधिसत्त्वस्य सर्व्वोऽसौ प्रासाद आ-
भया स्फुटोऽभूत्॥ तत्र राजा प्रतिविबुद्धस्तां प्रभामद्राक्षीत्।
दृष्ट्वा च पुनस्त्वरितं त्वरितं काञ्चुकीयमामन्त्रयति स्म । किं भोः
काञ्चुकीय सूर्य्योऽभ्युद्गतो येनेयं भा प्रविराजते ॥

---

१ "निषद्य" निषद्यः "शिष्यां कृताञ्जलिपुटानमरोनमन्तां" शिष्यान् कृता-ञ्जलिपुटांश्चानुनमतः "चन्द्राननश्च" चन्द्राननञ्च "यथु पश्यसि" अपश्यदद्राक्षीत् "आनन्दप्रश्रब्धमनरीं गगने सुवक्तः" आनन्दप्रश्रब्धमनरान् गगने सुवक्तः ।

२ "एवंविधा सुपिन पश्यसि" एवं विधान् स्वप्नान् अद्राक्षीत् "यानि पुरि" ये पूर्वं "यां श्रुत्व" यान् श्रुत्वा ।

काञ्चुकीय आह । अद्यापि तावद्देव रजन्या उपार्द्धं नातिक्रान्तमपि वा देव ।

सूर्य्यंप्रभाय भवते द्रुमगुल्मछाया
सन्तापयति च तनुम्प्रकरोति वर्णं ।
हंसामयूरशुककोकिलचक्रवाकाः
प्रत्यूषकालसमये स्वरुतां रवन्ति (१) ॥
आभा इयन्तु नरदेव सुखा मनोज्ञा
प्राह्लादनी शुभकरी न करोति दाहं ।
कुर्वीत इच्छा अभि भूय न चास्ति कायो
निःसंशयं गुणधरो इह अद्य प्राप्तः (२) ॥
सो प्रेक्षते इमदिशो नृपतिर्निषण्णो
वृक्षेषु सोऽन्तिकेऽमलशोभन शुद्धसत्त्वः ।
सोऽभ्युत्थितुं शयनमिच्छति न प्रभोति
पितु गौरवं जनयते यशशुद्धबुद्धिः (३) ॥

सो चालितो हि पुरतो नृपतिमवोचत्
मा भूयु विघ्न प्रकरोहि मा चैव खेदं ।
नैष्क्रम्यकालसमयो मम देव युक्तो

---

१ “ सूर्य्यंप्रभाय भवते ” सूर्य्यप्रभया भवति “ हंसामयूर ” हंसमयूर “ स्वरुतां रवन्ति ” स्वरुतीं रवन्ति ।

२ “ इच्छा अभि भूय न ” इच्छामभिभूयो न “ गुणधरो इह ” गुणधर इह ।

३ “ सो प्रेक्षते इमदिशो ” स प्रेक्षते इमदिशु “ अमलशोभन ” अमलशोभनः “ सोऽभ्युत्थितुं ” सोऽभ्युत्थातुं “ शयनमिच्छति ” शयनादिच्छति “ न प्रभोति ” न प्रभवति “ पितु गौरवं जनयते ” पितुर्गौरवं जनयति ;

क्षमस्व नृपते स्वजनः सराष्ट्रः (१) ॥
तमश्रुपूर्णनयनो नृपतिर्बभाषे
किञ्चित्प्रयोजन भवेद्विनिवर्त्तने ते ।
किं याचसे मम वरं वद सर्व्व दास्ये
अनुगृह्य राजकुल माञ्च इदञ्च राष्ट्रं (२) ॥
तद बोधिसत्त्व अवची मधुरप्रलापी
इच्छामि देव चतुरो वर तान्मि देहि ।
यदि शक्यसे ददितु मह्य वसोमि तत्र
तद्द्रक्ष्यसे सद गृहे न च निष्क्रमिष्ये (३) ॥
इच्छामि देव जर मह्य न आक्रमेया
शुभवर्णयौवनस्थितो भवि नित्यकालं ।
आरोग्यप्राप्तु भवि नो च भवेत व्याधि-
रमितायुषश्च भवि नो च भवेत मृत्युः (४) ॥
सम्पत्तितश्च विपुला न भवेद्विपत्ती
राजा श्रुणित्व वचनं परमं दुःखार्त्तो ।

---

१ "सो च" स च "मा भूयु विघ्न" मा भूयो विघ्नं "प्रकरोहि" प्रकुरु "नैष्क्रम्यकालसमयः" निष्क्रमणकालसमयः "यथ" यथा ।

२ "प्रयोजन" प्रयोजनं "मम" मत्त इत्यर्थः "सर्व्वदास्ये" सर्व्वं दास्ये "अनुगृह्य" अनुगृहाण "राजकुल" राजकुलं ।

३ "तद बोधिसत्त्व अवची" तदा बोधिसत्त्वोऽवोचत् "वर तान्मि" वरांस्तान्मे "ददितुं" दातुं "मह्य वसोमि" मम वसतिः "सद" सदा ।

४ "जर मह्य न आक्रमेया" जरा मां न आक्रमेत "भवि" भवानि "आरोग्यप्राप्तु भवि" आरोग्यप्राप्तो भवानि "भवेत" भवेत् "अमितायुषश्च भवि" अमितायुषश्च भवानि "भवेत" भवेत् ।

अस्थान याचसि कुमार न मेऽत्र शक्तिः
जरव्याधिमृत्युभयतश्च विपत्तितश्च (१) ॥
कल्पस्थितीय ऋषयो हि न जातु मुक्ताः
श्रुत्वा वचनमथ पितुः कुमारोऽवोची ।
यदिदानि देव चतुरो वर नो ददासि
जरव्याधिमृत्युभयतश्च विपत्तितश्च (२) ॥
हन्तं शृणुष्व नृपते अपरं वरैकं
अस्माच्च्युतस्य प्रतिसन्धि न मे भवेया ।
श्रुत्वैवमेव वचनं नरपुङ्गवस्य
तृष्णा तनुत्व करि छिन्दति पुत्रप्रेमं (३) ॥
अनुमोदमी हितकरा जगति प्रमोक्षं
अभिप्राय तुभ्य परिपूर्य्यतु यन्मतन्ते (४) ।

अथ खलु भिक्षवो बोधिसत्त्वः प्रतिक्रम्य स्वके प्रासादेऽभिरुह्य शयने निषसाद ॥ न चास्य कश्चिद्गमनं वा आगमनं वा जानीते स्म ॥ इति हि भिक्षवो राजा शुद्धोदनस्तस्या रात्र्या अत्ययेन सर्व्वः शाक्यगण. सन्निपत्यैनां प्रकृतिमारोच-

---

१ "शृणिम" श्रुत्वा "अस्थान याचसि" अस्थानमयोग्यं याचसे इत्यर्थः "जरव्याधिमृत्युभयतश्च" जराव्याधिमृत्युभयतश्च ।

२ "कल्पस्थितीय" कल्पपर्य्यन्तं तपस्तप्त्वा स्थिता ऋषि इत्यर्थः "कुमारोऽवोची" कुमारोऽवोचत् "यदि दानि" यदीदानीं "वर नो" वरान् "जरव्याधिमृत्युभयतश्च" जराव्याधिमृत्युभयतश्च ।

३ "हन्तं" हन्त "अस्माच्च्युतस्य प्रतिसन्धि नमे भवेया" अस्माच्च्युतस्य प्रतिसन्धिर्न मे भवेत् "तृष्णा तनुत्व करि" तृष्णां तनीं कृत्वा यः पुत्रप्रेमो जायते तं छिन्दति इत्यर्थः ।

४ "अनुमोदमी" अनुमोदनीयः "हितकरा" हे हितकर "प्रमोक्षं" प्रमोक्षः "अभिप्राय तुभ्य" अभिप्रायस्तव ।

यति स्म । अभिनिष्क्रमिष्यति कुमारस्तत् किं करिष्यामः ॥

शाक्या आहुः । रक्षां देव करिष्यामः । तत् कस्मात् ॥

अयञ्च महाञ्छाक्यगणः । स चैकाकी । तत् का तस्य शक्ति-रस्मादभिनिष्क्रमितुं ॥

तत्र तै राज्ञा शुद्धोदनेन च पञ्च शाक्यकुमारशतानि कृता-स्त्राणि कृतयोग्यानीष्वस्त्रशिक्षितानि महानग्नबलोपेतानि पूर्व्वे नगरद्वारे स्थापितान्यभवन् बोधिसत्त्वस्याऽऽरक्षणार्थं । एकैकश्च शाक्यकुमारः पञ्चरथशतपरिवारः एकैकश्च रथः पञ्चपत्ति-शतपरिवारः स्थापितोऽभूद्बोधिसत्त्वस्य रक्षणार्थं । एवं दक्षिणे पश्चिमे उत्तरे नगरद्वारे पञ्च पञ्च शाक्यकुमारशतानि कृता-स्त्राणि कृतयोग्यानि इष्वस्त्रशिक्षितानि महानग्नबलोपेतानि । एकैकश्च शाक्यकुमारः पञ्चरथशतपरिवारः एकैकश्चरथः पञ्चशतपत्तिपरिवारः स्थापितोऽभूद् बोधिसत्त्वस्य रक्षार्थं । महल्लकमहल्लिकाश्च शाक्याः सर्व्वचत्वरशृङ्गाटकयुगरथ्यास्वार-क्षार्थं स्थिता अभूवन् । राजा शुद्धोदनः पञ्चभिः कुमारशतैः सार्द्धं परिवृतः पुरस्कृतः स्वके गृहद्वारे हयेषु च गजेषु च समभिरुह्य जागर्त्ति स्म ॥

महाप्रजावती च गौतमी चेटीवर्गमामन्त्रयते स्म ।

द्वारे प्रदीप विमलां ध्वजाग्रि मणिरत्न विमल सर्व्वि स्थपेथा
ओलम्बयाथ हारां प्रभां कुरुत सर्व्व गेहेऽस्मिन् (१) ॥

---

१ "प्रदीपविमलां" प्रदीपान् विमलान् "ध्वजाग्रि मणिरत्न विमल सर्व्वि स्थपेथा" ध्वजाग्रे मणिरत्नानि विमलानि सर्व्वं स्थापयत "ओलम्बयाथ हारां" आलम्बयत हारान् "प्रभा" प्रभां "सर्व्व" सर्व्वस्मिन् ।

सङ्गीति योजयथा जागरथ अतन्द्रिता इमां रजनीं ।
प्रतिरक्षथा कुमारं यथाऽविदितो न गच्छेया (१) ॥
वर्मित कलापहस्ता असिधनुशरशक्तितोमरगृहीताः ।
प्रियतनयरक्षणार्थं करोथ सर्वे महायत्नं (२) ॥
द्वारां पिधेथ सर्वा सुयन्त्रितर्गडां दृढकपाटां ।
मुञ्चथ मा च अकाले मा चाप सत्व इति न व्रजेया (३) ॥
मणिहारमुक्ताहारान्मुक्तपुष्पके अर्द्धचन्द्रान् ।
घण्टाक्रमेखलकर्णिकमुद्रिक सुनिबद्धां नूपुरां कुरुत (४) ॥
यदि सहसा निष्क्रमेया नरमरुहित मत्तवारणविचारी ।
तथ तथ पराक्रमेथा यथा विघातं न विन्देया (५) ॥
या नारी शक्तिधारी नयनं परिवारयन्तु विमलाक्षम् ।
मा च भवथ सिद्धिविहताः पतङ्ग इव रक्षथा नेत्रैः (६) ॥
छादेथ रतनजालैरिदं गृहं पार्थिवस्य रक्षार्थं ।

---

१ "सङ्गीति योजयथा" सङ्गीतिं योजयत "जागरथ" जागृत "इमां रजनीं" अस्यां रजन्यां "प्रतिरक्षथा" प्रतिरक्षत "गच्छेया" गच्छेत्।

२ "वर्मित" वर्मिताः "असिधनु शरशक्ति" असिधनुः शरशक्ति "करोथ" कुरुत "सर्वे" सर्वाः ।

३ "द्वारां पिधेथ सर्वा" द्वाराणि पिधत्त सर्वाणि "सुयन्त्रितगंडां दृढकपाटां" सुयन्त्रितर्गलानि दृढकपाटानि "मुञ्चथ" मुञ्चत "व्रजेया" व्रजेत् ।

४ "मुक्तपुष्पके" मुक्तपुष्पकान् "घण्टाक्रमेखलकर्णिकमुद्रिक" घण्टाक्रमेखलाकर्णिकामुद्रिकान् "सुनिबद्ध" सुनिबद्धान् "नूपुरां" नूपुरान्।

५ "निष्क्रमेया" निष्क्रामेत् "नरमरुहित" नरमरुहितो "तथ तथ पराक्रमेथा" तथा तथा पराक्रमत "विन्देया" विन्देत्।

६ "नारी शक्तिधारिणी" नार्यः शक्तिधारिण्यः "भवथ" भवत "रक्षथा" रक्षत ।

वर्ष्टरवांश्च रवेथा इमां रजनीं रक्षथा विरजा (१) ॥
अन्योन्य बोधयथा मा वसेयथा रक्षथा इमां रजनीं ।
मा च अभिनिष्क्रमेथा विजस्य राजस्य राज्यस्य (२) ॥
एतस्य निर्गतस्य राजकुलं सर्व्विमं निरभिरम्यं ।
उच्छिन्नश्च भवेथा पार्थिववंशश्चिरानुबद्ध इति (३) ॥

अथ खलु भिक्षवोऽष्टाविंशतिमहायक्षसेनापतयः पाञ्चिकयक्षसेनापतिपूर्व्वङ्गमानि च पञ्चहारितीपुत्रशतान्येकस्मिन् सन्निपात्यैवं मतं विचारयन्ति स्म । अद्य मार्षा बोधिसत्त्वोऽभिनिष्क्रमिष्यति युष्माभिः पूजाकर्म्मणे औत्सुक्यमापत्तव्यं ॥

चत्वारश्च महाराजानो अडकवतीं राजधानीं प्रविश्य तां महतीं यक्षपर्षदमामन्त्रयते स्म । अद्य मार्षा बोधिसत्त्वोऽभिनिष्क्रमिष्यति । स युष्माभिर्हयचरणपरिगृहीतो निष्क्रामयितव्यः ॥
सा च यक्षपर्षदाह ।

वज्रदृढ अभेद्य नारायणो आत्मभावो
गुरुवीर्य्यबलउपेतु सोऽकम्पियो सर्व्वसत्त्वोत्तमः ।
गिरिरिव महामेरुरुत्पाद्य शक्यो नभ धारितुं केनचित्
न तु जिनगुणमेरुशैलेगुरुः पुण्यज्ञानाश्रितः शक्यते नेतुं काचित्(४)॥

---

१ "छादथ" छादयत "रतनजालैः" रत्नजालैः "रवेथा" रवीत "इमां रजनीं रक्षथ" अस्यां रजन्यां रक्षत "विरजा" विरजसं बोधिसत्त्वमित्यर्थः ।

२ "अन्योन्य बोधयथा" अन्योन्यं बोधयत "मा वसेयथा" मा वसत "रक्षथा इमां रजनीं" रक्षत अस्यां रजन्यां "अभिनिष्क्रमेथा" अभिनिष्क्रमेत् ।

३ "सर्व्विमं" सर्व्वमिदं "भवेथा" भवेत् ।

४ "अभेद्य नारायणो आत्मभावो" अभेद्यो नारायणतुल्यात्मभावो "गुरुवीर्य्यबलउपेतु" गुरुवीर्य्यबलोपेतः "सोऽकम्पियो" स अकम्प्यः "नभे धारितुं" नभसि धारयितुं ।

वैश्रवण आह ।

ये मानगर्व्वितनरा गुरुस्तेषु भ्रान्ता

ये प्रेमगौरवस्थिता लघु ते विज्ञाय ।

अध्याशयेन अभियुज्यथ गौरवेण

लघु तं हि वेत्स्यथ खगा इव द्रुमपक्षी (१) ॥

अहञ्च पुरतो यास्ये यूयञ्च व्रजथा वयं ।

नैष्क्रम्ये बोधिसत्त्वस्य पुण्यमार्गमो भवेत् (२) ॥

अथ खलु भिक्षवः शक्रो देवानामिन्द्रो देवांस्त्रयस्त्रिंशानामन्त्रयते स्म । अद्य मार्षा बोधिसत्त्वोऽभिनिष्क्रमिष्यति । तत्र युष्माभिः पूजाकर्म्मणे औत्सुक्येन भवितव्यं ॥

अहं तावत्कपिलवस्तुनि महानगरे सर्व्वस्त्रीपुरुषदारकदारिकाणामस्वापनं करिष्यामि । ललितव्यूहो नाम देवपुत्रः स एवमाह ॥

तत्र प्रशान्तसुमतिर्नाम देवपुत्रः स एवमाह । अहमपि सर्व्वहयगजखरोष्ट्रगोमहिषस्त्रीपुरुषदारकदारिकाणां शब्दमन्तर्द्धापयिष्यामि ॥

व्यूहमतिर्नाम देवपुत्रः स एवमाह । अहं गगनतले सप्तरथविस्तरप्रमाणरत्नवेदिकापरिवृतं सूर्य्यकान्तमणिरत्नप्रभोज्ज्वलितमुच्छ्रितच्छत्रध्वजपताकं नानापुष्पाभिकीर्णं नानागन्धधूप-

---

१ "मानगर्वित" मानगर्विताः "गुरुस्तु" गुरवोपां "अभियुज्यथ" अभियुज्यत ।
२ "व्रजथा" व्रजत "नैष्क्रम्ये" निष्क्रमणे "पुण्यमार्गमो" पुण्यमर्गविधायकः ।

वटिकानिर्धूपितं मार्गव्यूहं करिष्यामि । येन मार्गेण बोधिसत्त्वोऽभिनिष्क्रमिष्यति ॥

ऐरावणो नाम नागराजः स एवमाह । अहमपि च स्वस्यां शुण्डायां द्वात्रिंशद्योजनप्रमाणं कूटागारं मापयिष्यामि । यत्राप्सरसोऽभिरुह्य तूर्यसंगीतिसंप्रभणितेन महता गीतवादितेन बोधिसत्त्वस्योपस्थानपरिचर्यां कुर्वन्त्यो गमिष्यन्ति ॥

स्वयञ्च शक्रो देवानामिन्द्र एवमाह । अहं द्वाराणि विवरिष्यामि मार्गञ्च सन्दर्शयिष्यामि ॥

धर्मचारी देवपुत्र आह । अहं विकृतमन्तःपुरमुपदर्शयिष्यामि ॥

संचोदको देवपुत्र आह । अहं बोधिसत्त्वं शयनादुत्थापयिष्यामि ॥

तत्र वरुणश्च नाम नागराजो मनस्वी च नागराजः सागरश्च नागराजोऽनवतप्तश्च नागराजो नन्दोपनन्दौ नागराजावेवमाहुः । वयमपि बोधिसत्त्वस्य पूजाकर्मणे कालानुसारिमेघमभिनिर्माप्योरगसारचन्दनचूर्णवर्षमभिवर्षयिष्यामः ॥

इति हि भिक्षवो देवनागयक्षगन्धर्वैरायमेवंरूपाभिप्रायश्चिन्तितोऽभूत् व्यवसितश्च । बोधिसत्त्वस्यैव धर्मचिन्तामुपविष्टस्य संगीतिप्रासादेषु सुखशयनगतस्यान्तःपुरमध्यगतस्य पूर्वबुद्धचरितं विचिन्तयतः सर्वसत्त्वहितमनुचिन्तयतश्चत्वारि पूर्वप्रणिधानपदान्यामुखीभवन्ति स्म ॥

कतमानि चत्वारि । पूर्वं मया स्वयम्भुवामाधिपत्यमभि-

भवता सर्व्वज्ञतां प्रार्थयमानेनैवं सत्त्वार्थः सन्नद्धोऽभूत् । सत्त्वान् दुःखितान् दृष्ट्वा अहो बताहं संसारमहाचारकबन्धनप्रविष्टस्य लोकसन्निवेशस्य संसारचारकं भित्त्वा बन्धनप्रमोक्षशब्दमुदीरयेयं तृष्णायाः सन्निगडगाढबन्धनबद्धांश्च सत्त्वान् प्रमोचयेयं इदं प्रथमपूर्व्वप्रणिधानपदमामुखीभवति स्म ॥

अहो बताहं संसारमहाविद्यान्धकारगहनप्रविष्टस्य लोकस्याज्ञानपटलतिमिरावृतनयनस्य प्रज्ञाचक्षुर्विरहितस्याविद्यामोहान्धस्य महान्तं धर्म्मालोकं कुर्य्यां । ज्ञानप्रदीपश्चोपलम्भयेय त्रिविमोक्षसुखज्ञानवज्रौषधिसम्प्रयोगेण सोपायप्रज्ञाज्ञानसम्प्रयुक्तेन सर्व्वाविद्यान्धकारतमोमहत्तिमिरपटलकाचुकमपनीय प्रज्ञाचक्षुर्विशोधयेयं ॥ इदं द्वितीयं पूर्व्वप्रणिधानपदमामुखीभवति स्म ॥

अहो बताहं मानध्वजोच्छ्रितस्य लोकस्याहङ्कारममकाराभिनिविष्टस्यात्मीयग्राहानुगमाश्रयस्य सञ्ज्ञाचित्तदृष्टिविपर्य्यासविपर्य्यस्तस्याचक्षुरगृहीतस्यार्य्यमार्गोपदेशेनास्मिमानध्वजप्रपातनं कुर्य्यां ॥ इतीदं तृतीयं पूर्व्वप्रणिधानपदमामुखीभवति स्म ॥

अहो बताहं अनुपशान्तस्य लोकस्य तन्त्राकुलजातस्य गुणावगुण्ठितभूतस्याजवञ्जवसमापन्नस्याऽस्माल्लोकात् परं परलोकादिमं लोकं सन्धावतः संसरतः संसारादनिवृत्तस्याऽऽतप्तकमारुतस्योपशमकं प्रज्ञाह्लादकरं धर्म्मं प्रकाशयेयं ॥ इतीदं चतुर्थं पूर्व्वप्रणिधानपदमामुखीभवति स्म ॥ इमानि चत्वारि पूर्व्वप्रणिधानपदान्यामुखीभवन्ति स्म ॥

तस्मिंश्च क्षणे धर्मचारिणा देवपुत्रेण शुद्धावासकायिकैर्देवपुत्रैर्विकृतविगलितमन्तःपुरमुपदर्शितमभूत् ॥ विसंस्थितं बीभत्सरूपमुपदर्श्य च गगनतलस्थास्ते बोधिसत्त्वं गाथाभिरध्यभाषन्त ।

यथाब्रुवन् देवसुता महर्षयो विशुद्धपद्मायतलोचनं तं ।
कथं तवास्मिन्नुपजायते रतिः श्मशानमध्ये समवस्थितस्य ॥
प्रचोदितः सोऽथ सुरेश्वरेभिर्निरीक्ष्यतेऽन्तःपुरं मुहूर्त्तं ।
सम्प्रेक्षतः पश्यति तां विरूपां श्मशानमध्ये हि स्थितां च भूतां(१)॥

अद्राक्षीत् खल्वपि बोधिसत्त्वः सर्व्वावन्तं नारीगणं । अवलोकन् पश्यति । तत्र काश्चिद्व्यपकृष्टवस्त्राः काश्चिद्विधुतकेशाः काश्चिद्विकीर्णाभरणाः काश्चिद्विभ्रष्टमुकुटाः काश्चिद्वस्त्रैरंसैर्विनिपातितगात्र्यः काश्चिद्विसंस्थितमुखाः काश्चिद्विपरिवर्त्तितनयनाः काश्चित्प्रस्रवन्त्यो लालाभिः काश्चिद्रुदन्त्यः काश्चित् प्रहसन्त्यः काश्चित् प्रलपन्त्यः काश्चिद्दन्तान् कटकटायन्त्यः काश्चिद्विवर्णवदनाः काश्चिद्विसंस्थितरूपाः काश्चित् प्रलम्बितबाहवः काश्चिद्विक्षिप्तवदनाः काश्चिदुद्घाटितशीर्षाः काश्चिदवगुण्ठितशीर्षाः काश्चिद्विपरीतवर्त्तितमुखमण्डलाः काश्चित् प्रध्वस्तशरीराः काश्चिद्विभग्नगात्राः काश्चिन्निकुब्जाः घुरघुरायमाणाः काश्चिन्मृदङ्गमुपगूह्य परिवर्त्तितशीर्षशरीराः काश्चिद्वीणावल्लक्याद्यपरिगृहीतपाणयः काश्चिद्वेणुं दन्तैः कटकटायन्त्यः काश्चित्

१ "सुरेश्वरेभिः" सुरेश्वरैः । "निरीक्ष्यते" निरीक्षित । "स्थितां च भूतां" स्थिताम् भूताम् पश्यति स्मेति सान्वयार्थः ।

छिन्नवनमकुलसम्पताक्रान्तकर्णिकावातभग्नाः काश्चिन्निमेषोन्मेष-परिवर्तितनयना: काश्चिद्विवृत्ताक्षा एवं तद्विकृतं धरणीतल-गतमन्तःपुरं निरीक्षमाणो बोधिसत्त्वः श्मशानसंज्ञामुत्पादयति स्म ॥

तत्रेदमुच्यते।

तां दृष्ट्वा उद्विग्न स लोकनाथः करुणं विनिश्वस्य इदं जगाद।
अहो बता कृच्छ्रगता अमेयं कथं रतिं विन्दति राक्षसीगणैः(१)॥
अतिमोहतमावृते दुर्मतिकामगुणैर्निर्गुणबद्धमनः।
विहग पञ्जरमध्यगता यथा न हि लभन्ति कदाचिद्विनिः-सृतिं (२) ॥

अथ बोधिसत्त्वोऽनेन पुनरपि धर्मालोकमुखेनान्तःपुरं प्रत्यवेक्षमाणो महाकरुणापरिदेवितेन सत्त्वान् परिदेवते स्म ॥

इह ते बाला बध्यन्ते आघातिन इव वध्याः। इह ते बाला रज्यन्ते विचित्रघटेष्विवामेध्यपरिपूर्णेष्वविद्वांसः। इह ते बाला मज्जन्ति गजा इव वारिमध्ये। इह ते बाला रुध्यन्ते चौरा इव चारकमध्ये। इह ते बाला अभिरता वराहा इवाशुचिमध्ये। इह ते बाला अध्यवसिताः कुक्कुरा इवास्थिकरङ्कमध्ये। इह ते बालाः प्रपतिता दीपशिखास्विव पतङ्गाः। इह ते बाला बध्यन्ते कपय इव वलयेन। इह ते बालाः परि-

---

१ "दृष्ट्वा उद्विग्न" दृष्ट्वोद्विग्नः। "अहो बता कृच्छ्रगता" अहो बत कृच्छ्रगताः। "विन्दति" विन्दन्ति।

२ "विहग पञ्जरमध्यगताः" विहगाः पञ्जरमध्यगताः। "लभन्ति" लभन्ते।

दृश्यन्ते वातोत्क्षिप्ता इव कदल्यः । इह ते बालाः परिशु-
ष्यन्ते शुष्काष्ठेष्विवोरगाः । इह ते बाला अवबध्यन्ते किल्बिष-
कारिण इव शूलाग्रे । इह ते बालाः संसीदन्ति जीर्णगजा इव
पङ्के । इह ते बाला विपद्यन्ते भिन्नयानपात्रा इव महासमुद्रे ।
इह ते बालाः प्रपतन्ति महाप्रपात इव जात्यन्धाः । इह ते
बालाः पर्यवदानं गच्छन्ति पातालसन्धिगतमिव वारि । इह
ते बाला धूमायन्ते कल्पसंक्षय इव महापृथिवी । आभिर्बाला
भ्राम्यन्ते कुम्भकारचक्रमिवाविद्धं । इह ते बालाः परिभ्रा-
म्यन्ते शैलान्तर्गता इव जात्यन्धाः । इह ते बाला विपरिवर्तन्ते
कुक्कुरा इव सर्वच्छेदनबद्धाः । इह ते बाला म्लायन्ते ग्रीष्मकाल
इव तृणवनस्पतयः । इह ते बालाः परिहीयन्ते शशीव कृष्णपक्षे ।
आभिर्बाला भक्ष्यन्ते गरुडेनेव पन्नगाः । आभिर्बाला ग्रस्यन्ते म-
हामकरेणेव पोतकाः । आभिर्बाला लुप्यन्ते चोरसङ्घेनेव सार्थाः ।
आभिर्बाला भिद्यन्ते मारुतेनेव शालाः । आभिर्बाला हन्यन्ते
दुष्टविषैरिव जन्तवः । आस्वादसञ्ज्ञिनो बालाः क्षण्यन्ते मधुदि-
ग्धाभिरिव क्षुरधाराभिर्बालजातीयाः । आभिर्बाला उह्यन्ते
दारुस्कन्धा इव जलौघैः । आभिर्बालाः क्रीडन्ति दारका इव
स्वमूत्रपुरीषैः । आभिर्बाला वध्यन्ते अङ्कुशेनेव गजाः । आभि-
र्बाला बध्यन्ते धूर्तकैरिव बालजातीयाः । इह ते बाला कुशल-
मूलानि क्षपयन्ति द्यूताभिरता इव धनं । आभिर्बाला भक्ष्यन्ते
राक्षसीभिरिव वणिजः ॥

इत्येभिर्द्वात्रिंशताकारैर्बोधिसत्त्वोऽन्तःपुरं परिपूरयित्वा का-

षेऽशुभसंज्ञां विचारयन्नप्रतिकूलसंज्ञामुपसंहरन् जुगुप्ससंज्ञामुत्पादयन् सम्यगाधुः प्रतिविभावयन् कायस्यादीनवं सम्पश्यन् कायात् कायाभिनिवेशमुच्चारयच्छुभसंज्ञां विभावयन्नशुभसंज्ञामवक्रामयन् अधः पादतलाभ्यां यावदूर्द्ध्वं मस्तकपर्य्यन्तं पश्यति स्म । अशुचिसमुत्थितमशुचिसम्भवमशुचिस्रवन्नित्यं ॥ तस्यां च वेलायामिमां गाथामभाषत ।

कर्म्मक्षेत्ररुहं तृष्णासलिलजं सत्कायसंज्ञीकृतं
अश्रुस्वेदकफाद्रमूत्रविकृतं शोणीतबिन्दाकुलं ।
वस्तिपूयवसास्यमस्तकरसैः पूर्णं तथा किल्विषै-
र्नित्यं प्रस्रवितं ह्यमेध्यसकुलं दुर्गन्धि नानाविधं (१) ॥
अस्थीदन्तसकेशरोमविकृतं चर्म्मावृतं लोमशं
अन्तःप्लीहयकृद्वसोष्ठरसनैरेभिश्चितं दुर्ब्बलं ।
मज्जास्नायुनिबद्धयन्त्रसदृशं मांसेन शोभीकृतं
नानाव्याधिप्रकीर्णशोककलिलं क्षुत्तर्षसम्पीडितं (२) ॥
जन्तूनां निलयं अनेकसुषिरं मृत्युं जराधिष्ठितं
दृष्ट्वा को हि विचक्षणो रिपुनिभं मन्ये शरीरं स्वकं (३) ॥

एवञ्च बोधिसत्त्वः काये कायानुगतया स्मृत्या विहरति स्म॥
गगनतलगताश्च देवपुत्रा धर्म्मचारिणं देवपुत्रमेवमाहुः ।

---

१ "शोणीतबिन्दाकुलं" शोणितबिन्दाकुलं। "वस्तीपूयवसाकमस्तकरसैः" वस्तिपूयवसास्यमस्तकरसैः।

२ "अस्थीदन्त" अस्थिदन्तं।

३ "मन्ये" मन्येत्।

किमिदं मार्ष सिद्धार्थो विलम्बते । अन्तःपुरं व्यवलोकयति स्म । तस्योपदर्शयति चित्तमोदेजयति । भूयश्चक्षुर्निवेशयति । अथवा भवे जलनिधिगम्भीरोऽयं न शक्यमस्य प्रमाणं ग्रहीतुं अथवाऽसक्तस्य मा खलु विषये सज्यते मनः । मा खल्वमलैः सत्त्वोदितो विस्मरति पूर्व्वप्रतिज्ञामिति ॥

धर्म्मचार्य्याह । किमेवं कथयते(१) ॥ नूनमस्य प्रत्यक्षात् पूर्व्वमेव बोधाय चरतस्तथाविधा निःसक्तताऽभूत् । नैष्क्रम्यत्यागे च किमङ्ग पुनरेव तर्हि चरमभवावस्थितस्यासङ्गो भविष्यति ॥

अथ खलु भिक्षवो बोधिसत्त्वः कृतनिश्चयः संवर्षितमानसो व्यवसितबुद्धिः सलीलमवलम्बितपर्य्यङ्कादवतीर्य्य सङ्गीतिप्रासादे पूर्व्वाभिमुखः स्थित्वा दक्षिणेन पाणिना रत्नजालिकामवनाम्य(२) प्रासादकोटीगतो दशनखकृतकरपुटो भूत्वा सर्व्वबुद्धान् समन्वाहृत्य सर्व्वबुद्धेभ्यश्च नमस्कारं कृत्वा गगनतलमवलोकयति स्म ॥

सोऽद्राक्षीद् गगनतलगतममराधिपतिं दशशतनयनं देवशतसहस्रपरिवृतं पुष्पधूपगन्धमाल्यविलेपनचूर्णचीवरच्छत्रध्वजपताकावतंसकरत्नहारदामपरिगृहीतमवनतकायं बोधिसत्त्वं नमस्यमानं स्थितं ॥ चतुरश्च लोकपालान् यक्षराक्षसगन्धर्व्वभुजगगणसपरिवृतान् सन्नद्धदृढवर्म्मितकवचितान् असिधनुःशरशक्तितोमरत्रिशूलहस्तान् सलीलमणिमुकुटावलम्बितचूडान् बोधिसत्त्वं नमस्यमानान् स्थितान् पश्यति स्म ॥ चन्द्रसूर्य्यावपि

---

१ "कथयते" कथ्यते ।

२ "अवनाम्य" अपनमय्य ।

देवपुत्रौ वामदक्षिणयोः पार्श्वयोः स्थितावपश्यत् । पुष्यश्च नक्षत्राधिपतिरुत्थितोऽभूत् ॥ अर्द्धरात्रेच समयं सम्प्राप्तं दृष्ट्वा च बोधिसत्त्वश्छन्दकमामन्त्रयते स्म ॥

छन्दका च खलु माविलम्ब हे अश्वराज दद मे अलङ्कृतं ।
सर्व्वसिद्धि मम एति मङ्गला अर्थसिद्धि ध्रुवमद्य भेष्यते (१) ॥

अथ छन्दक इदं वचनं श्रुत्वोद्विग्नमना एवमाह । क गमिष्यसे विकसितभ्रु कमलदलशुभलोचन नृपसिंह शरदिन्दुपूर्ण कुमुदशशाङ्कपरिमुदित नवनलिनकोमलविशुद्धपद्मवदन हाटकबोधाम्बरितावर्णविमलशशितेजो घृतहुतार्चिरश्मिमणिविद्युत्प्रभोज्ज्वलिततेजो वारणमत्तलीलगजगामिन् गोवृषमृगेन्द्रहंसक्रमसुक्रमसुचरण ॥

बोधिसत्त्व आह ।

छन्दक यस्यार्थि मयि पूर्व्वत्यक्त करचरणनयना ।
तथ उत्तमाङ्ग भार्य्य प्रियाश्च राज्यधनकनकवसना (२) ॥
रत्नपूर्णगजतुरग अनिलजववेगविक्रमबलाः ।
शीलु मि रचि क्षान्तिपरिभावि वीर्य्यबलध्यानप्रज्ञानिरतश्चापि (३) ॥
बहुकल्पकोटि नियुता किन्तु स्पृशित्व बोधिशिवशान्तिं ।

---

१ "छन्दका च खलु माविलम्ब हे" हे छन्दक त्वं खलु माविलम्बस्वेत्यन्वयः। "अश्वराज दद मे" अश्वराजं देहि मे। "सर्व्वसिद्धि मम एति" सर्व्वसिद्धिर्मम चायाति। "अर्थसिद्धिध्रुवमद्य भेष्यते" अर्थसिद्धिर्ध्रुवमद्य भविष्यति।

२ "यस्यार्थे मयि पूर्व्वत्यक्त" यस्यार्थे मया पूर्व्वं एते त्यक्ताः। "करचरणनयना" करचरणनयनानि। "तथ उत्तमाङ्ग भार्य" तथा उत्तमाङ्गभार्या। "राज्यधनकनकवसना" राज्यधनकनकवसनानि।

३ "रत्नपूर्ण गजतुरग" रत्नपूर्णगजतुरगाः। "शीलु मि रचि" शीलं मया रचितं।

जरामरणपञ्जरनिरतसत्त्वपरिमोचनस्य समयोऽभ्युपस्थितु मम(१)॥

छन्दक आह। श्रुतं मया आर्य्यपुत्र यथा त्वं जातमात्र एव नैमित्तिकानां ब्राह्मणानामुपनामितो दर्शनाय॥ तैश्चापि राज्ञः शुद्धोदनस्याग्रतो व्याकृतः॥ देव वृद्धिस्ते राजकुलस्य॥ आह। किमिति॥ ते आहुः। अयं कुमारः शतपुण्यलक्षणो जातस्तवात्मजः पुण्यतेजितः। स चक्रवर्त्ती चतुर्द्वीपेश्वरो भविष्यति सप्तधनैरुपेतः॥ स चेत्पुनर्लोकमवेक्ष्य दुःखितं विजह्यान्तःपुरं(२) निष्क्रमिष्यति। अवाप्य बोधिमजरामरणं पदं तर्पयिष्यते धर्मजलैरिमां प्रजां॥ [छन्दार्य्यपुत्रास्ति तावदेतद्व्याकरणं नेदं नास्ति](३)॥ किन्तु शृणु तावन् ममार्थकामस्य वचनं॥ आह। किमिति॥ आह। देव यस्यार्थे इह केचिदनेकविधानि व्रततपांस्यारभन्तेऽजिनजटामुकुटचीवरवल्कलधरा दीर्घनखकेशश्मश्रुणानेकविधानि कायस्यातापनपरितापनानि समुत्सहन्ते। तीव्रञ्च व्रततपः समारभन्ते। किमिति। वयं देवमनुष्यसम्पत्तिं प्रतिलभेमहीति। सा च सम्पत्त्वयार्य्यपुत्र प्रतिलब्धा इदञ्च राज्यं समृद्धञ्च स्फुटञ्च क्षेमं सुभिक्षं रमणीयमाकीर्णबहुजनमनुष्यमिमानि चोद्यानानि वरप्रवराणि नानाविधपुष्पफलप्रतिमण्डितानि नानाशकुनिगणनिकूजितानि पुष्करिण्यश्चोत्पलपद्मकुमुदपुण्डरीकोपशोभिता हंसमयूरकोकिलक्रौञ्चसारसनिकूजिताः पुष्पितसहकाराऽ-

---

१ "बहुकल्पकोडिनियुता" बहुकल्पकोटिनियुतपर्य्यन्तं। "स्पृशित्व" स्पृष्ट्वा॥ "समयोऽभ्युपस्थितु" समयोऽद्य उपस्थितः॥

२ "विजह्यान्तःपुरं" विहायान्तःपुरं॥

३ [ ]एतच्चिह्नक्रोडीकृतपाठः द्वितीयसङ्ख्यके पुस्तके नोपलभ्यते॥

शोकचम्पककुरवकतिलककेशरादिनानाद्रुमतीरोपरिबद्धा ना-
नारत्नवृक्षवाटिकावनसञ्छन्ना अष्टापदानिबद्धा रत्नवेदिका-
परिवृता रत्नजालसञ्छन्ना षडर्त्तुकालपरिभोगा ग्रीष्मवर्षा-
शरद्धेमन्तसुखसंवासा इमे च शरदभ्रनिभाः कैलाशपर्व्वतस-
दृशा महाप्रासादा वैजयन्तसमा धर्म्मसुधर्म्मदेवसमा लोकविग-
तप्रख्यातयो वितर्द्दिनिर्य्यूहतोरणगवाक्षहर्म्यकूटागारप्रासादसम-
लङ्कृता रत्नकिङ्किणीजालसमीरिता इदञ्चार्य्यपुत्रान्तःपुरं
तूर्य्यपणववीणावेणुसम्पताडावचराकिम्पलनकुलसुघोषकमृदङ्ग-
पटहनृत्यगीतवादित्रसङ्गीतिसंयोगसुमिश्रितं हास्यलास्यक्रीडि-
तरमितसुखितमधुरोपचारं। त्वञ्च देवपुत्रो युवा नातिक्रान्त-
यौवनो नवोदग्रलक्षणः कोमलशरीरः शिशुः कृष्णकेशः अवि-
क्रीडितः कामैः। रमस्व तावदमराधिपतिरिव दशशतनयन-
स्त्रिदशाधिपतिः। ततः पश्चाद्वृद्धीभूता अभिनिष्क्रमिष्यामः॥

तस्यां च वेलायामिमां गाथामभाषत।

रमता च रतिविधिज्ञा अमराधिपतिर्य्यथा त्रिदशलोके।
ततः पश्चाद्वृद्धीभूता व्रततपसमारभिष्यामः(१)॥

बोधिसत्त्व आह।

अलं छन्दक अनित्याः खल्वेते कामा अध्रुवा अशाश्वता
विपरिणामधर्म्माणः प्रकृताश्चपला गिरिनदीवेगतुल्या अवश्या-
यबिन्दुवदचिरस्थायिन उल्लापनाः रिक्तमुष्टिवदसाराः कदली-
स्कन्धवद्दुर्बलाः आमभाजनवद्भेदनात्मकाः शरदभ्रनिभाः क्षणा-

---

१ "रमता" रमत। "व्रततपसं" व्रततपः व्रततपांसीति वा। "आरभिष्यामः" आरप्स्यामहे "आरमिष्यामः" "आभरिष्यामः" इति च क्वचिद्ग्रन्थे दृश्यते॥

ध्रुवा न भवन्ति अचिरस्थायिनो विद्युत इव नभसि विषभाज-
नमिव विपरिणामदुःखा मालतलतेवासुखदाः (१) अभिजि-
ह्विता बालबुद्धिभिरुदकबुद्बुदोपमाः क्षिप्रं विपरिणामधर्म्माणः
मायामरीचिसदृशाः संज्ञाविपर्य्याससमुत्थिताः मायासदृशाश्चि-
त्तविपर्य्यासतिचयिताः स्वप्नसदृशाः दृष्टिविपर्य्यासपरिग्रहयोगे-
नाप्तिकराः सागर इव दुःखपूराः लवणोदक इव तृषाकुलाः
सर्पशिरोवद्दुस्पर्शनीयाः महाप्रपातवत्परिवर्जिताः पण्डितैः स-
भयाः सरणाः सादीनवाः सदोषा इति ज्ञात्वा विवर्जिताः प्राज्ञैः
विगर्हिता विद्वद्भिः जुगुप्सिता आर्य्यैः विवर्जिता बुधैः परिगृहीता
अबुधैः निषेविता बालैः॥ तस्यां च वेलायामिमां गाथामभाषत।

विवर्जिताः सर्पशिरा यथा बुधै-
र्विगर्हिता मीढघटा यथाऽशुचिः।
विनाशकाः सर्व्वसुखस्य छन्दक
ज्ञात्वा हि कामान्न विजायते रतिः॥

तदा छन्दकः शल्यविद्धो यथा क्रन्दमानस्ततोऽश्रुनेत्रो दुःखी
एवं वाक्यमब्रवीत्।

देव यस्यार्थिं केचिदिहाऽऽतीव्रानेकविधान् आरभन्ते
व्रतान् अजिनजटाधरसुदीर्घकेशनखश्मश्रुपीवरास्तथा।

वल्कलधरा शुष्काङ्गानेके व्रतानाश्रिताः शाकश्यामाक-
गर्दुलभक्षाश्च ऊर्द्धमुण्डकाश्चापरे गोव्रतां संश्रिताः (२)॥

---

१ “मालतलतेव” मालुकलतेवेत्यनुमीयते॥

२ “यस्यार्थिं” यस्यार्थं। “वल्कलधरा” वल्कलधराः। “गर्दुल” गर्दभभक्षा।
“गोव्रतां” गोव्रताम्॥

किं तु वयञ्चवेम श्रेष्ठा विशिष्टा
अन्ने चक्रवर्त्तीवरा लोकपालास्तथा ।
शक्र वज्रधरा याम देवाधिपा निर्म्मिता
ब्रह्मलोके च ध्यानसुखाकाङ्क्षिणः (१) ॥
तदिदं नरवरिष्ठ राज्यं तवस्फीतमृद्धं सुभिक्षञ्च
तथाऽऽरामोद्यानप्रासाद उच्छ्रयितं वैजयन्तसमं ।
इस्त्रिागार स्ववेणुवीणारवैर्गीतवाद्यैरतिनृत्यचञ्चीति-
संयोगसंमिश्रितं भुञ्ज कामानिमान् मा व्रज स्मरत (२) ॥

बोधिसत्त्व आह ।

छन्दक शृणु यानि दुःखशतामर्षिता पूर्व्वजन्मान्तरे ।
बन्धनावन्धनाघाततर्ज्जनाः कामहेतोर्मया नो च निर्व्वि-
दभूत् (३) ॥
संक्रान्तमानसं प्रमदवशगतञ्च मोहाकुलं दृष्टिजालावृतं ।
अन्धभूतं पुरा आत्मसञ्ज्ञापहाकारका वेदनावीतिष्टन्ता
इमे (४) ॥
धर्म्माज्ञानतः सम्भूता चपलचला-

---

१ "अन्ने" अन्नति "चक्रवर्त्तिवरा" चक्रवर्त्तिवराः । "शक्र" शक्राः ॥

२ "आरामोद्यानप्रासाद" आरामोद्यानप्रासादैः" । "उच्छ्रयितं" उच्छ्रितं उन्नी-कृतमित्यर्थः । "इस्त्रिागार" स्त्र्यागारं । "भुञ्ज" भुङ्क्ष्व ॥

३ "दुःखशतामर्षिता" दुःखशतानि बन्धनादीनि मर्षितानि मया । "नो च" न च ॥

४ "आत्मसञ्ज्ञापहाकारका" आत्मसञ्ज्ञापहाकार इव आकारो येषां । "वेदनावी-तिष्टन्ता" वेदनावीतिष्टन्तानि । "इमे" इमानि बन्धनादीनि । एवं परत्रापि छिन्दोऽन विपरिणेयानि ॥

ऽनित्यमेघैः समा विद्युद्भिः सदृशाः।
ओसविन्दूपमा रिक्ततुच्छा असाराः
अनात्मा च शून्यस्वभावा इमे सर्व्वशः (१)॥
न च मम विषयेषु संरज्यते मानसं
देहि मे छन्दक कण्ठकाश्वकृतमश्वराजोत्तमं।
पूर्णमेवं मन्नथाये पुरा चिन्तिता भेष्यि
सर्व्वाभिभूः सर्व्वधर्म्मेश्वरो धर्म्मराजो मुनिः (२)॥

छन्दक आह।

इमां विबुद्धाम्बुजपत्रलोचनां
विचित्रहारां मणिरत्नभूषितां।
घनप्रमुक्तामिव विद्युतां नभे
नापेक्षसे प्रथमगतां विरोचनां (३)॥
इमांश्च वेणुपणवां सुघोषकां
मृदङ्गवंशांश्च सङ्गीति वादितां।
चकोरस्वरां कलविङ्कनादितां
यथाऽऽलयं किन्नरीणां कथं विहास्यसे (४)॥
सुमनोत्पलां वार्षिकचम्पकोत्तया
सुगन्धमालां गुणपुष्पसञ्चयां।

---

१ "ओस शब्देन" तुषार उच्यते। "अनात्मा" अनात्मानः॥
२ "चिन्तिता" चिन्तितः। "भेष्यि" भविष्यामि॥
३ "नभे" नभसि। "विरोचनां" प्रथमे पुस्तके द्वितीये च पुस्तके "विरोचतां" इति पाठो दृश्यते॥
४ "वेणुपणवां" वेणुपणवान् एवमेव अनुस्वारस्य स्थाने "न्" कारो बोध्यः॥

कालागुरूनुत्तमगन्धधूपना

नोऽपेक्षसे ताननुलेपनाम्बरान् (१) ॥

सुगन्धगन्धांश्च रसान् प्रणीतान्

सुसाधितान् व्यञ्जनभोजनांस्तथा ।

सशर्करान् पानरसान् सुसंस्कृतान्

नोपेक्षसे देव कचिन्नमिच्छसि (२) ॥

शीते च उष्णाननुलेपनान् वरान्

उष्णे च तानुरगसारचन्दनान् ।

तान् काशिकवस्त्रवराम्बरान् शुभान्

नोपेक्षसे देव कचिन्नमिच्छसि (३) ॥

इमे च ते देव कामगुणा हि पञ्च

सम्यङ्कुदेवेष्विव देवतानां ।

रमस्व तावद्रतिसौख्यसन्वितः

ततो वनं यास्यति शाक्यपुङ्गवः (४) ॥

बोधिसत्त्व आह ॥

अपरिमितानन्तकल्पा मया छन्दक

भुक्ता कामानिमां रूपाश्च शब्दाश्च ।

गन्धा रसास्पर्शता नानाविधा

---

१ "सुमनोत्पलां" सुमनोत्पलानि । "अनुलेपनाम्बरान्" अनुलेपनान् अम्बरान् अनुलेपनान् वरान् वा ॥

२ "कचिं" कुच ॥

३ "कचिं" कुच ॥

४ "रतिसौख्यसन्वितः" रतिसौख्यसमन्वित इत्यर्थः ॥

दिव्य ये मानुषा नो च तृप्तिरभूत् (१)॥
नृपतिवरसुतेनैश्वर्य्यंकारार्पितं चातु-
र्द्वीपे महाराज्येऽभूच्चक्रवर्त्ती समन्वागतः।
सप्तभिरत्नभिः इस्त्रिगारस्य मध्ये गतः
चिदशपतिषु यामाधिपत्यश्च कारार्षितं (२)॥
येभ्यश्चाहश्च्यविला इह गतो निर्म्मिता निर्म्मितेषु
मानात्मिका च श्रिया उत्तमा भुक्त पूर्व्वे मया।
सुरपतिवशवर्त्तिमानेश्वरत्वं च कारार्पितं
भुक्तं कामाः समृद्धा मनाक्षो च तृप्तीरभूत् (३)॥
किं पुनरद्य मां हीनसंसेवितस्तृप्तिं
गच्छेदहं स्थानमेतन्न संविद्यत्।
अपि च इदं जगं उपेक्षाम्यहं
छन्दक दुःखितं शोककान्तारमध्ये स्थितं (४)॥
क्लेशव्यालाकुले दह्यमानं सदा
अशरणमपरायणं मोहविद्यान्धकारे।
जरव्याधिमृत्युभयैः पीडितं

---

१ "भुक्ता" भुक्ताः। "कामानिमां" इमे कामाः। "स्वर्गता" स्वर्गाः। "दिव्य" दिव्याः॥

२ "ऐश्वर्य्यं" ऐश्वर्य्यं। "कारार्पितं" अकार्षं कृतं वा। "अभूत्" अभूवं। "इस्त्रिगारस्य" स्त्र्यागारस्य। "कारार्पितं" अकार्षं॥

३ "च्यविला" च्युतो भूत्वा। "भुक्त" भुक्ताः। "कारार्पितं" अकार्षं कृतं वा। "भुक्तं" भुक्ताः॥

४ "हीनसंसेवितः" हीनसंसारः इति वा पाठः। "गच्छेत्" गमयेत। "स्थानमेतत्" स्थाने एतस्मिन्। "संविद्यत्" संविद्येयं। "जगं" जगत॥

जन्मदुःखैः समन्ताहतं व्याहतं शत्रुभिः (१) ॥
अहमिमं समुदानीया धर्मनावं
महाशीलव्रतक्षान्तिवीर्य्यदृढां ।
दानसम्भारसङ्घातां सारमध्या-
शयैर्वज्रकैः संगृहीतां दृढां (२) ॥
स्वयमहमभिरुह्य नावामिमात्मनाऽवतीर्य्य
संसार ओघैरहं तारयिष्येऽनन्तं जगत् ।
शोकसंसारकान्ताररोषोर्मिरागग्रहा-
व्याकुले वैराकुले दुस्तरे एव चित्तं मम (३) ॥
तदात्मनोत्तीर्य्य इदं भवार्णवं
सवैरदृष्टिग्रहक्लेशराक्षसं ।
स्वयं तरित्वा च अनन्तकं जगत्
स्थलेऽन्तरीक्षे अजरामरे शिवे (४) ॥

तदा छन्दकोभूयस्या मात्रया प्ररुदन्नेवमाह ॥ देव एष व्यवसायस्य निश्चयः ॥

बोधिसत्व आह । शृणु छन्दक मह्य निश्चयं मोक्षसत्वार्थं हितार्थमुद्यतं अचलाचलमव्ययं दृढं मेरुराजेव (५) यथा सुदुश्चलं ॥

---

१ "मोहविद्यान्धकारे" मोहाविद्यान्धकारे। "जरव्याधिं" जराव्याधिं ॥
२ "समुदानीया" समुदानीय ॥
३ "नावां" नावं। "इमा" इमां। "चित्तं मम" उद्युक्तं इति भावः ॥
४ निवेशयामि इत्यध्याहार्य्यं ॥
५ "मह्य" मम। "मोक्षसत्वार्थं" सत्वमोक्षार्थं। "मेरुराजेव" मेरुराजमिव ॥

छन्दक आह। कीदृश आर्य्यपुत्रस्य निश्चयः॥

बोधिसत्त्व आह।

वज्राशनिपरशुशक्तिशराश्मवर्षं
विद्युत्प्रभाप्रज्वलितं क्वथितञ्च लोहं।
आदीप्तशैलशिखराः प्रपतेयु मूर्द्ध्नि
नो वा अहं पुनर्जनेय गृहाभिलाषं (१)॥

तदा अमरनभगताः किलिकिला मुञ्चिषु कुसुमवृष्टिं।
जय हे परममतिधरा जगति अभयदायका नाथ (२)॥

न रज्यते पुरुषवरस्य मानसं
नभो यथा तमरजधूमकेतुभिः।
न लिप्यते विषयसुखेषु निर्म्मल
जले यथा नवनलिनं समुद्भवं (३)॥

अथ खलु भिक्षवो बोधिसत्त्वस्य निश्चयं विदित्वा शान्तमतिश्च देवपुत्रो ललितव्यूहश्च देवपुत्रः कपिलवस्तुनि महानगरवरे(४)सर्व्वस्त्रीपुरुषदारकदारिकाणां अपस्वापनं अकुरुतां सर्व्वशब्दांश्चान्तर्द्धापयामासतुः॥

अथ खलु भिक्षवो बोधिसत्त्वः सर्व्वं नगरजनं प्रसुप्तं विदित्वाऽर्द्धरात्रिसमयं चोपस्थितं ज्ञात्वा पुष्यञ्च नक्षत्राधिपतिं

---

१ "प्रपतेयु" प्रपतेयुः। "जनेय" जायेय। "गृहाभिलाषं" गृहाभिलाषी॥

२ "किलिकिला" किलिकिलध्वनिभिः। "मुञ्चिषु" मुमुचुः आहुः "जय हे" इत्यादि। "परममतिधरा" परममतिधर। "अभयदायका" अभयदायक॥

३ "तमरजधूमकेतुभिः" तमोरजोधूमकेतुभिः। "निर्म्मल" निर्म्मलं॥

४ "नगरेऽपि" इति क्वचित् पाठः॥

युक्तं ज्ञात्वा साम्प्रतं निष्क्रमणकालमिति ज्ञात्वा छन्दकमामन्त्रयते स्म ॥

छन्दक मा मेदानीं खेदय । प्रयच्छ मे कण्ठकं समलङ्कृत्य मा च विलम्बिष्ठाः ॥ समनन्तरोदाहृताऽस्य बोधिसत्त्वेनेयं वाक् ॥

अथ तत्क्षणमेव चत्वारो लोकपालाः बोधिसत्त्वस्य वचनमुपश्रुत्य स्वकस्वकानि च भवनानि गत्वा बोधिसत्त्वस्य पूजाकर्म्मणे स्वैः स्वैर्व्यूहैस्त्वरितं पुनरपि कपिलवस्तुमहानगरमागच्छन्ति स्म ॥

तत्र धृतराष्ट्रो महाराजो गन्धर्व्वाधिपतिः पूर्व्वस्यान्दिशि आगतोऽभूत् । सार्द्धमनेकैर्गन्धर्व्वकोटीनियुतशतसहस्रैर्नानातूर्य्यसङ्गीतिसम्प्रवादितेन ॥ आगत्य कपिलवस्तुमहानगरं प्रदक्षिणीकृत्य यथागतः पूर्व्वां दिशमुपनिश्रित्यास्थात् । बोधिसत्त्वं नमस्यमानः ॥

दक्षिणस्यान्दिशि विरूढको महाराजोऽभ्यागतोऽभूत् । सार्द्धमनेकैः कुम्भाण्डकोटिनियुतशतसहस्रैर्नानामुक्ताहारपाणिप्रलम्बितैर्नानामणिरत्नपरिगृहीतैर्विविधगन्धोदकपूर्णघटपरिगृहीतैः ॥ आगत्य च कपिलवस्तुनि महानगरं प्रदक्षिणीकृत्य यथागत एव दक्षिणां दिशमुपनिश्रित्यास्थात् । बोधिसत्त्वं नमस्यमानः ॥

एवं पश्चिमाया दिशो विरूपाक्षो महाराजाऽऽ(१)गतोऽभूत् । सार्द्धमनेकैर्नागकोटीनियुतशतसहस्रैर्नानामुक्ताहारप्रलम्बितैर्नानामणिरत्नपरिगृहीतैर्गन्धचूर्णपुष्पवर्षमेघसमुत्थितै-

१ "महाराजाऽऽगतोभूत्" महाराज आगतोऽभूत् इति युक्तं ।

श्च मृदुभिः सुगन्धिभिर्नानावातैः प्रवायद्भिः ॥ आगत्य च कपिलवस्तुमहानगरं प्रदक्षिणीकृत्य यथागत एव पश्चिमां दिशमुपनिश्रित्यास्थात् । बोधिसत्त्वं नमस्यमानः ॥

उत्तरस्या दिशः कुवेरो महाराजाऽऽ (१) गतोऽभूत् । सार्द्धमनेकैः यक्षकोटिनियुतशतसहस्रैर्ज्योतीरसमणिरत्नपरिगृहीतैर्दीपिकापाणिपरिगृहीतैर्ज्वलितोल्कापाणिपरिगृहीतैः (२) धनुरसिशरशक्तितोमरत्रिशूलचक्रकनयभिन्दिपाल(३)नानाप्रहरणपरिगृहीतैर्दृढसन्नद्धवर्म्मितकवचितैः ॥ आगत्य कपिलवस्तुमहानगरवरं प्रदक्षिणीकृत्य यथागत एवोत्तरां दिशमुपनिश्रित्यास्थात् । बोधिसत्त्वं नमस्यमानः ॥

शक्रश्च देवानामिन्द्रः सार्द्धन्त्रायस्त्रिंशद्भिर्देवैरागतोऽभूत् । दिव्यपुष्पधूपगन्धमाल्यविलेपनचूर्णचीवरच्छत्रध्वजपताकाभरणपरिगृहीतैः ॥ आगत्य कपिलवस्तुमहानगरं प्रदक्षिणीकृत्य यथागत एव सपरिवारः पर्य्यन्तरीक्षेऽस्थात् । बोधिसत्त्वं नमस्कुर्व्वन् ॥

इति हि भिक्षवः छन्दको बोधिसत्त्वस्य वचनमुपश्रुत्याश्रुपूर्णनयनो बोधिसत्त्वमेवमाह । आर्य्यपुत्र त्वञ्च कालज्ञो वेलज्ञश्च समयज्ञः अयं कालोऽसमयो गन्तुं । तत्किमाज्ञापयसीति॥

बोधिसत्त्व आह । छन्दकायं स कालः ॥

छन्दक आह । कस्यार्य्यपुत्र कालः ॥

बोधिसत्त्व आह ।

---

१ अत्र सन्धिः पूर्व्ववत् ॥

२ अत्र समासे प्राग्भावस्य वैपरीत्यं ॥

३ "भिन्दिपाल" भिन्दपालः ॥

यत्तन्मया प्रार्थितु दीर्घरात्रं सत्त्वानामर्थं परिमार्गता हि ।
अवाप्य बोधिमजरामरं पदं मोचेम्यगत्तस्य सखा उपस्थितः (१)॥

इयमत्र धर्म्मता ॥

तत्रेदमुच्यते ।

भौमाऽऽन्तरीक्षाश्च तथैव पाला शक्रश्च देवाधिपतिः सयामः ।
यामाश्च देवा तुषिताश्च निर्म्मिताःपरनिर्म्मिताश्चुक्त तथैव देवाः(२)॥
वरुणो मनस्वी अपि नागराजा अनवोत्तप्तश्च तथैव सागरः ।
अभियुक्त ते चाप्यभिपूजनार्थं नैष्क्रम्यकाले नरपुङ्गवस्य (३) ॥
ये चापि रूपावचरेषु देवाः प्रशान्तचारी सद ध्यानगोचराः ।
अभियुक्त ते चाप्यभिपूजनार्थं त्रैलोक्यपूज्यस्य नरोत्तमस्य (४) ॥
दशद्दिशोऽभ्यागतबोधिसत्त्वाः सहायकाः पूर्व्वचरिस्य रत्नाः ।
द्रक्ष्यामहे निष्क्रमणं जिनस्य पूजां करिष्यामि तथानुरूपां (५) ॥
स चापि गुह्याधिपतिर्महात्मा आदीप्तवज्रो नभसि प्रतिष्ठितः ।
सन्नद्धगात्रो बलवीर्य्यविक्रमः करेण गृह्य ज्वलमानवज्रं (६) ॥
चन्द्रश्च सूर्य्यो उभि देवपुत्रौ प्रदक्षिणवामकेषु प्रतिष्ठितौ ।

---

१ "प्रार्थितु" प्रार्थितं । "सत्त्वानामर्थं" इत्यपि क्वचित् पाठः । "परिमार्गता" परिमृगयता । "मोचेत्"मुच्येत् । "सखा" सखः ॥

२ "भौमाऽऽन्तरीक्षाश्च" भौमाः चान्तरीक्षाश्च । "पाला" पालाः । "निर्म्मिता-द्यः" मतभेदाः । "परनिर्म्मिताश्चुक्त"परनिर्म्मिताद्युक्ताः तिब्बद्भाषानुवादितललितविस्तरे बहुवचनप्रयोगात् ॥

३ ग्रन्थभेदे "अनोवतप्तः" "अनवतप्तश्चेति" पाठः । "अभियुक्त" अभियुक्ताः मिलिता इत्यर्थः । "नागराजा" नागराजः ॥

४ "रूपावचरेषु" वा पाठः । "प्रशान्तचारी" प्रशान्तचारिणः । "सद" सदा । "अभियुक्त" अभियुक्ताः ॥

५ "अभ्यागत"अभ्यागताः । "पूर्व्वचरित्र"पूर्व्वचारिणः ।"करिष्यामि"करिष्यामः ॥

६ "आदीप्तवज्रः" "प्रदीप्तवज्रः" वा पाठः । "गृह्य" गृहीत्वा ॥

दशाङ्गुलीश्चाञ्जलि प्रगृहीत्वा नैष्क्रम्यशब्दाऽनुविचारयन्ति (१)॥
पुष्यस्य गच्छे सपारिषद् यो औदारिकनिर्म्मितश्चात्मभावं।
स्थिताग्रतस्तस्य नरोत्तमस्य मनोज्ञघोषाभिरुतं प्रमुञ्चत् (२)॥
सर्व्वेऽद्य सिद्धाः शुभ तुभ्य मङ्गलाः पुष्यस्य युक्तः समयश्च गन्तुं।
अहं प्रयास्यामि त्वयैव सार्द्धमनुत्तरायो भव रागसूदनः (३)॥
सञ्चोदकश्चोदयि देवपुत्र उत्तिष्ठ शीघ्र बलवीर्यउद्गतः।
दुःखैर्दितांस्तारय सर्व्वसत्त्वान्नैष्क्रम्यकालः समुपस्थितस्ते (४)॥
समागता देवसहस्रकोट्यः प्रवर्षमाणाः कुसुमान्मनोज्ञान्।
स चापि पर्य्यङ्कवरे निषण्णो देवैर्वृतो भ्राजति दीप्ततेजाः॥
नगरे इस्त्रिका दारकाश्च पुरुषा यावाभवन् दारिकाः
सर्व्वे ते शयिताः क्लिशान्तमनसो ईर्षापथेभ्यश्च्युताः।
हस्त्यश्वाश्च गवाश्च सारिकशुकाः क्रौञ्चा मयूरास्तथा
सर्व्वे ते शयिता क्लिशान्तमनसः पश्यन्ति रूपं न ते (५)॥
ये वा ते दृढवज्रतोमरधराः शाक्यैः सुताःस्थापिताः
हस्त्यश्वरथेषु तोमरवरे ते चाप्यवस्थापिताः।

---

१ "स्रुर्व्यौ" स्रुर्व्यः। "उभि" उभौ। "प्रदक्षिणवामकेषु" दक्षिणवामयोःपार्श्वयोः॥ "दशाङ्गुलीश्चाञ्जलि" दशाङ्गुलिभिः रचिताञ्जलिं। "प्रगृहीत्वा" प्रगृह्य। "नैष्क्रम्यशब्दानुविचारयन्ति" नैष्क्रम्यशब्दान् च विचारयन्तः॥

२ "औदारिकनिर्म्मितश्चात्मभावं" औदारिकनिर्म्मितात्मभावं। "प्रमुञ्चत्" प्रामुञ्चत्॥

३ "सर्व्वे" सर्व्वाणि "शुभ" शुभवतः। "तुभ्य" तव। "मङ्गलाः" मङ्गलानि। "युक्त" उदित इति भावः॥

४ "चोदयि" चोदयति। "शीघ्र" शीघ्रं॥

५ "इस्त्रिका" स्त्रियः। "क्लिशान्तमनसो ईर्षापथेभ्यः" इत्यत्र तेषां रीत्या विसर्गस्थाने उकारः अस्माकन्तु मते लुप्तात्॥

राजा राजकुमारपार्थिवजनः सर्व्वे प्रसुप्ताभवन्
अपि च नारीगणा विस्रस्तवसना सुप्ता न ते बुद्धिषु (१) ॥
सो च अन्तःपुरतो मनोज्ञवचनः कलविङ्कघोषस्वरो
रात्रौ निर्गतु अर्द्धरात्रसमये तं छन्दकमब्रवीत्।
साधु च्छन्दक देहि कण्ठक मम स्वालङ्कृतं शोभनं
मा विघ्नं कुरु मे ददाहि चपलं यदि मे प्रियं मन्यसे (२) ॥
श्रुत्वा च्छन्दक अश्रुपूर्णनयनस्तं स्वामिनमब्रवीत्
क त्वं यास्यसि सत्त्वसारथिवर किमस्यकार्य्यञ्च ते।
कालश्च समयश्च धर्म्मचरणे कालो न गन्तुं क्वचित्
द्वारास्ते पिहिता दृढार्गलकृताः को दास्यते तान् तव ॥
शक्रेण मनसाऽथ चेतनवशात् ते द्वार मुक्ताः कृताः
दृष्ट्वा च्छन्दको हर्षितः पुन दुःखी अश्रूणि सोऽवर्त्तयी।
हा धिक् कोऽसि सहाय किन्नु कुरुमि धावामिकां वा दिशं
ज्ञयं तेजवरेण वाक्य भणितं शक्यं न सन्धारितुं (३) ॥
सा सेना चतुरङ्गिनी बलवती किन्नु (४) करोतीह हा
राजा राजकुमारपार्थिवजना नेमं हि बुध्यन्ति ते।
स्त्रीसङ्घाः शयितस्तथा यशवती ओस्वापिता देवतैः

---

१ "प्रसुप्ताभवन्" इत्यत्र सन्धिरार्षः। "विस्रस्तवसना" विस्रस्तवसनाः। "न ते बुद्धिषु" ते बुद्धिषु न। न जागरिताः इत्यर्थः॥

२ "सो च" स च। "निर्गतु" निर्गन्तुं। "कण्ठक" कण्ठकं। "ददाहि" देहि॥

३ "द्वार" द्वाराः। "पुन" पुनः। "वर्त्तयी" अवर्त्तयत्। "कोसि सहाय" किं सहायः। "कुरुमि" करोमि। "तेजवरेण" वरतेजसा। इत्यर्थः क्वचित् मन्ये "तेजोधरेण" इति पाठः। "वाक्य" वाक्यं। "सन्धारितुं" सन्धारयितुं॥

४ "किन्नु" किं न वा पाठः॥

वा धिगच्छतु सिध्यतेऽस्य प्रणिधिर्यश्चिन्तितः पूर्व्वशः (१) ॥

देवाः कोटिसहस्रहृष्टमनसस्तं छन्दकमब्रुवन्

साधु छन्दक देहि कण्ठकवरं मा खेदयी नायकं ।

भेरीशङ्खमृदङ्गतूर्य्य नयुता देवासुरैस्ताडिताः

नैवेदं प्रतिबुध्यते पुरवर ओस्वापितं देवतैः (२) ॥

पश्य छन्दक अन्तरीक्षे विमलं दिव्या प्रभा शोभते

पश्य त्वं बहुबोधिसत्त्वनयुतां ये पूजनायागताः ।

शक्रं पश्य शचीपतिं बलवृतं द्वारस्थितं भ्राजते

देवाश्चाप्यसुराश्च किन्नरगणा ये पूजनार्थागताः (३) ॥

श्रुत्वा छन्दको देवतान वचनं त कण्ठकं आखपी

एषागच्छति सत्त्वसारथिवरः त्वं ताव हेषिष्यसे ।

सो तं वर्षिसुवर्ण काञ्चनखुरं स्वालङ्कृतं क्रन्तना

उपनेति गुणसागरस्य वहनं रोदन्तको दुर्मना (४) ॥

एषो ते वरलक्षणो हितकरो अश्वः सुजातः शुभो

गच्छ सिध्यतु तुभ्य एष प्रणिधिर्यश्चिन्तितः पूर्व्वशः ।

ये ते विघ्नकरा व्रजन्तु प्रशमं या या व्रतं सिध्यतां

---

१ "यमयती" यमावती । "ओस्वापिताः" प्रस्वापिताः इत्यनुमीयते ॥

२ "खेदयो" खेदय । "नयुता" नियुताः । "ओस्वापितं" प्रस्वापितं इत्यर्थः ॥

३ "नयुतां" नियुतां । "शक्रं" प्रचलितव्याकरणानुसारे "शक्रो भ्राजते पश्य" इत्यत्र प्रथमा विभक्तिरेव प्रशस्ता ॥

४ "देवतान" देवतानां । "आखपी" आलपत् कथयामास । "एषागच्छति" इत्यत्र सन्धिरार्षः । "ताव" तावत् । "सो तं" स तं । "वर्षिसुवर्ण" मेघवर्णं । "क्रन्तना" क्रान्त्वा । "उपनेति" उपनयति । "वहनं" वहनं वोढुं वा । "रोदन्तकः" रुदन् ॥

देवो भव हि सर्व्वजगस्य सौख्यददनः स्वर्गस्य शान्त्यास्तथा (१)॥
सर्व्वा कम्पिता षड्विकारा धरणी शयनाद्यदा सोत्थितः
आरूढः शशिपूर्णमण्डलनिभं तमश्वराजोत्तमं।
माला पाणिविशुद्धपद्म विमला न्यस्तश्च अश्वोत्तमे (?)
शक्रो ब्रह्मा उभौ च तस्य पुरतो दर्श्यन्ति मार्गोत्तमं (२)॥
आभा तेन प्रमुक्त अच्छविमला ओभासिता मेदिनी
सर्व्वे शान्तमपायसत्त्व सुखिता क्लेशैर्न बाधा तदा।
पुष्पा वर्षिषु तूर्य्यकोटि रणिषु देवासुरास्तुष्टुवुः
सर्व्वे कृत्य प्रदक्षिणं पुरवरं गच्छन्ति हर्षान्विताः (३)॥

पुरवरोत्तमी दैवतलक्ष्मी दीनमना
उपगम्य गच्छति महापुरुषे।
पुरतः स्थिता करुणदीनमना
गिरया समालपति पद्ममुखं (४)॥
तमसाकुलं भूमिषु सर्व्वपुरं
नगरं न शोभति त्वया रहितं।

---

१ "एषो ते" एष ते। "हितकरो ऽस्यः" हितकरोऽस्यः। "तुभ्यं" तव। "सा सा मतं" तत्तद् मतं। "सर्व्वजगस्य" सर्व्वजगतः। समस्तस्यापि "ददन" शब्दस्य विशेष्यान्वयः कार्य्यः॥

२ "सोत्थितः" स उत्थितः। "पाणिविशुद्धपद्म" पाणिरेव विशुद्धपद्मं तेन विमलां मालां। "दर्शयन्ति" दर्शयतः॥

३ "प्रमुक्त" प्रमुक्ता। "ओभासिता" आभासिता अवभासिता वा। "शान्तं" शान्ताः। "अपायसत्त्व" अपायसत्त्वाः। "सुखिता" सुखिताः। "बाधा" बाधाः। "पुष्पा" पुष्पाणि। "वर्षिषु" ववृषुः। "तूर्य्यकोटि" तूर्य्यकोट्यः। "रणिषु" रेणुः। "देवासुरा" देवासुराः। "कृत्य" कृत्वा॥

४ "गिरया" गिरा॥

न ममाऽच काचिरति प्रीतिकरी
त्यक्तं त्वया यदिदं भवनं । न पुनः (१) ॥
श्रुणिष्यि इतु पक्षिगणेऽन्तःपुरे मधुरवेणुरवं
मङ्गलशब्द तथ गीतरवं प्रतिबोधनन्तत्रावक्तशर्मैः (२) ॥
द्रक्षे च भूय सुरसिद्धगणाः
कुर्व्वन्तु पूजा तव रात्रिदिवं ।
घ्रायिष्यि गन्धं न च दिव्य पुनः
त्वयि निर्गते निहतक्लेशगणे (३) ॥
निर्भुक्तमाल्यमिव पर्य्युषिशिखितं
त्यक्तं त्वयाद्यभवनं हि तथा ।
नटरङ्गकल्प प्रतिभायति मे
त्वयि निर्गते च भूयु तेजश्शिरी (४) ॥
ओजो बलं हरसि सर्व्वपुरे
न च शोभतेऽटवितुल्यमिदं ।
वितथं ऋषीण वचनाद्य भूतं
ये हि व्याकृतु भुवि चक्रबला (५) ॥

---

१ "सोभति" शोभते। "काचिरति" काचिरति इति वा पाठः। काचिरति इति पाठे कापि रतिः इत्यर्थः काचिर्रति इति पाठे काचिद्रतिः इत्यर्थौ ज्ञेयः ॥

२ "श्रुणिष्यि" श्रोष्यामि। "इतु" इतं। "मङ्गलशब्द" मङ्गलशब्दं। "तथ" तथा। "चानन्तशर्मैः" चानन्तयशोभिः ॥

३ "द्रक्षे च भूय" भूयो न द्रक्ष्यामि। "पूजा" पूजां। "घ्रायिष्यि" घ्रास्यामि। "दिव्य" दिव्यं।

४ "पर्य्युषिशिखितं" पर्य्युषितं। "नटरङ्गकल्प" नटरङ्गकल्पं। "प्रतिभायति" प्रतिभाति। "भूयु" भूयः। "तेजश्शिरी" तेजःशरीरी ॥

५ "ऋषीण" ऋषीणां। "वचनाद्य" वचनं अद्य। "व्याकृतु" व्याचक्रुः। "चक्रबला" ये चक्रबलाः ॥

अचलं बलन्तु विपु शाक्यबलं
उच्छिन्नवंश इह राजकुले।
आशा अनष्टा इह शाक्यगणे
त्वयि निर्गते महति पुण्यद्रुमे ॥
अहमेव तुभ्य गति गच्छयमी
अथ त्वं प्रयासि अमला विमला ।
अपि च कृपाकरुणा सञ्जनिय्य
व्यवलोकयस्व भवनं स्वमिदं (१)॥
व्यवलोक्य चैव भवनं मतिमान्
मधुरस्वरो गिरमुदीरितवान् ।
नाहं प्रवेक्षि कपिलस्य पुरं
अप्राप्य जातिमरणान्तकरं (२)॥
स्थानासनं शयनचङ्क्रमणं
न करिष्येऽहं कपिलवस्तुमुखं।
यावन्नलब्धं वरबोधि मया
अजरामरं पदवरं ह्यमृतं ॥

यदसौ जगत्प्रधानो निष्क्रान्तु बोधिसत्त्वो
तस्मा नभे प्रजल्पा स्तवयिंसु अप्सराणि।
एष मह दक्षिणीयो एष महत् पुण्यक्षेत्र

---

१ "तुभ्य" तव। "गति" गतिं। "गच्छयमी" गच्छामि। "अमला विमला" हे अमल हे विमल। "करुणा" हे करुण। "सञ्जनिय्य" सञ्जनयिष्यन्॥

२ "प्रवेक्षि" प्रवेक्ष्यामि॥

पुण्यार्थिकान् छेवं अमृतफलस्य दाता (१)॥
एष बहुकल्पकोटीदानदमसंयम-
समुदानीतस्य बोधिः सत्त्वकरुणायमानो हि।
एष परिशुद्धशीलो सुव्रतोऽखण्डचारी
न च काम नैव भोगं प्रार्थेन्तु शीलरची (२) ॥
एष सद क्षान्ति वादी छिन्दन्तो अङ्गमङ्गेन
न च क्रोधु न चैव रोषः सत्त्वपरित्रायणार्थः।
एष सद वीर्य्यवन्तोऽविच्छिन्नःकल्पकोट्याः
समुदानीतस्य बोधिर्यष्टा च यज्ञकोटीः (३) ॥
एष सद ध्यानध्यायी शान्तप्रशान्त-
चित्तो ध्यायित्व सर्व्वक्लेशान् मोचयिष्यति सत्त्वकोटीः।
एषोऽसङ्गप्राज्ञः कल्पैर्विकल्पमुक्तो
विमुक्तचित्तो जिन भेष्यते स्वयम्भूः (४) ॥
एष सद मैत्रचित्तो करुणाय पारप्राप्तो
मुदितो प्रेचध्यायी शास्त्रपथे विधिज्ञः।
एषोऽति देवदेवो देवेभिः पूजनीयो

---

१ "तस्या नभे" तस्य नभसि। "प्रजन्ता" प्रजन्त्यः। "स्तवयिसु" तुष्टुवुः। "चम्पराणि" चम्परसः। "मन दर्शनीयः" मनो दर्शनीयः मनोऽनुकूल इति वा। "पुण्यचेन" पुण्यचेनं। "पुण्यार्थिकान्" पुण्यार्थिकानां ॥

२ "काम" कामं। "प्रार्थेन्तु" प्रार्थयते ॥

३ "सद" सदा। "क्रोध" क्रोधः। "सद" सदा वीर्य्यवान्। "समुदानीतस्य" समुदानीतस्य दानादिभिः। "निष्क्रान्तु" निष्क्रान्तः ॥

४ "सद" सदा। "ध्यायित्व" ध्यात्वा। "जिन" जिनः। "भेष्यते" भविष्यति ॥

शुभविमलविशुद्धचित्तो गुणनियुतपारमिप्राप्तः (१) ॥

*शरणं भयार्दितानां दीपोऽचक्षुषाणां नयनो उपद्रुतानां वैद्यश्चिरातुराणां राजा वरधर्मराज इन्द्रः सहस्रनेत्रो ब्रह्मस्व-यम्भूतः (२) ॥

*कायप्रश्रब्धचित्तो धीरः प्रभूतप्रज्ञो वीरो विनिर्मुक्तचित्तः शूरः क्लिशघाती अजितं जयो जितारिः (३) ॥

सिंहो भयप्रहीनो नागः सुदान्तचित्तो
ऋषभो गणप्रधानः प्रहीनकोपः ।
चन्द्रः प्रभासयन्तः सूर्य्योवभाषकरो
उल्काप्रद्योतकरो सर्व्वतमोविमुक्तः (४) ॥

*पद्मं अनोपलिप्तं पुष्पं सुशीलगन्धं मेरुरकम्पि शास्ता पृथिवी यथोपजीव्यो रत्नाकरोऽक्षोभ्यः (५) ॥

एतञ्चितु क्लेशमारो एतञ्चितु स्कन्धमारो
एतञ्चितु मृत्युमारो निहतोऽस्य देवपुत्रमारो ।
एष महासार्थवाहः कुपथप्रस्थितानां

---

१ "सद" सदा। "कषाय" कषायाः। "मुदितो" मुदितः। "देवभि" देवैः। "पूजनीयो" पूजनीयः। "पारमि" पारमिता ॥

*एतेषां श्लोकानां छन्दः नात्माभिर्गम्यं ॥

२ "अचक्षुषाणां" इत्यादावचक्षुष्काणां। "नयनो" नयनं। स्वरेषु उत्क्रमकु अन्थकाराणां मते ॥

३ "क्लिशघाती" क्लेशघाती ॥

४ "सुदान्तचित्तो" अत्रापि सन्धिः पूर्ववत्। "प्रभासयन्तः" प्रभासयन्। "सूर्य्यो-वभाषकरो" सूर्य्यावभासकरः। "उल्का प्रद्योतकरो" उल्काप्रद्योतकरः ॥

५ "मेरुरकम्पि" मेरुरकम्प्यः। "रत्नाकरः" रत्नाकरः ॥

अष्टाङ्गमार्गश्रेष्ठं देशयिष्यते नचिरेण (१) ॥
जरामरणक्लेशघाती तमतिमिरप्रमुक्तो
भुवि दिवि च सघुष्टो जिनो भेष्यति स्वयम्भूः ।
स्तुतस्तवितु अप्रमेयो वरपुरुषरूपधारी
यत्पुण्यं त्वां स्तविता भवामो यथा वादिसिंहः (२) ॥

इति हि भिक्षवो निष्क्रान्तो बोधिसत्त्वोऽतिक्रम्य शाक्यान् अतिक्रम्य कोड्यान् अतिक्रम्य मल्लान् मैनेयानामनुवैनेयेनिर्गमे षट्सु योजनेषु तत्र बोधिसत्त्वस्य रात्रिः प्रभाताभूत् ॥ ततो बोधिसत्त्वो कण्ठकादवतीर्य्य धरणीतले स्थित्वा तं महान्तं देवनागयक्षगन्धर्व्वासुरगरुडकिन्नरमहोरगसङ्घं विसर्जयति स्म॥ विसृज्य च अस्यैतदभूत्। इमान्याभरणानि कण्ठकस्य च्छन्दकस्य हस्ते विसर्जयामीति॥

अथ बोधिसत्त्वश्छन्दकमामन्त्र्यैतदवोचत्॥ गच्छ त्वं च्छन्दक इमान्याभरणानि कण्ठकञ्च गृहीत्वा निवर्त्तयस्व॥

यत्र च प्रदेशे च्छन्दको निवृत्तस्तत्र चैत्यं स्थापितमभूत्॥ अद्यापि तच्चैत्यं च्छन्दकनिवर्त्तनमिति ज्ञायते॥

पुनरस्य बोधिसत्त्वस्यैतदभवत्॥ कथं हि नामचूडा च प्रव्रज्या चेति॥ स खड्गेन चूडां छित्त्वा अन्तरीक्षे चिपति स्म॥ सा च त्रायस्त्रिंशता देवैः परिगृहीताऽभूत् पूजार्थं। अद्यापि च

---

१ अस्मिन् श्लोके "स्वष्मितु" स्थाने एतेन जित इत्यर्थः ज्ञेयः। "नचिरेण" अचिरेण।

२ "तमतिमिर-" तमस्तिमिर-। "भेष्यति" भविष्यति। "स्तुतस्तवितु" स्तुतिं कुर्व्वतः। "स्तविता" स्तुत्वा॥

चायस्त्रिंशत्सु देवेषु पूजा महो वर्त्तते॥ तत्रापि चैत्यं स्थापितमभूत्॥ अद्यापि च तत्पूजाप्रतिग्रहणमिति ज्ञायते॥

पुनरपि बोधिसत्त्वस्यैतदभूत्॥ कथं हि नाम प्रव्रज्या च काशिकानि (१) वस्त्राणि। स चेद्वनवासानुरूपाणि काषायाणि वस्त्राणि लभेयं शोभनं स्यात्॥

अथ शुद्धावासकायिकानां देवानामेतदभूत्। काषायैर्बोधिसत्त्वस्य कार्य्यमिति॥ तत्रैको देवपुत्रो दिव्यं रूपमन्तर्द्धाप्य लुब्धकरूपेण काषायवस्त्रप्रावृतो बोधिसत्त्वस्य पुरतोऽस्थात्॥

अथ बोधिसत्त्वस्तमेतदवोचत्॥ (२) मे लभ्यार्षं काषायाणि वस्त्राणि दद्यात् (३)। इमानि तेहं काशिकानि वस्त्राणि दद्यां॥

सावोचत् (४)॥ एतानि वस्त्राणि तव शोभन्ते। इमानि मम॥

बोधिसत्त्व आह॥ अहन्त्वां याचामि॥

ततस्तेन लुब्धकरूपेण देवपुत्रेण बोधिसत्त्वाय काषायाणि वस्त्राणि दत्तान्यभूवन्। काशिकानि गृहीते स्म॥

अथ स देवपुत्रो गौरवजातस्तानि वस्त्राणि उभाभ्यां शिरसि कृत्वा तत एव देवलोकमगमत् तेषां पूजार्थं॥ तच्छन्दकेन दृष्टमभूत्॥ तत्रापि चैत्यं स्थापितं अद्यापितचैत्यं काषायग्रहणमित्येवं ज्ञायते॥

---

१ क्वचित् ग्रन्थे "कौशिकानि" इति पाठः वर्त्तते।

२ प्रथमसंख्यके पुस्तके द्वितीये च "स चेत्" इति शब्दो नाव वर्त्तते।

३ "दद्यात्" दद्याः॥

४ "सावोचत्" स अवोचत्।

५ "गौरवजात" आत्मनै.रवः॥

यदा बोधिसत्त्वेन चूडां च्छित्वा काषायाणि वस्त्राणि प्रावृ-तानि तस्मिन् समये देवपुत्रशतसहस्रा हृष्टाः तुष्टा उदग्रा आत्तमनसः परममुदिताः प्रीतिसौमनस्यजाता हीहीकारकिलिकिला प्रक्ष्वेडितनिनादितनिर्घोषशब्दान् अकार्षुः ॥ सिद्धार्थः भो मार्षा कुमारः प्रव्रजितः । सोऽयमनुत्तरां सम्यक्सम्बोधिमभिसम्बुध्य धर्म्मचक्रं प्रवर्त्तयिष्यति ॥ असंख्येयान् जातिधर्म्मान् सत्वाञ्जात्याः परिमोचयिष्यति । यावज्जराव्याधिमरणशोकपरिदेवदुःखदौर्म्मनस्योपायासेभ्यः परिमोच्य संसारसागरात् पारमुत्तार्य्यानुत्तरे क्षेमेऽभयेऽशोके निरुपद्रवे शिवे विरजस्केऽमृते धर्म्मधातौ प्रतिष्ठापयिष्यतीति ॥ स च शब्दः शब्दपरम्परया यावदकनिष्ठभवनमभ्युद्गतोऽभूत् ॥

ततोऽन्तःपुरिकाभिः कुमारमपश्यन्तीभिः(१) ग्रैष्मिकवार्षिकहैमन्तिकेषु प्रासादेष्वासनेषु च गृहेषु परिमार्गमाणा यदा न पश्यन्ति स्म तदैकीभूताभिः कुररीभिरिवोत्क्रुष्टमभूत् ॥ तत्र काश्चित्ताः स्त्रियः परमशोकार्त्ता हा तातेति क्रन्दन्ति स्म ॥ काश्चिद्भ्रातः काश्चिद्भर्त्तरिति क्रन्दन्ति स्म ॥ काश्चिन्नाथेति क्रन्दन्ति स्म । काश्चिद्वा स्वामिन्निति ॥ काश्चिन्नानाप्रियवचनप्रलापैः काश्चिन्नाना कायपरिसर्पिकया रुदन्ति स्म ॥ काश्चिच्छिरोपकर्षया काश्चिदन्योन्यमुखावलोकितया रुदन्ति स्म ॥ काश्चिच्चतुपरिवर्त्तिकया काश्चित्स्ववदनानि वस्त्रैराच्छाद्य रुदन्ति स्म ॥ काश्चिदूरू पाणिभिः प्रस्फोटयन्त्यः काश्चिद्धृदयं पाणिभिस्ताड-

१ "कुमारमपश्यन्तीभिः" इति तृतीयसङ्ख्यके पुस्तके नास्ति ।

यन्त्यः। काश्चिद्गात्राणि पाणिभिः प्रस्फोटयन्त्यः काश्चिच्छिरांसि काश्चिच्छिरः पांशुभिरवकिरन्त्यो रुदन्ति स्म॥ काश्चिद्विक्षिप्तकेश्यः काश्चित् केशं विलुञ्चन्त्यः काश्चिदूर्द्ध्ववाहवः उच्चैरुत्क्रोशन्ति स्म॥ काश्चिन्मृग्य इव दिग्धविद्धाः सहसा प्रधावन्त्यो रुदन्ति स्म॥ काश्चित् मारुतकम्पिता इव कदल्यः प्रविकम्पमाना रुदन्ति स्म॥ काश्चिद्धरणीतले निपतिताः किञ्चित्प्राणाः काश्चित् जालोत्क्षिप्तमत्स्या इव पृथिव्यां परिवर्त्यमाना रुदन्ति स्म॥ काश्चिन्मूलच्छिन्ना इव वृक्षाः सहसाधरणीतले निपत्य रुदन्ति स्म॥

तच्च शब्दं राजा श्रुत्वा शाक्यानामन्त्रयते स्म॥ किमेतदुच्चैरन्तःपुरे शब्दः श्रूयते॥

ते शाक्या विज्ञाय कथयन्ति स्म॥ कुमारः किल महाराजाऽन्तःपुरे न दृश्यते॥

राजाऽऽह॥ क्षिप्रं नगरद्वाराणि पिधयत। कुमारमभ्यन्तरे मृगयामः॥

ते सान्तर्बहिर्मृगयन्ते। सान्तर्बहिर्मृगयमाणा न पश्यन्ति स्म॥

महाप्रजावत्यपि गौतमी परिदेवमाना महीतले परिवर्त्तते स्म राजानं शुद्धोदनमेवमाह॥ क्षिप्रं मां महाराज पुत्रेण सङ्गिनीं कुरुष्वेति॥

ततो राजा चतुर्द्दिशमश्वारोहदूतान् प्रेषयति स्म॥ गच्छत यावत्कुमारं न पश्यत तावन्मा निवर्त्तयथ॥

यत् नैमित्तिकैर्वैपञ्चिकैश्च (१) व्याहृतमभूत्। मङ्गलद्वारेण

१ पञ्चसंख्यके पुस्तके "वैपञ्चिकः" शब्दो न दृश्यते॥

बोधिसत्त्वोऽभिनिष्क्रमिष्यतीति ॥ ते मङ्गलद्वारेण गच्छन्तः पश्यन्ति स्म। अन्तरापथे पुष्पवर्षं प्रपतितम्॥ तेषामेतदभूत्॥ अनेन पथा कुमारोऽभिनिर्गत इति॥

ते स्वल्पमन्तरं गत्वा तं देवपुत्रं पश्यन्ति स्म (१)। बोधिसत्त्वस्य काशिकवस्त्राणि शिरसि कृत्वा आगच्छन्तं॥ तेषामेतदभूत्। इमानि खलु कुमारस्य काशिकवस्त्राणि। मा खलु अनेनैषां वस्त्राणामर्थे कुमारो जीविताद्व्यवरोपितः स्यात्। गृह्णीतैनमिति॥ भूयः पश्यन्ति स्म तस्य पृष्ठतः छन्दकं कण्ठकमाभरणानि चादायागच्छन्तं॥ ततस्ते परस्परमूचुः। मा तावद्भोः साहसं कार्षीः एष छन्दकोऽभ्यागच्छति कण्ठकमादाय यावदेनं प्रक्ष्यामः॥

ते छन्दकं परिपृच्छन्ति स्म। हे छन्दक मा खल्वनेनैव पुरुषेण काशिकानां वस्त्राणामर्थे कुमारो जीविताद्व्यवरोपितः स्यात्॥

छन्दक आह। नह्येतत्। अपि त्वनेन कुमाराय काषा-

---

१ अत्र प्रकरणे प्रथमसङ्ख्यके पुस्तके देवपुत्रस्यागमनं न दृश्यते। छन्दकेनैव तत्कृत-वस्त्रविनिमयादिवृत्तान्तं उक्तं। तत्र पाठो यथा। "ते स्वल्पमन्तरं गत्वा (एव) छन्दको ऽभ्यागतं पश्यन्ति स्म॥ छन्दक कुत्र गच्छति कुमारः इत्युक्ते कुमारेण कण्ठकं आभरणं त्यक्त्वा मह्यं हस्ते दत्वा मातापितरयोः मम जीविताद्व्यवरोपितःस्यात् इत्युक्त्वा त्वं स्वपुरं गच्छेत्। तस्य पृष्ठतः दृष्ट्वा कण्ठकमाभरणानि चादायागच्छामि।" परस्परमूचुः। तं पुनः छन्दकं वृत्तान्तं परिपृच्छन्ति स्म। कुमारेण स्वचूडाः छित्त्वा गगने क्षिपन्ति। एतत् मया पश्यति स्म। ततः बोधिसत्त्वाय काषायाणि वस्त्राणि देवपुत्रेण शिरसि कृत्वा आगच्छन्तं। तेषामेतदभूत्। इमानि काषायाणि देवपुत्रेण कुमाराय दत्तानि। कुमारेण चास्मै काशिकवस्त्राणि दत्तानि। अथ स देवपुत्रस्तानि वस्त्राण्युभाभ्यां पाणिभ्यां शिरसि कृत्वा तत एव देवलोकमगमत् तेषां पूजार्थं॥ ते पुनश्छन्दकं परिपृच्छन्त। तत्किं मन्यसे छन्दक" इत्येवं। अत्र तु अविकलः पाठ एव धृतः नास्माभिः परिशोधितः।

यवस्त्राणि दत्तानि । कुमारेण चास्मै काशिकवस्त्राणि दत्तानि ॥ अथ स देवपुत्रस्तानि वस्त्राणुभाभ्यां पाणिभ्यां शिरसि कृत्वा तत एव देवलोकमगमत् तेषां पूजार्थं ॥

ते भूयश्छन्दकं परिपृच्छन्ति । तत्किं मन्यसे छन्दक गच्छामो वयं । शक्यः कुमारः प्रतिनिवर्त्तयितुं ॥

स आह । मा खलु । अनिवर्त्त्यः कुमारो दृढवीर्य्यपराक्रमः ॥ एवञ्च तेनोक्तं । न तावदहं पुनरपि कपिलवस्तुमहानगरं प्रवेक्ष्यामि । यावन्मे (१) नानुत्तरा सम्यक्सम्बोधिरभिसम्बोध्येति ॥ यथा कुमारेणोक्तं तथैव तद्भविष्यति ॥

तत्कस्मात् अनिवर्त्त्यः कुमारः ॥

दृढवीर्य्यपराक्रमतः (२) ॥

ततश्छन्दकः कण्ठकमाभरणानि चादायान्तःपुरं प्राविशत् ॥ ततस्तान्याभरणानि चिरेण कालेन भद्रिकस्य शाक्यकुमारस्य महानाम्नोऽनिरुद्धस्य चावाधन्ते स्म (३) ॥ तानि महानारायण सङ्घातनकायस्यार्थं । नारायणसङ्घातन (४) न शक्नुवन्ति स्म धारयितुं । यदा न कश्चित्तानि धारयितुं शक्नोति स्म तदा प्रजापत्या (५) गौतम्या चिन्तितमभूत् । यावदहमिमान्याभरणानि पश्यामि तावन्मम हृदये शोको भविष्यति । नन्वहमि-

१ "मे" मया । चतुर्थंऽंश्लकपुस्तके यावन्नानुत्तरा सम्यक्सम्बोधिमभिसम्भुध्यते इति पाठः वर्त्तते ॥

२ "दृढवीर्य्यपराक्रमः" इति वा पाठः ॥

३ "चावाध्यन्ते स्म" च चावाध्यन्ते स्म । भद्रिकस्येत्यादौ कृतोऽशार्थे षष्ठी ॥

४ "सङ्घातन" सङ्घाता ॥

५ "प्रजापत्या" प्रजापत्येति वा पाठः ॥

माल्याभरणानि पुष्करिण्यां प्रक्षिपेयमिति ॥ ततो महाप्रजापती गौतमी तान्याभरणानि पुष्करिण्यां प्रक्षिपति स्म ॥ अद्यापि सा आभरणपुष्करिणीत्येवं सञ्ज्ञायते (१) ॥ तत्रेदमुच्यते ।

निष्क्रान्तु शूरो यद विदु बोधिसत्त्वो
नगरं विबुद्धं कपिलपुरं समन्तं ।
मन्यन्ति सर्व्वे शयनगतः कुमारो-
ऽन्योन्य हृष्टाः प्रमुदिता आलपन्ते (२) ॥
गोपा विबुद्धा तथापि दृष्टिगारे
शयनं निरिक्षी न दर्शि बोधिसत्त्वं ।
उत्क्रोशमुक्ता नरपतिनोऽगारे
हा वञ्चिता स्मः कहिंनु बोधिसत्त्वः (३) ॥
राजा श्रुणित्वा धरणितले निरस्तो
उत्क्रोशु कृत्वा अहो मम एकपुत्रो ।
सो क्षोभितो ही जलघटसंप्रसिक्तो
आश्वासयितो बहुशतशाकियानां (४) ॥
गोपा सयातो धरणितले निपत्य

१ आभरणप्रक्षेपणप्रकरणं प्रथमसंख्यके पुस्तके नास्ति। तत्स्थाने एतद्वाक्यं वर्त्तते। तद्यथा "इति श्रुत्वा ते सर्व्वेऽमात्याः कपिलवस्तुनि महानगरे प्रत्यागत्य राज्ञः शुद्धोदनस्याग्रे एतद्वृत्तान्तं नैवेदयेत् (न्यवेदिषुः)। राजा श्रुणित्वा (श्रुत्वा) तदा दुःखार्तोऽभूत् ॥

२ "निष्क्रान्तु" निष्क्रान्तः। "यद" यदा। "विदु" विद्वान्। "अन्योन्य" अन्योन्यं॥

३ "दृष्टिगारे" शय्यागारे। "निरीक्षी" निरीक्ष्य। "दर्शि" दृष्टवती। "नरपतिनः" नरपतेः। "कहिंनु" कुत्र गतः ॥

४ "श्रुणित्वा" श्रुत्वा। "उत्क्रोशु" उत्क्रोशं। "एक पुत्रो सो" अत्र गाथारीत्या विसर्गस्थाने उकारः। "आश्वासयितो बहुशतशाकियानां" बहुशतशाक्यैः आश्वासितः॥

केशां लुनाति अवशिरि भूषणानि ।
अहो सुभ्रष्टं मम पुरि नायकेन
सर्व्वप्रियेभि नचिरे तु विप्रयोगः (१) ॥
रूपा सुरूपा सुविमलविचित्रिताङ्गा
अच्छा विशुद्धा जगति प्रिय मनापा ।
धन्या प्रशस्ता दिवि भुवि पूजनीया
क्व त्वं गतोऽसि मम शयि च्छोरयित्वा (२) ॥
न पास्ये पानं नचात्स्ये सुप्रसादं
भूमौ शयिष्ये जटामुकुटं धरिष्ये ।
स्नानं जहित्वा व्रततपा चाचरिष्ये
यावन्न द्रक्ष्ये गुणधरबोधिसत्त्वं (३) ॥
उद्यान सर्व्वे अफलपत्रपुष्पा
हारा विशुद्धा तमरजपांशुतुल्याः ।
वेश्मं न शोभि अटविपुरप्रकाशं
यत्तेन त्यक्तं नरवरपुङ्गवेन (४) ॥
हा गीतवाद्याः सुमधुरमञ्जुघोषाः
हा इस्त्रिगारा विगलित भूषणाभिः ।

---

१ "शयानो" शय्यातः । "अवशिरि" अवधारणाति । "पुरि नायकेन" परिणायकेन वा पाठः । "सर्व्वप्रियेभि" सर्व्वप्रियैः ॥

२ "रूपा" इत्यादिसम्बोधनान्तं पदं । "शयि" शय्यां । "च्छोरयित्वा" त्यक्त्वा इत्यर्थः ॥

३ "जहित्वा" हित्वा । "व्रततपा" व्रततपः ॥

४ "उद्यान सर्व्वे" सर्व्वाणि उद्यानानि । "अफलपत्रपुष्पा" अफलपत्रपुष्पाणि । "विशुद्धा" विशुष्काः । "तमरज-" तमोरजः । "वेश्मं" वेश्म । "शोभि" शोभते ॥

हा हेमजालैः परिस्फुटमञ्जरीचं
न भूय द्रक्ष्ये गुणधरविप्रहीणा (१)॥
मातृस्वसा च परमसुखदुःखप्राप्ता
आश्वासयाती मा रुद शाक्यकन्ये।
पूर्व्वे च उक्तं नरपुङ्गवेन
कर्त्तास्मि लोके जरमरणात् प्रमोक्षं (२)॥
सो च महर्षी कुशलसहस्रचीर्णः
षटयोजनानि प्रतिगन्तु रात्रिशेषे।
छन्दस्य देती हयवर भूषणानि
छन्दो गृहीत्वा कपिलपुरं प्रयाहि (३)॥
मातापितॄणां मम वचनेन पृच्छेः
गतः कुमारो न च पुनः शोचयेथा।
बुद्धित्व बोधिं पुनरहमागमिष्ये
धर्मं श्रुणित्वा भविष्यथ शान्तचित्ताः (४)॥
छन्दो रुदित्वा प्रतिभणि नायकस्य
न मेऽस्ति शक्ति बलपराक्रमो वा।
स्वनेषु मह्य नरवरज्ञातिसङ्घाः
छन्दा क नीतो गुणधरबोधिसत्त्वः (५)॥

---

१ "हस्तिमारा" क्यामाराः। "विगलित" विगलित। "भूषणाभिः" भूषणैः॥
२ "आश्वासयाती" आश्वासयति। "रुद" रुदिहि। "जरमरणात्" जरामरणात्
३ "सो" सः। "प्रतिगन्तु" प्रतिगतः। "देती" दत्त्वा। "हयवर" हयवरं॥
४ "पृच्छेः" पृच्छाः। "शोचयेथा" शोचय। "बुद्धित्व" बुद्ध्वा। "श्रुणित्वा" श्रुत्वा॥
५ "प्रतिभणि" प्रतिभणति। "शक्ति" शक्तिः। "स्वनेषु" स्वनुः। मह्य" मम॥

मा चापि छन्दो प्रतिभणि बोधिसत्त्वः
तुष्टा भवित्वा अपि मम ज्ञातिसङ्घाः ।
आज्ञा रसज्ञा त्वयि सद भविष्यन्ति
प्रमेण सर्वं त्वयि नो विवर्त्तिष्यन्ते (१) ॥
छन्दो ग्रहीत्वा हयवर भूषणानि
उद्यानप्राप्तो नरवर पुङ्गवस्य ।
उद्यानपालः प्रमुदितु वेगजातः
आनन्दशब्द प्रतिभणि शाकियानां (२) ॥
अयं कुमारो हयवर छन्दकश्च
उद्यानप्राप्तो नच पुनः शोचितव्यो ।
राजा श्रुणित्वा परिहृतु शाकियेभिः
उद्यानप्राप्तो प्रमुदितु वेगजातः (३) ॥
गोपा विदित्वा दृढमतिबोधिसत्त्वं
नो वापि हर्षी न च गिरं श्रद्दधाति ।
अज्ञानमेतद्विनिर्गतु यत् कुमारः
अप्राप्य बोधि पुनरिहागमेया (४) ॥
दृष्टा तु राजा हयवर छन्दकश्च

१ "मा चापि" चापं मा कुरु । "प्रतिभणि" प्रतिभणति । "भवित्वा" भूत्वा । "आज्ञा" आज्ञाकारः । "सद" सदा । "प्रमेण" प्रेम्णा ॥

२ "हयवर" हयवरं । "नरवर" नरवरस्य । "आनन्दशब्द" आनन्दशब्दं । "प्रमुदितु" प्रमुदितः । "वेगजातः जातवेगः । "प्रतिभणि" प्रतिभणति स्म । "शाकियानां" शाक्यानां ॥

३ "हयवर" हयवरः । "श्रुणित्वा" श्रुत्वा । "परिहृतु" परिहृतः । "शाकियेभिः" शाक्यैः । "प्रमुदितु" प्रमुदितः । "वेगजातः" जातवेगः ॥

४ "विनिर्गतु" विनिर्गतः । "आगमेया" आगच्छेत् ॥

उत्क्रोशु कृत्वा धरणितले निरस्तः ।
हा मह्य पुत्रा सुकुमारगीतवाद्या
क्व त्वं गतोऽसि विजहीय सर्व्वराज्यं (१) ॥
साधु भणाहि वचनं ममेह छन्द
को वा प्रयोगः क्व च गन्तु बोधिसत्त्वः ।
केनाथ नीतो विवरित केन द्वाराः
पूजा च तस्या कथं कृत देवसङ्घैः (२) ॥
छन्दो भणाति शृणु मम पार्थिवेन्द्र
रात्रौ प्रसुप्ते नगरिषु बालवृद्धे ।
सो मञ्जुघोषो मम भणि बोधिसत्त्वः
छन्दो ददाहि मम लघु अश्वराजं (३) ॥
सो बोधयामि नरगणनारीसङ्घं
सुप्ता प्रसुप्ताः न च गिरं ते शृणन्ति ।
सो रोदमानो ददिय ऊ अश्वराजं
हन्त व्रजाही हितकर येन कामं (४) ॥
शक्रेण द्वारा विवरित यन्त्रयुक्ताः
पालास्ततो हयचरणे विक्षिप्ताः ।

---

१ "चयचर-" चयचरं । "उत्क्रोशु" उत्क्रोशं । "मह्य" मम । "पुत्रा" हे पुत्र । "-वाद्या" -वाद्य । "विजहीय" विहाय ॥

२ "भणाहि" भण । "गन्तु" गतः । "विवरित" विवरिताः । "तस्या" तस्य । "कृत" कृता ॥

३ "भणाति" भणति । "नगरिषु" नगरेषु । "सो" सः । "भणि" अभणत् । "ददाहि" देहि ॥

४ "सो" सोऽहं । "शृणन्ति" शृण्वन्ति । "सो" सः । "रोदमानो" रुदन् । "ददिय" दत्वा । "व्रजाही" व्रज ॥

आरुढ शूरः प्रचलितत्रिसहस्रः
मार्गो नभेस्मिन् सुविपुल येन क्रान्तः (१) ॥
आभा प्रमुक्ता विहततमोऽन्धकारा
पुष्पा पतितः तुतुरियशता रणिषु ।
देवास्तुविंसु तथपि हि चाप्सराणि
नभसा प्रयातो परिवृतु देवसङ्घैः (२) ॥
छन्दो गृहीत्वा हयवरु भूषणानि
अन्तः ुरे सो उपगतु रोदमानः ।
दृष्ट्वा तु गोपा हयवरु छन्दकञ्च
संमूर्च्छयित्वा धरणितले निरस्ता (३) ॥
उद्युक्त सर्व्वो सुविपुलनारिसङ्घः
वारि गृहीत्वा स्नपयिसु शाक्यकन्यां ।
अद्यैव कालं करिष्यसि शोकप्राप्ता
द्वाभ्यां प्रियाभ्यां बहु भवि विप्रयोगः (४) ॥
क्षामं जनित्वा सुदुःखितु शाक्यकन्या
कण्ठे बलं व्याहरय वराम्बराजं ।
अनुस्मरित्वा पुरिमूक कामक्रीडां

---

१ "विचरित" विचरिताः । "चतस्रः" चत्वारः । "आरुढ" आरूढः । "सुविपुल" सुविपुलः ॥

२ "पुष्पा पतितः" पुष्पाणि पतितानि । "तुतुरियशता" तूर्य्यशतानि । "रणिषु" रेणुः । "स्तुविंषु" तुष्टुवुः । "तथपि" तथापि । "चाप्सराणि" चाप्सरसः । "प्रयातो" प्रयातः । "परिवृतु" परिवृतः ॥

३ "हयवरु" हयवरं । "सो" सः । "उपगतु" उपगतः । "रोदमानः" रुदन् । "हयवरु" हयवरं ॥

४ "उद्युक्त" उद्युक्तः । "सर्व्वो" सर्व्वः । "स्नपयिसु" स्नापयामासुः । "भवि" भवति ॥

नानाप्रकारो प्रलपति शोकप्राप्ता (१) ॥

हा मह्य प्रीतिजनना हा मम नरपुङ्गवा विमलचन्द्रमुखा ।

हा मम सुरूपरूपा हा मम वरलक्षणा विमलतेजधरा (२) ॥

हा मम अनिन्दिताङ्ग सुजात अनुपूर्व्वउद्गता असमा ।

हा मम गुणाग्रधारि नरमरुभिः पूजिता परमकारुणिका (३) ॥

हा मम बलोपपेता नारायणस्थामवान् निहतशत्रुगणा ।

हा मम सुमञ्जुघोषा कलविङ्करुतस्वरा मधुरब्रह्मरुता (४) ॥

हा मम अनन्तकीर्त्ति शतपुण्यसमुद्गता विमलपुण्यधरा ।

हा मम अनन्तवर्णा गुणगणप्रतिमण्डिता ऋषिगणप्रीतिकरा (५) ॥

हा मम सुजातजाता लुम्बिनीवनोत्तमे भ्रमरगीतरुते ।

हा मम विघुष्टशब्दा दिवि भुवि अभिपूजिता विमलपुण्यज्ञान-
द्रुमा (६) ॥

---

१ "स्थामं जनित्वा" बलं कृत्वा इत्यर्थः । "सुदुःखितु" सुदुःखिता । "कण्ठे बलं बाहय" बलं यथास्यात् तथा कण्ठे अपाय । "अनुस्मरित्वा" अनुस्मृत्य । "पुरिमुक" पूर्व्वतनीं ॥

२ "मह्य" मम । "प्रीतिजनना" हे प्रीतिजनन । "नरपुङ्गवा" हे नरपुङ्गव । "सुरूपरूपा" हे सुरूपरूप । "वरलक्षणा" हे वरलक्षण । "विमलतेजधरा" हे विमलतेजोधर ।

३ "अनुपूर्व्वउद्गता" हे अनुपूर्व्वोद्गत । "असमा" हे असम । "गुणाग्रधारि" हे गुणाग्रधारिन् । "नरमरुभिः" नरामरैः । "पूजिता" हे पूजित । "परमकारुणिका" हे परमकारुणिक ॥

४ "बलोपपेता" हे बलोपेत । "नारायणस्थामवान्" हे नारायणस्थामवन् । "निहतशत्रुगणा" हे निहतशत्रुगण । "सुमञ्जुघोषा" हे सुमञ्जुघोष । "कलविङ्करुत-स्वरा" हे कलविङ्करुतस्वर । "मधुरब्रह्मरुता" हे मधुरब्रह्मरुत ॥

५ "शतपुण्यसमुद्गता" हे शतपुण्यसमुद्गत । "विमलपुण्यधरा" हे विमलपुण्यधर । "अनन्तवर्णा" हे अनन्तवर्ण । "गुणगणप्रतिमण्डिता" हे गुणगणप्रतिमण्डित । "ऋषि-गणप्रीतिकरा" हे ऋषिगणप्रीतिकर ॥

६ "सुजातजाता" हे सुजातजात । "विघुष्टशब्दा" हे विघुष्टशब्द । "अभिपू-जिता" हे अभिपूजित । "विमलपुण्यज्ञानद्रुमा" हे विमलपुण्यज्ञानद्रुम ॥

हा मम रसरसाया बिम्बोष्ठा कमललोचना कनकवर्णनिभा।

हा मम शुद्धदन्ता गोक्षीरतुषारसन्निभासहितदन्ता (१)॥

हा मम सुनास ऊर्णाभ्रुमुखान्तरेस्थिता तेजविमला।

हा मम सुवृत्तस्कन्धा चापोदर एनेयजङ्घवृत्तकटी (२)॥

हा मम गजहस्तोरुकरचरणविशुद्धशोभना ताम्रनखा।

इति तस्य भूषणानि पुण्याहृतानि पार्थिवे प्रीतिकरा (३)॥

हा मह्य गीतवाद्या वरपुष्पविलेपना शुभऋतुप्रवरा।

हा मह्य पुष्पगन्धा अन्तःपुरि गीतवादितैर्हर्षकरा (४)॥

हा कण्ठका सुजाता मम भर्त्तुः सहायक त्वया क्व नीतो।

हा छन्दका निकरुणा न बोधयसि गच्छमानके नरवरिष्ठे (५)॥

गच्छत्ययं हितकरो एका गिरं तस्मिन्नन्तरे न भणसि कस्मात्।

इतु अद्य पुरवरतो गच्छति नरदम्यसारथिः कारुणिकः (६)॥

कथं वा गतो हितकरो केन वा निष्क्रामितो इतु स राजकुलात्।

कतमां दिशमनुगतो धन्या वनगुल्मदेवता याऽस्य समुखी (७)॥

---

१ "रसरसाया" से रसरसाय। "बिम्बोष्ठा" से बिम्बोष्ठ। "कमललोचना" से कमललोचन। "कनकवर्णनिभा" से कनकवर्णनिभ। "शुद्धदन्ता" से शुद्धदन्त। "गोक्षीरतुषारसन्निभासहितदन्ता" से गोक्षीरतुषारसन्निभसहितदन्त॥

२ "ऊर्णाभ्रुमुखान्तरेस्थिता" ऊर्णाभ्रुमुखान्तरेस्थित। "तेजविमला" से विमलतेजः। "सुवृत्तस्कन्धा" से सुवृत्तस्कन्ध। "एनेयजङ्घवृत्तकटी" से ऐणेयजङ्घवृत्तकटे॥

३ "-शोभना" से शोभन। "ताम्रनखा" से ताम्रनख। "प्रीतिकरा" प्रीतिकराणि।

४ "मह्य" मम। "मह्य" मम। "हर्षकरा" से हर्षंकर।

५ "कण्ठका" कण्ठक। "सुजाता" से सुजात। "छन्दका" से छन्दक। "निकरुणा" से निष्करुण। "गच्छमानके इत्यादि" गच्छन्तं नरवरिष्ठं इत्यर्थः॥

६ "हितकरो" हितकरः। "एका" इत्येकां। "इतु" इतः।

७ "हितकरो" हितकरः। "निष्क्रामितो" निष्क्रामितः। "इतु" इतः। "समुखी" सम्मुखस्थिता। "सखी" इत्ययमपि क्वचित् पाठः॥

अतिदुःख मह्य छन्दा निधि दर्शय मेव उद्धृता चक्षुर्दद ।
सर्व्वजनैस्त्व छन्दा मातापितृनित्यवर्त्तिता पूजनीया (१) ॥
तानपि अहित्व निर्गतु किं पुनरिमं स्त्रिकामरतिं ।
हा धिक् प्रियैर्व्वियोगो नटरङ्गस्वभावसन्निभो अनित्यः (२) ॥
संज्ञाग्रहेण बाला दृष्टिविपर्य्यास निश्रिता अज्ञच्युति ।
प्रागेव तेन भणितं नास्ति जरामरणं संस्कृते काश्चित् (३) ॥
सखा परिपूर्य्यतोऽस्य आशा स्पृशतु वरबोधिमुत्तमां ।
द्रुमवरिष्टे बुद्धित्व बोधिविरजां पुनरपि एति (४) ॥
पुरवरेऽस्मिन् छन्दकः परमदीनमानसो गोपिकाय ।
वचनं श्रुणित्वैनां साश्रुकण्ठकगिरं सम्प्रभाषते (५) ॥
साधु गोपिनि शृणोहि मे वचः रात्रिये रहसि यामि मध्यमे ।
सर्व्वनारीगणसंप्रसुप्तके सो तदा च शतपुण्यउद्गतः (६) ॥
आलपति मम देहि कण्ठकं तन्निशम्य वचनं तदन्तरं ।
तुभ्यप्रेक्षेमि शयानसुप्तिकमुखैर्घोषं अङ्ग तव मुञ्चयी (७) ॥
उत्थि गोपि अमु याति ते प्रियो देवता वचनं तं निरोधयी ।

---

१ "मह्य" मम। "छन्दा" हे छन्दक। "निधि" निधिं। "मेव उद्धृता" मेवं उद्धृतं। "दद" ददस्व। "छन्दा" हे छन्दक। "नित्यवर्त्तिता" नित्यानुवर्त्तिता ॥

२ "तानपि" तावपि। "अहित्व" हित्वा। "निर्गतु" निर्गतः। "इमं" इमां "स्त्रिकामरतिं" स्त्रीकामरतिं। "-सन्निभो अनित्यः" सन्निभोऽनित्यः ॥

३ "दृष्टिविपर्य्यास" दृष्टिविपर्य्यासात्। "काश्चित्" किञ्चित् ॥

४ "सखा" हे सखे। "परिपूर्य्यतो" परिपूर्य्यतां। "बुद्धित्व" बुद्धा ॥

५ "गोपिकाय" गोपायाः। "श्रुणित्वा" श्रुत्वा ॥

६ "शृणोहि" शृणु। "रात्रिये" रात्र्याः। "यामि" यामे। "सो" सः ॥

७ "मम" मह्यं। "तुभ्य प्रेक्षेमि" त्वां पश्यामि। "शयानसुप्तिकं" शयने सुप्तां "अङ्ग" अङ्गं। "मुञ्चयी" अमुञ्चं ॥

एका इस्त्रि न कापि विबुध्यते चोद्यमानः समलङ्कारिस्वना (१)॥
अश्वराजं ददमी नरोत्तमे कण्ठको हि पति उग्रतेजवां।
ओम्रमाव स्वर तस्य गच्छति नो कश्चिच्छृणुते पुरोत्तमे (२)॥
देवताभिः ओस्वापनं कृतं स्वर्णरूप्यमणिकोटिता मही।
कण्ठकस्य चरणैः पराहता सो रणी मधुरभीष्मशोभनो (३)॥
नो च केचिच्छृणुवन्ति मानुषाः पुष्य युक्त अभूत्तस्मिन् अन्तरे।
चन्द्रज्योतिष नभे प्रतिस्थिताः देवकोटि गगणे कृताञ्जली (४)॥
ओनमन्त शिरसाऽभिवन्दिषु यक्षराक्षसगणैरुपस्थिताः।
लोकपालाः चतुरो महर्द्धिकाः कण्ठकस्य चरण करे न्यसी
पद्मकेसर (५)॥
विशुद्धनिर्मलं सो च पुण्यतेजउद्गतो आरुही कुमुदवर्षिकोपमं।
षड्विकारधरणी प्रकम्पिता बुद्धक्षेत्र स्फुटाभनिर्मलाः (६)॥
शक्रो देवगुरुः शचीपतिः स्वाम द्वारांश्च विवरी तदन्तरे।

---

१ "उत्थि" उत्तिष्ठ। "वयु" एव। "याति" गच्छति। "प्रियो" प्रियः। "निरोधयां" न्यवध्नत्। "इस्त्रि" स्त्री। "समलङ्कारिस्वना" समलङ्कृत्य॥

२ "ददमि" ददामि। "नरोत्तमे" नरोत्तमाय। "पति" पतिः। ओम्रमाव" ओम्रमाभं। "स्वर" स्वरः॥

३ "ओस्वापनं" प्रस्वापनं। "सो रणी" सोऽरणत्॥

४ "शृणुवन्ति" शृण्वन्ति। "पुष्य युक्त" पुष्यः युक्तः उदितः इत्यर्थः। "चन्द्रज्योतिष" चन्द्रज्योतींषि। "नभे" नभसि। "प्रतिस्थिता" प्रतिष्ठितानि। "देवकोटी" देवकोट्यः। "कृताञ्जली" कृताञ्जलयः॥

५ "ओनमन्त" प्रणमन्तः। "अभिवन्दिषु" अभ्यवादिषुः अपूजयन् इत्यर्थः। "चरण" चरणान्। "न्यसी" निदधुः। "पद्मकेसर" पद्मकेसरान्॥

६ "विशुद्धनिर्मलं" विशुद्धनिर्मलान्। "सो च" स च। "पुण्यतेज" पुण्यमततेजो वा पाठः। "आरुहि" आरोहत्। "बुद्धक्षेत्र" बुद्धक्षेत्राणि। "स्फुटाभनिर्मलाः" स्फुटाभनिर्मलानि।

देवकोटिनियुतैः पुरस्कृतः सोऽव्रजी अमरनागपूजितः (१) ॥
संग्रामाच इह आति कण्ठको लोकनाथं वहति नभोऽन्तरे ।
देवदानवगणाः सइन्द्रिका ये वहन्ति सुगतस्य गच्छतः (२) ॥
अप्सराः कुशलगीतवादिते बोधिसत्त्वगुणभाषमाणिकाः ।
कण्ठकस्य बल ते ददन्तिकाः मुञ्चि घोष मधुरं मनोरमं (३) ॥
कण्ठको वहति लोकनायकं शीघ्रशीघ्रमजनेहि खेदतां ।
नास्ति ते भयमपायदुर्गतिं लोकनाथमभिधारयित्वना (४) ॥
एकमेकमभिनन्दते सुरो वाहनस्मि अह लोकनायके ।
नो च किंचिदिह देवेषु विद्यते देवकोटिचरणैर्न मर्दितं (५) ॥
पश्य कण्ठक नभोऽन्तरे इमं मार्ग संस्थितु विचित्रशोभनं ।
रत्नवेदिकविचित्रमण्डितं दिव्यसारवरगन्धधूपितं (६) ॥
एन कण्ठक शुभेन कर्मणा त्रायस्त्रिंशभवने सुनिर्मिते ।
अप्सरैः परिवृतः पुरस्कृतो दिव्यकामरतिभी रमिष्यसि (७) ॥
साधु गोपि मा खलु भूय रोदिहि तुष्टु भोहि परमप्रहर्षिता ।
द्रक्ष्यसे नचिरतो नरोत्तमं बोधिप्राप्तं अमरैः पुरस्कृतं (८) ॥

---

१ "स्वाम" स्वयं। "विचरो" अहरोत्। "सोऽव्रजो" सोऽव्रजत् ॥

२ "सङ्ग्रामाच" सङ्ग्रामात्। "आति" याति गच्छति। "स इन्द्रिकाः" सेन्द्रकाः। "सुगतस्य गच्छतः" गच्छन्तं सुगतं ॥

३ "अप्सराः" अप्सरसः। "बल" बलं। "ते" ताः। "मुञ्चि" अमुञ्चन्। "घोष" घोषं। "ददन्तिकाः" ददत्यः ॥

४ "वहति" वह। "अजनेहि" मा जनय। "अपायदुर्गतिं" अपायदुर्गतिः। लोकनाथं अभिधृत्य स्थितस्य ते भयं अपायेन सह दुर्गतिश्च नास्तीत्यर्थः ॥

५ "एकमेकं" प्रत्येकं। "सुरः" सुरः। "वाहनस्मि" वाहनोऽस्मि। "अह" अहं ॥

६ "मार्ग संस्थितु" मार्गं संस्थितं ॥

७ "एन" एतेन। "अप्सरैः" अप्सरोभिः। "रमिष्यसि" रंस्यसे ॥

८ "साधु" हे साध्वि। "भूय" भूयः। "रोदिहि" रुदिहि। "तुष्टु" तुष्टा। "भोहि" भव ॥

ये नराः सुकृतकर्म्मकारकास्ते न गोपि सद रोदितव्यकाः ।
सो च पुण्यशततेजउद्गतो हर्षितव्य न स रोदितव्यकः (१) ॥
सप्तराचिभणमानु गोपिके सो वियूह नपि शक्य शोपितुं ।
यो वियूह अभूत्तच पार्थिवे निष्क्रमन्ति नरदेवपूजिते (२) ॥
लोभ तुभ्य परमा अचिन्तिया यत्तुपस्थितु जगे हितङ्करे ।
मह्य सञ्ज्ञि स्वकमेव वर्त्तते त्वं हि भेष्यषि यथा नरोत्तम(३)इति ॥

इति अभिनिष्क्रमणपरिवर्त्तो नाम पञ्चदशः ॥ १५ ॥

षोडशाध्यायप्रारम्भः ॥

एवं खलु भिक्षवः छन्दको बोधिसत्त्वाधिष्ठानेन राज्ञः शुद्धोदनस्य गोपायाः शाक्यकन्यायाश्च सर्व्वस्य चान्तःपुरस्य सर्व्वस्य च शाक्यगणस्य शोकविनोदनकथामकार्षीत् ॥

इति हि भिक्षवो बोधिसत्त्वो लुब्धकरूपाय देवपुत्राय काशिकानि वस्त्राणि दत्त्वा तस्य सकाशात् काषायाणि वस्त्राणि गृहीत्वा स्वयमेवं प्रव्रज्यां लोकानुवर्त्तनामुपादाय सत्त्वानुकम्पायै सत्त्वपरिपाचनार्थं ॥

अथ बोधिसत्त्वो येनैव शाक्या ब्राह्मणी आश्रमस्तेनोपसङ्क्रा-

---

१ "सद" सदा। "सो च" स च। "हर्षितव्य" हर्षितव्यः। "न स रोदितव्यकः" न शोचितव्यः।

२ "सप्तराचिभणमानु" सप्तरात्रिं भणमानेन। "सो वियूह" स व्यूहः। "नपि" नापि। "शक्य" शक्यः। "शोपितुं" शापयितुं। "वियूह" व्यूहः। "निष्क्रमन्ति" निष्क्रामति ॥

३ "लोभ तुभ्य" लब्धा त्वया। "अचिन्तिया" अचिन्तनीया शान्तिरितिशेषः। "यत्तुपस्थितु" यदुपस्थितः। "जगे" जगति। "हितङ्करो" हितकरः। "मह्य" मम। "सञ्ज्ञि" ज्ञानं। "भेष्यषि" भविष्यसि।

मत्(१)॥ सा बोधिसत्त्वं वासेन भक्तेन चोपनिमन्त्रयते स्म ॥ ततो बोधिसत्त्वः पद्मायाः ब्राह्मण्या आश्रमं गच्छति स्म ॥ तयाऽपि बोधिसत्त्वो वासेन भक्तेन चोपनिमन्त्रितोऽभूत् ॥ ततो रैवतस्य ब्रह्मर्षेराश्रममगमत् ॥ असावपि बोधिसत्त्वं तथैवोपनिमन्त्रयते स्म ॥ तथैव राजकोऽपि त्रिमदण्डिकपुत्रो (२) बोधिसत्त्वमुपनिमन्त्रयते स्म ॥ इति हि भिक्षवो बोधिसत्त्वोऽनुपूर्व्वेण वैशालीं महानगरीमनुप्राप्तोऽभूत् ॥

तेन खलु पुनः समयेनाऽऽराडः कालामो (३) वैशालीमुपनिश्रित्य प्रतिवसति स्म । महता श्रावकसङ्घेन सार्द्धं त्रिभिः शिष्यशतैः ॥ स शिष्येभ्यः आकिञ्चन्यायतनसहव्रतायै (४) धर्म्मं देशयति स्म ॥ स बोधिसत्त्वं दूरत एवागच्छन्तं दृष्ट्वाऽऽश्चर्य्यप्राप्तः शिष्यानामन्त्रयते स्म ॥ पश्यत पश्यत भो रूपमस्येति ॥

तेऽब्रुवन् । एवं ह्येतं पश्यामः । एनमतिविस्मयनीयं ॥

ततोऽहं भिक्षवो येनाराडः कालामस्तेनोपसङ्क्रम्याराडं कालाममेतदवोचत् (५) ॥ चरेयमहं भो आराडे कालामे ब्रह्मचर्य्यं ॥ सोऽवोचत् । चर भो गौतम तथा रूपे धर्म्माख्याने यस्मिन् श्राद्धं कुलपुत्रोऽल्पकृच्छ्रेणाज्ञामाराधयति ॥

तस्य मे भिक्षवः एतदभूत् । अस्ति मे छन्दः । अस्ति

---

१ "उपसङ्क्रामत्" उपसमक्रामत् ॥
२ दविमदण्डिक वा पाठः ॥
३ आराडः कारामो वा पाठः ॥
४ आकिञ्चन्याऽऽयतनसहव्रतायै ॥
५ "अवोचत्" अवोचं ॥

वीर्य्यं। अस्ति स्मृतिः। अस्ति समाधिः। अस्ति प्रज्ञा यन्न्वह-मेकोऽप्रमत्तः आतापी व्यपकृष्टो विहरेयं। तस्यैव धर्म्मस्य प्राप्तये साक्षात्क्रियायै॥ अथ खल्वहं भिक्षवो एकोऽप्रमत्तः आतापी व्यपकृष्टो विहरन्नल्पकृच्छ्रेणैवं तं धर्म्मं अध्यगच्छं साक्षादकार्षं॥

अथ खल्वहं भिक्षवो येनाराडःकालामस्तेनोपसङ्क्रम्यैतद-वोचत्(१)। एतावद्भोः(२)त्वयाऽऽराड धर्म्मोऽधिगतः साक्षात्कृतः॥

सोऽवोचत्। एवमेतद्भो गौतम॥

तमहमवोचत् (३)। मयापि भो एष धर्म्मः साक्षात्कृतो-ऽधिगतः॥

सोऽवोचत्। तेन हि भो गौतम यदहं धर्म्मं जानामि भ-वानपि तं जानाति यं भवान् जानाति अहमपि तं जानामि॥ तेन आवामुभावपीमं शिष्यगणं परिहारावः (४)॥

इति हि भिक्षवोऽऽराडः कालामः परमया पूजया मां पूज-यति स्म॥ अन्तेवासिषु च मां समानार्थतया स्थापयति स्म॥

तस्य मे भिक्षव एतदभूत्। अयं खल्वाराडस्य धर्म्मो न नैर्य्या-णिको न निर्य्याति॥ तत् कतरस्य सम्यक् दुःखक्षयाय यन्न्वह-मुत्तरे पर्य्येषमाणश्चरेयं॥ अथ खल्वहं भिक्षवो यथाभिरामं वैशाल्यां विहृत्य मगधेषु च प्रक्रान्तोऽभूत् (५)॥ सोऽहं मगधेषु

१ "अवोचत्" अवोचम्॥
२ "एतावत्" एतावन्॥
३ "अवोचत्" अवोचम्॥
४ "परिहारावः" शिक्षयाव इत्यर्थः॥
५ "अभूत्" अभवं॥

चर्य्यां चरन्॥ येन मागधकानां राजगृहं नगरं तदनुसृतो येन च पाण्डवः पर्व्वतराजस्तेनोपसङ्क्रान्तोऽभूवं॥ तत्राहं पाण्डवपर्व्वतराजपार्श्वे व्याहार्षं। एकाक्यद्वितीयोऽनेकैर्देवकोटिनियुतशतसहस्रैः संरक्षितः॥

ततोऽहं काल्यमेव सन्निवास्य पात्रचीवरमादाय तप्तोद्द्वारेण (१) राजगृहं महानगरं पिण्डाय प्राविशत् (२)। प्रासादिकेनाभिक्रान्तेन प्रतिक्रान्तव्यवलोकितेन सम्मिञ्जितेन प्रसारितेन प्रासादिकेन सङ्घाटीपटपात्रचीवरधारणेनाविक्षिप्तैरिन्द्रियैरबहिर्गतेन मानसेन निर्म्मितवत्तैलपात्रधरवद्युगमात्रं पश्यन्॥ तत्र मां राजगृहका मनुष्याः दृष्ट्वा विस्मिता अभूवन् किंस्विदयं ब्रह्मा भविष्यति शक्रो देवानामिन्द्र आहोस्विद्वैश्रवण आहोस्वित् किञ्चित् गिरिदैवतं॥

तत्रेदमुच्यते।

अथ विमलधरो ह्यनन्ततेजाः
स्वयमिह प्रव्रजियान् बोधिसत्त्वः।
शान्तमनु दान्त ईर्यवन्तो
विहरति पाण्डवशैलराजपार्श्वे (३)॥
रजनि विविर्गतु ज्ञात्व बोधिसत्वः
परमसुदर्शनीयं निवासयित्वा।

१ "ततपोत" "तपोत" द्वारेणेति क्वचिद्ग्रन्थे दृश्यते। चतुर्थखण्डके पुस्तके द्वारस्य नाम न दृश्यते॥

२ "प्राविशत्" प्राविशं॥

३ "प्रव्रजियान्" प्रव्रजन्। "शान्तमनु" शान्तमनाः। "ईर्य्यवन्तो" ईर्य्यावान्॥

पाच प्रतिग्रहीय स्थिरमानसेन
प्रविशति राजगृहं सपिण्डपात्रं (१) ॥
कनकमिव सुधातुजातरूपं
कवचितु लक्षणत्रिंशताद्वितिस ।
नरगण तथ नारि प्रेक्षमाणो
न च भवत काचित्तृप्ति दर्शनेन (२) ॥
वीथि रचितं रत्नवस्त्रधार्य्यैः
अवशिरिया अनु याति पृष्ठतोऽस्य ।
को नु अयु अदृष्टपूर्व्वसत्वो
यस्य प्रभा पुरं विभाति सर्व्वं (३) ॥
उपरिस्थिहिय नारीणां सहस्राः
तथ सिद्धारि तथैव वातयाने ।
रथ्य भरित गेहं शून्न कृत्वा
नरवरु प्रेक्षिषु ते अनन्यकामा (४) ॥
न च भूयु क्रयविक्रय करोति
न च पुनः सौण्ड पिबन्ति पानं ।

---

१ "रजनि" रजनीं । "विनिर्गतु" विनिर्गतां । "स्नात्व" स्नात्वा । "निवास-यित्वा" निवस्य परिधाय इत्यर्थः । "पात्र" पात्रं । "प्रतिगृह्णीय" प्रतिगृह्य ।

२ "कवचितु" कवचितं । "लक्षणत्रिंशताद्वितिस" द्वात्रिंशल्लक्षणैः । "नरगण" नरगणः । "तथ" तथा । "नारि" नारी । "भवत" भवतः । "तृप्ति" तृप्तिः ।

३ "वीथि" वीथी । "रचितं" रचिता । "रत्नवस्त्रधार्य्यैः" रत्नवस्त्रधारकैः । "अवशिरिया" अवनतशीर्षा । "अनु" जनः । "अयु" अयं । "विभाति" विभा-सयति ॥

४ "उपरिस्थिहिय" उपरि स्थित्वा । "तथ" तथा । "रथ्य" रथ्यां । "भरित" भरितं । "शून" शून्यं । "नरवरु" नरवरं । "प्रेक्षिषु" ददृशुः ॥

न च गृहि न च विथीये रमन्ते
पुरुषवरस्य निरीक्षमाण रूपं (१) ॥
पुरुष त्वरित गच्छित राजगेहं
अवचिषु राज स बिम्बिसार तुष्टः।
देव परम तुभ्य लब्ध लाभा
स्वयमिह ब्रह्म पुरे चरोति पिण्डं (२) ॥
केचित् अवचि शक्र देवराजो
अपरि भणन्ति सुयाम देवपुत्रः।
तथाऽपि सन्तुषितनिर्म्मितश्चाप्य-
परि भणन्ति सुनिर्म्मितिषु देवः (३) ॥
केचित् पुनर्भणन्ति चन्द्रसूर्य्यौ
तथापि च राहुर्बलिश्च वेमचित्री।
केचित् पुनर्भणन्ति वाचमेवं
अयु सो पाण्डवशैलराजवासी (४) ॥
वचनमिमु श्रुणित्वा पार्थिवोऽसौ
परम उदग्रमनाः स्थितो गवाक्षे।

---

१ "भूयु" भूयः। "क्रयविक्रय" क्रयविक्रयं। "शौण्ड" शौण्डाः मद्यपाः। "विथिये" विथिकाः पथिकाः। "निरीक्षमाण" निरीक्षमाणाः॥

२ "पुरुष" कश्चित् पुरुषः। "त्वरित" त्वरां कृत्वा। "गच्छित" गत्वा। "अवचिषु" अवोचत्। "राज" राजानं। "बिम्बिसार" बिम्बिसारं। "बिम्बसार" वा पाठः। "परम" परमाः। "तुभ्य" त्वया। "लब्ध" लब्धाः। "लाभा" लाभाः। "चरोति" चरति॥

३ "अवचि" अवोचन्। "शक्र" शक्रः। "सुयाम" सुयामः। "अपरि" अपरे॥

४ "अयु" अयं॥

प्रेक्षति वरमल्लबोधिसत्त्वं
ज्वलतु शिरीय सुधातुकाञ्चनं वा (१)॥
पिण्डं ददिय राजबिम्बसारः
पुरुषमवोचच्छिरीच क प्रयाति।
दृष्ट्वा गिरिवरं स गच्छमानः
अवचिषु देव गतः स शैलपार्श्वं (२)॥
रजनि विनिर्गतु शाल बिम्बसारो
महतिजनैः परिवारितो नरेन्द्रः।
उपगमि पाण्डवशैलराजमूले
शिरीय ज्वलन्तु तमद्दशाति शैलं (३)॥
धरणि व्रजित यानि ओरुहित्वा
परमसुगौरव प्रेक्षि बोधिसत्त्वं।
मेरुरिव यथा ह्यकम्प्यमानो
न्यषिय तृणानि निषण्ण स्वस्तिके नरेन्द्रः (४)॥
शिरसि चरण वन्दयित्व राजा
विविधकथा समुदाहरित्वाऽवोचत्।

---

१ "दृशु" दृष्टं। "शुचित्वा" शुक्ला। "ज्वलतु" ज्वलत्। "शिरीय" श्रेष्ठं॥

२ "ददिय" दत्वा। "राज" राजा। "शिरीच" शिरीचस। "गच्छमानः" गच्छन्। "अवचिषु" अवोचत्॥

३ "रजनि" रजनीं। "विनिर्गतु" विनिर्गतां। "शाल" शाला। "उपगमि" उपागमत्। "शिरीय" श्रेष्ठं। "ज्वलन्तु" ज्वलन्तं। "अद्दशाति" अद्दशत॥

४ "धरणि" धरण्यां। "व्रजित" गतः। "यानि" यानात्। "ओरुहित्वा" अवरुह्य। "परमसुगौरव" परमसुगौरवं। "प्रेक्षि" प्रेक्षित। "न्यषिय" न्यस्य आस्तीर्य्येत्यर्थः। "निषण्ण" निषण्णः॥

ददमि तव उपार्द्धं सर्व्वराज्या-
द्रम इह कामगुणैरहं च पिण्डं (१) ॥
प्रभणति गिरि बोधिसत्त्वः श्लक्ष्णं
धरणिपते चिरमायु पालयस्व ।
अहमपि प्रविजह्य राज्यमिष्टं
प्रव्रजितो निरपेक्षि शान्तिहेतोः (२) ॥
दहरतरुणयौवनैरुपेतः
शुभतनुवर्णनिभोऽसि वेगप्राप्तः ।
विपुलधन प्रतीच्छ नारिसङ्घं
तु इह मम राज्यि वसाहि भुङ्क्ष्व कामान् (३) ॥
परमप्रमुदितोऽस्मि दर्शनात्ते
अवचिषु स मागधराज बोधिसत्त्वं ।
भव हि मम सहायु सर्व्वराज्यं
अहु तव दास्ये प्रभूतं भुङ्क्ष्व कामान् (४) ॥
मा च पुनर्वने वसाहि शून्ये
मा भूयु तृणेषु वसाहि भूमिवासं ।
परमसुकुमारु तुभ्य कायः

---

१ "शिरषि" शिरसा। "विविधकथा" विविधकथां। "समुदाचरित्वा" समुदाचर्य। "ददमि" ददामि। "उपार्द्ध" उपार्द्धं ॥

२ "गिरि" गिरं। "चिरमायु" चिरमायुः सर्व्वकालमित्यर्थः। "प्रविजह्य" प्रविहाय। "निरपेक्षि" निरपेक्षः ॥

३ "विपुलधन" विपुलधनं। "राज्यि" राज्ये। "वसाहि" वस ॥

४ "मागधराज" मागधराजः। "सहायु" सहायः। "अहु" अहं ॥

इह मम राज्यि वसाहि भुङ्क्ष्व कामान् (१) ॥

प्रभणति गिरि बोधिसत्त्वः सत्त्वं

अकुटिलप्रेमणीयां हितानुकम्पी ।

स्वस्ति धरणीपाल तेऽस्तु नित्यं

न च अहं कामगुणेभिरर्थिकोऽस्मि (२) ॥

कामं विषसमा अनन्तदोषा

नरके प्रपातन प्रेततिर्य्यग्योनौ ।

विदुभिर्विगर्हिता च्यथनार्यकामाः

जहित मया यथ पक्वखेटपिण्डं (३) ॥

काम द्रुमफला यथा पतन्ति

यथा इव अभ्र बलाहका व्रजन्ति ।

अध्रुव चपलगामिमारुतं वा

विकिरण सर्व्वशुभस्य वञ्चनीयाः (४) ॥

काममलभमाना दह्यन्ते तथाऽपि

लब्धा न तृप्ति विन्दयन्ति ।

यदा पुरे अवशस्य तज्जयन्ते

---

१ "वसाहि" वस । "भूयु" भूयः । "वसाहि" वस । "परमसुकुमार" परमसुकुमारः । "तुभ्य" तव । "राज्यि" राज्ये । "वसाहि" वस ॥

२ "गिरि" गिरं । "गुणेभिः" गुणैः ॥

३ "कामं" कामाः । "प्रपातन" प्रपातनाः । "विदुभिः" विद्वद्भिः । "विगर्हिता" विगर्हिताः । "जहित" त्यक्ताः । "यथ" यथा ॥

४ "काम" कामा । "द्रुमफला" द्रुमफलानि । "अभ्र" अभ्रे । "अध्रुव" अध्रुवं । "विकिरण" विक्षेपकाः । "वञ्चनीयाः" वञ्चका ॥

तद मद्दुःख जनेन्ति घोरकामाः (१) ॥
काम धरणिपाल ये च दिव्याः
तथ अपि मानुष काम ये प्रणीताः ।
एकु नरु लभेति सर्व्वकामां
न च सो तृप्ति लभेत भूय एषः (२) ॥
ये तु धरणीपाल शान्तदान्ताः
आर्यानास्रवधर्म्मपूर्णसञ्ज्ञाः (?) ।
प्रज्ञविदुष तृप्त ते सुतृप्ताः
न च पुन कामगुणेषु काचित्तृप्तिः (३) ॥
काम धरणीपाल सेवमाना
पुरिमनु न विद्यातिकोटिसंस्कृतस्य ।
लवणजल यथा हि नर पित्वा
भूय तृषु वर्द्धति कामसेवमाने (४) ॥
अपि च धरणिपाल पश्य कायं
अध्रुवमसारकु दुःखयन्त्रमेतत् ।
नवभिर्व्रणमुखैः सदा स्रवन्तं

---

१ "तृप्ति" तृप्तिं । "विन्दयन्ति' प्राप्नुवन्ति । "तत्" ते । "तद" तदा । "दुःख" दुःखं । "जनेन्ति" जनयन्ति ॥

२ "काम" कामाः । "तथ" तथा । "मानुष" मानुषाः । "काम" कामाः । "एकु" एकः । "नर" नरः । "लभेति" लभते । "सो तृप्ति" स तृप्तिं ॥

३ "प्रज्ञविदुष" प्रज्ञाविद्वांसः । "तृप्त" तृप्ताः । "पुन" पुनः ॥

४ "काम" कामा । "सेवमाना" सेव्यमानाः । "पुरिमनु" मनःपूरकाः । "लवण-जल" लवणजलं । "नरो" नरः । "भुयु" भुयः । "तृषु" तृष्णां । "वर्द्धति" वर्द्धयति ॥

न मम नराधिप कामच्छन्दरागः (१) ॥

अहमपि विपुलान् विजह्य कामान्
तथाऽपि च इस्त्रिसहस्रान् दर्शनीयान् ।
अनभिरनुभवेषु निर्गतोऽहं
परमशिवां वर बोधि प्राप्तुकामः (२) ॥

राजा प्राह ॥

कतमदिशं कुतो गतोऽसि भिक्षो
क च तव जन्म क ते पिता क माता ।
क्षत्रिय अथ ब्राह्मणोऽथ वा राजा
परिकथ भिक्षुय हीनभारसञ्ज्ञा (३) ॥

बोधिसत्त्व आह ॥

श्रुतेति धरणीपाल शाकियानां
कपिलपुरं परमं सुसृद्धिस्फीतं ।
पितु मम शुद्धोदनेति नाम्ना
सुतु अहु प्रव्रजितो गुणाभिलाषी (४) ॥

राजा आह ॥

साधु तव सुदृष्टदर्शनं ते यत्तु
तव जन्म वयं पितस्य शिष्याः ।

---

१ "कामारकु" कामारकं ॥

२ "विजह्य" विहाय । "इस्त्रि" स्त्री । "अनभिरनुभवेषु" एभिरनुभवैः । "वर बोधि" वरबोधिं ॥

३ "कतमदिशं" कतमां दिशं । "क्षत्रिय" क्षत्रियः । "परिकथ" परिकथय । "भिक्षुय" भिक्षुकः ॥

४ "श्रुतेति" शृणु इति । "पितु" पिता । "सुतु" सुतः । "अहु" अहं ।

अपि च मम वयस्य आशयेन
वयमपि निमन्त्रितुकाम वीतरागः (१) ॥
यदि त्वय अनुप्राप्तु भोति बोधिः
तद मम सेति भोति धर्म्म स्वामिन्।
अपि च मम पुरा सुलब्ध लाभा
मम विजिते वसथीह यत् स्वयम्भो (२) ॥
पुनरपि चरणानि वन्दयित्वा
कृत्वा प्रदक्षिणु गौरवेण राज्ञा।
स्वकजनपरिवारितो नरेन्द्रः
पुनरपि राजगृहमनुप्रविष्टः (३) ॥
मगधपुरी प्रवेशि लोकनाथो
विहरिय शान्तमना यथाभिप्रायम्।
अर्थं करिये देवमानुषाणा-
मुपगतु तीर निरञ्जना नरेन्द्रः (४) ॥

इति ललितविस्तरे बिम्बसारोपसङ्क्रमपरिवर्त्तो नाम षोडशः ॥ १६ ॥

---

१ "वयं पितस्य" वयं पितुः वयमपि तस्य इति वा। "निमन्त्रितुकाम" निमन्त्रितुकामो ॥

२ "त्वय" त्वया "अनुप्राप्तु" अनुप्राप्तो "भोति" भवति "तद" तदा "सेति" स इति स एवेत्यर्थः। "भोति" भवति "धर्म" धर्मः "मम" मया "सुलब्ध" सुलब्धाः ॥

३ "चरणानि" चरणान् "वन्दयित्वा" वन्दित्वा "प्रदक्षिणु" प्रदक्षिणं ॥

४ "प्रवेशि" प्रविश्य। "विहरिय" विहृत्य "अर्थं करिये" अर्थं कृत्वा "उपगतु" उपगतः। "तीर निरञ्जना" तीरं निरञ्जनाया इत्यर्थः ॥

सप्तदशाध्यायप्रारम्भः

तेन खलु पुनर्भिक्षवः समयेन रुद्रको नाम रामपुत्रो राजगृहं नाम महानगरमुपनिःसृत्य विहरति स्म । महता शिष्यगणेन सार्द्धं सप्तभिः शिष्यशतैः ॥ स तेभ्यो नैवसंज्ञानासंज्ञायतनसहव्रतायै धर्मं देशयति स्म ॥ अद्राक्षीत् खल्वपि भिक्षवो बोधिसत्त्वो रुद्रकं रामपुत्रं सङ्घेगणिनं गणाचार्यं ज्ञातमभीप्सितं बहुपूजितं पण्डितजनसम्मतम् ॥ दृष्ट्वा चास्यैतदभूत् । अयं खल्वपि रुद्रको रामपुत्रः सङ्घेगणिगणाचार्यो ज्ञातोऽभीप्सितो बहुजनपूजितः पण्डितसम्मतः स चेदहमस्यान्तिकमुपसङ्क्रम्य व्रततपमारभेयं (१) ॥ नैष ममान्तिके विशिष्टसंज्ञो भवेत् । नापि प्रत्यक्षज्ञानेन (२) ज्ञातो भवेत् । यानातिसंस्कृतानां साश्रवाणां सोपादानानां ध्यानसमाधिसमापत्तीनां दोषो दृष्टो भवेत् ॥ यन्न्वहं तथारूपमुपादाय उपसन्दर्शयेयम् । येनैते च प्रत्यक्षा भवेयुः ॥ ध्यानगोचराणां च समापत्त्यालम्बनानां लौकिकसमाधीनामनिःसरणदर्शिता (३) भवेत् ॥ यन्न्वहं रुद्रकस्य रामपुत्रस्य सकाशमुपसङ्क्रम्य स्वसमाधिगुणविशेषोद्भावनार्थं शिष्यत्वमभ्युपगम्य संस्कृतसमाधीनामसारतामुपदर्शयेयम् ॥

अथ खलु भिक्षवो बोधिसत्त्व इदमर्थवशमधिकृत्य येन रुद्रको रामपुत्रस्तेनोपसङ्क्रामत् (४) ॥ उपसङ्क्रम्य रुद्रकरामपुत्र-

---

१ "व्रततपमारभेयं" व्रततपश्चारभेयम् ।

२ "प्रत्यक्षज्ञानेन"। "१ संख्यके पुस्तके बोधिप्रत्यक्षज्ञानेन" इति पाठो वर्त्तते ॥

३ "अनिःसरण दर्शिता" अनिःसरणं दर्शितं ॥

४ "उपसङ्क्रामत्" उपसमक्रामत् ।

मेतदवोचत्। कस्ते मार्ष शास्ता कस्य वा धर्म्मं देशितमाजानासि॥

इत्येवमुक्ते रुद्रको रामपुत्रो बोधिसत्त्वमेवमाह। न मे मार्ष कश्चिच्छास्ता। अपि तु खलु पुनः स्वयमेव मयेदं सम्यगधिगतम्॥

बोधिसत्त्व आह। किं भवताऽधिगतम्॥

आह। नैवसञ्ज्ञानासञ्ज्ञायतनसमापत्तेर्मार्गः॥

बोधिसत्त्व आह। वयं लभेमहि भवतः सकाशादववादानुशासनीयस्य समाधेर्मार्गम्॥

स ह्याहाढमस्त्विति यावद्दत्तोववादोऽभूत्।

ततो बोधिसत्त्व एकान्तं गत्वा पर्य्यङ्कमाबध्योपविशति स्म॥ समनन्तरोपविष्टस्य च बोधिसत्त्वस्य पुण्यविशेषेण ज्ञानविशेषेण पूर्व्वसुचरितचर्य्याफलविशेषेण सर्व्वसमाधिपरिचयविशेषेण च ध्यानप्रमुखानि सर्व्वाणि लौकिकानि लोकोत्तराणि समापत्तिशतान्यामुखीभवन्ति स्म साकाराणि सादेशानि यथापि तच्चित्तवशवर्त्तित्वात्॥ अथ च बोधिसत्त्वः स्मृतः सम्प्रजानन् उत्थायासनाद्येन रुद्रको रामपुत्रस्तेनोपसङ्क्रामत्(१)। उपसङ्क्रम्य रुद्रकं रामपुत्रमेवमाह। अस्त्यन्योऽपि मार्ष कश्चिदुत्तरे नैवसञ्ज्ञानासञ्ज्ञायतनसमापत्तेर्मार्गः॥

सोऽब्रवीत्। नास्तीति॥

ततो बोधिसत्त्वस्यैतदभवत्। न खलु रुद्रकस्यैवास्ति श्रद्धा वीर्य्यं स्मृतिः समाधिः प्रज्ञा। ममाप्यस्ति श्रद्धा वीर्य्यं स्मृतिः

१ "उपसङ्क्रामत्" उपसमक्रामत्॥

समाधिः प्रज्ञा ॥ अथ बोधिसत्त्वो रुद्रकं रामपुत्रमेवमाह । मयाप्येष मार्ष धर्मोऽधिगतो यत्र त्वन्निर्य्यातः ॥

सोऽवोचत् । तेन ह्यागच्छ त्वं चाहञ्चेमं गणं परिहरावः (१) ॥

समानार्थे च बोधिसत्त्वं स्थापयति स्म आचार्य्यस्थाने च ॥

बोधिसत्त्व आह ॥ नैष मार्ष मार्गो निर्विदे न विरागाय न विरोधाय नोपशमाय नाभिज्ञायै न सम्बोधाय न श्रमणाय न ब्राह्मणाय न निर्व्वाणाय संवर्त्तते ॥

इति हि भिक्षवो बोधिसत्त्वो रुद्रकस्य रामपुत्रस्य सन्निश्रस्यावर्जनीकृत्य यावदलमिति कृत्वा प्रक्रामत् (२) । अलं ममानेनेति ॥

तेन खलु पुनः समयेन पञ्चका भद्रवर्गीया रुद्रके रामपुत्रे ब्रह्मचर्य्यं चरन्ति स्म ॥ तेषामेतदभूत् । यस्य खलु वयमर्थाय दीर्घरात्रं घटामहे उद्युञ्जामहे (३) न च शक्नुमोऽन्तं वा पर्य्यन्तं वाधिगन्तुं तच्छ्रमणेन गौतमेनाल्पकृच्छ्रेणाधिगतं साक्षात्कृतं तच्चास्य न रोचते ॥ अथ चोत्तरि (४) पर्य्येषते निःसंशयमेष शास्ता लोके भविष्यति। यच्चैष साक्षात्करिष्यति। तदस्मभ्यं संविभक्ष्यतीति ॥ एवं विमृश्य पञ्चका भद्रवर्गीया रुद्रकरामपुत्रसकाशादपक्रम्य बोधिसत्त्वमनुबन्ध (५) ॥

---

१ "परिहरावः" शिक्षयावः ।
२ "प्रक्रामत्" प्राक्रामत् ।
३ "उद्युञ्जामहे" उद्यतामहे ।
४ "उत्तरि" उत्तरे ।
५ "अनुबन्ध" अनुबन्धुः अन्वागमन् इत्यर्थः ।

इति हि भिक्षवो बोधिसत्त्वो यथाभिप्रेतं राजगृहं (१) विहृत्य मगधेषु चारिकां प्राक्रामत्। सार्द्धं पञ्चकैर्भद्रवर्गीयैः॥

तेन खलु पुनः समयेनान्तरा च राजगृहस्यान्तरा च गयायां अन्यतमो गण उत्सवं करोति स्म॥ तेन च गणेन बोधिसत्त्वोऽभिनिमन्त्रितोऽभूत्। वासेन भक्तेन च सार्द्धं पञ्चकैर्भद्रवर्गीयैः॥

अथ खलु भिक्षवो बोधिसत्त्वो मगधेषु चर्य्यां चरन् येन मागधकानां गया तामनुसृत्य तामनुप्राप्तोऽभूत्॥ तत्र खल्वपि भिक्षवो बोधिसत्त्वः प्रहाणार्थी विहरति स्म गयाशीर्षपर्व्वते॥ तत्रास्य विहरतस्तिस्र उपमाः प्रतिभान्ति स्म अश्रुतपूर्व्वा अविज्ञातपूर्व्वाः॥ कतमास्तिस्रः। ये केचित्ते खल्वपि श्रमणब्राह्मणाः कामेभ्योऽनवकृष्टकाया विहरन्ति स्म। कामेभ्योऽनवकृष्टचित्ताश्च विहरन्ति स्म। याऽपि चैषां कामेषु नन्दी कामेषु रागः कामेषु छन्दः कामेषु तृष्णा कामेषु पिपासा कामेषु परिदाहः कामेषु अध्यवसानता सा व्यवशान्ता॥ किं चापि ते आत्मोपक्रमिकां शरीरोपक्रमिकां दुःखां तीव्रां खरां कटुकाममनापां वेदनां वेदयन्ते॥ अथ तर्ह्यभव्या एव ते उत्तरि(२) मनुष्यधर्म्मादलमार्य्यज्ञानविशेषं साक्षात्कर्त्तुम्॥ तद्यथाऽपि नाम पुरुषोऽग्न्यर्थी ज्योतिः पर्य्येषमाणः स आर्द्रकाष्ठमादाय चार्द्रीं चोत्तरारणीमुदके प्रक्षिप्य मथ्नीयात्। अभव्योऽसावग्निमुत्पादयितुं तेजः प्रादुष्कर्त्तुम्॥ एवमेव इमे श्रमणब्राह्मणाः

---

१ "राजगृहं" राजगृहे।

२ "उत्तरि" उत्तरे।

कामेभ्योऽनवकृष्टकायचित्ताश्च विहरन्ति स्म । याप्येषां कामेषु नन्दी कामेषु रागः कामेषु च्छन्दः कामेषु तृष्णा कामेषु पिपासा कामेषु परिदाहः कामेषु अध्यवसानता तदप्युपशान्तम् ॥ किञ्चापि ते आत्मोपक्रमिकां दुःखां तीव्रां खरां कटुकां शरीरोपतापिकां वेदनां वेदयन्ते । अथ तर्ह्यभव्या एवोत्तरि (१) मनुष्यधर्मादलमार्य्यज्ञानदर्शनविशेषं साक्षात्कर्त्तुम् । इयं बोधिसत्त्वस्य प्रथमा उपमा प्रतिभाति स्म ॥

भूयश्चास्यैतदभूत् । य इमे श्रमणब्राह्मणाः कामेभ्यो व्यपकृष्टकायचित्ता विहरन्ति स्म ॥ याऽपि तेषां कामेषु नन्दीति पूर्व्ववत् सर्व्वं कर्त्तव्यं यावत् ज्योतिःपर्य्यंपत इति । स आर्द्रकाष्ठमादाय स्थले स्थापयित्वा आर्द्रां चोत्तरारणीं मथ्नीयात् । अभव्योऽसावग्निमुत्पादयितुम् ॥ एवमेव य इमे श्रमणब्राह्मणा इति सर्व्वं पूर्व्ववत्कार्य्यं यावदभव्या उत्तरि (२) मनुष्यधर्म्मादलमार्य्यज्ञानदर्शनविशेषं साक्षात्कर्त्तुम् । इयं द्वितीया उपमा प्रतिभाति स्म ॥

पूर्व्वमश्रुता चाविज्ञाता च पुनरपरे च इमे श्रमणब्राह्मणा भवन्तः कामेभ्यो व्यपकृष्टकायचित्ता विहरन्ति । याऽपि तेषां कामेषु नन्दीति सर्व्वं पूर्व्ववत् । तदप्येषामुपशान्तम् । किञ्चापि ते आत्मोपक्रमिकां शरीरोपतापिकां दुःखां तीव्रां खरां कटुकां वेदनां वेदयन्ते । अथ खलु अभव्या एव ते उत्तरिमनुष्यधर्म्मादलमार्यज्ञानदर्शनविशेषं साक्षात्कर्त्तुम् ॥ तद्यथापि नामैव

१ "उत्तरि" उत्तरे ।

२ "उत्तरि" उत्तरे एवं सर्व्वत्र ।

स्यात्पुरुषोऽग्न्यर्थी ज्योतिर्गवेषी ज्योतिःपर्य्येषमाणः स शुष्कं काष्ठमादाय शुष्कां चोत्तरारणिं स्थले प्रतिष्ठाप्य मथ्नीयात्। स भव्योऽग्निमभिनिर्वर्त्तयितुं तेजः प्राविष्कर्त्तुम्॥ एवं च इमे भवन्तः श्रमणब्राह्मणा इति सर्व्वं यावद्वेदनां वेदयन्त इति। अथ च पुनर्भव्या एव ते उत्तरि (१) मनुष्यधर्म्मादलमार्य्यज्ञानदर्शनविशेषं साक्षात्कर्त्तुम्। इयं तृतीया उपमा प्रतिभाति स्म। अश्रुतपूर्व्वा चाविज्ञातपूर्व्वा च॥

अथ खलु भिक्षवो बोधिसत्त्वस्यैतदभूत्। अहं खल्वेतर्हि कामेभ्यो व्यपकृष्टकायो विहरामि व्यपकृष्टचित्तश्च। यापि मे कामेषु नन्दीति सर्व्वं यावत्तदपि मे उपशान्तम्। किञ्चाप्यहमात्मोपक्रमिकां शरीरोपतापिकां दुःखामिति पेयालं यावद्वेदनां वेद्मि॥ अथ खल्वहं भव्य एवोत्तरि (२) मनुष्यधर्म्मादलमार्य्यज्ञानदर्शनविशेषं साक्षात्कर्त्तुम्॥

इति हि भिक्षवो बोधिसत्त्वो यथाभिप्रेतं गयायां विहृत्य गयाशीर्षपर्व्वते जङ्घाविहारमनुचङ्क्रम्यमाणो येनोरुविल्वासेनापतिग्रामकस्तदनुसृतस्तदनुप्राप्तोऽभूत्॥ तत्राद्राक्षीन्नदीं नैरञ्जनामच्छोदकां सूपतीर्थ्यां प्रासादिकैश्चद्रुमगुल्मैरलङ्कृतां समन्ततश्च गोचरग्रामाम्॥ तत्र खल्वपि बोधिसत्त्वस्य मनोऽतीव प्रसन्नमभूत्। समो वतायं भूमिप्रदेशो रमणीयः प्रति संलयनानुरूपः पर्य्याप्तमिदं प्रहाणार्थिककुलपुत्रस्याहञ्च प्रहाणार्थी यन्वहमिहैव तिष्ठेयम्॥

---

२ "उत्तरि" उत्तरे।

१ "उत्तरि" उत्तरे॥

इति हि भिक्षवो बोधिसत्त्वस्यैतदभूत्। पञ्चकषायकालेऽस्-
मिन् जम्बुद्वीपेऽवतीर्णो हीनाधिमुक्तिकेषु सत्त्वेष्वाकीर्णतीर्थ्यवर्गेषु
नानादृष्टिप्रस्कन्नेषु कायपिण्डग्राहाभिनिविष्टेषु नानाविधैरा-
तापनपरितापनैः कायशुद्धिं पर्य्येषन्ते प्रज्ञापयन्ति च मूढाः॥
तद्यथा मन्त्रनिर्विचारकैर्हस्तप्रलेहकैर्नापावनकैरनामन्त्रकैर-
नेकमूलिकैरमत्स्यमांसकैर्वार्षिकैः सुरातुषोदकविसर्जनैरेक-
त्रिपञ्चसप्तकुलभिक्षाचर्यैर्मूलफलशैवालकुशपत्रगोमयगोमू-
त्रपायसदधिसर्पिःफाणितामपिष्टकभक्षणपानैः सारथिकापो-
तकसन्देशिकोत्कुटसम्प्रक्षालकैः ग्राम्यारण्याभिश्च वृत्तिभिः
गोव्रतमृगाश्ववराहवानरहस्तिव्रतैश्च स्थानमौनवीरासनैश्चैका-
लापकैर्यावत्सप्तालापकैरेकभक्ता एकाहोरात्रचातुर्थ्यपञ्चषड्-
कालान्तराश्च पक्षक्षपणचान्द्रायणैश्च गृध्रोलूकपक्षधारणैश्च
फलमुञ्जासनवल्कलदर्भवल्वजोष्ट्रकम्बलाजकम्बलकेशकम्बलचर्म-
निवेशनैश्च आर्द्रपटश्लोकजालशयनैश्च भस्मशर्करापाषाणफल-
कण्टकतृणमुसलशयनावाक्शिरःकुट्टकस्थण्डिलशयनैश्च एक-
वासद्वित्रिचतुष्पञ्चषट्सप्तबहुवासोभिर्नग्नभावैश्च स्नानास्नानवि-
धिभिश्च दीर्घकेशनखश्मश्रुजटामुकुटवल्कलधारणैश्च एककाले
तिलतण्डुलाहारैश्च भस्ममपि * निर्माल्योद्धृततमोरजःपांशु-
पङ्कपरिमर्षणैश्च रोममञ्जुकेशनखचीवरपट्टकरङ्कधारणैश्च
उष्णोदकतण्डुलोदकपरिश्रावितकम्बलिकस्थालीपानीयपानैश्च

* पुस्तकपञ्चकानां प्रमाणात्। किन्तु भस्मनिर्माल्येत्याद्युचितं।

अङ्गारधातुकषायचित्रदण्डमुण्डिककुण्डिककपालखट्वाङ्गधारणै-
श्च शुद्धिं प्रत्यवगच्छन्ति सम्मूढाः। धूमपानाग्निपानाऽऽदित्य-
निरीक्षणपञ्चतपैकपादो(१)र्द्ध्वबाहुस्थानैकचरणैश्च तपः सञ्चि-
न्वन्ति। तुषाद्यङ्गारदाहनिकुम्भसाधनपच्छिलापचनाग्निजल-
प्रवेशनमरुत्तीर्थगमनमरणैश्चेष्टां गतिं मृगयन्ते। ओङ्कार-वष-
ट्कार-स्वधाकार-स्वाहाकाराऽऽशीःस्तुतिचयनावाहनजप्यमन्त्रा-
ध्ययनधारणकरणैश्च शुद्धिं प्रत्यवगच्छन्ति॥

शुद्धश्चात्मानं मन्यमाना इमाश्चाश्रयन्ते। तद्यथा ब्रह्मेन्द्ररु-
द्र-विष्णु-देवी-कुमार-मातृ-कात्यायनी-चन्द्राऽऽदित्य-वैश्रवण-
वरुण-वासवाऽश्विन-नाग-यक्ष-गन्धर्वाऽसुर-गरुड-किन्नर-महो-
रग-राक्षस-प्रेत-भूत-कुष्माण्ड-पार्षद-गणपति-पिशाचांश्च देव-
र्षि-राजर्षि ब्रह्मर्षींश्च नमस्यन्ति। तेषु च सारषङ्गिनो भवन्ति।
पृथिव्यप्तेजोवाय्वाकाशांश्चाश्रयन्ते। गिरि-नदी-नद्युत्स-सरो-ह्र-
द-तडाग-सागर-सरःपल्वल-पुष्करिणी-कूप-वृक्ष-गुल्म-लता-
तृण-स्थाणु-गोष्ठ-श्मशान-चत्वर-शृङ्गाटकाऽन्तरापणमुखानि
चाश्रयन्ते। गृहस्तम्भोपल-मुषलाऽसि-धनुः-परशु-शर-शक्ति-
चिह्नांश्च नमस्यन्ते। दधि-घृत-सर्षप-यव-प्रतिसरा+दूर्वा-
मणि-कनक-रजतादिभिश्च मङ्गलं प्रत्यवगच्छन्ति। एवं विधानि
इमे तीर्थानि कुर्व्वन्ति आश्रयन्ते च संसारभयभीताः॥

इह केचित्पुनैर्मन्यन्ते स्वर्गापवर्गावस्माकमेतेभ्यो निर्व्वर्त्स्येते
इति मिथ्यामार्गप्रयाता अशरणे शरणसङ्गिनोऽमङ्गल्ये मङ्ग-

१ "पञ्चतपैकपादो" पञ्चतप एकपादो।

सम्भिन्नेनोऽयुक्ते मुक्तिं मन्यन्ते ॥ यन्न्वहं तादृशं व्रततपोविशेषमारभेयं यथासर्व्वपरप्रवादिनो निर्गृहीताः स्युः । कर्म्मक्रियाप्रनष्टानाञ्च सत्त्वानां कर्म्मक्रियाविप्रणाशमभिदर्शयेयम् । ध्यानगोचराणां च रूपावचराणां च देवानां ध्यानविशेषोपदर्शनादावर्जनं कुर्य्यामिति ॥

इति हि भिक्षवो बोधिसत्त्व एवं चिन्तयित्वा षड्वार्षिकं* महाघोरं व्रततपःसुदुष्करात्सुदुष्करचर्य्यामारभते स्म ॥ केन कारणेन । उच्यते । दुष्करकारिका एषा तेन उच्यते दुष्करचर्य्येति ॥ न स कश्चित् सत्त्वः सत्त्वनिकाये संविद्यते । मनुष्यो वा अमनुष्यो वा यः समर्थस्तथारूपं दुष्करं चरितुम् । अन्यत्र चरमभविकात् बोधिसत्त्वात् । य आस्फानकं ध्यानं समापद्यते स्म ॥ केन कारणेन उच्यते आस्फानकमिति । तर्हि चतुर्थध्यानस्यादित एव समापद्यमान आश्वासप्रश्वासानुपरोधयति सन्निरोधयति । अकल्पं तद्ध्यानमविकल्पमनिञ्जनमपनीतमस्पन्दनं सर्व्वत्रानुगतं च सर्व्वत्र चानिःसृतम् । न च तद्ध्यानं जातु केनचित्समापन्नं पूर्व्वं वा शैक्ष्येण वा अशैक्ष्येण वा प्रत्येकबुद्धेन वा चर्य्याऽप्रतिपन्नेन वा बोधिसत्त्वेन अतश्च आस्फानकं नामोच्यते ॥ आकाशमस्फुरणमविकरणं तच्च सर्व्वं स्फुरतीति आकाशसमं तद्ध्यानं तेनोच्यते आस्फानकमिति ॥

अथ खलु भिक्षवो बोधिसत्त्वः लोकस्याश्चर्य्यसन्दर्शनार्थन्तीर्थिकानाञ्च दर्पनिर्घातनार्थं परप्रवादिनाञ्च निग्रहार्थं देवाना-

---

* षड्वर्षिकं वा पाठः ।

श्चावर्जनार्थमुच्छेदशाश्वतवादिनाञ्च सत्त्वानां कर्मक्रियाप्रणष्टानां कर्मक्रियावतारणार्थं पुण्यफलोद्भावनार्थं ज्ञानबलसन्दर्शनार्थं ध्यानाङ्गविभजनार्थं कायबलस्थामसन्दर्शनार्थं चित्तशौर्य्यसञ्जननार्थञ्चासंस्कृतायां पृथिव्यां पर्य्यङ्कमाबध्य निषीदति स्म। निषद्य च स्वकायं चेतसा निगृह्णीते स्म निष्पीडयति स्म ॥

ततो मे भिक्षवो हेमन्तिकास्वष्टकरात्रिषु तथा कायं निगृह्णतो निष्पीडयतः कक्षाभ्यामपि स्वेदाः प्रस्रवन्ति स्म। ललाटादपि स्वेदाः प्रस्रवन्ति स्म। भूमौ निपतन्ति स्म। अवश्यायन्तो ऊष्मायन्तो वाष्पायन्तः (१)। तद्यथाऽपि नाम बलवान् पुरुषः दुर्बलतरं पुरुषं ग्रीवायां गृहीत्वा निष्पीडयेत्। एवमेव भिक्षव इमं कायं चेतसा निगृह्णतो निष्पीडयतः कक्षाभ्यामपि स्वेदाः प्रस्रवन्ति स्म्। ललाटादपि स्वेदाः प्रस्रवन्ति स्म भूमौ निपतन्ति स्म। अवश्यायन्त ऊष्मायन्तो वाष्पायन्तः ॥

तस्य मे भिक्षव एतदभूत्। यन्न्वहमास्फानकं ध्यानं ध्यायेयम्। ततो मे भिक्षव आस्फानकं ध्यायतो मुखतो नासिकातश्चाश्वासप्रश्वासावुपनिरुद्धावभूताम्। कर्णच्छिद्राभ्यामुच्चैःशब्दमहाशब्दा निश्चरन्ति स्म। तद्यथाऽपि नाम कर्मारगर्गरायां मथ्यमानायामुच्चशब्दो महाशब्दो निश्चरति। एवमेव मे भिक्षवो मुखनासिकाभ्यामाश्वासप्रश्वासावुपरुद्धावभूताम्। श्रोत्रच्छि-

---

१ "अवश्यायन्त ऊष्मायन्तो वाष्पायन्तः" अवश्यायीयन्त ऊष्मीयन्तो वाष्पीयन्तः एवमन्यत्रापि बोध्यम्।

2 R 2

त्राभ्यामुच्चैःशब्दो महाशब्दो निश्चरति स्म । तस्य मे भिक्षव एतदभूत् । यन्न्वहमभूय आस्फानकं ध्यानं ध्यायेयमिति ॥ ततो मे भिक्षवो मुखनासिकाश्रोत्राण्युपरुद्धानि अभूवन् ॥ तेषूपरुद्धेषु वायुरूर्ध्वं शिरःकपालमुपनिहन्ति स्म । तद्यथाऽपि नाम भिक्षवः पुरुषः कुण्ठया शक्त्या शिरःकपालमुपहन्यात् ॥ एवमेव भिक्षवः मुखनासिकाश्रोत्रेषूपरुद्धेषु आश्वासप्रश्वासा ऊर्ध्वं शिरःकपाल-मुपनिघ्नन्ति स्म ॥

तां चावस्थां दृष्ट्वा बोधिसत्त्वस्य तत्र केचिद्देवा एवमाहुः । कष्टं भोः कालगतो बताऽयं सिद्धार्थः कुमारः ॥

अपरे एवमाहुः । नाऽयं कालगतोऽपितु ध्यानविहार-एषोऽर्हतामेवंविध इति ॥

* [तस्यां च वेलायामिमे गाथे अभाषत ।

मा खल्वयं शाक्यनरेन्द्रगर्भो
अपूर्णसङ्कल्प इहैवारणे ।
त्राता त्रिलोकं दुःखितं ह्यनाथं
कालं करिष्यत्यकृतार्थ एव (१) ॥
हा सत्त्वसार दृढप्रतिज्ञा
सद्धर्मयज्ञेन निमन्त्रिताऽभूत् ।
वयं पुरा ते तुषिते नाथ उक्ता

* एतच्चिह्नद्वयप्रयोजनं १।८ पत्रे व्यक्तीभविष्यति ।

१ "इहैवारणे" इहैवारण्ये। "त्रिलोकं दुःखितं ह्यनाथं" त्रिलोकीं दुःखितां ह्यनाथामित्यर्थः ।

दृढप्रतिज्ञा तव शुद्धसत्त्व (१) ॥

अथ ते देवपुत्रास्त्रयस्त्रिंशद्देवेषु गत्वा मायादेव्या एतमर्थं श्रावयन्ति स्म कालगतः कुमारः ॥

अथ मायादेवी अप्सरोगणपरिवृता अर्द्धरात्रसमये नैरञ्जनायास्तीरे येन बोधिसत्त्वः तेन उपसंक्रम्य सा पश्यति स्म बोधिसत्त्वं शुष्कगात्रम्। कालगतमिव दृष्ट्वा बाष्पगद्गदकण्ठया* रोदितुमारब्धा ॥

तस्याञ्च वेलायामिमा गाथा अभाषत।

यदा जातोऽसि मे पुत्र वने लुम्बिनिसाह्वये।
सिंहवच्चागृहीतस्त्वं प्रक्रान्तः सप्तपदान् स्वयम् ॥
दिशश्चालोक्य चतुरो वाचा ते प्रव्याहृता शुभा।
इयं मे पश्चिमा जातिः सा ते न परिपूरिता (२) ॥
असितेनाभिनिर्द्दिष्टो बुद्धो लोके भविष्यसि।
क्षुण्णं व्याकरणं तस्य न दृष्टा तेन नित्यता ॥
चक्रवर्त्तिश्रियं पुत्र नापि भुक्ता मनोरमा।
न च बोधिमनुप्राप्तो जातोऽसि निधनं वने ॥
पुत्रार्थे कं प्रपद्यामि कस्य क्रन्दामि दुःखिता।
कामश्चैवैकपुत्रस्य किञ्चित् प्राणस्य जीवितम् ॥

बोधिसत्त्व आह।

---

१ वयं पुरा ते तुषिते तुषितलोके यां दृढप्रतिज्ञामपश्याम इति च शेषमापूर्य्य समन्वयः कार्य्यः।

* बाष्पगद्गदकण्ठा।

२ "दिशश्चालोक्य" दिशश्चालोक्य। "चतुरो" चतस्रः। "वाचा" वाक्।

केषातीव करुणं रुदते
प्रकीर्णकेशी च विनष्टशोभा ।
पुत्रं ह्यतीव परिदेवयन्ती
विचेष्टमाना धरणीतलस्था (१) ॥

मायादेवी आह ।

मया तु दशमासान् वै कुक्षौ वज्र इव धृतः ।
सा तेऽहं पुत्रका माता विलपामि सुदुःखिता (२) ॥

अथ बोधिसत्त्व आश्वासयन्नुवाच। नभेतव्यम्। पुत्रं लाभसे(३)। श्रमन्ते सफलं करिष्यामि। अमोघं बुद्धपरित्यागं असितनिर्देशस्य व्यक्तं करिष्यामि। दीपङ्करस्य व्याकरणं व्यक्तीकरिष्यामि॥

अपि शतधा वसुधा विकीर्य्यतः मेरुः प्लवे चाम्भसि रत्नशृङ्गः।
चन्द्रार्कतारागण भू पतेत पृथग् जनो नैव अहं म्रियेयम् (४) ॥

यस्मान्न शोको त्वयि * अत्र कार्य्यो न वै चिराद्द्रक्ष्यसि बुद्धबोधिम् ।

सहश्रवणादेव देवी माया सम्प्रहर्षितरोमकूप-जाता बोधिसत्त्वं मान्दारपुष्पैरभ्यवकीर्य्य त्रिःप्रदक्षिणीकृत्य दिव्यतूर्य्यैः-सम्प्रवाद्यमानैर्येन स्वभवनं तेन उपजगाम] † ॥

तत्र मे भिक्षव एतदभूत्। सन्त्येके श्रमणब्राह्मणा येऽ-

---

१ "रुदते" रोदिति ।

२ "पुत्रका" पुत्रक ।

३ "लाभसे" लाभाय इत्यर्थः ।

४ "विकीर्यतः" विदीर्णा भवेदित्यर्थः। "प्लवे" प्लवेत् काष्ठवत्तरेदित्यर्थः। "चन्द्रार्कतारागण" चन्द्रार्कतारागणो। "भू" भूवि। "पतेत" पतेत्।

* त्वयि त्वया ।

† एतचिह्न [ ] क्रोडीकृतपाठस्तु चक्रवर्त्तिहस्तपुस्तकानां मध्ये पुस्तकद्वये नास्ति।

ल्पाहारतया शुद्धिं मन्यन्ते। यन्न्वहमल्पाहारतया प्रतिपद्येय-मिति ॥ अभिजानाम्यहं भिक्षव एकमेवाद्वितीयं कोलमाहार-माहर्त्तुं स्यात् ॥

खलु पुनर्भिक्षवो युष्माकं एषा बुद्धिः। महत्तरं तत्र काले कोलमासीदिति। न खल्वेवं द्रष्टव्यम्। अथ खल्विदमेव तत्रकाले कोलमभूत्। तस्य मे भिक्षव एकमेव कोलमाहारमाहरतोऽद्वि-तीयं कायोऽत्यर्थं कर्शितोऽभूद्-दुर्ब्बलः। तद्यथापि नाम भिक्षव आसीतकीपर्व्वाणि (१) वा। एवमेव अङ्गप्रत्यङ्गान्यभूवन्। तद्यथा-ऽपि नाम कर्कटकपर्शुका एवमेव पर्शुका अभूवन् ॥ तद्यथापि नाम वाहनकारशालायां वा हस्तिशालायां वा जीर्णायामुभयतो विवृत्तायां गोपानस्यान्तरिकाश्च विराजन्ते व्यवभासन्ते। एवमेव मे पर्शुका अन्तःकाय (२) उभयतो विराजन्ते स्म। व्यवभासन्ते स्म ॥ तद्यथापि नाम वर्त्तनी वा वेण्युन्नताऽवनता भवति समवि-षमा एवं मे पृष्ठकाण्डकोऽभूदुन्नतावनतः समविषमः। तद्यथा तिक्तकालाबुस्तरुणो लून अम्लानो भवति सम्म्लानः सम्पुटक-जातः। एवमेव शिरोऽम्लानमभूत्सम्म्लानं समुत्पुटकजातं। तद्यथापि नाम ग्रीष्माणां पश्चिमे मासे कूपतारका दूरगता भवन्ति। कृच्छ्रेण सम्प्रकाशन्ते। एवमेव मेऽक्षितारकौ दूरगतावभूतां कृ-च्छ्रेण सम्प्रकाशेते स्म॥ तद्यथापि नामाजपदं वोष्ट्रपदं वा। एवमेव मे कक्षाकुक्षिवक्षआदीन्यभूवन्। ततो यदाऽहं भिक्षवः पाणिना

---

१ आसीतको वा।

२ "अन्तःकायः" कायस्यान्तरित्यर्थः।

कुक्षिं स्पृशामीति। पृष्ठकण्टकमेवाम्र्गाय्मुत्तिष्ठामीति (१) चाभिसंस्कुर्वंस्तथैव कुब्जाः प्रापतन्तः कृच्छ्रेणोत्थितोऽपि पांशुकृतानि गात्राणि पाणिना प्रमृजतो मे पूतिरोमाणि कायाच्छीर्य्यन्ते स्म॥ यापि मेऽभूत् पौराणी शुभवर्णा तनुः साप्यन्तर्धात् तथापीदं रक्षःप्रधानप्रहितात्मकत्वात् (२)। सामन्ताश्च मे गोचरग्रामवासिन एवं सञ्जानन्ते स्म॥ कालको बत भोः श्रमणो गौतमः श्यामको बत भोः श्रमणो गौतमः। मद्गुरच्छविर्वत भोः श्रमणो गौतमः। याप्यस्याभूत् पौराणी शुभवर्णा तनुः साप्यन्तर्हिता॥

तस्य मे भिक्षव एतदभूत्। यन्न्वहं भूयस्या मात्रयाऽव्याहारतायै प्रतिपद्येयमिति॥ अभिजानाम्यहं भिक्षव एकमेव तण्डुलमद्वितीयमाहारमाहारयितुं स्यात्। भिक्षवो युष्माकमेवं मनस्तर स्यात् तण्डुलस्तस्मिन्काले ऽभूदिति। न खल्वेवं द्रष्टव्यम्। यथैतावानेव तस्मिन् काले तण्डुलोऽभूत्। तस्य मे भिक्षवः एकं तण्डुलमाहर्तुः क्षिप्रं कामोऽभूदिति। पूर्ववद्यावन्मद्गुरच्छविर्वत भोः श्रमणो गौतम इति॥ याप्यस्याऽभूत्पौराणी शुभवर्णा तनुः साप्यन्तर्हितेति॥ तस्य मे भिक्षव एतदभूत्। यन्न्वहं भूयस्या मात्रयाऽव्याहारतायै प्रतिपद्येयमिति॥ अभिजानाम्यहं भिक्षव एकमेव तिलमद्वितीयमाहारमाहारयितुं पेयालं यावत्साऽप्यस्य शुभवर्णा तनुरन्तर्हितेति॥ तस्य मे भिक्षव एतदभूत्। सन्त्येके श्रमणब्राह्मणा ये अनाहारतया शुद्धिं मन्यन्ते। यन्न्वहं सर्वेण

१ "पृष्ठकण्टकमेवाम्र्गायमुत्तिष्ठामि" पृष्ठकाण्टकमेवाप्योत्थातुमुत्तिष्ठामि इत्यर्थः।
२ श्लोकार्थो न ज्ञायते।

यन्वहं अनाहारतायै प्रतिपद्येयमिति ॥ ततोऽहं भिक्षवोऽनाहारस्थितोऽभूवम्। तस्य मे भिक्षवोऽनाहारस्य कायोऽतीवशुष्कोऽभूत् कृशो दुर्बलः। तद्यथापि नामासितकीपर्व्वाणि वाऽकालपर्व्वाणि वा। ततो द्विगुणत्रिगुणचतुर्गुणपञ्चगुणदशगुणानि मे कृशाङ्गप्रत्यङ्गानि अभूवन् तद्यथा कर्कटकपर्शुका वाहनशालाया इव गोपानसीपार्श्वे द्विपरिवर्त्तना वेणीवत्। प्रथितकण्टकतिक्तालाबुवच्छिरःकपालम्। कूपतारका इवाऽक्षि तारके सोऽहं भिक्षवः साधुकमुत्तिष्ठामीति। गात्राण्यभिसङ्कुर्ब्बन् च कुब्जः प्रपतन् कृच्छ्रेणापि चोत्थितः। पांशुकृतानि मे गात्राणि प्रम्लानतः पूतिमूलानि रोमाण्यशीर्य्यन्त ॥ याऽपि मे साऽभूत् शुभवर्णा तनुनिभा साप्यन्तरधात्। तद्यथापि तद्रूक्षःप्रधानप्रहितात्मकत्वात्। सामन्ताश्च मे गोचरग्रामवासिनो जना एवं सञ्जानन्ते स्म। कालको बत भोः श्रमणो गौतमः श्यामको बत भोः श्रमणो गौतमो मद्गुरच्छविर्वत भोः श्रमणो गौतमः। याप्यस्याऽभूत् पौराणी शुभवर्णनिभा साप्यन्तर्हितेति ॥

राजापि तदा शुद्धोदनः प्रतिदिवसं बोधिसत्त्वस्यान्तिके दूतं प्रेषयति स्म ॥

इति हि भिक्षवो बोधिसत्त्वो लोकस्याद्भुतक्रियासन्दर्शनार्थं पूर्व्ववद्यावत् कर्म्मक्रियाप्रणष्टानां सत्त्वानां कर्म्मक्रियाऽवतारणार्थं पुण्यसञ्चयानां चोद्भावनार्थं महाज्ञानस्य च गुणसन्दर्शनार्थं ध्यानाङ्गानाञ्च विभजनार्थमेकतिलकोलतण्डुलेन षड्वर्षाणि दुष्करचर्य्यामुपदर्शयति स्म ॥ अदीनमानसः षड्वर्षाणि बोधि-

सत्त्वो यथाऽनिषण्ण एवास्थात् पर्य्यङ्के। न चेर्य्यापथाच् च्यवते स्म। नातपाच्छायायामगमन्नच्छायाया आतपन्न च वातातपवृष्टिपरित्राणमकरोन्न च दंशमशकसरीसृपानपनयति स्म। न चोच्चारप्रस्रावखेटसिङ्घाणकानुत्सृजति स्म। न च सम्यग् जानुप्रसारणमकरोत्। न च पार्श्वोदरपृष्ठस्थानेऽनाच्छादितेऽपि (१) च ते महामेघा दुर्दिनवर्षाशरद्ग्रीष्महैमन्तिका बोधिसत्त्वस्य काये निपतन्ति स्म॥ न चान्ततो बोधिसत्त्वः पाणिनाऽपि प्रच्छादनमकरोत्। नचेन्द्रियाणि विपथयति स्म। न चेन्द्रियार्थान् गृह्णीते स्म। ये च तत्रागमन् ग्रामकुमारका वा ग्रामकुमारिका वा गोपालका वा पशुपालका वा तृणहारिका वा काष्ठहारिका वा गोमयहारिका वा ते बोधिसत्त्वं पांशुपिशाचमिति मन्यन्ते स्म। तेन च क्रीडन्ति स्म। पांशुभिश्चैनं म्रक्षयन्ति स्म॥

तत्र बोधिसत्त्वस्तैः षड्भिर्व्वर्षैस्तावन्मूनं दुर्ब्बलकायः संवृत्तोऽभूत्॥ यदस्य कर्णस्रोतोभ्यां तृणतूलकं प्रक्षिप्य नासास्रोतोभ्यां निष्कास्यते स्म। नासास्रोतोभ्यां प्रक्षिप्य कर्णस्रोतोभ्यां निष्कास्यते स्म। कर्णस्रोतोभ्यां प्रक्षिप्य मुखद्वारेण निष्कास्यते स्म। मुखद्वारेण प्रक्षिप्य कर्णनासिकास्रोतोभ्यो निष्कास्यते स्म॥ नासायां प्रक्षिप्य कर्णनासिकामुखद्वारेण निष्कास्यते स्म॥ ये च ते देवनागयक्षगन्धर्व्वासुरगरुडकिन्नरमहोरगमनुष्यामनुष्या बोधिसत्त्वस्य गुणेषु प्रत्यक्षास्ते रात्रिन्दिवमधिष्ठाय बोधिसत्त्वस्य पूजां कुर्व्वन्ति स्म प्रणिधानानि च कुर्व्वन्ति स्म॥ तत्र बोधिसत्त्वेन

१ "अनाच्छादितेपि" अनाच्छादितेपि अनाच्छादिते एव इत्यर्थः।

तैः षड्भिर्व्वर्षैर्दुष्करचर्य्यां सन्दर्शयता परिपूर्णानि द्वादशनियुतानि देवमनुष्याणां त्रिभिर्यानैः परिपाचितान्यभूवन् ॥

तत्रेदमुच्यते ।

तस्य च गुणान्वितस्य पुरो विनिष्क्रम्य बोधिसत्त्वस्य ।
चिन्ताउपाययुक्ताः सत्त्वार्थहिताय उत्पन्नाः (१) ॥
पञ्चकषायकाले हीने धर्म्माधिमुक्तिके ।
जातोऽस्मिं जम्बुद्वीपे धर्म्मक्रिय उद्धुरे लोके (२) ॥
आकीर्ण तीर्थिकगणैः कौतूहलमङ्गलैरिमे युक्ताः ।
कायोपक्रमकरणैर्मन्यन्ते बालिशाः शुद्धिम् (३) ॥
अग्निप्रवेशनमेरुप्रपातपांशुभस्मादिसञ्चिता नग्नाः ।
कायपरितापनार्थं पञ्चातपयोगमनुयुक्ताः ॥
मन्त्राविचारकरणाः (४) केचिद्धस्तावलेहका अबुधाः ।
न च कुम्भमुखकरोटाग्रद्वारकुशलान्तराच्च गृह्णन्ति ॥
न च यत्र श्वानुभवती न च हितं तेन तिष्ठवाक्यस्य ।
कुलभिक्षु एकगृहिकाः शुद्धिं मन्यन्तिहात्मानम् (५) ॥
वर्जेन्ति सर्पितैलं मधुफाणितदधिदुग्धमत्स्यमांसानि ।
श्यामाकशाकभक्षा मृणालगर्दूलकणभक्षाः (६) ॥
मूलपत्रफलभक्षाः कुशचीवरचर्म्मकम्बलधराश्च ।

१ "चिन्ता उपाय" चिन्तोपाय ।

२ "जातोऽस्मिं" जातोऽस्मिन् । "धर्म्मक्रिय" धर्म्मक्रियया । "उद्धुरे" उद्धारायेत्यर्थः ।

३ "आकीर्ण" आकीर्णाः ।

४ "मन्त्राविचारकरणाः" मन्त्रविचारकरणाः ।

५ "कुलभिक्षु" कुलभिक्षवः । "मन्यन्तिहात्मानं" मन्यन्तीहात्मन इत्यर्थः ।

६ "वर्जेन्ति" वर्जयन्ति । "सर्पितैलं" सर्पिस्तैलं ।

अपरे भ्रमन्ति नग्नाः सत्यमिदं मोघमन्यदिति मूढाः॥
धारेन्ति ऊर्द्धं हस्ता ऊर्द्धं केशा जटाश्च धारेन्ति।
मार्गाननुप्रविष्टाः सुमार्गसंस्थाः सुगतिगमनकामाः (१)॥
तृणमुशलभस्मशयना: कण्टकशयनाश्च उत्कटध्यायि।
स्थित केचिदेकपादे ऊर्द्धमुखाश्चन्द्रसूर्य्यमपश्यन्तः (२)॥
उत्सां सरस्तडागां सागरसरितश्चन्द्रसूर्य्यौ च।
वृक्षगिरिशैलशिखरां कुम्भं धरणीं नमस्यन्ते (३)॥
विविधैश्च कारणैस्ते कायं परिशोधयन्ति सम्मूढाः।
मिथ्यादृष्टिपरीताः क्षिप्रं प्रपतन्त्यपायेषु॥
यन्नूनमहं व्रततपोदुष्करचर्यां समारभे घोराम्।
यद्दुष्करं न शक्यश्चरितुं देवैर्मनुष्यैर्वा (४)॥
आस्फानकञ्च ध्यानं ध्यायेयं वज्रकल्पदृढस्थानम्।
यद्ध्यानं न समर्थाः प्रत्येकजिनापि दर्शयितुम् (५)॥
सन्तीह देवमनुजास्तीर्थिक लोभव्रतेन लय्यन्ते।
तेषां परिपाचनहेतो दुष्करव्रततप आरभेयं तीव्रम् (६)॥

---

१ "धारेन्ति" धारयन्ति। "ऊर्द्धं" ऊर्द्धं। "हस्ता" हस्तौ। "ऊर्द्धं केशा" ऊर्द्धंकेशान्। "धारेन्ति" धारयन्ति।

२ "उत्कटध्यायि" उत्कटध्यायिन इत्यर्थः। "स्थितकेचिदेकपादे" स्थिताः केचिदेकपादेनेत्यर्थः। "चन्द्रसूर्य्यमपश्यन्तः" चन्द्रसूर्य्यावपश्यन्त इत्यर्थः।

३ "उत्सां" उत्साम् स्वयमुत्पन्नजलधारादिस्रोतांसीत्यर्थः। "तडागां" तडागान्। "वृक्षगिरिशैलशिखरां" वृक्षगिरिशैलशिखराणि।

४ "समारभे" समारभेयम्।

५ "प्रत्येकजिनापि" प्रत्येकजिना अपि।

६ "तीर्थिक" तीर्थिकाः। "परिपाचनहेतो" परिपाचनहेतवे।

पर्य्यङ्कमाभुजित्वा उपविष्टोऽभूत् स्थले असंस्तीर्णे ।
कोलतिलतण्डुलेनाहारविधिं निदर्शयति (१) ॥
आश्वासविप्रहीनः प्रश्वासविवर्जितो न चेङ्गते बलवान् ।
षड्वर्षाणि प्रवर ध्यायत्यास्फानकं ध्यानम् (२) ॥
अल्पको नधिकल्पन न चेञ्जना नाऽपि मन्ये प्रचारम् ।
आकाशधातुस्फुरणं ध्यायत्यास्फानकं ध्यानम् (३) ॥
न च आतपाच्छायां छायाया नातपकृतस्वाशी ।
मेरुरिव निष्प्रकम्पो ध्यायत्यास्फानकं ध्यानम् ॥
न च वातवृष्टिच्छदन न दंशमशकासरीसृपात्राणम् ।
अविकोपतया चर्य्यां ध्यायत्यास्फानकं ध्यानम् (४) ॥
न च केवलमात्मार्थं ध्यायत्यास्फानकं ध्यानम् ।
अन्यच्च करुणचित्तो भाविलोकस्य विपुलार्थम् ॥
ये ग्रामदारकाश्च गोपालाः काष्ठाहारतृणहाराः ।
पांशुपिशाचकमिति मन्यन्ते पांशुना च म्रक्षन्ति (५) ॥
अशुचिना विकिरन्ते विविधांश्च ते कारणां करोन्ति ।
न चेङ्गते भ्रमति च ध्यायत्यास्फानकं ध्यानम् (६) ॥

---

१ "पर्य्यङ्कमाभुजित्वा" पर्य्यङ्कमाभुज्य पर्य्यङ्कमास्तीर्य्येतिभावः ।

२ "प्रवर ध्यायति" प्रवरो ध्यायति ।

३ "नधिकल्पन" नाधिककल्पनं । "न चेञ्जना" न चेङ्गना । चल कल्पं नो च विकल्पमित्यपि पाठः ।

४ "वातवृष्टिच्छदन" वातवृष्ट्याच्छादनम् चन सर्व्वंच चकरोदिति शेषः । "दंशमशकासरीसृपात्राणं" दंशमशकसरीसृपात्राणम् ।

५ "पांशुपिशाचकमिति मन्यन्ते" पांशुपिशाचकमिति मत्वा पांशुना म्रक्षन्तीत्यर्थः ।

६ "विकिरन्ते" विकिरन्ति । "विविधांश्च" विविधानि च । "कारणां" कारणानि । "करोन्ति" कुर्व्वन्ति ।

न च नमति नो विनमते न कायपरिरक्षणां स्मरति।
किञ्चिन्नोच्चारप्रस्रावं शब्देषु न सन्त्रसीन परप्रेषी (१) ॥
संशुष्कमांसरुधिरचर्म्मस्नाय्वस्थिकाश्च अवशिष्टाः।
उदरश्च पृष्ठिवंशो विनिर्दृश्यते वर्त्तिता यथा वेणी (२) ॥
ये ते कृताधिकारा देवाः सुरनागयक्षगन्धर्व्वाः।
प्रत्यक्षा गुणधरस्य करोन्ति ते वा दिवा रात्रौ (३) ॥
प्रणिधिञ्च कुर्व्वते ते वयमपि एतादृशा भवेमहि क्षिप्रम्।
यथैष गगणचित्तो ध्यायत्यास्फानकं ध्यानम् (४) ॥
न च केवलमात्मार्थो न ध्यानास्वादनाच्च सुखबुद्ध्या।
अन्यत्र करुणबुद्ध्या करिष्यत्यर्थं विपुल लोके (५) ॥
निहताः परप्रवादा ध्यामीकृत तीर्थिका मतिविहीनाः।
कर्म्मक्रिया च दर्शिता या प्रोक्ता काश्यपे वाचा (६) ॥
ककुच्छन्दकस्य बोधिसत्त्वस्य सुदुर्लभं बहुभिः कल्पैः।
जनताहितार्थं ध्यायत्यास्फानकं ध्यानम्॥
द्वादशनियुताः पूर्णा विनीत मानुषास्त्रिभिर्यानैः।
एतदधिकृत्य सुमतिर्ध्यायत्यास्फानकं ध्यानम् (७) ॥

इति दुष्करचर्य्यापरिवर्त्तो नाम सप्तदशः॥ १७ ॥

---

१ "न सन्त्रसीन" न सन्त्रसः।
२ "पृष्ठिवंशो" पृष्ठवंशो।
३ "प्रत्यक्षा" प्रत्यक्षं साक्षात्कारं दर्शनमिति यावत् "करोन्ति" कुर्व्वन्ति।
४ "गगणचित्तो" गगनचित्तो।
५ "केवलमात्मार्थो" केवलमात्मार्थं। "विपुल" विपुलं।
६ "ध्यामीकृत" ध्यामीकृताः। "काश्यपे वाचा" काश्यपेन वाचा।
७ "द्वादशनियुताः पूर्णा" द्वादशनियुतेषु पूर्णेषु सत्सु। "विनीत" विनीता यत्र पूर्व्वार्द्धे भविष्यन्तीत्युक्तम्।

अष्टादशाध्यायप्रारम्भः ॥

मारश्च भिक्षवः पापीयान् बोधिसत्त्वस्य षड्वर्षाणि दुष्करचर्य्यां चरतः पृष्ठतः पृष्ठतः समनुबद्धोऽभूत्। अवतारप्रेक्षी अवतारगवेषी न च कदाचित् किञ्चिदवतारमध्यगच्छत्। सोऽवतारमधिगच्छन्निर्विवर्णो विप्रतिसारी प्रकामत् (१) ॥

तत्रेदमुच्यते ॥

रमणीयान्यरण्यानि वनगुल्माश्च वीरुधः।
प्राचीनउरुविल्वायां यत्र नैरञ्जना नदी (२) ॥
प्रहाणायोद्यतं तत्र सततं दृढविक्रमम्।
पराक्रमन्तं वीर्य्येण योगक्षेमस्य प्राप्तये ॥
नमुचिर्मधुरां वाचं भाषमाण उपागमत्।
शाक्यपुत्र समुत्तिष्ठ कायखेदेन किं तव ॥
जीवतो जीवितं श्रेयो जीवन् धर्म्मं चरिष्यसि।
जीवं हि तानि कुरुते यानि कृत्वा न शोचति (३) ॥
कृशो विवर्णो दीनस्त्वमन्तिके मरणं तव।
सहस्रभागे मरणमेकभागे च जीवितम् (४) ॥
दद तं सततं दानमहोरात्रञ्च जुह्वते।
भविष्यति महत्पुण्यं किं प्रहाणे करिष्यसि (५) ॥

---

१ प्राकामत ।

२ प्राचीन उरुविल्वायां" प्राचीनोरुविल्वायाम् ।

३ "जीवितो जीवितं श्रेयो" जीवितोऽजीविताच्छ्रेयान् इत्युचितम् । "धर्म्मं" धर्म्मं । "जीवं हि" जीवन् हि ।

४ "सहस्रभागे मरणमेकभागे च" सहस्रभागो मरणमेकभागश्च ।

५ "दद" देहि । "महत्पुण्यं" महापुण्यं । "प्रहाणे" प्रहाणेन ।

दुःखो मार्गः प्रहाणस्य दुष्करश्चित्तनिग्रहः ।
इमां वाचं तदा मारो बोधिसत्त्वमथाब्रवीत् ॥
तं तथावादिनं मारं बोधिसत्त्वस्ततोऽब्रवीत् ।
प्रमत्तबन्धो पापीयां स्वेनार्थेन समागतः (१) ॥
अणुमात्रं हि मे पुण्यैरर्थो मार न विद्यते ।
अर्थो येषान्तु पुण्येन तानेवं वक्तुमर्हसि ॥
नैवाहं मरणं मन्ये मरणान्तं हि जीवितम् ।
अनिवर्त्ती भविष्यामि ब्रह्मचर्यापरायणः ॥
स्रोतांस्यपि नदीनां हि वायुरेव विशोषयेत् ।
किं पुनः शोषयेत् कायं शोणितप्रहितात्मनाम् ॥
शोणिते तु विशुष्के वै ततो मांसं विशुष्यति ।
मांसेषु चीयमाणेषु भूयश्चित्तं प्रसीदति ॥
भूयश्छन्दश्च वीर्य्यञ्च समाधिश्चावतिष्ठति ।
* * * * * * * * * *
तस्यैवं मे विहरतः प्राप्तस्योत्तमवेदनाम् ।
चित्तं नावेक्षते कायं पश्य सत्त्वस्य शुद्धताम् ॥
अस्ति च्छन्दस्तथा वीर्य्यं प्रज्ञापि मम विद्यते ।
तं न पश्याम्यहं लोके वीर्य्याद्यो मां विचालयेत् ॥
वरं मृत्युः प्राणहरो धिग्ग्राम्यं नो च जीवितम् ।
सङ्ग्रामे मरणं श्रेयो न च जीवेत्पराजितः ॥

---

१ "पापीयां" पापीयः ।

न शूरो जयते सेनां जित्वा चैनां न मन्यते।
शूरस्तु जयते सेनां लघु मार जयामि ते (१)॥
कामास्ते प्रथमा सेना द्वितीया ते रतिस्तथा।
तृतीया क्षुत्पिपासा ते तृष्णा सेना चतुर्थिका॥
पञ्चमी स्त्यानमिद्धन्ते भयं षष्ठी निरुच्यते।
सप्तमी विचिकित्सा ते क्रोधम्रक्षौ तथाष्टमी॥
लोभश्लोकौ च संस्कारो मिथ्यालब्धश्च यद्यशः।
आत्मानं यश्च उत्कर्षेद्यश्च वै ध्वंसयेत्परान्॥
एषा हि नमुचेः सेना कृष्णबन्धोः प्रतापिनः।
अत्रावगाढा दृश्यन्त एते श्रमणब्राह्मणाः॥
या ते सेना प्रधर्षयति लोकमेनं सदेवकम्।
भेत्स्यामि प्रज्ञया तां त आमपात्रमिवाम्बुना॥
स्मृतिं सूपस्थितां कृत्वा प्रज्ञां चैव सुभाविताम्।
सम्प्रजानं चरिष्यामि किं करिष्यसि दुर्मते॥

एवमुक्ते मारः पापीयान् दुःखितो दुर्मना अनात्तमना विप्रतिसारी तत्रैवान्तरधात्॥

अथ खलु भिक्षवो बोधिसत्त्वस्यैतदभूत्। ये केचिच्छ्रमणा ब्राह्मणा वा अतीतानागतप्रत्युत्पन्नेष्वध्वस्वात्मोपक्रमिकां शरीरोपतापिकां दुःखां तीव्रां कटुकाममनापां वेदनां वेदयन्त्येतावत्परमन्ते दुःखमनुभवन्ति॥

तस्य मे भिक्षव एतदभूत्। अनयाऽपि खलु मया चर्ययाऽ-

---

१ "जयामि ते" जयामि त्वाम्।

नयाऽपि प्रतिपादकः कश्चिदुत्तरिमनुष्यधर्म्मा(१)दलमार्य्यज्ञान-
दर्शनविशेषः साक्षात्कृतः । नायं मार्गो बोधेर्नायं मार्ग आयत्यां
जातिजरामरणसम्भवानामस्तङ्गमाय न स्यात्तदन्यो मार्गो
बोधेरायत्यां जातिजरामरणदुःखसमुदायानामस्तङ्गमाय ॥

तस्य मे भिक्षव एतदभवत् । यन्न्वहं पितुरुद्याने जम्बु-
च्छायायां निषण्णो विविक्तं कामैर्व्विविक्तं पापकैरकुशलैर्धर्मैः
सवितर्कं सविचारं विवेकजं प्रीतिसुखं प्रथमं ध्यानमुपसम्पद्य
व्याहार्षं यावच्चतुर्थध्यानमुपसम्पद्य व्याहार्षम् । स्यात् स मार्गो
बोधेर्जातिजरामरणदुःखसमुदयानामसम्भवायास्तङ्गमायेति ॥
तदनुसारि च मे विज्ञानमभूत् । स मार्गो बोधेरिति ॥ तस्य म-
एतदभूत् । नासौ मार्गः शक्य एवं दौर्ब्बल्यप्राप्तेनाभिसम्बोद्धुम् ।
स चेत्पुनरहमभिज्ञाज्ञानबलेनैवाहं दुर्ब्बलकाय एव बोधिम-
ण्डमुपसङ्क्रमेयम् ॥ न मे पश्चिमा जनतानुकम्पिता स्यान्न चैव
मार्गो बोधेः ॥

यन्न्वहमौदरिकमाहारमाहृत्य कायबलस्थामं सञ्जनय्य
पश्चाद्बोधिमण्डमुपसङ्क्रमेयम् । तत्र भिक्षवो ये ते लुब्धाधिमुक्ता
देवपुत्रास्ते मम चेतश्चेतसैव परिवितर्कमाज्ञाय येनाहं तेनोप-
सङ्क्रम्य मामेवमाहुः । यस्य त्वं सत्पुरुषौदरिकमाहारमाहरेर्वयं
ते रोमकूपे ओजः प्रक्षेप्स्यामः ॥

तस्य मे भिक्षव एतदभूत् । अहं खल्वनशन इत्यात्मानं प्रति-
जाने सामन्ता मे गोचरग्रामवासिनो जना एवं सञ्जानन्ते स्म ।

---

१ "उत्तरिमनुष्यधर्म्मा" उत्तरमनुष्यधर्म्मा ।

यथानशनः श्रमणो गौतम इतीव मे लुब्धाधिमुक्ता देवपुत्रा रोमकूप ओजः प्रक्षिपन्ति स मम परमो मृषावादः स्यात्। ततो बोधिसत्त्वो मृषावादपरिहारार्थं तान्देवपुत्रान् प्रतिक्षिप्यौदारिकाहारे चित्तं नामयति स्म। इति हि भिक्षवः षड्वर्षव्रततपःसमुत्तीर्णो बोधिसत्त्वस्तस्मादासनादुत्थायौदारिकमाहारमाहरिष्यामीति वाचं निश्चारयति स्म। तद्यथा फाणीकृतं मुद्गयूषं यथौदनकुल्माषमिति (१)॥

अथ खलु भिक्षवः पञ्चकानां भद्रवर्गीयाणामेतदभूत्। तयापि तावच्चर्य्यया तयापि प्रतिपदा श्रमणेन गौतमेन न शकितं (२) किञ्चिदुत्तरिमनुष्यधर्म्मादलमार्य्यज्ञानदर्शनविशेषं साक्षात् कर्त्तुम्। किं पुनरेतर्ह्यौदारिकमाहारमुत्खनिकायोगमनुयुक्तो विहरन्नव्यक्तो बालोऽयमिति च मन्यमाना बोधिसत्त्वस्यान्तिकात्प्रक्रामन्तस्ते वाराणसीं गत्वा ऋषिपतने मृगदावे व्याहार्षुः॥

तत्र बोधिसत्त्वमादित एव दुष्करचर्य्यां चरन्तं दशग्रामिकदुहितरः कुमार्य्य उपतस्थुर्दर्शनाय वन्दनाय पर्य्युपासनाय च॥ एककोलतिलतण्डुलप्रदानेन च प्रतिपादितोऽभूत्॥ बला च नाम दारिका बलगुप्ता च प्रिया च सुप्रिया च विजयसेना च अतिमुक्तकमला च सुन्दरी च कुम्भकारी च उलुविल्लिका च जटिलिका च सुजाता च नाम ग्रामिकदुहिता आभिः कुमारिकाभिर्बोधिसत्त्वाय सर्व्वे ते यूषविधयः कृत्वोपनामिता

---

१ "फाणीकृतं मूगयूषं हरेणुकयूषमथौदनकुल्माषमितीति वा पाठः।

२ "न शकितं" न शक्तमित्यर्थः।

अभूवन्। तांश्चाभ्यवहृत्य बोधिसत्त्वः क्रमेण गोचरग्रामे पिण्डा-
यभ्याचरन् वर्णरूपबलवानभूत्। तदग्रेण बोधिसत्त्वः सुन्दरः
श्रमणो महाश्रमण इत्याचख्यते॥ तत्र भिक्षवः सुजाता ग्रामि-
कदुहिता बोधिसत्त्वस्य दुष्करचर्य्यां चरत आदित एव बोधि-
सत्त्वस्य व्रततपःसमुत्तरणार्थं शरीराप्यायनहेतोश्च प्रतिदिव-
समष्टशतं ब्राह्मणानां भोजयतिस्म। एवञ्च प्रणिदधाति स्म।
मम भोजनं भुक्त्वा बोधिसत्त्वोऽनुत्तरां सम्यक्सम्बोधिमभिसम्बु-
ध्यतामिति॥ तस्य मे भिक्षवः षड्वर्षव्यतिक्रान्तस्य काषायाणि
वस्त्राणि परिजीर्णान्यभूवन्॥ तस्य मे भिक्षव एतदभूत्। स
चेदहं कौपीनं प्रच्छादनं लभेयं शोभनं स्यात्॥

तेन खलु पुनर्भिक्षवः समयेन सुजाताया ग्रामिकदुहितुर्दासी
राधा नाम्नी कालगताऽभूत्। सा शाणकैः परिवेष्ट्य श्मशानम-
पनीय त्यक्ताऽभूत्। तदहमेवाद्राक्षं पांशुदकूलम्। ततोऽहं तत्
पांशुदकूलं वामेन पादेनाक्रम्य दक्षिणहस्तं प्रसार्य्यावनतोऽभू-
वमुद्ग्रहीतुम्॥ अथ भौमा देवा अन्तरिक्षाणां देवानां घोषमनु-
श्रावयन्ति स्म। आश्चर्य्यं मार्षा अद्भुतमिदं मार्षाः। यत्र हि नामैवं
महाराजकुलप्रसूतस्य चक्रवर्त्तिराज्यपरित्यागिनः पांशुदकूले
चित्तप्रणतमिति अन्तरिक्षा देवा भौमानां देवानां शब्दं श्रुत्वा
चातुर्महाराजिकानां देवानां घोषमुदीरयन्ति स्म। चातु-
र्महाराजिकास्त्रयस्त्रिंशतः, त्रयस्त्रिंशा यामानां, यामास्तुषि-
तानां, तुषिता निर्म्माणरतीनां, निर्म्माणरतयः परनिर्म्मितवश-
वर्त्तिनां, परनिर्म्मितवशवर्त्तिनो यावद्ब्रह्मकायिकानाम्॥

इति हि भिक्षवस्तत्क्षणं तत्रैवं तन्मुहूर्त्तं यावदकनिष्ठभुवनादेकघोष एकः सन्निर्नादोऽभ्युद्गतोऽभूत्। आश्चर्यमिदं मार्षा अद्भुतमिदम्। यत्र हि नामैवं महाराजकुलप्रसूतस्य चक्रवर्त्तिराज्यपरित्यागिनः पांशुदकूले चित्तं नतमिति॥

अथ बोधिसत्त्वस्य पुनरप्येतदभवत्। लब्धं मया पांशुदकूलं स चेदुदकं लभेयं शोभनं स्यात्। ततस्तत्रैव देवताः पाणिना महीं पराहन्ति स्म। तत्र पुष्करिणी प्रादुरभूत्। अद्यापि सा पाणिहतेति पुष्करिणी सञ्ज्ञायते॥ पुनरपि बोधिसत्त्वस्यैतदभूत्। लब्धं मया पानीयं स चेच्छिलां लभेयम्। यत्रेदं पांशुदकूलं प्रक्षालयेयं शोभनं स्यात्॥ तत्रैव शक्रेण शिला तत्क्षणमेवापनिक्षिप्ताऽभूत्॥ ततो बोधिसत्त्वस्तत्पांशुदकूलं प्रक्षालयति स्म॥ अथ शक्रो देवराजो बोधिसत्त्वमेवमाह। ददेहं (१) सत्पुरुष मह्यमहं प्रक्षालयामीति॥

ततो बोधिसत्त्वः स्वयङ्कारितां प्रव्रज्यायाः सन्दर्शयितुं तत्पांशुदकूलं शक्रस्यादत्वा स्वयमेव प्रक्षालयति स्म। स श्रान्तः क्लान्तकायोऽवतीर्य्य पुष्करिणीमुत्तरिष्यामीति॥ मारेण च पापीयसा ईर्ष्याधर्म्मपरीतेन पुष्करिण्या अत्युच्छ्रितानि तटानि निर्म्मितान्यभूवन्। तस्याश्च पुष्करिण्यास्तीरे महान्ककुभपादपस्तत्र देवतां बोधिसत्त्वो लोकानुवृत्त्या देवतानुग्रहार्थं चाब्रवीत्। आह। हे देवते वृक्षशाखाम्। तया वृक्षशाखावनामिताऽभूत्तां बोधिसत्त्वोऽवलम्ब्योत्तरति स्म। अवतीर्य्य च तत्ककुभपादप-

१ "ददेहं" देहीदम्।

स्याधस्तात् तत्पांशुकूलं सङ्गृह्य सीव्यति स्म ॥ अद्यापि तत्पांशुकूलसीवनमित्येवं सञ्ज्ञायते स्म ॥ अविमलप्रभो नाम शुद्धावासकायिको देवपुत्रः स दिव्यानि चीवराणि काषायरङ्गरक्तानि श्रमणसारूप्याणि बोधिसत्त्वायोपनामयति स्म। बोधिसत्त्वश्च तानि गृहीत्वा पूर्वाह्णे निवास्य सङ्घाटीप्रावृत्य गोचराभिमुखोऽभूत्। तत्र देवताभिरुरुविल्वासेनापतिग्रामके नन्दिकग्रामिकदुहितुः सुजातायाः आरोचितमभूत्। अर्द्धरात्रसमये यदर्थं त्वं महायज्ञं यजसे स तस्माद् व्रतादुत्तीर्णः स शुभमौदारिकमाहारमाहरिष्यति। त्वया च पूर्वं प्रणिधानं कृतं मम भोजनं भुक्त्वा बोधिसत्त्वोऽनुत्तरां सम्यक्सम्बोधिमभिसम्भोत्स्यत इति। यत्ते करणीयं तत् कुरुष्वेति ॥

अथ खलु भिक्षवः सुजाता नन्दिकग्रामिकदुहिता तासां देवतानां तद्वचनं श्रुत्वा शीघ्रं गोसहस्रस्य क्षीरं सप्तकृतसारोद्धृतादग्र्यमोजोमण्डं गृह्णीते स्म। गृहीत्वा च सा तत्क्षीरमभिनवमभिनवैस्तण्डुलैरभिनवायां स्थाल्यामभिनवां चुल्लीमुपलिप्य तद्भोजनं साधयति स्म। तस्मिंश्च साध्यमाने इमानि पूर्वनिमित्तानि सन्दृश्यन्ते स्म ॥ तस्मिन् खल्वपि क्षीरे श्रीवत्सस्वस्तिकनन्द्यावर्त्तपद्मवर्द्धमानादीनि मङ्गल्यानि सन्दृश्यन्ते स्म ॥ ततस्तस्या एतदभूत्। यादृशानीमानि पूर्वनिमित्तानि सन्दृश्यन्ते निःसंशयमिदं भोजनं भुक्त्वा बोधिसत्त्वोऽनुत्तरां सम्यक्सम्बोधिं प्राप्स्यति। सामुद्रिकज्ञानविधिज्ञश्च नैमित्तिकस्तं प्रदेशं प्राप्तोऽभूत्। सोऽपि तथैवामृताधिगमनमेव व्याकृतवान्। ततः

सुजाता तं पायसं पक्त्वा स्थण्डिलमुपलिप्य पुष्पैरवकीर्य गन्धोदकेनाभ्युक्ष्यासनं प्रज्ञप्य सत्वरयोत्तरां नाम चेटीमामन्त्रयते स्म। गच्छोत्तरे ब्राह्मणमानयाहमिदं मधुपायसमवलोकयामि॥ साध्वार्येति प्रतिश्रुत्य पूर्वां दिशमगमत्॥ सा तत्र बोधिसत्त्वं पश्यति स्म। एवं पश्चिमामुत्तरामेव दिशं गच्छति स्म। तत्र तत्र बोधिसत्त्वमेवाद्राक्षीत्। न कश्चित् सन्दृश्यते स्म॥ ततः सा गत्वा स्वामिनीमेवमाह। न खल्वार्येऽन्यः कश्चिद्दृश्यते श्रमणो ब्राह्मणो वाऽन्यत्र यदा यत एव गच्छामि तत्र तत्र श्रमणमेव सुन्दरं पश्यामि॥ सुजाता आह।

गच्छोत्तरे स एव ब्राह्मणः स एव श्रमणस्तस्यैवार्थेऽयमारम्भस्तमेवानय॥ साध्वार्ये इत्युत्तरा गत्वा बोधिसत्त्वस्य चरणयोर्निपत्य सुजाताया नाम्नोपनिमन्त्रयते स्म॥ ततो भिक्षवो बोधिसत्त्वः सुजाताया ग्रामिकदुहितुर्निवेशनं गत्वा प्रज्ञप्त एवासने न्यसीदत्॥

अथ खलु भिक्षवः सुजाता ग्रामिकदुहिता सुवर्णमयीं पात्रीं मधुपायससम्पूर्णां बोधिसत्त्वस्योपनामयति स्म॥ अथ बोधिसत्त्वस्यैतदभवत्। यादृशमिदं सुजातया भोजनमुपनामितं निःसंशयमहमद्यैनं भुक्त्वानुत्तरां सम्यक्सम्बोधिमभिसम्भोत्स्ये॥

अथ बोधिसत्त्वस्तद्भोजनं प्रतिगृह्णन् सुजातां ग्रामिकदुहितरमेतदवोचत्। इयं भगिनि सुवर्णपात्री किं क्रियताम्॥ साऽऽह। तवैव भवत्विति॥

बोधिसत्त्व आह । न ममेदृशेन भाजनेन प्रयोजनम् ।

सुजाता आह । यथेष्टं क्रियताम् । नाहं विना भाजनेन कस्यचिद्भोजनं प्रयच्छामि ॥

अथ बोधिसत्त्वस्तं पिण्डपात्रमादायोरुविल्वाया निष्क्रम्य नागनदीं पूर्व्वाह्णकालसमये नदीं नैरञ्जनामुपसङ्क्रम्य तं पिण्डपात्रं चीवराणि चैकान्ते निक्षिप्य नदीं नैरञ्जनामवतरति स्म गात्राणि शीतलीकर्त्तुम् । बोधिसत्त्वस्य खलु पुनर्भिक्षवः स्नायतोऽनेकानि देवपुत्रशतसहस्राणि दिव्यागुरुचन्दनचूर्णविलेपनैर्नदीमालोकयन्ति स्म । दिव्यानि च नानावर्णानि कुसुमानि जले क्षिपन्ति स्म । यदुत बोधिसत्त्वस्य पूजाकर्म्मणे ॥

तेन खलु पुनः समयेन नदी नैरञ्जना दिव्यैर्गन्धैः पुष्पैश्च समाकुला भवति स्म । येन च गन्धोदकेन बोधिसत्त्वः स्नातोऽभूत् । तेन खलु पुनः समयेन शुद्धावासकायिकैर्देवपुत्रैः सर्व्वे अन्यतीर्थिका निगृहीता अभूवन् । तं देवपुत्रकोटीनियुतशतसहस्राणि अभ्युत्क्षिप्य स्वकस्वकानि भवनानि नयन्ति स्म चैत्यार्थं पूजार्थञ्च ॥ यानि च बोधिसत्त्वस्य केशश्मश्रूण्यभवन् तानि सर्व्वाणि सुजाता ग्रामिकदुहिता मङ्गल्यानीति चैत्यार्थं च परिगृह्णीते स्म । नद्युत्तीर्णश्च बोधिसत्त्वः पुलिनं निरीक्षते स्म उपवेष्टुकामः । अथ या नैरञ्जनायां नद्यां नागकन्या सा धरणीतलादभ्युद्गत्य मणिमयं मनोरमं भद्रासनं बोधिसत्त्वायोपनामयति स्म ॥ तत्र बोधिसत्त्वो निषद्य यावदर्थं तं मधुपायसं परिभुङ्क्ते स्म ॥ सुजाताया ग्रामिकदुहितुरनुकम्पामुपादाय

परिभुज्य तां सुवर्णपात्रीमनपेक्षो वारिणि प्रक्षिपति स्म। क्षिप्तमात्राञ्च तां सागरो नागराजो चित्रीकारबहुमानजातो गृहीत्वा स्वभवनाभिमुखः प्रस्थितोऽभूत् पूजार्हेति कृत्वा॥ अथ दशशतनयनः पुरन्दरो गरुडरूपमभिनिर्माय वज्रतुण्डो भूत्वा सागरस्य नागराजस्यान्तिकात्तां सुवर्णपात्रीं हर्त्तुमारब्धो यदा न शक्नोति स्म तदा स्वरूपेणादरेण याचित्वा त्रयस्त्रिंशद्भवनं नीतवान् चैत्यार्थं पूजार्थञ्च। नीत्वा पात्रीयात्रां नाम पर्व्वणि प्रवर्त्तितवान्। अद्यापि च त्रयस्त्रिंशेषु देवेषु प्रतिसंवत्सरं पात्रीमहो वर्त्तते। तच्च भद्रासनं तयैव नागकन्यया परिगृहीतं चैत्यार्थं पूजार्थञ्च॥ समनन्तरपरिभुक्तश्च भिक्षवो बोधिसत्त्वेनौदारिक आहारोऽथ तत्क्षणमेव बोधिसत्त्वस्य पुण्यबलेन प्रज्ञाबलेन पूर्व्विककायशुभवर्णपुष्करतया प्रादुरभूत्। द्वात्रिंशच्च महापुरुषलक्षणानि अशीतिश्चानुव्यञ्जनानि व्योमप्रभता च॥ तत्रेदमुच्यते।

षड्वर्ष व्रततप उत्तरित्व भगवान् एवं मतिं चिन्तयेत्
स चेदहं ध्यानअभिज्ञज्ञानबलवानेवं कृशाङ्गोऽपि सन्।
गच्छेयं द्रुमराज मूल विटपी सर्व्वज्ञतां बुध्यतुं
नो मे स्यादनुकम्पिता च जनता एवं भवेत् पश्चिमा (१)॥
यन्नौदारिक भुक्त भोजनवरं काये बलं कृत्व ना

१ "षड्वर्ष" षड्वर्षं। "व्रततप उत्तरित्व" व्रततपोभिरुत्तीर्य्य। "चिन्तयेत्" अचिन्तयत्। "ध्यानअभिज्ञज्ञानबलवान्" ध्यानाभिज्ञाज्ञानबलवान्। "द्रुमराज मूल" द्रुमराजस्य मूले। "विटपी" विटपिनः। "बुध्यतुं" बोद्धुं।

गच्छेयं द्रुमराज मूल विटपी सर्व्वज्ञतां बुध्यितुम् ।
आरैवं ते च पुत्र देवमनुजा सूत्रेण ज्ञानेषिणा
ये प्रस्थावि च बुद्धिना च अमृतं कायेन ते दुर्ब्बलाः (१) ॥
सा च ग्रामिक धीतपूर्व्वचरिता नाम्ना सुजाता इति
यज्ञं नित्यं यजति एवमनसा सिद्धे व्रतं नायके ।
सा देवान् निशम्य चोदन तदा गृह्य मधूपायसं
उपगम्य नदितीरि हृष्टमनसा नैरञ्जनानाम्निता (२) ॥
सो चाकल्पसहस्रचीर्णचरितः शान्तप्रशान्तेन्द्रियो
देवैर्नागगणैर्ऋषीपरिवृतो आगत्य नैरञ्जनाम् ।
तीर्णस्या च कुमार सत्त्व मतिमां स्नाने मतिं चिन्तयन्
ओतरिया नदि स्नापि शुद्ध विमलो लोकानुकम्पी मुनिः (३) ॥
देवाः कोटिसहस्र हृष्टमनसा गन्धानि चूर्णानि च
ओरत्वा नदि ओदयन्ति सलिलं स्नानार्थ सत्त्वोत्तमे ।
स्नाना स्नात्व च बोधिसत्त्व विमलस्तीरे स्थितः सूरतो

---

१ "चलोदरिक भुक्त्व" चलोदरिकं भुक्त्वा। "कलना" कला नेति पादपूरणार्थमेव। "द्रुमराज मूल विटपी" द्रुमराजस्य मूले विटपिनः। "बुध्यितुं" बोद्धुं। "आरैवं" आऊरेयं। "पुत्र" पुत्राः। "ज्ञानेषिणा" ज्ञानेषणा। "ये प्रस्थावि च" येऽप्रस्ता आसन् ये। "बुद्धिना च" बुद्ध्या ये। "अमृतं" अमृतं प्राप्तुमित्यर्थः।

२ "ग्रामिक" ग्रामिका। "धीतपूर्व्वचरिता" अधीतपूर्व्वचरिता। "एवमनसा" एवंमनसा इतिबुद्ध्या इत्यर्थः। "सिद्धे व्रतं नायके" सिद्धेद्व्रतं नायके नायकस्येत्यर्थः। "चोदन" चोदनं। "गृह्य" गृहीत्वा। "मधूपायसं" मधुपायसम्। "उपगम्या" उपगम्य। "नदितीरि" नदीतीरं। "नैरञ्जनानाम्निता" नैरञ्जनानाम्निता।

३ "सो चाकल्प" स चाकल्प। "ऋषीपरिवृतो" ऋषिपरिवृतो। "तीर्णस्या च कुमार सत्त्व मतिमां" "तीरस्थश्च कुमारः सत्त्वो मतिमान्। "ओतरिया नदि स्नापि" अवतरस्य नद्यां स्नातः। "शुद्ध" शुद्धो।

मरुर्दैवसहस्र स्नान सलिल पूजार्थ सत्त्वोत्तमे (१) ॥
काषायाणि च वस्त्राणि निर्मल शुभां तां देवपुत्रोऽददत्
कल्पीयानि च संनिवास्य भगवांस्तीरे हि नद्यां स्थितः ।
नागाकन्योदग्रहृष्टमनसा भद्रासनं साऽनयीत्
यत्रासौ निषसाद शान्तमनसो लोकस्य चक्षुष्करः (२) ॥
दत्वा भोजनं सुजात मतिमां स्वर्णामये भाजने
वन्दित्वा चरणानि सा प्रमुदिता परिभुङ्क्ष्व मे सारथे ।
भुक्त्वा भोजन यावदर्थ मतिमां पात्रीं जले प्राक्षिपेत्
तां जग्राह पुरन्दरः सुरगुरुः पूजां करिष्याम्यहम् (३) ॥
यद्भुक्तञ्च जिनेन भोजनवरमौदारिकं तत्क्षणे
तस्य कायबलञ्च तेजश्शिरिया पूर्व्वं यथा संस्थितम् ।
धर्म्मीं कृत्य कथा सुजात मरुणां क्षमा च सर्वं वज्रं
सिंहाहंसगतिर्गजेन्द्रगमनो बोधिद्रुमं सम्प्रस्थितः (४) ॥

इति नैरञ्जनापरिवर्त्तो नामाष्टादशः ॥ १८ ॥

---

१ "कोटीसहस्र" कोटिसहस्राणि । नमान्ति इति पदेन एवं पाठः । यत्र नमान्ति इति पाठे अर्थः सङ्गच्छति । "चोदत्स्या" चोदत्स्याः । "नदि शोदयन्ति" नद्योमायो-दयन्ति च । "स्नानार्थ सत्त्वोत्तमे" स्नानार्थं सत्त्वोत्तमस्य । "स्नाना स्नान" स्नानं स्नाना । "बोधिसत्त्व विसृतः" बोधिसत्त्वो विसृतः । "चूरतो" चूरतो । "मरुर्दै-वसहस्र" मरुद्भिर्देवसहस्राणि । "स्नान सलिल पूजार्थ सत्त्वोत्तमे" स्नानात् सलिले पूजार्थं सत्त्वोत्तमस्य ।

२ "निर्मल शुभां तां" निर्मलानि शुभानि तानि । "कल्पीयानि" चाकल्पनी-यानि परित्यागयोग्यानीति भावः । "नद्यां" नद्याः । "नागाकन्यो॰" नागकन्या॰ । "शान्तमनसो" शान्तमनाः ।

३ "सुजात मतिमां" सुजाता मतिमती । "स्वर्णामये" स्वर्णमये । "भोजन या-वदर्थ मतिमां" भोजनं यावदर्थं मतिमान् । "प्राक्षिपेत्" प्राक्षिपत् ।

४ "औदारिकं" औदरिकं । "तेजश्शिरिया" तेजःश्रिया । "धर्म्मीं कृत्य" धर्म्यां कृत्वा । "कथा" कथां । "सुजात" सुजातायाः । "मरुणां" मरुतां । "वज्रं" वज्र । "सिंहाहंसगतिः" सिंहहंसगतिः "गजेन्द्रगमनः" यत्र प्रस्थित इति पाठे न छन्दोभङ्गः ।

ऊनविंशाध्यायप्रारम्भः ।

इति हि भिक्षवो बोधिसत्त्वो नद्यां नैरञ्जनायां स्नात्वा च भुक्त्वा कायबलस्थामं सञ्जनय्य येन षोडशाकारसम्पन्नपृथिवीप्रदेशे महाबोधिद्रुमराजमूलं तेन प्रतस्थे विजयाय तया च गत्या । याऽसौ महापुरुषाणां गतिरनुचरितगतिः । इन्द्रयष्टिगतिः सुसंस्थितगतिः । मेरुराजगतिरजिह्मगतिरकुटिलगतिरनुपद्रुतगतिरविलम्बितगतिरलुलितगतिरस्खलितगतिरसङ्घट्टितगतिरलीनगतिरविलम्बित(१)गतिरचपलगतिः सलीलगतिर्विमलगतिः शुभगतिरदोषगतिरमोहगतिररक्तगतिः सिंहगतिर्हंसराजगतिर्नागगतिर्नारायणगतिर्धरणीतलासंसृष्टगतिः सहस्रारचक्रधरणीतलचित्रगतिः । जालाङ्गुलिताम्रनखगतिः । धरणीतलनिर्नादगतिः । शैलराजसङ्घट्टनगतिः । उत्कूलनिकूलसमकरचरणगतिः । जालाङ्कराभारश्म्युत्सर्जनसत्त्वसंस्पृशनसुगतिगमनगतिः । विमलपद्मक्रमनिक्षेपणगतिः । पूर्व्वशुभसुचरितगमनगतिः । पूर्व्वबुद्धसिंहाभिगमनगतिः । वज्रदृढाभेद्याशयगतिः । सर्व्वापायगतिः । सर्व्वापायदुर्गतिपिधनगतिः । सर्व्वसुखसञ्जननगतिः । मोक्षपथसन्दर्शनगतिः । मारबलापकरणगतिः । कुगतिगणपरप्रवादिसहधर्म्मनिग्रहणगतिः । कर्म्मपटलक्लेशविधमनगतिः । संसारपक्षापक्षकरणगतिः । शक्रब्रह्ममहेश्वरलोकपालाभिभवगतिः । त्रिसाहस्रमहासाहस्रैकशूर-

१ द्वितीयाविलम्बितशब्दस्यार्थवैलक्षण्यं न ज्ञायते ।

गतिः। स्वयम्भूरभिभूगतिः (१)। सर्व्वशास्त्रागाभिगमनगतिः। स्मृतिमतिगतिः। समभिगमनगतिर्जरामरणप्रशमगतिः। शिव-वीजामराभयनिर्व्वाणपुरगमनगतिः। ईदृश्या गत्या बोधिसत्त्वो बोधिमण्डं सम्प्रस्थितोऽभूत्॥

इति हि भिक्षवो यावच्च नद्या नैरञ्जनाया यावच्च बोधिमण्डादेतस्मिन्नन्तरे वातबलाहकैर्देवपुत्रैः संमृष्टमभूत्। वर्षबलाहकैर्देवपुत्रैर्गन्धोदकेन सिक्तमभूत् पुष्पैश्चावकीर्णमभूत्। यावदेव त्रिसाहस्रलोकधातौ वृक्षास्ते सर्व्वे येन बोधिमण्डस्तेनाभिनताया अभूवन्। येऽपि च तदहोजातबालदारकास्तेऽपि बोधिमण्डशीर्षकाः स्वपन्ति स्म॥ येऽपि चेह त्रिसाहस्रमहासाहस्रलोकधातौ सुमेरुप्रमुखाः पर्व्वतास्तेऽपि सर्व्वे येन बोधिमण्ड-प्रणता (२) अभूवन्। नदीं नैरञ्जनामुपादाय यावद्बोधिमण्डोऽस्मिन्नन्तरे कामावचरैर्देवपुत्रैः क्रोशविस्तारैकप्रमाणो मार्गोऽभिव्यूहितोऽभूत्। तस्य च मार्गस्य वामदक्षिणपार्श्वयोः सप्तरत्नमयी वेदिका(३)ऽभिनिर्म्मिताऽभूत्। सप्ततालाश्च उच्चैस्त्वेन उपरिष्टाद्रत्नजालसञ्छन्ना दिव्यच्छत्रध्वजपताकासमलङ्कृता। द्वयोश्चापि सप्तरत्नमयास्ताला अभिनिर्म्मिता अभूवन्॥ तस्या वेदिकाया अभ्युद्गतात् सर्व्वस्माच्च तालाद्रत्नसूत्राद् द्वितीयतालमवसक्तमभूत्। द्वयोश्च तालयोर्मध्ये पुष्करिणी मापिताऽभूत्ता गन्धो-

---

१ स्वयम्भुवोऽभिभूमतिरिति शुद्धः पाठः।
२ "येन बोधिमण्डप्रणता" येन बोधिमण्डस्तेनप्रणता अभूवन् इत्यर्थः।
३ वेदिका-पुष्करिणी- विशेषणे सर्वत्र बहुत्वमपेक्षितम्।

उदकपरिपूर्णा सुवर्णवालुकासंस्तृता उत्पलपद्मकुमुदपुण्डरीकसंछन्ना रत्नवेदिकापरिवृता वैदूर्य्यमणिरत्नसोपानप्रत्युप्ता आतिवकाहका(१)हंसचक्रवाकमयूरोपकूजिता । तं च मार्गमशीत्यप्सरःसहस्राणि गन्धोदकेन सिञ्चन्ति स्म ॥ अशीत्यप्सरःसहस्राणि मुक्तकुसुमैरभ्यवकिरन्ति स्म दिव्यैर्गन्धवद्भिः । सर्व्वस्य च तालवृक्षस्य पुरतो रत्नव्योमकः संस्थितोऽभूत् । सर्व्वस्मिंश्च रत्नव्योमके अशीत्यप्सरःसहस्राणि चन्दनागरुचूर्णकपुटापरिगृहीतानि कालानुसारिधूपघटिकापरिगृहीतानि स्थितान्यभूवन् । सर्व्वस्मिंश्च रत्नव्योमके पञ्चपञ्चाप्सरःसहस्राणि दिव्यसङ्गीतिसम्प्रवादितस्थितान्यभूवन् ॥

इति हि भिक्षवो बोधिसत्त्वः प्रकम्पमानैः क्षेत्रै रश्मिकोटीनियुतशतसहस्राणि निश्चारयंस्तूर्य्यशतसहस्रैः प्रवाद्यमानैर्महता पुष्पाभ्रेण प्रवर्षता अप्सरस्सहस्रैर्भ्राम्यमाणैर्दुन्दुभिशतसहस्रैः पराहन्यमानैर्गर्ज्जद्भिः प्रगर्ज्जद्भिर्हयगजवृषभैः प्रदक्षिणीकुर्व्वद्भिः शुकशारिकाकोकिलकलविङ्कजीवञ्जीवकहंसक्रौञ्चमयूरचक्रवाकशतसहस्रैरुपनाम्यमानैर्मङ्गल्यशतसहस्रैरनेनैवं रूपेण मार्गव्यूहेन बोधिसत्त्वो बोधिमण्डं गच्छति स्म ॥ यां च रात्रिं बोधिसत्त्वो बोधिमभिसम्बोद्धुकामोऽभूत् । तामेव रात्रिं वशवर्त्ती नाम त्रिसाहस्रमहासाहस्राधिपतिर्ब्रह्मा सहाम्पतिं पार्षद्यमामन्त्र्यैवमाह । यत् खलु मार्ष जानीयाः । एष स बोधिसत्त्वो महासत्त्वो महासन्नाहसन्नद्धो महाप्रतिज्ञानुगतो दृढ-

१ बलाका· इति पाठः ।

सन्नाहसन्नद्धोऽपरिखिन्नमानसः सर्व्वबोधिसत्त्वचर्य्यासु निर्य्यातः सर्व्वपारमितासु पारङ्गतः सर्व्वबोधिसत्त्वभूमिषु वशिताप्राप्तः सर्व्वबोधिसत्त्वाशयसुविशुद्धः सर्व्वसत्त्वेन्द्रियेष्वनुगतः सर्व्वतथागतगुह्यस्थानेषु सुप्रविष्टः सर्व्वमारकर्म्मपथसमतिक्रान्तः सर्व्वकुशलमूलेष्वपरप्रत्ययः सर्व्वतथागतैरधिष्ठितः सर्व्वसत्त्वेषु प्रमोक्षमार्गदेशयिता महासार्थवाहः सर्व्वमारमण्डलविध्वंसनकरः त्रिसाहस्रमहासाहस्रैकशूरः सर्व्वधर्म्मभैषज्यसमुदानीतो महावैद्यराजो विमुक्तिपट्टाबद्धो महाधर्म्मराजो महाप्रज्ञाप्रभोत्सर्जनकरो महाकेतुराजोऽष्टलोकधर्म्मानुपलिप्तो महापद्मभूतः सर्व्वधर्म्मधारण्या सम्मुखितो महासागरभूतोऽनुनयप्रतिघापगतोऽचलोप्रकम्पी महासुमेरुभूतः सुनिर्म्मलः सुपरिशुद्धः सर्व्ववलयितबुद्धिर्महामणिरत्नभूतः सर्व्वधर्म्मवशवर्त्ती सर्व्वकर्म्मण्यचित्तो महाब्रह्मभूतो बोधिसत्त्वो बोधिमण्डमुपसङ्क्रामति मारसैन्यप्रधर्षणार्थमनुत्तरां सम्यक्सम्बोधिमभिसम्बोद्धुकामो दशबलवैशारद्याष्टादशावेणिकबुद्धधर्म्मपरिपूरणार्थं महाधर्म्मचक्रप्रवर्त्तनार्थं महासिंहनादनादनार्थं सर्व्वसत्त्वान् धर्म्मदानेन सन्तर्पणार्थं सर्व्वसत्त्वानां धर्म्मचक्षुर्विशोधनार्थं सर्व्वपरप्रवादीनां सहधर्म्मेण निग्रहार्थं पूर्व्वप्रतिज्ञापरिपूरि (१) सन्दर्शनार्थं सर्व्वधर्म्मैश्वर्य्यवशिताप्राप्त्यर्थम् । तत्र युष्माभिर्मार्षाः सर्व्वैरेव बोधिसत्त्वस्य पूजोपस्थानकर्म्मण्युत्सुकैर्भवितव्यम् ॥ अथ खलु वशवर्त्ती महाब्रह्मा तस्यां वेलायामिमा गाथा अभाषत ॥

---

१ "परिपूरि-" परिपूर्णता- ।

यस्या तेजेन पुण्यतश्च श्रिरिये आशाः पथो ज्ञायते
मैत्री वा करुणा उपेचमुदिताध्यानान्यभिज्ञा तथा ।
सोऽयं कल्पसहस्रचीर्णचरितो बोधिद्रुमं प्रस्थितः
पूजां साधु करोथ तस्य मुनिना आशाप्रते साधनाम् (१) ॥
यं गत्वा शरणं न दुर्गतिभयं प्राप्नोति नैवाक्षणं
देवेष्विष्टसुखञ्च प्राप्य विपुलां ब्रह्मालयं गच्छति ।
षड्वर्षाणि चरित्व दुष्करचरिं यात्येष बोधिद्रुमं
साधू सर्व्वि उदग्रहृष्टमनसः पूजास्य कुर्व्वामहे (२) ॥
राजाऽसौ त्रिसहस्र ईश्वरवरो धर्म्मेश्वरः प्रार्थिवः
शक्रो ब्रह्मपुरे च चन्द्रसूर्य्यौ नास्त्यस्य कश्चित्समः ।
यस्या जाते क्षेत्रकोटिनियुताः सङ्कम्पिता षड्विधा
सैषोऽद्य व्रजते महाद्रुमवरं मारस्य जेतुं चमून् (३) ॥
मूर्द्ध्नि यस्य न शक्यमीक्षितुमिह ब्रह्मालयेऽपि स्थितैः
कायो यस्य वराग्रलक्षणधरो द्वात्रिंशताऽलङ्कृतः ।
वाग्यस्येह मनोज्ञवल्गुमधुरा ब्रह्मस्वरा सुस्वरा
चित्तं यस्य प्रशान्त (४) दोषरहितं गच्छाम तत्पूजने ॥

---

१ "यस्या तेजेन पुण्यतश्च श्रिरिये" यस्य तेजसा पुण्येन श्रिया । "पथो" पन्थाः । "उपेचमुदिताध्यानान्यभिज्ञा" उपेक्षामुदिताध्यानान्यभिज्ञाः । "करोथ" कुरुत । "मुनिना आशाप्रते साधनाम्" मुनीनां आशाप्रतस्य साधिकाम् इत्यर्थः ।

२ "विपुलां" विपुलं । "चरित्व दुष्करचरिं" चरित्वा दुष्करचर्यां । "साधू सर्व्वि" साधु सर्व्वे ।

३ "त्रिसहस्र ईश्वरवरो" त्रिसहस्रेश्वरवरो "यस्या जाते क्षेत्रकोटिनियुताः सङ्कम्पिता षड्विधा" यस्मिञ्जाते क्षेत्रकोटिनियुतानि सङ्कम्पितानि षड्विधानि "चमून्" चमूः ।

४ "प्रशान्त" प्रशान्तं ।

येषां वा मति ब्रह्मशक्रभवने नित्यं सुख चेयितुं
अथवा सर्व्वक्लेशबन्धनलतां छेत्तुं हि तां जालिनीम्।
अश्रुत्वा परतः स्वयम्भेयमम्तं प्रत्येकबोधि शिवां
बुद्धत्वं यदि वेच्छितं त्रिभुवने पूजेत्वसौ नायकम् (१)॥
त्यक्ता येन ससागरा वसुमती रत्नान्यनन्तान्यथो
प्रासादाश्च गवाक्षहर्म्यकलिका युग्यानि यानानि च।
भूम्यालङ्कृत पुष्पदाम रुचिरा उद्यानकूपामला
हस्ता पादशिरोत्तमाङ्गनयना: सो बोधिमण्डोन्मुख: (२)॥

इति हि भिक्षवस्त्रिसाहस्रमहासाहस्रिको महाब्रह्मा इमं त्रिसाहस्रमहासाहस्रं लोकधातुं तत्क्षणं समभ्यतिष्ठत। पाणितलजातमपगतशकठिलमुत्सदमणिमुक्तावज्रवैदूर्य्यशङ्खशिलाप्रवालरजतजातरूप्यनीलमृदुककुण्डकजातप्रदक्षिणनन्द्यावर्त्तकाचिलिन्दिकसुखसंस्पर्शैश्च तृणैरिमं त्रिसाहस्रमहासाहस्रं लोकधातुं सञ्छादितमभ्यतिष्ठत। सर्व्वे च तदा महासमुद्रा धरणीतलसंस्थिता अभूवन्॥ न च जलचराणां सत्त्वानां कश्चिद्विहेठोऽभूत्। इमं चैव लोकधातुमलङ्कृतं दृष्ट्वा च दशसु दिक्षु शक्रब्रह्मलोकपालैर्बोधिसत्त्वस्य पूजाकर्म्मणे बुद्धक्षेत्रशतसहस्राणि

---

१ "मति ब्रह्मशक्रभवने" मतिर्ब्रह्मशक्रभवने। "सुख चेयितुं" सुखं चयितुं। "सर्व्वक्लेशबन्धनलतां" सर्व्वक्लेशबन्धनलतां। "प्रत्येकबोधि शिवां" प्रत्येकबोधेः शिवं। "वेच्छितं" विविदिष्टं। "पूजेत्वसौ" पूजयतु इमं।

२ "भूम्यालङ्कृत पुष्पदामरुचिरा" भूम्यलङ्कृता पुष्पदामानि रुचिराणि। "उद्यानकूपामला" उद्यानकूपा अमला। "पादशिरोत्तमाङ्गनयनाः" पादशिरउत्तमाङ्गनयनानि। "सो बोधिमण्डोन्मुखः" स बोधिमण्डोन्मुखः।

समलङ्कृतान्यभूवन्॥ बोधिसत्त्वैश्च दिव्यमानुष्यकातिक्रान्तैः पूजा-व्यूहैर्दशसु दिक्ष्वप्रमेयाणि बुद्धक्षेत्राणि प्रतिमण्डितान्यभूवन् बोधिसत्त्वस्य पूजाकर्म्मणे। सर्व्वाणि च तानि बुद्धक्षेत्राण्येकस्मि-न्नेव सन्दृश्यन्ते नानाव्यूहालङ्कारालङ्कृतानि च। न च भूयो लोकान्तरिका न च कालपर्व्वता न चक्रवाडमहाचक्रवाडाः प्रज्ञायन्ते स्म। सर्व्वाणि च तानि बुद्धक्षेत्राणि बोधिसत्त्वस्या-भया स्फुटानि सन्दृश्यन्ते स्म॥

षोडश च बोधिमण्डपरिपालका देवपुत्राः। तद्यथा उत्खली च नाम देवपुत्रमुत्खली च नाम प्रजापतिश्च शूरबलश्च केयूरबलश्च सुप्रतिष्ठितश्च महीधरश्च अवभासकरश्च विमलश्च धर्म्मेश्वरश्च धर्म्मकेतुश्च सिद्धपात्रश्चाप्रतिहतनेत्रश्च महाव्यूहश्च शीलविशुद्धनेत्रश्च पद्मप्रभश्च। इतीमे षोडश बोधिमण्डप्र-तिपालदेवपुत्राः सर्व्वेऽवैवर्त्त्यचान्तिप्रतिलब्धास्ते बोधिसत्त्वस्य पूजार्थं बोधिमण्डं मण्डयन्ति स्म समन्तादशीतियोजनानि सप्तरत्नवेदिकाभिः परिवृतं सप्तभिस्तालपङ्क्तिभिः सप्तभी रत्न-किङ्किणीजालैः सप्तरत्नसूत्रैः परिवृतं सप्तरत्नप्रत्युप्तैश्च जाम्बू-नदसुवर्णपटैः सुवर्णसूत्रैर्जाम्बूनदसुवर्णपद्मैश्चावकीर्णं सारवर-गन्धनिर्धूपितं रत्नजालसञ्छन्नम्। ये च दशसु दिक्षु नाना-लोकधातुषु विविधा वृक्षाः सन्त्यभिजाता दिव्यमानुष्यका-स्तेऽपि सर्व्वे तत्र बोधिमण्डे सन्दृश्यन्ते स्म। याश्च दशसु दिक्षु नानाप्रकारा जलजस्थलजपुष्पजातयस्ता अपि सर्व्वास्तत्र बोधि-मण्डे सन्दृश्यन्ते स्म। येऽपि च दशसु दिक्षु नानालोकधातुषु

बोधिसत्त्वा बोधिमण्डालङ्कुर्व्वन्त्य(१)प्रमाणपुण्यज्ञानसम्भारव्यूहैस्तेऽपि तत्र बोधिमण्डे सन्दृश्यन्ते स्म ॥

इति हि भिक्षवो बोधिमण्डपरिपालकैर्देवपुत्रैस्तादृशा व्यूहा बोधिमण्डाभिनिर्म्मिता (२) अभूवन् । यान् दृष्ट्वा देवनागयक्षगन्धर्व्वासुराः स्वभवनानि श्मशानसञ्ज्ञामुत्पादयामासुः । तांश्च व्यूहान् दृष्ट्वाऽत्यर्थं चित्रीकारमुत्पादयामासुः । उदानञ्चोदानयामासुः साध्वहोऽचिन्त्यः पुण्यविपाकनिष्यन्द इति ॥ चत्वारश्च बोधिवृक्षदेवताः । तद्यथा वेणुश्च वल्गुश्च सुमनश्च ओजोपतिश्च एते चत्वारो बोधिवृक्षदेवता बोधिसत्त्वस्य पूजार्थं बोधिवृक्षमाययन्ति (३) स्म मूलसम्पन्नं स्कन्धसम्पन्नं शाखापत्रपुष्पफलसम्पन्नमारोहपरिणाहसम्पन्नं प्रासादिकं दर्शनीयमशीतिस्तालमुच्चैस्तेन तदनुरूपेण परिणाहेन चित्रं दर्शनीयं मनोरमं सप्तभी रत्नवेदिकाभिः परिवृतं सप्तभी रत्नतालपङ्क्तिभिः सप्तभी रत्नकिङ्किणीजालैः सप्तभी रत्नसूत्रैः समनुपरिवृतं पारिजातककोविदारप्रकाशमतृप्तचक्षुर्दर्शनम् ॥ स च पृथिवीप्रदेशस्त्रिसाहस्रमहासाहस्रलोकधातुवंशेणाभिरूढः सारो(४)ऽभेद्यवज्रमयः संस्थितोऽभूत् । यत्र बोधिसत्त्वो निषण्णोऽभूद् बोधिमभिसम्बोद्धुकामः ॥

इति हि भिक्षवो बोधिसत्त्वेन बोधिमण्डमुपसङ्क्रमता तथा-

१ "बोधिमण्डालङ्कुर्वन्त्य-" बोधिमण्डमलङ्कुर्वन्त्य- ।
२ "बोधिमण्डाभिनिर्मिता" बोधिमण्डमभितोऽभिनिर्मिता इत्युचितम् ।
३ "माययन्ति" मायान्ति ।
४ "वंशेणाभिरूढः सारो" वज्रादपि दृढसारो ।

रूपा कायात्प्रभा मुक्ताऽभूद् यया प्रभया सर्व्वेऽपायाः स्फुटा अभूवन्। सर्व्वाण्यक्षराणि पिथिनितान्यभूवन् (१)। सर्व्वदुर्गतिवेदनाश्चापश्रोषिता अभूवन्। ये च सत्त्वा विकलेन्द्रिया अभूवन् ते सर्व्वे परिपूर्णेन्द्रियाण्यनुप्राप्नुवन्। व्याधिताश्च व्याधिभ्यो व्यामुच्यन्त। भयार्द्दिताश्चाश्वासप्राप्ता अभूवन्। बन्धनबद्धाश्च बन्धनेभ्यो व्यामुच्यन्त। दरिद्रसत्त्वाश्च भोगवन्तोऽभूवन्। क्लेशसन्तप्ताश्च सत्त्वा निष्परिदाहका अभूवन्। बुभुक्षिताश्च सत्त्वाः पूर्णोदरा अभूवन्। पिपासिताश्च तृषापगता अभूवन्। गुर्व्विण्यश्च सुखेन प्रसूयन्ते स्म। जीर्णदुर्व्वलाश्च बलसम्पन्ना अभूवन्। न च कस्य चित् सत्त्वस्य तस्मिन् समये रोगो बाधते द्वेषो वा मोहो वा क्रोधो वा लोभो वा खिलं वा व्यापादो वा ईर्ष्या वा मात्सर्य्यं वा। न कश्चित्सत्त्वस्तस्मिन् समये म्रियते स्म न च्यवते स्म नोपपद्यते स्म। सर्व्वसत्त्वाश्च तस्मिन् समये मैत्रचित्ता हितचित्ताः परस्परं मातापितृसञ्ज्ञिनोऽभूवन् ॥ तत्रेदमुच्यते।

यावन्तावीचिपर्य्यन्तं नरका घोरदर्शनाः।
दुःखं प्रशान्तं सत्त्वानां क्षिप्रं विहन्ति वेदनाम् (२) ॥
तिर्य्यग्योनिषु यावन्तः सत्त्वा अन्योन्यघातकाः।
मैत्रचित्ता हितचित्ता जाताः स्पृष्टा भाभिर्महामुनेः ॥
प्रेतलोकेषु यावन्तः प्रेताः क्षुत्तर्षपीडिताः।
प्राप्नुवन्त्यन्नपानानि बोधिसत्त्वस्य तेजसा ॥

---

१ "पिथिनितान्यभूवन्" प्रथितान्यभूवन्।
२ क्षिप्रं विहन्ति वेदनामित्यस्य क्षिप्रं विहता वेदना समभवदित्यर्थः।

अप्सरा पिथिताः सर्व्वे (१) दुर्गतिस्रोपशोषिता ।
सुखिताः सर्व्वसत्त्वाश्च दिव्यसौख्यसमर्पिताः ॥
चक्षुःश्रोत्रविहीनाश्च ये चान्ये विकलेन्द्रियाः ।
सर्व्वेन्द्रियैः सुसम्पूर्णा जाताः सर्व्वाङ्गशोभनाः ॥
रागद्वेषादिभिः क्लेशैः सत्त्वा बाधन्त ये सदा (२) ।
शान्तक्लेशास्तदा सर्व्वे जाताः सुखसमर्पिताः ॥
उन्मत्ताः स्मृतिमन्तश्च दरिद्रा धनिनस्तथा ।
व्याधिता रोगनिर्म्मुक्ता मुक्ता बन्धनबद्धकाः ॥
न खिलं न च मात्सर्य्यं व्यापादो न च विग्रहः (३) ।
अन्योन्यं सम्प्रकुर्व्वन्ति मैत्रचित्ताः स्थितास्तदा ॥
मातुः पितुस्तैकपुत्रे हि यथा प्रेम प्रवर्त्तते ।
तथान्योन्येन (४) सत्त्वानां पुत्रप्रेम तदाऽभवत् ॥
बोधिसत्त्वप्रभाजालैः स्फुटाः क्षेत्रा ह्यचिन्तियाः ।
गङ्गावालुकसङ्ख्याताः समन्ताद्दै दिशो दश (५) ॥
न भूयश्चक्रवालाश्च दृश्यन्ते कालपर्व्वताः ।
सर्व्वे ते विपुला क्षेत्रा दृश्यन्त्येकं यथा तथा (६) ॥
पाणितलप्रकाशाश्च दृश्यन्ते सर्व्वरत्निकाः ।

---

१ "अप्सरा पिथिताः सर्वे" अप्सराधि प्रथितानि सर्वाणि ।

२ "बाधन्त ये सदा" बाध्यन्ते ये सदा इत्यर्थः ।

३ "व्यापादो न च विग्रहः" व्यापादं न च विग्रहमित्यर्थः ।

४ "तथान्योन्येन" तथान्योन्यं ।

५ "स्फुटाः क्षेत्रा ह्यचिन्तियाः गङ्गावालुकसङ्ख्याताः" स्फुटानि क्षेत्राणि ह्यचिन्तितानि गङ्गावालुकासङ्ख्यातानि इत्यर्थः ।

६ "सर्वे ते विपुला क्षेत्राः" सर्वाणि तानि विपुलानि क्षेत्राणि । उत्तरत्रापि विशेषणे नपुंसकत्वं योज्यम् यथा "सर्वरत्निकाः" सर्वरत्नकानि ।

बोधिसत्त्वस्य पूजार्थं सर्व्वक्षेत्रा अलङ्कृताः (१) ॥
देवाश्च येऽत्र तथा बोधिमण्डोपचारकाः ।
अलञ्चक्रुर्बोधिमण्डमशीतियोजनायतम् ॥
ये च केचिन्महाव्यूहाः क्षेत्रकोटीष्वनन्तकाः ।
ते च सर्व्वंच दृश्यन्ते बोधिसत्त्वस्य तेजसा ॥
देवा नागास्तथा यक्षाःकिन्नराश्च महोरगाः ।
स्वानि स्वानि विमानानि श्मशानानीव मेनिरे ॥
तान्व्यूहान् समिरीक्ष्येह विस्मिताः सुरमानुषाः ।
साधुः पुण्यस्य निस्यन्दः सम्पद्यस्येयमीदृशी ॥
करोति वै ततो योगं कायवाङ्मनसा तथा ।
सर्व्वार्थास्तस्य सिद्ध्यन्ति येऽभिप्रेता मनोरमाः ॥
अभिप्राया यथान्येषां पूरितास्तरता पुरा ।
विपाकः कर्म्मणस्तस्य सम्पज्जातेयमीदृशी ॥
अलङ्कृतो बोधिमण्डस्तुर्भिर्बोधिदेवतैः (२) ।
पारिजातो दिवि यथा तस्मादपि विशिष्यते ॥
गुणाः शक्या न ते वाचा सर्व्वे सम्परिकीर्त्तितुम् ।
ये व्यूहा बोधिमण्डस्य देवतैरभिसंस्कृताः (३) ॥

इति हि भिक्षवस्तया बोधिसत्त्वस्य कायप्रमुक्तया प्रभया कालिकस्य नागराजस्य भवनमवभासितमभूद् विशुद्धया विम-

१ "सर्व्वक्षेत्रा अलङ्कृताः" सर्व्वक्षेत्राणि अलङ्कृतानि ।
२ "बोधिदेवतैः" बोधिदेवताभिरिति साधुः ।
३ "देवतैरभि" देवताभिरभि ।

तया कायचित्तप्रह्लादोद्विल्यजनन्या (१) सर्व्वक्लेशापकर्षिण्या स-र्व्वसत्त्वसुखप्रीतिप्रसादप्रामोद्यजनन्या। दृष्ट्वा च पुनः कालिको नागराजस्तस्यां वेलायां स्वपरिवारस्य पुरतः स्थित्वेमा गाथा अभाषत।

क्रकुच्छन्दे यथा आभ दृष्ट रुचिरा दृष्टा च कनकाह्वयं
यद्वत् काश्यपधर्म्मराजमुनि दृष्टाः प्रभा निर्म्मलाः।
निःसंशयं वरलक्षणो हितकरो उत्पन्नज्ञानप्रभो
येनेदं भवनं विरोचति हि मे स्वर्णप्रभालङ्कृतम् (२) ॥
नास्मिंश्चन्द्ररविप्रभा सुविपुला सन्दृश्यते वेश्मनि
नो चाग्नेर्न मणेर्न विद्युदमला नो च प्रभा ज्योतिषाम्।
नो वा शक्रप्रभा न ब्रह्माण प्रभा (३) नो च प्रभा आसुरी
एकान्तं तमसाकुलं मम गृहं प्रादुष्कृतैः कर्म्मभिः॥
अद्येदं भवनं विराजति शुभं मध्येरविं दीप्तिमत्
चित्ते प्रीति जनेति कायु सुखितो गात्रोऽङ्कुता शीतलाः।
तप्ताबालुकया शरीर निपती जातो स मे शीतलं
सुव्यक्तं बहुकल्पकोटिचरितो बोधिद्रुमं गच्छति (४)॥

---

१ "प्रह्लादोद्विल्यजनन्या" प्रह्लादोत्सुकजनन्या इत्थं सम्भाव्यते।

२ "आभ दृष्ट" आभा दृष्टा। "कनकाह्वयं" कनकाह्वये इत्युचितम्। "काश्यप धर्म्मराजमुनि" काश्यपधर्मराजमुनौ "विरोचति" विरोचितं।

३ "ब्रह्माण प्रभा" ब्रह्मणः प्रभा।

४ "मध्येरविं" मध्येरवि। "प्रीति जनेति" प्रीतिं जनयति। "कायु सुखितो गा-त्रोऽङ्कुता शीतलाः" कायः सुखितः गात्रमङ्कुतं शीतलं। "तप्ताबालुकया शरीर-निपती जातो स मे" तप्तबालुकायां शरीरं निपतितं यद्वत् शीतोपायेन शीतलं भवति तद्वत् जातम्मे शरीरमित्यर्थः।

क्षौमं गृह्णत नागपुष्प रुचिरां वस्त्रां सुगन्धां शुभां
मुक्ताहारपिनद्धतांश्च वलयांश्चूर्णानि धूपोत्तमान्।
सङ्गीतिं प्रकुरुध्व वाद्य विविधां भेरीमृदङ्गैः शुभै-
र्हन्तं गच्छथ पूजना हितकरं पूजार्ह सर्व्वे जगे (१)॥
सोऽभ्युत्थाय च नागकन्यसहितश्चतुरो दिशः प्रेक्षते
अद्राक्षीदथ मेरुपर्व्वतनिभं ज्वालकृतं तेजसा।
देवैर्दानवकोटिभिः परिवृतं ब्रह्मेन्द्रयक्षैस्तथा
पूजां तस्य करोति हृष्टमनसः दर्शेन्ति मार्गं शुभम् (२)॥
संहृष्टः स हि नागराज सुमुदितश्चाभ्यर्च्य लोकोत्तमं
वन्दित्वा चरणौ च गौरवकृतस्तस्थौ मुनेरग्रतः।
नागाकन्य उदग्र हृष्टमनसः कुर्वन्ति पूजां मुनेः
पुष्पं गन्धविलेपनांश्च क्षिपिषुस्तूर्याणि निर्नादयन् (३)॥
कृत्वा चाञ्जलि नागराट् सुमुदितः तुष्टाव तथ्यैर्गुणैः
साधु दर्शतु पूर्णचन्द्रवदने लोकोत्तमे नायके।
यथा मे दृष्टं निमित्तं पूर्वऋषीणां पश्याम तानेव मे

---

१ “नागपुष्प रुचिरां” नागपुष्पाणि रुचिराणि। “वस्त्रां सुगन्धां शुभां” वस्त्राणि सुगन्धाम् शुभाम्। “मुक्ताहारपिनद्धतांश्च” मुक्ताहारपिनद्धांश्च। “प्रकुरुध्व वाद्य विविधां” प्रकुरुध्वं वाद्यानि विविधानि। “हन्तं गच्छथ पूजना” हन्त गच्छत पूजनार्थं। “पूजार्ह सर्वे जगे” पूजार्हं सर्वस्मिन् जगति।

२ “नागकन्यसहित-” नागकन्यासहित-। “प्रेक्षते” प्रेक्षते स्म। “ज्वालकृतं” ज्वल-कृतं। “करोति” कुर्वन्ति। “दर्शेन्ति” दर्शयन्ति।

३ “नागराज सुमुदित” नागराजः सुमुदितः। नागराजो मुदित इति पाठे न छन्दोभङ्गः। “नागकन्य उदग्रहृष्टमनसः” नागकन्या उदग्रहृष्टमनसः। “गन्ध-विलेपनांश्च क्षिपिषु” गन्धं विलेपनानि च क्षिपन्ति- “निर्नादयन्” निर्नादयन्त्यः।

अद्य त्वं विनिहत्य मारं बलवानिष्टं पदं लप्स्यसे (१) ॥

यस्यार्थे दमदानसंयमपुरे सर्वास्तित्यागी अभूद्
यस्यार्थे दमशीलमैत्रकरुणाक्षान्तिबलं भावितम्।
यस्यार्थे दृढवीर्य ध्याननिरतः प्रज्ञाप्रदीपः कृतः
सैषा ते परिपूर्ण सर्व प्रणिधि अद्यो जिनो भेष्यसे (२) ॥

यद्वृक्ष सपत्रपुष्प सफला बोधिद्रुमं सन्नता
यद्वत् कुम्भसहस्र पूर्णसलिला कुर्वन्ति प्रादक्षिणम्।
यद्वाप्सरगणाश्च सम्प्रमुदिताः स्निग्धस्तं कुर्वते
हंसाः क्रौञ्चगणा यथा च गगणे गच्छन्ति लीलान्विताः ॥
कुर्वन्ते सुखिना प्रदक्षिण ऋषिं भावि त्वमद्यार्हवान् (३) ॥

यथा वा काञ्चनवर्ण आभ रुचिरा क्षेमाश्रतां गच्छते
शान्ताश्चापि यथा अपाय निखिला दुःखैर्विमुक्ताः प्रजाः।
यद्वदुत्थित चन्द्रसूर्यभवना वायू मृदुर्वायते
अद्या भेष्यसि सार्थवाह त्रिभवे जातीजरामोचको (४) ॥

---

१ "चाञ्जलि" चाञ्जलिं। "दृश्यंतु" दृश्यन्ते। "पूर्वश्रपीत्वं" पूर्वर्षीणां। "पश्यामि" पश्यामि। मे इत्यत्र मतिरिति अध्याहार्यं तेन इष्टं पदं लप्स्यसे इति मे मतिरित्यर्थः।

२ "परिपूर्ण सर्व प्रणिधि अद्यो जिनो भेष्यसे" परिपूर्णा सर्वा प्रणिधिरद्य जिनो भविष्यसि।

३ "यद्वृक्ष सपत्रपुष्प" यद्वृक्षाः सपत्रपुष्पाः। "कुम्भसहस्र पूर्णसलिला" कुम्भसहस्राणि पूर्णसलिलानि। "प्रादक्षिणम्" प्रदक्षिणम्। "यद्वाप्सरगणाश्च" यद्वाप्सरोगणाश्च। "कुर्वन्ते" कुर्वन्ति। "सुखिना" सुखेन। "प्रदक्षिण ऋषिं" प्रदक्षिणमृषिं। "भावि त्वमद्यार्हवान्" भावी त्वमद्यार्हवान्।

४ "काञ्चनवर्ण आभ रुचिरा क्षेमाश्रतां गच्छते" काञ्चनवर्णा आभा रुचिरा क्षेमश्रतं गच्छति। "अपाय निखिला" अपाया निखिला। "यद्वदुत्थित चन्द्रसूर्यभवना वायू मृदुर्वायते" यद्वदुत्थितानि चन्द्रसूर्यभवनानि वायुर्मृदुर्वाति। "अद्या भेष्यसि सार्थवाह त्रिभवे" अद्य भविष्यसि सार्थवाहस्त्रिभवे। "जातीजरामोचको" जातिजरामोचकः।

यद्वत्कामरती विहाय च सुरास्त्वत्पूजनेऽभ्यागता
ब्रह्मा ब्रह्मपुरोहिताश्च अमरा उत्सृज्य ध्यानं सुखम्।
ये केचित्त्रिभवे तथैव च पुरे सर्वे इहाभ्यागता
अद्यो भेष्यसि वैद्यराज त्रिभवे जातीजरामोचको (१) ॥
मार्गश्चापि यथा विशोधितु सुरैर्येनाद्य त्वं गच्छसे
एतेनागतु क्रकुच्छन्द भगवान् कनकाह्वयः काश्यपः।
यथ वा पद्म विशुद्ध निर्मल शुभा भित्वा महीमुद्गता
यस्मिन् विक्षिपसे क्रमानतिबलाद् भावि त्वमर्घार्हवान् (२)॥
माराः कोटिसहस्रनेकनियुतं गङ्गा यथा वालिका-
स्ते तुभ्यं न समर्थ बोधिविटपाच्चालेतु कम्पेतु वा।
यज्ञा नैकविधाः सहस्रनियुताः गङ्गा यथा वालिका
यष्टास्ते चरता हिताय जगतस्तेनेक विभ्राजसे (३) ॥
नक्षत्राः सशशी सतारकरवी भूमौ पते अम्बरात्
स्वस्थानाच्च चलेन्महागिरिवरः शुष्येद्द्यो सागरः।

---

१ "ध्यानं सुखं" ध्यानसुखमित्यर्थः। "अद्यो भेष्यसि वैद्यराज त्रिभवे" अद्य भविष्यसि वैद्यराजस्त्रिभवे। "जातीजरामोचको" जातिजरामोचकः।

२ "विशोधितु सुरै-" विशोधितः सुरै-। "गच्छसे" गच्छसि। "एतेनागतु" एतेनागतः। "क्रकुच्छन्द भगवान्" क्रकुच्छन्दो भगवान्। "यथ वा पद्म विशुद्ध निर्मल" यथा वा पद्मा विशुद्धा निर्मलाः। "विक्षिपसे" विक्षिपसि। "भावि त्वमर्घार्हवान्" भावी त्वमर्घार्हवान्।

३ "कोटिसहस्रनेकनियुतं" कोटिसहस्रानेकनियुतं। "गङ्गा यथा वालिका" गाङ्गा यथा वालुका। "तुभ्यं न समर्थ बोधिविटपाच्चालेतु कम्पेतु" त्वां न समर्था बोधिविटपाच्चालयितुं कम्पयितुं। "गङ्गा यथा वालिका" गाङ्गा यथा वालुका। "जगतस्तेनेक विभ्राजसे" जगतस्तेनैको विभ्राजसे। अथ तेनेह विभ्राजसे इत्यपि पाठः।

चतुरो धातवः कश्चिद्दिशपुरुषो दर्शय एकैकशो
नैव त्वं द्रुमराजमूलुपगतो अप्राप्य बोध्युत्थिहेत् (१) ॥
लाभा मह्य सुलब्ध वृद्धि विपुला दृष्टोऽसि यत् सारथे
पूजा चैव कृता गुणाश्च कथिता बोधाय चोत्साहिताः ।
सर्वा नागवधूरहं च ससुता मुच्येमितो योनित-
स्त्वं यासी यथ मत्तवारणगते गच्छाम एवं वयम् (२) ॥

इति हि भिक्षवः कालिकस्य नागराजस्याग्रमहिषी सुवर्णप्रभासा नाम सम्बहुलाभिर्नागकन्याभिःपरिवृता पुरस्कृता नानारत्नच्छत्रपरिगृहीताभिर्नानाद्रव्यपरिगृहीताभिर्नानामुक्ताहारपरिगृहीताभिर्नानारत्नपरिगृहीताभिर्दिव्यमानुष्यकमाल्यविलेपनगुणपरिगृहीताभिर्नानातूर्यसङ्गीतिसम्प्रवादितैर्नानारत्नपुष्पवर्षैर्बोधिसत्त्वं गच्छन्तमभ्यवकिरन्तिस्माभिश्च गाथाभिस्तुष्टुवुः (३) ।

अभ्रान्ता अचला अभीररम्भी
अलीना अदीना प्रहृष्टा दुधर्षा ।
अरक्ता अदुष्टा अमूढा अलुब्धा
विरक्ता विमुक्ता नमस्ते महर्षे (४) ॥

---

१ "नक्षत्राः सग्रहो सतारकरवो" नक्षत्राणि सग्रहाणि सतारकरवीणि । "पतेच्चवरात्" पतेदम्बरात् । "धातवः" धातून् । "दर्शय एकैकशो" दर्शयेदेकैकशो । "द्रुमराजमूलुपगतो-" द्रुमराजमूलमुपगत- । "बोध्युत्थिहेत्" बोधिमुत्तिष्ठेत् ।

२ "मह्य सुलब्ध वृद्धि विपुला" मया सुलब्धा वृद्धिर्विपुला । "नागवधूरहं" नागवध्वोऽहं । "मुच्येमितो" मुच्ये इतो । "यासी यथ" यासि यथा ।

३ अभ्यवकिरन्ति तुष्टुवुः इत्यत्र वचनमनुचितम् ।

४ "अभीररम्भी" अभीरा अदम्भिन् अभ्रान्ता इत्यादौ सर्व्वत्र अभ्रान्त इतिवत् सम्बोधनैकवचनान्तं बोध्यम् ।

भिषक्का विश्रुत्वा विनेयादिमैषो
सुवैद्या जगत्ता दुःखेभ्यः प्रमोचो ।
अखेना अनाथा अदीना त्रिदिता
भवाखे गुणाथा त्रिलोकेऽस्मि जात: (१) ॥

प्रसन्ना प्रहृष्टा ययुर्देवसङ्घा:
प्रवर्षी नभस्था महत्पुष्पवर्षम् ।
महाचैलक्षेपं करोन्ति यथेमे
जिनो भेष्यसे व्याकुरुष्व प्रहर्षम् (२) ॥

उपेहि द्रुमेन्द्रं निषीद अच्छम्भी
जिता मारसेना पुनः क्लेशजालम् ।
विबुध्य प्रशान्तां वरामग्रबोधिं
यथा पौर्विकैस्तद्विबुद्धा जिनेन्द्रैः (३) ॥

त्वया यस्य अर्थे बहुकल्पकोट्यः
कृता दुष्कराणि जगन्मोचनार्थम् ।
प्रपूर्णा ति आशा अयं प्राप्तु कालो

---

१ "भिषक्का" भिषक् "विश्रुत्वा विनेयादिमैषी" विश्रुतश्च विनीतादिमीन। "जगत्ता" जगतः। "प्रमोचो" प्रमोचिन्। "अखेना अनाथा अदीना" अक्लीनमनाथमदीनं। "भवाखे गुणाथा त्रिलोकेस्मि" भवाखणमनुथातुं त्रिलोकेऽस्मिन्।

२ प्रवर्षी नभस्था" प्रवर्षं नभस्स्थात्। "महत्पुष्पवर्षं" महापुष्पवर्षं। "करोन्ति" कुर्वन्ति। "भेष्यसे व्याकुरुष्व" भविष्यसि व्याकुरु।

३ "अच्छम्भी" अदम्भी अनाथर्यंमाम् वा। "पौर्विकैस्तद्विबुद्धा" पौर्विकैः वा वि- बुद्धा। यस्मिन् ग्रन्थे सर्वत्र बोधिशब्दस्य स्त्रीलिङ्गत्वं समर्थितम्।

उपेहि द्रुमेन्द्रं स्पृश स्वायम्बोधिम् (१)॥

अथ खलु भिक्षवो बोधिसत्त्वस्यैतदभवत् कुत्र निषण्णैस्तैः पौर्विकैस्तथागतैरनुत्तरा सम्यक्सम्बोधिरभिसम्बुद्धा इति॥ ततोऽस्यैतदभूत्। तृणसंस्तरनिषण्णैरिति॥

अथ खलु अन्तरीक्षगतानि शुद्धावासकायिकदेवपुत्रशत-सहस्राणि बोधिसत्त्वस्य चेतोभिरेव चेतःपरिवितर्कमाज्ञायैवं चाभाषन्त। एवमेतत् सत्पुरुषैवमेतत्। तृणसंस्तरे सत्पुरुष निषद्य तैः पौर्विकैस्तथागतैरनुत्तरा सम्यक्सम्बोधिरभिसम्बुद्धा॥

अद्राक्षीत् खल्वपि भिक्षवो बोधिसत्त्वो मार्गस्य दक्षिणे पार्श्वे स्वस्तिकं यावसिकम्। तृणानि लुनाति स्म नीलानि मृदुकानि सुकुमाराणि रमणीयानि कुण्डलकजातानि प्रदक्षिणावर्त्तानि मयूरग्रीवसन्निभानि काचिलिन्दिकसुखसंस्पर्शानि सुगन्धानि वर्णवन्ति मनोरमाणि॥ दृष्ट्वा च पुनर्बोधिसत्त्वो मार्गादपक्रम्य येन स्वस्तिको यावसिकस्तेनोपसङ्क्रामदुपसङ्क्रम्य स्वस्तिकं मधुरया वाचा समालपति स्म। याऽसौ वागाज्ञापनी विज्ञापनी विस्पष्टा अनेकलोकैकवर्णसुखा वल्गुश्रवणीया स्निग्धा स्मार-णीया चोदनी तोषप्रेमणी अकर्कशा अगद्गदा अपरुषा अचपला श्लक्ष्णा मधुरा कर्णसुखा कायचित्तोद्बिल्यकरणी (२) रागद्वेष-मोहकलिकलुषविनोदनी कलविङ्करुतस्वरा कुणालजीवञ्जीव-

---

१ "बहुकल्पकोट्यः" बहुकल्पकोटिपर्य्यन्तमित्यर्थः। "हृता" हृतानि। "प्रपूर्णा नि" प्रपूर्णा ते। "प्राप्तु कालो उपेहि" प्राप्तः काल उपेहि।

२ "कायचित्तोद्बिल्यकरणी" काय-चित्तौत्सुक्यकरणी इत्यनुमीयते।

काभिनदितघोषा दुन्दुभिसङ्गीतिरुतरवितनिर्घोषवती अनुपहता सत्त्वश्रद्धाभूता (१) ब्रह्मस्वररुतरवितनिर्घोषा समुद्रस्वरवेगनिभा शैलसङ्घट्टनवती देवेन्द्रासुरेन्द्राभिष्टुता गम्भीरा दुरवगाहा नमुचिबलाबलकरणी परप्रवादमथनी सिंहस्वरवेगा हयगजगर्ज्जितघोषा नादनिर्नादनी मेघस्तनिताभिगर्ज्जितस्वरा दशदिक्सर्व्वबुद्धक्षेत्रस्फुरणी विनेयसत्त्वसञ्चोदनी अनुपद्रुता अनुपहता अविलम्बितासहिता (२) युक्ता कालवादिनी समयानतिक्रमणी धर्म्मशतसहस्रसुग्रथिता सौम्या अशक्ता अधिष्ठितप्रतिभाना (३) एकरुता सर्व्वरुतरमणी सर्व्वाभिप्रायज्ञापनी सर्व्वसुखसञ्जननी मोक्षपथसन्दर्शिता (४) मार्गसम्भारचोदनी पर्षदनतिक्रमणी सर्व्वबुद्धभाषिता अनुकूला ॥ ईदृश्या वाचा बोधिसत्त्वः स्वस्तिकं गाथाभिरध्यभाषत ।

शृणु देहि मि स्वस्तिक शीघ्रं अद्य ममार्थं तृणैः ।
सुमहान्त सबलं नमुचिं निहनित्वा बोधिमनूत्तर प्राप्तिं स्पृशिष्ये(५)।
यस्य कृते मयि कल्पसहस्रा दानु दमोपि च संयमत्यागा ।
शीलव्रतश्च तपश्च सुचीर्णा तस्य निष्पद्दि भेष्यति अद्य (६) ॥

---

१ "सत्त्व श्रद्धाभूता" सत्त्वाश्रद्धाभूता ।

२ अविलम्बिता अनुपहता सहिता इति वा पाठः ।

३ अधिष्ठितप्रणिधाना इति वा पाठः ।

४ "मोक्षपथसन्दर्शिता" मोक्षपथसन्दर्शयित्री इति साधुः पाठः ।

५ "देहि मि" देहि मह्यं । "शीघ्रं अद्य" शीघ्रमद्य । "ममार्थं तृणैः" ममार्थं तृणैः । "निहनित्वा" निहत्य । "बोधिमनुत्तर प्राप्तिं" बोधिमनुत्तरां प्राप्तिं । "स्पृशिष्ये" स्प्रक्ष्यामि ।

६ "मयि" मया । "कल्पसहस्रा" कल्पसहस्रपर्य्यन्तमित्यर्थः । "दानु" दानं । "संयमत्यागा" संयमत्यागौ । "सुचीर्णा" सुचीर्णं । "निष्पद्दि भेष्यति" निष्पत्तिर्भविष्यति ।

क्षान्तिबलन्तथ वीर्यबलञ्च ध्यानबलं तथ प्रज्ञबलञ्च ।
पुण्यअभिज्ञविमोक्षबलञ्च तस्य मि निष्पदि भेष्यति अद्य (१) ॥
प्रज्ञाबलञ्च उपायाबलञ्च ऋद्धिसमङ्गतमैत्रबलञ्च ।
प्रतिसंविदसत्वबलं च तस्य निष्पदि भेष्यति अद्य (२) ॥
पुण्यबलञ्च तवापि अनन्तं यन्मम दास्यसि अद्य तृणानि ।
नष्टवरं तव एतु निमित्तं त्वमपि अनन्तरु भेष्यसि शास्ता (३) ॥

श्रुत्वा स्वस्तिकु वाच नायके सुरुचिर मधुरां
तुष्टो आत्तमनाश्च हर्षितः प्रमुदितमनसः ।
गृह्णीत्वा तृणमुष्टि स्पर्शनवती मृदुतरुणशुभां
पुरतः स्थित्व वाच भाषते प्रमुदितहृदयः (४) ॥
यदि तावत् तृण केचि लभ्यते पदवरममृतं
बोधिमुत्तम प्राप्त दुर्दृशा पुरिमजिनपथस्थिहता ।
तावन्महागुणोदधे अपरिमितयशा
अहमेव प्रथमे बुध्यमि पदवरममृतम् (५) ॥

---

१ "क्षान्तिबलन्तथ" क्षान्तिबलन्तथा । "तथ प्रज्ञबलञ्च" तथा प्रज्ञाबलञ्च । "पुण्यअभिज्ञविमोक्षबलञ्च तस्य मि निष्पदि भेष्यति" पुण्याभिज्ञाविमोक्षबलञ्च तस्य मे निष्पत्तिर्भविष्यति ।

२ "तस्य निष्पदि भेष्यति" तस्य निष्पत्तिर्भविष्यति ।

३ "एतु निमित्तं" एतन्निमित्तं । "अनन्तरु भेष्यसि" अनन्तरूपा भविष्यसि ।

४ "स्वस्तिकु वाच नायके सुरुचिर" स्वस्तिको वाचं नायकस्य सुरुचिरां । "तुष्टो आत्तमना-" तुष्ट आत्तमना- । "प्रमुदितमनसः" प्रमुदितमानसः । "गृह्णीत्वा तृणमुष्टि स्पर्शनवती" गृहीत्वा तृणमुष्टिं स्पर्शवतीं । "स्थित्व वाच भाषते" स्थित्वा वाचं भाषते ।

५ "तृण केचि लभ्यते" तृणेन कश्चिल्लभ्यते । 'बोधिमुत्तम प्राप्त' बोधिरुत्तमा प्राप्ता । "दुर्दृशा पुरिमजिनपथस्थिहता" दुर्दृशा पुरातनजिनपथि तिष्ठता । "अपरिमितयशा" अपरिमितयशः । "प्रथम बुध्यमि" प्रथमं बुध्यामि भोत्स्यामि इत्यर्थः ।

बोधिसत्त्व आह।

एषा स्वस्तिक बोधि लभ्यते तृणवरग्रहणे-
श्चरित्वा बहुकल्पदुष्करी व्रततप विविधां।
प्रज्ञापुण्यउपायउद्गतो यद भवि मतिमां-
स्तत्पश्चाज्जिन व्याकरोति मुनयो भविष्यसि विरजः (१)॥
यदि बोधि इयं शक्यु स्वस्तिका परजनि ददितु
पिण्डीकृत्य च देय पाणिना म भवतु विमतिः।
यद बोधि मय प्राप्त जानसे विभजामि अमृतं
आगत्या शृणु धर्मयुक्तं सम्भविष्यसि विरजः (२)॥

गृह्णीत्वा तृणमुष्टि नायकः परमसुमृदुकां
सिंहहंसगतिश्च प्रस्थितः प्रचलित धरणी।
देवनागगणे कृताञ्जली प्रमुदितमनस
अद्यो मारबलं निहत्य यं स्पृशिष्यति अमृतम् (३)॥

इति हि भिक्षवो बोधिसत्त्वस्य बोधिवृक्षमूलमुपसंक्रामतो-ऽष्टौ तिबोधिवृक्षसहस्राणि देवपुत्रैश्च बोधिसत्त्वैश्च मण्डितान्य-

---

१ "बोधि लभ्यते" बोधिर्लभ्यते। "बहुकल्पदुष्करी व्रततप विविधां" बहुकल्पे दुष्कराणि व्रततपांसि विविधानि।"प्रज्ञापुण्यउपायउद्गतो यद भवि" प्रज्ञापुण्योपायोद्गतो यदा भवति।"तत्पश्चाज्जिन व्याकरोति मुनयो भविष्यसि विरजः" तत्पश्चाज्जिनं व्याकरोति मुनिर्भविष्यति विरजाः।

२ "बोधि इयं शक्यु स्वस्तिका परजनि ददितु" बोधिरियं शक्यते स्वस्तिक परजनाय दातुं।"देय पाणिना म भवतु" देहि पाणिना मा भवतु।"यद बोधि मय प्राप्त जानसे" यदि बोधिर्मया प्राप्ता जानासि।"आगत्या" आगत्य।"विरजः" विरजस्का।

३ "गृह्णीत्वा तृणमुष्टि" गृहीत्वा तृणमुष्टिं। "सिंहहंसगतिश्च" सिंहहंसगतिश्च। "प्रचलित" प्रचलिता। "देवनागगणे कृताञ्जली" देवनागगणाः कृताञ्जलयः। "अद्यो" अद्य। "यं स्पृशिष्यति" अयं स्प्रक्ष्यति।

भूवन्। इह निषद्य बोधिसत्त्वो बोधिं प्राप्स्यत्यभिसम्भोत्स्यत इति॥ सन्ति तत्र केचिद्बोधिवृक्षाः पुष्पमयाः पञ्चयोजनशतसहस्राण्युच्चैस्त्वेन। केचिद्बोधिवृक्षा गन्धमया योजनशतसहस्राण्युच्चैस्त्वेन। केचिद्बोधिवृक्षाश्चन्दनमया योजनशतसहस्रोद्विद्धाः। केचिद्बोधिवृक्षा वस्त्रमयाः पञ्चयोजनशतसहस्राण्युच्चैस्त्वेन। केचिद्बोधिवृक्षा रत्नमया दशयोजनशतसहस्राण्युच्चैस्त्वेन। केचिद्बोधिवृक्षा रत्नमया दशयोजनकोटिनियुतशतसहस्राण्युच्चैस्त्वेन। केचिद्बोधिवृक्षा रत्नमया कोटीनियुतशतसहस्रसमुद्विद्धाः। सर्वेषु तेषु बोधिवृक्षमूलेषु यथानुरूपाणि सिंहासनानि प्रज्ञप्तान्यभूवन् नानादिव्यपुष्पसंस्तृतानि। कचिद्बोधिवृक्षे पद्मासनं प्रज्ञप्तमभूत्। कचिद्गन्धासनं कचिन्नानाविधरत्नासनम्॥ बोधिसत्त्वश्च ललितव्यूहं नाम समाधिं समापद्यते स्म॥ समनन्तरसमापन्नस्य च बोधिसत्त्वस्येदं ललितव्यूहं नाम बोधिसमाधिम्(१)। अथ तत्क्षणमेव बोधिसत्त्वाः सर्वेषु तेषु बोधिवृक्षमूलेषु सिंहासनेषु संनिषण्णाः सन्दृश्यन्ते स्म लक्षणानुव्यञ्जनसमलङ्कृतेन कायेन। एकैकश्च बोधिसत्त्वो देवपुत्रैश्चैवं सञ्जानीते स्म। ममैव सिंहासने बोधिसत्त्वो निषण्णो नान्येषामिति॥ यथा च ते सञ्जानते स्म तथास्यैव ललितव्यूहस्य बोधिसत्त्वसमाधेरनुभावेन सर्व्वनिरयतिर्य्यग्योनियमलौकिकाः सर्व्वे देवा मनुष्याश्च सर्व्वगत्युपपन्नाः सर्व्वसत्त्वा बोधिसत्त्वं पश्यन्ति स्म बोधिवृक्षमूले सिंहासने निषण्णम्। अथ च पुनर्हीनाधिमुक्ति-

१ बोधिवृक्षसमाधिमिति वा पाठः।

कानां सत्त्वानां मतिपरितोषणार्थं बोधिसत्त्वस्तृणमुष्टिमादाय येन बोधिवृक्षस्तेनोपसङ्क्रामदुपसङ्क्रम्य बोधिवृक्षं सप्तकृत्वः प्रदक्षिणीकृत्य स्वयमेवाभ्यन्तराग्रं बहिर्मूलं समन्तभद्रं तृणसंस्तरं संस्तीर्य्य सिंहवच्छूरवद्बलवद्दृढवद्वीर्य्यवत्स्थामवन्नागवदैश्वर्य्यवत्स्वयम्भूवज्ज्ञानिवदनुत्तरवद्विशेषवदभ्युद्गतवद्यशोवत्कीर्त्तिवद्दानवच्छीलवत्क्षान्तिवद्वीर्य्यवद्ध्यानवत्प्रज्ञावज्ज्ञानवत्पुण्यवन्निहतमारप्रत्यर्थिकवत्सम्भारवत्पर्य्यङ्कमाभुज्य तस्मिंस्तृणसंस्तरे न्यषीदत् प्राङ्मुख ऋजुकायं प्रणिधाय । अभिमुखां स्मृतिमुपस्थाप्य ईदृशञ्च दृढसमादानमकरोत् ।

इहासने शुष्यतु मे शरीरं
त्वगस्थिमांसं प्रलयञ्च यातु ।
अप्राप्य बोधिं बहुकल्पदुर्लभां
नैवासनात् कायमतश्चलिष्यते इति ॥

इति श्रीललितविस्तरे बोधिमण्डगमनपरिवर्त्तो नाम एकोनविंशतमः ॥ १९ ॥

विंशाध्यायप्रारम्भः ।

इति हि भिक्षवो बोधिसत्त्वस्य बोधिमण्डनिषण्णस्य पूर्वस्यां दिशि षट्कामावचरा देवाः स्थिता अभूवन् । मा बोधिसत्त्वस्य कश्चिदन्तरायं कार्षीदित्येवं दक्षिणपश्चिमोत्तरा दिशो देवैः परिगृहीता अभूवन् ॥ इति हि भिक्षवो बोधिसत्त्वो बोधिमण्डनिषण्णस्तस्यां वेलायां बोधिसत्त्वसञ्चोदनीं नाम रश्मिं प्रामुञ्चत् ॥ यया

स्पृष्ट्वा (१) समन्ताद्दशसु दिक्ष्वप्रमेयाण्यसङ्ख्येयानि धर्म्मधातुपरमा-
न्याकाशधातुपर्य्यवसानानि सर्व्वबुद्धक्षेत्राण्यवभासितान्यभूवन् ॥

अथ खलु पूर्व्वस्यां दिशि विमलायां लोकधातौ विमलप्रभासस्य तथागतस्य बुद्धक्षेत्राल्ललितव्यूहो नाम बोधिसत्त्वस्तया प्रभया सञ्चोदितः सन् गणनासमतिक्रान्तैर्बोधिसत्त्वैः परिवृतः पुरस्कृतो येन बोधिमण्डस्तेनोपसङ्क्रामदुपसङ्क्रम्य च तस्यां वेलायां बोधिसत्त्वस्य पूजाकर्म्मणे तथारूपमृद्ध्यभिसंस्कारमभिसंस्करोद्येनार्द्ध्यभिसंस्कारेणाभिसंस्कृतेन दशसु दिक्ष्वाकाशधातुपर्य्यवसानानि सर्व्वबुद्धक्षेत्राणि एकं मण्डलमात्रमादर्शयति। शुद्धस्य नीलवैडूर्य्यस्य पञ्चगत्युपपन्नानां सर्व्वसत्त्वानां पुरतो बोधिमण्डनिषण्णं बोधिसत्त्वमुपदर्शयति स्म ॥ ते च सत्त्वाः परस्परमेकाङ्गुलिभिर्बोधिसत्त्वमुपदर्शयन्ति स्म । कोऽयमेवंरूपः सत्त्वलक्षितः कोऽयमेवंरूपसत्त्वो विराजत इति॥ तेषाञ्च सत्त्वानां पुरतो बोधिसत्त्वानां बोधिसत्त्वं निर्म्मिमीते स्म ॥ तत्र ते बोधिसत्त्वविग्रहा इमां गाथामभाषन्त ॥

यस्य क्लिष्ट न रागदोषकलुषा वासना उद्धृता
यस्या कायप्रभा कृता दशदिशे सर्व्वे प्रभा निःप्रभाः ।
यस्या पुण्यसमाधिज्ञानविचयः कल्पौघसंवर्द्धितः
सोयं शाक्यमुनिर्महामुनिवरः सर्व्वा दिशो भ्राजते (२) ॥

अथ खलु भिक्षवो दक्षिणस्या दिशो रत्नव्यूहाया लोकधातो

---

१ षच लोलमनुचितम् ।

२ "उद्धृता" उद्धृणा। "यस्या कायप्रभा" यस्य कायप्रभया। "दशदिशे सर्व्वे" दशदिशि सर्व्वाः "यस्या" यस्य। "सर्व्वा दिशो" सर्व्वासु दिक्षु।

रत्नार्चिषस्तथागतस्य बुद्धक्षेत्राद् रत्नछत्रकूटसन्दर्शनो नाम बोधिसत्त्वो महासत्त्वस्तया प्रभया सञ्चोदितः सन् गणनासमतिक्रान्तैर्बोधिसत्त्वैः परिवृतः पुरस्कृतो येन बोधिमण्डो येन च बोधिसत्त्वस्तेनोपसङ्क्रामदुपसङ्क्रम्य बोधिसत्त्वस्य पूजाकर्म्मणे एकरत्नच्छत्रेण तं सर्व्वावन्तं मण्डलमात्रं सञ्छादयति स्म ॥ तत्र शक्रब्रह्मलोकपालाः परस्परमेतदवोचन्। कस्येदं फलं केनायमेवंरूपो रत्नछत्रव्यूहः सन्दृश्यते ॥ अथ तस्माद्रत्नछत्रादियं गाथा निश्चरति स्म।

येन कल्पसहस्रकोटिनयुता गन्धान रत्नान च
दत्ता अप्रतिमेषु मैत्रमनसा तिष्ठन्ति के निर्वृते।
सो एषो वरलक्षणो हितकरो नारायणस्थामवान्
बोधेर्मूलमुपागतो गुणधरस्तस्यैष पूजा कृता (१) ॥

अथ खलु पश्चिमाया दिशश्चम्पकवर्णाया लोकधातोः पुष्पावलिवनराजिकुसुमिताभिज्ञस्य तथागतस्य बुद्धक्षेत्रादिन्द्रजाली नाम बोधिसत्त्वो महासत्त्वस्तया प्रभया सञ्चोदितः सन् गणनासमतिक्रान्तैर्बोधिसत्त्वैः परिवृतः पुरस्कृतो येन बोधिमण्डो येन च बोधिसत्त्वस्तेनोपजगाम। उपेत्य च बोधिसत्त्वस्य पूजाकर्म्मणे सर्वावन्तं मण्डलमात्रमेकरत्नजालेन सञ्छादयति स्म॥ तत्र दशसु दिक्षु देवनागयक्षगन्धर्वाः परस्परमेवमाहुः। कस्यायमेवंरूपो प्रभाव्यूहः॥ अथ तस्माद्रत्नजालादियं गाथा निश्चरति स्म।

---

१ "कल्पकोटिनयुता" कल्पकोटिनियुतानि। "गन्धान रत्नान" गन्धा रत्नानि। "निर्वृते" निर्वृतौ। "सो एषो" स एष। "गणधरस्तस्यैष" गुणधरस्तस्यैषा।

रत्नाकरो रत्नकेतुरतिस्त्रिलोके
रत्नोत्तमो रत्नकीर्त्ति रतः सुधर्म्मे ।
रत्नानि चीणि न च छेत्स्यति वीर्य्यप्राप्तः
सो बोधि प्राप्स्यति करोमि तस्य पूजा (१) ॥

अथ खलु उत्तरस्या दिशः सूर्य्यावर्त्ताया लोकधातोश्चन्द्र-सूर्य्यजिह्मीकरप्रभस्य तथागतस्य बुद्धक्षेत्राद्व्यूहराजो नाम बोधिसत्त्वो महासत्त्वस्तया प्रभया सञ्चोदितः सन् गणनासमतिक्रान्तैर्बोधिसत्त्वैः परिवृतः पुरस्कृतो येन बोधिमण्डो येन च बोधिसत्त्वस्तेनोपसङ्क्रामदुपसङ्क्रम्य बोधिसत्त्वस्य पूजाकर्म्मणे यावन्तो दशसु दिक्षु सर्व्वलोकधातुषु बुद्धक्षेत्रगुणव्यूहास्तान् सर्व्वांस्तस्मिन्मण्डलमात्रे सन्दर्शयति स्म ॥ तत्र केचिद्बोधिसत्त्वा एवमाहुः । कस्य एवंरूपा व्यूहाः ॥ अथ तेभ्यः सर्व्वव्यूहेभ्य इयं गाथा निश्चरति स्म ॥

कायो येन विशोधितः सुबहुशः पुण्येन ज्ञानेन च
येन वाच विशोधिता व्रततपैः सत्येन धर्म्मेण च ।
चित्तं येन विशोधितं ह्रिरिधृतीकरुणायमैत्र्या तथा
सो एष द्रुमराजमूलोपगतः शाक्यप्रभुः पूज्यते (२) ॥

अथ खलु पूर्व्वदक्षिणस्या दिशो गुणाकराया लोकधातो-र्गुणराजप्रभासस्य तथागतस्य बुद्धक्षेत्राद्गुणमतिर्नाम बोधिसत्त्वो महासत्त्वस्तया प्रभया सञ्चोदितः सन् गणनासमतिक्रान्तैर्बोधि-

१ "रत्नकीर्त्ति रतः" रत्नकीर्त्तौ रतः । "सो बोधि" स बोधिं । "पूजा" पूजाम् ।
२ "वाच" वाक् । "व्रततपैः" व्रततपोभिः । "ह्रिरीधृतीकरुणायमैत्र्या" ह्रीधृतीकारुण्यमैत्र्या । "सो एष द्रुमराजमलोपगतः" स एष द्रुमराजमूलमुपगतः ।

सत्त्वैः परिवृतः पुरस्कृतो येन बोधिमण्डो येन च बोधिसत्त्वस्तेनोपसङ्क्रामदुपसङ्क्रम्य बोधिसत्त्वस्य पूजाकर्म्मणे सर्व्वगुणव्यूहं कूटागारं तस्मिन् मण्डलमात्रेऽभिनिर्म्मिमीते स्म। ततस्तु कूटागारादियं गाथा निश्चरति स्म।

यस्य गुणैः सततं गुणगन्धिका
भान्ति सुरासुरयक्षमहोरगाः।
सो गुणवान् गुणराजकुलोदितो
बोधिविटप उपविष्टु गुणोदधिः (१)॥

अथ खलु दक्षिणपश्चिमाया दिशो रत्नसम्भवाया लोकधातो रत्नयष्टेस्तथागतस्य बुद्धक्षेत्राद्रत्नसम्भवो नाम बोधिसत्त्वो महासत्त्वस्तया प्रभया सञ्चोदितः सन् गणनासमतिक्रान्तैर्बोधिसत्त्वैः परिवृतः पुरस्कृतो येन बोधिमण्डो येन च बोधिसत्त्वस्तेनोपसङ्क्रामदुपसङ्क्रम्य बोधिसत्त्वस्य पूजाकर्म्मणे अप्रमेयासङ्ख्येयान् रत्नव्योमकांस्तस्मिन्मण्डलमात्रेऽभिनिर्म्मिमीते स्म॥ तेभ्यश्च रत्नव्योमकेभ्य इदं गाथा निश्चचार।

त्यक्ता येन ससागरा वसुमती रत्नान्यथानेकशः
प्रासादाश्च गवाक्षहर्म्मिकवरा युग्यान्ययानानि च।
व्योमालङ्कृत पुष्पदाम रुचिरा उद्यानकूपाः सभा
हस्तापादशिरोत्तमाङ्गनयनाः सो बोधिमण्डे स्थितः (२)॥

---

१ "गुणगन्धिका" इत्यत्र गुणवर्विका इति वा पाठः। "सो गुणवान्" स गुणवान्। "उपविष्टु गुणोदधिः" उपविष्टो गुणोदधिः।

२ "गवाक्षहर्म्मिकवरा" गवाक्षहर्म्यकवरा। "व्योमालङ्कृत पुष्पदाम रुचिरा" व्योमालङ्कृतानि पुष्पदामानि रुचिराणि। "हस्तापादशिरोत्तमाङ्गनयनाः सो" हस्तपादशिरउत्तमाङ्गनयनानि स।

अथ खलु पश्चिमोत्तरस्या दिशो मेघवत्या लोकधातोर्मेघराजस्य तथागतस्य बुद्धक्षेत्रान् मेघकूटाभिगर्जितेश्वरो नाम बोधिसत्त्वो महासत्त्वस्तया प्रभया सञ्चोदितः सन् गणनासमतिक्रान्तैर्बोधिसत्त्वैः परिवृतः पुरस्कृतो येन बोधिमण्डो येन च बोधिसत्त्वस्तेनोपसङ्क्रामदुपसङ्क्रम्य बोधिसत्त्वस्य पूजाकर्म्मणे कालानुसार्य्यगुरुमेघमभिनिर्म्मायोरगसारचन्दनचूर्णं वर्षन्ति स्म॥ तस्माच्च कालानुसारिमेघमण्डलमाच्चादियं गाथा निश्चरति स्म।

धर्म्मामेघ स्फुरित्व सर्वत्रिभवे विद्याधिमुक्तिप्रभः
सद्धर्म्मस्य विराग वर्षि अमृतं निर्वाणसम्प्रापकम्।
सर्वा रागक्लिशेशबन्धनलतां सो वासना च्छेत्स्यति
ध्यानर्द्धिबलइन्द्रियैः कुसुमितः श्रद्धाकरं दास्यते (१)॥

अथ खलूत्तरपूर्व्वस्या दिशो हेमजालप्रतिच्छन्नाया लोकधातो रत्नच्छत्राभ्युद्गतावभासस्य तथागतस्य बुद्धक्षेत्राद्धेमजालालङ्कृतो नाम बोधिसत्त्वो महासत्त्वस्तया प्रभया सञ्चोदितः सन् गणनासमतिक्रान्तैर्बोधिसत्त्वैः परिवृतः पुरस्कृतो येन बोधिमण्डो येन च बोधिसत्त्वस्तेनोपसङ्क्रामदुपसङ्क्रम्य बोधिसत्त्वस्य पूजाकर्म्मणे सर्व्वेषु तेषु कूटागारेषु रत्नव्योमकेषु द्वात्रिंशल्लक्षणसमलङ्कृतान् बोधिसत्त्वविग्रहानभिनिर्म्मिमीते स्म॥ सर्व्वे च ते बोधिसत्त्वविग्रहा दिव्यमानुष्यकपुष्पदामपरिगृहीता

---

१ "धर्म्मामेघ स्फुरित्व" धर्ममेघं स्फुरयित्वा। "विराग वर्षि" विरागं वर्षित्वा। "सर्वा रागक्लिशेशबन्धनलतां" सर्वां रागक्लेशबन्धनलतां। "सो वासना" स वासनां। "ध्यानर्द्धिबलइन्द्रियैः कुसुमितः" ध्यानर्द्धिबलेन्द्रियैः कुसुमितं श्रद्धाकरमिति सर्वत्र पाठः परन्त्वत्र श्रद्धाफलमिति पाठे रूपकसङ्गतिः।

येन बोधिसत्त्वस्तेनाभिनतकायास्तानि पुष्पदामान्यभिप्रासम्-
यन्ति स्म॥ इमां गाथामभाषन्त।

येन बुद्धनयुता स्तवित गौरवेण महता जनिय श्रद्धान्।
ब्रह्मघोषवचनं मधुरवाणिं बोधिमण्डोपगतं शिरसि वन्दे (१)॥

अथ खल्वधस्ताद्दिशः समन्तविलोकितायां लोकधातोः
समन्तदर्शिनस्तथागतस्य बुद्धक्षेत्राद्रत्नगर्भो नाम बोधिसत्त्वो
महासत्त्वस्तया प्रभया सञ्चोदितः सन् गणनासमतिक्रान्तैर्बो-
धिसत्त्वैः परिवृतः पुरस्कृतो येन बोधिमण्डो येन च बोधि-
सत्त्वस्तेनोपसङ्क्रामदुपसङ्क्रम्य बोधिसत्त्वस्य पूजाकर्मणे तस्मिन्
वैदूर्यमयमण्डलमात्रे जाम्बूनदसुवर्णपद्मान्यभ्युद्गतान्युपदर्शयति
स्म॥ तेषाञ्च पद्मानां कर्णिकास्वर्द्धकायिका नार्यो वर्णरूपसम्पन्ना
सर्वालङ्कारप्रतिमण्डिता उपदर्शयति स्म॥ वामदक्षिणपाणि-
भिर्हर्षकटककेयूरसुवर्णसूत्रमुक्ताहारादिविविधाभरणानि प-
रिगृहीताः पुष्पपट्टदामानि चाभिप्रासम्यन्त्यो येन बोधिमण्डो
येन बोधिसत्त्वस्तेनोपर्यभिनतकायास्ताश्चेमां गाथाम् भाषन्त।

यो आगमिष्ट सदा गुरूणां बुद्धश्रावकप्रत्येकजिनानाम्।
निर्माणसुशील: सदोज्ज्वलप्रष्टो तस्य आगमया गुणधरस्य(२)॥

अथ खलूपरिष्टाद्दिशो वरगणाया लोकधातोर्गणेन्द्रस्य
तथागतस्य बुद्धक्षेत्राद्गगनगञ्जो नाम बोधिसत्त्वो महासत्त्वस्तया

१ "बुद्धनियुतास्तुवित" बुद्धनियुतानि स्तुतानि। "जनिय महान्" जनयित्वा महान्।
"शिरसि" शिरसा।

२ "यो आगमिष्ट" य आगमत्। "सदोज्ज्वल प्रष्टो" सदोज्ज्वलः पुष्टो प्रष्टा वा।
"आगमया" आगमत। अथ वा षष्ठी वा कर्मणि षष्ठी बोध्या।

प्रभया सञ्चोदितः सन् गणनासमतिक्रान्तैर्बोधिसत्त्वैः परिवृतः पुरस्कृतो येन बोधिमण्डो येन च बोधिसत्त्वस्तेनोपसङ्क्रामदुपसङ्क्रम्य बोधिसत्त्वस्य पूजाकर्म्मणे गगणतलस्थ एव यावन्तो दशसु दिक्षु सर्व्वबुद्धक्षेत्रेष्वदृष्टाश्रुतपूर्व्वाः सन्ति पुष्पधूपगन्धमाल्यविलेपनचूर्णचीवरवस्त्रालङ्कारच्छत्रध्वजपताकावैजयन्तीरत्नमणिकनकरजतमुक्ताहारहयगजरथपङ्क्तिवाहनपुष्पवृक्षफल(१)दारकदारिकादेवनागयक्षगन्धर्व्वासुरगरुडकिन्नरमहोरगशक्रब्रह्मलोकपालमानुषाः सर्व्वे गगणतलादभ्यन्तं पुष्पवर्षमभिप्रवर्षयन्ति स्म। सर्व्वसत्त्वप्रीतिसञ्जननञ्च न कस्यचित्सत्त्वस्य भयञ्चोत्पीडां वा करोति (२) स्म ॥ तत्रेदमुच्यते।

प्रेयात्समेव दिशताश्च जिनौरसा ये
सम्पूजितं हितकरं अनुप्राप्तबोधिम्।
तेषां वियूहक्रमविक्रमसुक्रमाणा-
मौपम्यमात्र निर्दिशेय जिनौरसानाम् (३) ॥
के चागता नभसि मेघ इव स्तनन्तो
हाराः सहस्रनियुतानि प्रलम्बयन्तः।
के चागता मुकुटरत्नविलम्बचूडाः
पौर्ण्यं विमान गगणे उपदर्शयन्तः (४) ॥

---

१ "पुष्पवृक्षफल" सर्वत्र एतादृशः पाठः। किन्तु पुष्पवृक्षफलानि एतादृशपाठे समन्वयो भवति।

२ "करोति" कुर्वन्ति इति उचितम्।

३ "प्रेयात्समेव" प्रियमन्नमेते प्रेयांसमेते वा। "हितकरं अनुप्राप्त" हितकरमनुप्राप्त। "वियूहक्रम" व्यूहक्रम। "औपम्यमात्र निर्दिशेय" औपम्यमात्रं निर्दिशेत।

४ "हाराः" हारान्। "मुकुटरत्नविलम्बचूडाः" मुकुटरत्नविलम्बिचूडाः। "पौर्ण्यं विमान" पौर्ण्यं विमानं।

के आगता धरणिसिंह इवानदन्त.
शून्या निमित्तप्रणिधीरवमुच्चमानाः।
के आगता यथ वृषा अभिनर्दमाना
न च दृष्टपूर्व्व रुचिराणि क्षिपन्ति पुष्पां (१) ॥
के आगता नभसि सार इवा रवन्ते
वर्णसहस्रि स्वकि मात्मनि दर्शयन्तः।
के आगता शशिरिवा गगणे सुपूर्णाः
सुगतात्मजस्य गुणमालमुदीरयन्तः (२) ॥
के आगता रविरिव प्रभ मुञ्चमानाः
सर्व्वाणि मारभवनानि करोन्ति जिह्मां।
के आगता विमलकेतु यथेन्द्रयष्टः
सम्भारपुण्यनिचितास्तथि बोधिमण्डे (३) ॥
केचित्क्षिपन्ति गगणान्मणिरत्नजालां
चन्द्राः सुचन्द्रस्तथ बाल विरोचमानाम्।
मान्दारवां सुमन वार्षिकचम्पकमाल्यदामां
सम्बोधिसत्त्व द्रुमराज स्थिते क्षिपन्ति (४) ॥

---

१ "प्रणिधीरव" प्रणिधीनिव। "यथ" यथा। "दृष्टपर्व" दृष्टपूर्वाणि। "पुष्पां" पुष्पाणि।

२ "सार इवा" सारस इव। "वर्णसहस्रि स्वकि मात्मनि-" वर्णसहस्रं स्वके आत्मनि "शशिरिवा" शशीव। "गुणमालमुदीरयन्तः" गुणमालामुदीरयन्तः।

३ "प्रभ" प्रभां। "करोन्ति जिह्मां" कुर्वन्ति जिह्मानि। "विमलकेतु यथेन्द्रयष्टः" विमलकेतुर्यथेन्द्रयष्टिः। "तथि बोधिमण्डे" तथ बोधिमण्डे।

४ "मणिरत्नजाला" मणिरत्नजालानि। "चन्द्राः सुचन्द्रस्तथ बाल" यथा चन्द्रो विरोचते सुचन्द्रो बालचन्द्रश्च तथा विरोचमानानि मणिरत्नजालानीत्यर्थः। "मान्दरवां सुमन वार्षिकचम्पकमाल्यदामां" मान्दाराणि सुमनांसि वार्षिकचम्पकमाल्यदामानि। "सम्बोधिसत्त्व द्रुमराज" सम्बोधिसत्त्वे द्रुमराजे।

के चागता धरणि कम्पयमान पद्भ्यां
सङ्कम्पिता च वसुधा प्रीतिकरी जनस्या।
के चागता ग्रहिय मेरु करेतलेभिः
उत्सृष्टपुष्पपुट संस्थित अन्तरिक्षे (१)॥
के चागताश्चतुर सागर गृह्य मूर्ध्ना
उत्सृष्ट सिञ्चि वसुधा वरगन्धतोयैः।
के चागता रतनयष्टि ग्रहील चित्रां
सम्बोधिसत्त्वमुपदर्शय स्थित दूरे (२)॥
के चागता भविय ब्रह्म प्रशान्तरूपाः
शान्ताः प्रशान्तमनसः स्थित ध्यानध्यायी।
रोमेभ्यस्तेष स्वर निश्चरते मनोज्ञा
मैत्रीउपेक्षकरुणामुदिताप्रमाणाः (३)॥
के चागता मरुतशक्र दृवा तथैव
देवैः सहस्रनयुतैश्च पुरस्कृतास्ते।
उपगम्य बोधिविटप प्रगृह्य कृताञ्जलीभिः

---

१ "धरणि कम्पयमान" धरणिं कम्पयमानाः। "जनस्या" जनस्य। "ग्रहिय मेरु करेतलेभिः" गृहीत्वा मेरुं करतलैः। "उत्सृष्टपुष्पपुट संस्थित" उत्सृष्टपुष्पपुटाः संस्थिताः।

२ "चतुर सागर गृह्य" चतुरः सागरान् गृहीत्वा। "उत्सृष्ट सिञ्चि" उत्सृज्य सिञ्चिता। रतनयष्टि ग्रहीत" रत्नयष्टिं गृहीत्वा। "मुपदर्शय स्थित" मुपदर्शयन्ति स्थिता।

३ "भविय" भूत्वा। "स्थित ध्यानध्यायी" स्थिता ध्यानध्यायिनः। "रोमेभ्यस्तेष स्वर निश्चरते मनोज्ञा" रोमेभ्यस्तेषां स्वरा निश्चरन्ति मनोज्ञा। "मैत्रीउपेक्षकरुणा मुदिताप्रमाणाः" मैत्र्युपेक्षाकरुणामुदिताप्रमाणाः।

शाखोऽभिलम्बमणिरत्न क्षिपन्ति चित्राम् (१)

के चागताश्चतुर्दिशा च यथैव पाला

गन्धर्वराक्षस परिवृत: किन्नरेभि: ।

विद्युत्स्फुटान्त कुसुमानि प्रवर्षमाणा

गन्धर्वकिन्नररुतेन स्तुवन्ति वीरम् (२) ॥

के चागता: कुसुमितां प्रगृहीत्व वृक्षान्

सफलां सुपुष्पवरगन्धप्रमुञ्चमानान् ।

जातेषु तेषु स्थित बुद्ध ऋजुकाया

अवलम्बमान प्रतिमण्डित क्षिपन्ति पुष्पाम् (३) ॥

के चागता: कुसुमिता: पद्मिनीर्गृहीत्वा

पद्मोत्पलै: कुसुमितैस्तथ पुण्डरीकै: ।

द्वात्रिंशलक्षणधरा: स्थितु पद्मगर्भे

स्वविष्ट अश्लिष्टमनसं विदु बोधिसत्त्वम् (४) ॥

---

१ "नवतमम इवा" नवच्छत्रमिव। "सपवनयुतैव पुराकृतास्ते" सपवनियुतैव पुरस्कृतास्ते। "बोधिविटप" बोधिविटपं। "कृताञ्जलीभि:" कृताञ्जलिभि:। "शाखोऽभिलम्बमणिरत्न क्षिपन्ति चित्रां" शाखोऽभिलम्बमणिरत्नानि क्षिपन्ति चित्राणि।

२ "चतुर्दिशा च" चतुर्दिशाश्च। "गन्धर्वराक्षस परिवृत: किन्नरेभि: "गन्धर्वराक्षसै: परिवृता: किन्नरै:। "विद्युत्स्फुटान्त" विद्युत्स्फुटान्तानि।

३ "कुसुमितां प्रगृहीत्व" कुसुमितान्प्रगृह्य। "सफलां सुपुष्पवरगन्धप्रमुञ्चमानां" सफलान् सुपुष्पवरगन्धप्रमुञ्चमानान्। "जातेषु" ये एतेषु। "स्थित बुद्ध" स्थिता बुद्धा:। "अवलम्बमान प्रतिमण्डित" अवलम्बमाना: प्रतिमण्डिता:।'पुष्पाम्' पुष्पाणि।

४ "पद्मिनीर्गृहीत्वा" पुष्करिणीर्गृहीत्वा। अथ पुष्करिणीर्गृहीत्वेति वा पाठ:। "तथ" तथा। "द्वात्रिंशलक्षणधरा: स्थितु" द्वात्रिंशल्लक्षणधरं स्थितं। "स्वविष्ट अश्लिष्ट-" स्वाविपुराश्लिष्ट-। "विदु बोधिसत्त्वम्" विदुर्बोधिसत्त्वम्। विदित्वा बोधिसत्त्वमित्यर्थो वा।

के आगता विपुलकाय तथैव मेरु
स्थित्वान्तरीक्ष स्वकमात्मनमुत्सृजन्ति ।
उत्सृज्यमाश्च भविया नवपुष्पदामाः
सञ्छादयन्ति त्रिसहस्रि जिनस्य क्षेत्रम् (१) ॥
के आगता उभय चतुर्थि कल्प दाहं
सन्दर्शयन्ति विभवं तथ सम्भवञ्च ।
तेषां शरीरि बहुधर्ममुखा रणन्ति
तां श्रुत्व सत्त्वनियुताः प्रजहन्ति तृष्णाम् (२) ॥
के आगता रचितकिन्नरतुल्यघोषा
विम्बोष्ठ चारुवदना परिपूर्णवक्त्रा ।
कन्या यथैक अलङ्कृत चित्रहारा
प्रेक्षन्त यां सुरगणा न लभन्ति तृप्तिम् (३) ॥
के आगता वजिरिकाय इवा अभेद्या
हेष्टा प्रस्कन्धचरणैः प्रतिपाद्यमानाः ।
के आगता रविरिवा शशिपूर्णवक्त्रा
ज्योत्स्नाकराः प्रभकरा हतक्लेशदोषाः (४) ॥

---

१ "विपुलकाय" विपुलकायाः । "स्थित्वान्तरीक्ष स्वकमात्मनमुत्सृजन्ति" स्थित्वान्तरीक्षे स्वकमात्मानमुत्सृजन्ति । "उत्सृज्यमाश्च भविया नवपुष्पदामाः" उत्सर्जनमानेन भूत्वा नवपुष्पदामानि । "त्रिसहस्रि" त्रिसाहस्रं ।

२ "कल्प" परिकल्प्य । "दाहं" गुप्तपदार्थदर्शकमज्ञानविशेषमिति सम्भाव्यते । "तथ" तथा । "शरीरि" शरीरे । "तां श्रुत्व" ताञ्छ्रुत्वा । "सत्त्वनियुताः" सत्त्वनियुतानि । "प्रजहन्ति" प्रजहति ।

३ "विम्बोष्ठ" विम्बोष्ठा । "यथैक अलङ्कृत" यथैका अलङ्कृता । "प्रेक्षन्त यां" प्रेक्षन्तो यां ।

४ "वजिरिकाय इवा" वज्रकाय इव । "हेष्टा" हृष्टाः । "रविरिवा" रविरिव । "प्रभकरा" प्रभाकरा ।

के चागता रतनमण्डित रत्नपाणी
वज्राद्धयिल वज्रक्षेत्रसहस्रकोट्यः।
वर्षन्ति रत्नवर पुष्प सुगन्ध गन्धां
सन्तोषणार्थं बहुसत्त्वहितं सुखार्थम् (१)॥
के चागता मरुति धारणि रत्नकोशा
रेमेति सूत्रनियुतानि प्रभाषमाणाः।
प्रतिभानवन्त मतिवन्त सुबुद्धिवन्तो
मत्तप्रमत्तजनतां प्रतिबोधयन्तः (२)॥
के चागता प्रहिय भेरि यथैव मेरु
राकोट्यमानु गगणे चरणी सुमनोज्ञघोषाम्।
यस्या चैवं दशदिशो व्रजि क्षेत्रकोट्या
अद्यावबोद्धुममृतं अनुबुद्धि प्राप्तेरिति (३)॥
दशदिग्देवाः सर्वे यथागतास्तथा च स्वालये ययुः। (४)

इति ललितविस्तरे बोधिमण्डव्यूहपरिवर्तो नाम विंशतितमः॥ २०॥

---

१ "रतनमण्डित रत्नपाणी" रत्नमण्डिता रत्नपाणयः। "वज्राद्धयिल वज्रक्षेत्रसहस्रकोट्यः" वज्राच्च वज्रक्षेत्रसहस्रकोटीम्। "रत्नवर पुष्प सुगन्ध गन्धां" रत्नवराणि पुष्पाणि सुगन्धीनि गन्धान्। "सन्तोषणार्थं" सन्तोषणार्थं। "बहुसत्त्वहितं" बहुसत्त्वहिताय।

२ "मरुति धारणि रत्नकोशाः" मरुतीं धारणीं रत्नकोशान्। "प्रतिभानवन्त मतिवन्त सुबुद्धिवन्तो" प्रतिभानवन्तो मतिमन्तः सुबुद्धिमन्तो।

३ "प्रहिय भेरि" प्रहीणा भेरीं। "राकोट्यमानु" पताकोट्यमानां। "चरणी" चारिणीं। "यस्याचैवं" यस्याश्चैवं। चच मध्ये इत्यध्याहार्यम्। "दशदिशो व्रजि क्षेत्रकोट्या" दशदिशि व्रजत् क्षेत्रकोटिपर्यन्तम्। "अमृतं अनुबुद्धि प्राप्तेरिति" अमृतमनुबुध्यते प्राप्तेति।

४ चतुर्हस्तपुस्तकानां सर्वां मध्ये एकस्मिन्नेवैतादृशः पाठः।

एकविंशाध्यायप्रारम्भः॥

इति हि भिक्षवो बोधिसत्त्वैरेवंरूपा व्यूहा बोधिसत्त्वस्य पूजाकर्म्मणे बोधिमण्डेऽभिसंस्कृता अभूवन्॥ स्वयञ्च बोधिसत्त्वो यावन्तो दशसु दिक्ष्वतीतानागतप्रत्युत्पन्नानां भगवतां सर्व्व-बुद्धक्षेत्रेषु बोधिमण्डालङ्कारव्यूहास्तान् सर्व्वांस्तस्मिन् बोधि-मण्डे सन्दर्शयति स्म॥

अथ खलु भिक्षवो बोधिमण्डनिषण्णस्य बोधिसत्त्वस्यैतदभ-वत्। इह खलु कामधातौ मारः पापीयानधिपतिरीश्वरो वशवर्त्ती नैतन्मम प्रतिरूपं भवेत्। यदहं तेनाविदितोऽनुत्तरां सम्यक्सम्बोधिमभिसम्बुध्येयम्। यन्वहं मारस्य पापीयसः स-ञ्चोदनां कुर्य्याम्। तस्मिन् विजिते सर्व्वे कामावचरा देवादयो निग्टहीता भविष्यन्ति। ततश्च मारपर्षदः पूर्व्वावरोपितकुशल-मूला मारकायिका देवपुत्रा मम सिंहविक्रीडितं दृष्ट्वाऽनुत्त-रायां सम्यक्सम्बोधौ चित्तमुत्पादयिष्यन्ति॥

अथ खलु भिक्षवो बोधिसत्त्व एवमनुविचिन्त्य तस्यां वेलायां भ्रूविवरान्तरादूर्णाकोशात् सर्व्वमारमण्डलविध्वंसनकरीं नामै-कां रश्मिमुत्सृजत्(१)। यया रश्म्या सर्व्वस्मिंस्त्रिसाहस्रमहासा-हस्रे लोकधातौ सर्व्वमारभवनान्यवभास्य जिह्मीकृतानि सम्प्र-कम्पितानि चाभूवन्। सर्व्वश्चायं त्रिसाहस्रमहासाहस्रलोकधा-तुर्महतावभासेन स्फुटोऽभूत्॥ तस्याः प्रभाया मारः पापीया-निदमेवंरूपं शब्दमश्रौषीत्।

१ "अस्मिन्नेव ग्रन्थे रश्मिशब्दस्य क्लीबं व्यवहृतम्। "मुत्सृजत्" मुदसृजत्।

कल्पौघचीर्णचरितो ह्यतिशुद्धसत्त्वः
शुद्धोदनस्य तनयः प्रविजह्य राज्यम्।
सो निर्गतो हितकरो ह्यमृताभिलाषी
बोधिद्रुमं ह्युपगतोऽद्य कुरु प्रयत्नम् (१)॥

सोत्तीर्ण आत्मन परानपि तारयिष्ये
मोचेष्यते स च परां स्वयमेव मुक्तः।
आश्वासप्राप्त स परानपि आश्वसेया
निर्व्वापयिष्यति परां परिनिर्वृतश्च (२)॥

शून्यां करिष्यति अपायचयोऽप्यशेषां
पूर्णां करिष्यति पुरीं सुरमानुषाणाम्।
ध्यानानभिज्ञ परमं अमृतं सुखञ्च
दास्यत्यसौ हितकरो अमृतं स्पृशित्वा (३)॥

शून्यं करिष्यति पुरं तव कृष्णबन्धो
अबलाबलो बलविहीन अपक्षपक्षो।
न ज्ञास्यसे क्व नु व्रजासि करोषि किंवा
यद्धर्म्मवर्षमभिवर्षि स्वयं स्वयम्भूः (४)॥

---

१ "प्रविजह्य" प्रविहाय। "सो निर्गतो" स निर्गतो।

२ "सोत्तीर्ण" स उत्तीर्ण। "आत्मन" आत्मना। "मोचेष्यते स च परां" मोचयिष्यति स च पराम्। "आश्वासप्राप्त" आश्वासप्राप्तः। "आश्वसेया" आश्वासयिष्यति। "परां" पराम्।

३ "शून्यां करिष्यति अपायचयोऽप्यशेषां" शून्याम् करिष्यत्यपायचयानशेषान्। "ध्यानानभिज्ञा" ध्यानमभिज्ञां। "परमं अमृतं" परमममृतं। "स्पृशित्वा" स्पृष्ट्वा।

४ "अबलाबलो" अबलाबल। "अपक्षपक्षो" अपक्षपक्ष। "न ज्ञास्यसे क्व नु व्रजासि" न ज्ञास्यसि क्व नु व्रजसि। "अभिवर्षि" अभिवर्षसि। यः स्वयं स्वयम्भूः तदुपरि इत्यर्थः।

इति हि भिक्षवो मारः पापीयानाभिः संचोदनाभिर्गाथाभिः संचोदितः सन् द्वात्रिंशदाकारं स्वप्नमपश्यत्॥ कतमद्द्वात्रिंशदाकारम्। तद्यथा।

तमसाकुलञ्च स्वभवनमपश्यत्। रजसाकुलञ्चाकीर्णशर्कराकठिलञ्च स्वभवनमपश्यत्। भीतत्रस्तोद्विग्नं(१)दिशो दश प्रपलायमानञ्चात्मानमपश्यत्। विभ्रष्टमुकुटमपविद्धकुण्डलञ्चात्मानमपश्यत्। शुष्कोष्ठगलतालुकञ्चात्मानमपश्यत्। सन्तप्तहृदयञ्चात्मानमपश्यत्। शीर्णपत्रपुष्पफलानि चोद्यानान्यपश्यत्। अपगतजलाः परिशुष्काश्च पुष्करिणीरपश्यत्। हंसक्रौञ्चमयूरकलविङ्ककुणालजीवञ्जीवकादींश्च पक्षिगणांश्छिन्नपक्षानपश्यत् (२)। भेरीशङ्खमृदङ्गपटहतुणववीणावल्लकीताडसम्यादींश्च वाद्यभाण्डांश्छिन्नविच्छिन्नान् भूमौ निपतितानपश्यत्। प्रियजनपरिवाराश्च मारमुत्सृज्य दीनमुखा एकान्ते गत्वा प्रध्यायन्तमपश्यत् (३)। अग्रमहिषीञ्च मालिनीं शयनभ्रष्टां धरण्यामुभाभ्यां पाणिभ्यां शीर्षमभिपीडयन्तीमपश्यत्। ये च ते मारपुत्रा वीर्यवत्तमाश्च बलवत्तमाश्च तेजोवत्तमाश्च तं बोधिसत्त्वं बोधिमण्डवराग्रगतं नमस्यन्त एवमपश्यत्। आत्मनीया च दुहिता (४) हा तात हा तातेति क्रन्दन्तीमपश्यत्। मलिनचेलगात्रञ्चात्मानमपश्यत्। अवकीर्णपांशुशिरस्कञ्च पाण्डुदुर्बलमोजोऽपहृतञ्चा-

---

१ "भीतत्रस्तोद्विग्नं" भीतं त्रस्तमुद्विग्नमित्युचितम्।

२ पक्षिगणाननुशोचंपक्षानपक्षानपश्यदिति वा पाठः।

३ "प्रध्यायन्तमपश्यत्" प्रध्यायन्ति इत्यपश्यत्।

४ "आत्मनीया च दुहिता" आत्मीयां च दुहितरं।

त्मानमपश्यत्। हर्म्यकूटागारगवाक्षतोरणांश्च रजसावकीर्णान्पततोऽपश्यत्। ये चास्य ते सेनापतयो यक्षराक्षसकुम्भाण्डगन्धर्वाधिपतयस्तान् सर्वान् हस्ताञ्छिरसि कृत्वा रुदतः क्रन्दतः पलायमानांश्चापश्यत्। ये च ते कामावचरेषु देवाधिपतयः। तद्यथा। धृतराष्ट्रविरूढकविरूपाक्षवैश्रमणशक्रसुयामसन्तुषितसुनिर्मितवशवर्त्तिप्रभृतयः। तान् सर्वांश्छुश्रूषमाणान् मारः पापीयान् बोधिसत्त्वाभिमुखानपश्यत्। रणमध्ये चास्यासिर्विकोषो न भवति स्म। विक्रोशन्तमशिवञ्चात्मानमपश्यत्। स्वेन च परिवारेणात्मानं परित्यक्तमपश्यत्। मङ्गलपूर्णकुम्भांश्च द्वारपतितानपश्यत्। नारदं च ब्राह्मणं माङ्गल्यशब्दं श्रावयन्तमपश्यत्। आनन्दितं च दौवारिकमनानन्दं श्रावयन्तमपश्यत्। तमसाकुलञ्च गगणतलमपश्यत्। कामभवननिवासिनीञ्च श्रियं रुदन्तीमपश्यत्। स्वानैश्वर्यनष्टानपश्यत्। स्वपक्षञ्चापक्षमपश्यत्। मणिमुक्ताजालानि ध्वस्तीभूतानि छिन्नविच्छिन्नानि भूमौ पतितान्यपश्यत्। सर्वं च मारभवनं प्रचलितमपश्यत्। वृक्षांश्छिद्यमानान्निर्यूहांश्च पततोऽद्राक्षीत्। सर्वं च मारसेनाव्यूहमभिमुखम्पात्यमानमपश्यत्॥ इति हि भिक्षवो एवं द्वात्रिंशदाकारं मारः पापीयान् स्वप्नमपश्यत्।

स प्रतिबुद्धः सन् भीतस्त्रस्तः संविग्नः सर्वमन्तर्जनं सन्निपात्य सबलपार्षद्यसेनापतिदौवारिकान् सन्निपतितांश्च तान् विदित्वाऽऽभिर्गाथाभिरध्यभाषत।

दृष्ट्वा नु तां स सुपिनां नमुची दुःखार्त्तो

आमन्त्रयाभिस्तुत येऽपि च पारिषद्या ।
सेनापतिं नमुचि सिंहहनुश्च नाम्ना
सर्वेषु तेषु परिपृच्छति कृष्णबन्धुः (१) ॥
गाथाभि गीत रचितोऽद्य श्रुतोऽस्मरीया-
च्छाक्येषु जातु वरलक्षणविचिताङ्गः ।
षड्वर्ष दुष्करव्रतानि चरित्व घोरान्
बोधिद्रुमं ह्युपगतः प्रकुरुष्व यत्नम् (२) ॥
सोऽभूद्विबुद्ध स्वयमेव हि बोधिसत्त्वो
बहुसत्त्वकोटिनियुतानि विबोधयेत ।
शून्यं करिष्यति स मे भवनं ह्यशेषं
यद लप्स्यते ह्यमृतु स्पर्शि नमोति भावम् (३) ॥
हन्त व्रजाम सहिता महता बलेन
घातेम तं श्रमणु एक द्रुमेन्द्रमूले ।
उद्योजयध्वं चतुरङ्गिणि शीघ्र सेनां
यदिच्छथा मम प्रियमचिरं करोथ (४) ॥

---

१ "न तां च सुपिनां नमुची दुःखार्त्तो" न तान् च स्वप्नान्नमुचिर्दुःखार्त्तः । "आमन्त्रयाभिस्तुत" आमन्त्र्याभिस्तुतं । "पारिषद्या" पारिषद्याः । "नमुचि सिंहहनुश्च" नमुचिं सिंहहनुश्च । अथवा नमुचिसिंहहनुमिति एकं नाम ।

२ "गाथाभि गीत रचितोऽद्य" गाथाभिर्गीतं रचितमद्य । "श्रुतोऽस्म" श्रुतमस्म । "जातु" जातो । "षड्वर्षं" षड्वर्षं । "चरित्व घोरान्" चरित्वा घोराणि । "प्रकुरुष्व" प्रकुरुत ।

३ "विबुद्ध स्वय-" विबुद्धः स्वय । "यद लप्स्यते" यदा लप्स्यते । "ह्यमृतु स्पर्शि" ह्यमृतं स्पृष्टुं "नमोति भावम्" नंक्ष्यति भावम् ।

४ "घातेम तं" घातयिष्यामस्तं । "श्रमणु एक" श्रमणमेकं । "उद्योजयध्वं चतुरङ्गिणि शीघ्र" उद्योजयत चतुरङ्गिणीं शीघ्रं । "यदिच्छथा" यदीच्छत । "करोथ" कुरुत ।

प्रत्येकबुद्ध अर्हंति च पूर्व लोके
निर्वायमाण न बलं मम दुर्बलं स्यात्।
सो भूयु एकु जिन भेष्यति धर्मराजो
गणनाव्यतिवृत्तु जिनवंश न जातु च्छिद्येत् (१)॥

अथ खलु भिक्षवः सार्थवाहो नाम मारपुत्रः स मारं पापीयसं गाथयाध्यभाषत।

किं तात भिन्नवदनोऽसि विवर्णवक्त्रो
हृदयं समुत्प्लवति वेधति अङ्गमङ्गम्।
किं ते श्रुतं अथ च दृष्टु भणाहि शीघ्रं
ज्ञास्याम तत्त्व तु विचिन्त्य तथा प्रयोगम् (२)।

निर्माण माह अब्रवी शृणु मह्य वत्स
पापं मि दृष्ट सुपिनं परमं सुघोरम्।
भाषेय सर्वमिह पर्षदि अशेषं
सम्मूर्छिताः क्षितितले प्रपतेथ यूयम् (३)॥

सार्थवाह आह।

रणकालि प्राप्ति यदि नाम जयो न दोष-

---

१ "प्रत्येकबुद्ध अर्हंति च पूर्व" प्रत्येकबुद्धोऽर्हंति च पूर्वो। "निर्वायमाण" निर्वायमाणं। "सो भूयु एकु जिन भेष्यति" स भूय एको जिनो भविष्यति। "गणना-व्यतिवृत्तु जिनवंश न" गणनाव्यतिवृत्तो जिनवंशो न।

२ "भिन्नवदनोऽसि" अत्र छिन्नवदनोऽसि इति पाठ उचितः। "समुत्प्लवति" समुत्प्लवति। "दृष्टु भणाहि" दृष्टं भण। "ज्ञास्याम तत्त्व" ज्ञास्यामस्तत्त्वं।

३ "निर्माण माह अब्रवी शृणु मह्य" निर्माणो मारोऽब्रवीत् शृणु मत्तः। "मि दृष्ट सुपिनं" मया दृष्टं स्वप्नं। "भाषेय" भाषेयं। "अशेषं" अशेषं। "प्रपतेथ" प्रपतेत।

स्थानैव यस्तु निहतो भवते न दोषः ।
स्वप्नान्तरे तु यदि ईदृश ते निमित्ता
श्रेयो उपेक्षण रणे परिभावु गच्छेत् (१) ॥

मारोऽब्रवीत् ।

व्यवसायबुद्धि पुरुषस्य रणे प्रसिद्धि-
रवलम्ब्य धैर्यमतुलं यदि नो जयं स्यात् ।
का तस्य भक्ति मम दृष्ट सपारिषद्यं
नोत्थातु मह्य चरणे शिरसा प्रवर्त्त (२) ॥

सार्थवाह आह ।

विस्तीर्णमस्ति हि बलं च सुदुर्बलं च
अस्त्येक शूर बलवांश्च रणञ्जहश्च ।
खद्योतकैर्यदि भवेत्त्रिसहस्र पूर्णा
एको रविर्ग्रसति निष्प्रभतां करोति (३) ॥

अपि च ।

यस्य मानश्च मोहश्च मीमांसा च न विद्यते ।
विलोमयति विद्वांसो (४) नासौ शक्यश्चिकित्सितुम् ॥

इति हि भिक्षवो मारः पापीयान् सार्थवाहस्य वचनम-

---

१ "रणकालि प्राप्ति" रणकाले प्राप्ते। "भवते" भवति। "ईदृश ते निमित्ता" ईदृशानि ते निमित्तानि। "उपेक्षण" उपेक्षणं। "परिभावु" परिभावं।

२ "व्यवसायबुद्धि पुरुषस्य" व्यवसायबुद्धेः पुरुषस्य। "जयं" जयः। "भक्ति मम दृष्ट सपारिषद्यं" भक्तिर्मां दृष्ट्वा सपारिषदं। "नोत्थातु" नोत्थाय। "मह्य" मम। "प्रवर्त्त" प्रवर्त्तेत्।

३ "अस्त्येक शूर" अस्त्येकः शूरो। "त्रिसहस्र पूर्णा" त्रिसहस्रं पूर्णं।

४ "विद्वांसो" विदुषो।

कृत्वा महतीं चतुरङ्गिणीं सेनामुद्योजयति स्म महाबलरणशौण्डां भीषणिकां रोमहर्षणीं दृष्टाश्रुतपूर्वां देवमनुष्यैर्बहुविधमुखवि- कारकोटिनियुतशतसहस्रविकारप्रकारां भुजगशतसहस्रकरच- रणकुटिलपरिवेष्टितशरीरामसिधनुःशरशक्तितोमरकुठारपट्टि- शभुशुण्डीमुसलदण्डपाशगदाचक्रवज्रबाणधराम्बरचर्मकवर्मितश- रीरां विपरीतशिरःकरचरणनयनां ज्वलितशिरोनयनवदनां दुःसंस्थितोदरपाणिपादामुग्रतेजोवदनां परमविकृतवदनदर्शनां विकरालविकृतदंष्ट्रां घनविपुलप्रलम्बजिह्वां शुण्डिककिलिञ्जसदृ- शजिह्वां ज्वलनसदृशकृष्णसर्पविषपूर्णरक्तनेत्राम्। केचित्तत्र ते आशीविषान् वमन्ति स्म। केचित् करतलैराशीविषान् परि- गृह्य भक्षयन्ति स्म। गरुड इव सागरादभ्युत्क्षिप्य केचिन्नर- मांसरुधिरकरचरणशिरो(१)यकृदन्त्रपुरीषादींश्च भक्षयन्ति स्म। केचिज्ज्वलितपिङ्गलकृष्णनीलरक्तकद्रुकरालविचित्ररूपाः। के- चिद्विकृतकूपप्रज्वलितोत्पाटितविकृतकटाक्षाः। केचित् परि- वृत्तज्वलितविकृतनयनाः। केचिज्ज्वलितान् पर्वतान् परि- गृह्य सलीलमपरेषु पर्वतेषु अभिरूढा आगच्छन्ति स्म। केचित् समूलं वृक्षमुत्पाट्य बोधिसत्त्वाभिमुखा अभिधावन्ति स्म। केचिदजकर्णशूर्पकर्णहस्तिकर्णलम्बकर्णवराहकर्णाः। केचि- दकर्णाः। केचिदेकोदरिणो दुर्बलकाया अस्थिकङ्कालसङ्घात- मभिनिर्माय भग्ननासाः कुम्भोदराः करोटपादा उच्छुष्कत्व-

---

१ "शिरोयकृत" शिरउयकृत।

मांसरुधिरच्छिन्नकर्णनासाकरचरणनयनोत्तमाङ्गाः। केचि-
द्रुधिरपिपासया शिरांसि परस्परं निकृन्तन्ति स्म। केचिद्भि-
न्नविकृतभैरवरूक्षस्वरा हुंहुङ्कारपिचुत्कारहुलुहुलुप्रक्ष्वेडिता-
नि कुर्वन्ति स्म। केचिदाहुः। आहरत हरत हनत हनत
बध्नत गृह्णत छिन्दत भिन्दत मथयतोत्क्षिपत नाशयतेमं
श्रमणं गौतमं सार्द्धं द्रुमेणेति ब्रुवन्ति स्म। केचिद्भेरण्डकशृ-
गालशूकरगर्दभगोहस्त्यश्वोष्ट्रमहिषखरशशचमरखड्गशरभनाना-
प्रतिभयरौद्रविकृतवक्त्राः। केचित्सिंहव्याघ्रर्क्षवराहवानरद्वी-
पिविडालच्छागलोरभ्रसर्पनकुलमत्स्यमकरशिशुमारकूर्मकाकगृ-
ध्रोलूकगरुडादिसदृशात्मभावाः। केचिद्विरूपरूपाः। केचि-
देकशीर्षा द्विशीर्षा यावच्छतसहस्रशीर्षाः। केचिदशीर्षाः।
केचिदेकभुजा यावच्छतशतसहस्रभुजाः। केचिदभुजाः।
केचिदेकपादकाः। केचिद्बहुपादा अपादकाः। केचित्
कर्णमुखनासिकाक्षिनाभिश्रोतोभिराशीविषान्निश्चारयन्ति स्म।
केचिदसिधनुःशरशक्तिपट्टिशपरशुचक्रतोमरकुणपवज्रभुशुण्डी-
भिन्दिपालादीनि नानाप्रहरणानि भ्रामयन्तो नृत्यन्तो बो-
धिसत्त्वं सन्तर्जयन्ति स्म। केचिन्नराङ्गुलिं छित्वा मालागुणं
कृत्वा धारयन्ति स्म। केचिच्छिरोभिरस्थिकरकान् शीर्ष-
कटाहकांश्च मालागुणमिव कृत्वा धारयन्ति स्म। केचि-
दाशीविषपरिवेष्टितशरीराः। केचिच्छीर्षकटाहकान् परि-
गृह्य हस्त्यश्वोष्ट्रगोगर्दभमहिषारूढाः। केचिदधःशिरस ऊर्द्ध-
पादाः। केचित्स्थूलरोमाणः। केचिद्गोगर्दभवराहनकुलच्छा-

गर्दभोरभ्रखरभविडालकपिद्रकद्रुगात्ररोमाश्च आशीविषान् व-
मन्तोऽयोगुडानि निर्गिलन्तो धूमकेतूनुत्सृजन्तो ज्वलितता-
म्रलोहवर्षं प्रवर्षन्तो विद्युद्वर्षां क्षिपन्तो वज्राशनिं प्रमुञ्चन्त-
स्तप्तामयोवालुकां प्रवर्षन्तः कालमेघान् सञ्जनयन्तो वातवृष्टि-
मुत्पादयन्तः शरमेघवर्षानुत्सृजन्तः कालरात्रीं दर्शयन्तो रावं
सञ्जनयन्तो बोधिसत्त्वमभिधावन्ति स्म। केचित् पाशान् भ्रा-
मयन्तो महापर्वतान् प्रपातयन्तो महासागरान् क्षोभयन्तो
लङ्घयन्तो महापर्वतांश्चालयन्तो मेरुपर्वतराजमभिधावन्तः
पलायमाना विक्षिपन्तोऽङ्गप्रत्यङ्गानि भ्रामयन्तः शरीराणि
हसन्तो महाहास्यमुरांसि प्रस्फोटयन्त उरांसि ताडयन्तः
केशान् धुन्वन्तः पीतमुखानि च (१) नीलशरीरा ज्वलितशिरस
ऊर्ध्वकेशा इतस्ततो वेगेन परिधावन्तो गहडाचाक्ष बोधिसत्त्वं
भीषयन्ति स्म। जीर्णाः स्त्रियश्च रुदन्त्यो बोधिसत्त्वमुपसङ्क्रम्यैवं
वदन्ति स्म। हा पुत्र हा मम पुत्रोत्तिष्ठोत्तिष्ठ शीघ्रं प्रपला-
यस्व। राक्षसरूपाः पिशाचीरूपाः काणखञ्जदुर्बलाश्च प्रेताः
क्षुत्क्षामाश्च ऊर्ध्वबाहवो विकृतास्याः क्रन्दन्तो भयमुपदर्शयन्त-
स्त्रासञ्जनयन्तो बोधिसत्त्वस्य पुरतोऽभिधावन्ति स्म (२)॥ तया
चैवंरूपया मारसेनया समुदितया समन्तादशीतियोजनान्या-

---

१ केशान् इत्यादौ केचाचिद्बुद्बुदपीतमुखानि इति पाठः। परन्तु चत्र पूर्वक्रमानु-
सारेण केचिद्बुद्बुदपीतमुखा इति उचितम्। अत्रापि पीतमुखानि इत्यत्र पीतमुख
इत्युचितम्।

२ "बोधिसत्त्वस्य पुरतोऽभिधावन्ति स्म" इत्यत्र बोधिसत्त्वस्य पुरतोऽभिधावन्ति इत्यु-
चितम्।

यामेन विस्तारेण स्फुटमभूत्। यथा चैकस्य मारस्यैवं कोटी-शतानां त्रिसाहस्रपर्यापन्नानां माराणां पापीयसां सेनाभि-स्तिर्यगूर्द्धं च परिस्फुटमभूत् ॥

तत्रेदमुच्यते।

यक्षकुम्भाण्डमहोरगरूपा
राक्षसप्रेतपिशाचकरूपाः।
यत्तु विलोकि विरूप सुरौद्रा:
सर्वि त निर्मित तत्र शठेभिः (१) ॥
एकशिरा द्विशिरा त्रिशिराश्च
यावत् सहस्रशिरा बहु अन्ये।
एकभुजा द्विभुजा त्रिभुजाश्च
यावत् सहस्रभुजा बहुभुजाः (२) ॥
एकपदा द्विपदा त्रिपदाश्च
यावत् सहस्रपदा बहु अन्ये।
नीलमुखाश्च पीतशरीराः
पीतमुखानि च नीलशरीराः (३) ॥
अन्यमुखानि च अन्यशरीराः
सर्व एवमुपागतु किङ्करसैन्यम्।

---

१ "यत्तु विलोकि विरूप" ये तु विलोकिता विरूपाः। "सर्वि त निर्मित तत्र शठेभिः" सर्वे ते निर्मितास्तत्र शठैः।

२ "एकशिरा द्विशिरा त्रिशिराश्च" एकशिरसो द्विशिरसस्त्रिशिरसश्च। "सहस्रशिरा बहु अन्ये" सहस्रशिरसो बहवोऽन्ये।

३ "बहु अन्ये" बहवोऽन्ये। "पीतमुखानि च" पीतमुखाश्च।

वातं प्रवायति वर्षति वर्षं
विद्युत्घटशतानि पतन्ति (१) ॥
देव गुडायति वृक्ष लुडन्ति
बोधिवटस्य मर्द्दयति पत्रम्।
वर्षदेव प्रवर्षति वर्षं
ओघवहन्ति जलाकुल भूमिम् (२) ॥
ईदृश भीषणिका बहुराशी
यत्र अचेतन वृक्ष पतन्ति।
दृष्ट्वा च तानतिभीषणरूपान्
सर्वि विसंस्थित रूपविरूपान् (३) ॥
श्रीगुणलक्षणतेजधरस्य
चित्त न कम्पित मेरु यथैव।
मायसमास्तथ स्वप्नसमाश्च
अभ्रनिभा समुदीक्षति धर्म्मान् (४) ॥

---

१ "अन्यमुखानि च" अन्यमुखाश्च। "सर्व एवमुपागतु" सर्वमेवमुपागतं। सर्व-मुखागतु इति वा पाठः। "वातं प्रवायति" वातं प्रवायन्ति। "वर्षति वर्षं" वर्ष-यन्ति वर्षां। "पतन्ति" पातयन्ति।

२ "देव गुडायति वृक्ष लुडन्ति" देवाम् लुठयन्ति वृक्षं लुनन्ति। "मर्द्दयति पत्रम्" मर्दयन्ति पत्राणि। "वर्षदेवः प्रवर्षति वर्षं" वर्षदेवः प्रवर्षयति वर्षां। "ओ-घवहन्ति जलाकुल" ओघावयन्ति जलाकुलां।

३ "ईदृश भीषणिका बहुराशी" ईदृशा भीषणका बहुराशयः। "अचेतन वृक्ष" अचेतने वृक्षे। "सर्वि विसंस्थित" सर्वान् विसंस्थितान्।

४ "तेजधरस्य" तेजोधरस्य। "चित्त न कम्पित मेरु यथैव" चित्तं न कम्पितं मेरुर्यथैव। "मायसमास्तथ स्वप्नसमाश्च अभ्रनिभा" मायासमांस्तथा स्वप्नसमांश्च अभ्रनिभान्।

ईदृश धर्मनयं विम्हयन्तो
सुस्थितु ध्यायति संस्थितु धर्मे।
यस्य भवन्ति ममहन्ति ममेति
भाव समुच्छ्रयि सत्त्वनिविष्टाः (१)॥
सो विभियादबुधः स्थितु पाशे
आत्मनि सम्भ्रम गच्छ गिरीच्छ।
शाक्यसुतस्तु स्वभावमभावं
धर्म प्रतीत्य समुत्थित बुद्धाः (२)॥
गगणोपमचित्त सुयुक्तो
न भ्रमते सबलं साधु दृष्ट्वा (३)॥

इति हि भिक्षवो मारस्य पापीयसः पुत्रसहस्रं तत्र ये मारपुत्रा बोधिसत्त्वेऽभिप्रसन्नाः सार्थवाहपूर्वङ्गमास्तेमारस्य दक्षिणे पार्श्वे स्थिता अभूवन्। ये मारपाक्षिकास्ते वामपार्श्वे स्थिता अभूवन् मारस्य पापीयसः। तत्र मारः पापीयांस्तान् स्वान्पुत्रानामन्त्रयते स्म। कीदृशेन बलेन वयं बोधिसत्त्वं धर्षयिष्यामः। तत्र दक्षिणे पार्श्वे सार्थवाहो नाम मारपुत्रः स पितरं गाथया प्रत्यभाषत।

सुप्तं प्रबोधयितुमिच्छति पन्नगेन्द्रं

---

१ "ईदृश" ईदृशं। "विम्हयन्तो" विस्मयम्। "सुस्थितु" सुस्थितः। "संस्थितु" संस्थितः। "ममहन्ति" ममहमिति। "भाव समुच्छ्रयि" भावाः समुच्छ्रयिनः।

२ "सो विभियादबुधः" स विभियादबुधः। "स्थितु पाशे" स्थितो पाशे। "पाशे आपदे इत्यर्थः। "सम्भ्रम गच्छ" सम्भ्रमं गच्छति। "धर्म प्रतीत्य समुपत्थित बुद्धाः" धर्मं प्रत्येत्य समुत्थितं बुद्धा। "गगणोपमचित्त" गगणोपमचित्तः। एतच्छ्लोकस्य उत्तरार्द्धमन्यपुस्तकेषु नास्ति।

सुप्तं प्रबोधयितुमिच्छति यो गजेन्द्रम् ।
सुप्तं प्रबोधयितुमिच्छति यो मृगेन्द्रं
सुप्तं प्रबोधयितुमिच्छति सो नरेन्द्रम् (१) ॥

वामपार्श्वे दुर्मतिर्नाम मारपुत्रः स एवमाह ।

सम्प्रेक्षणेन हृदयान्यभिसंस्फुटन्ति
लोकेषु सारमहतामपि पादपानाम् ।
का शक्तिरस्ति मम दृष्टिहतस्य तस्य
सञ्जीवितुं जगति मृत्युहतस्य वास्तु ॥

दक्षिणे मधुरनिर्घोषो नामाह ।

वृक्षेषु सार क इहास्ति ततो ब्रवीषि
दृष्ट्वा भिनन्मि मनुजेष्वथ का अवस्था ।
मेरुं गिरिं यदि भिनत्सि निरीक्षणेन
नैवास्य तुभ्यमयनेभिहतोन्मिषेरन् (२) ॥

अपिच ।

यः सागरं तरितुमिच्छति वै भुजाभ्यां
तोयञ्च तस्य पिबितुं मनुजेष्वसन्तु ।
शक्यं भवेदिदमतस्तु वदामि दुःखं
यस्तस्य वक्त्रमभितोप्यमलं निरीक्षेत् (३) ॥

---

१ "सो नरेन्द्रम्" स नरेन्द्रम् ।

२ "भिनन्मि" भिनद्मि । "भिनत्सि" भेत्स्यसि । "नैवास्य तुभ्यमयनेभिहतोन्मिषे-रन्" नैवायं तव नयनाभिहतो क्षियेत इत्यर्थः ।

३ "तरितु" तर्तुं । "पिबितुं" पातुं । "मनुजेष्वसन्तु" एतादृशो जनो मनुजेषु नास्ति इत्यर्थः ।

वामे शतबाहुर्नामाह।

ममेह देहेऽस्मि शतं भुजानां
क्षिपामि चैकेन शतं शराणाम्।
भिनद्मि कायं श्रमणस्य तात
सुखी भव त्वं व्रज मा विलम्बम् (१)॥

दक्षिणे सुबुद्धिराह।

शतं भुजानां यदि को विशेषो
भुजा किमर्थं न भवन्ति रोमाः।
भुजैकमेकेन च तथैव शूरा-
स्तैश्चापि कुर्यान्न हि तस्य किञ्चित् (२)॥

किं कारणं मैत्रीव्रतस्य मुनेः शरीरे
विषं न शस्त्रं क्रमते न चाग्निः।
क्षिप्तानि शस्त्राणि व्रजन्ति पुष्पतां
मैत्रीविहलोकोत्तरभावितस्य (३)॥

अपिच।

दिवि भुवि च जले च ये बलाढ्या
असिपरशुधराश्च गुह्यका नरा वा।
शमबलमिमु प्राप्य ते नरेन्द्रं

---

१ "देहेऽस्मि" देहेऽस्मिन्। "भिनद्मि" भेत्स्यामि। मा विलम्बम्, चल कुरु इत्य-ध्याहार्य्यं मा विलम्बं कुरु इत्यर्थः।

२ "रोमाः" रोमाणो रोमतुल्या रोमसङ्ख्यका वा। "भुजैकमेकेन" भुजैकेनैकेन एकैकेन भुजेनेत्यर्थः। "तैश्चापि कुर्य्यान्न" ते चापि कुर्य्युर्न।

३ "किं कारणम्" यस्मात्कारणादित्यर्थः। "मैत्रीविहलोकोत्तरभावितस्य" मैत्री-बलस्य लोकोत्तरभावितस्य इत्यर्थः सम्भाव्यते पाठस्तु चस्तुतः।

प्रबलबलान्यबला भवन्ति सर्वे (१) ॥

वामे उग्रतेजा आह ।

अन्तर्गतोऽहं धक्ष्यामि प्रविशास्य तनुं शुभाम् ।
वृक्षं सकोटरं शुष्कं दावाग्निरिव सूक्ष्मतः (२) ॥

दक्षिणे सुनेत्र आह ।

मेरुं दहेत्सं यदि वापि कृत्स्नं प्रविश्य चान्तर्गतु मेदिनीं वा ।
दग्धुं न शक्यः स हि वज्रबुद्धिस्त्वत्सन्निभैर्बालिकगङ्गतुल्यैः (३) ॥

अपि च ॥

चलेयुर्गिरयः सर्वे क्षयं गच्छेन्महोदधिः ।
चन्द्रसूर्यौ पतेद्भूमौ मही च विलयं व्रजेत् (४) ॥
लोकस्यार्थे कृतारम्भः प्रतिज्ञाकृतनिश्चयः ।
अप्राप्यैव वरां बोधि नोत्थास्यति महाद्रुमात् (५) ॥

वामे दीर्घबाहुर्गर्वित आह ।

आलयं चन्द्रसूर्याणां नक्षत्राणां च सर्वशः ।
पाणिनाहं प्रमर्दामि तवेह भवने स्थितः (६) ॥
चतुर्भ्यः सागरेभ्यश्च जलं घटामि लीलया ।
तं घट्य श्रमणं तात सागरस्य परं क्षिपेत् (७) ॥

---

१ "क्षमबलमिमु" क्षमबलमिमं। "प्रबलबलान्यबला" प्रबलबला अबला इत्यर्थः।

२ "प्रविशास्य" प्रविश्यास्य ।

३ "चान्तर्गतु" चान्तर्गतो। "बालिकगङ्गतुल्यैः" गङ्गावालुकातुल्यैरित्यर्थः।

४ "पतेद्भूमौ" पतेतां भूमौ।

५ "बोधि" बोधिं।

६ "चन्द्रसूर्याणां" चन्द्रसूर्ययोः। "प्रमर्दामि" प्रमर्दितुं समर्थोऽस्मि इत्यर्थः।

७ "घटामि" मक्षीतुं समर्थोऽस्मि इत्यर्थः। "घट्य" घटित्वा। "परं क्षिपेत्" पारे क्षेप्स्यामि।

तिष्ठतां तात सैन्येयं मा त्वं शोकार्दितो भव ।
सबोधिवृक्षमुत्पाट्य क्षेप्स्ये पाण्या दिशो दशः (१) ॥

दक्षिणे प्रसादप्रतिलब्ध आह ।

सदेवासुरगन्धर्वां ससागरनगां महीम् ।
त्वं मर्षिता प्रकुर्य्याश्च पाणिभ्यां मदगर्वितः (२) ॥
त्वद्विधानां सहस्राणि गङ्गावालिकया समाः ।
रोम तस्य न चालेतुं बोधिसत्त्वस्य धीमतः (३) ॥

वामे भयङ्कर आह ।

भयं हि ते तात भृशं किमर्थं सेनाथ मध्ये समवस्थितस्य ।
सेना न तस्यास्ति कुतः सहायाः कस्माद्भयं ते भवतीह तस्मात् (४)॥

दक्षिण एकाग्रमतिराह ।

यूथं न लोकेस्ति शशीरवीनां न चक्रवर्त्ती न च केशरीणाम् ।
न बोधिसत्त्वानिह तात यूथमेकः समर्थो नमुचिन्निहन्तुम् (५) ॥

वामेऽवतारप्रेक्ष्याह ।

न शक्तिशूला न गदा न खड्गाः न हस्तिनोऽश्वा न रथा न पत्तिः ।
तं शौण्डमेकं श्रमणं निषण्णं हन्येत मा सम्भ्रम तात किञ्चित् (६)॥

---

१ "सैन्येयं" सैन्यमिदं । "सबोधिवृक्षमुत्पाट्य" सबोधिं वृक्षमुत्पाट्य सम्बोधिवृक्षमुत्पाट्य इति वा । "क्षेप्स्ये पाण्या" क्षेप्स्यामि पाणिना ।

२ "त्वं मर्षिता" त्वममर्षितः ।

३ "त्वद्विधानां" त्वद्विधाः । "गङ्गावालिकया" गङ्गावालुकयाः । "चालेतुं" चालयितुं न समर्थाः इति शेषः ।

४ "सेनाथ" सेनायाः ।

५ "शशीरवीणां" शशिरवीणां । "चक्रवर्त्ती" चक्रवर्त्तिनां । "केशरीणां" केशरिणां । "बोधिसत्त्वानिह" बोधिसत्त्वानामिह ।

६ "शक्तिशूला" शक्तिशूलौ । "पत्ति" पत्तयः । "हन्येत" हन्ति ।

दक्षिणे पुण्यालङ्कृत आह।

नारायणस्य यथ काय अच्छेद्यभेद्या

क्षान्तिबलैः कवचितो दृढवीर्यखङ्गः।

त्रिविमोक्षवाहन त्रिप्रज्ञाधनुः स तात

पुण्यबलेन स हि जेष्यति मारसेनाम् (१) ॥

वामे अनिवर्त्याह।

न निवर्त्तते व्रणगतः प्रदहन्दवाग्निः

क्षिप्तः शरो न च निवर्त्त विज्ञिक्षिते न।

वज्रं नभे निपतितं न निवर्त्तते च

न स्थानमस्ति मम प्राप्यसुतं अजित्वा (२) ॥

दक्षिणे धर्मकाम आह।

आर्द्रतृणं प्राप्य निवर्त्ततेऽग्नि-

र्गिरिकूटमासाद्य निवर्त्तते शरः।

वज्रं महीं प्राप्य अधः प्रयाति

अप्राप्य शान्तममृतं न निवर्त्ततेऽयम् (३) ॥

किं कारणं शक्यतु तात अन्तरीक्ष लेख्यचित्रितुं

यावन्तः केचित् सर्वसत्त्व एकचित्ता स्थापितुम्।

चन्द्रसूर्य मारुतं च शक्यं पाश बन्धितुं

---

१ "यथ काय अच्छेद्यभेद्या" यथा कायोऽच्छेद्योऽभेद्यः। "वाहन त्रिप्रज्ञाधनुः" वाहनः शुभ्रज्ञाधनुः। अत्र स तात स हि इत्यत्र कर्तृपदस्य पुनरुक्तिरनुचिता।

२ "निवर्त्त" निवर्त्तते। "नभे" नभसि। न स्थानमस्तीत्यस्य यत्र स्थितस्य प्राप्यसुतस्याजयो भवेदेताहशं स्थानं मम सम्बन्धे नास्ति इत्यर्थः।

३ "न निवर्त्ततेऽयं" न निवर्त्तिष्यत्ययम्।

न बोधिसत्त्व शक्य तात बोधिमण्ड चालितुम् (१)॥

वामेऽनुपशान्त आह ।

दृष्टीविषेण महता प्रदहामि मेरुं
भस्मीकरोमि सलिलञ्च महोदधीनाम् ।
बोधिञ्च पश्य श्रमणञ्च अहं हि तात
दृष्ट्वा यथाद्य उभयं हि करोमि भस्मां (२) ॥

दक्षिणे सिद्धार्थ आह ।

विषेण पूर्णो यदिवेष सर्वो भवेत्त्रिसाहस्रवरः प्रदीप्तः ।
निरीक्षणादेव गुणाकरस्य मुनिर्विषत्वं विषमभ्युपेयात् ॥
विषाणमुग्र त्रिभवेह यस्य
रागस्य द्वेषस्य तथैव मोहः ।
ते तस्य काये च तथैव चित्ते
नभे यथा पङ्करजो न सन्ति (३) ॥
तस्मान्निवर्त्तामह तात सर्वे (४)

---

१ "किं कारणं शक्यथु" केन कारणेन शक्येत । "चलरोष" चलरोषे । "लेख्य" लिखिता, लेख्यं वा । "सर्वसत्त्व" सर्वसत्त्वाः । "ताम् एकचित्ता" एकचित्ताम् इत्यर्थः । "स्थापितुं" स्थापयितुं । "शक्य पाश बन्धितुं" शक्यः पाशेन बद्धुं । "बोधिसत्त्व शक्य तात बोधिमण्ड चालितुं" बोधिसत्त्वः शक्यस्तात बोधिमण्डाच्चालयितुम् ।

२ "दृष्टीविषेण" दृष्टिविषेण । "प्रदहामि" प्रदग्धुं समर्थोऽस्मि इति स्पष्टार्थः । "यथाद्य उभयं" यथाद्योभयं । "भस्मां" भस्म ।

३ "विषाणमुग्र त्रिभवे" विषाणामुग्रस्त्रिभवे । "नभे" नभसि । पङ्करजो न सन्ति" पङ्करजसी न स्तः । यथा पङ्को रजश्च नभसि न लिप्यते तद्वद्बोधिसत्त्वस्य काये चित्ते च विषादयो न लिप्यन्ते इत्यर्थः अस्मिन् श्लोके पादैकमधिकम् । पाठोऽपि सर्वत्रैवमेव ।

४ "निवर्त्तामह" निवर्त्तामहै ।

वामे रतिलोलो नामाह।

अद्य तूर्यसहस्र प्रवादितै-

रप्सरशतसहस्रालङ्कृतैः।

लोभयित्वमु नेष्यि पुरोत्तमं

कामरतिं हि करोमि वशे भवत् (१)॥

दक्षिणे धर्मरतिराह।

धर्मरती सद तस्य रतीहा

ध्यानरती अमृतार्थरतिश्च।

सत्त्वप्रमोक्षणमैत्ररतिश्च

रागरतिं च रतिं न करोति (२)॥

वामे वातजवो नामाह।

जवेनाहं चन्द्ररवी ग्रसेयं

प्रवायमानं गगने च वायुम्।

अद्यैव तात श्रमणं गृहीत्वा

वेगस्य मुष्टिं विकिरामि वायुवत् (३)॥

दक्षिणे अचलमतिर्नाम मारपुत्रः स एवमाह।

---

१ "अद्य" अद्यं। "तूर्यसहस्र" तूर्यसहस्रैः। "रप्सरशत" रप्सरःशत-। "लोभयित्वमु नेष्यि" लोभयित्वाऽमुमानेष्यामि। "करोमि वशे भवत्" करिष्यामि वशे भविष्यति।

२ "धर्मरती सद" धर्मरतिः सदा। "रतीहा" रतिरिह। "ध्यानरती अमृतार्थ" ध्यानरतिरमृतार्थ-।

३ "ग्रसेयं" ग्रसीयां। अत्र ग्रसेयमिति वा पाठः। "वेगस्य" वेगेन। "विकिरामि" विकीर्तुं समर्थोऽस्मि इति स्वाद्यर्थः। प्रसह्य मुष्टिं विकिरामि वायुं। यद्वैव मुष्टिं विकिरामि वायुवत्। इति चाच पाठान्तरे।

यथा तवैषो अव वेग उग्रस्तदस्यदि स्यात् सुरमानुषाणाम्।
सर्वे समग्रापि न ते समर्थाः कर्त्तुं रजाम प्रतिपुङ्गवस्य (१)॥

वामे अन्नमतिराह।

श्रान्ताद्‌भ्रान्तामपि वृन्दमुग्र-
कुर्य्यान्न किञ्चित्तव मानघातम्।
प्रागेव सैकः प्रकरोति किं ते
वृन्देन साध्यन्ति हि सर्व्वकार्य्यम् (२)॥

दक्षिणे सिंहमतिराह।

न सिंहवृन्दं भुवि दृष्टपूर्वं दृष्टी-
विषाणामपि (३) नास्ति वृन्दम्।
तेजस्विनां सत्यपराक्रमाणां
पुरुषर्षभाणामपि नास्ति वृन्दम्॥

वामे सर्वचण्डालो नामाह।

न ते श्रुता तात गिरोऽभिदीप्ता यथा नदन्ते(४)तनयस्तवेमे।
वीर्य्येण वेगेन बलेन युक्ता श्रजाम शीघ्रं श्रमणं हि हन्तुम्॥

दक्षिणे सिंहनादी नामाह।

बहवः शृगाला हि वनान्तरेषु
नर्द्दन्ति नादान्न सन्तीह सिंहे।
ते सिंहनादन्तु निशम्य भीमं

---

१ "अव वेग" अवो वेग। "समग्रापि" समग्रा अपि। "रजाम" रोचामः।
२ "साध्यन्ति" साध्यते।
३ "दृष्टीविषाणामपि" दृष्टिविषाणामपि।
४ "नदन्ते" नदन्ति।

त्रस्ता पलायन्ति दिशो दशासु (१) ॥
मारीरसाखदद्‌मी अपण्डिता
अश्रुत्य नादं पुरुषोत्तमस्य।
नदन्ति तावत् स्वमतातिहृष्टा
मनुष्यसिंहे नदिते न सन्ति (२) ॥

वामपार्श्वे दुश्चिन्तितचिन्त्याह।

यच्चिन्तयामि तदिहाशु भोति
कथं न एषो इमु वीक्षते च।
मूढो च एषो अनभिज्ञ किन्वा
यदुत्थिहित्वा न पलायते लघुं (३) ॥

दक्षिणात् पार्श्वात् सुचिन्तितार्थो नामाह।

मूढो न चायमविधिज्ञमपराक्रमो वा
युष्मेव मूढाश्च असंयताश्च।
न युष्मि जानाथ इमस्य वीर्यं
प्रज्ञाबलेनास्य जिताः स्म सर्वे (४) ॥
मारात्मजानां यथ गङ्गबालिका
एतेन वीर्येण यथैव यूयम्।

---

१ "मनुष्य सिंहे" सिंहे नदिते सति ते स्थिरा न भवन्ति इत्यर्थः। "दिशो दशासु" दिक्षु दशसु।

२ "न सन्ति" न स्थिरा भविष्यन्ति इत्यर्थः।

३ "भोति" भवति। "एषो इमु" एष इमं। "मूढो च एषो अनभिज्ञ" मूढश्चैषोऽनभिज्ञः। "यदुत्थिहित्वा" यदुत्थाय। "लघु" लघु।

४ "अविधिज्ञमपराक्रमो" अविधिज्ञोऽपराक्रमो। "युष्मेव" यूयमेव। "युष्मि" यूयम्। "जानाथ" जानीथ। "इमस्य" अस्य।

क्षोभाय एकं न समर्थ चालितुं
प्रागेव यच्चिन्तयि घातयिष्ये (१) ॥

मा यूयमत्र च्छिणुयात मानसं
प्रसन्नचित्ता भवथा सगौरवाः ।
विवर्त्तमाना प्रकरोथ विग्रहं
भविष्यतेऽसौ त्रिभवेऽस्मि राजा (२) ॥

प्रेयालमेवं (३) ते सर्वे मारपुत्राः परिपूर्णपुत्रसहस्रं शुक्लपाक्षिकाश्च मारं पापीयसं पृथक् पृथग् गाथाभिरध्यभाषन्त ।

अथ खलु मारपापीयसः सेनापतिर्भद्रसेनो नाम स मारपापीयसं गाथाभिरध्यभाषत ।

ये ते तवानुयात्राः शक्रलोकपालाश्च ।
किन्नरगणाश्चासुरेन्द्राः कृताञ्जलिपुटाः प्रणते तस्मै (४) ॥

किं पुनरनुयात्रा ब्रह्मा आभास्वराश्च सुरदेवपुत्राश्च ।
शुद्धावासकास्तेपि च सर्वे प्रणते तस्मै (५) ॥

ये च तवेमे पुत्राः प्रज्ञामेधाविनो बलिनश्च ।

---

१ "यथ गङ्गवालिका" यथा गङ्गावालुकाः । मारात्मजानां सङ्ख्या यथा गङ्गावालुकास्तद्वदित्यर्थः । "समर्थ चालितुं" समर्थाश्चालयितुं । "यच्चिन्तयि" यदचिन्तयिष्ट । "घातयिष्ये" घातयिष्याम इति इत्यर्थः ।

२ "च्छिणुयात" च्छिणुत । "भवथा" भवत । "प्रकरोथ" प्रकुरुत । स्वच्छन्दकृत्या मामव्यवस्यान्वयात्मा कुरुत इत्यर्थः । "भविष्यतेऽसौ त्रिभवेऽस्मि" भविष्यत्यसौ त्रिभवेऽस्मिन् ।

३ "प्रेयालमेवं" प्रियमलमेवं प्रेयांसोऽलमेवमिति वार्थः सम्भाव्यते ।

४ "तवानुयात्राः" तवानुयातारः । "प्रणते तस्मै" प्रणमन्ति तम् ।

५ "पुनरनुयात्रा" पुनरनुयातारः । "ब्रह्मा आभास्वराश्च" ब्रह्माभास्वराश्च । "प्रणते तस्मै" प्रणमन्ति तम् ।

ते बोधिसत्त्वहृदयमनुप्रविष्टा नमस्यन्ति (१) ॥

याव्येष मारसेना अभीतिस्फुटयोजनानि यत्राद्यैः ।
भूयिष्ठ सर्वप्रेक्षी प्रसन्नमनसो हि निर्दोषम् (२) ॥

दृष्ट्वा यथा सुभीमां रौद्रां विकृतां चमुमिमां घोराम् ।
न च विस्मितो न चलितो ध्रुवमस्य जयो भवत्यद्य (३) ॥

स्थित यत्र च सेनेयं तत्र उलूकाः शिवाश्च विचरन्ति ।
वायसगर्दभरवितं निवर्त्तितव्यं चम शीघ्रम् (४) ॥

वीक्षस्व बोधिमण्डे विहतं पटशोभहंसकोकिलमयूराः ।
अभिप्रदक्षिणं करोन्ति ध्रुवमस्य जयो भवत्यद्य (५) ॥

यत्र स्थित सेनेयं तत्रमषिपांशवश्च वर्षन्ति ।
महिमण्डि कुसुमवृष्टिः कुरुष्व वचनं निवर्त्तयस्व (६) ॥

यत्र स्थित सेनेयं उत्कुलनिकुल तत्र कण्टकाकीर्णम् ।
महिमण्ड कनकनिर्मलु निवर्त्तितव्यं चमं प्राज्ञैः (७) ॥

---

१ "नमस्यन्ति" नमन्ति ।

२ "याव्येष" याव्येषा । "अभीतिस्फुटयोजनानि" अशीतिस्फुटयोजनविस्तीर्णा इत्यर्थः । "भूयिष्ठ सर्वप्रेक्षी" भविष्यति सर्वप्रेक्षिणां । "प्रसन्नमनसो हि निर्दोषम्" प्रसन्नमनसां हि निर्दोषा ।

३ "चमुमिमा" चमूमिमां । "भवत्यद्य" भविष्यत्यद्य ।

४ "स्थित" स्थिता । "निवर्त्तितव्यं" निवर्त्तयितव्यं । "चम" चमूः ।

५ "विहतं" विहगमाः "पट" कस्य पक्षिणः पट इति नाम तन्न जाने । "करोन्ति" कुर्वन्ति । "भवत्यद्य" भविष्यत्यद्य ।

६ "स्थित" स्थिता । "तत्रमषिपांशवश्च" तत्राषिपांशूंश्च । "महिमण्डि कुसुमवृष्टि कुरुष्व" महीमण्डले कुसुमवृष्टिं कुरु ।

७ "स्थित" स्थिता । "उत्कुलनिकुल" उत्कूलनिकूलं । "महिमण्ड कनकनिर्मलु" महीमण्डलं कनकनिर्मलं । अत्र कर्त्तव्यमित्यध्याहार्यम् । "चमं" चमूमित्यर्थः ।

दृष्ट्वा ति सुपिनि पूर्वे भेष्यसि प्रत्यसु यदि न गच्छसि ।
भस्म यमूष करिष्यति ऋषिभिरीर्ष्याः कृता यथा भस्म (१) ॥
राजायनो ऋषिवरो रोषितु आसीत् स ब्रह्मदत्तेन ।
उद्दग्ध दण्डकवने वर्षैर्बहुभिस्तृणं न जाता (२) ॥
ये केचित्सर्व लोके ऋषयो सुधाभव्रतचारिणस्तपोयुक्ताः ।
तेषामयं प्रधानो ह्यहिंसकः सर्वभूतानाम् (३) ॥
किं ते न श्रुत पूर्वा काये दीप्ताः सुलक्षणा यस्य ।
निष्क्रामति चागारात्सभवति बुद्धो जितक्लेशः (४) ॥
इम ईदृशी विभूति पूजार्थं निर्मिता जिनसुतेभिः ।
तं नूनमयसत्त्वो ह्ययाकृतिसम्प्रतिग्राही (५) ॥
ऊर्णा यथा सुविमला विराजते क्षेत्रकोटिनयुतेषु ।
जिह्मीकृता स्म प्रततपा निःसंशयमेष मारवराहन्ता (६) ॥
मूर्द्धं यथास्य देवैर्द्रष्टुं न शक्यं न वै भवग्रस्थैः ।

---

१ "ति सुपिनि" त्वया स्वप्नानि । "भेष्यति" भयं प्राप्स्येत्यर्थः । "प्रत्यसु" प्रत्यहो । "गच्छसि" गमिष्यति ।

२ "राजायनो ऋषिवरो रोषितु आसीत्" राजायन ऋषिवरो रोषित आसीत् । "उद्दग्ध दण्डकवने वर्षैर्बहुभिस्तृणं न जाता" उद्दग्धं दण्डकवनं (चर्यानेनर्षिणा) पुनस्तत्र बहुवर्षपर्यन्तं तृणानि न जातानि इत्यर्थः ।

३ "सर्व लोके" सर्वस्मिंल्लोके । "ऋषयो सुधाभव्रतचारिण" ऋषयः सुधाशव्रत-चारिणः ।

४ "न श्रुत पूर्वा" न श्रुतं पूर्वं । "दीप्ताः सुलक्षणा" दीप्तानि सुलक्षणानि । "निष्क्रामतिचागारात्" निष्क्रान्तश्चागारात् ।

५ "इम ईदृश विभूति" इमा ईदृश्यो विभूतयः । "जिनसुतेभिः" जिनसुतैः । "तं नून" त्वं नून ।

६ "क्षेत्रकोटिनयुतेषु" क्षेत्रकोटिनियुतेषु । "जिह्मीकृता स्म प्रततपा" जिह्मीकृतानि च प्रततपांसि ।

नूनं सर्वज्ञत्वं प्राप्स्यत्यन्यैरनुप्रविष्टैः (१) ॥
यथ मेरुचक्रवाडचन्द्रसूर्यशक्रब्रह्माणो वृचाश्च ।
पर्व्वतवराः प्रणते सर्वे महीमण्डम् (२) ॥
निःसंशयु पुण्यबली प्रज्ञाबलवांश्च ज्ञानबलवांश्च ।
चान्तिबलवांश्च वीर्य्यबलवानबलं कर्त्ता नमुचिपचान् (३) ॥
हस्ती यथा मत्यण्डं प्रमर्दते क्रोष्टुकान्यथा सिंहः ।
खद्योतां वा यथादित्यो भेत्स्यति सुगतस्तु तथा सेनाम् (४) ॥

एवं श्रुत्वाऽपरो मारपुत्रोऽतीव रोषात् संरक्तनयनोऽब्रवीत् ।

एकस्य वर्णानतिअप्रमेया
प्रभाषसे तस्य त्वमेककस्य ।
एको हि कर्त्तुं खलु किं समर्थो
महाबलं पश्यसि किं न भीमाम् (५) ॥

अथ दक्षिणपार्श्वान्मारप्रमर्दको मारपुत्र आह ।

सूर्य्यस्य लोके (६) न सहायकृत्यं
चन्द्रस्य सिंहस्य च चक्रवर्त्तिनः ।

---

१ "मूर्द्धं" मूर्द्धा । "प्रशु न शक्यं" द्रष्टुं न शक्यः ।

२ "यथ" यथा । "प्रणते सर्वे महीमण्डम्" प्रणमति सर्वो महीमण्डलः ।

३ "निःसंशयु" निःसंशयं । "नबलं" नबलान् ।

४ "मत्यण्डं" मर्त्यमण्डलं । "क्रोष्टुकान्यथा" क्रोष्टून्यथा । "खद्योतां" खद्योताम् ।

५ "वर्णानतिअप्रमेया" वर्णानामत्यप्रमेयां । "महाबलं" महाबलां । तस्य बोधिसत्त्वस्यैकस्यैव प्रशंसा क्रियते महाबलां भीमां मम सेनां त्वं किं न पश्यसि इति स्वहार्थः ।

६ "लोके" लोकेन इत्यर्थः ।

बोधौ निषण्णस्य च निश्चितस्य
न बोधिसत्त्वस्य सहायकृत्यम् ॥

अथ बोधिसत्त्वो मारस्य दुर्बलीकरणहेतोर्विकसितशतपत्त्रनिभं वदनं सञ्चारयति स्म । यं दृष्ट्वा मारः प्रपलायमानोऽभूत् । मम चमूर्बोधिसत्त्वस्य वदनं प्रविष्टेति मन्यमानः प्रपलायमानः पुनरेव प्रतिनिवृत्य सपरिवारो विविधानि प्रहरणानि बोधिसत्त्वस्योपर्युत्सृजति स्म सुमेरुमात्रांश्च पर्वतान् । ते च बोधिसत्त्वस्योपरि क्षिप्ताः पुष्पवितानानि विमानानि सन्तिष्ठन्ते स्म । ये च दृष्टिविषा आशीविषाः श्वासविषास्त्वाग्निज्वालामुत्सृजन्ति स्म । तच्चाग्निमण्डलं बोधिसत्त्वस्य प्रभामण्डलमिव सन्तिष्ठते स्म ।

अथ पुनरेव बोधिसत्त्वो दक्षिणेन पाणिना शीर्षं प्रमार्ष्टि स्म । मारश्च पश्यति स्म । बोधिसत्त्वस्य हस्ते खड्ग इति दक्षिणाभिमुखः प्रपलायते स्म । न किञ्चिदिति पुनरेव निवर्त्तते स्म । निवृत्य च बोधिसत्त्वस्योपरि नानाविधानि प्रहरणानि उत्सृजति स्म असिधनुःशरशक्तितोमरपरश्वधभुशुण्डीमुषलकणय(१) गदाचक्रवज्रमुद्गरपादपशिलापाशायोगुडानतिभयानकान् । ते चोत्क्षिप्तमात्रा नानाविधानि पुष्पदामानि पुष्पवितानानि इव सन्तिष्ठन्ते स्म । मुक्तकुसुमानि च महीं विकिरन्तो (२) माल्यदामानि चावलम्बमानानि बोधिवृक्षं विभूषयन्ति स्म ।

---

१ कणय इति सर्वत्रैवादर्शः पाठः । परन्तु अर्थो न बुध्यते कीदृशस्यायुधस्येदं नाम ।

२ "विकिरन्तो" विकीर्यमाणानि ।

तांश्च व्यूहविभूतिं दृष्ट्वा बोधिसत्त्वस्य मारः पापीयानीर्ष्यामा-त्सर्य्योपहतो बोधिसत्त्वमब्रवीत्। उत्तिष्ठोत्तिष्ठ हे राजकुमार राज्यं भुङ्क्ष्व तावत्तव पुण्यं कुतस्ते मोक्षप्राप्तिः।

अथ बोधिसत्त्वो धीरगम्भीरोदारश्लक्ष्णमधुरया वाचा मारं पापीयसमेतदवोचत्। त्वया तावत्पापीयन्नेकेन निरर्गलेन य-ज्ञेन कामेश्वरत्वं प्राप्तम्। मया त्वनेकानि यज्ञकोटिनियुतशत-सहस्राणि निरर्गलानि यष्टानि। करचरणनयनोत्तमाङ्गानि च निकृत्यार्थिभ्यो दत्तानि गृहधनधान्यशयनवसनं चङ्क्रमोद्या-नानि चानेकशो याचकेभ्यो निसृष्टानि सत्त्वानां मोक्षार्थिना॥

अथ खलु मारः पापीयान् बोधिसत्त्वं गाथया प्रत्यभाषत।

यज्ञो मया यष्टस्त्वमिहात्र साक्षी
निरर्गडः (१) पूर्व्वभवेऽनवद्यः।
तवेह साक्षी तु न कश्चिदस्ति
किञ्चित्प्रलापेन पराजितस्त्वम्॥

बोधिसत्त्व आह। इयं पापीयन्मम भूतधात्री प्रमाणमिति॥ अथ बोधिसत्त्वो मारं मारपर्षदञ्च मैत्रीकरुणापूर्व्वङ्गमेन चि-त्तेन स्फुरित्वा सिंहवदभीतोऽनुत्त्रस्तोऽत्रस्तो (२) ऽदीनोऽलीनो-ऽसंक्षुभितोऽलुलितो विगतभयलोमहर्षः शङ्खध्वजमीनकलश-स्वस्तिकाङ्कुशचक्राङ्कमध्येन जालावितानावनद्धेन सुरुचिरताम्र-

---

१ "निरर्गडः" निरर्गलः।

२ अनुत्रस्तोऽत्रस्तो इति वा पाठः। अत्रस्तो इत्यस्य अनायासं मन्यमान इत्यर्थं अभ्यस्यते।

नामवनखालङ्कृतेन मृदुतरुणसुकुमारेणानन्तकल्पापरिमितकु-शलमूलसम्भारोपचितेन दक्षिणेन पाणिना सर्व्वं कायं परि-मार्ज्य सलीलं महीं पराहन्ति स्म। तस्यां च वेलायामिमां गाथामभाषत।

इयं मही सर्व्वजगत्प्रतिष्ठा

अपक्षपाता सचराचरे समा।

इयं प्रमाणं मम नास्ति मे मृषा

साक्षीत्वमस्मिन् मम सम्प्रयच्छतु ॥

संस्पृष्टमात्रा चेयं महापृथिवी बोधिसत्त्वेन षड्विकारमक-म्पत सम्प्राकम्पत। अरणत् प्रारणत् सम्प्रारणत्। तद्यथापि नाम मागधिकानां कांस्यपात्री काष्ठेनाभ्याहता रणत्यनुरणत्येवमेवेयं महापृथिवी बोधिसत्त्वेन पाणिनाऽऽहता रणत्यनुरणति स्म।

अथ खलु यस्यां त्रिसाहस्रमहासाहस्रलोकधातौ स्थावरा नाम महापृथिवीदेवता सा कोटीशतपृथिवीदेवतापरिवारा सर्व्वां महापृथिवीं सम्प्रकम्प्य नातिदूरे बोधिसत्त्वस्य पृथिवीतलं भित्वाऽर्द्धकायमुन्नाम्य सर्व्वालङ्कारप्रतिमण्डिता येन बोधिसत्त्व-स्तेनावनतकाया प्राञ्जलीकृता बोधिसत्त्वमेतदवोचत्। एवमेवं महापुरुषैवमेतद् यथा त्वयाभिहितं वयमत्र प्रत्यक्षाः। अपि-तु भगवंस्त्वमेव सदेवकस्य लोकस्य परमसाक्षीभूतश्च। एवमुक्त्वा स्थावरा महापृथिवीदेवता मारपापीयांसमनेकप्रकारं निर्भर्त्स्य बोधिसत्त्वं चाभ्यर्च्य स्तुत्वा विविधञ्च स्वकं प्रभावं सन्दर्श्य सप-रिवारा तत्रैवान्तर्दधे।

तं श्रुत्वा भेदमीरवं स शठः ससैन्य-
उत्त्रस्त भिन्नहृदयः प्रपलान सर्व्वे ।
श्रुत्वैव सिंहनदितं वने हि शृगालाः
काकेव लोष्टुपतने सहसा प्रणष्टाः (१) ॥

अथ खलु मारः पापीयान् दुःखितो दुर्म्मना अनात्तमना अपत्रपमाणरूपो मानाभिभवान्न गच्छति स्म न निवर्त्तते स्म न पलायते स्म। पश्चान्मुखं स्थित्वा उत्तरोसेना(२) मामन्त्रयते स्म। सहिताः समग्रास्तावद्भवन्तस्तिष्ठन्तु मुहूर्त्तं यावद्वयं ज्ञास्यामो यदि तावच्छक्यतेऽयमनुनयेनोत्थापयितुम्। मा खल्वेवंरूपस्य सत्त्वरत्नस्य सहसा विनाशो भूदिति॥

अथ खलु मारः पापीयान् स्वा दुहितृरामन्त्रयते स्म। गच्छध्वं यूयं कन्यका बोधिमण्डमुपसङ्क्रम्य बोधिसत्त्वस्य जिज्ञासनां कुरुत। किं सरागोऽथ वीतरागः किं मूढोऽथ प्राज्ञः किं तत्त्वार्थदेशज्ञोऽथा(३) पलायनो दीनो वा धीरो वेति॥ इदं खलु वचनं श्रुत्वा अप्सरसो येन बोधिमण्डो येन च बोधिसत्त्वस्तेनोपसङ्क्रामन्नुपसङ्क्रम्य बोधिसत्त्वस्य पुरतः स्थित्वा द्वात्रिंशदाकारां स्त्रीमायामुपदर्शयन्ति स्म। कतमा द्वात्रिंशदाकारा। तद्यथा। काश्चित्तत्रार्द्धवदनमाच्छादयन्ति स्म। काश्चिदुन्नतान् कठिनान् पयोधरान्दर्शयन्ति स्म। काश्चिदर्द्धविहसितैर्दन्तावलीर्दर्शयन्ति

१ "उत्त्रस्त" उत्त्रस्तो। "प्रपलान सर्व्वे" इत्यस्य स मारः प्रपलायमानोऽभूत् सर्व्वे चानुचराः प्रपलायमाना बभूवुरित्यर्थः। "काकेव लोष्टुपतने" काका इव लोष्टपतने।

२ "उत्तरोसेनां" उत्तरसेनां उत्तीर्थं च सेनां पूर्व्वमुत्तीर्णां सेनां उत्तरसाधिकां सेनां चेत्यर्थः सम्भाव्यते।

३ यत्र किमथ देशश्च इति पाठान्तरम्।

स्म । काश्चिद्बाहूनुत्क्षिप्य विजृम्भमाणकक्षं दर्शयन्ति स्म । काश्चिद्बिम्बफलोपमोष्ठान्दर्शयन्ति स्म । काश्चिदर्द्धनिमीलितैर्नयनैर्बोधिसत्त्वं निरीक्षन्ते स्म । दृष्ट्वा च शीघ्रं शीघ्रं निमीलयन्ति स्म । काश्चिदर्द्धप्रावृतान् पयोधरान्दर्शयन्ति स्म । काश्चिच्छिथिलाम्बरमेखलां श्रोणिं दर्शयन्ति स्म । काश्चित् सुमेखलां तदनुकूलां निर्व्वासितां श्रोणिं दर्शयन्ति स्म । काश्चिद् रणुरणुशब्दान्नूपुरैः कुर्व्वन्ति स्म । काश्चिदेकाङ्गुलीं स्तनान्तरेषूपदर्शयन्ति स्म । काश्चिद्विनग्नानर्द्धोरूनुपदर्शयन्ति स्म । काश्चिच्छिरःस्कंऽसेषु च पत्रगुप्ताः शुकशारिकाश्चोपविष्टा उपदर्शयन्ति स्म । काश्चिदर्द्धकटाक्षैर्बोधिसत्त्वं निरीक्षन्ते स्म । काश्चित् सुनिर्व्वस्त्रा अपि दुर्न्निर्व्वस्त्राः कुर्व्वन्ति स्म । काश्चिज्जघनरसनाः कम्पयन्ति स्म । काश्चित्सम्भ्रान्ता इव सविलासमितस्ततश्चङ्क्रमन्ते स्म । काश्चिन्नृत्यन्ते स्म । काश्चिद्गायन्ति स्म । काश्चिद्विलपन्ति स्म । काश्चिल्लज्जन्ते स्म । काश्चित्कदलीमिव वायुविधुतामूरूं कम्पयन्ति स्म । काश्चिद्गम्भीरं स्तनन्ति स्म । काश्चिदंशुकाप्रावृतां सघण्टां रसनां विहृत्य चङ्क्रमन्ते स्म । काश्चिद्वस्त्राण्याभरणानि च पृथिव्यां छारयन्ति (१) स्म । काश्चिद्गुह्यकाप्रकाशानि सर्व्वाभरणान्युपदर्शयन्ति स्म । काश्चिद्गन्धानुलिप्तबाहूनुपदर्शयन्ति स्म । काश्चिद्गन्धानुलेपन(२)कुण्डलान्युपदर्शयन्ति स्म । काश्चिदवगुण्ठितकया वदनान्याच्छादयन्ति स्म क्षणेन चोपदर्शयन्ति स्म ।

---

१ "छारयन्ति" विमुच्य स्थापयन्ति इत्यर्थः ।
२ "अनुलेपन" अनुलिप्त- ।

काश्चित् पूर्व्वहसितरमितक्रीडितान्यन्योन्यं स्मारयन्ति स्म पुनरपि लज्जिता इव तिष्ठन्ति स्म। काश्चित्कुमारीरूपाण्यप्रसूतिरूपाणि मध्यस्त्रीरूपाणि चोपदर्शयन्ति स्म। काश्चित्कामोपहितेन बोधिसत्त्वं निमन्त्रयन्ते स्म। काश्चिन्मुक्तकुसुमैर्बोधिसत्त्वमवकिरन्ति स्म पुरतश्च स्थित्वा बोधिसत्त्वस्याशयं मीमांसन्ते स्म वदनञ्च निरीक्षन्ते स्म। किमयं रक्तेन्द्रियैः पश्यत्याहोस्विद्दूरीकरोति नयने ईर्ष्यते वा नवेति ताः पश्यन्ति स्म। बोधिसत्त्वस्य वदनं शुद्धविमलं चन्द्रमण्डलमिव राहुविनिर्मुक्तं सूर्य्यमिव प्रोद्यमानं यूपमिव कनकमयं विकसितमिव सहस्रपत्रं हव्यावसिक्तमिवानलं मेरुमिवाचलं चक्रवाडमिवाभ्युद्गतं गुप्तेन्द्रियं नागमिव सुदान्तचित्तम्॥

अथ ता मारदुहितरो भूयस्या मात्रया बोधिसत्त्वस्य सुलोभार्थमिमा गाथा अभाषन्त।

सुवसन्तके ऋतुवरे आगतके
रतिमो प्रिया फुल्लितपादपके।
तव रूप सुरूप सुशोभनको
वशवर्त्तिसुलक्षणविचित्रितको (१)॥

वयं जात सुजात सुसंस्थितिकाः
सुखकारण देवनराणसम्भूतिकाः।
उत्थि लघु परिभुञ्ज सुयौवनकं

---

१ "रतिमो प्रिया" रमाम हे प्रिय इत्यर्थः। "रूपसुरूपसुशोभनको" रूपं सुरूपं सुशोभनकं। तव रूपमयं सुशोभनको इति वा पाठः। "वशवर्त्तिसुलक्षणविचित्रितको" वशवर्त्तिसुलक्षणविचित्रितकं।

दुर्लभ बोधि निवर्त्तय मानसकम् (१) ॥
पेक्षसि ताव इमा मरुकन्य सुलङ्कृतिका-
स्तव कारण सज्जित भूषित आगतिकाः ।
को रूपमिमं समवेक्ष्य न रज्यति रागरतो
अपि जर्जरकाष्ठवशोषितजीवितकः (२) ॥
केश मृदू सुरभीवरगन्धिनिका
मुकुटकुण्डलपत्त्रविबोधितआननिकाः ।
सुललाट सुलेपनआननिकाः
पद्मविशुद्धविशालसुलोचनिकाः (३) ॥
परिपूरितचन्द्रनिभाननिका
बिम्बसुपक्वनिभाधरिकाः ।
शङ्खकुन्दहिमशुक्लसुदन्तिनिकाः
प्रेक्ष कान्त रतिलालसिकाः (४) ॥

---

१ "जात सुजात" जाताः सुजाताः । "सुखकारण देवनराणवसन्तुतिकाः" सुखकारणार्थं देवनराणामवसन्तोषिका इत्यर्थः । "उत्थि" उत्थाय । "परिभुञ्ज" परिभुङ्क्ष्व । "दुर्लभ बोधि" दुर्लभाद्बोधेः ।

२ "पेक्षसि ताव इमा मरुकन्य सुलङ्कृतिकाः" प्रेक्षसे तावदिमा मरुत्कन्याः स्वलङ्कृताः । "कारण सज्जित भूषित आगतिकाः" कारणाय सज्जिता भूषिता आगताः । "जर्जरकाष्ठवशोषितजीवितकः" जर्जरकाष्ठावशोषितजीवितकः ।

३ "केश मृदू सुरभीवरगन्धिनिका" केशा मृदवः सुरभिवरगन्धिकाः । "मुकुटकुण्डलपत्त्रविबोधितआननिकाः" मुकुटकुण्डलपत्त्रविबोधिताननकाः । "सुललाट सुलेपनआननिकाः" सुललाटाः सुलिप्ताननकाः । "पद्मविशुद्धविशालसुलोचनिकाः" विशुद्धपद्मविशालसुलोचनका इत्यर्थः ।

४ "चन्द्रनिभाननिकाः" चन्द्रनिभाननकाः । "बिम्बसुपक्वनिभाधरिकाः" सुपक्वबिम्बनिभाधरका इत्यर्थः । "दन्तिनिकाः" दन्तकाः । "प्रेक्ष" प्रेक्षस्व ।

कठिनपीनपयोधरउद्गतिका-
त्रिवलीकृतमध्यसुसुन्दरिका: ।
जघनाङ्गणचारुसुविस्फुरिका:
प्रेक्षसु नाथ सुकामिनिका: (१) ॥
गजभुजसन्निभऊरुणिका
वलयनिरन्तरबाहुनिका: ।
काञ्चीवरश्रोणिसुमण्डितिका:
प्रेक्ष हि नाथ इमास्तव दासिनिका: (२) ॥
हंसगतिसुविलम्बितगामिनिका
मञ्जुमनोज्ञसुमन्मथभाषिणिका: ।
ईदृशरूपसुभूषिणिका
दिव्यरतीषु सुपण्डितिका: (३) ॥
गीतकवादितनृत्यसुशिक्षितिका
रतिकारणजातिसुरूपिणिका: ।
यदि नेच्छसि कामसुलालसिका:

---

१ "कठिनपीनपयोधरउद्गतिका" उद्गतकठिनपीनपयोधरा इत्यर्थः। "जघनाङ्गणचारुसुविस्फुरिका:" चारुजघनाङ्गणसुविस्फुरिता इत्यर्थः। "प्रेक्षसु" प्रेक्षस्व।

२ "गजभुजसन्निभऊरुणिका" गजभुजसन्निभोरुका:। "बाहुनिका:" बाहुका:। "काञ्चीवरश्रोणिसुमण्डितिका:" काञ्चीवरसुमण्डितश्रोणिका इत्यर्थः। "प्रेक्ष" प्रेक्षस्व। "दासिनिका: दासिका:।

३ "मञ्जुमनोज्ञसुमन्मथभाषिणिका:" मन्मथमञ्जुमनोज्ञसुभाषिका इत्यर्थः। मन्मथमञ्जुमनोज्ञसुमनोज्ञभाषिका इति वा पाठः। "ईदृशरूपसुभूषिणिका:" ईदृशरूपसुभूषिता:। "दिव्यरतीषु सुपण्डितिका:" दिव्यरतिषु सुपण्डितका:।

सुष्ठु सुवस्त्रितकोऽसि भृशं खलु लोके (१) ॥

निधि दृष्टि यथा हि पलायति को

कोपि नरो धनसौख्यमजानक मूढमना: ।

त्वमपि तथैव हि रागमजानमको यः

स्वयमागतिकास्त्र हि भुञ्जसि कामिनिका: (२) ॥

अथ खलु भिक्षवो बोधिसत्त्वोऽनिमिषनयन: प्रहसितवदन: स्मितमुखोऽविकोपितैरिन्द्रियैरनभिसंस्कृतैर्गात्रैरजिह्मोऽरक्तोऽदुष्टोऽमूढ: शैलेन्द्रवदकम्प्योऽनवलीनो नावदीर्णोऽसम्पीडित: सुसंस्थितया च बुद्ध्या स्वाधीनेन ज्ञानमुखेनात्यन्तसुप्रहीणत्वात् क्लेशानां श्लक्ष्णया मधुरया वाचा ब्रह्मातिरेकेण घोषेण कलविङ्करुतेन स्वरेण वल्गुना मनोज्ञेन ता मारदुहितॄन् (३) गाथाभि: प्रत्यभाषत ।

कामा भो बहुदुःखसञ्चया दुःखमूला

ध्यानाधीततपस्स भ्रंसनी अदृढानाम् ।

न स्त्रीकामगुणेभिस्तृप्तिकां विदुराहुः

प्रज्ञा तृप्तिकरो भविष्यमबुधानाम् (४) ॥

---

१ "गीतकवादितनृत्यसुशिक्षितिका" गीतवादितनृत्यसुशिक्षितकाः । "रतिकारणजातसुकल्पितिका" रतिकारणार्थं जाताः सुकल्पितिका इत्यर्थः ।

२ "निधि दृष्टि" निधिं दृष्ट्वा । "पलायति को" पलायति कः । "धनसौख्यमजानक:" धनसौख्याज्ञानवान् इत्यर्थः । "रागमजानमको" रागाज्ञानवान् इत्यर्थः । "स्वयमागतिकास्त्र हि भुञ्जसि" स्वयमागता न हि भुङ्क्ते ।

३ "दुहितॄन्" दुहितॄः ।

४ "ध्यानाधीततपस्स भ्रंसनी" ध्यानाधीततपसश्च भ्रंशका इत्यर्थः । "स्त्रीकामगुणेभिस्तृप्तिकां विदुराहुः" स्त्रीकामगुणैस्तृप्तिः (न भवति इति) विद्वांस आहुः । "प्रज्ञा तृप्तिकरो भविष्यमबुधानाम्" प्रज्ञया तृप्तिकरो भविष्यामि अबुधानामित्यर्थः ।

कामां सेवयतो विवर्द्धते पुनस्तृष्णा
पीत्वा वै लवणोदकं यथा नरु कश्चि।
नात्मार्थे न परार्थि भोतिहा प्रतिपन्नो
आत्मार्थे च परार्थि उत्सुको भविताऽहम् (१)॥
फेनबुद्बुदतुल्यसन्निभं तव रूपं
मायारङ्गमिवा वितथावितथ स्वमतेन।
क्रीडा वै सुपिनेव अध्रुवा अपिनित्या
बालानां सद चित्तमोहना अबुधानाम् (२)॥
नेत्रा बुद्बुदतुल्यसादृशा तुम
त्वचनद्धाः कठिनशोणितपिण्डमुद्गतम्।
यथा गण्डउदरो मूत्रपुरीषसञ्चयोऽ-
शुचोक्षः कर्मक्लेशसमुत्थितो दुःखयन्त्रः (३)॥
सम्मूढा ये हि बालबुद्धयो न तु विज्ञाः
शुभतो कल्पयमान आशयं वितथेन।
संसारे बहुकालसंसरी दुःखमूले

---

१ "कामां" कामान्। "नरु कश्चि" नरस्य कस्यचिदित्यर्थः। "परार्थि भोतिहा प्रतिपन्नो" परार्थं भवतीह प्रतिपन्नः। "भविताहम्" भवाम्यहमित्यर्थः।

२ तुल्यसन्निभमिति शब्दद्वये अन्यतरस्यैकस्याभावश्चकला। "मायारङ्गमिवा" मायारङ्ग इव। "वितथावितथ" वितथावितथं। "सुपिनेव" स्वप्नमिव। "अपिनित्या" अप्यनित्या इत्यर्थः। "सद" सदा।

३ "नेत्रा बुद्बुदतुल्यसादृशा तुम" नेत्रे बुद्बुदतुल्ये सादृशा तुम इति अनयोरप्यत्र। "त्वचनद्धाः" त्वङ्नद्धे। "कठिनशोणितपिण्डमुद्गतम्" उद्गतकठिनशोणितपिण्डे एव इत्यर्थः। "गण्डउदरो मूत्रपुरीषसञ्चयो" गुह्योदरौ मूत्रपुरीषसञ्चयौ। "अशुचोक्षः कर्मक्लेशसमुत्थितो दुःखयन्त्रः" अशुची उक्षौ कर्मक्लेशसमुत्थितौ दुःखयन्त्रौ।

अनुभोक्ता निरयेषु वेदनां बहुदुःखाम् (१) ॥

शोणिः प्रस्रवते विगन्धिका प्रतिकूला
जरजर्ज्जरमाश्रु संस्थिता यथ यन्त्रम्।
भूतं युष्मि निरीक्षिमि यथ माया-
हेतुः प्रत्ययतः प्रवर्त्तथावितथेन (२) ॥

दृष्ट्वा कामगुणांश्च निर्गुणां गुणहीना-
नार्य्यज्ञानपथस्य उत्पथां वितथा च।
विषपत्राग्निसमांश्च महोरगां यथ क्रुद्धां
बाला अत्र हि मूर्च्छिता ताः सुखसञ्ज्ञा (३) ॥

कामदासु भवीति यो नरः प्रमदानां
शील उत्पथि ध्यायि उत्पथि मतिहीनो।
ज्ञान सो हि सुन्दरि तिष्ठते लोको
योऽसौ धर्म्मरतिं जहित्व नो रमित कामैः (४) ॥

---

१ "भ्रमतो कल्पयमान" भ्रमं कल्पयमानाः। "बहुकालसंसरी" बहुकालसंसारिणि। "अनुभोक्ता" अनुभोक्तारः।

२ "शोणिः प्रस्रवते विगन्धिका प्रतिकूला जरजर्ज्जरमाश्र" शोणितः प्रस्रवन्ति विगन्धकाः प्रतिकूला जरजर्ज्जरपादाश्च। "यथ यन्त्रम्" यथा यन्त्रम्। "भूतं युष्मि निरीक्षिमि" यथार्थभूतानि युष्मान् निरीक्षामि इत्यर्थः। "यथ मायाहेतुः" यथा मायाहेतुः। "प्रवर्त्तथावितथेन" प्रवर्त्तध्वेऽवितथेन।

३ "निर्गुणां" निर्गुणान्। "उत्पथां वितथा च" उत्पथान् वितथांश्च। "महोरगां यथ क्रुद्धां" महोरगान् यथा क्रुद्धान्। "मूर्च्छिता ताः सुखसञ्ज्ञा" मूर्च्छितास्तेषु सुखसञ्ज्ञिनः।

४ "कामदासु भवीति" कामदासो भवति। "शील उत्पथि ध्यायि उत्पथि" शीलमुत्पथमिति (येन ज्ञानेन) ध्यायति उत्पथे। "ज्ञान सो हि" ज्ञानं तद्धि। "तिष्ठत लोको" तिष्ठति लोकम्। "योऽसौ धर्मरतिं जहित्व नो रमित कामैः" योऽसौ धर्मरतिं त्यक्त्वा नो रमति कामैः। यः कोऽपि जनः धर्मरतिं त्यक्त्वा कामैर्नो रमति अपि तु रमत्येव इति भावः। अत्र नो इत्यनेन काकुः सूच्यते।

नो रागेण सखी वशाम्यहं न च दोषै-
र्नो तैर्नित्याशुभात्मभिर्वसि सार्द्धम्।
अरतीयरतीयसंवसेन च सार्द्धं
निर्मुक्तं मम चित्तु मारुतो गगणेवा (१) ॥
पूर्णं सर्व्व जगत्त्वमीदृशैर्यदिह स्यात्
कल्पन्ताभिः सह समाश्रितो विचरयेयम्।
नो वा मह्य खिलं न रज्यना न च मोहो
आकाशसमतुल्यमानसा जिन भोन्ति (२) ॥
यद्यपीह रुधिरास्थिवर्जिता
देवअप्सर सुनिर्मलाः शुभाः ।
तेऽपि सर्व्वि सुमहद्भये स्थिता
नित्यभावरहिता अशाश्वताः (३) ॥

अथ खलु ता मारदुहितरः सुशिक्षिताः स्त्रीमायासु भूयस्या मात्रया रागमदद्दर्पं सञ्जनय्य चेष्टामुपदर्श्य गात्राणि विभूषयित्वा स्त्रीमायामुपदर्श्य बोधिसत्त्वं प्रलोभयन्ति स्म । तत्रेदमुच्यते ।

तृष्णारतीरतिश्च सहिता प्रमद मधुरा
मारसमीरिताः सुलक्षिताश्चरितमुपगताः ।

---

१ "सखी" सख। "नित्याशुभात्मभिर्वसि" नित्यमशुभात्मभिर्वसामि। "अरतीयरतीयसंवसेन" अरतिरतसंवासकेन। "चित्तु" चित्तं। "गगणेवा" गगने इव।

२ "पूर्णं सर्वं जगत्त्वमीदृशैर्यदिह" पूर्णं सर्वं जगत् त्वादृशीभिर्यदीह। "विचरयेयम्" विचरेयम्। "मह्य" मम। "रज्यना न च मोहो" रञ्जना न च मोहः। "जिन भोन्ति" जिना भवन्ति।

३ "देवअप्सर" देवाप्सरसः। "तेऽपि सर्वि" ता अपि सर्वाः।

वायुसमीरिता इव किसलयास्तरुणतरुलता
नृत्यत लोभयं नृपसुतं द्रुमविटपगतम् (१) ॥
एष वसन्तकालसमयः प्रवर ऋतुवरो
नारीनराण हर्षण करोति निहततमरजः ।
कोकिलहंसमयूररविता द्विजगणकलिलः
काल उपस्थितोऽनुभवितुं मदनगुणरतिम् (२) ॥
कल्पसहस्रशीलनिरतो व्रततपचरितो
निश्चल शैलराजसदृशस्तरुणरविवपुः ।
मेघनिनाद वल्गुवचनो मृगपतिनिनदो
वचनमुवाच सोऽर्थसहितं जगति हितकरः (३) ॥
कामविवादवैरकलहाः
मरणभयकरा बालजनोपसेविताः ।
सदा बुद्धजनरहिताः प्राप्नुयु
कालु यत्र सुगतैरमृतमधिगतम् (४) ॥
अद्य भविष्य मारु जिनिया
दशबल अर्हन् माय निदर्शयन्ति ।
अवदन् प्रणु कमलमुखा

---

१ "हल्लरतीरतिष चषिता प्रमद" हल्लारतिरतिचषिताः प्रमदाः । "तरुण-तरुलता" तरुणतरुलताया इत्यर्थः । "नृत्यत लोभयं" नृत्यन्ति स्म लोभयन्त्यः ।

२ "नारीनराण हर्षण" नारीनराणां हर्षं । "निहततमरजः" निहततमो-रजाः । "मयूररविता" मयूररुतं ।

३ "व्रततपचरितो" चरितव्रततपा इत्यर्थः । "निश्चल" निश्चलः । "मेघनिनाद" मेघनिनादः ।

४ "प्राप्नुयु कालु" प्राप्ताः कालं प्रसह्य इति भावः ।

राज भविष्यसेश्वरवरः क्षितिपति बलवान् (१)॥

तूर्य्यसहस्र सम्प्रभणिते प्रमदवरगणे

किं मुनिवेशकेण भवतो विरम तिभजे (२)॥

बोधिसत्त्व उवाच।

भेष्यि अहं हि राजा त्रिभवे दिवि भुवि महितो

ईश्वर धर्म्मचक्रकरणो दशबलु बलवान्।

शैक्ष्याशैक्ष्यपुत्रनयुतैः सतत समितमभिनतो

धर्म्मरती रमिष्य विषयैर्न रमति मनः (३)॥

ता आहुः।

यावच्च यौवनं सुललितं प्रथमवयधरो

यावच्च व्याधि नाक्रमते न च जरं।

अस्मि च यावच्च रूपयौवनधरो वयमपि च

---

१ "भविष्य" भविष्यसि। "मार जिनिया" मारं जित्वा। "दशबल चर्मम्" दशबलोऽचर्मम्। "माय निदर्शयन्ति" मायां निदर्शयिष्यति। "अवदन्" मारदुःखितोऽवदन् इति शेषार्थः। "कमलमुखा" हे कमलमुख। "राज भविष्यसेश्वरवरः क्षितिपति बलवान्" राजा भविष्यसीश्वरवरः क्षितिपतिर्बलवान् इति। अत्र राज भविष्यसे चक्रवर्त्तीश्वरवरः क्षितिपति बलवानिति वा पाठः।

२ "तूर्यसहस्र सम्प्रभणिते" तूर्यसहस्रे सम्प्रध्वनिते सति इत्यर्थः। "प्रमदवरगणे" प्रमदावरगणेन इत्यर्थः। "मुनिवेशकेण" मुनिवेशेनेत्यर्थः। "तिभजे" त्रिभवे त्रिलोके इति यावत्। अस्मिन् श्लोके उत्तरार्द्धं नास्ति। पाठोऽपि अन्यपुस्तकेषु सर्वत्रैतादृशः। अन्वयस्तु पूर्वश्लोके।

३ "भेष्यि अहं" भविष्याम्यहं। "महितो ईश्वरधर्मचक्रकरणो" महित ईश्वरो धर्मचक्रकरणो, धर्मचक्रकारको धर्मचक्रप्रवर्त्तक इति यावत्। "दशबलु" दशबलः। "शैक्ष्याशैक्ष्यपुत्रनयुतैः" शिक्ष्याशिक्ष्यपुत्रनियुतैः। "सतत समितमभिनतो" सततं समन्तादभिनत इत्यर्थः। अत्र सततमभिनता इति वा पाठः। "धर्मरती रमिष्य" धर्मरतिभी रमिष्यामि। विषयैर्न रमति मन इत्यत्र ममेत्यध्याहार्यं यतो मम मनो विषयैर्न रमति इत्यर्थः।

सुखी तावदनुभुङ्क्ष्व कामरतयः प्रहर्षितवदनः (१)॥

बोधिसत्त्व आह।

यावच्च दुर्लभोऽद्य लभितः क्षणवर अमृतो
यावच्च वर्जिता क्षणदुःखा असुरसुरपुरो।
यावज्जराव्याधिमरणं न कुपितं रिपव-
स्तावद्ध भावयिष्ये सुपथमभयपुरगमनम् (२) ॥

ता आहुः।

देवपुरालयेऽप्सरवृतस्त्रिदशपतिरिव
यामसुयामसन्तुषितको अमरवरस्तुतो।
मारपुरे च कामरतयः प्रमदवशगतः
क्रीडयनुभुङ्क्ष्व अस्माभिर्महाविपुलरतिकर (३) ॥

बोधिसत्त्व आह।

काम तृणाग्रबिन्दुचपलाः शरदघनसमा
पन्नगकन्यरोषसदृशा भृशभयकरणाः।
शक्रसुयामदेवस्तुषिता नमुचिवशगताः

---

१ "प्रथमवयधरो" प्रथमवयोधारि। "व्याधि नाक्रमते" व्याधिर्नाक्रमते। "न च जरं" न च जरा। "सुखी" सुखं। "कामरतयः" कामरतीन्।

२ "लभितः क्षणवर अमृतो" लब्धं क्षणवरेणामृतं। "असुरसुरपुरो" सुरासुरपुरी। "कुपितं रिपवस्तावद्ध" कुपिता रिपवस्तावत्। अत्र सेत्यस्य देवलोकोदीपकन्यायेनोभयत्रान्वयः। "भावयिष्ये" चिन्तयिष्यामि इत्यर्थः।

३ "अप्सरवृतः" अप्सरोवृतः। "अमरवरस्तुतो" अमरवरस्तुतः। "कामरतयः" कामरतीन् कामरत्यात्मिकां क्रीडामनुभोक्ष्यसीति भावः। "प्रमदवशगतः" प्रमदावशगतः। क्रीडयनुभुङ्क्ष्व अस्माभिः" क्रीडामनुभुङ्क्ष्वास्माभिरेवेति सङ्क्षेपार्थः। अत्र क्रीडामनुभुङ्क्ष्व अस्माभिरिति वा पाठः।

कोऽत्र रमेत नार्य्यभिलषिते व्यसनपरिगते (१) ॥

ता आहुः।

पुष्पित पद्मोमां तरुवरां तरुणकिशलयां
कोकिलजीवञ्जीवकरुतां मधुकरविरुताम्।
स्निग्धसुनीलकुञ्चितमृदुधरणितलरुहे
किन्नरसिंहसेवित वने रम सुयुवतिभिः (२) ॥

बोधिसत्त्व उवाच।

कालवशात् पुष्पित द्रुमे किशलय तरवो
भृङ्गा पिपासिता मधुकरा कुसुममभिगताः।
भास्कर शोषयिष्यति यदा धरणितलरुहां
पूर्व्वजिनोपभुक्तममृतं व्यवसितमिह मे (३) ॥

मारदुहितर आहुः।

प्रेक्ष हि तावचन्द्रवदनावदनावलिनिभा
वाच मनोज्ञ श्लक्ष्ण दशना हिमरजतनिभाः।
ईदृश दुर्लभाः सुरपुरे कुत मनुजपुरे

१ "काम" कामाः। "शरदघनसमाः" शरद्घनसमाः। "पन्नगकन्यरोषसदृशा भयभयकरकाः" पन्नगकन्यारोषसदृशा भयभयकारका इत्यर्थः। "नार्य्यभिलषिते" अनार्याभिलषिते इत्यर्थः। "व्यसनपरिगते" व्यसनापरिगते व्यसनयुक्ते इति यावत्।

२ "पुष्पित पद्मोमां तरुवरकिशलयां" पुष्पितानि पद्मोमानि तरुवानि किशलयानि "जीवञ्जीवकरुतां" जीवञ्जीवकरुतानि। "मधुकरविरुतां" मधुकरविरुतानि। "धरणितलरुहे" धरणीतलरुहे। "सिंहसेवित" सिंहसेविते।

३ "पुष्पित द्रुमे" पुष्पिता द्रुमे। "किशलय तरवो" किशलयास्तरवो। "भास्कर" भास्करः। "धरणितलरुहां" धरणीतलरुहाम् इत्यल्पगुणादीनिति भावः।

ते त्वया लब्ध ये सुरवरैरभिलषित सदा (१) ॥

बोधिसत्त्व आह ।

पश्यामि कायममेध्यमशुचिं क्रिमिकुलभरितं
जर्जरभिन्धनस्य भिदुरमसुखपरिगतम् ।
यत्सचराचरस्य जगतः परमसुखकरं
तत्पदमच्युतं प्रतिलभे बुधजनमहितम् (२) ॥

ता आहुः ।

चतुःषष्टिकामकलितानि चानुभविया
नूपुरमेखला अभिहनो विगलितवसना: ।
कामशराहता: समदना: प्रहसितवदना:
किं तव आर्य्यपुत्र विकृतं यदि न भजसे (३) ॥

बोधिसत्त्व आह ।

सर्व्वभवेषु दोष विदितोऽवविधुतरजा
कामासिशक्तिशूलसदृशाः समधुक्षुरसमा: ।
सर्पशिरोऽग्निकर्षुसदृशा: सुविदित इह मे ते

---

१ "प्रेष" प्रेषस्व। "वदननिभा" (आसां) वदननिभास्व प्रेषस्वेति स्पष्टार्थः। "वाच मनोज्ञ श्लक्ष्ण" वाचो मनोज्ञा श्लक्ष्णाः। "ईदृश" ईदृश्यः। "कुत मनुजपुरे" कुतो मनुजपुरे। "ते त्वया लब्ध ये" तास्त्वया लब्धा याः। "अभिलषित सदा" अभिलषिताः सदा।

२ "क्रिमिकुलभरितं" क्रिमिकुलपूर्णमित्यर्थः। "असुखपरिगतम्" असुखपरिगतमित्यर्थः। "प्रतिलभे" प्रतिलप्स्यामि।

३ "चानुभविया" चानुभूय अनुभवायेति भावः। "अभिहनो" अभिहता आहताः शब्दायमाना इति स्पष्टार्थः। "किन्तव आर्य्यपुत्र विकृतं यदि न भजसे" हे आर्य्यपुत्र अस्मान् दृष्ट्वा तव मनः किं विकृतं न जातं (यदि) यतोऽस्मान्न भजसे इति समग्रस्पष्टार्थः।

बहुनारिसङ्घं त्यजामि गुणचर प्रमदाः (१)॥

ता बहुभिः प्रकारनयुतैः प्रमद गुणकरै-

र्लोभयितुं न शक्तुः सुगतराज करभगतिम्।

लज्जिभि राचपलं मुनिनं प्रपतित चरणे

गौरवु तुष्ट प्रेम जनिया स्तुविषु हितकरम् (२)॥

निर्मलपद्मगर्भसदृशा शरदिशशिमुखा

सर्पिहुतार्चितेजसदृशा कणकगिरिनिभा।

सिध्यतु चिन्तितानि प्रणिधिर्भव व्रतचरिता-

त्मानु पतारय जगत् व्यसनपरिगतम् (३)॥

ताः कर्णिकारचम्पकनिभं स्तविय बहुविधं

कृत्व प्रदक्षिणमतिशयं गिरिरिव अचलम्।

गत्य पितुर्निपत्य शिरसा इदमवचि गिरं

---

१ "दोष विदितोऽवविधुतरजा" दोषो विदितोऽवविधुतरजाश्च इत्यर्थः। "कामाग्निशिखज्वलसदृशाः" कामा अग्निशिखाज्वलसदृशाः। "सर्पशिरोग्निकर्षुसदृशाः" सर्पशिरोऽग्निकर्षूसदृशाः। "सुविदित इह" सुविदिता इह। "बहुनारिसङ्घ" (अत एव) बहुनारीसङ्घं। "गुणचर" (यतो) गणचारिकाः प्रमदा इत्यर्थः।

२ "प्रकारनयुतैः प्रमद गुणकरैः" प्रकारनियुतैः प्रमदा गुणनिकरैः। "न शक्तु" नाशक्नुवन्। "सुगतराज" सुगतराजं। "लज्जि भि राचपलं मुनिनं प्रपतित चरणे" लज्जिता चपलं मुनिं प्रपतिताश्चरणे। यत्र लज्जा शब्दस्तत्रापि लज्जार्थस्य विधानेः प्रयोगात्तं मुनिं प्रति ता चलितरां लज्जिता भूता इति भावः। "गौरवु तुष्ट प्रेम जनिया स्तुविषु" गौरवेण तुष्टाः प्रेम जनयित्वा अस्तौषुः।

३ "निर्मलपद्मगर्भसदृशा" हे निर्मलपद्मगर्भसदृश। "शरदिशशिमुखा" हे शारदशशिमुख। "सर्पिहुतार्चितेजसदृशा" हे सर्पिर्हुतार्चिस्तेजःसदृश। "कनकगिरिनिभा" हे कनकगिरिनिभ। "सिध्यतु" सिध्यन्तु। "प्रणिधिर्भव व्रतचरितात्म प्रतारय" प्रणिधिर्भवतु व्रतचरिताद्धि आत्म प्रतारय।

साध्वसं न तात प्रतिघममरनरगुरोः (१)॥

पश्यति पद्मपत्त्रनयनः प्रहसितवदनो

नापि स वक्तु प्रेक्षिति जनमपि च सभ्रुकुटिः।

मेरु चलेय शुष्य उदधिः शशिरवि प्रपते

नैव स दोषदर्शि त्रिभवे प्रमदवश गमिया (२)॥

अथ खलु मारः पापीयानिदं वचनं श्रुत्वा भूयस्या मात्रया दुःखितो दुर्मना अनात्तमनाः प्रदुष्टमनास्तां स्वदुहितॄनामन्त्रयते स्म (३)। कथं भो न शक्यते स बोधिमण्डादुत्थापयितुम्। मा खलु मूढः प्राज्ञोऽथ युष्माकं रूपाकृतिम् पश्यति।

अथ खलु मारदुहितरः स्वपितरं गाथाभिः प्रत्याभाषन्त।

श्लक्ष्णा मधुरस्य भाषते न च रक्तो

गुह्यगुह्यस्य निरीक्षते न च दुष्टः।

ईर्याचर्य प्रेक्षते न च मूढकायः

सर्वं पनेति आशयो सुगम्भीरः (४)॥

निःसंशयेन विदिताः पृथु दृष्टिदोषाः

---

१ "स्त्रुविय" सुत्वा। "छत्व" छत्वा। "गिरिरिव" गिरिमिव। "गत्य पितुः" गत्वा पितुर्निकटे इत्यर्थः। "इदमवचि गिरं" इमामवोचम् गिरं। "प्रतिघं" प्रतिघः, क्रोध इत्यर्थः।

२ "स वक्तु प्रेक्षिति" स वक्ति प्रेक्षते। "मेरु चलेय शुष्य उदधिः" मेरुश्चलेत् शुष्येदुदधिः। "शशिरवि प्रपते" शशिरवी प्रपतेताम्। "दोषदर्शि" दोषदर्शी। "प्रमदवशगमिया" प्रमदावशङ्गमिष्यति इत्यर्थः।

३ "स्वां स्वदुहितॄनामन्त्रयते स्म" स्वाः स्वदुहितॄरामन्त्रयते स्म।

४ "श्लक्ष्णा" श्लक्ष्णं। गुह्यगुह्यस्य" जघगुह्यस्येति यावत्। "मूढकायः" मुग्धकाय इत्यर्थः। "सर्वं पनेति" सर्वामपनयति। "आशयो सुगम्भीरः" तस्य आशयः सुगम्भीर इत्यर्थः।

कामैर्विमुक्तमनसो न च रागरक्तः।
नैवाख्यसौ दिवि भुवीह नरः सुरो वा
यस्तस्य चित्तचरितं परिजानयेया (१) ॥

या इस्त्रिमाय उपदर्शित तत्र तात
प्रचलेयु तस्य हृदयं भवियः सरागः।
तन्दृष्ट एकमपि कम्पितु नास्य चित्तं
शैलेन्द्रराज इव तिष्ठति सोऽप्रकम्पः (२) ॥

शतपुण्यतेजभरितो गुणतेजपूर्णः
शीलतपस्मि चरितो बहुकल्पकोट्यः।
ब्रह्मा च देव शुभतेज विशुद्धसत्त्वा
मूर्ध्ना निपत्य चरणेषु नमन्ति तस्मै (३) ॥

निःसंशयेन विनिहत्य स मारसैन्यं
पूर्वं जिनानुमत प्राप्स्यति अग्रबोधिम्।
ताता न रोचति हि मनोऽपि रणे विवादो

---

१ “स्त्रिषु इस्त्रिदोषाः” स्त्रियः स्त्रीदोषाः। “विमुक्तमनसो” विमुक्तमनाः। “नैवाख्यसौ” नैवैतादृश इत्यर्थः। “परिजानयेया” परिजानीयात्।

२ “इस्त्रिमाय उपदर्शित तत्र” स्त्रीमाया उपदर्शितास्तत्र। “प्रचलेयु” प्रचलेत्। “भवियः सरागः” भूत्वा सरागं। तस्य हृदयं सरागं भूत्वा प्रचलेदित्यस्माकं मनसि स्थितमिति समेषार्थः। “तन्दृष्ट” ता दृष्ट्वा। “एकमपि” एकांशमपि, किञ्चिदपि अणुमात्रमपीति निष्कृष्टार्थः। “कम्पितु” कम्पितं।

३ “शतपुण्यतेजभरितः” शतगुणितपुण्यतेजःपूर्ण इत्यर्थः। “गुणतेजपूर्णः” गुणतेजःपूर्णः। “शीलतपस्मि चरितः” चरितशीलतपा इत्यर्थः। “बहुकल्पकोट्यः” बहुकल्पकोटिपर्यन्तमित्यर्थः। “देव शुभतेज विशुद्धसत्त्वा” देवः शुभतेजा विशुद्धसत्त्वः। “नमन्ति तस्मै” नमति तं बोधिसत्त्वमित्यर्थः।

बलवन्तु विग्रह सुडुष्कु अयं प्रयोगः (१) ॥

प्रेचस्व तात गगणे मणिरत्नचूडाः
सम्बोधिसत्त्वनयुताः स्थित गौरवेण ।
रत्नाकरा कुसुमदामविचित्रिताङ्गाः
सम्प्रेक्षिता दशबलैरिह पूजनार्थम् (२) ॥

ये चेतना अपि च ये च अचेतना च
वृक्षाश्च शैलेन्द्रसुरेन्द्रयक्षाः ।
अभ्यानता अभिमुखा गुणपर्वतस्य
श्रेयो भवेत् प्रतिनिवर्त्तितुमद्य तात (३) ॥

अपिच ।

न तत्तरेद्यस्य न पारमुत्तरे-
न्न तत्खणेद्यस्य न मूलमुद्धरेत् ।
न कोपयेत्तं चमयेत्पुनोपि तं
कुर्य्यान्न तं येन भवेच्च दुर्म्मनाः (४) ॥

अथ खलु भिक्षवस्तस्मिन् समयेऽष्टौ बोधिवृक्षदेवताः । तद्यथा । श्रीवृद्धिः, तपा, श्रेयसी, विदुः, ओजो, बला, सत्यवादिनी, समङ्गिनी च ताः । ता बोधिसत्त्वं सम्पूज्य षोड-

---

१ "पूर्वं जिनानुमत" पूर्वजिनानुमतमित्यर्थः । "ताता" हे तात । "मनोऽपि" मम मनस्यपीत्यर्थः । "विग्रह सुडुष्कु अयं" विग्रहः सुडुष्कोऽयं ।

२ "सम्बोधिसत्त्वनयुताः स्थित" सम्बोधिसत्त्वनियुतानि स्थितानि । "रत्नाकरा" रत्नाकराः । "सम्प्रेक्षिता दशबलैरिह" सम्प्रेषणे दशबलैः प्रहिता इव इत्यर्थः । "पूजनार्थं" बोधिसत्त्वस्य पूजनार्थमित्यर्थः ।

३ "अचेतना च" अचेतनाश्च ।

४ "तत्खणेद्यस्य" तत्खनेद्यस्य । "चमयेत् पुनोपि" चमापयेत् पुनरपि ।

अभिराकारैर्बोधिसत्त्वं श्रिया वर्द्धयन्ति स्म, अभिष्टुवन्ति स्म।

उपशोभसे त्वं विशुद्धसत्त्व चन्द्र इव शुक्लपक्षे।
अभिविरोचसे त्वं विशुद्धबुद्ध सूर्य्य इव प्रोद्गच्छमानः॥
प्रस्फुटितस्त्वं विशुद्धसत्त्वः पद्ममिव वारिमध्ये।
नदसि त्वं विशुद्धसत्त्व केशरीव वने राजवनचारी॥
विभ्राजसे त्वं अग्रसत्त्व(१)पर्व्वतराज इव सागरमध्ये।
अभ्युद्गतस्त्वं विशुद्धसत्त्व चक्रवाड इव पर्व्वते॥
दुरवगाहस्त्वमग्रसत्त्व जलधर इव रत्नसम्पूर्णः।
विस्तीर्णबुद्धिरसि लोकनाथ गगणमिवापर्य्यन्तम्॥
सुस्थितबुद्धिरसि विशुद्धसत्त्व
धरणितलवत् सर्व्वसत्त्वोपजीव्यः।
अकलुषबुद्धिरसि अग्रसत्त्वा (२)
न च तप्त इव सरः सदा प्रसन्नः॥
अनिकेतबुद्धिस्त्वमग्रसत्त्व
मारुत इव सर्व्वलोके सदा प्रसक्तः।
दुरासदस्त्वमग्रसत्त्व
तेजोराजा इव सर्व्वमन्यमनाप्रहीनो (३)॥
बलवानसि त्वमग्रसत्त्व
नारायण इव दुर्धर्षः।

---

१ "त्वं अग्रसत्त्व" त्वमग्रसत्त्व।

२ "अग्रसत्त्वा" हे अग्रसत्त्व इत्यर्थः।

३ "तेजोराजा इव" तेजोराज इव। "सर्व्वमन्यमनाप्रहीनो" सर्व्वमन्यमना अप्रहीणः।

दृढसमादानस्त्वं लोकनाथा
अनुत्थितो बोधिमण्डात् (१) ॥
नानिवर्त्यस्त्वमग्रसत्त्व
दृढकरोत्सृष्टमिव वज्रम्।
सुलब्धलाभस्त्वमग्रसत्त्व
दृशबलसमग्र्याऽचिरात् भविष्यसि (२) इति ॥

एवं खलु भिक्षवो बोधिवृक्षदेवताः षोडशाकारं बोधिसत्त्वं श्रिया वर्द्धयन्ति स्म। तत्र भिक्षवः शुद्धावासकायिका देवपुत्राः षोडशभिराकारैर्मारं पापीयांसं दुर्बलं कुर्वन्ति ॥ कतमैः षोडशभिः। तद्यथा।

ध्वस्तस्त्वं पापीयं बोधिसत्त्वेन जीर्णक्रौञ्च इव ध्यायसे।
दुर्बलस्त्वं पापीयं जीर्णगज इव पङ्कमग्नः (३) ॥
एकोऽसि त्वं पापीयं निर्जित इव शूर प्रतिज्ञा।
अद्वितीयस्त्वं पापीयं अटव्यां त्यक्त इव रोगार्त्तः (४) ॥
अबलस्त्वं पापीयं भारक्लृष्ट इव बलीवर्द्दः।
अपविद्धस्त्वं पापीयं वातक्षिप्त इव तरुः ॥
कुपथस्थितस्त्वं पापीयं मार्गभ्रष्ट इव सार्थिको।

१ "लोकनाथा अनुत्थितो" हे लोकनाथ अनुत्थितो भविष्यसि इत्यर्थः।

२ "नानिवर्त्यः" अनिवर्त्यः। "दृशबलसमग्र्या" दृशबलसामग्र्या (सम्पन्नः) इत्यर्थः।

३ "पापीयं" हे पापीयन्। इत्यमेव सर्वत्र बोध्यम्। "ध्यायसे" ध्यायसि।

४ "शूर प्रतिज्ञा" शूरः प्रतिज्ञयेत्यर्थः। "पापीयं अटव्यां" पापीयन्नटव्यां।

दीनदीनस्त्वं पापीयं मत्सरिण इव दरिद्रपुरुषः (१) ॥
मुखरस्त्वं पापीयं वायस इव प्रगल्भः ।
मानाभिभूतस्त्वं पापीयं अकृतज्ञ इव दुर्व्विनीतः ॥
पलायिष्यसे त्वमद्य पापीयं क्रोष्टुक इव सिंहनादेन ।
विधुनिष्यसे त्वमद्यपापीयं बोधिसत्त्वेन वैरम्भवाय विक्षिप्त इव पक्षी॥
अकालज्ञस्त्वं पापीयं पुण्यक्षीण इव भैक्षुकः (२) ।
विवर्जिष्यसे त्वमद्य पापीयं भिन्नभाजनमिव पांशुप्रतिपूर्णम् ॥
निगृहिष्यसे त्वमद्य पापीयं बोधिसत्त्वेन मन्त्रेण चोरगाः (३) ।
सर्व्वबलप्रहीणोऽसि पापीयं छिन्नकरचरण इवा षण्ढः (४) ॥

एवं खलु भिक्षवः शुद्धावासकायिका देवपुत्राः षोडशभिराकारैर्मारं पापीयांसं दुर्बलमकार्षुः । तत्र भिक्षवो बोधिपरिचारका देवपुत्राः षोडशभिराकारैर्मारं पापीयांसं विच्छेदयन्ति स्म । कतमैः षोडशभिः । तद्यथा ।

अद्य त्वं पापीयं निर्जेष्यसे
बोधिसत्त्वेन परसैन्यं (५) इव शूरेण ।
निष्टहिष्यसे त्वमद्य पापीयं
बोधिसत्त्वेन दुर्बलमल्ल इव महामल्लेन ॥
अभिभविष्यसे त्वमद्य पापीयं

१ "सार्थिको" सार्थिकः पथिको वा। "मत्सरिण इव" मत्सरीव।
२ "पुण्यक्षीण इव" क्षीणपुण्य इव। भैक्षुकः" भिक्षुकः।
३ "चोरगाः" चोरा इवेत्यर्थः।
४ "इवा षण्ढः" इव षण्ढः।
५ "परसैन्यं इव" परसैन्यमिव।

बोधिसत्त्वेन खद्योतमिव (१) सूर्य्यमण्डलेन।
विध्वंसिष्यसे त्वमद्य पापीयं
बोधिसत्त्वेन बुसमुष्टिरिव महामारुतेन॥
विचसिष्यसे त्वमद्य पापीयं
बोधिसत्त्वेन केशरिणेव शृगालः।
प्रपातिष्यसे त्वमद्य पापीयं
बोधिसत्त्वेन महाशाल इव मूलच्छिन्नः॥
विलोप्स्यसे त्वमद्य पापीयं
बोधिसत्त्वेनामित्रनगरमिव महाराजेन।
विशोषिष्यसे त्वमद्य पापीयं
बोधिसत्त्वेन गोष्पदवारीव महाऽऽतपेन॥
पलायिष्यसे त्वमद्य पापीयं
बोधिसत्त्वेन बन्धनिर्मुक्त इव धूर्त्तपुरुषः।
उत्त्रसिष्यसे त्वमद्य पापीयं
बोधिसत्त्वेनाग्निदाहेनेव मधुकरवृन्दम्॥
उद्भ्रमिष्यसे (२) त्वमद्य पापीयं
बोधिसत्त्वेन राष्ट्रभ्रष्ट इव धर्म्मराजः।
ध्यायिष्यसे त्वमद्य पापीयं
बोधिसत्त्वेन जीर्णक्रौञ्च इव लूनपक्षः॥
विहनिष्यसे (३) त्वमद्य पापीयं

---

१ "खद्योतमिव" खद्योत इव।
२ रोपिष्यसे इति वा पाठः।
३ अत्र विभर्त्स्यसे इति वा पाठः। परन्तु पूर्वपाठेऽर्थः समीचीनः सम्भाव्यते।

बोधिसत्त्वेन चीणपथ्योदन इवाटवीकान्तारे ।
विलयिष्यसे त्वमद्य पापीयं
बोधिसत्त्वेन भिन्नयानपात्र इव (१) महार्णवे ॥
आश्वास्यसे त्वमद्य पापीयं
बोधिसत्त्वेन कल्पदाह इव वनस्पतयः ।
विकिरिष्यसे त्वमद्य पापीयं
बोधिसत्त्वेन महावज्रेणेव गिरिकूटम् (२) ॥

एवं खलु भिक्षवो बोधिपरिचारका देवपुत्राः षोडशाकारैर्मारं विच्छेदयन्ति स्म । न च मारः पापीयान् विनिवर्त्तते स्म तत्रेदमुच्यते ।

भूताक्षोदन श्रुत्व दैवतगणा न निवर्त्तते सोऽन्तको
उच्छेया हनथा विलुम्पथ इमा मा दास्यथा जीवितम् ।
एषोत्तीर्ण स्वयं ममापि विषयात्तारिष्यते चापरां
नान्यं मोक्ष वदेमि किञ्चि श्रमणे उत्थापयेत्प्रक्रमेत् (३) ॥

बोधिसत्त्व आह ।

मेरुःपर्व्वतराज स्थानतु चलेत्सर्व्वं जगन्नो भवेत्

---

१ "भिन्नयानपात्र इव" भिन्नयानपात्रमिव ।

२ "गिरिकूटम्" गिरिकूटः ।

३ "भूताक्षोदन श्रुत्व दैवतगणा" एवम्भूताक्षोदनां श्रुत्वा दैवतगणानामित्यर्थः । "सोऽन्तको" सोऽन्तकः । "उच्छेया हनथा विलुम्पथ इमा मा दास्यथा जीवितम्" उच्छिन्त हत विलुम्पत इमं मा दत्त जीवितुम् । "एषोत्तीर्ण स्वयं ममापि" एष उत्तीर्णः स्वयं मामपि । "तारिष्यते चापरां" तारयिष्यति चापराम् । "मोक्ष वदेमि" मोक्षं वदामि बोधिसत्त्वद्वारा जनानां मोक्षं पश्यामीति तात्पर्य्यम् । "किञ्चि श्रमणे उत्थापयेत् प्रक्रमेत्" केनचित् प्रकारेण श्रमणमुत्थाप्य प्रक्रामयेत् यदि कोपि तदा मङ्गलादिति तात्पर्य्यार्थः ।

सर्व्वे तारकसङ्घ भूमि प्रपतेत्सज्योतिषेन्द्रा नभात् ।
सर्व्वे सत्त्व करेय एकमतयः शुष्येन्महासागरो
नत्वेव द्रुमराजमूलोपगतश्चाल्येत अस्मद्विधः (१) ॥

मार आह ।

कामेश्वरोऽस्मि वशिता इह सर्व्वलोके
देवाश्च दानवगणा मनुजाश्च तीर्य्या ।
व्याप्ता मया मम वशेन च यान्ति सर्व्वे
उत्तिष्ठ मह्य विषयस्थ वचं कुरुष्व (२) ॥

बोधिसत्त्व आह ।

कामेश्वरोऽसि यदि व्यक्तमनीश्वरोऽसि
धर्म्मेश्वरोऽहमपि पश्यसि तत्त्वतो माम् ।
कामेश्वरोऽसि यदि दुर्गति न प्रयासि
प्राप्स्यामि बोधि च समक्षतु पश्यतस्ते (३) ॥

मार आह ।

एकात्मकः श्रमण किं प्रकरोषि रण्यं
यं प्रार्थयस्यसुलभः खलु सम्प्रयोगः (४) ।

---

१ "पर्वतराज स्थानतु" पर्वतराजः स्थानतः । "तारकसङ्घ भूमि" तारका-सङ्घेन भूमौ । "सज्योतिषेन्द्राः" सज्योतिरिन्द्राः । "सत्त्व करेय एकमतयः" सत्त्वाः कुर्युरेकमतं ।

२ "वशिता" वशिताऽस्मि । "देवाश्च दानवगणा" अथ देवाः सदानवगणा वा पाठः । "तीर्य्या" तीर्यञ्चः । "मह्य विषयस्थ वचं" मम विषयस्थां वाचं ।

३ "दुर्गति" दुर्गतिं । "बोधि च" बोधिञ्च । "समक्षतु" समक्षमे इत्यनुमीयते ।

४ "रण्यं" रण्यं । "सम्प्रयोगः" स प्रयोगः ।

अथाङ्गिरःप्रभृतिभिस्तपसा प्रयत्ना-
त्प्राप्तं न तत्पदवरं मनुजः कुतस्त्वम् ॥

बोधिसत्त्व आह ।

अज्ञानपूर्वं कुतपो ऋषिभिः प्रतप्तः
क्रोधाभिभूतमतिभिर्दिवलोककामैः (१) ।
नित्यमनित्यमिति चात्मनि संश्रयद्भि-
र्मोक्षश्च देशगमनस्थितमाश्रयद्भिः ॥
ते तत्त्वतोऽर्थरहिताः पुरुषं वदन्ति
व्यापिं प्रदेशगत शाश्वतमाहुरेके ।
मूर्त्तिं न मूर्त्तिमगुणं गुणिनं तथैव
कर्त्ता न कर्त्ता इति चाप्यपरे ब्रुवन्ति (२) ॥
प्राप्याद्य बोधि विरजामिह चासनास्थ-
स्त्वां जित्व मार विहतं सबलं ससैन्यम् ।
वर्त्तिष्यमस्य जगतः प्रभवोद्भवश्च
निर्व्वाणदुःखशमनं तथ सीतिभावम् (३) ॥

मारः क्रुद्धो दुष्टो रुष्टः परुषगिरं पुनस्तु भणति गृहाण सुगौतमं
एषो ह्यकारणे न्यस्तो पश्यिय मम पुरस्तु व्रजता लघुं वशकुर्व्वंताम् ।

---

१ "अज्ञानपूर्वं कुतपो ऋषिभिः प्रतप्तः" अज्ञानपूर्वं कुतप ऋषिभिः प्रतप्तं । "दिवलोककामैः" द्युलोककामैः ।

२ "व्यापिं प्रदेशगत" व्याप्तं प्रदेशगतं । "मूर्त्तिं न मूर्त्तिमगुणं" मूर्त्तममूर्त्तमगुणं ।

३ "बोधि विरजामिह" बोधिं विरजस्कामिह । "जित्व मार विहतं" जित्वा मार विहत्य । "वर्त्तिष्यमस्य" वर्त्तयिष्येऽस्य प्रवर्त्तयिष्येऽस्येत्यर्थः । "प्रभवोद्भवश्च" प्रभवमुद्भवञ्च । "तथ सीति भावम्" तथास्तीति भावम् ।

शीघ्रं गत्वा मह्यं गेहे दृढनिगडयुगलविहितं कुरोथ दुवारिकायामं द्रक्ष्ये दुःखेनार्त्तं बहुविधजवितरवितं मरुदण्व चेटकम् (१) ॥

बोधिसत्त्व आह ।

शक्याकाशे लेख्यं चित्रं बहुविधविततपदशः पृथक् पृथक् प्रकर्त्तुं

शक्यो वायुः पाशैर्बद्धुं दिशविदिशं गमनजविनो नरेण सुयत्नतः ।

शक्यो कर्त्तुं चन्द्रादित्यौ तमतिमिरं वितिमिरकरौ नभोद्य महीतलं

शक्यो नाहं त्वत्सादृश्यैर्बहुभिरपि गणेन विहतैर्द्रुमात् प्रतिचाल

लयितुम् (२) ॥

मार आह ।

अभ्युत्थिता बलवती नमुचेश्चमू सा

हाहाकारशङ्खभेरीमृदङ्गशब्दैः ।

हा पुत्र वत्स दयिता किमसि प्रणष्टो

१ "पुनतु" पुनस्तु पुनरपि इत्यर्थः । "स्टहाण" स्टह्णन । "एषो ह्यकारणे न्यस्तो" अत्र एषो ह्यकारणन्यस्त इति वा पाठः । एषो हि अकारणेन न्यस्तः । निष्कारणमेवात्र न्यस्त इति पाठद्वयमिष्कृष्टार्थः । "प्रस्थिय" स्टस्थित्वा । "पुरस्तु" अत्र पुरतु इति वा पाठः । अग्र पुरत इत्यर्थः । "अज्ञाता लघु वध कुर्वताम्" अज्ञात लघु वधं कुरुत । "मह्यं" मम । "करोथ" कुरुत । "दुवारिकायामं द्वौवारिकायाम् । "बहुविधजवितरवितं" बहुविधजवेन रुदन्तमिति तात्पर्यार्थः । "मरुदण्व चेटकम्" मरुतामिव देवविशेषाणामिव चेटकम् ।

२ "शक्याकाशे लेख्यं" शक्यमाकाशे लेखितुं । "विततपदशः" विततपदांशः । "दिशविदिशं" दिग्विदिशि । "गमनजविनो" गमनजविना गमनार्थं जवयुक्तेनेति स्पष्टार्थः । अत्र गमने जविन इति वा पाठः । "शक्यो" शक्यौ । "तमतिमिरं" तमस्तिमिरौ । "त्वत्सादृश्यैः" त्वत्सदृशैः । त्वत्सदृशानामित्युचितम् । अत्र त्वत्सादृशैरिति च पाठः । "गणेन" गणैः । त्वत्सदृशानां बहुभिरपि गणैः हतैर्विहतैर्द्रुमात् प्रतिचालयितुं नाहं शक्य इति साम्वयार्थः ।

दृष्ट्वा निमां नमुचिसेनमतीव भीमाम् (१) ॥
जाम्बूनदकनकचम्पकगर्भगौर
सुकुमार देवनरसंस्तुत पूजनीय ।
अद्य प्रयास्यसि विनाश्यु महारणेऽस्मिं
मारस्य एष्यसि वशं असुरस्य चन्द्रः (२) ॥
  अथ मधुस्वरेण कलविङ्करुतस्वरेण
तान् यक्षराक्षसगणां सुगतोऽवभाषते ।
आकाश चाशयितुमिच्छति यो ह्यविद्वान्
योऽस्मद्विधं द्रुमवराद्धरणाय इच्छेत् (३) ॥
भित्वा च यो रजु गणेय महासहस्रे
सोत्वा च सागरजलस्य समुद्धरेद्यः ।
वज्रमयां गिरिवरां विकिरेत्क्षणाच्च
सो चापि मां तरुगतं न विहेठयेच्च (४) ॥
  युगमन्तरस्मिं स्थित मार प्रदुष्टचित्तो
निष्कोष पाणिनमसिं प्रगृहील तीक्ष्णम् ।
उत्तिष्ठ शीघ्र श्रमणास्ममतेन गच्छ

---

१ "दयिता" "हे दयित। निमां नमुचिसेनमतीव" इमां नमुचिसेनामतीव ।

२ "विनाश्यु महारणेऽस्मिं" विनाशं महारणेऽस्मिन्। "वशं असुरस्य चन्द्रः" वशमसुरस्य चन्द्र इवेत्यर्थः ।

३ "यक्षराक्षसगणां" यक्षराक्षसगणान्। "सुगतोऽवभाषते" सुगतोऽवभाषते । "आकाश" आकाशं ।

४ "रजु गणेय" रजांसि गणयेत्। "महासहस्रे" महासहस्रं। "वज्रमयां गिरिवरां" वज्रमयान् गिरिवरान्। "सो चापि" स चापि। "विहेठयेच" विघा-तयेचेति भावः ।

मा वेणुयष्टि हरि तास्र छिनद्मिऽतेऽस्य (१) ॥

बोधिसत्त्व आह।

सर्व्वेयं त्रिसाहस्र मेदिनी यदि मारैः प्रपूर्णा भवेत्
सर्व्वेषां यथ मेरु पर्व्वतवरः पाणीषु खड्गो भवेत्।
ते मह्यं न समर्थ लोम चलितुं प्रागेव मां घातितुं
कुर्य्याश्चापि हि विग्रहे स्म वर्मितेन दृढम् (२) ॥

विध्यन्ति शैलशिखरां ज्वलिताग्निवर्णां
वृक्षां समूलक क्षिपी तथ ताम्रलोहम्।
उष्ट्राश्च गोगजमुखास्तथ भैरवाक्षा
आशीविषा भुजग दृष्टिविषाश्च घोराः (३) ॥
मेघाश्च उत्थित चतुर्दिश गर्जमाना
वज्राशनी तथ अयोगुड वर्षमाणाः।
कुन्तासिशक्ति तीक्ष्णपरशु सविषाश्च वाणां

---

१ "युगमन्तरस्मिं" युगान्तरस्मिन् कल्पान्तरस्मिन्निति स्पष्टार्थः। "स्थित मार" स्थितो मारः। "निष्कोष पाणिनमसिं" निष्कोषं पाणिनाऽसिं। "प्रगृह्योत्व" प्रगृह्य। "शीघ्र अमर्षाक्रमतेन" शीघ्रं अमर्षाक्रान्तेन। "वेणुयष्टि हरि" वेणुयष्टिं प्रहर।

२ "त्रिसाहस्र" त्रिसाहस्रा। "यथ मेरु" यथा मेरुः। "पाणीषु" पाणिषु। "मह्यं" मम। "समर्थ" समर्थाः। "चलितुं" चालयितुं। प्रागेव इत्यत्र प्रागपि च इति वा पाठः। "घातितुं" घातयितुम्। "कुर्य्याश्चापि हि विग्रहे स्म वर्मितेन दृढं" यद्यपि विग्रहेऽपि प्रदत्तं कुर्य्यास्तथापि मां वर्मितत्वेन दृढं विद्धीति तात्पर्यार्थः।

३ "शैलशिखरां ज्वलिताग्निवर्णां" शैलशिखराम्, ज्वलिताग्निवर्णान्। "वृक्षां समूलक क्षिपी" वृक्षान् समूलकान् क्षिपन्ति। "तथ" तथा। "गोगजमुखास्तथ" गोगजमुखास्तथा। "भुजग" भुजगाः। युद्धस्य साहाय्याय उष्ट्रादयोऽपि समाजग्मुरिति समेतार्थः।

भिन्दन्ति मेदनितलं प्रमथन्ति वृक्षां (१)॥
बाहुशतैः शरशतानि क्षिपन्ति केचित्
आशीविषां ज्वलवशांश्च मुखोत्सृजन्ति।
मकरादिकांश्च अखजानुदधेर्ग्रहीला
विध्यन्ति केचिद्भुजगां गरुडाश्च भूत्वा (२)॥
केचित् सुमेरुसदृशानयसो गुडानि
तप्ताग्निवर्णशिखराणि क्षिपन्ति हृष्टाः।
आच्छाद्य मेदनितलं क्षुभयन्ति बोधि
ऐष्टापस्कन्द सलिलस्य विलोडयन्ति (३)॥
केचित् पतन्ति पुरतस्तथ पृष्ठतोऽपि
वामे च दक्षिण पतन्ति अहो विवस्त्राः।
विपरीतहस्तचरणोज्वलितोत्तमाङ्गा
नेत्रेभि निश्चरति विद्युदिव प्रदीप्ता (४)॥

---

१ "उत्थित चतुर्दिश" उत्थिताश्चतुर्दिक्षु। "तथ चयोगुड" तथायोगुडान्। "कुन्तासिशक्ति तोमरपरश्च सविषांश्च बाणां" कुन्तासिशक्तितोमरपरश्वधान् सविषांश्च बाणान्। अत्र केचित् उत्सृजन्ति इत्यध्याहार्य्य समन्वयः कार्यः। "मेदिनितलं" मेदिनीतलं। "वृक्षां" वृक्षान्।

२ "आशीविषां" आशीविषान्। "मुखोत्सृजन्ति" मुखादुत्सृजन्ति। "केचिद्भुजगां" केचिद्भुजगान्।

३ "गुडानि" गुडान्। "मेदिनितल" मेदिनीतलं। "क्षुभयन्ति बोधि" क्षोभयन्ति बोधिं। "केष्टापस्कन्द सलिलस्य विलोडयन्ति" केष्टाः स्कन्दं (तटं) सलिलस्य विलोडयन्ति (विदारयन्ति) इति स्पष्टार्थः।

४ "पुरतस्तथ" पुरतस्तथा। "दक्षिण पतन्ति" दक्षिणे आपतन्ति इत्यर्थः। "चरणोज्वलितो-" चरणा उज्वलिता-। "नेत्रेभि" नेत्रैः, नेत्रेभ्य इत्यर्थः। "प्रदीप्ता" प्रदीप्तिः।

दृष्ट्वा विकारविकृतां नमुचेस्तु सेनां
मायाकृतश्च यथ प्रेक्षति शुद्धसत्त्वः ।
नैवात्र मारुतबलं न जगच्च चात्मो-
दकचन्द्ररूपसदृशं भ्रमति त्रिलोकः (१) ॥
चक्षुना इस्त्रिपुरुषो न चात्मनीयं
श्रोतश्च घ्राण तथ जिह्व तथैव कायाः ।
अध्यात्मशून्यबहिर्शून्यप्रतीत्यजाता
धर्मा इमे कारकवेदकवीतिवृत्ताः (२) ॥
सो सत्य वाक्यमकरोत् सद सत्यवादी
येनेह सत्यवचनेनेम शून्यधर्माः ।
ये केचित् सौम्य विनयेऽनुकूल यक्षा-
स्ते शक्तपाणिषु निरीक्षिषु पुष्पदामान् (३) ॥

---

१ "यथ प्रेक्षति" यथा प्रेक्षते । "शुद्धसत्त्वः" अत्र शुद्धसत्त्वस्य स्थानात् सप्तरत्नप्रभासं चाप्तं परिज्ञातमभूत् इति वा पाठः । परन्तु श्लोकपादानुरूपो नास्ति । दृश्यतेऽप्ययमेकस्मिन्नेव पुस्तके । "-रूपसदृशं" रूपसदृशो । "त्रिलोकः" त्रिलोकी । अत्र त्रिलोकनाथ इति वा पाठः । अस्मिन् पक्षे रूपसदृशमित्यत्र रूपसदृश इति बोध्यम् ।

२ "चक्षुना इस्त्रिपुरुषो न चात्मनीयं" चक्षुषा स्त्रीपुरुषौ न चात्मीयं पश्यति इति शेषः । "श्रोतश्च घ्राण तथ जिह्व तथैव कायाः" श्रोत्रञ्च घ्राणं तथा जिह्वा तथैव कायः, एतानीन्द्रियाण्यपि बोधिसत्त्वस्य स्वस्वविषयेभ्यो निवृत्तानि इति तु श्रोत्रादीनामध्यात्मशून्येति विशेषणदानाल्लभ्यते । "अध्यात्मशून्यबहिर्शून्यप्रतीत्यजाताः" अध्यात्मशून्यबहिःशून्यप्रतीतिं प्राप्तानि । अर्थात् बोधिसत्त्वस्य आत्मा सुखदुःखादिप्रतीतिशून्यः श्रोत्रादीनि तु शब्दादिबहिर्विषयप्रतीतिशून्यानि इति स्पष्टार्थः । "कारकवेदकवीतिवृत्ताः" इत्यस्य कर्त्ता वेदितव्या वीतवृत्तयश्चेति स्पष्टार्थः ।

३ "सो सत्य" स सत्यं । "सद" सदा । "सत्यवचनेनेम" सत्यवचनेनेमे । "सौम्य" सौम्याः । "विनयेऽनुकूल" विनयानुकूलाः । "निरीक्षिषु पुष्पदामान्" अनिरीक्षन् पुष्पदामानि ।

सो दक्षिणे करतले रचिताग्रजाले
ताम्रैर्नखैः सुरुचिरैः सह मारचक्रैः।
जाम्बूनदार्चिसदृशैः शुभपुण्यजुष्टै-
र्मूर्द्धा तु यावत् स्पृशते चरणां सलीलम् (१) ॥

बाहुं प्रसार्य्य यथ विद्युदिवा नभस्था-
दाभाषते वसुमतीमियमत्र साक्षी।
चित्राणि यज्ञनयुतानपि यष्ट पूर्व्वे
न मि जातु याचनक वन्ध्य कृता न दाशे (२) ॥

आपोऽपि साक्षि तथ तेज तथैव वायु-
र्ब्रह्मा प्रजापति सज्योतिष चन्द्रसूर्य्याः।
बुद्धा मि साक्षि दशसु स्थित ये दिशासु
यथ मह्य शील व्रत उद्गत बोधिअङ्गाः (३) ॥

दानञ्च साक्षि तथ शील तथैव क्षान्ति
र्वीर्य्यञ्च साक्षि तथ ध्यान तथैव प्रज्ञा।

---

१ "सो" स। "दक्षिणे करतले रचिताग्रजाले" दक्षिणेन करतलेन रचिताग्रजालेनेत्यर्थः। "जाम्बूनदार्चिसदृशैः" जाम्बूनदार्चिःसदृशैः। "मूर्द्धा तु यावत् स्पृशते" मूर्द्धानं तु यावत् स्पृशति स्मेत्यर्थः। "चरणां" चरणानि। चरणारविन्दमिति वाच पाठः।

२ "यथ" यथा। "विद्युदिवा नभस्थादाभाषते वसुमतीमियमत्र साक्षी" विद्युदिव नभस्थात् आभाषते (स्म) वसुमती इयं मम साक्षिणी इतीत्यर्थः। "यज्ञनयुतानपि यष्ट" यज्ञनियुतान्यपि यष्टानि। "न मि जातु याचनकवन्ध्य कृता न दाशे" चरं न दाशे इत्युपार्थे न मे जातु याचका वन्दिनश्च दूरीकृता इत्यर्थः।

३ "आपोऽपि साक्षि तथ" आपः सन्ति साक्षिण्यस्तथा। "तेज तथैव" तेजस्तथैव। "प्रजापति सज्योतिष चन्द्रसूर्य्याः" प्रजापतिः सज्योतिषौ चन्द्रसूर्य्यौ। "बुद्धा मि साक्षि दशसु स्थित ये दिशासु" बुद्धा मे साक्षिणो दशसु स्थिता ये दिक्षु। "यथ मह्य शील व्रत उद्गत बोधि अङ्गाः" यथा मम शीलं व्रत उद्गता बोध्यङ्गाः।

चतुर प्रमाण मम साक्षि तथा अभिज्ञा
अनुपूर्व्व बोधिचरि सर्व्व ममेह साक्षी (१) ॥
यावन्ति सत्त्व निखिला दशसु दिशासु
यत्तेषु पुण्य बल शील तथैव ज्ञानम् ।
यस्मा निरर्गड यष्ट शतः कलाभि-
स्ते मह्य रोम सति मां कलमोपयान्ति (२) ॥
सो पाणिना धरणि आहनते सलीलं
रणते इयं वसुमती यथ कंसपात्री ।
मारो निशाम्य रिपु मेदिनीये निरस्तः
शृणुतेवं रवं हनत गृह्णत कृष्णबन्धुम् (३) ॥
प्रस्विन्नगात्र हततेज विवर्णवक्त्रो
मारो जराभिहतु आत्मनि सम्प्रपश्यत् ।
उर राड क्रन्दतु भयार्त्त अनाथभूतो
भ्रान्तमना नमुचि सो गतु चित्तमोहम् (४) ॥

---

१ "शील तथैव" शीलन्तथैव । "तथ ध्यान" तथा ध्यानं । "चतुर प्रमाण मम साक्षि" चत्वारि प्रमाणानि मम साक्षीणि । "अनुपूर्व बोधिचरि सर्व" आनुपूर्विकं बोधिचर्यारतं सर्वं । "साक्षी" साक्षि ।

२ "यावन्ति सत्त्व" यावन्तः सत्त्वाः । "दिशासु" दिक्षु । "यत्तेषु पुण्यबल शील" यत्तेषु पुण्यं बलं शीलं । अथ पुण्यबलमित्येकपदं वा । "निरर्गड यष्ट शतः कलाभिः" निरर्गडा यष्टाः शतकलाभिः शताहुतिभिरुपलक्षिता इति समुदायार्थः । "मह्य रोम सति मां कलमोपयान्ति" मम रोमस्तु सन्ति मां कलमायोपयान्ति ।

३ "सो" स । "धरणि आहनते" धरणीमाहन् । "रणते" रणति स्वनत्यर्थः । "यथ कंसपात्री" यथा कांस्यपात्रम् । "निशाम्य रिपु मेदिनिये" निशम्य रिपुर्मेदिन्यां । "शृणुतेवं" शृण्वन्तिस्वैवं ।

४ "प्रस्विन्नगात्र हततेज" प्रस्विन्नगात्रो हततेजाः । "जराभिहतु आत्मनि सम्प्रपश्यत्" जराभिहतमात्मानं सम्प्रपश्यत् । "उर राड क्रन्दतु भयार्त्त अनाथभूतो" उरस्ताडयन् क्रन्दति स भयार्त्तोऽनाथभूतो । "नमुचि सो गतु" नमुचिर्सो गतः ।

हस्त्यश्वयानरथ भूमितले निरस्ताः
धावन्ति राक्षसकुम्भाण्डपिशाच भीताः ।
सम्मूढ मार्ग न लभन्ति अलेनात्राणाः
पक्षी दवाग्निपतनेव निरीक्ष्य क्रान्ताः (१) ॥
माता स्वसा पितर पुत्र तथैव भ्राता
पृच्छन्ति तत्र कहि दृष्टु कहिं गता वा ।
अन्योन्य विग्रह करोन्ति तथैव हेतोः
प्राप्ता वयं व्यसन जीवित नावकाशः (२) ॥
सा मारसेन विपुला महती अक्षोभ्या
विभ्रष्ट सर्व्व विरलीकृत नैव सन्धिः ।
दिवसानि सप्त अभिजानि परस्परेण
आभासि दृष्ट्व यदि जीवसि बन्धु पीता (३) ॥
सा वृक्षदेवत तदा करुणां हि कृत्वा
वारीघटां ग्रहिय सिञ्चति कृष्णबन्धुम् ।

---

१ "हस्त्यश्वयानरथ" हस्त्यश्वयानरथाः। "राक्षसकुम्भाण्डपिशाच" राक्षसकुम्भाण्डपिशाचाः। "सम्मूढ मार्ग न लभन्ति अलेनात्राणाः" सम्मूढा मार्गं न लभन्ति (ख) आलीना अत्राणा इत्यर्थः। "पक्षी दवाग्निपतनेव निरीक्ष्य क्रान्ताः" पक्षिणो दावाग्निपातमिव निरीक्ष्य प्रक्रान्ता इत्यर्थः।

२ "पितर पुत्र तथैव" पिता पुत्रस्तथैव। "कहि दृष्टु कहिं गता वा" किं दृष्टं किमागतो वा, अथवा केन दृष्टः केन आगत इत्यर्थः। "अन्योन्य विग्रह करोन्ति" अन्योऽन्यं विग्रहं कुर्वन्ति। "तथैव हेतोः" तस्यैव हेतोरित्यर्थः। "व्यसन जीवित नावकाशः" व्यसनं जीवितं (प्राप्तुं) नावकाश इति च वदन्ति इति समेषार्थः।

३ "मारसेन" मारसेना। "विभ्रष्ट सर्वं विरलीकृत नैव सन्धिः" विभ्रष्टा सर्वा विरलीकृता नैव सन्धिभूता इत्यर्थः। "दिवसानि सप्त अभिजानि" सप्तदिवसानि जातानि इति अभिप्रायेति समेषार्थः। "आभासि दृष्ट्व" आभाषि दृष्ट्वा। "जीवसि बन्धु पीता" जीवसि बन्धुः पिता। अयं मारोऽस्माकं बन्धुः पिता च यदि जीवति अस्माद्वा भद्रं स्यादिति भावः।

उत्तिष्ठ शीघ्र व्रज हेमपुर मा विलम्ब
एवं हि तेष भवते गुरु उद्धराणाम् (१) ॥

मार आह।

दुःखं भयं व्यसनशोकविनाशनञ्च
धिक्कारशब्दमवमानगतञ्च दैन्यम्।
प्राप्तोऽस्मि अद्य अपराध्य सुमुक्षसत्त्वे-
ऽश्रुत्व वाक्य मधुरं हितमात्मजानाम् (२) ॥

देवता आह।

भयञ्च दुःखं व्यसनञ्च दैन्यं
धिक्कारशब्दं वधबन्धनञ्च।
दोषाननेकां (३) लभते ह्यविद्वान्
निरापराधेष्वपराध्यते यः ॥
देवासुरा गरुडकिन्नरराक्षसेन्द्रा
ब्रह्माथ शक्र परनिर्मित साकनिष्ठाः।
भाषन्ति तस्य विजयं जय लोकवीर
यच्चेदृशी नमुचिसेन त्वया निरस्ता (४) ॥

---

१ "इच्छदेवत" इच्छदेवता। "वारीघटां घहिय सिञ्चति" वारिघटां गृहीत्वा सिञ्चति (ख)। "शीघ्र व्रज हेमपुर मा विलम्ब" शीघ्रं व्रज हेमपुरं मा विलम्बं कुरु इत्यर्थः। "एवं हि तेष भवते गुरु उद्धराणाम्" एवं हि तेषां भवति गुरवः उद्धतानाम्।

२ "अद्य अपराध्य सुमुक्षसत्त्वे" अद्यापराधी (अहं) शुभ्रसत्त्वविषये इत्यर्थः। "अश्रुत्व वाक्य" अश्रुत्वा वाक्यं।

३ "दोषाननेकां" दोषाननेकान्।

४ "शक्र परनिर्मित साकनिष्ठाः" शक्राः परनिर्मिताः सकनिष्ठाः अकनिष्ठा वार्थः। "भाषन्ति" भाषन्ते। "नमुचिसेन" नमुचिसेना।

हाराद्र्धहारध्वजच्छत्रपताकदन्ती
पुष्पागुरुतगरचन्दनचूर्णवर्षाम्।
तूर्यां पराहनिय वाक्यमुदीरयन्ते
आच्छा द्रुमे तव शूर जितारिसिंहा (१) ॥

अत्रैव चासनवरे लभसेऽद्य बोधि-
मावेणिकां दशबला प्रतिसंविदां च।
सर्व्वञ्च बुद्धविषयं लभतेऽद्य शूर
मैत्री विजित्य विपुलां शठमारपक्षां (२) ॥

इह मारधर्षणकृते च रणे प्रवृत्ते
सम्बोधिसत्त्वबलविक्रम येभि दृष्ट।
षट्त्रिंशकोटिनयुतां चतुरे च विंशा
येभिर्मनः प्रणिहितं वरबुद्धबोधाविति (३) ॥

इति श्रीललितविस्तरे मारधर्षणपरिवर्त्तो नामैकविंशतितमोऽध्यायः ॥ २१ ॥

---

१ "पताकदन्ती" पताकादन्यादीन्प्रयच्छन्ति स्नेत्याशयः। "तूर्यां पराहनिय" तूर्याणि पराहत्य। "वाक्यमुदीरयन्ते आच्छा द्रुमे" वाक्यमुदीरयन्ति (स्म) आस्था द्रुमे। "जितारिसिंहा" हे जितारिसिंह।

२ "लभसेऽद्य" लप्स्यसेऽद्य। "बोधिमावेणिकां दशबला प्रतिसंविदां च" बोधिं चासमन्तादेवीव इवीभूतां चे दशबल प्रतिसंविदश्च लप्स्यसे। अथवा बोधिं लप्स्यसे (वेणिकां) देवताऽहयं मा त्यज चे दशबल प्रतिसंविदश्च लप्स्यसे इति समेपार्थः। चव संविदाश्चेत्यत्र प्रतिसंविदश्चेति वा पाठः। "लभतेऽद्य" लप्स्यसेऽद्य। "मैत्री" मैत्र्या। "विपुलां शठमारपक्षां" विपुलाम् शठमारपक्षाम्।

३ "विक्रम येभि दृष्ट" विक्रमो यैर्दृष्टः। "षट्त्रिंशकोटिनयुतां चतुरे च विंशाः" षट्त्रिंशकोटिनियुतानि चतुर्विंशाश्च। "येभिर्मनः" यैर्मनः।

द्वाविंशाध्यायप्रारम्भः ॥

इति हि भिक्षवो बोधिसत्त्वो निहतमारप्रत्यर्थिको मर्दितकण्टको रणशिरसि विजितविजय उच्छ्रितच्छत्रध्वजपताको विविक्तं कामैर्विविक्तं पापकैरकुशलैर्धर्मैः सवितर्कं सविचारं विवेकजं प्रीतिसुखं प्रथमं ध्यानमुपसम्पद्य विहरति स्म। स वितर्कसविचाराणां व्युपशमादध्यात्मसम्प्रसादाच्चेतसः॥ एकोतिभावादवितर्कमविचारं समाधिजं प्रीतिसुखं द्वितीयं ध्यानमुपसम्पद्य विहरति स्म। स प्रीतिविरागादुपेक्षको विहरन् स्मृतिमान्सम्प्रजानन्सुखं कायेन प्रतिसंवेदयति स्म। यत्तदार्या आचक्षते स्म॥ उपेक्षकः स्मृतिमान्सुखविहारी निष्प्रीतिकं तृतीयं ध्यानमुपसम्पद्य विहरति स्म॥ स सुखस्य च प्रहाणाद्दुःखस्य च प्रहाणात् पूर्व्वमेव च सौमनस्यदौर्मनस्ययोरस्तङ्गमाददुःखासुखमुपेक्षास्मृतिविशुद्धं चतुर्थध्यानमुपसम्पद्य विहरति स्म॥

अथ बोधिसत्त्वस्तथासमाहिते चित्ते परिशुद्धे पर्य्यवदाते प्रभास्वरे अनिङ्गिते विगतोपक्लेशे मृदुनि कर्म्मण्यस्थिते आनिंज्यप्राप्ते (१) रात्र्यां प्रथमयामे दिव्यचक्षुषो ज्ञानदर्शनविद्यासाक्षात्क्रियायै चित्तमभिनिर्हरति स्म अभिनिर्णामयति स्म॥

अथ बोधिसत्त्वो दिव्येन चक्षुषा परिशुद्धेनातिक्रान्तमानुष्यकेण सत्त्वान् पश्यति स्म च्यवमानानुत्पद्यमानान्सुवर्णदुर्व-

---

१ "आनिंज्यप्राप्ते" अभिज्ञमतां प्राप्ते सर्वसिंहासन्नभूते इत्यनुमीयते।

र्णान् सुगतान्दुर्गतान् हीनान्प्रणीतान्यथाकामोपगान्सत्त्वान् ॥

प्रजानाति स्म इमे वत भोः सत्त्वाः कायदुश्चरितेन समन्वागता वाङ्मनोदुश्चरितेन समन्वागता आर्य्याणामपवादका मिथ्यादृष्टयस्ते मिथ्यादृष्टिकर्म्मधर्म्मसमादानहेतोः कायस्य भेदात् परं मरणादपायदुर्गतिविनिपातपर्य्यन्तं नरकेषु प्रपद्यन्ते ॥

इमे पुनर्भवन्तः सत्त्वाः कायसुचरितेन समन्वागता आर्य्याणामनपवादका वाङ्मनःसुचरितेन समन्वागताः सम्यग्दृष्टयस्ते सम्यग्दृष्टिकर्म्मधर्म्मसमादानहेतोः कायस्य भेदात् सुगतौ स्वर्गलोकेषूपपद्यन्ते ॥

इति हि दिव्येन चक्षुषा विशुद्धेनातिक्रान्तमानुष्यकेण सत्त्वान् पश्यति स्म च्यवमानानुत्पद्यमानान्सुवर्णान्दुर्वर्णान्सुगतान्दुर्गतान् हीनान्प्रणीतान्यथाकर्म्मोपभोगान् ।

एवं खलु भिक्षवो बोधिसत्त्वो रात्र्यां प्रथमे यामे विद्यां साक्षात्करोति स्म तमो निहन्ति स्म आलोकमुत्पादयति स्म ।

अथ बोधिसत्त्वस्तथासमाहिते चित्ते परिशुद्धे पर्य्यवदाते प्रभास्वरे निरिङ्गिते विगतोपक्लेशे मृदुनि कर्म्मण्यस्थिते आनिंज्यप्राप्ते रात्र्यां मध्यमे यामे पूर्व्वनिवासानुस्मृतिज्ञानदर्शनविद्यासाक्षात्क्रियायै चित्तमभिनिर्हरति स्म निर्णामयति स्म । स आत्मनः परसत्त्वानां चानेकविधपूर्व्वनिवासाननुस्मरति स्म । तद्यथा ।

एकामपि जातिं द्वे तिस्रश्चतस्रः पञ्चदश विंशतिर्व्विंशचत्वारिंशत्पञ्चाशच्छतिशतं जातिसहस्रं जातिशतसहस्रम् ।

अनेकान्यपि जातिशतसहस्राण्यपि जातिकोटिमपि जातिकोटिशतमपि जातिकोटीसहस्रमपि जातिकोटीनियुतमपि जातिकोटिशतान्यनेकान्यप्यनेकान्यपि जातिकोटीशतसहस्राण्यपि अनेकान्यपि जातिकोटीनियुतशतसहस्राणि यावत्संवर्त्तकल्पमपि विवर्त्तकल्पमपि संवर्त्तविवर्त्तकल्पमपि अनेकान्यपि संवर्त्तविवर्त्तकल्पान्यनुस्मरति स्म (१)॥ अमुत्राहमासन्नेवंनामा एवंगोत्र एवंजातिरेवंवर्ण एवमायुःप्रमाणमेवंचिरस्थितिक एवंसुखदुःखप्रतिवेदी सोऽहं ततश्च्युतः सन्नमुत्रोपपन्नस्ततश्च्युत्वाऽमुत्रोपपन्नस्ततश्च्युत्वेहोपपन्न इति साकारं सोद्देशमनेकविधमात्मनः सर्वसत्त्वानाञ्च पूर्व्वनिवासमनुस्मरति स्म॥

अथ बोधिसत्त्वस्तथासमाहितेन चित्तेन परिशुद्धेन पर्य्यवदातेन प्रभास्वरेण अनङ्गेन(२) विगतोपक्लेशेन मृदुना कर्म्मण्यस्थितेनानिंज्यप्राप्तेन (३) रात्र्यां पश्चिमे यामे अरुणोपघाटनकालसमये (४) नन्दीमुख्यां रात्रौ दुःखसमुदयास्तङ्गतायामाश्रयततज्ञानदर्शनविद्यासाक्षात्क्रियायै चित्तमभिनिर्हरति स्म अभिनिर्नामयति स्म॥

तस्यैतदभवत्। कृच्छ्रो वतायं लोक उत्पन्नो यदुत जायते जीयते म्रियते च्यवते उपपद्यते। अथ च पुनरस्य केवलस्य महतो दुःखस्कन्धस्य निःशरणं न प्रजानाति। जराव्याधिम-

---

१ अत्रानुस्मरतिस्मेत्यस्य पुनरुक्तिः।
२ "अनङ्गेन" अनिङ्गितेनेत्यर्थः। अत्र अनङ्गणेनेति वा पाठः।
३ "अनिंज्यप्राप्तेन" अनिङ्गनतां प्राप्तेनेत्यर्थः।
४ अरुणोद्घाटनकालसमये इति वा पाठः।

रणादिकस्य अहो बतास्य केवलस्य महतो दुःखस्कन्धस्या-न्तःक्रिया न प्रज्ञायते सर्व्वस्य जराव्याधिमरणादिकस्य ॥

ततो बोधिसत्त्वस्यैतदभूत्। कस्मिन् सति जरामरणं भवति। किं प्रत्ययं च पुनर्ज्जरामरणम् ॥

तस्यैतदभूत्। जात्यां सत्यां जरामरणं भवति। जाति-प्रत्ययं हि जरामरणम् ॥

अथ बोधिसत्त्वस्य पुनरेतदभवत्। कस्मिन् सति जातिर्भ-वति किम्प्रत्यया च पुनर्जातिः ॥

तस्यैतदभवत्। भवे सति जातिर्भवति भवप्रत्यया च पुन-र्जातिः ॥

अथ खलु बोधिसत्त्वस्यैतदभवत्। कस्मिन् सति भवो भवति किम्प्रत्ययश्च पुनर्भवः ॥

तस्यैतदभवत्। उपादाने सति भवो भवत्युपादानप्रत्ययो हि भवः ॥

अथ खलु बोधिसत्त्वस्यैतदभवत्। कस्मिन् सत्युपादानं भव-ति किम्प्रत्ययञ्च पुनरुपादानम् ॥

तस्यैतदभूत्। तृष्णायां सत्यामुपादानं भवति तृष्णाप्रत्ययो ह्युपादानम् ॥

अथ बोधिसत्त्वस्य पुनरेतदभवत्। कस्मिन् सति तृष्णा भ-वति किम्प्रत्यया च तृष्णा ॥

तस्यैतदभवत्। वेदनायां सत्यां तृष्णा भवति वेदनाप्रत्यया च तृष्णा ॥

अथ बोधिसत्त्वस्य पुनरेतदभूत्। कस्मिन् सति वेदना भवति किम्प्रत्यया पुनर्वेदना ॥

तस्यैतदभूत्। स्पर्शे सति वेदना भवति स्पर्शप्रत्यया हि वेदना ॥

अथ बोधिसत्त्वस्य पुनरेतदभवत्। कस्मिन् सति स्पर्शो भवति किम्प्रत्ययश्च पुनः स्पर्शः ॥

तस्यैतदभवत्। षडायतने सति स्पर्शो भवति षडायतनप्रत्ययो हि स्पर्शः ॥

अथ बोधिसत्त्वस्य पुनरेतदभवत्। कस्मिन् सति षडायतनं भवति किम्प्रत्ययञ्च पुनः षडायतनम् ॥

तस्यैतदभवत्। नामरूपे सति षडायतनं भवति नामरूपप्रत्ययं हि षडायतनम् ॥

अथ बोधिसत्त्वस्य पुनरेतदभवत्। कस्मिन् सति नामरूपं भवति किम्प्रत्ययञ्च पुनर्नामरूपम् ॥

तस्यैतदभवत्। विज्ञाने सति नामरूपं भवति विज्ञानप्रत्ययं हि नामरूपम् ॥

अथ बोधिसत्त्वस्य पुनरेतदभवत्। कस्मिन् सति विज्ञानं भवति किम्प्रत्ययञ्च विज्ञानम् ॥

तस्यैतदभवत्। संस्कारेषु सत्सु विज्ञानं भवति संस्कारप्रत्ययञ्च विज्ञानम् ॥

अथ बोधिसत्त्वस्य पुनरेतदभवत्। कस्मिन् सति संस्कारा भवन्ति किम्प्रत्ययाश्च संस्काराः।

तस्यैतदभवत्। अविद्यायां सत्यां संस्कारा भवन्ति अविद्या-प्रत्यया हि संस्काराः ॥

इति हि भिक्षवो बोधिसत्त्वस्यैतदभूत् (१)। अविद्याप्रत्ययाः संस्काराः संस्कारप्रत्ययं विज्ञानं विज्ञानप्रत्ययं नामरूपं नामरूपप्रत्ययं षडायतनं षडायतनप्रत्ययः स्पर्शः स्पर्शप्रत्यया वेदना वेदनाप्रत्यया तृष्णा तृष्णाप्रत्ययमुपादानमुपादानप्रत्ययो भवो भवप्रत्यया जातिर्जातिप्रत्यया जरामरणशोकपरिदेवदुःखदौर्मनस्योपायासाः सम्भवन्त्येव केवलस्य महतो दुःखस्कन्धस्य समुदयो भवति समुदयः ॥

इति हि भिक्षवो बोधिसत्त्वस्य (२) पूर्व्वमश्रुतेषु धर्मेषु योऽनिशो मनसिकाराद्बहुलीकाराज्ज्ञानमुत्पादि चक्षुरुत्पादि (३) विद्योदपादि भूरिरुदपादि मेधोदपादि प्रज्ञोदपादि लोकः प्रादुर्बभूव ॥

कस्मिन् सति जरामरणं न भवति कस्य वा निरोधाज्जरामरणनिरोध इति ॥

तस्यैतदभूत्। जात्यां सत्यां जरामरणं न भवति जातिनिरोधाज्जरामरणनिरोधः ॥

अथ बोधिसत्त्वस्य पुनरेतदभवत्। कस्मिन् सति जातिर्न भवति कस्य वा निरोधाज्जातिनिरोधः ॥

---

१ अथ बोधिसत्त्वस्यैतदभवत् इति वा पाठः।

२ "बोधिसत्त्वस्य" बोधिसत्त्वेनेत्यर्थः।

३ "ज्ञानमुत्पादि चक्षुरुत्पादि" ज्ञानमुदपादि चक्षुरुदपादि।

तस्यैतदभवत्। भवेऽसति जातिर्न भवति भवनिरोधाज्जातिनिरोधः॥

अथ बोधिसत्त्वस्य पुनरेतदभवत्। कस्मिन् सति विस्तरेण यावत्संस्कारा न भवन्ति। कस्य वा निरोधात्संस्कारनिरोधः।

तस्यैतदभवत्। अविद्यायामसत्यां संस्कारा न भवन्त्यविद्यानिरोधात्संस्कारनिरोधः। संस्कारनिरोधाद्विज्ञाननिरोधः। यावज्जातिनिरोधाज्जरामरणशोकपरिदेवदुःखदौर्मनस्योपायाऽऽसा निरुध्यन्ते। एवमस्य केवलस्य महतो दुःखस्कन्धस्य निरोधो भवतीति॥

इति हि भिक्षवो बोधिसत्त्वस्य पूर्व्वमश्रुतेषु धर्म्मेषु योऽनिशो मनसिकाराद्बहुलीकारा(१)ज्ज्ञानमुदपादि चक्षुरुदपादि विद्योदपादि भूरिरुदपादि मेधोदपादि प्रज्ञोदपादि आलोकः प्रादुर्बभूव।

सोऽहं भिक्षवो तस्मिन् समये इदं दुःखमिति यथाभूतमज्ञासिषमयमास्रवसमुदयोऽयमास्रवनिरोध इयमास्रवनिरोधगामिनी प्रतिपदिति॥ यथाभूतमज्ञासिषं कामास्रवोऽयं भवास्रवोऽयमविद्यास्रवोऽयं दृष्ट्यास्रव इहास्रवा निरवशेषतो निरुध्यन्ते इहास्रवो निरवशेषमनाभासमस्तं गच्छतीति॥ इयमविद्या अयमविद्यासमुदयोऽयमविद्यानिरोध इयमविद्यानिरोधगामिनी प्रतिपदिति यथाभूतमज्ञासिषम्। इहाविद्या अपरिशेषमनाभासमस्तं गच्छतीति॥ पेयालम्।

---

१ "योऽनिशो मनसिकाराद्बहुलीकारात्" यदनिशं मनोनियोगाद्बाहुल्यादित्यर्थः।

अमी संस्कारा अयं संस्कारसमुदयोऽयं संस्कारनिरोध इयं संस्कारनिरोधगामिनी प्रतिपदिति यथाभूतमज्ञासिषम्॥

इदं ज्ञानमयं विज्ञानसमुदयोऽयं विज्ञाननिरोध इयं विज्ञाननिरोधगामिनी प्रतिपदिति यथाभूतमज्ञासिषम् (१)॥

इदं नामरूपमयं नामरूपसमुदयोऽयं नामरूपनिरोध इयं नामरूपनिरोधगामिनी प्रतिपदिति यथाभूतमज्ञासिषम्॥

इदं षडायतनमयं षडायतनसमुदयोऽयं षडायतननिरोध इयं षडायतननिरोधगामिनी प्रतिपदिति यथाभूतमज्ञासिषम्॥

अयं स्पर्शोऽयं स्पर्शसमुदयोऽयं स्पर्शनिरोध इयं स्पर्शनिरोधगामिनी प्रतिपदिति यथाभूतमज्ञासिषम्॥

इयं वेदना अयं वेदनासमुदयोऽयं वेदनानिरोध इयं वेदनानिरोधगामिनी प्रतिपदिति यथाभूतमज्ञासिषम्॥

इयं तृष्णा अयं तृष्णासमुदयोऽयं तृष्णानिरोध इयं तृष्णानिरोधगामिनी प्रतिपदिति यथाभूतमज्ञासिषम्॥

इदमुपादानमयमुपादानसमुदयोऽयमुपादाननिरोध इयमुपादाननिरोधगामिनी प्रतिपदिति यथाभूतमज्ञासिषम्॥

अयं भवोऽयं भवसमुदयोऽयं भवनिरोध इयं भवनिरोधगामिनी प्रतिपदिति यथाभूतमज्ञासिषम्॥

इयं जातिरयं जातिसमुदयोऽयं जातिनिरोध इयं जातिनिरोधगामिनी प्रतिपदिति यथाभूतमज्ञासिषम्।

---

१ अस्मिन्नन्यत्रापरवाक्ये च यथा भूतमज्ञासिषमित्यत्र यथा भूतमभ्यज्ञासिषमिति वा पाठः। कस्मिन् पुस्तके तु सर्वत्रैव यथाभूतमाज्ञासिषमिति वा पाठः।

इयं जराऽयं जरासमुदयोऽयं जरानिरोध इयं जरानिरोधगामिनी प्रतिपदिति यथाभूतमज्ञासिषम् ॥

इदं मरणमयं मरणसमुदयोऽयं मरणनिरोध इयं मरणगामिनी प्रतिपदिति यथाभूतमज्ञासिषम् ॥

इमे शोकपरिदेवदुःखदौर्मनस्योपायासा एवमस्य केवलस्य महतो दुःखस्कन्धस्य समुदयो भवति यावन्निरोधो भवतीति यथाभूतमज्ञासिषम् ॥

इदं दुःखमयं दुःखसमुदयोऽयं दुःखनिरोध इयं दुःखनिरोधगामिनी प्रतिपदिति यथाभूतमज्ञासिषम् ॥

एवं खलु भिक्षवो बोधिसत्त्वेन रात्र्यां पश्चिमे यामेऽरुणोद्घाटनकालसमये नन्दीमुख्यां रात्रौ यत्किञ्चित् पुरुषेण सत्पुरुषेणातिपुरुषेण महापुरुषेण पुरुषर्षभेण पुरुषनागेन पुरुषसिंहेन पुरुषपुङ्गवेन पुरुषशूरेण पुरुषवीरेण(१) पुरुषयागेन पुरुषपद्मेन पुरुषपुण्डरीकेण पुरुषधौरेयेणानुत्तरेण पुरुषदम्यसारथिना एवम्भूतेनार्यज्ञानेन ज्ञातव्यं बोद्धव्यं प्राप्तव्यं द्रष्टव्यं साक्षात्कर्त्तव्यं सर्व्वं तदेकचित्तेक्षणसमायुक्तं प्रज्ञयाऽनुत्तरां सम्यक्सम्बोधिमभिसम्बुध्य चैविद्याऽधिगता ॥

ततो भिक्षवो देवता आहुः। अवकिरत मार्षाः पुष्पाण्यभिसम्बुद्धो भगवान् ॥

यत्तत्र देवपुत्राः पूर्व्वबुद्धदर्शिनस्तस्मिन् सन्निपतिता आसंस्तेऽवोचन्। तावन्मार्षाः पुष्पाण्यवकिरत यावत्तावद्भगवान्निमित्तं

---

१ अत्र पुरुषधौरेयेति वा पाठः।

प्रादुष्करोति। पूर्व्वका अपि सम्यक्सम्बुद्धा निमित्तमकार्षुर्नि-
मित्तानभिनिर्म्मिण्वन्ति (१) स्म॥

अथ खलु भिक्षवस्तथागतस्तान्देवपुत्रान् विमतिप्राप्तान् ज्ञात्वा सप्ततालमात्रं विहाय समभ्युद्गम्य तत्रस्थ इदमुदानमुदानयति स्म। छिन्न वर्त्मोपशान्त रजाः शुष्का आस्रवा न पुनः स्रवन्ति (२)। छिन्ने वर्त्मनि वर्त्तते दुःखस्यैषोन्त उच्यते इति।

ततस्ते देवपुत्रा दिव्यैः कुसुमैस्तथागतमभ्यकिरन्ति स्म। ततो जानुमात्रं दिव्यानां पुष्पाणां संस्तरोऽभूत्॥

इति हि भिक्षवस्तथागतेऽभिसम्बुद्धे विगतं तमोऽन्धकारं विशोषिता तृष्णा विवर्त्तिता दृष्टिर्विक्षोभिता क्लेशा विसारितं मानशल्यं मुक्तो ग्रन्थिः प्रपातितो मानध्वज उत्क्षेपितो धर्म्मध्वज उद्घाटितोऽनुशया ज्ञाता धर्म्मतथता (३) अवबुद्धा भूतकोटिः परिज्ञातो धर्म्मधातुर्व्यवस्थापितः धर्म्मधातुः संवर्णितः (४) सम्यक्त्वनियतो राशिर्विवर्णितो मिथ्यात्वनियतो राशिः परिगृहीतोऽनियतराशिर्व्यवस्थापितानि सर्व्वेन्द्रियाणि परिज्ञाता सत्त्वचरिता (५) अवबुद्धो सत्त्वव्याधिः सत्त्वसमुत्थानसिद्धोऽमृतभैषजप्रयोगः। उत्पन्नो वैद्यराजः प्रमोचकः सर्व्वदुःखेभ्यः प्रतिष्ठापको निर्वाणसुखे निषण्णस्तथागतगर्भे तथागतमहाधर्म्मराजा-

---

१ "निर्म्मिण्वन्ति" निर्मान्ति।

२ "छिन्नवर्त्मोपशान्त रजाः" छिन्नं वर्त्मोपशान्तं रजः। "स्रवन्ति" स्रूयन्ते।

३ "धर्म्मतथता" धर्म्मतथ्यता।

४ अत्र सत्त्वधातुः संवर्णित इति वा पाठः।

५ "परिज्ञाता सत्त्वचरिता" परिज्ञातानि सत्त्वचरितानि।

सने सर्वे आस्रवा विमुक्तिपक्षाः प्रविष्टः सर्व्वज्ञतानगरं समवसृतं सर्व्वदुःखै(१)रसम्भिन्नो धर्म्मधातुप्रसरानुबोधैः।

प्रथमे सप्ताहे भिक्षवस्तथागतस्तस्मिन्नेव बोधिमण्डे निषण्णोऽभूत्। इह मयाऽनुत्तरा सम्यक्सम्बोधिरभिसम्बुद्धा। इह मयाऽनवराग्रस्य जातिजरामरणदुःखस्यान्तः कृत इति।

समनन्तरप्राप्ते खलु पुनर्भिक्षवो बोधिसत्त्वेन सर्व्वज्ञत्वे अथ तत्क्षणमेव दशसु दिक्षु सर्व्वलोकधातुषु सर्व्वसत्त्वास्तत्क्षणं तल्लवं तन्मुहूर्त्तं परमसुखसमर्पिता अभूवन्। सर्व्वलोकधातवश्च महताऽवभासेनावभास्यन्त। या अपि ता लोकान्तरिका अघा अघस्फुटा(२)अन्धकारा इति पूर्व्ववत्। षड्विकारं च दशसु दिक्षु सर्व्वे लोकधातवोऽकम्पन्त प्राकम्पन्त सम्प्राकम्पन्त अवेधन्त प्रावेधन्त सम्प्रावेधन्त। अचलत् प्राचलत् सम्प्राचलत्। अक्षुभ्यत् प्राक्षुभ्यत् सम्प्राक्षुभ्यत्। अरणत् प्रारणत् सम्प्रारणत्। अगर्ज्जत्प्रागर्ज्जत् सम्प्रागर्ज्जत्(३)॥ सर्व्वबुद्धाश्च तथागतायाभिसम्बुद्धाय साधुकारं ददति स्म। धर्म्माच्छादांश्च सम्प्रेषयन्ति स्म। यैर्धर्म्माच्छादैरयं त्रिसाहस्रमहासाहस्रलोकधातुरनेकरत्नच्छत्रसञ्छन्नोऽभूत्। तेभ्यश्च रत्नच्छत्रेभ्य एवंरूपा रश्मिजाला निश्चरन्ति स्म। यैर्दशसु दिक्षु अप्रमेया असङ्ख्येया लोकधातवोऽवभास्यन्त। दशसु दिक्षु बोधिसत्त्वाश्च देवपुत्राश्चानन्दशब्दं निश्चारयामासुः। उत्पन्नः सत्त्वपण्डितपद्मो ज्ञानसरसि सम्भू-

---

१ अत्र सर्वबुद्धैरिति वा पाठः।

२ अत्यस्फुटा इति वा पाठः।

३ अत्र अचलदित्यत्सर्वत्र बहुवचनमपेक्षितम्।

तेाऽनुपलिप्तो लोकधर्म्मैः। समन्ततो महाकरुणामेघं स्फुरित्वा धर्म्मधातुभवनं(१) वर्षयिष्यति। धर्म्मवर्षं विनीय जनभैषजाङ्कुरप्ररोहणं सर्व्वकुशलमूलवीजानां विवर्द्धनं श्रद्धाङ्कुराणां दाता विमुक्तिफलानाम्। तत्रेदमुच्यते।

मारं विजित्य सबलं स हि पुरुषसिंहो
ध्यानसुखमभिमुखमभितोऽपि शास्ता।
त्रैविद्यता दशबलेन यदा हि प्राप्ता
सङ्कम्पिता दशदिशो बहुक्षेत्रकोट्यः॥
ये बोधिसत्त्व पुरि आगत धर्म्मकामा-
श्चरणौ निपत्य इति भाषिषु मासि क्लान्तः।
प्रत्यक्ष अस्मि चमु याडृशिका सुभीमा
सा प्रज्ञपुण्यबलवीर्य्यबलेन भग्ना (२)॥
मुञ्चेय क्षेत्रनयुतैः प्रहितानि च्छत्रा
साधो महापुरुष धर्षित मारसेना।
प्राप्तं त्वया पदवरममृतं विशोक
सद्धर्म्मवृष्टि त्रिभवेऽभिवर्ष शीघ्रम्(३)॥
बाहुं प्रसार्य्य दशदिशु च सत्त्वसारा
आभाषयिं सुकलविङ्करुताय वाचा।

---

१ "धर्मधातुभवनं" धर्मधातुभवने इत्यर्थः। अत्र धर्मधातुगमनमिति वा पाठः।

२ "बोधिसत्त्व पुरि आगत" बोधिसत्त्वाः पुरतः आगताः। "चरणौ" चरणे। "इति भाषिषु मासि क्लान्त" इत्यभाषिषुर्मा भव क्लान्त इत्यर्थः। "प्रत्यक्ष अस्मि चमु याडृशिका" प्रत्यक्षेऽस्माकं चमूर्याडृशीत्यर्थः। "प्रज्ञपुण्य" प्रज्ञापुण्य।

३ "क्षेत्रनयुतैः" क्षेत्रनियुतेषु इत्यर्थः। "छत्रा" छत्राणि। "धर्षित" धर्षिता। "विशोक" विशोकं। "सद्धर्मवृष्टि" सद्धर्मवृष्टिं।

बोधिर्यथामनुगता भवता विघुष्टा
तुल्यः समापि यथ सर्पिष सर्पिमण्डैः (१) ॥

अथ खलु भिक्षवः कामावचरा अप्सरसो बोधिमण्डनिषण्णं तथागतं प्राप्ताभिज्ञं परिपूर्णसङ्कल्पं विजितसङ्ग्रामं निर्जितमारप्रत्यर्थिकमुच्छ्रितच्छत्रध्वजपताकं शूरं जयोद्गतं पुरुषं महापुरुषं वैद्योत्तमं महाशल्यहर्त्तारं सिंहं विगतभयलोमहर्षं नागं सुदान्तचित्तं निर्मलं त्रिमलमलप्रहीणं वेदकं त्रैविद्यतामनुप्राप्तं पारगं चतुरौघोत्तीर्णं क्षत्रियमेकरत्नच्छत्रधारिणं त्रैलोक्यब्राह्मणं वाहितपापधर्माणं (२) भिक्षुं भिन्नाविद्याण्डकोषं श्रमणं सर्व्वसङ्गसमतिक्रान्तं स्वयम्भुवं (३) निःसृतक्लेशं शूरमप्रपातितध्वजं बलीयांसं दशबलधारिणं रत्नाकरमिव सर्व्वधर्मरत्नसम्पूर्णं विदित्वा बोधिमण्डाभिमुखास्तथागतमाभिर्गाथाभिरभ्यष्टाविषुः (४) ॥

एष द्रुमराजमूलेऽभिजित्य मारसैन्यम् ।
स्थितु मेरुवदकम्प्यो निर्भीरप्रत्रासी (५) ॥

अनेकबहुकल्पकोट्य दानदमसंयमेन ।

---

१ "सब्रह्मचारा वाभाषयि सुकलविवृद्धताय" सब्रह्मचार अभाषत सुकलविवृद्धतया। "यथामनुगता" यथानुगता। "तुल्यः समापि यथ सर्पिष सर्पिमण्डैः" यथा सर्पिषा सर्पिर्मण्डैर्वा तुल्यं सर्पिर्भवति तथा त्वमपि बोधितुल्य इत्यर्थः। तुल्यः समोऽसि यथ सर्पिष सर्पिमण्डे इति वाच पाठः। अत्र तुल्यसमयोरेकतरेण भाव्यम्।

२ वाहितपापकर्माणमिति वा पाठः ।

३ श्रोत्रिय, सोभिभूयमिति पाठद्वयमत्र ।

४ "अभ्यष्टाविषुः" अभ्यष्टौषुः ।

५ "स्थितु मेरुवदकम्प्यो" स्थितो मेरुवदकम्प्यो ।

समुदानार्थं प्रबोधितस्तेनैष सो भवेद्यः (१) ॥
अनेन बहुकल्पकोट्यः शीलव्रततपोऽभिः ।
जिह्मीकृत शक्रब्रह्मा बोधिवर एषता हि (२) ॥
अनेन बहुकल्पकोट्यः क्षान्तिबलवर्मितेन ।
अधिवासिता दुःखानि तेन प्रभ सुवर्णवर्णा (३) ॥
अनेन बहुकल्पकोट्यो वीर्यबलविक्रमेण ।
पश्चान्मुखीकृताश्चा तेन मार जित सेना (४) ॥
अनेन बहुकल्पकोट्यो ध्यानाभिज्ञाज्ञानैः ।
सम्पूजिता मुनीन्द्रास्तेनैव पूजितोऽद्य (५) ॥
अनेन बहुकल्पकोट्यः प्रज्ञाश्रुतसञ्चयेन ।
प्रगृहीत सत्त्वकोट्यस्तेन लघु बोधि प्राप्ता (६) ॥
अनेन जितु स्कन्ध मारस्तथ मृत्युमारक्लेशमाराः ।
अनेन जितु देवपुत्र मारस्तेनाद्य नास्ति शोकः (७) ॥

---

१ "अनेकबहुकल्पकोट्या" अनेकबहुकल्पकोटिपर्यन्तमित्यर्थः। "प्रबोधितस्तेनैष सो भवेद्यः" अनेन यो बोधिः प्रबोधितस्तेन हेतुना एष बोधिसत्त्वः स बोधिर्भवेदिति समुदायार्थः।

२ "बहुकल्पकोट्यः" बहुकल्पकोटिपर्यन्तमिति सर्वत्र बोध्यम्। "जिह्मीकृत शक्रब्रह्मा" जिह्मीकृताः शक्रब्रह्मादय इत्यर्थः। "बोधिवर एषता" (अत एव) बोधिवरमेष्यति, बोधिवरमन्वेष्यता वा।

३ "क्षान्तिबलवर्मितेन" क्षान्तिबलवर्मितत्वेन। "अधिवासिता" अधिवासितानि। "प्रभ" प्रभा (स्वदेहस्य) इत्यर्थः।

४ "पश्चान्मुखीकृताश्चा तेन मार जित सेना" पश्चान्मुखीकृतास्तेन मारो जिता सेना। अत्र पराङ्मुखीकृताश्चा तेन मार जित सेनेति वा पाठः।

५ "ध्यानाभिज्ञाज्ञानैः" ध्यानाभिज्ञाज्ञानैः।

६ "प्रगृहीत" प्रगृहीताः। "बोधि" बोधिः।

७ "जितु स्कन्ध मारस्तथ" जितः स्कन्धो मारस्तथा। "मृत्युमारक्लेशमाराः" इत्यत्र मृत्युक्लेशमारा इति वा पाठः। "जितु देवपुत्र" जितो देवपुत्रः।

एषोऽतिदेवदेवो देवैरपि पूजनीयः ।
पूजार्हस्त्रिलोके पुण्यार्थिकाम् क्षेत्रममृतफलस्य दाता (१) ॥
एष वरदक्षिणीयो उत्पातुदक्षिणा हि ।
नास्त्युत्तरेऽस्य नाथो यथा च वर बोधि लब्धा (२) ॥
ऊर्णा विभ्राजतेऽस्य स्फुरती बहुकल्पकोट्यः ।
जिह्मीकृत चन्द्रसूर्यौ सत्त्व आलोक प्राप्त (३) ॥
एवं हि सुरूपरूपो वररूपो साधुरूपो ।
वरलक्षणो हितैषी त्रैलोक्यपूजनीयः (४) ॥
एष सुविशुद्धनेत्रो बहु प्रेक्षते स्वयम्भूः ।
क्षेत्रांश्च सत्त्वकायां चित्तानि चेतनाश्च (५) ॥
सुविशुद्धश्रोत्रः शृणुतेऽनन्तशब्दां दिव्यांश्च ।
मानुष्यांश्च जिनशब्दं धर्मशब्दां (६) ॥
एष प्रभूतजिह्वः कलविङ्कमञ्जुघोषः ।
श्रोष्याम अस्य धर्ममममृतं प्रशान्तगामिं (७) ॥

---

१ "पुण्यार्थिकाम् क्षेत्रममृतफलस्य" पुण्यार्थिकेभ्यः पुण्यक्षेत्रस्यामृतफलस्य चेत्यर्थः।

२ "उत्पातुदक्षिणा हि" उपात्तदाक्षिण्यो हि इत्यर्थः। "नास्त्युत्तरेऽस्य" नास्त्युत्तरश्चास्य। "वर बोधि लब्धा" वरा बोधिर्लब्धा।

३ "स्फुरती बहुकल्पकोट्यः" स्फुरन्ती बहुकल्पकोटिपर्यन्तमित्यर्थः। "जिह्मीकृत चन्द्रसूर्यौ" जिह्मीकृतौ चन्द्रसूर्यौ। "सत्त्व आलोक प्राप्त" सत्त्वा आलोकं प्राप्ताः। अत्र सत्त्व आलोकप्राप्त इति वा पाठः।

४ "एवं हि" अत एवेत्यर्थः। "साधुरूपो" साधुरूपः।

५ "क्षेत्रांश्च सत्त्वकायां चित्तानि चेतनाश्च" क्षेत्राणि सत्त्वकायांश्चित्तानि चेतनांश्च। अत्र चित्तानचेतनांश्चेति वा पाठः। किन्त्वत्र चेतनानचेतनांश्चेत्युचितम्।

६ "शृणुतेऽनन्तशब्दां" शृणोत्यनन्तशब्दान्। "मानुष्यांश्च जिनशब्दं धर्मशब्दां" मनुष्यशब्दांश्च जिनशब्दान्धर्मशब्दांश्चेत्यर्थः।

७ "प्रशान्तगामिं" प्रशान्तगामि।

दृष्ट्वा च मारसैन्यं न क्षुभ्यति मनोऽस्य
पुनर्दृष्ट्वा देवसङ्घां न च हर्षते सुमेधो (१) ॥
शस्त्रेण चापि वाचैर्जित एनमारसेना ।
सत्यव्रततपोभिर्जितु एन दुष्टमल्लः (२) ॥
चलितो न चासना ना च काय बोधिमो ।
न चास्य खेऊर्नापि दोषस्तदनन्तरे अभूवन् (३) ॥
लाभा सुलब्धास्तेषां मरुणां नराणां चैवम् ।
ये तुभ्य धर्म श्रुत्वा प्रतिपत्तिमेष्यन्ति हि (४) ॥
यत्पुण्यं स्यान्तविदित्वा जिनपुण्यराशे ।
सर्व्वे भवेम क्षिप्र यथ त्वं मनुष्यचन्द्रः (५) ॥
बुद्धित्व बोधि पुरुषर्षभ नायकेन
सङ्कम्प्य क्षेत्रनियुतानि विजित्य मारम् ।
ब्रह्मस्वरेण कलविङ्करुतस्वरेण
प्रथमेन गाथ इमि भाषित नायकेन (६) ॥
पुण्यविपाकसुखसर्व्वदुःखापनेषी

---

१ "देवसङ्घां" देवसङ्घं । "हर्षते" हृष्यति ।

२ "जित एन" जिता अनेन । "जितु एन" जितोऽनेन ।

३ "न चासना ना च काय बोधिमो" न चासनात् न च कायो बोधेः । "खेऊ" खेदः । "तदनन्तरे अभूवन्" तस्मिन् समये अभूत् इत्यर्थः ।

४ "मरुणां" मरुतां । अत्र स्थानत्रये या षष्ठी सा कर्त्तरिषष्ठी बोध्या । "तुभ्य-धर्म" तव धर्मं ।

५ "स्यान्त" स्यान्तु । "भवेम क्षिप्र यथ" भविष्यामः क्षिप्रं यथा ।

६ "बुद्धित्व बोधि" बोधयित्वा बुद्धा वा बोधिं । "पुरुषर्षभ" पुरुषर्षभेण । "प्रथमेन गाथ इमि भाषित" प्रथमं गाथा इमा भाषिताः । "नायकेन" पुनरुक्तिस्त्वाक्षेपि-तमप्येतत्पदम् ।

अभिप्राउ चास्य सिध्यति च पुण्यवतो नरस्य।
क्षिप्रञ्च बोधि स्पृशते विनिहत्य मारं
शान्तापथो गच्छति च निर्वृत्तिशीतिभावम् (१) ॥

तस्मात्कः पुण्यकरणेन भवेत तृप्तः
शृण्वञ्च धर्ममसृतं भवि को वितृप्तः।
विजने च विहरे भवि को वितृप्तः
कः सत्त्व अर्थकरणेन भवेद्वितृप्तः (२) ॥

पाणिं प्रसार्य्य ममुवाच बोधिसत्त्वा
पूजा कृता भजत चेव खकस्वकानि।
सर्वेऽभिवन्द्य चरणौ च तथागतस्य
नानाविवूहगत चेव स्वकस्वकानि (३) ॥

दृष्ट्वा च तां नमुचिनो महतीमवस्थां
विक्रीडितास्य सुगतस्य तथा सलीलम्।
बोधाय चित्तमतुलं प्रणिधाय सत्त्वा
मारं विजित्य सबलममृतं स्पृशेम (४) ॥

अभिसम्बुद्धस्य भिक्षवस्तथागतस्य बोधिवृक्षमूले सिंहासनो-

---

१ "सर्वदुःखाप्रनेषी" सर्वदुःखापनयिता। "अभिप्राउ चास्य" अभिप्राय अस्य सिध्यति। "बोधि स्पृशते" बोधिं स्पृशति। "शान्तापथो" शान्तिपथे। "निर्वृत्तिशीतिभावम्" निर्वृत्तिभावमशीतिभावमित्यर्थः।

२ "शृण्वञ्च" शृण्वंश्च। "भवि" भवति। "विजने च विहरे" विजनविहारे चेत्यर्थः। "भवि" भवति।

३ "बोधिसत्त्वा" बोधिसत्त्वः। "चेव" चेमाणि। "नानाविवूहगत चेव" नाना व्यूहगतानि चेमाणि।

४ "नमुचिनो" नमुचेः। "विक्रीडितास्य" विक्रीडितस्य। "सत्त्वां" सत्त्वानां।

प्रविष्टस्य तस्मिन् क्षणेऽप्रमेयाणि बुद्धविक्रीडितान्यभूवन् । यानि न सुकरं कल्पेनापि निर्देष्टुम् । तत्रेदमुच्यते ।

करतलसदृशाऽभूत् सुस्थिता मेदनीयं
विकसितशतपत्राश्चोद्गता रश्मिमन्तः ।
अमरशतसहस्रा आगमी बोधिमण्ड
इमु प्रथम निमित्तं सिंहनादे हि दृष्टम् (१) ॥
द्रुमशत चिसहस्रो बोधिमण्डे नमन्ते
गिरिवर तथनैके शैलराजश्च मेरुः ।
दशबलमधिगम्य ब्रह्मशक्रा नमन्ते
इदमपि नरसिंहे विक्रीडितं बोधिमण्डे (२) ॥
रश्मिशतसहस्रां स्वशरीरात्मभावात्
स्फुरि जिनवरक्षेत्रां चोणि शान्ता अपायाः ।
तत्क्षण सुसमुद्धृर्त्तै शोधिताक्षाक्षणानि
न च खिलमददोषा बोधिषु किञ्चि सत्त्वा (३) ॥

---

१ "विकसितशतपत्राश्चोद्गता रश्मिमन्तः" विकसितशतपत्राणि चोद्गतानि रश्मिमन्ति । "अमरशतसहस्रा चागमी बोधिमण्ड" अमरशतसहस्राणि चागमन्नि बोधिमण्डं । "इमु प्रथम" इदं प्रथमं ।

२ "द्रुमशत चिसहस्रो बोधिमण्डे नमन्ते" द्रुमशतानि चिसहस्रस्य बोधिमण्डं नमन्ति । "गिरिवर तथनैके" गिरिवरास्तथाऽनैके । "ब्रह्मशक्रा नमन्ते" ब्रह्मशक्रौ नमतः । "इदमपि नरसिंहे" इदमपि नरसिंहस्य द्वितीयनिमित्तमित्यर्थः ।

३ "रश्मिशतसहस्रां स्वशरीरात्मभावात् स्फुरि जिनवरक्षेत्रां चोणी" रश्मिशतसहस्राणि स्वशरीरादात्मभावात् स्फुरयित्वा जिनवरक्षेत्राणि चयः । "तत्क्षण" तत्क्षणे । "शोधिताक्षाक्षणानि" शोधितान्यक्षणानि । "खिलमददोषाः" खिलमददोषवन्त इत्यर्थः । "बोधिषु" बोधिमण्डेषु बोधिसत्त्वसंबन्धेन सार्थः । "किञ्चि सत्त्वा" केचित् सत्त्वाः ।

इदमपि नरसिंहस्यासनस्थस्य क्रीडा
शशिरविमणिवह्निविद्युताभा च दिव्या ।
न तपति अभिभूता भासयन्त्युर्णकोशा
न च जगदिह कश्चित्प्रेक्षते शास्तु मूर्द्धम् (१) ॥
इदमपि नरसिंहस्यासनस्थस्य क्रीडा
करतलस्पृशनेनाकम्पिता मेदिनी सर्वा ।
येन नमुचिसेना क्षोभिता तूलभूता
नमुचि इपु गृहीत्वा मेदिनी व्यालिखेच्च (२) ॥

इदमपि नरसिंहस्यासने क्रीडितमभूदिति ।

इति श्रीललितविस्तरे अभिसम्बोधनपरिवर्त्तो नाम द्वा-
विंशतितमः ।

त्रयोविंशाध्यायप्रारम्भः ।

अथ खलु शुद्धावासकायिका देवपुत्रा बोधिमण्डे निषण्णं तथागतं प्रदक्षिणीकृत्य दिव्यैश्चन्दनचूर्णवर्षैरभ्यवकीर्य्याभिर्गाथाभिरभ्यष्टावीत् (३) ।

---

१ "वह्निर्विद्युताभा" वह्निविद्युदाभा । "तपति" तापयति । "भासयन्त्युर्णकोशा" भासयन्त्युर्णाकोशाम् । अत्र नाशयन्त्युर्णपाशा इति वा पाठः । "शास्तु मूर्द्धम्" शास्तुः (बोधिसत्त्वस्य) मूर्द्धानमित्यर्थः ।

२ "करतलस्पृशनेन" करतलस्पर्शेन । "मेदिनि" चार्वीत्यनुमीयते । "नमुचि इपु" नमुचिरिपुं । "मेदिनी व्यालिखेच्च" मेदिनीं व्यलिखद् यः ।

३ "रभ्यष्टावीत्" रभ्यष्टौषुः ।

उत्पन्नो लोकप्रद्योतो लोकनाथः प्रभङ्करः ।
अन्धभूतस्य लोकस्य चक्षुर्दाता रणञ्जहः ॥
भगवान् विजितसङ्ग्रामः पुण्यैः पूर्णमनोरथः ।
सम्पूर्णः शुक्लधर्म्मैस्त्वं जगन्ति तर्पयिष्यसि (१) ॥
उत्तीर्णपङ्को ह्यनिघः स्थले तिष्ठति गौतमः ।
अन्यां सत्त्वां महाऽघेन प्राज्ञस्तारयिष्यसि (२) ॥
उद्गतस्त्वं महाप्राज्ञ लोकेष्वप्रतिपुद्गल ।
लोकधर्म्मैरलिप्तस्त्वं जलस्थमिव पङ्कजम् ॥
चिरप्रसुप्तमिमं लोकं तमःस्कन्धावगुण्ठितम् ।
भवान् प्रज्ञाप्रदीपेन समर्थः प्रतिबोधितुम् ॥
चिरातुरे जीवलोके क्लेशव्याधिप्रपीडिते ।
वैद्यराट् त्वं समुत्पन्नः सर्व्वव्याधिप्रमोचकः ॥
भविष्यन्त्यक्षणाः शून्यास्त्वयि नाथे समुद्गते ।
मनुष्याश्चैव देवाश्च भविष्यन्ति सुखान्विताः ॥
येषां त्वद्दर्शनं सौम्य एष्यसे (३) पुरुषर्षभ ।
न ते कल्पसहस्राणि जातु यास्यन्ति दुर्गतिम् ॥
पण्डिताश्चाप्यरोगाश्च धर्म्मं श्रोष्यन्ति येऽपि ते ।
गम्भीराश्चोपधिक्षीणा (४) भविष्यन्ति विशारदाः ॥

---

१ "तर्पयिष्यसि" तर्पयिष्यति ।

२ "अन्यां सत्त्वां" अन्यान् सत्त्वान् । "महाघेन प्राज्ञस्तारयिष्यसि" महाघात् प्रज्ञानः (प्रज्ञया) तारयिष्यति ।

३ "एष्यसे" भविष्यति इत्यर्थः ।

४ "चोपधिक्षीणाः" चोपाधिक्षीणाः ।

मोक्षं ते च लघुं सर्व्वे छित्वा वै क्लेशबन्धनम् ।
यास्यन्ति निरुपादाना: फलप्राप्ति वरं शुभम् (१) ॥
दक्षिणीयाश्च ते लोके आहुतीनां प्रतिग्रहाः ।
न तेषु दक्षिणा न्यूना सत्त्वानिर्वाणहेतुकी (२) ॥

एवं खलु भिक्षवः शुद्धावासकायिका देवपुत्रास्तथागतमभिष्टुत्यैकान्ते प्राञ्जलयस्तस्थुः ॥

अथ खल्वाभास्वरा देवपुत्रास्तथागतं बोधिमण्डनिषण्णं दिव्यैर्नानाप्रकारैः पुष्पधूपमाल्यविलेपनचूर्णचीवरच्छत्रध्वजपताकाभिः सम्पूज्य त्रिःप्रदक्षिणीकृत्य चाभिर्गाथाभिरभ्यष्टाविषुः (३) ।

गम्भीरबुद्धे मधुरस्वरा मुने
ब्रह्मस्वरा मुनिवरगीत सुस्वरा ।
वराग्रबोधिपरमार्थप्राप्ता
सत्यस्वरे पारङ्गते नमस्ते (४) ॥
त्रातासि दीपोऽसि परायणोऽसि
नाथोऽसि लोके कृपामैत्रचित्तः ।
वैद्योत्तमस्त्वं खलु शल्यहर्त्ता
चिकित्सकस्त्वं परमं हितङ्करः ॥

---

१ "फलप्राप्ति वरं शुभम" फलप्राप्तिं वरां शुभाम् ।
२ "प्रतिग्रहाः" प्रतिग्राहका इत्यर्थः । "सत्त्वानिर्वाणहेतुकी" सत्त्वनिर्वाणहेतुकी ।
३ "अभ्यष्टाविषुः" अभ्यस्तोषुः ।
४ "मधुरस्वरा" मधुरस्वर । अत्र सर्वत्र सम्बोधने आकारान्तोऽकारान्तो बोध्यः ।
"सत्यस्वरे पारङ्गते" सत्यस्वर पारङ्गत ।

दीपङ्करस्य मह दर्शनं त्वया
समुदानितं मैत्रकृपाग्रजालम्।
प्रमुञ्चमाना अमृतस्य धारां
समेहि तापं सुरमानुषाणाम् (१) ॥

त्वं पद्मभूतस्त्रिभवेष्वलिप्त-
स्त्वं मेरुकल्पो विपुलो ह्यकम्प्यः।
त्वं वज्रकल्पो ह्यचलप्रतिज्ञ-
स्त्वं चन्द्रमाः सर्व्वगुणाग्रधारी ॥

एवं खलु भिक्षव आभास्वरा देवपुत्रास्तथागतमभिसंस्तुत्यैकान्ते तस्थुः प्राञ्जलयस्तथागतन्नमस्यन्तः (२)।

अथ खलु सुब्रह्मदेवपुत्रप्रमुखाः ब्रह्मकायिका देवास्तथागतं बोधिमण्डनिषण्णमनेकमणिरत्नकोटिनियुतशतसहस्रप्रत्युप्तेन रत्नजालेनाभिच्छाद्य त्रिःप्रदक्षिणीकृत्य आभिः सारूप्याभिर्गाथाभिरभ्यष्टाविषुः (३)।

शुभविमलप्रज्ञाप्रभतेजधरा
द्वात्रिंशल्लक्षणवराग्रधरा।
स्मृतिमां मतिमां गुणज्ञानधरा
अकिलान्तका शिरसा वन्दामि ते (४) ॥

---

१ "समुदानितं" समुदानीतं। "समेहि" शमय।

२ "नमस्यन्तः" नमस्यन्तः।

३ "रभ्यष्टाविषुः" अभ्यष्टौषुः।

४ "प्रभतेजधरा" प्रभातेजोधर। एवमग्र सर्वत्र सम्बोधनान्ताकारोऽकारो बोध्यः। स्मृतिमां मतिमां" स्मृतिमन्मतिमन्। "अकिलान्तका" अक्लान्तक। "वन्दामि ते" वन्दामहे त्वाम्।

अमला विमला त्रिमलैर्विमला
त्रैलोक्यविश्रुत त्रिविद्यगता।
त्रिविधाविमोक्षवरचक्षुददा
वन्दामि त्वां त्रिनयनं विमलम् (१) ॥
कलिकलुष उद्धृत सुदान्तमना
रूपकरुण उद्गत जगदर्थकरा।
मुनिमुदितोद्गतप्रशान्तमना
द्वयमतिमोचक उपेक्षरता (२) ॥
प्रततपसङ्गत जगार्थकरा
सुचरी विशुद्धचरिं पारङ्गता।
चतुःसत्यदेशक विमोक्षरता
मुक्तो विमोचयसि चान्य जगत् (३) ॥
बलवीर्यं आगतु दृढा नमुचि
प्रज्ञाय वीर्य तव मैत्र्य जितो।

---

१ "त्रिविद्यगता" त्रैविद्यगत। "त्रिविधाविमोक्षवरचक्षुददा" त्रिविधविमोक्षवरचक्षुर्द। "वन्दामि" वन्दामहे।

२ "उद्धृत" उद्धृतः। "रूपकरुण उद्गत" रूपाकरुणा उद्गता। "उद्गतप्रशान्तमना" उद्गतप्रशान्तमनः। "द्वयमतिमोचक उपेक्षरता" अज्ञानतिमोचय उपेक्षारत इत्यर्थः। सर्वापि सम्बोधनान्ताकारोऽकारो बोध्यः।

३ "प्रततपसङ्गत जगार्थकरा" प्रततपःसङ्गत जगदर्थकर। "सुचरी विशुद्धचरिं पारङ्गता" सुचरित विशुद्धचरित पारङ्गत। सुचर्याया विशुद्धचर्यायाः पारङ्गत इति वार्थः। "चतुःसत्यदेशक" चतुःसत्योपदेशक। अथ चतुःसत्यदर्शक इति वा पाठः। "विमोचयसि चान्य" विमोचयिष्यसि चान्यं।

प्राप्तं च ते पदवरमच्युतं
वन्दाम ते शठचमूमथना (१) ॥

एवं खलु भिक्षवः सुब्रह्मदेवपुत्रप्रमुखा ब्रह्मकायिका देवास्तथागतमाभिर्गाथाभिरभिष्टुत्यैकान्ते तस्थुः प्राञ्जलयस्तथागतं नमस्यन्तः (२)।

अथ खलु ते शुद्धावासकायिका देवपुत्रा येन तथागतस्तेनोपसंक्रामन्नुपसंक्रम्य महारत्नच्छत्रवितानैस्तथागतमभिच्छाद्य प्राञ्जलयस्तथागतमाभिः सारूप्याभिर्गाथाभिरभ्यष्टाविषुः (३)।

प्रत्यचेस्मिं बले भवातिविपुले मारस्य घोरा चमू
यथा सा मारचमू महाप्रतिभया एकक्षणेन ते जिता ।
न च तेऽउत्थितु नैव कायु भ्रमितो नो वा गिरा व्याहृता
त्वां वन्दामहि सर्व्वलोकमहितं सर्व्वार्थसिद्धं मुनिम् (४) ॥
माराः कोटिसहस्रनयुता गङ्गाणुभिः संस्थिता-
स्ते तुभ्यं न समर्थ बोधिसत्वटां सञ्चालिकं कम्पितुम् ।
यज्ञा कोटिसहस्रनयुता गङ्गा यथा वालिका

---

१ "बलवीर्यं आगतु दृष्ट्वा नमुचि प्रज्ञाय वीर्यं तव मैत्र्य जितो" बलवीर्यमागत दृष्ट्वा नमुचिः प्रज्ञया वीर्येण तथा मैत्र्या जितः। "वन्दाम ते शठचमूमथना" वन्दामहे त्वां शठचमूमथन ।

२ "नमस्यन्तः" नमस्यमानाः ।

३ "अभ्यष्टाविषुः" अभ्यस्तौषुः ।

४ "प्रत्यचेस्मिं" प्रत्यक्षमस्मिन्। "भवातिविपुले" भावातिविपुले अतिविपुलभावापन्ने इति यावत्। न च तेऽउत्थितु नैव कायु" न च समुत्थितो नैव कायः। "व्याहृता" व्याहृतम्। "वन्दामहि" वन्दामहे।

यष्टा बोधिगताश्रितेन भवता तेनाद्य विभ्राजसे (१) ॥
भार्य्याश्चेष्टतमां सुतांश्च दयितां दासांश्च दासीस्तथा
उद्यानानगराणि राष्ट्रनिगमाराज्यानि सान्तःपुरा।
हस्तापादशिरोत्तमाङ्गमपि वा चक्षूंषि जिह्वा तथा
त्यक्तास्ते वरबोधिचर्य्यचरिता तेनाद्य विभ्राजसे (२) ॥
उक्तं यद्वचनं त्वया सुबहुशो बुद्धो भविष्याम्यहं
तारिष्ये बहुसत्त्वकोटिनयुता दुःखार्णवेनोह्यता।
ध्यानाधीन्द्रियबुद्धिभिः कवचितः सद्धर्मनावा स्वयं
सा चैषा प्रतिपूर्ण तुभ्य प्रणिधिस्तारिष्यसे प्राणिनः (३) ॥
यत्पुण्यं स्तवित्व वादिवृषभं लोकस्य चक्षुर्ददं
सर्व्वे भूत्व उदग्रहृष्टमनसः प्रार्थेम ते सर्व्वज्ञताम्।
समुदानेत्व वराग्रबोधिमतुलां बुद्धैः सुसंवर्णिता-

---

१ "कोटिसहस्रनयुताः" कोटिसहस्रनियुतसङ्ख्याका इत्यर्थः। "गङ्गारेणुभिः संस्थिताः" गङ्गारेणुभिः परिमिता इत्यर्थः। "ते तुभ्यं न समर्थ बोधिद्रुमवटात् संचालितुं कम्पितुम्" ते त्वां न समर्था बोधिद्रुमवटात् संचालयितुं कम्पयितुम्। "कोटिसहस्रनयुता" कोटिसहस्रनियुतसङ्ख्याका इत्यर्थः। "गङ्गा यथा वालिका" गाङ्गा यथा वालुकाः।

२ "भार्य्याश्चेष्टमां" भार्याश्चेष्टतमाः। "दयितां" दयिताम्। "उद्यानानगराणि राष्ट्रनिगमाराज्यानि सान्तःपुरा" उद्याननगराणि राष्ट्रनिगमराज्यानि सान्तःपुराणि। "हस्तापादशिरोत्तमाङ्गमपि" हस्तपादशिरउत्तमाङ्गमपि। "वरबोधिचर्यचरिता" चाचरितवरबोधिचर्य वरबोधिचर्या चरिता चार्थः।

३ "तारिष्ये बहुसत्त्वकोटिनयुता दुःखार्णवे नोह्यता" तारयिष्ये बहुसत्त्वकोटिनियुतानि दुःखार्णवेनोह्यमानानि। "ध्यानाधीन्द्रिय" ध्यानधीन्द्रिय। "प्रतिपूर्ण तुभ्य" प्रतिपूर्णा तव। "तारिष्यसे" तारयिष्यसि।

मेवं तद्विनिहत्य मारपर्षद् बुध्येम सर्व्वज्ञताम् (१) ॥

एवं खलु भिक्षवो मारपुत्रास्तथागतमभिष्टुत्यैकान्ते तस्थुः प्राञ्जलयस्तथागतं नमस्यन्तः (२) ॥

अथ खलु परनिर्मितवशवर्त्ती देवपुत्रोऽनेकदेवपुत्रशतसहस्रैः परिवृतः पुरस्कृतो जाम्बूनदसुवर्णवर्णैः पद्मैस्तथागतमभ्यवकीर्य सम्मुखमाभिर्गाथाभिरभ्यष्टावीत् (३)।

अस्खलितअलुडितअवितथवचना
अपगततमरज अद्भुतगतिङ्गता ।
अर्हसि दिवि भुवि श्रिय श्रियमतुला-
मतिद्युति स्तुतिमति प्रणयति शिरसा (४) ॥

रतिकरण अव रजमलमथना
रमयसि सुरनर सुविषदवचनैः ।
विकसितसुविपुलवरतनुकिरणैः
सुरनरपतिरिव जयसि जगदिदम् (५) ॥

---

१ "स्थित्व" स्थित्वा। "चतुर्दं" चतुर्दं। "भूत्व" भूत्वा। "प्रार्थेम" प्रार्थयामः "समुदानीत" समुदानीय। "तद्विनिहत्य मारपर्षद् बुध्येम सर्वज्ञताम्" तद्विनिहत्य मारपर्षद् बुध्यामहे।

२ "नमस्यन्तः" नममानाः।

३ "अभ्यष्टावीत्" अभ्यस्तोषीत्।

४ "अस्खलितअलुडितअवितथवचना" हे अभिष्टुतानामस्खलितावितथवचन। "अपगततमरज अद्भुतगतिङ्गता" अपगततमोरजोऽद्भुतगतिङ्गत। "श्रिय श्रियमतुलाम्" श्रियं श्रियमतुलामाप्नुमित्यर्थः। अतिद्युति स्तुतिमति प्रणयति" अतिद्युते स्तुतिमते प्रणमामि। अस्खलित प्रणयति इत्यत्र अपिस्थित प्रणिपति इति वा पाठः। अस्खलितइत्यत्र अभिष्टुत इत्यपि पाठः।

५ "अव रजमथना" यथा रजोमथन। अथ अव अरमथन इति वा पाठः। "सुरनर" सुरनराम्।

परगणिप्रमथन वरचरिकुशला
प्रियु भव नरमरु परमति धुनता।
परचरि विभजसि सुनिपुणमतिमान्
पथि इह विचरतु दुमबलगमने (१)॥
त्यजि पृथु भवपथि वितथ दुःख महा
विनयसि सुरनर यथमति विनये।
विचरसि चतुर्दिशं शशिरिव गगणे
चतुर्भव परायणी इह भुवि विभवे (२)॥
प्रियु भव नरमरु न च स्खलि विषये
रमयसि शुभरति कामरतिविरतो।
दीनदर्शि पर्षदि न ति समु विभवे
नाथ गति परायणु त्वमिह हि जगतः (३)॥

एवं खलु भिक्षवो वशवर्तिदेवपुत्रप्रमुखाः परनिर्मितवश-

---

१ "परगणिप्रमथन" परगणप्रमथन। अथ परमतिप्रमथनेति वा पाठः। "वरचरिकुशला" वरचर्याकुशल। "प्रियु भव नरमरु परमति धुनता" प्रियो भव नरमरूणां परमतिं धुनीहि। "परचरि" परचर्यां। "सुनिपुणमतिमान्" सुनिपुणमतिमन्। "विचरतु" विचर।

२ "त्यजि पृथु भवपथि" त्यक्त्वा पृथुं भवपथं। "वितथ दुःख महा" वितथं महादुःखदमित्यर्थः। "सुरनर यथमति" सुरनराम् यथामति। "चतुर्दिशं शशिरिव" चतुर्दिक्षु शशीव। "परायणी" परायणं।

३ "प्रियु भव" प्रियो भव। "नरमरु" नरमरूणां। "न च स्खलि" न च स्खलितः। "शुभरति कामरतिविरतो" शुभरत्या कामरतिविरतमित्यर्थः। "दीनदर्शि" दीनदर्शिन्यां। "न ति समु विभवे" न ते समविभवे। "गति परायणु" गतिः परायणा।

वर्त्तिनो देवपुत्रास्तथागतमभिष्टुत्यैकान्ते तस्थुः प्राञ्जलयस्तथागतं नमस्यन्तः (१)।

अथ खलु सुनिर्मितो देवपुत्रो देवसङ्घपरिवृतः पुरस्तो नानारत्नपट्टदामैस्तथागतमभिच्छाद्य सम्मुखमाभिर्गाथाभिरभ्यष्टावीत्।

धर्म्मालोकभवान् समुद्गतस्त्रिविधमलमुच्छेदो
मोहादृष्टिरविद्यघातको ह्रिरिश्रिरिभरितो।
मिथ्यामार्गरतामिमां प्रजायमम्हते स्थापयित्वा
उत्पन्नो इह लोकि चेति यो दिवि भुवि महितः (२)॥
त्वं वैद्य कुशलचिकित्सको अमृतसुखददो
दृष्टिक्लेशमविद्यसञ्चयं रिपुमनुश्रयम्।
सर्व्वव्याध्यपनेसि देहिनां पुरिम जिनपथे
तस्माद्वैद्यतमोसि नायका विचरसि धरणीम् (३)॥
चन्द्रसूर्य्य प्रभाश्च ज्योतिषा मणि तथ ज्वलना
शक्रब्रह्मप्रभा न भासते पुरितु श्रिरिघने।

---

१ "नमस्यन्तः" नमस्यमानाः।

२ "त्रिविधमलमुच्छेदो" त्रिविधमलोच्छेदकः। "मोहादृष्टिरविद्यघातको ह्रिरिश्रिरिभरितो" मोहदृष्ट्यविद्याघातको ह्रीश्रीपरिपूर्ण इत्यर्थः। "प्रजायमम्हते स्थापयित्वा" प्रजाममृते स्थापनार्थमित्यर्थः। "उत्पन्नो इह लोकि" उत्पन्न इह लोके।

३ "वैद्य" वैद्यः। "अमृतसुखददो" अमृतसुखदायक इत्यर्थः। "अविद्यसञ्चयं" अविद्यासञ्चयं। "सर्व्वव्याध्यपनेसि" सर्व्वव्याधीनपनयसि। "पुरिम जिनपथे" पुरातने जिनपथे देहिनः स्थापयिष्यसि इति समेतार्थः। "नायका" हे नायक।

प्रज्ञालोककरा प्रभङ्करा प्रभश्रिरिभरिता
प्रत्यचास्तव शान्ति अद्भुते प्रणिपति शिरसा (१) ॥
सत्यासत्यकथी विनायका सुमधुरवचना
दान्तशान्तमना जितेन्द्रिय प्रणमित मनसा ।
शास्ता शासनीयां प्रशाससे नरमरुपरिषां
वन्दे शाक्यमुनिं नरर्षभं सुरनरमहितम् (२) ॥
शान्तिं शानकथाग्रधारका शापयसि विभवे
त्रैविद्य विमोचदेशका विमलममलगुदा ।
भव्याभव्य मुने प्रजानसे यथामति विनये
वन्दे त्वां चिरदृष्ट अद्भुतं दिवि भुवि महितम् (३) ॥

एवं खलु भिक्षवः सुनिर्मितो देवपुत्रः सपरिवारस्तथागतमभिष्टुत्यैकान्तेऽस्थात् प्राञ्जलीभूतस्तथागतं नमस्कुर्व्वन् ।

अथ खलु सन्तुषितो देवपुत्रः सार्द्धं तुषितकायिकैर्देवैर्येन तथागतस्तेनोपसङ्क्रामदुपसङ्क्रम्य महता दिव्यवस्त्रजालेन बोधि-

---

१ "चन्द्रसूर्यं" चन्द्रसूर्ययोः । "ज्योतिषा मणि तथ ज्वलना" ज्योतिषां मणेरग्ना ज्वलनस्येत्यर्थः । "भासते" भासन्ते । पुरितु शिरिघने" पूर्णे श्रीघने । "प्रज्ञालोककरा प्रभङ्करा प्रभश्रिरिभरिता" प्रज्ञालोककर प्रभङ्कर प्रभाश्रीपरिपूर्णेत्यर्थः । "प्रत्यचास्तव शान्ति अद्भुते प्रणिपति" प्रत्यक्षस्तव शान्तिर्हे अद्भुत त्वां प्रणिपतामीत्यर्थः ।

२ सत्यासत्यकथी" हे सत्य हे सत्यकथयिन् । "विनायका सुमधुरवचना" विनायक सुमधुरवचन । "दान्तशान्तमनाः" दान्तशान्तमनः । "प्रणमित" प्रणमामि । "शासनीयां" शासनीयान् । "नरमरुपरिषां" नरमरुत्पर्षदः ।

३ "शान्तिं शानकथाग्रधारका" शान्तिमं शानकथां हे अग्रधारक । "त्रैविद्य" त्रैविद्यां । "विमोचदेशका विमलममलगुदा" विमोक्षोपदेशक विमलममलगुत् । "भव्याभव्य मुन प्रजानसे" भव्यमभव्यं मुने प्रजानासि ।

मण्डलिवरं तथागतमभिसम्भाष्य सम्मुखमाभिर्गाथाभिरभ्य-
स्तौषीत्।

तुषितालयि यद्वसितस्त्वं तत्र निर्देशितु धर्म्म उदारो।
न च छिद्यति सा अनुशास्ति अद्यापि धर्म्मचरी सुरपुत्राः (१)॥
न च दर्शन तृप्ति लभामो धर्म्मशृण्वोतु न विन्दति तृप्तिम्।
गुणसागर लोकप्रदीप वन्दिम ते शिरसा मनसा च (२)॥
तुषितालये यद्वसितस्त्वं शोषित अपाय सर्वि सदा ते।
यद बोधिवटे उपविष्टः सर्व्वजगस्य क्लिशेस प्रशान्ताः (३)॥
यस्य कृते न च बोधि उदारा एषति प्राप्ति जिनस्य न मारम्।
प्रणिधितपस परिपूर्णा क्षिप्र प्रवर्त्तय धर्म्मचक्रमुदारम् (४)॥
मरुद्दिवु प्राणिसहस्रा धर्म्मरता शृणुयामथ धर्म्मम्।

---

१ "तुषितालयि यद्वसितः" तुषितालये यदा उषितः। "निर्देशितु धर्म उदारो" निर्दिष्टो धर्म उदारः। "छिद्यति सा अनुशास्ति" छिद्यते तदनुशासनं। "धर्म चरी" धर्मचारिणः।

२ "दर्शन तृप्ति" दर्शनातृप्तिं। "धर्मशृण्वोतु न विन्दति तृप्तिम्" धर्मश्रवणेऽपि न विन्दामि तृप्तिमित्यर्थः। अथवा भवान् धर्मं श्रावयतु नाहं विन्दामि तृप्तिमित्यर्थः। "वन्दिम ते" वन्दे त्वां।

३ "यद्वसितः" यदा उषितः। अत्र यत्रसित इति वा पाठः। "शोषित अपाय सर्वि" शोषिता अपायाः सर्वे। अत्र सदा ते इत्यत्र तदा ते इति वा पाठः। "यद" यदा। "सर्वजगस्य क्लिशेस" सर्वजगतः क्लेशाः।

४ "यस्य कृते" मारस्य संहारकरणनिमित्तायेत्यर्थः। "बोधि उदारा एषति प्राप्ति जिनस्य न मारम्" बोधिरुदारः (पुनरत्र) एषति प्राप्तिर्जिनस्य न मारस्यापि सम्भवो भविष्यति इति भावार्थः। "प्रणिधितपस परिपूर्णा क्षिप्र" प्रणिधितपसा परिपूर्णं क्षिप्रं।

क्षिप्र प्रवर्त्तय चक्रमुदारं मोचय प्राणिसहस्र भवेयुः (१) ॥

एवं खलु भिक्षवः सन्तुषितो देवपुत्रः सपरिवारस्तथागतमभिष्टुत्यैकान्तेऽस्थात् प्राञ्जलीकृतस्तथागतं नमस्यमानः(२) ॥

अथ खलु सुयामदेवपुत्रप्रमुखा यामा देवा येन तथागतस्तेनोपसङ्क्रामन्नुपसङ्क्रम्य नानापुष्पधूपगन्धमाल्यविलेपनैर्बोधिमण्डनिषण्णं तथागतं सम्पूज्य सम्मुखमाभिः सारूप्याभिर्गाथाभिस्तुष्टुवुः ।

सदृशोऽसि न ते कुरूत्तरे
शीलसमाधि तथैव प्रज्ञया ।
अधिमुक्तिविमुक्तिकोविदा
शिरसा वन्दिम ते तथागतम् (३) ॥

द्रुमासनविष्ट पुज्य शोभना
बोधिमण्डेऽस्मिन् महभि या कृता ।
न तमर्हति अन्य कश्चनो
यथ त्वं देवमनुष्य पूजितः (४) ॥

---

१ "प्राणिसहस्रा धर्मरता" प्राणिसहस्राणि धर्मरतानि। "शृणुयामस धर्मम्" वयमपि तं धर्मं शृणुयामित्यर्थः। "क्षिप्र" क्षिप्रं। "चक्रमुदारं" धर्मचक्रमुदारमित्यर्थः। "प्राणिसहस्र भवेयुः" प्राणिसहस्राणि भवेयु इत्यर्थः।

२ "नमस्यमानः" नममानः।

३ "कुरूत्तरे" उत्तरकुरावित्यर्थः। "शीलसमाधि" शीलसमाधिभ्यां। "कोविदा" कोविद। "वन्दिम ते" वन्दामहे त्वां। "तथागतम्" हे तथागत।

४ "द्रुमासनविष्ट" द्रुमासनोपविष्टं त्वां। "शोभना" शोभनमित्यर्थः। "महभि या" महर्भिर्या। "तमर्हति अन्य" तामर्हत्यन्यः। "यथ त्वं देवमनुष्य" यथा त्वं देवमनुष्यैः।

न सुधाय भवान् समुद्गतो
यस्य अर्थी बहु चीर्ण दुष्करा।
विजितो शठः ससैन्यकः
प्राप्ता बोधि अनुत्तरा त्वया (१)॥
आलोक कृतो दशदिशे
प्रज्ञाप्रदीपेन त्रिलोक ज्वालित।
तिमिरमपनामयिष्यसे
दास्य चक्षुरनुत्तरं जगे (२)॥
बहुकल्पकोटि स्तुति निभाषतो
रोमकूपस्य न चास्तु अस्ति ते।
गुणसागर लोकविश्रुता
शिरसा वन्दिम ते तथागतम् (३)॥

एवं खलु ते सुयामदेवपुत्रप्रमुखा देवास्तथागतमभिष्टुत्वैकान्ते तस्थुः प्राञ्जलयस्तथागतं नमस्यन्तः (४)।

अथ खलु शक्रो देवानामिन्द्रः सार्द्धं त्रयस्त्रिंशत्कायिकै-

---

१ "सुधाय" सुधा इत्यर्थः। "अर्थी बहु चीर्ण" अर्थो बहव आचरणीया इत्यर्थः। "बोधि अनुत्तरा" बोधिरनुत्तरा।

२ "आलोक कृतो दशदिशे" आलोकः कृतो दशदिक्षु। "त्रिलोक ज्वालित" त्रिलोक उज्ज्वलितः। "तिमिरमपनामयिष्यसे दास्य चक्षुरनुत्तरं जगे" तिमिरमपनयिष्यसि दास्यसि चक्षुरनुत्तमं जगति इत्यर्थः।

३ "बहुकल्पकोटि स्तुति निभाषतो" बहुकल्पकोटिपर्यन्तं स्तुतिर्निर्भाषिता। "न चास्तु" न चास्ति। बहुकल्पकोटिपर्यन्तमपि कृतया स्तुत्या तव रोमकूपस्यापि स्तुतिः कर्तुं न शक्यते कुतस्तव इति भावः। "लोकविश्रुता" लोकविश्रुत। "वन्दामि ते" वन्दामहे त्वामित्यर्थः।

४ "नमस्यन्तः" नममानाः।

र्दैवैर्नानापुष्पधूपदीपमाल्यविलेपनचूर्णचीवरछत्रध्वजपताकाव्यूहैस्तथागतं सम्पूज्याभिर्गाथाभिरभ्यस्तावीत्।

अस्खलिता अनवद्या सदासुस्थिता मेरुकल्पा मुने
दशदिशे सुविघुष्ट ज्ञानप्रभा पुण्यतेजान्विता।
बुद्धाः शतसहस्र सम्पूजिता च भुवि तुभ्यं मुने
तस्य विशेषु येन बोधिद्रुमे मारसेना जिता (१)॥

शीलश्रुतसमाधिप्रज्ञाकरा ज्ञानकेतुध्वजा
जरामरणनिर्घाति वैद्योत्तमा लोकचक्षुर्ददा।
त्रिमलमखिलप्रहीणा शान्तेन्द्रिया शान्तचित्ता मुने
शरण तव मुपेमु शाक्यर्षभा धर्मराजा जगे (२)॥

बोधीचरी अनन्ततुल्या अभूद्वीर्यस्थामोद्गता
प्रज्ञाबल उपायमैत्रीबलं शास्त्रपुण्यं बलम्।
एति बलमनन्ततुल्यो भवं बोधि सम्प्रस्थितो
दशबलबलधारो पुनर्बोधिमण्डे भूतो (३)॥

---

१ "अस्खलिता" हे अस्खलित। एवमपेषि सम्बोधनान्ताकारोऽकारो बोध्यः। "दशदिशे" दशदिक्षु। "सुविघुष्ट" सुविघुष्टा। "पुण्यतेजान्विता" पुण्यतेजोन्विता। "बुद्धाः शतसहस्र" बुद्धाः शतसहस्राणि। "भुवि तुभ्यं" भुवि त्वया। "विशेषु येन" विशेषो येन।

२ "प्रज्ञाकरा" प्रज्ञाकर। "ज्ञानकेतुध्वजा" ज्ञानकेतुध्वज। अत्र केतुध्वजयोरन्यतरेण भाव्यम्। "जरामरणनिर्घाति" जरामरणनिर्घातक। "वैद्योत्तमा" वैद्योत्तम। "लोकचक्षुर्ददा" लोकचक्षुर्द। "त्रिमलमखिलप्रहीणा" अखिलत्रिमलप्रहीण इत्यर्थः। "शान्तेन्द्रिया शान्तचित्ता" शान्तेन्द्रिय शान्तचित्त। "शरण तव मुपेमु शाक्यर्षभा धर्मराजा जगे" शरणं तवोपैमि शाक्यर्षभ धर्मराज जगति।

३ "बोधिचरी" बोधिचर्या। "प्रज्ञाबल उपाय-" प्रज्ञाबलमुपाय-। "एति बलमनन्ततुल्यो" इति बलेन अनन्ततुल्य इत्यर्थः। "बोधि" बोधिः। "भूतो" भूतः।

दृष्ट्वा चमु अनन्तसत्त्वे सुरा भीतत्रस्ताभवन्
मा खलु श्रमणुराचार्य्यो भविष्यते बोधिमण्डे स्थिते ।
न च भवत बभूव तेभ्यो भयं मा च कायेञ्जना
करऊत गुरुभारं सङ्ग्रमणा मारसेना जिता (१) ॥
यथ च पुरिमकेभिः सिंहासने प्राप्त बोधि वरा
तथ त्वया अनुबुद्ध तुल्या समा अन्यथा त्वम् ।
न हि समनस समचित्त सर्व्वज्ञता स्थाम प्राप्ता
त्वथागतेन भव स्वयम्भूर्लोकोत्तमः पुण्यक्षेत्रं जगे (२) ॥

एवं खलु भिक्षवः शक्रो देवानामिन्द्रः सार्द्धं देवपुत्रैस्त्रयस्त्रिंशैस्तथागतमभिष्टुत्यैकान्तेऽस्थात् प्राञ्जलीभूतस्तथागतं नमस्कुर्व्वन् ।

अथ खलु चत्वारो महाराजानः सार्द्धं चतुर्महाराजकायिकैर्देवपुत्रैर्येन तथागतस्तेनोपसङ्क्रामदुपसङ्क्रम्याभिमुक्तचम्पकसुमनोवार्षिकधातुमाल्यदामपरिगृहीता अप्सरःशतसहस्रपरिवृता दिव्यसङ्गीतिसम्प्रवादितेन तथागतस्य पूजां कृत्वा आभिः सारूप्याभिर्गाथाभिरभितुष्टुवुः ।

---

१ "चमु अनन्तसत्त्वे" चमूमनन्तसत्त्वस्य निकटे इत्यर्थः । "भीतत्रस्ताभवन्" भीतास्त्रस्ता अभवन् । "मा खलु श्रमणुराचार्यो भविष्यते" मा खलु (विघ्नं भूयात्) श्रमण आचार्यो भविष्यति इति समेपार्थः । "भवत बभूव" भवतु भवतु इत्यर्थः । "मा च कायेञ्जना" न च काये इञ्जना । "करऊत" करहूतं भूयादिति शेषः ।

२ "यथ च पुरिमकेभिः" यथा च पूर्वैः । "प्राप्त बोधि वरा" प्राप्ता बोधिर्वरा । "अनुबुद्ध" अनुबुद्धा । "अन्यथा त्वं नहि" अत्र विषये अन्यथात्वं नास्ति इत्यर्थः । "समनस समचित्त सर्वज्ञता स्थाम प्राप्ता" सौमनस्यं समचित्तत्वं सर्वज्ञता स्थाम प्राप्तं । "भव" भवे । "भूर्लोकोत्तमः" भूर्लोक उत्तमः । "जगे" जगति ।

सुमधुरवचना मनोज्ञघोषा
शशि इव प्रशान्तिकरा प्रसन्नचित्ता ।
प्रहसितवदना प्रभूतजिह्वा
परमसुप्रीतिकरा मुने नमस्ते (१) ॥

इत रचिता च अस्ति सर्वलोके
सुमधुर प्रेमणीया सुरमरूणाम् ।
भगवतः स्वरूप मुक्तमञ्जुघोषा-
ऽभिभवते इत सर्वि भाषमाणां (२) ॥

रागु शमयि दोषमोहक्लेशा
प्रीति जनेति अमानुषां विशुद्धाम् ।
अकलुषहृदया निशाम्य धर्मं
आर्य विमुक्ति लभन्ति ते हि सर्वे (३) ॥

न च भव अभिमन्यसेऽविद्वां
न च पुनर्विद्वमदेन जातु मत्तः ।
उन्नतु न च नैव चोन्नतत्वं

---

१ "सुमधुरवचना" सुमधुरवचन एवमन सर्वत्र सम्बोधनाम्नाकारोऽकारो बोध्यः । "शशि इव" शशीव ।

२ "इत रचिता च अस्ति" इतानि रचितानि यानि सन्ति । "सुमधुर प्रेमणीया" सुमधुरं प्रेमणीयानि । "मुक्तमञ्जुघोषा" मुक्तमञ्जुघोष । "इत सर्वि भाषमाणां" (तव) इतं सर्वान् भाषमाणान् इत्यर्थः ।

३ "रागु शमयि दोषमोहक्लेशा" (येषां) रागं शमयित्वा दोषमोहक्लेशाश्चे-त्यर्थः । "प्रीति जनेति अमानुषां" प्रीतिं जनयति अमानुषीं । "विमुक्ति" विमुक्तिं ।

गिरिरिव सुस्थितु सागरस्य मध्ये (१) ॥
लाभ इह सुलब्ध मानुषाणां
यत्र हि तादृशु जातु सत्त्व लोके ।
श्रीरिव परमेधनस्य दात्री
तथ भव दास्यति धर्म सर्व्वलोके (२) ॥

एवं खलु चतुर्महाराजप्रमुखा महाराजकायिका देवा बोधिमण्डे निषण्णं तथागतमभिष्टुत्यैकान्ते तस्थुः प्राञ्जलयस्तथागतं नमस्यन्तः (३) ।

अथ खलु अन्तरीक्षा देवास्तथागतस्यान्तिकमुपसङ्क्रम्याभिसम्बोधिपूजाकर्मणे सर्वमन्तरीक्षं रत्नजालेन रत्नच्छत्रै रत्नपताकाभी रत्नपट्टदामै (४) रत्नावतंसकैर्विविधमुक्ताहारपुष्पदामार्द्धं (५) कायिकदेवतापरिगृहीतैरर्द्धचन्द्रकैश्च समलङ्कृत्य तथागताय निर्यातयन्ति स्म । निर्यात्य च सम्मुखमाभिर्गाथाभिरभ्यष्टाविषुः ।

अस्माकं वासं गगणे ध्रुवं मुने
पश्याम सर्व्वा चर्या यथा अगे ।

---

१ "अभिमन्यसेऽविद्वां" अविद्वांसमुद्दिश्यापि तथा नाभिमन्यते इत्यर्थः । "विद्रुमदेन" विद्रुमामदेनेत्यर्थः । "उन्नतु न च" उन्नतो न च । "सुस्थितु" सुस्थितः ।

२ "सुलब्ध मानुषाणां" सुलब्धो मानुषैरित्यर्थः । "तादृशु जातु सत्त्व लोके" तादृशो जातः सत्त्वो लोके । "परमेधनस्य" परमधनस्य । "भव" भवे । "धर्म" धर्मं ।

३ "नमस्यन्तः" नममानाः ।

४ "रत्नपट्टदामै" रत्नपट्टदामभिः ।

५ "पुष्पदामार्द्धं" पुष्पदामभिरर्द्धं ।

भवतश्चरि प्रेक्षिम शुद्धसत्त्व
स्खलितं न पश्याम तवैकचित्ते (१) ॥
ये आगता पूजन बोधिसत्त्वा
गगनं स्फुटं तैर्नरनायकेभिः ।
ह्यानिर्विमाना न चा भवन्त
तथा हि ते वै गगनात्मभावाः (२) ॥
ये अन्तरीक्षात्तु प्रवर्षि पुष्पां
स्थाणूबन्धा हि महासहस्रे ।
ते तुभ्य काये पतिता अशेषा
नद्यो यथा सागरि सम्प्रविष्टाः (३) ॥
पश्याम छत्राण्यवतंसकांश्च
मालागुणांश्चम्पकपुष्पदामां ।
हारांश्च चन्द्रांश्च तथार्द्धचन्द्रां
क्षिपन्ति देवा न च संस्करोति (४) ॥

---

१ "वासं गगणे" वासो गगणे। "पश्याम सर्वा चर्या यथा जगे" पश्यामः सर्वां चर्यां यथा जगति जाता इत्यर्थः। सर्वा चर्या इन्यत्र सत्त्वचर्या इति वा पाठः। "भवतश्चिर प्रेक्षिम" भवन्तं चिरं प्रेक्षामहे। "पश्याम तवैकचित्ते" पश्यामस्तवैकचित्त्यमित्यर्थः।

२ "आगता पूजन बोधिसत्त्वा" आगताः पूजनार्थं बोधिसत्त्वा इत्यर्थः। "नरनायकेभिः" नरनायकैः। "विमाना न चा भवन्त" विमानानां न चाभवन्। "गगनात्मभावाः" गगनस्वभावा जाता इत्यर्थः।

३ "प्रवर्षि पुष्पां" प्रवर्षितानि पुष्पाणि। "स्थाणूबन्धा" स्थाणुबन्धतुल्यानि जातानि इत्यर्थः। "ते तुभ्य काये पतिता अशेषाः" तानि तव काये पतितान्यशेषाणि अपि तु न पुञ्जीभूतानि दृश्यन्ते इति शेषः। "सागरि" सागरं।

४ "पश्याम छत्राणि" पश्यामश्छत्राणि। "चम्पकपुष्पदामां" चम्पकपुष्पदामानि। "तथार्द्धचन्द्रां" तथार्द्धचन्द्रान्। "संस्करोति" संस्कुर्वन्ति।

बालस्य माभूद्वकाशमस्मिन्
देवैः स्फुटं सर्व्वत अन्तरीक्षम्।
कुर्व्वन्ति पूजां द्विपदोत्तमस्य
न च ते मदो जायति विस्मयो वा (१)॥

एवं खलु भिक्षवोऽन्तरीक्षा देवा बोधिमण्डनिषण्णं तथागतमभिष्टुत्यैकान्तेऽवस्थितवन्तः प्राञ्जलयस्तथागतं नमस्कुर्व्वन्ति स्म।

अथ खलु भौमा देवास्तथागतस्य पूजाकर्म्मणे सर्व्वावन्तं धरणीतलं सुगन्धितोपलिप्तं गन्धोदकपरिषिक्तं पुष्पावकीर्णञ्च कृत्वा नानापुष्पवितानविततञ्च तथागताय निर्य्यातयन्ति स्म आभिर्गाथाभिरभितुष्टुवुः।

वज्रमिव अभेद्या संस्थिता चित्तदृढा
वज्रमयेणावस्थितो बोधिमण्डे।
इह मम त्वचमांसं प्रध्यतामस्थि मज्जा
न च अङ्ग अस्पृशित्वा बोधिं उत्थेष्ये अस्मात् (२)॥
सर्वि भवनसत्त्वाः सर्व्विमं चित्तदृढा
न कर्तु अधिष्ठानं स्यादितीर्णा असेषा।
तावदुष्य महवेगा आगता बोधिसत्त्वा

---

१ "स्फुटं" स्फुटं परिपूर्णमिति तात्पर्यम्। "जायति विस्मयो वा" जायते विस्मयोऽपि तेन भवति इति भावः।

२ "वज्रमयेण" वज्रमयेणासनेनेत्यर्थः। "बोधिमण्डे" बोधिमण्डके। "त्वच मांसं" त्वग्मांसे। "अङ्ग अस्पृशित्वा" अप्राप्य। "बोधिं उत्थेष्ये" बोधिमुत्थास्ये।

येषां क्रमतलेभिः कम्पिताः क्षेत्रकोट्यः (१) ॥

लाभ इह सुलब्धा भूमिदेवैरुदारा
यत्र परमसत्त्वश्चङ्क्रमी मेदिनीये ।
यत्र भूरजु लोके सर्व्व शोभाषितस्ते
येति भू शिलाचयः किं पुनस्तुभ्य कायः (२) ॥

हस्तिशतसहस्रं यावतस्त्वास्य स्कन्धो
धरणितल जगस्था यावतस्त्वोपजीव्याः ।
सर्व्व वयु धरेमो मेदिनी शिलाचयं
सर्व्वं तव ददामो भुङ्क्ष्विमां त्वं यथेष्टम् (३) ॥

यत्र भव स्थितेद्वा चङ्क्रमेद्वाशयेद्वा
येऽपि सुगतपुत्राः श्रावका गौतमस्य ।
धर्म्मकथ कथेन्ती येऽपि वा तां शृणोन्ति
सर्व्वं कुशलमूलं बोधये नामयामः (४) ॥

---

१ "सर्वि" सर्वे । "सर्विय" सर्वेषं । "न कषु अधिष्ठानं" नाकार्षुरधिष्ठानं स्थानं दातुं समर्था नाभवत् इति भावः । "स्थाद्विलोर्णा" अभयद्विलीर्णा । "नाडम मरुवेगाः" एताहशा मरुद्वेगाः । "क्रमतलेभिः" पादतलैरित्यर्थः ।

२ "लाभ इह" लाभा इह । "चङ्क्रमी मेदिनीये" चचङ्क्रममेदिन्यां । "भूरजु लोके सर्व शोभासितः" भूरजसा लोकः सर्वं आभासितः । "भू शिलाचयः" शिलाचयात्मिका भूरपि आभासिता इत्यर्थः । "तुभ्य कायः" तव कायः ।

३ "यावतस्त्वास्य" यावांस्त्वास्य शिलाचयस्कन्धेत्यर्थः । "धरणितल जगस्था यावतः" धरणीतले जगति यावन्तः । "सर्व वयु धरेमो मेदिनी" ('एतत्) सर्वं वयं धारयामो मेदिनीं । "सर्व तव" एतत्सर्वं तुभ्यमित्यर्थः । "भुङ्क्ष्विमां" भुङ्क्ष्वेदं सर्वमित्यर्थः ।

४ "यत्र भव स्थितेद्वा चङ्क्रमेद्वा शयेद्वा" बोधिसत्त्वो यथाभवत् स्थितो वाऽचङ्क्रमेद्वाऽशेत वा । "धर्मकथ कथेन्ती" धर्मकथां कथयन्ति । "सर्वं कुशलमूलं बोधिये नामयामः" एतान् सर्वान् कुशलमूलान् बोधिस नमाम इत्यर्थः ।

एवं खलु भौमा देवा बोधिमण्डे निषण्णं तथागतमभिष्टुत्यैकान्ते तस्थुः प्राञ्जलयस्तथागतं नमस्यन्तः (१) ॥

इति श्रीललितविस्तरे संस्तवपरिवर्त्तो नाम त्रयोविंशतितमः ॥ २३ ॥

चतुर्व्विंशाध्यायप्रारम्भः ।

इति हि भिक्षवोऽभिसम्बुद्धस्तथागतो देवैरभिष्टूयमानः पर्य्यङ्कमभिन्दन्ननिमिषनयनो द्रुमराजं प्रेक्षते स्म । ध्यानप्रीत्याहारः सुखप्रतिसंवेदी सप्तरात्रं बोधिवृक्षमूलेऽभिनामयति स्म ।

अथ सप्ताहेऽतिक्रान्ते कामावचरा देवपुत्रा दशगन्धोदककुम्भसहस्राणि परिगृह्य येन तथागतस्तेनोपसङ्क्रामन्तिस्म । रूपावचरा अपि देवपुत्रा दशगन्धोदककुम्भसहस्राणि परिगृह्य येन तथागतस्तेनोपसङ्क्रामन्ति स्म । उपसङ्क्रम्य बोधिवृक्षं तथागतञ्च गन्धोदकैः स्नापयन्ति स्म । गणनासमतिक्रान्ताश्च देवनागयक्षगन्धर्व्वासुरगरुडकिन्नरमहोरगास्तेन तथागतकायपतितेन गन्धोदकेन स्वकस्वकान् कायानुपलिम्पन्ति स्म । अनुत्तरायाञ्च सम्यक्सम्बोधौ चित्तान्युत्पादयामासुः स्वभवने प्रविष्टाः ।

अपि च ते देवपुत्रादयोऽविरहिता अभूवंस्तेन गन्धोदकेन

---

१ "नमस्यन्तः" नममानाः ।

न चान्यस्मै गन्धाय स्पृहामुत्पादयामासुः। तेनैव च प्रीतिप्रामोद्येन तथागतगौरवमनसिकारनिर्जातेनावैवर्त्तिका अभूवन् अनुत्तरायाः सम्यक्सम्बोधेः।

अथ खलु भिक्षवः समन्तकुसुमो नाम देवपुत्रस्तस्यामेव पर्षदि सन्निपतितोऽभूत्। स तथागतस्य चरणयोर्निपत्य प्राञ्जलिस्तथागतमेतदवोचत्। को नामायं भगवन् समाधिर्येन समाधिना समन्वागतस्तथागतः सप्तरात्रं विहरत्यभिन्नपर्य्यङ्कः। एवमुक्ते भिक्षवस्तथागतस्तं देवपुत्रमेतदवोचत्। प्रीत्याहारव्यूहो नाम देवपुत्रायं समाधिर्येन समाधिना समन्वागतस्तथागतः सप्तरात्रं व्याहार्षीदभिन्नपर्य्यङ्कः।

अथ खलु भिक्षवः समन्तकुसुमो देवपुत्रस्तथागतं गाथाभिरभ्यष्टावीत्।

रथचरणनिचितचरणा दशशत अरजाः कमलदलतेजाः।
सुरमकुटघृष्टचरणा वन्दे चरणौ श्रिरिघनस्य (१) ॥
अभिवन्द्य सुगतचरणौ प्रमुदितचित्तः स सुरपुत्रः।
इदमवचि (२) विमतिहरणं प्रशान्तकरं नरमरूणाम् ॥
शाक्यकुलनन्दिजनना अन्तक रागदोषमोहानाम्।
अज्ञानअन्तःकरणा विनेहि काङ्क्षां नरमरूणाम् (३) ॥

---

१ "रथचरणनिचितचरणा" हे रथचरणनिचितचरण, चक्राङ्कितचरण इत्यर्थः। "चरजाः कमलदलतेजाः" हे चरजः कमलदलतेजः। "सुरमकुटघृष्टचरणा" सुरमुकुटघृष्टचरण। "श्रिरिघनस्य" श्रीघनस्य।

२ "इदमवचि" इदमवोचत्।

३ "नन्दिजनना" नन्दिजनन। "अज्ञानअन्तःकरणा" अज्ञानान्तःकरण। "विनेहि" परिपूरयेत्यर्थः।

किं कारणं दशबला बुद्धा सर्व्वगतामपरिमाणाम् ।
सप्ताहं महिमण्डे जिना न भिन्दन्ति पर्य्यङ्कम् (१) ॥
किन्तु खलु पश्यमानः सप्ताहमनिमेषेण नरसिंहः ।
प्रेक्षति विपुलद्रुमचक्षो विकसितशतपत्रतुल्याक्ष (२) ॥
किन्तु भवतेष प्रणिधि उताहु सर्व्वेष वादिसिंहानाम् ।
येन द्रुमराजमूले पर्य्यङ्कं न भिन्दि सप्ताहम् (३) ॥
साधु समभद्रुदन्ता सुगन्धगन्धमुखं दशबलस्य ।
प्रवद वचनमवितथं कुरुष्व प्रीतिं नरमरूणाम् ॥
तमुवाच चन्द्रवदनः शृणुष्व मे भाषतो ह्यमरपुत्र ।
अस्य प्रश्नस्याहं किञ्चिन्मात्रं प्रवक्ष्यामि ॥
राजा यद्वदभिनवभिषिक्तो भवति क्षातियाणेन ।
सप्ताह तं प्रदेशं न जहाति धर्म्मता राज्ञाम् (४) ॥
एवमेव दशबला अपि अभिषिक्ता भान्ति यद प्रणिधि पूर्णा ।
सप्ताह धरणिमण्डे जिना न भिन्दन्ति पर्य्यङ्कम् (५) ॥
शूरो यथारिसङ्घान् निरीक्षते निर्जिताश्चिरवशेषान् ।
बुद्धापि बोधिमण्डे क्लेशां निहता निरीक्षन्ते (६) ॥

---

१ "दशबला" हे दशबल। "महिमण्डे" महीमण्डले। "भिन्दन्ति" भिन्दन्ति स्मेत्यर्थः ।

२ "विपुलचक्षो" विपुलचक्षुः ।

३ "किन्तु भवतेष प्रणिधि उताहु सर्वेष" किन्तु भवत एषा प्रणिधिरुताहो सर्वेषां । "भिन्दि" भग्नं ।

४ "सप्ताह" सप्ताहं। "धर्मता राज्ञां" धर्मतो राज्ञा इत्यर्थः ।

५ "यद प्रणिधि" यदा प्रणिधिः। "सप्ताह धरणिमण्डे" सप्ताहं धरणीमण्डले। "भिन्दन्ति" भिन्दन्ति स्म ।

६ "बुद्धापि बोधिमण्डे क्लेशां निहता' बुद्धा अपि बोधिमण्डले क्लेशान्निहतान् ।

इह ते कामक्रोधा मोहप्रभवा जगत्परिभिकासाः ।
समूहता इव चौरा विनाशिता ये निरवशेषाः ॥
इह मे हता न विविधा(१)मानविधिमन्युना पुनर्निकेताः ।
सर्व्वास्रवाः प्रहीणा ज्ञानं चाग्र्यं समुत्पन्नम् ॥
इह सा अकार्य्यकर्त्री भवतृष्णाचारिणी मयाऽविद्या ।
सानुशयमूलजाला महाज्ञानाग्निना दग्धा (२) ॥
इह सा अहं ममेति च कालिपाशदुरानुगाढजितमूला ।
नीवरणकठिनग्रन्थिश्छिन्ना मम ज्ञानशस्त्रेण (३) ॥
इह ते चिरं ममायं त उत्तापनका विनाशपर्य्यन्ताः ।
स्कन्धाः सोपादाना ज्ञानेन मया परिज्ञाताः ॥
इह ते हृदयसञ्चोदा मिथ्याप्राणा महानरकनिष्ठाः ।
मया उद्धृता अशेषाः भूयश्च न जातु शाम्यन्ते ॥
इह नीवरणवनादी दग्धा मे कुशलमूलतेजेन ।
चतुरश्च विपर्य्यासा विदग्धा मया निरवशेषाः (४) ॥
इह सा वितर्कमाला सञ्ज्ञासक्ते सुगुम्फितानि उत्पन्नी ।
विनिवर्त्तिता अशेषा बोध्यङ्गविचित्रमालाभिः (५) ॥

---

१ "न विविधा" नु विविधा इत्यर्थः ।

२ "महाज्ञानाग्निना" पटुना ज्ञानाग्निना इति वा पाठः ।

३ "सा अहं" सोऽहं । "कालिपाशदुरानुगाढजितमूला" कालपाशदुरवगाढमूला । "नीवरणकठिनग्रन्थिः" नीवर एव प्रस्तरादिरेव कठिना ग्रन्थिरिति नीवरणकठिनग्रन्थिः ।

४ "नीवरणवनादी" नीवरणवनादयः । "कुशलमूलतेजेन" कुशलमूलतेजसा । "विदग्धाः" निर्दग्धा इति वा पाठः ।

५ "सुगुम्फितानि उत्पन्नी" सुगुम्फिता उत्पत्तिः ।

दुर्गाणि पञ्चषष्टि मोहानी षिंशति पञ्च मलिनानि।
चत्वारिंशद्व्यानि छित्त्वा मेऽस्मिं धरणिमण्डे (१)॥
षोडश असंस्कृतानी अष्टादश धातवश्च महिमण्डे।
छक्राणि पञ्चविंशति छिन्नानि मयेहसंक्षेन (२)॥
विंशति रजस्तराणि अष्टाविंशति जगस्य षिपाशाः।
इह मे समतिक्रान्ता वीर्य्यबलपराक्रमं करित्वा (३)॥
तथ बुद्धनर्दितानि पञ्चशताश्चिं मया समनुबुद्धा।
परिपूर्णशतसहस्रं धर्म्मान् मया समनुबुद्धम् (४)॥
इह मे अनुशय अशेषा अष्टानवतिः समूलपर्य्यन्ताः।
पर्य्युत्थानक्लिशलया निर्दग्धा ज्ञानतेजेन (५)॥
काङ्क्षा विमतिसमुद्या दृष्टीजटजन्तिता अशुभमूला।
तृष्णानदी तिवेगा प्रशोषिता मे ज्ञानसूर्य्येण (६)॥
कुहनलपनप्रहाणं मायामात्सर्य्यदोषदर्शायं।

---

१ "पञ्चषष्टि मोहानी" पञ्चषष्टिर्मोहाः। "षिंशति" विंशतिः। "मेऽस्मिं धरणिमण्डे" मेऽस्मिन् धरणीमण्डले।

२ "असंस्कृतानी" असंस्कृतानि। "महिमण्डे" महीमण्डले। "पञ्चविंशति" पञ्चविंशतिः।

३ "विंशति रजस्तराणि" विंशती रजोगुणस्य आवरणानि इत्यर्थः। "अष्टाविंशति जगस्य" अष्टाविंशतिर्जगतः। "समतिक्रान्ता" समतिक्रान्तानि वा। "करित्वा" कृत्वा।

४ "तथ" तथा। "पञ्चशताश्चिं मया समनुबुद्धा" पञ्चशतान्यश्चिन्मया समनुबुद्धानि। "परिपूर्णशतसहस्रं धर्मान् मया समनुबुद्धम्" परिपूर्णशतसहस्राणि धर्मा मया समनुबुद्धाः।

५ "अनुशय" अनुशयाः। "अष्टानवतिः" अष्टनवतिः। "ज्ञानतेजेन" ज्ञानतेजसा।

६ "दृष्टीजटजन्तिता" दृष्टिजटयन्त्रिता। "तिवेगा" त्रिवेगा अतिवेगा वार्थः।

इह ते क्लेशारण्यं छिन्नं विनयाग्निना दग्धम् (१) ॥
इह ते विवादमूला आकर्षणदुर्गतिषु विषमासु ।
आर्य्यापवादवचना ज्ञानवरविरेचनैर्वान्ताः (२) ॥
इह रुदितक्रन्दितानां शोचितपरिदेवितानपर्य्यन्तम् ।
प्राप्तं मया ह्यशेषं ज्ञानगुणसमाधिमागम्य (३) ॥
अघो योगगन्धाः शोकशल्या मदाः प्रमदाश्च ।
विजिता ममेह सर्व्वे सत्यनयसमाधिमागम्य (४) ॥
इह मया किलेशगहनाः सङ्कल्पविमूढमूल भवन्तकाः ।
स्मृतिपरशुना अशेषाश्छिन्ना ज्ञानाग्निना दग्धाः (५) ॥
इह शो मया ह्यतिबलाऽस्मिं मारस्त्रिलोकवशवर्त्ती ।
ज्ञानासिना शठात्मा हतो यथेन्द्रेण दैत्येन्द्रः (६) ॥
इन्द्रजालिनी अशेषा षट्त्रिंशति विचारिणी धरणिमध्ये ।
प्रज्ञासिना बलवता छित्त्वा ज्ञानाग्निना दग्धा (७) ॥
इह ते मूलक्लेशाः सानुशया दुःखशोकसम्भूताः ।

---

१ “दोषदृष्ट्याद्यं” दोषेर्ष्याद्यं। “इह स” इह तत्।

२ “विवादमूलाः” विवादमूलानि। “आर्य्यापवादवचना” आर्य्यापवादवचनानि। “वान्ताः” वान्तीकृतानि इत्यर्थः।

३ “शोचितपरिदेवितानपर्य्यन्तं” शोचितपरिदेवितपर्य्यन्तं। “समाधिमागम्य” समाधिं कृत्वेत्यर्थः।

४ “ममेह” मयेह। “समाधिमागम्य” समाधिं कृत्वेत्यर्थः।

५ “किलेशगहनाः” क्लेशगहनाः। “सङ्कल्पविमूढमूल” सङ्कल्पविमूढमूला इत्यर्थः। अत्र सङ्कल्पविरूढमूल इति वा पाठः।

६ “शो मया” स मया। “अतिबलाऽस्मिं” अतिबलोऽस्मिन्। “त्रिलोकवशवर्त्ती” त्रिलोकचक्रवर्त्तीति वाऽत्र पाठः।

७ “षट्त्रिंशति विचारिणी” षट्त्रिंशतिर्विचारिण्यः। विचारिणीत्यत्र चारिणीति वा पाठः। “धरणिमध्ये” धरणीमध्ये।

मया उद्धृता अशेषा प्रज्ञावरवज्रकुशलमुखेन ॥

इह मे प्रज्ञाचक्षुर्विशोधितं प्रकृतिविशुद्धसत्त्वानाम् ।

ज्ञानाञ्जनेन महता मोहपटलविस्तरं भिन्नम् (१) ॥

इह धातुभूत चतुरो मदमकरविलोडिता विपुलतृष्णा: ।

स्मृतिसमर्थभास्करकराग्रैर्विशोषिता मे भवसमुद्रा: (२) ॥

इह विषयकाष्ठनिचयो वितर्कसमो महामदवह्निः ।

निर्व्वापितो दीप्तो विमोक्षरसशीततोयेन ॥

इह मे अनुशयपटला आस्वादतडिद्वितर्कनिर्घोषाः ।

वीर्य्यबलपवनवेगैर्विधूय विलयं समुपनीताः ॥

इह मे हतो ह्यशेषश्चित्तचरि रिपु भवानुगत वैरी ।

प्रज्ञासिना बलवता स्मृतिविमलसमाधिमागम्य (३) ॥

इह सा ध्वजाग्रधारी (४) हस्त्यश्वरथोच्छ्रिता विकृतरूपा ।

नमुचिबलवीर्य्यसेना मैत्रीमागम्य विध्वस्ता ॥

इह पञ्चगुणसंछन्नाः षडिन्द्रियहया मदोन्मत्ताः ।

बद्धा मया ह्यशेषा समाधिमशुभं समागम्य (५) ॥

इहानुनयप्रतिघानां कलहविवादप्रहाणपर्य्यन्तः ।

प्राप्तो मया ह्यशेष अप्रणिहित समाधिमागम्य (६) ॥

इह मथिताश्च सर्व्वे अध्यात्मिक वाह्यकाः परिक्षीणाः ।

---

१ "इह मे" इह मया ।

२ "धातुभूत चतुरो" धातुभूताश्चत्वारो ।

३ "चित्तचरि रिपु भवानुगत" चित्तचारी रिपुर्भवानुगतो ।

४ "ध्वजाग्रधारी" अग्रे ध्वजाधारिणी इत्यर्थः ।

५ "समाधिमशुभं" समाधिं शुभमित्यर्थः ।

६ "अप्रणिहित" अप्रणिहितं । अप्रतिहतेति वाच पाठः ।

कल्पितविकल्पितानि च शून्यमिति समाधिमागम्य (१) ॥
इह शास्तृषिता (२) भवे मर्त्या दिव्या भवाग्रपर्य्यन्ताः ।
त्यक्ता मया सर्व्वेषा आगम्य समाधिमनिवर्त्तम् ॥
सर्व्वभवबन्धनानि च मुक्तानि मयेह तानि सर्वाणि ।
प्रज्ञाबलेन निखिलाखिलविधमिह (३) विमोक्षमागम्य ॥
इह हेतुदर्शनाद्वै जिता मया हेतुकाश्रयः ।
सञ्ज्ञा नित्यानित्ये सञ्ज्ञासुखदुःख चात्मनि च (४) ॥
इह मे कर्म्मविधानाः (५) समुदयमुदिताः षडायतनमूलाः ।
छिन्ना द्रुमेन्द्रमूले सर्व्वानित्यप्रहारेण ॥
इह मोहतमःकलुषैर्दुष्टीकृत दर्पदोषसङ्कीर्णम् ।
भित्वा चेचे सुचिरान्धकारं प्रभासितं ज्ञानसूर्य्येण (६) ॥
इह रागमदनमकरं तृष्णोर्म्मिजलं कुदृष्टिसङ्ग्राहम् (७) ।
संसारसागरमहं सन्तीर्णो वीर्य्यबलनावा ॥
इह तन्मयानुयुक्तं बद्ध्वा रागद्वेषमोहांश्च ।
प्रदहति चित्तवितर्कान्दावाग्निपतितानिव पतङ्गान् ॥
इह मञ्ज चिरप्रयातो ह्यपरिमितकल्पकोटिनयुतानि (८) ।

---

१ "आध्यात्मिक बाह्यकाः" आध्यात्मिका बाह्यका इमाः इति शेषः। "शून्य-मिति" शून्यमिति ज्ञातानि इत्यर्थः।

२ "शास्तृषिता" शास्तृषितारः।

३ "निखिलाखिलविधमिह" निखिलानि विविधान्येव।

४ "संज्ञा" संज्ञे। "संज्ञासुखदुःख" संज्ञासुखदुःखानि।

५ "कर्मभिधानाः" कर्माभिधानाः।

६ "दुष्टीकृत" दुष्टीकृतं। "चेचे" चेचं। "सुचिरान्धकारं" सुचिरमन्धकारं।

७ "कुदृष्टिसङ्ग्राहम्" कुदृष्टसङ्ग्राहम्।

८ "मञ्ज" मञ्जं। कल्पकोटिनयुतानि" कल्पकोटिनियुतपर्य्यन्तम्।

संसारपथा क्लिष्टो विश्रान्तो नष्टसन्तापः ॥
इह तन्मयाऽनुबुद्धं सर्व्वपरप्रवादिभिर्यदप्राप्तम्।
अमृतं लोकहितार्थं जरामरणशोकदुःखान्तम् ॥
यत्र स्कन्धैर्दुःखमायतनैः (१) तृष्णासम्भवं दुःखम्।
भूयो न चोद्भविष्यत्यभयपुरमिहाभ्युपगतोऽस्मि ॥
इह ते मयाऽनुबुद्धा रिपवोऽध्यात्मिका महाशत्रवः।
बद्धा च सम्प्रदग्धाः क्लेशाश्च ते मे पुनर्भवनिकेताः ॥
इह तन्मयाऽनुबुद्धं यस्यार्थे कल्पकोटिनयुतानि।
त्यक्ता समांसनयनानि रत्नानि बहून्यमृतहेतोः (२) ॥
इह तन्मयाऽनुबुद्धं यद्बुद्धं प्राक्तनैर्जिनैरपरिमाणैः।
यस्य मधुरोऽभिरम्यः शब्दो लोकेषु विख्यातः ॥
इह तन्मयाऽनुबुद्धं प्रतीत्यसमुत्पादागतम्।
जगच्छून्यं चित्तक्षणेऽनुयातं (३) मरीचिगन्धर्व्वपुरतुल्यम् ॥
इह मे तत् खलु बुद्धं वरनयनं येन लोकधातवः सर्व्वान्।
पश्यामि पाणिनिमध्ये न्यस्तानि यथा द्रुमफलानि (४) ॥
पूर्व्वनिवासस्मरणं तिस्रो विद्या मयेह सम्प्राप्ताः।
अपरिमितकल्पनयुता (५) स्मरामि स्वप्नादिव विबुद्धः ॥
यैरादीप्त सुरनरा विपरीतसञ्ज्ञिनो विपर्य्यस्ताः।

---

१ "दुःखमायतनैः" दुःखायतनैः।

२ "कल्पकोटिनयुतानि त्यक्ता" कल्पकोटिनियुतपर्य्यन्तं त्यक्तानि। "अमृतहेतोः" अमृतहेतवे इत्यर्थः।

३ "चित्तक्षणेऽनुयातं" चित्तक्षणेनानुयातं ज्ञातमित्यर्थः।

४ "बुद्धं" बोधितम्। "लोकधातवः" लोकधातून्। "पाणिनिमध्ये" पाणिमध्ये।

५ "अपरिमितकल्पनयुता" अपरिमितकल्पनियुतपर्य्यन्तम्।

सो पि च तथा अवितथा इह मया पीतो ह्यमृतमण्डः (१) ॥
यस्यार्था यद्दशबला मैत्री भावेन्ति (२) सर्व्वसत्त्वेषु ।
मैत्रीबलेन जित्वा पीतो मेऽस्मिन्नमृतमण्डः ॥
यस्यार्थाय दशबलाः करुणा भावेन्ति (३) सर्व्वसत्त्वेषु ।
करुणाबलेन जित्वा पीतो मेऽस्मिन्नमृतमण्डः ॥
यस्यार्थाय दशबला मुदितां भावेन्ति (४) सर्व्वसत्त्वेषु ।
मुदिताबलेन जित्वा पीतो ह्यस्मिन्नमृतमण्डः ॥
यस्यार्थाय दशबला उपेक्षा भावेन्ति कल्पनयुतानि ।
तमुपेक्षबलैर्जित्वा (५) पीतो मेऽस्मिन्नमृतमण्डः ॥
यत् पीतश्च दशबलैर्गङ्गानदीवालिकाबहुतरैः ।
प्राग्जिनसिंहैः पूर्व्वे पीतो इह मे ह्यमृतमण्डः (६) ॥
या भाषिता च वाग् मारस्येहागतस्य ससैन्यस्य ।
भेत्स्यामि भिन्नपर्य्यङ्कं अप्राप्य जरामरणपारम् (७) ॥
भिन्ना मया ह्यविद्या दीप्तेन ज्ञानकठिनवज्रेण ।
प्राप्तश्च दशबलत्वं तस्मात् भिन्नमिव पर्य्यङ्कम् ॥

---

१ "येराद्दीप्त" येनाद्दीप्ताः । "अवितथा" अवितथोक्त इत्यर्थः ।

२ "यस्यार्थाः" यस्यार्थाय । "मैत्री भावेन्ति" मैत्रीं भावयन्ति ।

३ "करुणा भावेन्ति" करुणां भावयन्ति ।

४ "भावेन्ति" भावयन्ति ।

५ "उपेक्षा भावेन्ति कल्पनयुतानि" उपेक्षां भावयन्ति कल्पनियुतपर्यन्तम् । "तमुपेक्षबलैः" तमुपेक्षाबलैः ।

६ "गङ्गानदीवालिकाबहुतरैः" गङ्गानदीवालुकाबहुतरैः । "पूर्व्वे पीतो इह" पूर्वं पीत इह ।

७ "मारस्येहागतस्य ससैन्यस्य" ससैन्यमिहागतं मारं प्रतीत्यर्थः । "भिन्नपर्यङ्कं अप्राप्य" भिन्नपर्यङ्कमप्राप्य ।

प्राप्तं महार्हत्वं क्षीणा मे आस्रवा निरवशेषाः ।
भग्ना नमुचिसेना भिनद्मि तस्माद्धि पर्य्यङ्कम् ॥
नीवरणकपाटाश्च पञ्च मयेह प्रदारिताः सर्वे ।
तृष्णालता विच्छिन्नाऽहं तेन भिनद्मि पर्यङ्कम् ॥
अथ सो मनुष्यचन्द्रः सविलम्बितमासनात् समुत्थाय ।
भद्रासनेन्यसीदन्महाभिषेकं प्रतीच्छंश्च ॥
रत्नघटसहस्रैरपि नानागन्धोदकैश्च सुरसङ्घाः ।
स्नापयन्ति लोकबन्धुं दशबलं गुणपारमिताप्राप्तम् ॥
वादित्रसहस्रैरपि सन्ततो देवकोटिनयुतानि ।
अतुलां करोति पूजां अप्सरानयुतैः सह समपाः (१) ॥
एवं खलु देवपुत्राः सहेतुप्रत्ययं च सनिदानम् ।
सप्ताह धरणिमण्डे जिना न भिन्दन्ति पर्यङ्कमिति (२) ॥

इति हि भिक्षवोऽभिसम्बुद्धबोधिस्तथागतः प्रथमे सप्ताहे तत्रैवासनेऽस्थात् । इह मयाऽनुत्तरा सम्यक्सम्बोधिरभिसम्बुद्धा । इह मयाऽनवराग्रस्य जातिजरामरणदुःखस्यान्तः कृत इति । द्वितीये सप्ताहे तथागतो दीर्घचङ्क्रमं चङ्क्रमते स्म । त्रिसाहस्र-महासाहस्रलोकधातुमुपस्तभ्य । तृतीये सप्ताहे तथागतोऽनिमिषं बोधिमण्डमीक्षते स्म । इह मयाऽनुत्तरा सम्यक्सम्बोधिरभि-

---

१ "सन्ततो देवकोटिनयुतानि" सन्ततं देवकोटिनियुतानि । "करोति पूजां अप्सरानयुतैः सह समपाः" कुर्वन्ति पूजामप्सरोनियुतैः सह सम्यगिति इत्यर्थः ।

२ "सप्ताह धरणिमण्डे" सप्ताहं धरणीमण्डे । "भिन्दन्ति" भिन्दन्ति स्मेत्यर्थः ।

समुद्रा अनवरतस्य जरामरणदुःखस्यान्तः कृत इति ॥ चतुर्थसप्ताहे तथागतो दीर्घचङ्क्रमं चङ्क्रमते स्म पूर्व्वसमुद्रात् पश्चिमसमुद्रमुपगम्य ।

अथ खलु मारः पापीयान् येन तथागतस्तेनोपसङ्क्रामदुपसङ्क्रम्य तथागतमेतदवोचत् । परिनिर्व्वातु (१) भगवन् परिनिर्व्वातु सुगत । समय इदानीं भगवतः परिनिर्व्वाणाय ॥

एवमुक्ते भिक्षवस्तथागतो मारपापीयांसमेतदवोचत् । न तावदहं पापीयन् परिनिर्व्वास्यामि यावन्मे न स्थविरा भिक्षवो भविष्यन्ति दान्ता व्यक्ता विनीता विशारदा बहुश्रुता धर्म्मानुधर्म्मप्रतिपन्नाः प्रतिबलाः स्वयमाचार्य्यकं ज्ञानं परिदीपयितुमुत्पन्नोत्पन्नानाञ्च परप्रवादिनां सह धर्म्मेण निगृह्याभिप्रायं संसाद्य सप्रातिहार्य्यं धर्म्मं देशयितुम् । न तावदहं पापीयन् परिनिर्व्वास्यामि यावन्मया बुद्धधर्म्मसङ्घवंशो लोके न प्रतिष्ठापितो भविष्यति । अपरिमिता बोधिसत्त्वा न व्याकृता भविष्यन्ति । अनुत्तरायां सम्यक्सम्बोधौ न तावदहं पापीयान् परिनिर्व्वास्यामि । यावन्मम चतस्रः पर्षदो दान्ता विनीता व्यक्ता विशारदा भविष्यन्ति यावत् सप्रातिहार्य्यं धर्म्मं देशयितुमिति ॥

अथ खलु मारः पापीयानिदं वचनं श्रुत्वा एकान्ते प्रक्रम्य स्थितोऽभूत् । दुःखी दुर्मना विप्रतिसारी अधोमुखः काष्ठेन महीं विलिखन् विषयमतिक्रान्त इति ।

---

१ "परिनिर्व्वातु" भगवन् परिनिर्व्वातु इति शब्दार्थः । एवमन्यत्र बोध्यम् ।

अथ खलु तास्तिस्रो मारदुहितरो रतिश्चारतिश्च तृष्णा च मारं पापीयांसङ्गाथयाऽध्यभाषन्त ।

दुर्मनाषि कथं तात प्रोच्यतां यद्यसौ नरः ।
नागपाशेन तं बध्वा कुञ्जरं वाऽऽनयामहे (१) ॥
आनयित्वा च तं शीघ्रं करिष्यामो वशे तव (२) ।

मार आह ।

अर्हन् सुगतो लोके न रागस्य वशं व्रजेत् ।
विषयं मे ह्यतिक्रान्तस्तस्माच्छोचाम्यहं भृशम् इति ॥

ततस्ताः स्त्रीचापल्यादविदितप्रभावा अपि बोधिसत्त्वभूतस्यैवं तथागतस्य पितुर्वचनमश्रुत्वैव प्रभूतयौवनमध्ययौवनधारिण्यो भूत्वा विचक्षुःकर्मणे तथागतस्यान्तिकमुपसङ्क्रान्ताः । ताश्च तथागतो न मनसि करोति स्म । भूयश्च ता जराजर्जरा अधितिष्ठन् । ततस्ताः पितुरन्तिके गत्वैवमाहुः ।

सत्यं वदसि नस्तात न रागेण स नीयते ।
विषयं मे ह्यतिक्रान्तस्तस्माच्छोचाम्यहं भृशम् ॥
वीक्षेत यद्यसौ रूपं यदस्माभिर्विनिर्मितम् ।
गौतमस्य विनाशार्थं ततोऽस्य हृदयं स्फुटेत् ॥
तत्साधु नस्तातेदं जराजर्जरशरीरमन्तर्धापय ।
मार आह ।

---

१ "दुर्मनाषि" दुर्मना असि । "यद्यसौ नरः" योऽसौ बोधिसत्त्वनामा नरोऽस्ति यदि तमिति परेणान्वयः । "कुञ्जरं वा" कुञ्जरमिव ।

२ अस्य उत्तरार्द्धं न लभ्यते । अन्यान्यपुस्तकेष्वपि एतावानेव पाठः ।

नाहं पश्यामि तं लोके पुरुषं सचराचरे।
बुद्धस्य यो ह्यधिष्ठानं प्रकुर्यात्कर्तुमन्यथा॥
ग्रामं गत्वा निवेदयन्तामत्ययं स्वकृतं मुनेः(१)।
सर्वं पौराणिकं कार्यं करिष्यति यथामतम्॥

ततस्ता गत्वा तथागतं क्षमापयन्ति स्म। अत्ययं नो भगवन् प्रतिगृह्णातु। अत्ययं नो सुगत यथा बालानां यथा मूढानां यथाव्यक्तानामकुशलानामक्षेत्रज्ञानाम्। यावद्वयं भगवन्तमासादयितव्यं मन्यामहे॥ ततस्तास्तथागतं गाथयाऽध्यभाषन्त।

गिरिं नखैर्विलिखत लोहं दन्तैर्विखादथ।
शिरसा विभेत्स्यथ गिरिमगाधे गाधमैषतः (२)॥

तस्माद्युष्माकं दारिका अत्ययं प्रतिगृह्णातु। तत्कस्माद्वृद्धिरेषा ये ऽत्ययमत्ययतो दृष्ट्वा प्रतिदेशयन्त्यायत्यां च सम्बरमापद्यन्ते।

पञ्चमे सप्ताहे भिक्षवस्तथागतो मुचिलिन्दनागराजभवने विहरति स्म। सप्ताहमेघे दुर्दिनेऽथ खलु मुचिलिन्दनागराजः स्वभवनान्निष्क्रम्य तथागतस्य काये सप्तकृद्भोगैः परिवेष्ट्य फणैश्छादयति स्म। मा भगवतः शीतं काये शीतवाताः प्राक्षुरिति। यथा पूर्वस्यामपीदृशोऽन्येऽपि सम्बहुला नागराजा आगत्य तथागतस्य कायं सप्तकृद्भोगैः परिवेष्ट्य फणैश्छादयन्ति

१ "निवेदयन्ताम्" निवेदयन्तु।
२ "विलिखत" विलिखेत्। "विखादथ" विखादेत्। "विभेत्स्यथ" विभेत्स्येत्। "गाधमैषतः" गाधमिच्छेत्।

स्म । मा भगवतः काये शीतवाताः प्राक्षुरिति । यथा पूर्व्वस्या दिश एवं दक्षिणपश्चिमोत्तराभ्यो दिग्भ्यो नागराजा आगत्य तथागतस्य कायं सप्तकृत्वोभोगैः परिवेष्ट्य फणैश्छादयन्ति स्म । मा भगवतः काये शीतवाताः प्राक्षुरिति । स च नागराजस्तैर्नागराजैः मेरुपर्व्वतेन्द्रवदुच्छ्रितत्वेन स्थितोऽभूत् । न च तैर्नागराजैस्तादृशं कदाचित्सुखं प्राप्तं पूर्वं यादृशं तेषां सप्तरात्रिन्दिवसानि तथा तथागतकायसन्निकर्षादासीत् । ततः सप्ताहस्यात्ययेन ततस्ते नागराजा व्यपगतदुर्द्दिनं विदित्वा तथागतस्य कायाद्भोगानपनीय तथागतस्य पादौ शिरोभिरभिवन्द्य चिःप्रदक्षिणीकृत्य स्वकस्वकानि भवनान्युपजग्मुः । मुचिलिन्दोऽपि नागराजस्तथागतस्य पादौ शिरसाभिवन्द्य चिःप्रदक्षिणीकृत्य स्वभवनं प्राविशत् ।

षष्ठे सप्ताहे तथागतो मुचिलिन्दभवनादजपालस्य न्यग्रोधमूलं गच्छति स्म । अन्तरे च मुचिलिन्दभवनस्यान्तरादजपालस्य नद्या नैरञ्जनायास्तीरे चेरकपरिव्राजकश्रावकगौतमनिर्ग्रन्थाजीवकादयस्तथागतं दृष्ट्वाऽभिभाषन्ते स्म । अपि भवता गौतमेनेव सप्ताहमकालदुर्द्दिनं सुखेन व्यतिनामितम् ।

अथ खलु भिक्षवस्तथागतस्तस्यां च वेलायामिदमुदानमुदानयति स्म ।

सुखो विवेकतुष्टस्य (१) श्रुतधर्म्मस्य पश्यतः ।
अव्याबध्यं सुखं लोके प्राणिभूतस्य संयमः ॥

---

१ "सुखा विवेकतुष्टस्य" सुखं विवेकतुष्टस्य ।

सुखा विरागता लोके पापानां समतिक्रमः।
अस्मिन् मानुष्यविषये एतद्वै परमं सुखम्॥

पश्यति स्म भिक्षवस्तथागतो लोकमादीप्तं प्रदीप्तं जात्या जरया व्याधिभिर्मरणेन शोकपरिदेवदुःखदौर्मनस्योपायासैः। तत्र तथागत इदमित्थोदानमुदानयति स्म।

अयं लोकः सन्तापजातः शब्दस्पर्शरसरूपगन्धैः।
भयभीतो भवमेव भूयो मार्गते भवतृष्णया॥

सप्तमे सप्ताहे तथागतो तारायणमूले विहरति स्म। तेन खलु पुनः समयेनोत्तरापथकौ द्वौ भ्रातरौ त्रपुषभल्लिकौ नाम वणिजौ पण्डितौ निपुणौ विविधपण्यं गृहीत्वा महा-लब्धलाभौ दक्षिणापथादुत्तरापथं गच्छतः स्म॥ महता सा-र्थेन पञ्चभी रथशतैः सुपरिपूर्णैः॥ तयोः सुजातः कीर्त्तिश्च नामा जात्यौ द्वौ बलीवर्द्दावास्तां नास्ति तयोर्लग्नभयं यत्रान्ये बलीवर्द्दा न वहन्ति स्म तत्र तौ युज्येते स्म। यत्र चायतो भयं भवति स्म तत्र तौ कीलबद्धाविव तिष्ठतः स्म। न च तौ प्रतो-देन वाह्येते स्म। उत्पलहस्तकेन वा सुमनोदामकेन वा तौ वाह्येते स्म। तेषां तारायणसमीपे क्षीरिकावननिवासिनीदेव-ताधिष्ठानात्ते च शकटाः अधिविष्ठिता न वहन्ति स्म। वरत्रा-दीनि च सर्व्वशकटाङ्गानि च छिद्यन्ते स्म। शकटचक्राणि च नाभिपर्यन्तं भूमौ निमग्नानि सर्व्वप्रयत्नैरपि ते शकटा न वहन्ति स्म। ते (१) विस्मिता भीतास्त्वाभूवन्। किं खल्वत्र

१ "ते" त्रपुषभल्लिकादयः।

कारणं कोऽयं विकारो यदि मे खलशकटा विष्ठिताः। तैस्तौ सुजातकीर्त्तिबलीवर्दौ योजितौ। तावपि न वहतः स्म उत्पलहस्तेन च सुमनोदामकेन च बाध्यमानौ। तेषामेतदभवत्। भयमयं पुरतः किञ्चिद्भयं येनैतावपि न वहतः॥ तैरश्वदूताः पुरतः प्रेषिताः। अश्वदूताः प्रत्यागताः प्राहुर्नास्ति किञ्चिद्भयमिति। तथापि देवतया स्वरूपं सन्दर्श्याश्वासिता न भेतव्यमिति। तावपि च बलीवर्दौ (१) येन तथागतस्तथा शकटा प्रकर्षिताः। यावत्ते पश्यन्ति स्म तथागतं वैश्वानरमिव प्रदीप्तं द्वात्रिंशन्महापुरुषलक्षणैः समलङ्कृतमचिरोदितमिव दिनकरं श्रिया देदीप्यमानम्। दृष्ट्वा च ते विस्मिता बभूवुः।

किन्नु खल्वयं ब्रह्माऽनुप्राप्त उताहो शक्रो देवानामिन्द्र उताहो वैश्रमण उताहो सूर्य्यचन्द्रौ वा उताहो किञ्चिद्गिरिदैवतं वा नदीदेवतं वा॥ ततस्तथागतः काषायाणि वस्त्राणि प्रकटयति स्म॥ ततस्ते प्राहुः।

प्रव्रजितः खल्वयं काषायसंवृतो नास्माद्भयमस्तीति ते प्रसादं प्रतिलभ्य अन्योन्यमेवमाहुः।

प्रव्रजितः खल्वयं कालभोजी भविष्यति। अस्ति किञ्चिदाहारोऽस्ति मधुतर्पणमिक्षुलिस्यातकाः। ते मधुतर्पणमिक्षुलिस्यातकांस्तादाय येन तथागतस्तेनोपसङ्क्रामन्नुपसङ्क्रम्य तथागतस्य

---

१ "तावपि च बलीवर्दौ" ताभ्यामपि च बलीवर्दाभ्यामित्यर्थः ।

पादौ शिरोभिर्वन्दित्वा चिःप्रदक्षिणीकृत्यैकान्ते तस्थुः। एकान्ते स्थितास्ते तथागतमेवमाहुः।

प्रतिगृह्णातु भगवन्निदं पिण्डपात्रमस्माकमनुकम्पामुपादाय।

अथ खलु भिक्षवस्तथागतस्यैतदभूत्। साधु खल्विदं स्याद्यदहं हस्ताभ्यां प्रति गृह्णीयाम्। कस्मिन् खलु पूर्वकैस्तथागतैः सम्यक्सम्बुद्धैः प्रतिगृहीतम्। पात्रेणेत्यज्ञासीत्।

इति हि भिक्षवस्तथागतस्य भोजनकाल इति विदित्वा तत्क्षणमेव चतसृभ्यो दिग्भ्यश्चत्वारो महाराजा आगत्य चत्वारि सौवर्णानि पात्राण्यादाय तथागतस्योपनामयन्ति स्म। प्रतिगृह्णातु भगवन्निमानि सौवर्णानि चत्वारि पात्राण्यस्माकमनुकम्पामुपादाय। तानि च श्रमणाप्रतिरूपाणीति कृत्वा तथागतो न प्रतिगृह्णाति स्म। एवं चत्वारि रूप्यमयानि वैदूर्य्यमयानि स्फटिकमयानि मुसारगल्वमयानि अश्मगर्भमयानि ॥ ततश्चत्वारि सर्व्वरत्नमयानि पात्राणि गृहीत्वा तथागतस्योपनामयन्ति। न श्रमणस्य सारूप्याणीतिकृत्वा तथागतो न प्रतिगृह्णाति स्म।

अथ खलु भिक्षवस्तथागतस्य पुनरेतदभूत्। एवं कतमद्विधैः पात्रैः पौर्वकैस्तथागतैरर्हद्भिः सम्यक्सम्बुद्धैः प्रतिगृहीतम्। शैलपात्रैरित्यज्ञासीत्। एवं चित्त उत्पन्नस्तथागतस्य।

अथ खलु वैश्रवणो महाराजस्तदन्यांस्त्रीन्महाराजानामन्त्रयते स्म। इमानि खलु पुनर्मार्षाश्चत्वारि शैलपात्राणि नील-

कायिकैर्देवपुत्रैरारब्धं भक्तानि । तथागतमेतदभूदेव वयं परिभोजयाम इति ॥ ततो वैरोचनो नाम नीलकायिको देवपुत्रः सोऽत्रानेवमाह ।

मा एष भोक्ष्यथ भो जनेषु
धारेति मोचेति समतीते भणिता जिनः ।
शाक्यमुनिरिति नाम्ना
तस्येति पात्राण्युपनामयेथा (१) ॥
अयं स कालः समयश्च मार्षा
उपनामितुं शाक्यमुनेह भोजनम् (२) ।
सङ्गीतितूर्यस्वरनादितेन
दास्यामि पात्राणि विधाय पूजाम् ॥
स भोजनं धर्ममयं लभेय-
मिमे च शैलामयमभेद्य भाजनाः ।
प्रतिग्रहीतुं क्षमते न चान्यः
प्रतिग्रहार्थाय प्रयाम हन्त (३) ॥

अथ खलु चत्वारो महाराजाः सस्वजनपार्षद्याः पुष्पधूप-माल्यगन्धविलेपनतूर्यताडावचरसङ्गीतिसम्प्रभणितेन स्वैः स्वैः

---

१ "मा एष" न एव इत्यर्थः । "भोक्ष्यथ" भोक्ष्यते । "भोजनेषु" भो जनेषु, भोजनकर्मसु चेत्यर्थः । "धारेति मोचेति" धारयति मोचयति, धारयितुं मोचयितुञ्च समर्थोऽयमिति भावः । "तस्येति" तस्यैतानि । "उपनामयेथा" उपनामयत ।

२ "उपनामितुं शाक्यमुनेह" उपनामयितुं शाक्यमुनये इह ।

३ "इमे च शैलामयमभेद्य भाजना" इमानि च शैलमयानि अभेद्यानि भाजनानि । "प्रयाम हन्त" प्रयामो हन्त ।

पाणिभिस्तानि पात्राणि परिगृह्य येन तथागतस्तेनोपसङ्क्रा-
मन्नुपसङ्क्रम्य तथागतस्य पूजां कृत्वा तानि पात्राणि दिव्यकुसु-
मपरि पूर्णानि तथागतायोपनामयन्ति स्म।

अथ खलु भिक्षवस्तथागतस्यैतदभूत्। इमे खलु पुनश्चत्वारो महाराजाः श्राद्धाः प्रसन्ना मम चत्वारि शैलपात्राण्युपनामयन्ति स्म। न च मे चत्वारि शैलपात्राणि कल्पन्ते। अथैकस्य प्रतिग्रहिष्यामि त्रयाणां वैमनस्यात्। यन्न्वहमिमानि चत्वारि पात्राणि प्रतिगृह्यैकपात्रमधिष्ठेयम्।

अथ खलु भिक्षवस्तथागतो दक्षिणपाणिं प्रसार्य्य वैश्रवणं महाराजं गाथयाऽध्यभाषत।

उपनामयस्व सुगतस्य भाजनं
त्वं भेष्यसे (१) भाजनमग्र्ययाने।
अस्मद्विधेभ्यो हि प्रदाय भाजनं
स्मृतिर्मतिश्चैव न जातु हीयते॥

अथ खलु भिक्षवस्तथागतो वैश्रवणस्यान्तिकात्तत्पात्रं प्रतिगृह्णीते स्म अनुकम्पामुपादाय। प्रतिगृह्य च धृतराष्ट्रं महाराजं गाथयाऽध्यभाषत।

यो भाजनं देति तथागतस्य
न तस्य जातु स्मृति प्रज्ञा हीयते।
अतिनाम्य कालञ्च सुखं सुखेन

---

१ "सुगतस्य" सुगतायेत्यर्थः। "भेष्यसे" भविष्यसि।

यावत्परं मुच्यति प्रीतिभावम् (१) ॥

अथ खलु भिक्षवस्तथागतो धृतराष्ट्रस्य महाराजस्यान्तिका-
त्तत्पात्रं प्रतिगृह्णाति स्म अनुकम्पामुपादाय। प्रतिगृह्य च विरू-
ढकं महाराजं गाथयाऽध्यभाषत।

ददासि यस्त्वं परिशुद्धभाजनं
विशुद्धचित्ताय तथागताय।
भविष्यसि त्वं लघु शुद्धचित्तः
प्रशंसितो देवमनुष्यलोके ॥

अथ खलु भिक्षवस्तथागतो विरूढकस्य महाराजस्यान्तिकात्त-
त्पात्रं प्रतिगृह्णाति स्म अनुकम्पामुपादाय। प्रतिगृह्य च विरू-
पाक्षं महाराजं गाथयाऽध्यभाषत।

अच्छिद्रशीलस्य तथागतस्य
अच्छिद्रवृत्तस्य अच्छिद्रभाजनम्।
अच्छिद्रचित्तः प्रददासि श्रद्धया
अच्छिद्र ते भेष्यति पुण्यदक्षिणा (२) ॥

प्रतिगृह्णाति स्म भिक्षवस्तथागतो विरूपाक्षस्य महाराजस्या-
न्तिकात्तत्पात्रमनुकम्पामुपादाय। प्रतिगृह्य चैकपात्रमधिति-
ष्ठति स्म अधिमुक्तिबलेन। तस्यां च वेलायामिदमुदानमुदान-
यति स्म।

---

१ "देति तथागतस्य" ददाति तथागताय। "स्मृति प्रज्ञा" स्मृतिः प्रज्ञा। "अभि-नाम्य" अभिनाम्येति वा पाठः।

२ "अच्छिद्र" अच्छिद्रा। "भेष्यति" भविष्यति।

इमानि पात्राणि पुराभवे मया
फलपूरिता प्रेमणीयाश्च कृत्वा ।
तेनेमि पात्राश्चतुरः सुसंस्थिता
ददन्ति देवाश्चतुरो महर्द्धिका: (१) ॥

तत्रेदमुच्यते ।

स सप्तरात्रं वरबोधिवृक्षं सम्प्रेक्ष्य धीरः परमार्थदर्शी ।
षड्भिः प्रकारैः प्रविकम्प्य चोर्व्वीमभ्युत्थितः सिंहगतिर्नृसिंहः ॥
समन्तनागेन्द्रविलम्बगामी क्रमेण तारायणमूलमेत्य ।
उपाविशन्मेरुवदप्रकम्प्यो ध्यानं समाधिश्च मुनिः प्रदध्यौ ॥
तस्मिंश्च काले त्रपुषश्च भल्लिको भ्रातृद्वयं वणिजगणेन सार्द्धम् ।
शकटानि ते पञ्च धनेन पूर्णाः सम्पुष्पितशालवने प्रविष्टाः (२) ॥
महर्षितेजेन च अर्द्धमात्रं चक्राणि भूमौ विविशुः क्षणेन ।
तां तादृशीं प्रेक्ष्य च ते अवस्थां महद्भयं वणिजगणस्य जातम् (३)॥
ते खड्गहस्ताः शरशक्तिपाणयो वने मृगं वा मृगयन् क एष ।
वीक्षन्त (४) शारदचन्द्रवक्त्रं जिनं सहस्रांशुमिवाभ्रमुक्तम् ॥
प्रहीनकोपा अपनीतदर्पाः प्रणम्य मूर्द्ध्ना विमृशुः क एष ।

---

१ "फलपूरिता प्रेमणीयाश्च" फलपूरितानि प्रेमणीयानि । "तेनेमि पात्राश्चतुरः सुसंस्थिता ददन्ति" तेनेमानि पात्राणि चत्वारि सुसंस्थितानि ददति स्म । "चतुरो महर्द्धिकाः" चत्वारि महर्द्धिकानि ।

२ "वणिजगणेन" वणिग्गणेन । "शकटानि ते" शकटांश्चानादाय । "पूर्णाः" पूर्णाम् । "प्रविष्टाः" प्रविष्टम् ।

३ "महर्षितेजेन" महर्षितेजसा । "ते अवस्थां" तदवस्थामित्यर्थः । "वणिजगणस्य" वणिग्गणस्य ।

४ "ते" त्रपुषभल्लिकादय इत्यर्थः । "वीक्षन्त" अवीक्षन् ।

नभस्तलाद्देवत वाच भाषते (१) बुद्धोऽयं लोकहितार्थकारी ॥
रात्रिन्दिवा सप्त न चान्नपानमनेन भुक्तं करुणात्मकेन ।
यदिच्छथा आत्मनः क्षेमशान्तिं भोजेथिमं भावितकायचित्तम्(२)॥
श्रुत्व ते तं मधुरं गिरस्य वन्दित्व(३)क्रमा च जिनं प्रदक्षिणम्।
प्रीतास्ततस्ते सहितैः सहायैः जिनस्य पिण्डाय मतिं प्रचक्रुः ॥

तेन खलु पुनर्भिक्षवः समयेन अपुत्रभक्तिकानां वणिजां प्रत्यन्तकर्वटे गोयूथं प्रतिवसति स्म ।

अथ ता गावस्तस्मिन् काले तस्मिन् समये सर्पिर्मण्डप्रदुग्धा अभूवन् । अथगोपालास्तं सर्पिर्मण्डमादाय येन अपुत्रभक्तिकौ वणिजौ तेनोपसङ्क्रामन्नुपसङ्क्रम्यैनौ प्रवृत्तिमारोचयन्ति स्म। यत् खलु यूयं भद्रा जानीयात सर्व्वास्ता गावः सर्पिर्मण्डप्रदुग्धास्तत्किमेतत्प्रशस्तमाहोस्विन्नेति।

तत्र लोलुपजात्या ब्राह्मणा एवमाहुः । अमङ्गल्यमेतद्ब्राह्मणानां महायज्ञो यष्टव्यमिति ।

तेन खलु पुनर्भिक्षवः समयेन अपुत्रभक्तिकानां वणिजां शिखण्डी नाम ब्राह्मणः पूर्व्वज्ञातीसालोहितो ब्रह्मलोके प्रत्याजातोऽभूत् । स ब्राह्मणरूपमभिनिर्माय तान् वणिजो गाथाभिरध्यभाषत ।

युष्माकं प्रणिधिः पूर्व्वं बोधिप्राप्तस्तथागतः ।

---

१ "विप्रघुष्टः" अभिघुष्टः। विरुद्ध इति वाऽस्य पाठः। "देवत वाच भाषते" देवता वाचं भाषते।

२ "यदिच्छथा" यदीच्छथ। "भोजेथिमं" भोजयतेमं।

३ "वन्दित्व" वन्दित्वा।

मच्छाकं भोजनं भुक्त्वा धर्मचक्रं प्रवर्त्तयेत् ॥
स चैव प्रणिधिः पूर्वो बोधिप्राप्तस्तथागतः ।
आहारमुपनामयत भुक्त्वा च धर्मचक्रं प्रवर्त्तयेत् ॥
सुमधुरं सुगन्धं गवाञ्च सर्पिर्दोहनम् ।
पुण्यकर्मविशेषोऽनुभावो महर्षिणः (१) ॥
एवं सम्बोध्य वणिजः श्रियस्वी भवनङ्गतः ।
उदग्रमनसः सर्व्वे बभूवुस्त्रपुषाह्वयाः ॥

क्षीरं यदासीच्च हि गोसहस्रादग्रेषु तत्तं समुदानयित्वा ।
अग्रञ्च तस्मात्परिगृह्य ओजः साधेन्तु ते भोजन गौरवेण (२) ॥
शतं सहस्रैकपलस्य मूल्यं या रत्नपात्री अभूचन्दनमिश्रिणिका ।
चोक्षांसुधौतां विमलाञ्च कृत्वा समतीर्थिकां पूरिषु भोजनेन(३)॥
मधुं गृहीत्वा तथ रत्नपात्री तारायणीमूलमुपेत्य शास्तुः ।
प्रतिगृह्य भक्तं अनुगृह्य चास्मादिदं प्रणीतं प्रतिभुञ्ज भोजनम्(४)॥
अनुकम्पार्थाय उभयोश्च भ्रातृणां पूर्वाश्रयं ज्ञात्व च बोधि प्रस्थितौ ।
प्रतिम्रदित्वा परिभुञ्जि शास्ता भुक्त्वा क्षिपी पात्रि नभस्तलेऽस्मिं(५)॥

---

१ "सर्पिर्दोहनम्" सर्पिर्दोहनम्। सर्पिर्दोहनमिति क्वच पाठः। "महर्षिणः" महर्षेः।

२ "साधेन्तु ते" साधयितवन्तो। "भोजन" भोजनं।

३ "चन्दनमिश्रिणिका" चन्दनमिश्रिता। "चोक्षांसुधौतां" चोक्षां सुधौतामिति योजना। "पूरिषु" अपूरयन्।

४ "मधुं" मधु। "तथ रत्नपात्री" तथा रत्नपात्रीं। "प्रतिगृह्य भक्तं" प्रतिगृहाण भक्तं। "अनुगृह्य चास्मादिदं" अनुगृहाण चास्मानिदं।

५ "भ्रातृणां" भ्रात्रोः। "ज्ञात्व च बोधि प्रस्थितौ" ज्ञात्वा च बोधिः प्रस्थितः। "प्रतिम्रदित्वा परिभुञ्जि" प्रतिगृह्य परिभुङ्क्ते। "क्षिपी पात्रि नभस्तलेऽस्मिं" अक्षिपत् पात्रीं नभस्तले इत्यर्थः।

सुब्रह्मनामा च हि देवराजो अधारयत्तां वररत्नपात्रीम् ।
अधुनाप्यसौ तां खलु ब्रह्मलोके सम्पूजयत्यन्यसुरैः सहायः (१) ॥

अथ खलु तथागतस्तस्यां वेलायां त्रपुषभल्लिकानां वणिजामिमां संहर्षणामकार्षीत् ।

दिशां स्वस्तिकरं दिव्यं माङ्गल्यं चार्थसाधकम् ।
अर्था वः सम्पताः सर्व्वे भवन्त्वाशु प्रदक्षिणाः ॥
श्रीर्वोऽस्तु दक्षिणे हस्ते श्रीर्वो वामे प्रतिष्ठिता ।
श्रीर्वोऽस्तु सर्व्वरोगेषु मालेव शिरसि स्थिता ॥
धनैषिणां प्रयातानां वणिजां वै दिशोदश: ।
लभन्तां महालाभास्ते च सन्तु सुखोदयाः ॥
कार्य्येण केनचिद्येन गच्छथा पूर्व्विकां दिशम् ।
नक्षत्राणि वः पालयन्तु ये तस्यां दिशि संस्थिताः (२) ॥
कृत्तिका रोहिणी चैव मृग आर्द्रा पुनर्वसुः ।
पुष्यश्चैव तथाऽश्लेषा इत्येषां पूर्व्विका दिशा (३) ॥
इत्येते सप्त नक्षत्रा लोकपाला यशस्विनः ।
अधिष्ठिताः पूर्व्वभागे देवा रक्षन्तु सर्व्वतः (४) ॥
तेषाञ्चाधिपती राजा धृतराष्ट्रेति विश्रुतः ।
स सर्व्वगन्धर्वपतिः सूर्य्येण सह रक्षतु ॥
पुत्रापि तस्य बहव एकनामा विचक्षणाः ।

---

१ "अधारयत्तां" अधारय तां । "अन्यसुरैः सहायः" अन्यसुरैः सहित इत्यर्थः ।

२ "गच्छथा" गच्छतो युष्मानित्यर्थः । "पूर्व्विकां" पूर्वां । "ये तस्यां" यानि तस्यां । "संस्थिताः" संस्थितानि ।

३ "पूर्व्विका दिशा" पूर्वा दिक् ।

४ "इत्येते सप्त नक्षत्रा" इत्येतानि सप्त नक्षत्राणि ।

अशीति दश चैकश्च इन्द्रनामा महाबलाः (१) ॥
तेऽपि च अधिपालेन्तु (२) आरोग्येण शिवेन च ।
पूर्व्वस्मिन्वै दिशोभागे अष्टौ देवकुमारिकाः ॥
जयन्ती विजयन्ती च सिद्धार्था अपराजिता ।
नन्दोत्तरा नन्दिसेना नन्दिनी नन्दवर्द्धनी ॥
तापि च अधिपालेन्तु आरोग्येण शिवेन च ।
पूर्व्वस्मिन्वै दिशो भागे चापलं नाम चेटिका (३) ॥
अवुत्तं जिनेभि ज्ञातमर्हन्तेभिश्च तायिभिः ।
साऽपि च अधिपालेन्तु आरोग्येण शिवेन च (४) ॥
क्षेमाश्च वो दिशः सन्तु मा च वः पापमागमत् ।
लब्धार्थाश्च निवर्त्तध्वं सर्व्वदेवेभि रक्षिताः (५) ॥
येन केनचित्कृत्येन गच्छथा दक्षिणां दिशं ।
नक्षत्राणि वः पालेन्तु ये तां दिशमधिष्ठिताः (६) ॥
मघा च द्वौ च फाल्गुण्यौ हस्ता चित्रा च पञ्चमी ।
स्वातिश्चैव विशाखा च एतेषां दक्षिणा दिशः (७) ॥

---

१ "पुत्रापि" पुत्रा अपि। "एकनामा" एकनामानः। "अशीति दश" अशीति-दंश। "इन्द्रनामा" इन्द्रनामानः।

२ "च अधिपालेन्तु' वोऽधिपालयन्तु।

३ "तापि च अधिपालेन्तु" ता अपि वोऽधिपालयन्तु। "चापलं नाम" चापला नाम।

४ "अवुत्तं जिनेभि ज्ञातमर्हन्तेभिश्च तायिभिः" अनुक्ता जिनैर्ज्ञाता अर्हद्भिश्च त्रायिभिः इति अनुमीयते। "अधिपालेन्तु" अधिपालयन्तु।

५ "लब्धार्थाः" लब्धार्थाश्च। "सर्व्वदेवेभि" सर्वदेवैः।

६ "गच्छथा" गच्छेत। "पालेन्तु ये" पालयन्तु यानि तानि। "दिशमधिष्ठिताः" दिशमधिष्ठितानि।

७ "दक्षिणा दिशः" दक्षिणा दिक्।

इत्येते सप्त नक्षत्रा (१) लोकपाला यशस्विनः।
आदिष्टा दक्षिणे भागे ते वो रक्षन्तु सर्व्वतः॥
तेषाञ्चाधिपती राजा विरूढक इति स्मृतः।
सर्व्वकुम्भाण्डाधिपतिर्यमेन सह रक्षतु॥
पुत्रापि तस्य बहव एकनामा विचक्षणाः।
अशीतिर्दश चैकश्च इन्द्रनामा महाबलाः (२)॥
तेऽपि च अधिपालेन्तु (३) आरोग्येण शिवेन च।
दक्षिणस्या दिशो भागे अष्टौ देवकुमारिकाः॥
श्रियामती यशमती यशःप्राप्ता यशोधरा।
सुउत्थिता सुप्रथमा सुप्रबुद्धा सुखावहा॥
तापि व अधिपालेन्तु आरोग्येण शिवेन च।
दक्षिणस्या दिशो भागे पद्मनामेन चेटिका (४)॥
नित्यं ज्वलिति तेजेन नित्यं सर्व्वं प्रकाशितं।
साऽपि व अधिपालेन्तु आरोग्येण शिवेन च (५)॥
क्षेमाश्च वो दिशः सन्तु मा च वः पापमागमत्।
लब्धार्थाश्च निवर्त्तध्वं सर्व्वदेवेभि रक्षिताः (६)॥
येन केनचित्कृत्येन गच्छेथा पश्चिमां दिशम्।

---

१ "इत्येते सप्त नक्षत्रा" इत्येतानि सप्त नक्षत्राणि।

२ "पुत्रापि" पुत्रा अपि। "एकनामा" एकनामानः।

३ "अधिपालेन्तु" अधिपालयन्तु।

४ "तापि व अधिपालेन्तु" ता अपि वोऽधिपालयन्तु। "पद्मनामेन" पद्मनाम्नी।

५ "ज्वलिति तेजेन" ज्वलति तेजसा। "प्रकाशितं" प्रकाशयति इत्यर्थः। "व अधिपालेन्तु" वोऽधिपालयतु।

६ "पापमागमत्" पापमागच्छेदित्यर्थः। "सर्व्वदेवभि" सर्व्वदेवैः।

नक्षत्राणि वः पालेन्तु ये तां दिशमधिष्ठिताः (१) ॥
अनुराधा च ज्येष्ठा च मूला च दृढवीर्यता ।
द्वावाषाढेऽभिजिच्च श्रवणा भवति सप्तमा (२) ॥
इत्येते सप्त नक्षत्रा लोकपाला यशस्विनः ।
आदिष्टाः पश्चिमे भागे ते वो रक्षन्तु सर्व्वदा (३) ॥
तेषां चाधिपती राजा विरूपाक्ष इति स्मृतः ।
स सर्व्वनागाधिपतिर्वरुणेन सह रक्षतु ॥
पुत्रापि बहवस्तस्य एकनामा विचक्षणाः ।
अशीतिर्दश चैकश्च इन्द्रनामा महाबलाः (४) ॥
तेऽपि व अधिपालेन्तु (५) आरोग्येण शिवेन च ।
पश्चिमेऽस्मिन्दिशो भागे अष्टौ देवकुमारिका: ॥
अलम्बुषा मिश्रकेशी पुण्डरीका तथाऽरुणा ।
एकादशा नवनामिका शीता कृष्णा च द्रौपदी ॥
तापि व अधिपालेन्तु आरोग्येण शिवेन च ।
पश्चिमेऽस्मिन्दिशो भागे अष्टमो नाम (६) पर्वतः ॥
प्रतिष्ठा चन्द्रसूर्य्याणामिष्टमर्थं ददातु वः ।

---

१ "नक्षत्रा" नक्षत्र । "पालेन्तु ये" पालयन्तु यानि । "दिशमधिष्ठिताः" दिशमधिष्ठितानि ।

२ "भवति सप्तमा" भवति सप्तमी ।

३ "इत्येते सप्त नक्षत्रा" इत्येतानि सप्त नक्षत्राणि ।

४ "पुत्रापि" पुत्रा अपि । "एकनामा" एकनामानः । "इन्द्रनामा" इन्द्रनामानः ।

५ "व अधिपालेन्तु" वोऽधिपालयन्तु ।

६ "तापि व अधिपालेन्तु" ता अपि वोऽधिपालयन्तु । "अष्टमो नाम" अष्टाङ्गो नाम इति वा पाठः ।

तेऽपि व अधिपालेन्तु (१) आरोग्येण शिवेन च ॥
क्षेमाश्च वो दिशः सन्तु मा च वः पापमागमत् ।
लब्धार्थाश्च निवर्त्तध्वं सर्व्वदेवेभि रक्षिताः (२) ॥
येन केनचित्कृत्येन गच्छथा उत्तरान्दिशम् ।
नक्षत्राणि वः पालेन्तु ये तान्दिशमधिष्ठिताः (३) ॥
धनिष्ठा शतभिषा चैव द्वौ च भाद्रपदे तथा ।
रेवती अश्विनी चैव भरणी भवति सप्तमी ॥
इत्येते सप्तनक्षत्रा (४) लोकपाला यशस्विनः ।
उद्दिष्टा उत्तरे भागे ते वो रक्षन्तु सर्व्वदा ॥
तेषाञ्चाधिपती राजा कुवेरो नरवाहनः ।
सर्व्वयक्षाणामधिपतिर्मणिभद्रेण सह रक्षतु ॥
पुत्राऽपि तस्य बहव एकनामा विचक्षणाः ।
अशीतिर्दश चैकश्च इन्द्रनामा महाबलाः (५) ॥
तेऽपि व अधिपालेन्तु (६) आरोग्येण शिवेन च ।
उत्तरस्मिन्दिशो भागे अष्टौ देवकुमारिकाः ॥

---

१ "तेऽपि" महाप्राणपर्वतेऽपि इत्यर्थः। "व अधिपालेन्तु" वोऽधिपालयन्तु ।

२ "पापमागमत्" पापमागच्छेत्। एवं पूर्वापरेऽपि सर्वत्र बोध्यम् । "सर्वदेवेभि" सर्वदेवैः ।

३ "गच्छथा" गच्छेत । "पालेन्तु ये तान्दिशमधिष्ठिताः" पालयन्तु यानि तान्दिशमधिष्ठितानि ।

४ "इत्येते सप्त नक्षत्रा" इत्येतानि सप्त नक्षत्राणि ।

५ "पुत्राऽपि" पुत्रा अपि। "एकनामा" एकनामानः। "इन्द्रनामा" इन्द्रनामानः ।

६ "व अधिपालेन्तु" वोऽधिपालयन्तु ।

इलादेवी सुरादेवी पृथ्वी पद्मावती तथा ।
उपस्थिता महाराजा आशा भद्रा हिरी शिरी (१) ॥
तापि च अधिपालेन्तु (२) आरोग्येण शिवेन च ।
उत्तरस्मिन्दिशो भागे पर्व्वतो गन्धमादनः ॥
आवासो यक्षभूतानां चित्रकूटः सुदर्शनः ।
तेऽपि च अधिपालेन्तु (३) आरोग्येण शिवेन च ॥
क्षेमाश्च वो दिशः सन्तु मा च वः पापमागमत् ।
लब्धार्थाश्च निवर्त्तध्वं सर्व्वदेवेभि रक्षिताः (४) ॥
अष्टाविंशति नक्षत्राः (५) सप्त सप्त चतुर्दिशम् ।
द्वात्रिंशद्देवकन्याश्च अष्टावष्टौ चतुर्दिशम् ॥
अष्टौ श्रमणाश्चाष्टौ ब्राह्मणा अष्टौ जानपदेषु नैगमाः ।
अष्टौ देवाः सेन्द्रकास्ते वो रक्षन्तु सर्व्वतः ॥
स्वस्ति वो गच्छतां भोन्तु स्वस्ति भोन्तु निवर्त्तताम् ।
स्वस्ति वोऽस्तु तथैव ज्ञाति स्वस्ति पश्यन्तु ज्ञातयः (६) ॥
सेन्द्रा यथा महाराजा अर्हन्तमनुकम्पिताः (७) ।
सर्व्वं च स्वस्ति गच्छध्वं प्राप्नुध्वममृतं शिवम् ॥

---

१ "हिरी शिरी" ह्रीः श्रीः ।
२ "तापि च अधिपालेन्तु" ता अपि वोऽधिपालयन्तु ।
३ "तेऽपि च अधिपालेन्तु" तेऽपि वोऽधिपालयन्तु ।
४ "पापमागमत्" पापमागच्छेत् । "सर्वदेवेभि" सर्वदेवैः ।
५ "अष्टाविंशति नक्षत्राः" अष्टाविंशतिर्नक्षत्राणि ।
६ "भोन्तु" भवन्तु । "भोन्तु" भवन्तु । "ज्ञाति" ज्ञातेः । "स्वस्ति वाऽस्तु तथैव ज्ञातिः" इत्यत्र स्वस्ति पश्यत वै ज्ञाति इति वा पाठः ।
७ "अर्हन्तमनुकम्पिताः" अर्हन्तोऽप्यनुकम्पितारः । भवन्तु इति शेषः ।

संरक्षिता ब्राह्मणा वा शिवेन
विमुक्तचित्तेषु अनाश्रवेषु ।
नागेषु यक्षेषु सदाऽनुकम्पिता:
पालेथ आयुः शरदां शतं समा (१) ॥
प्रदक्षिणं दक्षिणलोकनाथ-
स्तेषां दिशलेष प्रतिमं विनायकः ।
अनेन यूयं कुशलेन कर्म्मणा
मधुसम्भवा नाम जिना भविष्यथ ॥
प्रथमादिदं श्लोक विनायकस्य
असङ्कृतो व्याकरणं जिनस्य ।
पश्चादनन्ता बहुबोधिसत्त्वा
ये व्याकृता बोधये नो विवर्त्त्याः (२) ॥
श्रुत्वा इमं व्याकरणं जिनस्य
उदग्रचित्ता परमाय प्रीत्या (३) ।
तौ भ्रातरौ सार्द्धं सहायकैस्तै
बुद्धञ्च धर्म्मञ्च शरणं प्रपन्ना इति ॥

इति श्रीललितविस्तरे त्रपुषभल्लिकपरिवर्त्तो नाम चतुर्विंशतितमः ॥ २४ ॥

---

१ "पालेथ" पालयन्तु ।
२ "प्रथमादिदं श्लोक" प्रथममयं श्लोको । "असङ्कृतो" सुसङ्गमित्युचितम् ।
३ "इमं" इदं । "उदग्रचित्ता परमाय" उदग्रचित्तौ परमया ।

पञ्चविंशाध्यायप्रारम्भः।

इति हि भिक्षवस्तथागतस्य तारायणमूले विहरतः प्रथमाभिसम्बुद्धस्यैकस्य रहोगतस्य प्रतिसंलीनस्य लोकानुवर्त्तिनां प्रत्येतदभवत्। गम्भीरो वतायं मया धर्म्मोऽधिगतोऽभिसम्बुद्धः। शान्तः प्रशान्त उपशान्तः प्रणीतो दुर्द्दृशो दुरनुबोधोऽतर्को वितर्कोऽचलो अलमार्य्यः पण्डितवेदनीयः। यदुत सर्व्वोपधिनिसर्ग आवेदितो निवेदितः सर्व्ववेदितनिरोधः परमार्थोऽनालयः। शीतिभावोऽनादानोऽनुपादानो विज्ञप्तो विज्ञापनीयोऽसंस्कृतः षड्विषयः समतिक्रान्तः अकल्पोऽविकल्पोऽनभिलाप्यः। अरुतो घोषोऽनुदाहारः। अनिदर्शनोऽप्रतिघः सर्व्वालम्बनसमतिक्रान्तः। समर्थो धर्म्मोपच्छेदः। शून्यतानुपलम्भतृष्णानिरोधविरागनिरोधो निर्व्वाणम्। अहं चेदिमं परेभ्यो धर्म्मं देशयेयं ते चेन्नाजानीयुः। स मे स्यात्कुपथो मिथ्याव्यायामः क्षणधर्म्मदेशनता च। यन्न्वहमल्पोत्सुकस्तूष्णीभावेन विहरेयम्॥

तस्यां च वेलायामिमा गाथा अभाषत।

गम्भीर शान्तो विरजः प्रभास्वरः प्राप्तो मि धर्म्मो ह्यमृतोऽसंस्कृतः।
देशेय चाहं न परस्य जाने यन्नून तूष्णी पवने चरेयम् (१)॥
अपगतगिरि वाक्पथो ह्यलिप्तो यथ गगणन्तथा स्वभावधर्म्मम्।

---

१ "गम्भीर" गम्भीरः। "विरज" विरजाः। "प्राप्तो मि" प्राप्तो मया। "देशेय" देशयिषं, इमं धर्ममुपदेशयेयमिति वार्थः। "यन्नून तूष्णी पवने" यन्नूनं तूष्णीमुपवने। अथ यन्नूनं तूष्णीं उपवसेयम् इति वा पाठः।

चित्तमनं त्विचारविप्रमुक्तं परमश्चाश्चर्य्यं परो विजाने (१) ॥
न च पुनरयु शक्य अक्षरेभ्यः प्रविशतु अनर्थयोगत्विप्रवेशः ।
पुरिमजिनकृताधिकारः सत्त्वास्ते इमु श्रुणित्व हि धर्म्मं श्रद्दधन्ति (२) ॥
न च पुनरिह कश्चिदस्ति धर्म्मः सोऽपि न विद्यति यस्य नास्ति भावाः ।
हेतुक्रियपरम्परा जानेत तस्य न भोतीह अस्तिनास्तिभावाः (३) ॥
कल्पशतसहस्र अप्रमेया अहु चरितः पुरिमजिनप्रकाशे ।
न च मया प्रतिलब्ध एष क्षान्ती यत्र न आत्म न सत्त्व नैव जीवः (४) ॥
यद् मय प्रतिलब्ध एष क्षान्ति म्रियति न चेह कश्चिज्जायते वा ।
प्रकृति इमि निरात्म सर्व्वधर्म्मास्तद मां व्याकरि बुद्धदीपनामा (५ ॥
करुण मम अनन्त सर्व्वलोके परमनु चानर्थरतामहं प्रतीक्ष्य ।
इयं पुनर्जनता प्रसन्न ज्ञात्व तेन अधीष्य प्रवर्त्तयि चक्रम् (६) ॥

---

१ "वाक्पथो ह्यतिगो यथ" वाक्पतो ह्यतिगं यथा । "चित्तमनं" चित्तमनः । "परम आश्चर्यं" परमाश्चर्यमिति । "विजाने" विजानाति ।

२ पुनरयु शक्य अक्षरेभ्यः" पुनरयं शक्योऽक्षरेभ्यः । "प्रविशतु अनर्थ-" प्रवेशयितुमनर्थ- । "पुरिमजिन-" पूर्वजिन- । "इमु श्रुणित्व धर्म श्रद्दधन्ति" इमं श्रुत्वा धर्मं श्रद्दधति ।

३ "नास्ति" न सन्ति । "हेतुक्रियपरम्परा जानेत" हेतुक्रियापरम्परां जानाति । "न भोतीह" न भवन्तीह ।

४ "कल्पशतसहस्र अप्रमेया अहु चरितः" कल्पशतसहस्रमप्रमेयमहं चरितवानित्यर्थः । "पुरिमजिनप्रकाशे" पूर्वजिनप्रकाशात् । "प्रतिलब्ध एष क्षान्तो यत्र" प्रतिलब्धा एषा क्षान्तिर्यत्र । "न आत्म न सत्त्व नैव" आत्मा न सत्त्वो नैव ।

५ "यद् मय प्रतिलब्ध एष क्षान्ति" यदा मया प्रतिलब्धा एषा क्षान्तिः । "म्रियति" म्रियते । "प्रकृति इमि निरात्म" प्रकृतिरियं निरात्मनः अनात्मनो देहादेरित्यर्थः । "तद मां व्याकरि बुद्धदीपनामा" तदा मां व्याकरिष्यन्ति बुद्धदीपनामानम् ।

६ "करुण मम अनन्त" करुणा मम अनन्ता । "चानर्थरतामहं" चानर्थरतमहं । "इयं पुनर्जनता प्रसन्न" इयं पुनर्जनता प्रसन्ना । यद् पुनर्जनता प्रसन्न इति वाच पाठः । "ज्ञात्व तेन अधीष्य प्रवर्त्तयि" ज्ञात्वापि तेनाधिष्ठाय प्रवर्त्तयिष्यामि ।

एवञ्च अयु धर्म्म याच्य मे स्वात च मम ब्रह्म क्रमे निपत्य याचेत्।
प्रवदति विरजा विप्रणीतधर्म्मा सन्ति विज्ञानक सत्त्वसारकाश्च(१)॥

इति हि भिक्षवस्तथागतस्तस्मिन् समये ऊर्णाकोशात् प्रभामुत्सृजति स्म। यया प्रभया त्रिसाहस्रमहासाहस्रलोकधातुर्महता सुवर्णवर्णावभासेन स्फुटोऽभूत्॥

अथ खलु दशत्रिसाहस्रमहासाहस्राधिपतिः शिखी महाब्रह्मा बुद्धानुभावेनैव तथागतस्य चेतसैव चेतःपरिवितर्कमाज्ञायाल्पोत्सुकतायै भगवतश्चित्तमभिनतं धर्म्मदेशनायामिति तस्यैतदभवत्। यन्न्वहमुपसङ्क्रम्य तथागतमध्येषयेयं धर्म्मचक्रप्रवर्त्तनतायै॥

अथ खलु शिखी महाब्रह्मा तस्यां वेलायां तदन्यान् ब्रह्मकायिकान्देवपुत्रानामन्त्रयते स्म। नश्यति बतायं मार्षा लोको विनश्यति। यत्र हि नाम तथागतोऽनुत्तरां सम्यक्सम्बोधिमभिसम्बुद्धाल्पोत्सुकतायै चित्तमभिनामयति न च धर्म्मदेशनायाम्। यन्नु वयमुपसङ्क्रम्य तथागतमर्हन्तं सम्यक्सम्बुद्धमध्येष्यामहे धर्म्मचक्रप्रवर्त्तनाय॥

अथ खलु भिक्षवः शिखी महाब्रह्माऽष्टषष्ट्या ब्राह्मणशतसहस्रैः परिवृतः पुरस्कृतो येन तथागतस्तेनोपसङ्क्रामदुपसङ्क्रम्य तथागतस्य पादौ शिरसाभिवन्द्य प्राञ्जलिस्तथागतमेतदवो-

---

१ "अयु धर्म याच्य मे" अयं धर्मो याच्यो मे। "स च" तच। "क्रमे" पदे इत्यर्थः। "प्रवदति विरजा" प्रवदन्ति विरजस्काः। "विज्ञानक सत्त्वसारकाश्च" विज्ञानकाः सत्त्वसारकाश्च।

षत् । नश्यति बतायं भगवन् लोकः प्रणश्यति बतायं भगवन् लोकः । यत्र हि नाम तथागतोऽनुत्तरां सम्यक्सम्बोधिमभिसम्बुध्याऽल्पोत्सुकतायै चित्तमभिनामयति न धर्म्मदेशनायाम् । तत्साधु देशयतु भगवन् देशयतु सुगत धर्म्मम् । सन्ति सत्त्वाः स्वाकाराः सुविज्ञापकाः प्राज्ञा भव्याः प्रतिबला भगवता भाषितस्यार्थमाज्ञातुम् ॥ तस्यां वेलायामिमा गाथा अभाषत ।

समुदानिय ज्ञानमहाप्रभमण्डलं विसृज्य रश्मिन्दशदिक्षु चैव ।
तदन्यशास्त्रासु नृपद्मबोधका उपेक्षकस्तिष्ठसि वादिभास्करः (१)॥
निमन्त्रयित्वाऽऽर्यधनेन सत्त्वानाश्वासयित्वा बहुप्राणिकोट्यः ।
न युक्तमेतत्तव लोकबन्धो यं तुष्णिभावेन उपेक्षसे जगत् (२)॥
पराहनस्वोत्तमधर्म्मदुन्दुभिं सद्धर्म्मशङ्खञ्च प्रपूरयाशु ।
उच्छ्रेपयस्वोत्तमधर्म्मयूपं प्रज्वालयस्व महधर्म्मदीपम् (३)॥
प्रवर्ष वै धर्म्मजलं प्रधानं प्रतारयेमां भवसागरस्थाम् ।
प्रमोचयेमां महव्याधिक्लिष्टां क्लेशाग्नितप्ते प्रशमं कुरुष्व (४)॥
निदर्शय त्वं खलु शान्तिमार्गं क्षेमं शिवं निर्जरतामशोकम् ।
निर्वाणमार्गागमनादृनाथे विपथस्थिते नाथ कृपां कुरुष्व ॥
विमोक्षद्वाराणि अपावृणुष्व प्रवच्च तं धर्म्मनयं ह्यकोप्यम् ।

---

१ "समुदानिय ज्ञानमहाप्रभमण्डलं" समुदानीय महाज्ञानप्रभमण्डलमित्यर्थः । "तदन्यशास्त्रासु नृपद्मबोधका" तदन्यशास्त्रेषु नृपद्मबोधक ।

२ "बहुप्राणिकोट्यः" बहुप्राणिकोटीः । "यं तुष्णिभावेन" यत्तूष्णीभावेन ।

३ "पराहनस्व" पराहन । "उच्छ्रेपयस्व" उत्क्षेपय । "प्रज्वालयस्व महधर्मदीपम्" प्रज्वालय महाधर्मदीपम् ।

४ "प्रतारयेमां भवसागरस्थां प्रमोचयेमां महव्याधिक्लिष्टां" प्रतारयेमान् भवसागरस्थान् प्रमोचयेमान्महाव्याधिक्लिष्टान् । "क्लेशाग्नितप्ते" क्लेशाग्नितप्तानामित्यर्थः ।

आत्यन्धभूतस्य जनस्य नाथ त्वमुत्तमं शोधय धर्म्मचक्षुः ॥
न ब्रह्मलोके न च देवलोके न यक्षगन्धर्व्वमनुष्यलोके।
लोकस्य जातिजरापनेता नान्योऽस्ति त्वत्तो हि मनुष्यचन्द्र ॥
अध्येषकोऽहं तव धर्म्मराज अध्यावदाहत्व न सर्व्वदेवान्।
अनेन पुण्येन अहंपि क्षिप्रं प्रवर्त्तयेयं वरधर्म्मचक्रम्(१) ॥

अधिवासयति स्म भिक्षवस्तथागतः शिखिनो ब्रह्मणस्तूष्णीभावेन सदेवमानुषासुरस्य लोकस्यानुग्रहार्थमनुकम्पामुपादाय ॥

अथ खलु शिखी महाब्रह्मा तथागतस्य तूष्णीभावेनाधिवासनां विदित्वा दिव्यैश्चन्दनचूर्णैरगुरुचूर्णैश्च तथागतमभ्यवकीर्य्य प्रीतिप्रामोद्यजातस्तत्रैवान्तरधात्।

अथ खलु भिक्षवस्तथागतस्य धर्म्मालोकस्यादरोत्पादनार्थं शिखिनस्य महाब्रह्मणः पुनः पुनस्तथागताध्येषणया कुशलमूलविवृद्ध्यर्थं धर्म्मस्य चातिगम्भीरोदारतामुपादाय पुनरप्येकस्य रहोगतस्य प्रतिसंलीनस्यायमेवंरूपश्चेतोवितर्कोऽभूत्। गम्भीरः खल्वयं मया धर्म्मोऽभिसम्बुद्धः सूक्ष्मो निपुणो दुरनुबोधः अतर्को तर्कावचरः पण्डितविज्ञो वेदनीयः सर्व्वलोकविप्रत्यनीकको दुर्द्दशः सर्व्वोपधिनिःसर्गः सर्व्वसंस्कारोपशमः सर्व्वतमोपच्छेदः(२) शून्यतानुपलम्भः तृष्णाक्षयो विरागो निरोधो निर्व्वाणम्। अहञ्चेदिदं धर्म्मं देशयेयं परे च मे न विभावयेयुः।

---

१ "अध्यावदाहत्व" अध्यवस्य कुरु इत्यर्थः। "अहंपि" अहमपि।
२ "सर्व्वतमोपच्छेदः" समतमउपच्छेदः।

सा मे परमा विहेठा (१) भवेत्। यन्न्वहमल्पोत्सुकविहारेणैव विहरेयम् ॥

अथ खलु भिक्षवः शिखी महाब्रह्मा बुद्धानुभावेन पुनरपि तथागतस्येदमेवंरूपं चेतःपरिवितर्कमाज्ञाय येन शक्रो देवानामिन्द्रस्तेनोपसङ्क्रामदुपसङ्क्रम्य शक्रं देवानामिन्द्रमेतदवोचत्। यत् खलु कौशिक जानीयास्तथागतस्यार्हतः सम्यक्सम्बुद्धस्याल्पोत्सुकतायै चित्तं नतं न धर्मदेशनायाम्। न ह्यन्तो वतायं कौशिक लोको विनङ्क्ष्यति। वतायं कौशिक लोको महान्धकारप्रक्षिप्तो वतायं कौशिक लोको भविष्यति। यत्र हि नाम तथागतस्यार्हतः सम्यक्सम्बुद्धस्याल्पोत्सुकतायै चित्तं नतं न धर्मदेशनायाम्। कस्मादयं न गच्छामस्तथागतमर्हन्तं सम्यक्सम्बुद्धं धर्मचक्रप्रवर्त्तनायाध्येषितुम्। तत्कस्मात्। न ह्यध्येषितास्तथागता धर्मचक्रं प्रवर्त्तयन्ति। साधु मार्षेति शक्रो ब्रह्मा भौमाश्च देवा अन्तरीक्षाश्चातुर्महाराजकायिकास्त्रयस्त्रिंशा यामास्तुषिता निर्म्माणरतयः परनिर्म्मितवशवर्त्तिनो ब्रह्मकायिका आभास्वरा बृहत्फलाः शुभकृत्स्नाः सम्बहुलानि च शुद्धावासकायिकदेवपुत्रशतसहस्राण्यतिक्रान्तवर्णा (२) अतिक्रान्तायां रात्रौ केवलं तारायणमूलं दिव्येन वर्णेन दिव्येनावभासेनावभास्य येन तथागतस्तेनोपसङ्क्रामदुपसङ्क्रम्य तथागतस्य पादौ शिरसाऽभिवन्द्य प्रदक्षिणीकृत्यैकान्ते तस्थुः।

---

१ "सा मे परमा विहेठा" सो मे परमो विहेठो।

२ "अतिक्रान्तवर्णाः" अतिक्रान्तवर्णानि।

अथ खलु शक्रो देवानामिन्द्रो येन तथागतस्तेनाञ्जलिं प्रणम्य तथागतं गाथयाऽभिष्टुष्टाव।

उत्तिष्ठ विजितसङ्ग्राम प्रज्ञाकराद्य यो चर लोके।
चित्तं हि ते विमुक्तं शशिरिव पूर्णो ग्रहविमुक्तः (१) ॥

एवमुक्ते तथागतस्तूष्णीमेवाख्यात्।

अथ खलु शिखी महाब्रह्मा शक्रं देवानामिन्द्रमेतदवोचत्। नैव कौशिक तथागता अर्हन्तः सम्यक्सम्बुद्धा अध्येष्यन्ते धर्म्मचक्रप्रवर्त्तनतायै यथा समध्येष्यते।

अथ खलु शिखी महाब्रह्मा एकांसमुत्तरासङ्गं कृत्वा दक्षिणजानुमण्डलं पृथिव्यां प्रतिष्ठाप्य येन तथागतस्तेनाञ्जलिम्प्रणम्य तथागतं गाथयाऽध्यभाषत।

उत्तिष्ठ विजितसङ्ग्राम प्रज्ञाकाराद्य यो विचर लोके।
देशय त्वं मुने धर्म्ममाज्ञातारो भविष्यति (२) ॥

एवमुक्ते भिक्षवस्तथागतः शिखिनं महाब्रह्माणमेतदवोचत्। गम्भीरः खल्वयं महाब्रह्मन् मया धर्म्मोऽभिसम्बुद्धः सूक्ष्मो निपुणः। पेयालम्। यावत्सा मे स्यात्परमा विहेठा (३)। अपि च मे ब्रह्मन् इमे गाथे अभीक्ष्णं प्रतिभासतः।

प्रतिश्रोतगामिको मार्गो गम्भीरो दुर्दृशो मम।
न तं द्रक्ष्यति रागान्धा अलं तस्मात्प्रकाशितुम् (४) ॥

---

१ "प्रज्ञाकराद्य" प्रज्ञाकर्णः। "यो चर" मो चर। "शशिरिव" शशीव।

२ "प्रज्ञाकराद्य" प्रज्ञाकर्णः। "यो विचर" मो विचर। "भविष्यति" भविष्यन्तीत्यर्थः।

३ अत्र विहेठविशेषणेऽपि पुंस्त्वं।

४ "प्रतिश्रोतगामिको" प्रतिश्रोतोगामी। "द्रक्ष्यति" पश्यन्तीत्यर्थः।

अनुस्रोतं प्रवाह्यन्ते कामेषु पतिताः प्रजाः।

कृच्छ्रेण मेऽयं सम्प्राप्तमलं तस्मात् प्रकाशितुम् (१)॥

अथ खलु भिक्षवः शिखी महाब्रह्मा शक्रश्च देवानामिन्द्रस्तथागतं तूष्णीभूतं विदित्वा सार्द्धं तैर्देवपुत्रैः दुःखिता दुर्मनास्तत्रैवान्तरधायिषुः। चिरपि (२) न तथागतस्याल्पोत्सुकतायै चित्तं नामयति (३) स्म।

तेन खलु पुनर्भिक्षवः समयेन मागधकानां मनुष्याणामिमान्येवंरूपाणि पापकानि अकुशलानि दृष्टिगतान्युत्पन्नान्यभूवन्। तद्यथा। केचिदेवमाहुः। वाता न वास्यन्ति॥ केचिदेवमाहुः। अग्निर्न ज्वलिष्यति॥ केचिदाहुः। देवो न वर्षिष्यति॥ केचिदाहुः। नद्यो न वक्ष्यन्ति (४)॥ केचिदाहुः। शस्यानि न प्रजायन्ते (५)॥ केचिदाहुः। पक्षिण आकाशे न क्रमिष्यन्ति॥ केचिदाहुः। गुर्विण्यो नारोग्येण प्रसविष्यन्ति॥

अथ खलु भिक्षवः शिखी महाब्रह्मा तथागतस्येममेवंरूपं चित्तवितर्कमाज्ञाय मागधकानाञ्च मनुष्याणामिमानि दृष्टिगतानि विदित्वाऽतिक्रान्तायां रात्रावतिक्रान्तेन वर्णेन सर्व्वावन्तं तारायणमूलं दिव्येनावभासेनावभास्य येन तथागतस्तेनोपसङ्क्रामदुपसङ्क्रम्य तथागतस्य पादौ शिरसाऽभिवन्द्यैकांशमुत्तरा-

---

१ "अनुस्रोतं" अनुस्रोतः। "सम्प्राप्तमलं" सम्प्राप्तोऽलं।

२ "दुःखिता दुर्मनास्तत्रैवान्तरधायिषुः चिरपि" दुःखितौ दुर्मनसौ भूत्वा तत्रैवान्तर्दधतुश्चिरमपि इत्यर्थः।

३ "नामयति" नामयतः।

४ "वक्ष्यन्ति" वहिष्यन्ति।

५ "प्रजायन्ते" प्रजनिष्यन्ति।

सङ्गं कृत्वा दक्षिणं जानुमण्डलं पृथिव्यां प्रतिष्ठाप्य येन तथा-
गतस्तेनाञ्जलिं प्रणम्य तथागतं गाथाभिरध्यभाषत ।

वादो बभूव समलैर्विचिन्तितो
धर्म्मो विशुद्धो मगधेषु पूर्व्वम् ।
अमृतं मुने तद्विवृणीष्व द्वारं
शृण्वन्ति (१) धर्म्मंविपुलं विमलेन बुद्धम् ॥
कृतस्वकार्य्योऽसि भुजिष्यतां गतो
दुःखाभिसंस्कारसमापकृष्टः ।
न हानिवृद्धी कुशलस्य तेऽस्ति
त्वमग्रधर्म्मेष्विह पारमिं गतः (२) ॥
न ते मुने सदृश इहास्ति लोके
कुतोऽधिकः स्यादिह ते महर्षे ।
भवानिहायस्त्रिभवे विरोचसे
गिरिर्यथाऽसा च (३) सुरालयस्थः ॥
महाकृपां विजनय दुःखिते जने
न त्वादृशा जातु भवन्त्युपेक्षकाः ।
भगवन्वैशारद्यबलैः समन्वित-
स्त्वमेव शक्तो जनतां प्रतारितुम् (४) ॥

---

१ “शृण्वन्ति” श्रोष्यन्ति ।
२ “पारमिं गतः” पारङ्गतः ।
३ “सा च” स च ।
४ “प्रतारितुम” प्रतारयितुम् ।

इयं सुभक्षा सुचिरातुरा प्रजा
सदेवकाः सश्रमणा द्विजाखिलाः (१)
अरोगिणी भवतु निरातुरज्वरा
न चापरः शरणमिहास्य विद्यते ॥
चिरानुबद्धास्तव देवमानुषाः
कल्याणचित्ता अमृतार्थिनश्च ।
धर्मं यमेवाधिगमिष्यते जिनो
यथावदन्यूनमुदाहरिष्यति (२) ॥
तस्माद्धिया चापि सुविक्रमत्ता
विनयस्व सत्त्वाश्चिरनष्टमार्गान् ।
अपि श्रुतार्थाः श्रमणाय काङ्क्षिता
इयं ह्यपार्त्ता जनता महामुने (३) ॥
उदीक्षते धर्मजलं तवान्तिके
मेघो यथा सन्तृषितां वसुन्धराम् ।
कुरु तर्पणां नायक धर्मवृष्टिं
चिरप्रणष्टा विचरन्ति मानवाः ॥
भवे कुदृष्टिगहने सकण्टके
अकण्टकं मार्गमनुप्रयच्छ तम् ।

---

१ "द्विजाखिलाः" द्विजा अखिलाः ।

२ धर्मं यमेवाधिगमिष्यते" धर्मेण येनैवाधिगमिष्यते । "उदाहरिष्यति" उदाहरिष्यसि ।

३ "सुविक्रमत्ता विनयस्व" सुविक्रमवत्त्वाद्विनयवत्त्वाच्चेत्यर्थः । "चिरनष्टमार्गान" चिरनष्टमार्गाः । "श्रमणाय काङ्क्षिता" श्रमणमिकाङ्क्षायस्य इत्यर्थः ।

यं भावयित्वा ह्यमृतं लभेयं (१)

अन्धप्रपाते पतिता ह्यनायका

नोद्धर्त्तुमन्यैरिह शक्यमेते ।

महाप्रपाते पतितां समुद्धर

च्छन्दं समुत्पाद्य हृषोऽसि बुद्धिमान् (२) ॥

न सन्न तिष्ठेति सदा मुने चिरं

कदाचिदौदुम्बरपुष्पसन्निभो ।

जिनाः पृथिव्यां प्रभवन्ति नायकाः

प्राप्तक्षणो मोचय नाथ सत्त्वान् (३) ॥

अभूच्च ते सर्व्वभवेष्वियं मति-

स्तीर्णः स्वयं तारयिता भवेयम् ।

असंशयं पारगतोऽसि साम्प्रतं

सत्यां प्रतिज्ञां कुरु सत्यविक्रम ॥

धर्म्मोल्कया विधम मुनेऽन्धकार-

मुत्क्षेपय त्वं हि तथागतध्वजम् ।

अयं स कालः प्रतिभात्युदीरणे

मृगाधिपो वा नद दुन्दुभिस्वरः (४) ॥

अथ खलु भिक्षवस्तथागतः सर्व्वावन्तं लोकं बुद्धचक्षुषा-व्यवलोकयन् सत्त्वान् पश्यति स्म । हीनमध्ये प्रणीतानुच्चनीच-

---

१ चस्य चतुर्थपादो नापत्यपत्रपुस्तकेष्वपि ।

२ "शक्यमेते" शक्या एते । "पतितां" पतिताम् ।

३ "सन्न तिष्ठेति" सन्ने तिष्ठसि । "पुष्पसन्निभो" पुष्पसन्निभः ।

४ "मृगाधिपो वा" मृगाधिप इवेत्यर्थः ।

मध्यमान् स्वाकारान् दुराकारान् सुविज्ञोधकान् दुर्विज्ञोधकानुद्घाटिताज्ञान् विपञ्चिताज्ञान् पदपरमांस्त्रीन् सत्त्वराशीनेकं मिथ्यात्वनियतमेकं सम्यक्त्वनियतमेकमनियतम्। तद्यथापि नाम भिक्षवः पुरुषः पुष्करिण्यास्तीरे स्थितः पश्यति अम्बुरुहाणि कानिचिदुदकान्तर्गतानि कानिचिदुदकसमानि कानिचिदुदकाभ्युद्गतानि। एवमेव भिक्षवस्तथागतः सर्व्वावन्तं लोकं बुद्धचक्षुषा व्यवलोकयन् पश्यति स्म सत्त्वांस्त्रिषु राशिषु व्यवस्थितान्।

अथ खलु भिक्षवस्तथागतस्यैतदभवत्। देशयेयमहं धर्म्मं न वा देशयेयम्। स एष मिथ्यात्वनियतो राशिर्नैवायं धर्म्ममाजानीयात्। देशयेयञ्चाहं धर्म्मं न वा देशयेयम् योयं सम्यक्त्वनियतो राशिराज्ञास्यत्येवैष धर्म्मम्। यत् खलु पुनरनियतो राशिराज्ञास्यत्येवैष धर्म्मम्। यत् खलु पुनरनियतो राशिस्तस्मै स चेद्धर्म्मं देशयिष्याम्याज्ञास्यत्युत न देशयिष्यामि नाज्ञास्यामीति।

अथ खलु भिक्षवस्तथागतोऽनियतराशिव्यवस्थितान् सत्त्वान् दृष्ट्वाऽऽरभ्य महाकरुणामवक्रामयति स्म।

अथ खलु तथागत आत्मनस्तेमं सम्यग्ज्ञानमधिकृत्य शिखिनश्च महाब्रह्मणोऽध्येषणां विदित्वा शिखिनं महाब्रह्माणं गाथाभिरध्यभाषत (१)।

अपावृतास्तेषाममृतस्य द्वारा
ब्रह्मन्निति सततं ये श्रोतवन्तः।

---

१ "गाथाभिरध्यभाषत" गाथयाऽध्यभाषत।

प्रविशन्ति श्रद्धा न विहेठसञ्ज्ञा

श्रोष्यन्ति धर्मं मगधेषु सत्त्वाः (१) ॥

अथ खलु शिखी महाब्रह्मा तथागतस्याधिवासनां विदित्वा तुष्ट उदग्र आत्तमना प्रमुदितः प्रीतिसौमनस्यजातस्तथागतस्य पादौ शिरसाऽभिवन्दित्वा तत्रैवान्तरधात् ।

अथ खलु भिक्षवो भौमा देवास्तस्यां वेलायामन्तरीक्षेभ्यो देवेभ्यो घोषमुदीरयन्ति स्म शब्दमनुश्रावयन्ति स्म । अद्य मार्षा तथागतेनार्हता सम्यक्सम्बुद्धेन धर्म्मचक्रप्रवर्त्तनतायै प्रतिश्रुतम् । तद्भविष्यति बहुजनहिताय सुखाय लोकानुकम्पायै महतो जनकायस्यार्थाय हिताय सुखाय देवानाञ्च मनुष्याणाञ्च ॥ परिहास्यन्ते बत भो मार्षा असुराः काया दिव्याः कायाः परिपूरं गमिष्यन्ति । बहवश्च सत्त्वा लोके परिनिर्व्वास्यन्ति ॥ एवमेवान्तरीक्षा देवा भौमेभ्यः प्रतिश्रुत्य चातुर्महाराजिकानां देवानां (२) घोषमुदीरयन्ति स्म । चातुर्महाराजिकास्त्रयस्त्रिंशानां त्रयस्त्रिंशा यामानां यामा तुषितनिर्म्माणरतीनां निर्म्माणरतयः परनिर्म्मितवशवर्त्तिनां तेऽपि ब्रह्मकायिकानां घोषमुदीरयन्ति स्म शब्दमनुश्रावयन्ति स्म । अद्य मार्षास्तथागतेनार्हता सम्यक्सम्बुद्धेन धर्म्मचक्रप्रवर्त्तनतायै प्रतिश्रुतम् । तद्भविष्यति

---

१ "श्रोतवन्तः" श्रुतवन्तः । "श्रद्धा" श्रद्धावन्त इत्यर्थः । "विहेठसञ्ज्ञा" विहेठसञ्ज्ञिन इत्यर्थः ।

२ "चातुर्महाराजिकानां देवानां" चातुर्महाराजिकान् देवान् प्रतीत्यर्थः । एवं परेऽपि बोध्यम् ।

बहुजनहिताय बहुजनसुखाय लोकानुकम्पायै महतो जनकायस्यार्थाय हिताय सुखाय देवानाञ्च मनुष्याणाञ्च ॥ परिहास्यन्ते बत भो मार्षा असुराः कायाः दिव्याः कायाः । विवर्द्धिष्यन्ते बहवश्च सत्त्वा लोके परिनिर्वास्यन्तीति ॥

इति हि भिक्षवस्तत्क्षणं तन्मुहूर्त्तं तलवं यावद्ब्रह्मकायिका देवास्तस्मादेवारभ्यैकनिर्नाद एकनिर्घोषोऽभ्युद्गतोऽभूत् । अद्य मार्षास्तथागतेनार्हता सम्यक्सम्बुद्धेन धर्मचक्रप्रवर्त्तनाय प्रतिश्रुतमिति ॥

अथ खलु भिक्षवो धर्मरुचिश्च नामा बोधिवृक्षदेवता धर्मकायश्च धर्ममतिश्च धर्मचारी च एते चत्वारो बोधिवृक्षदेवतास्तथागतस्य चरणयोर्निपत्यैवमाहुः । क्व भगवन् धर्मचक्रं प्रवर्त्तयिष्यसीति ।

एवमुक्ते भिक्षवस्तथागतस्ता वृक्षदेवता एतदवोचत् । वाराणस्यां ऋषिपतने मृगदावे ॥ ता आहुः । परीतजनकाया भगवन् वाराणसी महानगरी परीतद्रुमच्छायश्च मृगदावः । सन्त्यन्यानि भगवन् महानगराणि ऋद्धानि स्फीतानि क्षेमाणि सुभिक्षाणि रमणीयानि आकीर्णबहुजनमनुष्याणि उद्यानोपवनपर्व्वतप्रतिमण्डितानि । तेषां भगवन्नन्यतमे धर्मचक्रं प्रवर्त्तयतु । तथागतोऽवोचत् । एवम् ॥ भद्रमुखोऽवोचत् । तत्कस्मात् ।

षष्टि यज्ञकोटिसहस्रनयुता ये तत्र यष्टा मया
षष्टिबुद्धकोटिनयुतसहस्रा ये तत्र सम्पूजिताः ।
पौराण ऋषिणामिहालय वरा वाराणसी नाम वरा

सा देवानागाभिष्टुतो महीतलो धर्म्माभिनिम्नः सदा (१) ॥

बुद्धकोटिसहस्र चैकनवतिः पूर्व्वे स्मरामि अहं

ये तस्मिन्नृषिसाह्वयेवनवरे वर्त्ति सुचक्रोत्तमम् ।

शान्तं चाप्युपशान्त ध्यानाभिमुखं नित्यं मृगैः सेवितं

इत्यर्थे ऋषिसाह्वये वनवरे वर्त्तिष्य चक्रोत्तमम् (२) ॥ इति

इति श्रीललितविस्तरे अध्येषणापरिवर्त्तो नाम पञ्चविंशतितमः ॥

षड्विंशाध्यायप्रारम्भः ।

अथ खलु भिक्षवस्तथागतः कृतकृत्यः कृतकरणीयः सर्व्वबन्धनसमुच्छिन्नः सर्व्वक्लेशोद्धृतो निर्व्वान्तमलक्लेशो निहतमारप्रत्यर्थिकः सर्व्वबुद्धधर्म्मनयानुप्रविष्टः सर्व्वज्ञः सर्व्वदर्शी दशबलसमन्वागतश्चतुर्वैशारद्यप्राप्तोऽष्टादशावेणिकबुद्धधर्म्मप्रतिपूर्णः पञ्चचक्षुःसमन्वागतोऽनावरणेन बुद्धचक्षुषा सर्व्वावन्तं लोकमवलोक्यैवञ्चिन्तयति स्म । कस्मादहं सर्व्वप्रथमं धर्म्मं देशयेयम् । कतमः सत्त्वः शुद्धः स्वाकारः सुविनेयः सुविज्ञापकः सुविबोधको

---

१ "यदि" यदापि । "सहस्रनयुता ये तव यदा" सहस्रनियुतानि यानि तव यदानि। अत्र यच्छब्दस्य पुनरुक्तिः । "नयुतसहस्रा ये तव सम्पूजिताः" नियुतसहस्राणि यानि तव सम्पूजितानि । "पौराण ऋषिणाम" पुराणानामृषीणाम् । "व्यासव वरा" व्यासया वराः । "देवानामाभिष्टुतो" देवनागाभिष्टुतो ।

२ "बुद्धकोटिसहस्र चैकनवतिः पूर्वे" एकनवत्यधिकबुद्धकोटिसहस्राणि च पूर्वाणि इत्यर्थः । "ये तस्मिन्" येऽस्मिन् । "वर्त्ति" प्रवर्त्तितम् । "चाप्युपशान्त" चाप्युपशान्तं । "इत्यर्थे ऋषिसाह्वये" इत्यर्थमृषिसाह्वये । "वर्त्तिष्य" मयं प्रवर्त्तयिष्याम इत्यर्थः ।

मन्दरागदोषमोहोऽपरोक्षविज्ञानः सः श्रद्धावान् धर्म्मस्यापरिहीयते (१)। तस्मादहं सर्व्वप्रथमं धर्मं देशयेयम्। स च मे धर्मं देशितमाजानीयान्न च मां च विहेठयेत्॥

अथ खलु भिक्षवस्तथागतस्यैतदभूत्। रुद्रकः खलु रामपुत्रः शुद्धः स्वाकारः सुविज्ञापकः सुविशोधको मन्दरागमोहोऽपरोक्षविज्ञानः स श्रवणाद् धर्म्मस्यापरिहीयते। यः श्रावकेभ्यो नैवसंज्ञानासंज्ञायतनसहव्रतायै धर्मं देशयति। कुत्रासावेतर्हि प्रतिवसतीत्याज्ञासीदद्य सप्ताहकालगत इति। देवता अपि तथागतस्य चरणयोर्निपत्यैवमाहुः। एवमेतद्भगवन्नेवमेतत्सुगत। अद्य सप्ताहकालगतो रुद्रको रामपुत्रः॥ तस्य मे भिक्षव एतदभूत्। महाहानिर्व्वर्त्तते रुद्रकस्य रामपुत्रस्य। य इममेवं सुप्रणीतं धर्म्ममश्रुत्वा कालगतः। सचेदसाविमं धर्मं श्रोष्यत्याज्ञास्यति तस्यैवाहं प्रथमं धर्मं देशयिष्ये न च मां स विहेठयेत्॥

पुनरपि भिक्षवस्तथागतस्यैतदभूत्। कोन्यः सत्त्वः शुद्धः सुविनयः पूर्व्ववद्यावन्न च धर्म्मदेशनां विहेठयेदिति॥ ततो भिक्षवस्तथागतस्यैतदभवत्। अयं खल्वाराडः कालामः शुद्धो यावन्न च मे धर्म्मदेशनां विहेठयेदिति॥ समन्वाहरति स्म भिक्षवस्तथागतः कुत्रासावेतर्हि इति। समन्वाहरंश्चाज्ञासीदद्य त्रीण्यहानि कालगतस्येति॥ शुद्धावासकायिका अपि च देवता एतमर्थं तथागतस्यारोचयन्ति स्म। एवमेव भगवन्नेवमेतत्सुगत। अद्य त्र्यहं

१ "सः श्रद्धावान्" अत्र सः अवधान् इति चात्र सर्वत्र पाठः। "धर्म्मस्यापरिहीयते" धर्म्मात्र परिहास्यति इत्यर्थः। एवं सर्वत्र बोध्यम्। अत्र धर्म्मस्यापरिहीयते इति वा पाठः।

कालगतमाराडस्य कालामस्य ॥ ततस्तथागतस्यैतदभवत् । महाहानिर्वर्त्ततेऽराडस्य कालामस्य । य इममेवं सुप्रणीतं धर्ममश्रुत्वा कालगत इति ॥

पुनरपि भिक्षवस्तथागतस्यैतदभूत् । कः सत्त्वः शुद्धः ऋजुः स्वाकारो यावन्न च मे देशनां विहेठयेदिति ।

अथ खलु भिक्षवस्तथागतस्यैतदभवत् । ते खलु पञ्चका भद्रवर्गीयाः शुद्धाः ऋजुकाः स्वाकाराः सुविज्ञापकाः सुविबोधका मन्दरागदोषमोहा अपरोक्षविज्ञानास्ते श्रवणात् धर्मस्यापरिहीयन्ते । तैश्चाहं दुष्करचर्य्यां चरन्नुपतिष्ठोऽभूत् (१) ते मया धर्म्मं देशितमाज्ञास्यन्ति । न च मेऽव विहेठयिष्यन्ति ॥

अथ खलु भिक्षवस्तथागतस्यैतदभवत् । योऽन्वहं पञ्चकेभ्यो भद्रवर्गीयेभ्यः प्रथमं धर्मं देशयेयम् ॥

अथ खलु भिक्षवस्तथागतस्यैतदभवत् । कस्मिन्नेतर्हि पञ्चकाः भद्रवर्गीयाः प्रतिवसन्ति ॥ अथ तथागतः सर्व्वावन्तं लोकं बुद्धचक्षुषा व्यवलोकयन् पश्यति स्म । अद्राक्षीत् पञ्चकान् भद्रवर्गीयान् वाराणस्यां विहरत ऋषिपतने मृगदावे ॥ दृष्ट्वा च तथागतस्यैतदभवत् । यन्वहं पञ्चकेभ्यो भद्रवर्गीयेभ्यः सर्व्वप्रथमं धर्मं देशयेयं तर्हि मम सर्व्वप्रथमं धर्मं देशितमाज्ञास्यन्ति । तत्कस्य हेतोश्चरिता विना (२) हि ते भिक्षवः सुपरिपाचितशुक्लधर्माणो मोक्षमार्गाभिमुखा निर्बन्धापनीताः (३) ॥

---

१ "उपतिष्ठोऽभूत्" उपस्थितोऽभूवम् ।

२ "चरित्वा विना" आचरणं विना ।

३ "निबन्धापनीताः" अपनीता निर्बन्धात् ।

अथ खलु भिक्षवस्तथागत एवमनुविचिन्त्य बोधिमण्डादुत्थाय त्रिसाहस्रमहासाहस्रं लोकधातुं सम्प्रकम्प्यानुपूर्वेण मगधेषु चर्य्यां चरन्काशीषु जनपदेषु चर्य्यां सम्प्राक्रामत्॥ अथ गयायां बोधिमण्डस्य चान्तरादन्यतम आजीवकोऽद्राक्षीत्तथागतं दूरत एवागच्छन्तम्। दृष्ट्वा च पुनर्येन तथागतस्तेनोपजगामोपेत्यैकान्तेऽस्थात्॥ एकान्ते स्थितश्च भिक्षव आजीवकस्तथागतेन सार्द्धं विविधां सम्मोदनीं कथां कृत्वा एवमाह। विप्रसन्नानि ते आयुष्मन् गौतम इन्द्रियाणि परिशुद्धः पर्य्यवदातः पीतनिर्भासश्च ते छविवर्णः। तद्यथापि नाम शारदः कालः पाण्डुरवर्णः प्रभास्वरः पीतनिर्भासो भवत्येवमेव भगवतो गौतमस्य परिशुद्धानीन्द्रियाणि परिशुद्धं मुखमण्डलं पर्य्यवदातम्। तद्यथापि नाम तालफलस्य पक्वस्य समनन्तरवृन्तच्युतस्य बन्धनाश्रयः पीतनिर्भासो भवति। परिशुद्धः पर्य्यवदात एवमेवं भगवतो गौतमस्य परिशुद्धानीन्द्रियाणि परिशुद्धं मुखमण्डलं पर्य्यवदातम्। तद्यथापि नाम जाम्बूनदवर्णनिष्क उल्कामुखप्रविष्टो दक्षिणकर्मारपुत्रेण सुपरिकर्म्मकृतः पाण्डुकम्बलोपरि निःक्षिप्तो वर्णवान् भवति परिशुद्धः पर्य्यवदातः पीतनिर्भासोऽतीवप्रभास्वरः। एवमेव भगवतो गौतमस्य विप्रसन्नानीन्द्रियाणि परिशुद्धः छविवर्णः पर्य्यवदातं मुखमण्डलम्॥ कस्मिन्नायुष्मन् गौतम ब्रह्मचर्य्यमुष्यते। एवमुक्ते भिक्षवस्तथागतस्तमाजीवकं गाथया प्रत्यभाषत॥

आचार्य्यो न हि मे कश्चित् सदृशो मे न विद्यते।

एकोऽहमस्मिं सम्बुद्धः (१) शीतिभूतो निराश्रवः ॥

सोऽवोचत् ।

अर्हन् खलु गौतममात्मानम्प्रतिजानीषे ॥

तथागतोऽवोचत् ।

अहमेवार्हं लोके शास्ता ह्यहमनुत्तरः ।

सदेवासुरगन्धर्व्वे नास्ति मे प्रतिपुद्गलः ॥

सोऽवोचत् ।

जिनं खलु गौतममात्मानम्प्रतिजानीषे ॥

तथागतोऽवोचत् ।

जिना हि मा दृशा ज्ञेया ये प्राप्ता आश्रवक्षयम् ।

जिता मे पापका धर्म्मास्तेनोपजिनो ह्यहम् ॥

सोऽवोचत् ।

क तर्ह्यायुष्मन् गौतम गमिष्यसि ।

तथागतोऽवोचत् ।

वाराणसीं गमिष्यामि गत्वा वै काशिकां पुरीम् ।

अन्धभूतस्य लोकस्य कर्त्तास्म्यसदृशीं प्रभाम् ॥

वाराणसीं गमिष्यामि गत्वा वै काशिकां पुरीम् ।

शब्दहीनस्य लोकस्य ताडयिष्ये ऽमृतदुन्दुभिम् (२)॥

वाराणसीं गमिष्यामि गत्वा वै काशिकां पुरीम् ।

धर्म्मचक्रं प्रवर्त्तिष्ये लोकेष्वप्रतिवर्त्तितम् ॥

---

१ "अस्मिं सम्बुद्धः" अस्मि सम्बुद्धः ।

२ लोकस्य" लोकं । "अमृतदुन्दुभिम्" अमृतदुन्दुभिमेत्यर्थः ।

गमिष्यामि गौतम इत्युक्त्वा स आजीवको दक्षिणामुखः प्राक्रामत्। तथागतोऽप्युत्तरामुखः प्राक्रामत्॥

इति हि भिक्षवस्तथागतो गयायां सुदर्शनेन नागराजेन निमन्त्रितोऽभूत् वासेन भक्तेन च॥ ततस्तथागतो रोहितवस्तुमगमत्तस्मादुरुविल्वाकल्पं तस्मादनालमनमत्। ततः सारथिपुरिमेषु च सर्व्वेषु भिक्षवस्तथागतो गृहपतिभिर्भक्तेन वासेन चोपनिमन्त्र्यमाणोऽनुपूर्वेण गङ्गाया नद्यास्तीरमुपागमत्। तेन खलु पुनर्भिक्षवः समयेन गङ्गा महानदी सुपरिपूर्णा समतीर्थिका वहति स्म॥

अथ खलु भिक्षवस्तथागतो नाविकसमीपमुपागमत् पारसन्तरणाय॥ स प्राह। प्रयच्छ गौतम तरपण्यम्॥ न मेऽस्ति मार्ष तरपण्यमित्युक्त्वा तथागतो विहायसा स्थातीरात्परं तीरमगमत्॥ ततः स नाविकस्तं दृष्ट्वाऽतीव विप्रतिसार्य्यभूदेवंविधो दक्षिणीयो मया न तारित इति। हा कष्टमिति कृत्वा मूर्च्छितः पृथिव्यां पतितस्तत एतामप्रवृत्तिं नाविको राज्ञे बिम्बिसारायारोचयामास। श्रमणः स्वामिन् गौतमस्तरपण्यं याच्यमानो नास्ति तरपण्यमित्युक्त्वा विहायसा परतीरात्परं तीरङ्गत इति॥ तच्छ्रुत्वा तद्देव राज्ञा बिम्बिसारेण सर्व्वप्रव्रजितानां तरपण्यमुत्सृष्टमभवत्।

इति हि भिक्षवस्तथागतोऽनुपूर्वेण जनपदचर्य्यां चरन् येन वाराणसी महानगरी तेनोपसङ्क्रामदुपसङ्क्रम्य कालमेव निवास्य पात्रचीवरमादाय वाराणसीं महानगरीं पिण्डाय प्राविशत्।

तस्यां पिण्डाय चरित्वा कृतभक्तकृत्यः पश्चाद्भक्तपिण्डपातप्रतिक्रान्तो येन ऋषिपतनो मृगदावो येन च पञ्चका भद्रवर्गीयास्तेनोपसंक्रामति स्म। अद्राक्षुः खलु पुनः पञ्चका भद्रवर्गीयास्तथागतं दूरत एवागच्छन्तम्। दृष्ट्वा च क्रियाबन्धमकार्षुः। एष स आयुष्मान् श्रमणो गौतम आगच्छति स्म(१) शैथिलिको बाहुलिको प्रहाणविभ्रष्टः। अनेन खल्वपि तयापि तावत्पूर्व्विकया दुष्करचर्य्यया न शकितं (२) किञ्चिदुत्तरिमनुष्यधर्म्मादलमार्य्यज्ञानदर्शनविशेषं साक्षात्कर्त्तुम्। किं पुनरेतर्ह्यौदारिकमाहारमाहरन् सुखल्लिकायोगमनुयुक्तो विहरन्नभव्यः। खल्वेष शैथिलिको बाहुलिको नास्य केनचित्प्रत्युद्गन्तव्यं न प्रत्युत्थातव्यम्। न पात्रचीवरम्प्रतिग्रहीतव्यं न आसनं दातव्यं न पानीयं परिभोग्यं न पादप्रतिष्ठानं स्थापयित्वाऽतिरिक्तान्यासनानि वक्तव्यञ्च न संविद्यते। इमान्यायुष्मन् गौतमातिरिक्तान्यासनानि स चेदाकाङ्क्षति निषीदति। तत्र आज्ञातकौण्डिन्य एकोऽस्ति तेन स्वतम्। आयुष्मांस्त्वज्ञातकौण्डिन्यश्चित्ते नाधिवासयति स्म। वाचा च न प्रतिक्षिपति स्म। यथा यथा च भिक्षवस्तथागतो येन पञ्चका भद्रवर्गीयास्तेनोपसंक्रामति स्म। तथा तथा ते स्वकस्वकेष्वासनेषु न रमन्ते स्म। उत्थातु कामा अभूवन्। तद्यथापि नाम पक्षी शकुनिः पञ्जरगतः स्यात्तस्य च पञ्जरगतस्याधोऽग्निर्दग्धो भवेत्(३)। सोऽग्निसन्तप्तस्त्वरितमूर्द्धमुत्पतितुकामो भवेत् प्रक्र-

---

१ "आगच्छति स्म" आगच्छति इत्यु इत्युचितम्।

२ "न शकितं" न शक्तं।

३ "अग्निर्दग्धो भवेत्" अग्निर्दीप्तो भवेदित्युचितम्।

नितुकामश्चैव। यथा यथा तथागतः पञ्चकानां भद्रवर्गीयाणां सकाशमुपसंक्रामति स्म। तथा तथा पञ्चका भद्रवर्गीयाः स्वकस्वकेष्वासनेषु न रमन्ते स्म। उत्थातुकामा अभूवन्। न च कश्चित्सत्त्वः सत्त्वनिकाये संविद्यते यस्तथागतं दृष्ट्वा आसनान्न प्रत्युत्तिष्ठेत्(१)। यथा यथा च तथागतः पञ्चकान् भद्रवर्गीयानुपसंक्रामति स्म। तथा तथा पञ्चका भद्रवर्गीयाः तथागतस्य श्रियन्तेजश्चासहमानाः आसनेभ्यः प्रकम्पमानाः सर्व्वे क्रियां भित्त्वोत्थायासनेभ्यः कश्चित्प्रत्युद्गच्छति स्म। कश्चित्प्रत्युद्गम्य पात्रचीवरम्प्रतिगृह्णाति स्म। कश्चिदासनमुपनामयति स्म। कश्चित्पादप्रतिष्ठापनं कश्चित्पादप्रक्षालनोदकमुपस्थापयति स्म। एवं चावोचत्। स्वागतन्ते आयुष्मन् गौतम स्वागतन्ते आयुष्मन् गौतम निषीदेदमासनं। प्रज्ञप्तं न्यषीदत्। खल्वपि भिक्षवस्तथागतप्रज्ञप्त एवासने पञ्चकापि (२) भद्रवर्गीयास्ते तथागतेन सार्द्धं विविधाः सम्मोदनीः संरञ्जनीः कथाः कृत्वैकान्ते निषेदुः। एकान्ते निषण्णाश्च ते पञ्चका भद्रवर्गीयास्तथागतमेतदवोचन्। विप्रसन्नानि ते आयुष्मन् गौतमेन्द्रियाणि परिशुद्धश्छविवर्णः [इति हि सर्व्वं पूर्व्ववत्] अस्ति ते आयुष्मन् गौतम कश्चिदुत्तरिमनुष्यधर्म्मादलमार्य्यज्ञानदर्शनविशेषः साक्षात्कृतः। एवमुक्ते भिक्षवस्तथागतः पञ्चकान् भद्रवर्गीयानेवमाह। मा यूयं भिक्षवस्तथागतमायुष्मद्वादेन समुदाचरिष्ट (३)। मा वोऽभूद्दीर्घरात्रमर्थाय हिताय

---

१ "संविद्यते" "प्रत्युत्तिष्ठेत्" इत्यत्र संविद्यते स्म प्रत्युदतिष्ठदित्युचितम्।
२ "पञ्चकापि" पञ्चका अपि।
३ "आयुष्मद्वादेन समुदाचरिष्ट" आयुष्मन्तो वादेन समुदाचरेतेत्युचितम्।

सुखाय। अमृतं मया भिक्षवः साक्षात्कृतोऽमृतगामीय (१) मार्गः। बुद्धोऽहमस्मि भिक्षवः सर्व्वज्ञः सर्व्वदर्शी शीतिभूतोऽनास्रवः। वशी सर्व्वधर्म्मेषु धर्म्मसहं भिक्षवो देशयिष्याम्यागच्छत शृणुत प्रतिपद्यध्वं श्रोतमवदधताहमेव (२) वदाम्यनुशास्मि । यथा मया सम्यगववेदिताः सम्यगनुशिष्टा यूयमप्यास्रवाणां चेतो-विमुक्तिं दृष्ट एव धर्म्मे साक्षात्कृत्वोपसम्पद्य प्रवेदयिष्यथ (३) क्षीणा नो जातिरुषितञ्च ब्रह्मचर्य्यं कृतं करणीयं नापरमित-मन्यद्भवं प्रजानाम इति। ननु च युष्माकं भिक्षव एतदभूत्। अयं खल्वायुष्मन्त आगच्छति श्रमणो गौतमः शैथिलिको बाहु-लिकः प्रधानविभ्रष्ट [इति पूर्व्ववत्] यावत् स चेदाकाङ्क्षति निषीदेति (४)। तेषाञ्च भिक्षव इत्युक्ते यत्किञ्चित्तीर्थिकलि-ङ्गतीर्थिकध्वजः सर्व्वोऽसौ तत्क्षणमेवान्तरधात्। त्रिचीवरञ्च पात्रञ्च प्रादुरभूत्तदनुच्छिन्नाश्च केशाः। तद्यथापि नाम वर्ष-शतोपसम्पन्नस्य भिक्षोरीर्य्यापथः संवृत्तोऽभूत् सैव च तेषां प्रव्र-ज्याऽभूत् सैवोपसम्पद्भिक्षुभावः ।

अथ खलु भिक्षवस्तस्यां वेलायां पञ्चका भिक्षवस्तथागतस्य चरणयोर्निपत्यात्ययं देशयन्ति स्म। तथागतस्यान्तिके शास्तृ-सञ्ज्ञां प्रेम च प्रसादञ्च गौरवञ्चोत्पादयन्ति स्म। गौरवजाताश्च वज्रविचित्रपुष्करिण्यां तथागतस्य स्नानपरिकर्म कुर्व्वन्ति स्म।

१ "अमृतगामीय" अमृतगाम्ययं।
२ "श्रोतमवदधताहमेव" शृणुतावदधताहमेव।
३ "प्रवेदयिष्यथ" प्रवेदिष्यथ।
४ "निषीदेति" निषीदति।

ध्यानप्रत्युत्तीर्णस्य भिक्षवस्तथागतस्यैतदभूत्। कस्मिन् खलु पूर्वकैस्तथागतैरर्हद्भिः सम्यक्सम्बुद्धैर्भिक्षव धर्मचक्रं प्रवर्त्तितम्। यस्मिंश्च भिक्षवः पृथिवीप्रदेशे पूर्वकैस्तथागतैरर्हद्भिर्धर्मचक्रं प्रवर्त्तितमभूत्। अथ तस्मिं पृथिवीप्रदेशे सप्तरत्नमयमासनशतं (१) प्रादुरभूत्।

अथ तथागतः पूर्वकाणां तथागतानां गौरवेण त्रीण्यासनानि प्रदक्षिणीकृत्य सिंह इव निर्भीः चतुर्थ आसने पर्यङ्कमाभुज्य निषीदति स्म। पञ्चका अपि भिक्षवस्तथागतस्य पादौ शिरोभिरभिवन्द्य तथागतस्य पुरतो निषेदुः (२)।

अथ खलु भिक्षवस्तस्यां वेलायां तथारूपां कायात् प्रभां तथागतः प्रामुञ्चत्। यया प्रभयाऽयं त्रिसाहस्रमहासाहस्रो लोकधातुर्महतावभासेन स्फुटोऽभूत्। तेन चावभासेन या अपि लोकान्तरिका अघा अघस्फुटा अन्धकारतमिस्रा यत्रेमौ चन्द्रसूर्यौ एवंमहर्द्धिकौ एवंमहानुभावावेवंमहेशाख्यौ आभया आभां वर्णेन वर्णं तेजसा तेजो नाभितपतो न विरोचतः। तत्र ये सत्त्वा उपपन्नास्ते स्वकस्वकमपि बाहुं प्रसारितं न पश्यन्ति स्म। तत्रापि तस्मिं समये महत उदारस्यावभासस्य लोके प्रादुर्भावोऽभूत्। ये च तत्र सत्त्वा उपपन्नास्ते च तेनावभासेन परिस्फुटाः समाना अन्योन्यं पश्यन्ति स्म अन्योन्यं सञ्जानन्ते स्म॥ एवं चाहुः। अन्येऽपि किल भोः सत्त्वा इहोपपन्ना अन्येपि किल

१ सहस्रं इति वा पाठः।
२ “निषेदुः” अपीदम्।

भोः सत्त्वा इहोपपन्ना इति। अयञ्च त्रिसाहस्रमहासाहस्र-लोकधातुः षड्विकारमष्टादशमहानिमित्तमकम्पत् प्राकम्पत् सम्प्राकम्पत्। अवेधत प्रावेधत सम्प्रावेधत। अचलत् प्राचलत् सम्प्राचलत्। अक्षुभ्यत् प्राक्षुभ्यत् सम्प्राक्षुभ्यत्। अरणत् प्रारणत् सम्प्रारणत्। अगर्ज्जत् प्रागर्ज्जत् सम्प्रागर्ज्जत्। अन्तेऽवनमति स्म मध्येऽवनमति स्म अन्ते उन्नमति स्म। मध्ये उन्नमति स्म। पूर्व्वस्यां दिश्यवनमति स्म। पश्चिमायां दिश्युन्नमति स्म। पश्चिमायामवनमति स्म। पूर्व्वस्यां दिश्युन्नमति स्म। दक्षिणस्यां दिश्यवनमति स्म। उत्तरस्यां दिश्युन्नमति स्म। उत्तरस्यां दिश्यवनमति स्म। दक्षिणस्यां दिश्युन्नमति स्म। तस्मिंश्च समये हर्षणीयास्तोषणीयाः प्रसादनीया अवलोकनीयाः प्रह्लादनीया वर्णनीया अप्रतिवर्णनीया असेचनका अप्रतिकूला अनुचासकराः शब्दा श्रूयन्ते स्म। न च कस्यचित् सत्त्वस्य तस्मिन् क्षणे विहेठा वा त्रासो वा भयं वा स्तम्भितत्वं वाऽभूत्। न च भूयः सूर्य्यचन्द्रमसोः शक्रब्रह्मलोकपालानां तस्मिन् क्षणे प्रभाः प्रज्ञायन्ते स्म। सर्व्वनरकतिर्य्यग्योनियमलोकोपपन्नाश्च सत्त्वास्तस्मिन् क्षणे विगतदुःखा अभूवन् सर्व्वसुखसमर्पिताः। न च कस्यचित् सत्त्वस्य रागो बाधते स्म द्वेषो वा मोहो वा ईर्ष्या वा मात्सर्य्यं वा मानो वा म्रक्षो वा मदो वा क्रोधो वा व्यापादो वा परिदाहो वा। सर्व्वसत्त्वास्तस्मिन् क्षणे मैत्रचित्ता हितचित्ताः परस्परमातृपितृसञ्ज्ञिनोऽभूवन्। ततश्च प्रभाव्यूहादिमा गाथा निश्चरन्ति स्म।

योऽसौ तुषितालयाच्च्युत्वा आक्रान्त मातृकुक्षौ हि (१)।
जातश्च लुम्बिनिवने प्रतिगृहीतः शचीपतिना ॥
यो हि सिंहविक्रमगतिः सप्तपदां विक्रमी (२) असंमूढः।
ब्रह्मस्वरामथ गिरं मुमोच जगत्यहं श्रेष्ठः ॥
चतुरो द्वीपांस्त्यक्त्वा प्रव्रजितः सर्व्वसत्त्वहितहेतोः।
दुष्करतपश्चरित्वा उपागमद्येन महिमण्डः (३) ॥
सबलं निहत्य मारं बोधिः प्राप्तो हिताय लोकस्य।
वाराणसीमुपागतो धर्म्मचक्रप्रवर्त्तनाय (४) ॥
समभ्यर्थ्या सह सुरैरधिष्ठो वर्त्तयास्य इमं चक्रम् (५)।
अधिवासितश्च मुनिना लोके कारुण्यमुत्पाद्य ॥
सोऽयं दृढप्रतिज्ञा वाराणसीमुपगतो मृगदावम्।
चक्रं अनुत्तरमसौ प्रवर्त्तयिताद्भुतं श्रीमान् (६) ॥
यः श्रोतुकामो धर्म्मं यः कल्पनयुतैः समार्जितु जिनेन।
शीघ्रमसौ त्वरमाणो आगच्छतु धर्म्मश्रवणाय (७) ॥
दुरवाप्यं मानुष्यं बुद्धोत्पादः सुदुर्लभः श्रद्धा।
श्रेष्ठं धर्म्मश्रवणमष्टाक्षणविवर्जनं दुरापः ॥

---

१ "आक्रान्त मातृकुक्षौ" आक्रान्तो मातृकुक्षौ।
२ "सप्तपदां विक्रमी" सप्तपदानि अक्रमत्।
३ "महिमण्डः" महीमण्डः।
४ "धर्मचक्रप्रवर्त्तनाय" धर्मचक्रं प्रवर्त्तयिता इति वाच पाठः।
५ "अधिष्ठो वर्त्तयास्य" अधिष्ठितः प्रवर्त्तयिता।
६ "दृढप्रतिज्ञा" दृढप्रतिज्ञः।
७ "कल्पनयुतैः समार्जितु" कल्पनियुतैः समर्जितः। "शीघ्रमसौ" शीघ्रं च इत्यर्थः।

प्राप्तश्च तेऽद्य सर्व्वबुद्धोत्पादः क्षणस्तथा श्रद्धा ।
धर्म्मश्रवणञ्च वरः प्रमादमखिलं विवर्ज्जयत (१) ॥
भवति कदाचिदवस्था यः कल्पनयुतैर्न (२) श्रूयते धर्म्मः ।
सम्प्राप्तः स चैवाद्य प्रमादमखिलं विवर्ज्जयत ॥
भौमादीन् देवगणान् सञ्चोदयतीयं ब्रह्मपर्य्यन्तां (३) ।
आयात लघु सर्व्वे वर्त्तयिता नायको ह्यमृतचक्रम् ॥
सञ्चोदिताश्च महता देवघोषेण तत्क्षणं सर्व्वे ।
त्यक्त्वा देवसमृद्धिं प्राप्ता बुद्धस्य ते पार्श्वे ॥

इति हि भिक्षवो भौमैर्देवैर्वाराणस्यां ऋषिपतने मृगदावे धर्म्मचक्रप्रवर्त्तनार्थं तथागतस्य महामण्डलमात्रोऽधिष्ठितो ऽभूत् । चित्रो दर्शनीयो विपुलो विस्तीर्णः सप्तयोजनशतायामो विस्तारेण ॥ उपरिष्टाच्च देवैश्छत्रध्वजपताकावितानसमलङ्कृतं गगणतलसमलङ्कृतमभूत्। कामावचरै रूपावचरैश्च देवपुत्रैश्चतुरशीतिसिंहासनशतसहस्राणि तथागतायोपनामितान्यभूवन् । इह निषद्य भगवान् धर्म्मचक्रप्रवर्त्तयत्वस्माकमनुकम्पामुपादायेति ॥

अथ खलु भिक्षवस्तस्मिन् समये पूर्व्वदक्षिणपश्चिमोत्तराभ्यो दिग्भ्य ऊर्द्ध्वमधः समन्ताद्दशभ्यो दिग्भ्यो बहुबोधिसत्त्वकोट्यः पूर्व्वप्रणिधानसमन्वागता आगत्य तथागतचरणयोर्निपत्य धर्म्मचक्रप्रवर्त्तनायाध्येषन्ते स्म । ये चेह त्रिसाहस्रमहासाहस्रलोकधातौ शक्रो वा ब्रह्मा वा लोकपाला वा तदन्येऽपि

१ "धर्म्मश्रवणञ्च" धर्म्मश्रवणञ्च ।
२ "कल्पनयुतैर्न" कल्पनियुतैर्न ।
३ "सञ्चोदयतीयं ब्रह्मपर्य्यन्तां" सञ्चोदयतीदं ब्रह्मपर्य्यं तान् इत्यर्थः ।

महेशाख्यमहेशाख्या देवपुत्रास्तेऽपि सर्व्वे तथागतस्य चरणयोः शिरोभिः प्रणिपत्य तथागतमध्येषन्ते स्म धर्म्मचक्रप्रवर्त्तनाय। प्रवर्त्तयतु भगवान् धर्म्मचक्रं प्रवर्त्तयतु सुगतो धर्म्मचक्रं बहुजनहिताय बहुजनसुखाय लोकानुकम्पायै महतो जनकायस्यार्थाय हिताय सुखाय देवानाञ्च मनुष्याणाञ्च यजस्व (१) भगवन्धर्म्मयज्ञं प्रवर्ष (२) महाधर्म्मवर्षमुच्छ्रेपय(३)महाधर्म्मध्वजम्। प्रपूरय महाधर्म्मशङ्खं प्रताडय महाधर्म्मदुन्दुभिम्। तत्रेदमुच्यते।

निषाद्य इतो बहुब्रह्मस्वरैश्च पाल तथा
उपगम्य जिनस्य क्रमेऽभिनिपत्य उदाहरिषुः।
स्मर पूर्व्वप्रतिज्ञां महामुनि या त्वय वाच कृता
बहु ज्येष्ठ विशिष्ट प्रजाय करिष्ये दुःखस्य क्षयम् (४)॥
त्वयि धर्षितु मार ससैन्य द्रुमेन्द्रि स्थिहित्व मुने
वरबोधि विबुद्धः सुशान्ति निपातित क्लेशद्रुमाः।
अभिप्रायु पूर्ण अशेष य चिन्तित कल्पशता
जनतां प्रसमीक्ष्य अनाधिक वर्त्तय धर्म्मचक्रवरम् (५)॥

---

१ "यजस्व" यज।

२ "प्रवर्ष" प्रवर्षय।

३ "उच्छ्रेपय" उत्क्षेपय।

४ "निषाद्य इतो" निषाद्यवादितो। "पाल तथा" पालास्तथा। "उदाहरिषुः" उदाहरन्। "महामुनि" महामुने। "त्वय वाच" त्वया वाक्। "बहु ज्येष्ठ विशिष्ट प्रजाय" बहुं ज्येष्ठो विशिष्टो प्रजानां।

५ "त्वयि धर्षितु मार ससैन्य द्रुमेन्द्रि स्थिहित्व" त्वया धर्षितो मारः ससैन्यो द्रुमेन्द्रे स्थित्वा। "वरबोधि विबुद्धः" वरबोधिर्विबुद्धः। "सुशान्ति" सुशान्तिः कृता इत्यर्थः। "निपातित" निपातिताः। "अभिप्रायुपूर्ण अशेष च विचिन्तित कल्पशता" अभिप्रायः पूर्णोऽशेषो यो विचिन्तितः कल्पशतात् पूर्वमित्यर्थः। "अनाधिक" आज्ञापिकं। "धर्मचक्रवरं" चक्र चक्रवरमिति वा पाठः।

सुगतस्य प्रभाय सुभाषित चोदनसञ्चोदिता
बहवः शत बुद्धसुतास्य उपागत ऋद्धिबलैः।
विविधां सुगतस्य करित्व पूज महाऋषिचर्यां
स्तवयित्सु तथागतु भूतगुणेभि अध्येषिषु कारुणिकम् (१) ॥
करुणाघन विद्युतप्रभ विपश्यन् वायुसमा
अभिगर्जितु कल्पसहस्र निमन्त्रितु सर्वजगत्।
अष्टाङ्गिकमार्गजलोधर वर्ष समेहि जगस्य इमां
बल इन्द्रियध्यानविमोच विवर्द्धय सत्त्वधनम् (२) ॥
बहुकल्पसहस्र सुभिचितु शून्यतयलक्षिता
समुदानितु धर्म्मज भैषज आनितु सत्त्वचरी।
जनता इयं व्याधिशतेभिरुपद्रुत क्लेशगण-
जिनवैद्य प्रमोचक वर्त्तय धर्म्मचक्रवरम् (३) ॥
न हि पारमिते चिरराव विवर्द्धितु काल त्वया
अशमं तु चराणु प्रणीतु सुसञ्चितु धर्म्मधनम्।
अञ सत्त्व अनाथ दरिद्र अनायिक दृष्ट इमां

---

१ "प्रभाय सुभाषित चोदनसञ्चोदिता" प्रभया सुभाषितानि चोदनसञ्चोदितानि। "बहवः शत" बहुशतसङ्ख्यका इत्यर्थः। "उपागत" उपागताः। "करित्व पूज" कृत्वा पूजां। "स्तवयित्सु तथागतु भूतगुणेभि अध्येषिषु" अस्तुवंस्तथागतं एवम्भूतगुणैरध्येषितुं।

२ "विद्युतप्रभ विपश्यन्" विद्युत्प्रभ विपश्य। "वायुसमा" वायुसमम्। "अभिगर्जितु कल्पसहस्र निमन्त्रितु" अभिगर्जितं कल्पसहस्रपर्य्यन्त निमन्त्रितं। "अष्टाङ्गिकमार्गजलोधर वर्ष समेहि जगस्य" अष्टाङ्गिकमार्गस्वरूपं जलधरं वर्षय समस्त जगतः। "बल इन्द्रियध्यानविमोच" बलमिन्द्रियध्यानविमोचं।

३ "बहुकल्पसहस्र सुभिचितु शून्यतयलक्षिता" बहुकल्पसहस्रपर्य्यन्तं सुभिचित शून्यतयालक्षित। "समुदानितु धर्म्मज भैषज आनितु सत्त्वचरी" समुदानितं धर्म्मजं भैषज्यं ज्ञाता सत्त्वचर्य्यां। "व्याधिशतेभिरुपद्रुत" व्याधिशतैरुपद्रुता।

विचरन्धन सप्त विनायक चक्रं प्रवर्त्तय हे (१) ॥
धनधान्यहिरण्यसुवर्णस्तथैव च वस्त्र शुभा
वरपुष्पविलेपनधूपनचूर्ण गृहाश्च वराः ।
अन्तःपुर राज्य प्रियात्मज त्यक्त प्रहर्षयतो
जिनबोधिगवेषत शान्तिविशुद्धं प्रवर्त्तय चक्रवरम् (२) ॥
तथ शील अखण्ड अकल्मषु रक्षितु कल्पशतां
सद क्षान्तिसुभावितवीर्य अलीन अभूषितका ।
वरध्यानअभिज्ञ विपश्यन् प्रज्ञ उपेक्षत मुने
परिपूर्णमनोरथ निर्जर वर्त्तय चक्रवरम् (३) ॥

अथ खलु भिक्षवः सहचित्तोत्पादधर्म्मचक्रप्रवर्त्ती नाम बोधिसत्त्वो महासत्त्वस्तस्यां वेलायां सर्वरत्नप्रत्युप्तं सर्वरत्नप्रशोभितं नानारत्नालङ्कारव्यूहविभूषितं सहस्रारं सहस्ररश्मिं सनाभिकं सनेमिकं सपुष्पदामं सहेमजालं सकिङ्किणीजालं सगन्धहस्तं सपूर्णकुम्भं सनन्दिकावर्त्तं स्वस्तिकालङ्कृतं नानारङ्गरक्तं दि-

---

१ "चिरराच विवर्द्धितु कालु मया" चिररात्रं विवर्द्धितः कालस्त्वया । "वचासु प्रणीतु सुभाषितु" वचांस्यं प्रणीतं सुभाषितं । "धन्य धनाथ दरिद्र अनाथिक दृष्ट्व" धन्यमनाथं दरिद्रमनाथकं दृष्ट्वा । अत्र धन्य धनाथ इत्यत्र धनं धनाथ इति वा पाठः । "विचरन्धन सप्त" वितरन् धनानि सप्त इत्युचितमित्यनुमीयते । "हे" चि इति वा पाठः ।

२ "धनधान्यहिरण्यसुवर्णस्तथैव च वस्त्र शुभा" धनधान्यहिरण्यसुवर्णानि तथैव च वस्त्राणि शुभानि । "वरपुष्पविलेपनधूपनचूर्ण" वरपुष्पविलेपनधूपनचूर्णानि । "अन्तःपुर राज्य प्रियात्मज त्यक्त" अन्तःपुरं राज्यं प्रियात्मजास्त्यक्ताः । "जिनबोधिगवेषत शान्तिविशुद्ध" जिनबोध्यन्वेषणेन शान्तिमयविशुद्धमित्यर्थः ।

३ "तथ शील अखण्ड अकल्मषु रक्षितु कल्पशतां" तथा शीलमखण्डमकल्मषं रक्षितं कल्पशतपर्य्यन्तमित्यर्थः । "सद" सदा "अभूषितका" आत्मनो अभूषितक इत्यर्थः । "वरध्यानअभिज्ञ" वरध्यानाभिज्ञ । "प्रज्ञ उपेक्षत" प्राज्ञ उपेक्षक ।

ध्वजोपशोभितं दिव्यपुष्पगन्धधूपमाल्यविलेपनानुलिप्तं सर्व्वा-
कारवरोपेतं तथागताय धर्म्मचक्रप्रवर्त्तनाय पूर्व्वप्रणिधानाभि-
निर्हृतं बोधिसत्त्वाशयविशोधितं तथागतपूजार्हं सर्व्वतथागतस-
मन्वाहृतं सर्व्वबुद्धाधिष्ठानाविकोपितं पौर्वकैस्तथागतैरर्हद्भिः
सम्यक्सम्बुद्धैः प्रेषितं प्रवर्त्तितं पूर्व्वं धर्मचक्रमुपनामयति स्म।
उपनाम्य च कृताञ्जलिपुटस्तथागतमाभिर्गाथाभिरभ्यष्टावीत्।

दीपङ्करेण यद व्याकृत शुद्धसत्त्वो
बुद्धो भविष्यसि हि त्वं नरसिंहसिंहः।
तस्मिं समासि प्रणिधी इयमेवरूपा
सम्बोधि प्राप्त अहु धर्म्म अध्येषयेयम् (१)॥
न च शक्य सर्व्व गणनाय अनुप्रवेष्टुं
ये आगता दशदिशेभिरिहाग्रसत्त्वाः।
अध्येषि शाक्यकुलनन्दन धर्म्मचक्रं
शक्राः कृताञ्जलिपुटाश्चरणे निपत्य (२)॥
या बोधिमण्डे मरुताश्च सुरैर्वियूहा
या च वियूहाः कृत सर्व्वजिनात्मजेभिः।
सा सर्व्व संस्थित वियूह धर्म्मचक्रे

---

१ "यद व्याकृत" यदा व्याकृतम्। "तस्मिं समासि" तस्मिन् समासे। "इयमेव-रूपा" इयमेवंरूपा। "सम्बोधि प्राप्त अहु धर्म अध्येषयेयम्" सम्बोधिः प्राप्ता अहं धर्ममध्येषयेयम्।

२ "शक्य सर्वगणनाय अनुप्रवेष्टु" शक्याः सर्वे गणनायामनुप्रवेष्टुं। "दशदिशेभिः" दशदिग्भिः। "अध्येषि शाक्यकुलनन्दन धर्मचक्रं" अध्येषयिष्यति शाक्यकुलनन्दनो धर्मचक्रम्। अत एव ते चरणयोर्निपतिता इति भावः। "निपत्य" निपतिता इत्यर्थः।

परिपूर्णकल्प भ्रममानु चर्यं न गच्छेत् (१) ॥
चित्तरत्नलोक गगनं स्फुट सर्विदेवै-
र्धरणीतलमसुरकिन्नरमानुषैश्च ।
उल्काग्रशब्दमपि श्रूयति तन्मुहूर्तं
सर्वे प्रसन्नमनसो जिनमभ्युदीक्षन् (२) ॥

इति हि भिक्षवस्तथागतो रात्र्याः प्रथमे यामे तूष्णीं-भावेनातिनामयति स्म। रात्र्या मध्यमे यामे संरञ्जनीयां कथां प्रवर्त्तयति स्म ॥ रात्र्याः पश्चिमे यामे पञ्चकान् भद्रवर्गीयानामन्त्र्यैतदवोचत्। द्वाविमौ भिक्षवः प्रव्रजितस्य तावत् ऽन्तौ। यश्च कामेषु कामसुखल्लिकायोगो हीनो ग्राम्यः पार्थग्जनिको(३) नालमार्योऽनर्थोपसंहितो नायत्यां ब्रह्मचर्याय न निर्विदे न विरागाय न निरोधाय नाभिज्ञाय न सम्बोधये न निर्वाणाय संवर्त्तते। या चेयं मध्यमा प्रतिपदात्मकायक्लमथानुयोगो दुःखोऽनर्थोपसंहितो दृष्टधर्मदुःखायत्यां च दुःखविपाकः। एतौ च भिक्षवो द्वावन्तावनुपगम्य मध्यमयैव प्रतिपदा तथागतो धर्मं देशयति। यदुत सम्यग्दृष्टिः सम्यक्सङ्कल्पः सम्यग्वाक्सम्यक्कर्मान्तः

---

१ "या" ये। "सुरैर्विंयूहाः" सुरैर्व्यूढाः। "या च वियूहाः" ये च व्यूढाः। "जल सर्वजिन तजेभिः" जलाः सर्वजिनात्मजैः। "ता सर्व संस्थित वियूह" ते सर्वे संस्थिता व्यूढाः। "परिपूर्णकल्प भ्रममानु चर्यं न गच्छेत्" (ये व्यूढाः) परिपूर्णकल्पपर्यन्तं भ्रमणात् चर्यं न गच्छेयुः।

२ "चित्तरत्नलोक गगनं स्फुट" चित्तरत्नलोकं गगनस्थं स्फुटमभूदित्यर्थः। "सर्विदेवैः" सर्वदेवैः। अत्र देवसङ्घैरिति वा पाठः। "उल्काग्रशब्दमपि श्रूयति तन्मुहूर्तं" उल्काग्रशब्दोऽपि श्रूयते स्म तन्मुहूर्त्तं इत्यर्थः। "जिनमभ्युदीक्षन्" जिनमभ्युदीक्षन्त।

३ "पार्थग्जनिकः" पार्थग्जनकः।

सम्यगाजीवः सम्यग्व्यायामः सम्यक्स्मृतिः सम्यक्समाधिरिति ॥
चत्वारीमानि भिक्षव आर्य्यसत्यानि। कतमानि चत्वारि। दुःखं दुःखसमुदयो दुःखनिरोधो दुःखनिरोधगामिनी प्रतिपत् ॥ तत्र कतमद्दुःखम्। जातिरपि दुःखं जरापि व्याधिरपि मरणमपि अप्रियसम्प्रयोगोऽपि प्रियविप्रयोगोऽपि दुःखम्। यदपि इच्छन् पर्य्येषमाणो न लभते तदपि दुःखम्। सङ्क्षेपतः पञ्चोपादानस्कन्धो दुःखमिदमुच्यते दुःखम् ॥ तत्र कतमो दुःखसमुदयः। येयं तृष्णा पौनर्भविकी नन्दिरागसहगता तत्र तत्राभिनन्दिन्यायमुच्यते दुःखसमुदयः ॥ तत्र कतमो दुखनिरोधः। योऽस्या एव तृष्णायाः पुनर्भविक्या नन्दिरागसहगतायास्तत्र तत्राभिनन्दिन्या अनिकाया निवर्त्तिकाया अशेषो विरागो निरोधोऽयं दुःखनिरोधः ॥ तत्र कतमा दुःखनिरोधगामिनी प्रतिपत्। एष एवार्य्याष्टाङ्गमार्गः। तद्यथा। सम्यग्दृष्टिर्यावत् सम्यक्समाधिरिति। इदमुच्यते। दुःखनिरोधगामिनी प्रतिपदार्य्यसत्यमिति। इमानि भिक्षवश्चत्वार्य्यसत्यानि ॥ दुःखमिति मे भिक्षवःपूर्व्वमश्रुतेषु धर्म्मेषु योनिशो मनसिकाराद्बहुलीकाराज्ज्ञानमुत्पन्नं चक्षुरुत्पन्नं विद्योत्पन्ना भूरिरुत्पन्ना मेधोत्पन्ना आलोकःप्रादुर्भूतः। अयं दुःखनिरोध इति मे भिक्षवः सर्व्वं पूर्व्ववद्यावदालोकः प्रादुर्भूतः। इयं दुःखनिरोधगामिनी प्रतिपदिति मे भिक्षवः पूर्व्ववदेव पेयालं यावदालोकः प्रादुर्भूतः। तत्र (१) खल्विदं दुःखं परिज्ञेयमिति मे भिक्षवः पूर्व्ववदेव याव-

---

१ तत इति वा पाठः।

दालोकः प्रादुर्भूतः। स खल्वयं दुःखसमुदयः प्रहातव्य इति मे भिक्षवः पूर्व्वमश्रुतेषु सर्व्वं यावदालोक इति। स खल्वयं दुःखनिरोधः साक्षात्कर्त्तव्य इति मे भिक्षवः पूर्व्ववद्यावदालोक इति। सा खल्वियं दुःखनिरोधगामिनी प्रतिपदिति भावयितव्येति पूर्व्ववद्यावदालोक इति। तत् खल्विदं दुःखं परिज्ञातमिति मे भिक्षवः पूर्व्वमश्रुतेषु इति पेयालम्। स खल्वयं दुःखसमुदयप्रहाण इति मे भिक्षवः पूर्व्वमश्रुतेति पेयालम्। स खल्वयं दुःखनिरोधः साक्षात्कृत इति मे भिक्षवः पूर्व्वमश्रुतेति पेयालम्। सा खल्वियं दुःखनिरोधगामिनी प्रतिपद्भावितेति मे भिक्षवः पूर्व्वमश्रुतेषु धर्म्मेषु योनिशो मनसिकाराद्बहुलीकाराज्ज्ञानमुत्पन्नं चक्षुरुत्पन्नं विद्योत्पन्ना मेधोत्पन्ना आलोकः प्रादुर्भूतः।

इति हि भिक्षवो यावदेव मे एषु चतुर्ष्वार्य्यसत्येषु योनिशो मनसि कुर्व्वते एवं त्रिपरिवर्त्तितं द्वादशाकारं ज्ञानदर्शनमुत्पद्यते न तावदहं भिक्षवोऽनुत्तरां सम्यक्सम्बोधिमभिसम्बुद्धोऽस्मि इति प्रतिज्ञासिषम्(१)। न च मे ज्ञानदर्शनमुत्पद्यते(२)। यतश्च मे भिक्षव एषु चतुर्ष्वार्य्यसत्येष्वेवं त्रिपरिवर्त्तं द्वादशाकारं ज्ञानदर्शनमुत्पन्नम्। अकोप्या च मे चेतोविमुक्तिः प्रज्ञाविमुक्तिश्च साक्षात्कृता। ततोऽहं भिक्षवोऽनुत्तरां सम्यक्सम्बोधिमभिसम्बुद्धोऽस्मीति प्रत्यज्ञासिषम्॥ ज्ञानदर्शनं मे उदपादि

१ "प्रतिज्ञासिषम्" प्रत्यज्ञासिषम्।
२ "उत्पद्यते" उत्पद्यते स्म।

क्षीणा मे जातिरुषितं ब्रह्मचर्य्यं कृतं करणीयं नापरस्मादभवं प्रजानामि ॥

तत्रेदमुच्यते ।

वाचाय ब्रह्मरुत किन्नरगर्जिताय
अङ्गैः षष्टस्तनयुतेभि समुद्गताय ।
बहुकल्पकोटि सद सत्यसुभाविताय
कौण्डिन्यमालपति शाक्यमुनिः स्वयम्भूः (१) ॥

चक्षुरनित्यमध्रुवं तथ श्रोतघ्राणं जिह्वापि
काय मन दुःखा अनात्म अपि रिक्तस्वभावशून्याः ।
जडास्वभाव तृणकुड्य इवा निरीहा
नैवात्र आत्म न नरो न च जीवमस्ति (२) ॥

हेतुप्रतीत्य इमि सन्तु त सर्व्वधर्म्मा
अत्यन्तदृष्टिविगता गगणप्रकाशाः ।
न च कारकोस्ति तथ नैव च वेदकोस्ति
न च कर्म्म नश्यति कृतं शुभमशुभं शुभं वा (३) ।

स्कन्धाः प्रतीत्य समुदेति हि दुःखमेवं

---

१ "वाचाय" वाचा । "ब्रह्मरुत किन्नरगर्जिताय" ब्रह्मरुतया किन्नरगर्जितया । "षष्टस्तनयुतेभि समुद्गताय" षष्टस्तनियुतैः समुद्गतया । "बहुकल्पकोटि सद सत्य-सुभाविताय" बहुकल्पकोटिपर्यन्तं सदा सत्यसुभावितया ।

२ "तथ श्रोतघ्राणं" तथा श्रोत्रघ्राणे । "काय मन दुःखा अनात्म" कायो मनश्च (एते) दुःखरूपा अनात्मानः । "जडास्वभाव तृणकुड्य इवा" जडस्वभावास्तृणकुड्या-विव । "आत्म न" आत्मा न । "जीवमस्ति" जीवोऽस्ति ।

३ "हेतुप्रतीत्य इमि सन्तु त" हेतुप्रतीत्यजाता इमे सन्ति त इत्यर्थः । "तथ" तथा ।

सम्भोन्ति तृष्णसलिलेन विवर्द्धमानाः
मार्गेण धर्म्मसमताय विपश्यमाना
अत्यन्तक्षीणक्षयधर्म्मतया निरुद्धाः (१) ॥
सङ्कल्पकल्पजनितेन अयोनिशेन
भवते अविद्यमपि सम्भवकोऽस्य कश्चित् ।
संस्कारहेतु ददते न च सङ्क्रमोऽस्ति
विज्ञानमुद्भवति सङ्क्रमणं प्रतीत्य (२) ॥
विज्ञान नाम तथ च रूप समुत्थितोऽस्ति
नामे च रूपे समुदेन्ति षडिन्द्रियाणि ।
षडिन्द्रियैर्निपतितो इति स्पर्श उक्तः
स्पर्शेन तिस्र अनुवर्त्तति वेदना च (३) ॥
यत्किञ्चिद्वेदयितु सर्व्व सतृष्ण उक्ता
तृष्णात सर्व्व उपजायति दुःखस्कन्धः ।
उपादानतो भवति सर्व्व भवप्रवृत्ति-
र्भवप्रत्यया च समुदेति हि जातिरस्य (४) ॥

---

१ "प्रतीत्य समुदेति" प्रतीत्य समुद्यन्ति। "तृष्णसलिलेन" तृष्णासलिलेन। "धर्म्मसमताय" धर्म्मसमतायोगेनेत्यर्थः।

२ "भवते अविद्यमपि" भवत्यविद्यापि। "सम्भवकोऽस्य" सम्भावकोऽस्याः। "संस्कारहेतु ददते" संस्कारहेतुं ददाति।

३ "विज्ञान नाम" विज्ञानं नाम। "तथ" तथा। "रूपसमुत्थितोऽस्ति" रूपं समुत्थितमस्ति। "नामे च रूपि समुदेन्ति" नाम्नि च रूपे समुद्यन्ति। "निपतितो इति" निपातित इति। "तिस्र अनुवर्त्तति वेदना च" तिस्रोऽनुवर्त्तन्ते वेदनाश्च।

४ "वेदयितु" वेदयितुं। "सर्व्व सतृष्ण उक्ता" सर्वे सतृष्णाः उक्ताः। "तृष्णात सर्व्व उपजायति" तृष्णातः सर्वं उपजायते। "सर्व्व भवप्रवृत्तिः" सर्वा भवप्रवृत्तिः। भव भवप्रवृत्तिरिति पाठे सम्यक्।

जातीनिदानजरव्याधिदुःखानि भोन्ति
उपपत्ति नैक विविधा भवपञ्जरेऽस्मिन्।
एवमेव सर्व्व इति प्रत्ययतो जगच्च
न च आत्मपुद्गल न सङ्क्रमकोऽस्ति कश्चित् (१) ॥
यस्मिन्न कल्प न विकल्प न योनिमाज्ञा
अयोनिशो भवति न तत्र अविद्य काचित्।
यस्मिन्निरोध भवतीह अविद्यतायाः
सर्व्वे भवाङ्ग क्षयक्षीण क्षयं निरुद्धाः (२) ॥
एवमेव प्रत्ययत बुद्ध तथागतेन
तेन स्वयम्भु स्वकमात्मन व्याकरोति।
न स्कन्ध आयतन धातु वदेमि बुद्धं
नान्यत्र हेत्ववगमाद्भवतीह बुद्धः (३) ॥
भूमिर्न चात्र परतीर्थिकनिर्मितानां
शून्यप्रवादि इह ईदृश धर्म्मयोगे।
ये पूर्व्वबुद्धचरिताः सुविशुद्धसत्त्वाः

---

१ "जातीनिदानजरव्याधिदुःखानि भोन्ति" जातिनिदानजराव्याधिदुःखानि भवन्ति। "उपपत्ति नैक" उपपत्तिर्नैका। "भवपञ्जरेऽस्मिं" भवपञ्जरेऽस्मिन्। "जगच्च" जगतः। "आत्मपुद्गल" आत्मपुद्गलस्य जीवात्मन इत्यर्थः।

२ "कल्प न विकल्प न योनिमाज्ञा" कल्पो न विकल्पो न योनिराज्ञा। "अविद्य काचित्" अविद्याः काचित्। "निरोध भवतीह" निरोधो भवतीह। "अविद्यतायाः" अविद्यायाः। "भवाङ्ग क्षयक्षीण" भवाङ्गाः क्षयक्षीणाः। "क्षयं निरुद्धाः" क्षयो निरुद्धः।

३ "प्रत्ययत बुद्ध तथागतेन" प्रत्ययतो बुद्धतथागतेन। "स्वयम्भु स्वकमात्मन" स्वयम्भुवं स्वकमात्मानं। "स्कन्ध आयतन धातु वदेमि" स्कन्धमायतनं धातुं वदामि।

ते प्रकुर्वन्ति इमि धर्म विजानताथ (१) ॥
एवं हि द्वादशाकारं धर्मचक्रं प्रवर्त्तितम् ।
कौण्डिन्येन च आज्ञातं निर्हृत्ता रत्नाश्रयः (२) ॥
बुद्धो धर्मश्च सङ्घश्च इत्येते रत्नत्रयम् (३) ।
परम्परागतः शब्दो यावद्ब्रह्मपुरालयम् ॥
वर्त्तितं विरजं चक्रं लोकनाथेन तायिना ।
उत्पन्ना रत्नाश्चोपि लोके परमदुर्लभाः (४) ॥
कौण्डिन्यं प्रथमं कृत्वा पञ्चकाश्चैव भिक्षवः ।
षष्टीनां देवकोटीनां धर्मचक्षुर्विशोधितम् (५) ॥
अन्ये चाशीतिकोट्यस्तु रूपधातुकदेवताः ।
तेषां विशोधितं चक्षुर्धर्मचक्रं प्रवर्त्तिते (६) ॥
चतुरशीतिसहस्राणि मनुष्याणां समागताः ।
तेषां विशोधितं चक्षुर्मुक्ताः सर्वेभि दुर्गति (७) ॥
दशदिशन्तु अनन्तां बुद्धस्वरो गच्छि तस्मिं क्षणे
रुत मधुर मनोज्ञः संश्रूयते चाम्बरीच शुभ ।

---

१ "प्रत्यप्रवादि इव ईडम" प्रत्यप्रवादे इव ईडबे । "इमि धर्म विजानताथ" इमं धर्मं विज्ञातुम् ।

२ "निर्हृत्ता रत्नाश्रयः" निर्हृत्तानि रत्नानि त्रीणि ।

३ "इत्येते रत्नत्रयम्" इत्येतानि रत्नत्रयाणि ।

४ "विरजं" विरजस्कं । "तायिना" विभुतेन । "उत्पन्ना रत्नाश्चोपि" उत्पन्नानि रत्नानि त्रीणि । "परमदुर्लभाः" परमदुर्लभानि ।

५ "कौण्डिन्यं प्रथमं कृत्वा पञ्चकाश्चैव भिक्षवः" कौण्डिन्यमग्रतः कृत्वा पञ्चकानाश्चैव भिक्षूनभिलक्ष्य ।

६ "अन्ये" अन्याः । "तेषां" तासां । "धर्मचक्रं" धर्मचक्रे ।

७ "समागताः" समागतानि । "सर्वेभि दुर्गति" सर्वदुर्गतेः ।

एष दशबलेन शाक्यर्षभेण धर्म्मचक्रोत्तमं
ऋषिपतनमुपेत्य वाराणसी वर्त्तितो नान्यथा (१) ॥
इमदिशिम ये केचिद् बुद्धशता: सर्व्वे तूष्णीभूता-
स्तेषु मुनिनये उपस्थायका: सर्व्वि पृच्छिषु जनां ।
किमिति दशबलेभि धर्म्मा कथाच्छिन्न मुत्वा इतं
साधु भणत शीघ्रं किं कारणं तूष्णीभावेन स्थिता: (२) ॥
पूर्व्वभवशते वीर्य्यबलैर्बोधि: समुदानीत्व
बहव: शतसहस्र पराङ्मुखा बोधिसत्त्वा गता: ।
तेन हितकरेण उत्पन्ना प्राप्त बोधि: शिवा
चक्र विपरिवर्त्तितो तेन तूष्णीभूता: (३) ॥
इमु वचन श्रुणित्वा तेषां मुनी शक्रकोट्य: शता
मैत्रबलजनित सम्प्रस्थिता अग्रबोधिं शिवाम् ।

---

१ "इमदिशमनु चमन्तं" इमदिशु चलन्तं। "गच्छि तस्मिं" अगच्छत् तस्मिन्। "हत मधुर मनोज्ञः" हतं मधुरं मनोज्ञं। "संश्रूयसे चान्तरीक्ष शुभ" असंश्रूयत चान्तरीक्षे शुभम्। "एष" एतत्। "धर्मचक्रोत्तमं" धर्मचक्रमुत्तमम्। "वाराणसी वर्तितो नान्यथा" वाराणस्याः प्रवर्तितं (अत्र विषये) अन्यथा नेत्यर्थः।

२ "इमदिशिम" इमदिशु। "ये केचित् बुद्धशताः सर्वे तूष्णीभूताः" यानि कानिचित् बुद्धशतानि सर्वाणि तूष्णीभूतानि। "मुनिनये उपस्थायकाः सर्वि पृच्छि जनां" मुनिनयोपस्थापकाः सर्वे अपृच्छन्नित्यर्थः। "दशबलेभि धर्मा कथाच्छिन्न" दशबलैर्धर्म्मां कथामच्छिन्नामित्यर्थः। "तूष्णीभावेन स्थिताः" तूष्णीभावेन स्थितानि (बुद्धशतानि इत्यर्थः)।

३ "बोधिः समुदानीत्व" बोधिं समुदानीय। "बहवः शतसहस्र" बहुशतसहस्रसंख्यकाः। "पराङ्मुखाः" पराङ्मुखा इत्यर्थः। "उत्पन्ना" उत्पन्नम्। "प्राप्त बोधिः" प्राप्ता बोधिः। "चक्र विपरिवर्तितो" चक्रं निःपरिवर्तितं। "तूष्णीभूता" तूष्णीभूताः।

वयमपि अनुशिक्षि तस्या मुने वीर्य्यस्थामोद्गतं
क्षिप्र भवेम लोकि लोकोत्तमा धर्म्मचक्षुद्ददा इति (१)॥

अथ खलु मैत्रेयो बोधिसत्त्वो महासत्त्वो भगवन्तमेतदवोचत्। इमे भगवन् दशदिग्लोकधातुसन्निपतिता बोधिसत्त्वा महासत्त्वा भगवतः प्रकाशाद्धर्म्मचक्रप्रवर्त्तनविकुर्व्वितस्य प्रश्नं श्रोतुकामास्तत्साधु भगवन् देशयतु तथागतोऽर्हन् सम्यक्सम्बुद्धः कियद्रूपं तथागतेन धर्म्मचक्रं प्रवर्त्तितम्।

भगवानाह। गम्भीरं मैत्रेय चक्रं ग्राह्यानुपलब्धित्वात्। दुर्द्दर्शनं तच्चक्रं द्वयविगतत्वात्। दुरनुबोधं तच्चक्रं मनसिकारामनसिकारत्वात्। दुर्विज्ञेयं तच्चक्रं ज्ञानविज्ञानसमतानुबद्धत्वात्। अनाविलं तच्चक्रमनावरणविमोक्षप्रतिलब्धत्वात्। सूक्ष्मं तच्चक्रमुपन्यासविगतत्वात्। सारं तच्चक्रं वज्रोपमज्ञानप्रतिलब्धत्वात्। अभेद्यं तच्चक्रं पूर्व्वान्तासम्भवत्वात्। अप्रपञ्चं तच्चक्रं सर्व्वप्रपञ्चोपारम्भविगतत्वात्। अकोप्यं तच्चक्रमत्यन्तनिष्ठत्वात्। सर्व्वत्रानुगतं तच्चक्रमाकाशसदृशत्वात्। तत् खलु पुनर्म्मैत्रेय धर्म्मचक्रं सर्व्वधर्म्मप्रकृतिस्वभावसन्दर्शनविभवचक्रम्। अनुत्पादानिरोधासम्भवचक्रम्। अनालयचक्रम्। अकल्पाविकल्पधर्म्मनयविस्तीर्णचक्रम्। शून्यताचक्रम्। अनिमित्तचक्रम्। अप्रणिहित-

---

१ "इमु वचन सुणित्वा तेषां मुनी" इदं वचनं श्रुत्वा तेषां मुनीनां। "सत्त्वकोटः शता" सत्त्वकोटिशतानि इत्यर्थः। "मैत्रवस्य जनित्वा सम्प्रस्थिता" मैत्रवर्ण जनयित्वा सम्प्रस्थितानि। "अनुशिक्षि तस्या मुने" अनुशिक्षाम तस्य मुनेः सकाशात् इत्यर्थः। "वीर्यस्थामोद्गतं" वीर्यस्थामोद्गताः। "क्षिप्र" क्षिप्रं। "लोकि" लोके। "लोकोत्तमा धर्मचक्षुद्दा" हे लोकोत्तम धर्मचक्षुर्दायक इत्यर्थः।

चक्रम्। अनभिसंस्कारचक्रम्। विवेकचक्रम्। विरागचक्रम्। विबोधचक्रम्। तथागतानुबोधचक्रम्। धर्म्मधात्वसम्भेदचक्रम्। भूतकोट्यविकोपनचक्रम्। असङ्गानावरणचक्रम्। प्रतीत्यवतारोभयान्तदृष्टिसमतिक्रमणचक्रम्। अनन्तमध्यधर्म्मधात्वविकोपनचक्रम्। अनाभोगबुद्धकायाप्रतिप्रश्रब्धचक्रम्। अप्रवृत्त्यनभिनिर्वृत्तिचक्रम्। अत्यन्तानुपलब्धिचक्रम्। अनायूहनिर्य्यूहचक्रम्। अनभिलाप्यचक्रम्। प्रकृतियथावच्चक्रम्। एकविषयसर्व्वधर्म्मसमतावतारचक्रम्। अक्षणसत्त्वविनयाधिष्ठानप्रत्युदावर्त्यचक्रम्। अद्वयासमारोपपरमार्थनयप्रवेशचक्रम्। धर्म्मधातुसमवसरणचक्रम्। अप्रमेयं तच्चक्रम्। सर्व्वप्रमाणातिक्रान्तमसङ्ख्येयं तच्चक्रम्। सर्व्वसङ्ख्यापगतमचिन्त्यं तच्चक्रम्। चित्तपथसमतिक्रान्तमतुल्यं तच्चक्रम्। अतुल्यापगतमनभिलाप्यं तच्चक्रम्। सर्व्वरुतघोषवाक्पथातीतमप्रमाणमनुपममुपमापगतमाकाशसदृशमनुच्छेदमशाश्वतं प्रतीत्यवताराविरुद्धमात्मात्यन्तोपशमं तत्त्वं तथावितथानन्यथान्यथाभावं सर्व्वसत्त्वरुतचरणनिर्घोषो माराणां पराजयस्तीर्थिकानां समतिक्रमणं संसारविषयावतारणं बुद्धविषयपरिज्ञातमार्य्यपुद्गलैरनुबुद्धं प्रत्येकबुद्धैः परिगृहीतं बोधिसत्त्वैःस्तुतं सर्व्वबुद्धैरभिमभिन्नं सर्व्वतथागतैरेवंरूपं मैत्रेय तथागतेन धर्म्मचक्रं प्रवर्त्तितम्॥ यस्य प्रवर्त्तनात् तथागत इत्युच्यते। सम्यक्सम्बुद्ध इत्युच्यते। स्वयम्भूरित्युच्यते। धर्म्मस्वामीत्युच्यते। नायक इत्युच्यते। विनायक इत्युच्यते। परिणायक इत्युच्यते। सार्थवाह इत्युच्यते।

सर्व्वधर्म्मवशवर्त्तीत्युच्यते। धर्म्मेश्वर इत्युच्यते। धर्म्मचक्रप्रवर्त्ती-त्युच्यते। धर्म्मदानपतिरित्युच्यते। यज्ञस्वामीत्युच्यते। विद्रु-प्रत इत्युच्यते। पूर्णाभिप्राय इत्युच्यते। दैशिक इत्युच्यते। आश्वासक इत्युच्यते। क्षेमङ्कर इत्युच्यते। शूर इत्युच्यते। रण-ञ्जह इत्युच्यते। विजितसङ्ग्राम इत्युच्यते। उच्छ्रितच्छत्रध्वज-पताक इत्युच्यते। आलोककर इत्युच्यते। प्रभङ्कर इत्युच्यते। तमोनुद इत्युच्यते। उल्काधारीत्युच्यते। महावैद्यराज इत्यु-च्यते। भूतचिकित्सक इत्युच्यते। महाशल्यहर्त्ता इत्युच्यते। वितिमिरज्ञानदर्शन इत्युच्यते। समन्तदर्शीत्युच्यते। समन्त-विलोकित इत्युच्यते। समन्तचक्षुरित्युच्यते। समन्तप्रभ इत्यु-च्यते। समन्तालोक इत्युच्यते। समन्तमुख इत्युच्यते। सम-न्तप्रभाकर इत्युच्यते। समन्तचन्द्र इत्युच्यते। समन्तप्रासा-दिक इत्युच्यते। अप्रतिष्ठितानायूहानिर्य्यूह इत्युच्यते। धर-णीसम इत्युच्यते अनुन्नतावनतत्वात्। त्रैलोक्यवृषभ इत्युच्यते अप्रकम्प्यत्वात्। सर्व्वलोकश्रीरित्युच्यते सर्व्वगुणसमन्वागतत्वात्। अनवलोकितमूर्द्ध इत्युच्यते सर्व्वलोकाभ्युद्गतत्वात्। समुद्रकल्प इत्युच्यते गम्भीरदुरवगाहत्वात्। धर्म्मरत्नाकर इत्युच्यते सर्व्व-बोधिपाक्षिकधर्म्मरत्नप्रतिपूर्णत्वात्। वायुसम इत्युच्यते अनि-केतत्वात्। असङ्गबुद्धिरित्युच्यते सर्व्वत्रासङ्गमुक्तचित्तत्वात्। अवैवर्त्तिकधर्म्म इत्युच्यते सर्व्वधर्म्मनिर्व्विरोधिकज्ञानत्वात्। तेजःसम इत्युच्यते दुरासदसर्व्वमननाप्रहीणसर्व्वक्लेशदाहप्रत्यु-पस्थानत्वात्। अप्सम इत्युच्यते अनाविलसङ्कल्पनिर्म्मलकाय-

चित्तवाचितपापत्वात्। आकाशसम इत्युच्यते असङ्गज्ञानविषयानन्तमध्यधर्म्मधातुगोचरज्ञानाभिज्ञाप्राप्तत्वात्। अनावरणज्ञानविमोक्षविहारीत्युच्यते नानावरणीयधर्म्मसुप्रदीपत्वात्। सर्व्वधर्म्मधातुप्रसृतव्याप्तकाय इत्युच्यते गगणसमचक्षुःपथसमतिक्रान्तत्वात्। उत्तमसत्त्व इत्युच्यते सर्व्वलोकविषयासङ्क्लिष्टत्वात्। असङ्गसत्त्व इत्युच्यते। अप्रमाणबुद्धिरित्युच्यते। लोकोत्तरधर्म्मदेशिक इत्युच्यते। लोकचैत्य इत्युच्यते। लोकवैद्य इत्युच्यते। लोकाभ्युद्गत इत्युच्यते। लोकधर्म्मानुपलिप्त इत्युच्यते। लोकनाथ इत्युच्यते। लोकज्येष्ठ इत्युच्यते। लोकश्रेष्ठ इत्युच्यते। लोकेश्वर इत्युच्यते। लोकमहित इत्युच्यते। लोकपरायण इत्युच्यते। लोकपारङ्गत इत्युच्यते। लोकप्रदीप इत्युच्यते। लोकोत्तर इत्युच्यते। लोकगुरुरित्युच्यते। लोकार्थंकर इत्युच्यते। लोकानुवर्त्तक इत्युच्यते। लोकविदित्युच्यते। लोकाधिपतेयप्राप्त(१) इत्युच्यते। महादक्षिणीय इत्युच्यते। पूजार्ह इत्युच्यते। महापुण्यक्षेत्र इत्युच्यते। अग्रसत्त्व इत्युच्यते। वरसत्त्व इत्युच्यते। प्रवरसत्त्व इत्युच्यते। उत्तमसत्त्व इत्युच्यते। अनुत्तरसत्त्व इत्युच्यते। असदृशसत्त्व इत्युच्यते। सतत-समाहित इत्युच्यते। सर्व्वधर्म्मसमताविहारीत्युच्यते। मार्गप्राप्त इत्युच्यते। मार्गदर्शक इत्युच्यते। मार्गदेशिक इत्युच्यते। सुप्रतिष्ठितमार्ग इत्युच्यते। मारविषयसमतिक्रान्त इत्युच्यते। मारमण्डलविध्वंसनकर इत्युच्यते। अजरामरणशीतिभावप्राप्त-

१ "ले काधिपतेय प्राप्तः" लोकाधिपत्यप्राप्तः।

इत्युच्यते। विगततमोऽन्धकार इत्युच्यते। विगतकण्टक इत्युच्यते। विगतकाङ्क्ष इत्युच्यते। विगतक्लेश इत्युच्यते। विनीतसंशय इत्युच्यते। विमतिसमुद्घाटित इत्युच्यते। विमुक्त इत्युच्यते। विरक्त इत्युच्यते। विशुद्ध इत्युच्यते। विगतराग इत्युच्यते। विगतद्वेष इत्युच्यते। विगतमोह इत्युच्यते। क्षीणास्रव इत्युच्यते। निःक्लेश इत्युच्यते। वशीभूत इत्युच्यते। सुविमुक्तचित्त इत्युच्यते। सुविमुक्तप्रज्ञ इत्युच्यते। आजानेयचित्त इत्युच्यते। महानाग इत्युच्यते। कृतकृत्य इत्युच्यते। कृतकरणीय इत्युच्यते। अपहृतभार इत्युच्यते। अनुप्राप्तस्वकार्थ इत्युच्यते। परिक्षीणभवसंयोजन इत्युच्यते। सम्यगाज्ञानविमुक्तिरित्युच्यते। सर्व्वचेतोवशिपरमपारमिताप्राप्त इत्युच्यते। दानपारगत इत्युच्यते। शीलाभ्युद्गत इत्युच्यते। क्षान्तिपारग इत्युच्यते। वीर्य्याभ्युद्गत इत्युच्यते। ध्यानाभिज्ञप्राप्त (१) इत्युच्यते। प्रज्ञापारगत इत्युच्यते। सिद्धप्रणिधान इत्युच्यते। महामैत्रीविहारीत्युच्यते। महाकरुणाविहारीत्युच्यते। महामुदिताविहारीत्युच्यते। महोपेक्षाविहारीत्युच्यते। संग्रहवस्तुप्रयुक्त इत्युच्यते। अनावरणप्रतिसंवित्प्राप्त इत्युच्यते। प्रतिशरणभूत इत्युच्यते। महापुण्य इत्युच्यते। महाज्ञानीत्युच्यते। स्मृतिमतिगतिबुद्धिसम्पन्न इत्युच्यते। स्मृत्युपस्थानसम्यक्प्रहाणर्द्धिपादेन्द्रियबलबोध्यङ्गसमर्थविदर्शनालोकप्राप्त इत्युच्यते। उत्तीर्णसंसारार्णव इत्युच्यते। पारग इत्युच्यते। स्थलगत इत्युच्यते।

१ "ध्यानाभिज्ञप्राप्त" ध्यानाभिज्ञाप्राप्तः ।

शमप्राप्त इत्युच्यते। अभयप्राप्त इत्युच्यते। मर्दितमारक्लेशकण्टक (१) इत्युच्यते। पुरुष इत्युच्यते। महापुरुष इत्युच्यते। पुरुषसिंह इत्युच्यते। विगतभयलोमहर्षण इत्युच्यते। नाग इत्युच्यते। निर्मल इत्युच्यते। त्रिमलप्रहीण इत्युच्यते। वेदक इत्युच्यते। त्रैविद्यानुप्राप्त इत्युच्यते। चतुरोघोत्तीर्ण इत्युच्यते। पारग इत्युच्यते। (२) क्षत्रिय इत्युच्यते। ब्राह्मण इत्युच्यते। एकरत्नच्छत्रधारीत्युच्यते। वाहितपापधर्म इत्युच्यते। भिक्षुरित्युच्यते। भिन्नाविद्याण्डकोष इत्युच्यते। श्रमण इत्युच्यते। सर्वसङ्गपथसमतिक्रान्त इत्युच्यते। श्रोत्रिय इत्युच्यते। निःसृतक्लेश इत्युच्यते। बलवानित्युच्यते। दशबलधारीत्युच्यते। भगवानित्युच्यते। भावितकाय इत्युच्यते। राजातिराज इत्युच्यते। धर्मराज इत्युच्यते। प्रवरवर इत्युच्यते। वरप्रवरधर्मचक्रप्रवर्त्यनुशासक इत्युच्यते। अकोप्यधर्मदेशक इत्युच्यते। सर्वज्ञज्ञानाभिषिक्त इत्युच्यते। असङ्गमहाज्ञानविमलविमुक्तिपट्टाबद्ध इत्युच्यते। सप्तबोध्यङ्गरत्नसमन्वागत इत्युच्यते। सर्वधर्मविशेषप्राप्त इत्युच्यते। सर्वार्य्यश्रावकमार्य्यावलोकितमुखमण्डल इत्युच्यते। बोधिसत्त्वमहासत्त्वपुत्रपरिवार इत्युच्यते। सुविनीतविनय इत्युच्यते। सुव्याकृतबोधिसत्त्व इत्युच्यते। वैश्रवणसदृश इत्युच्यते। सप्तार्य्यधनविश्राणितकोश इत्युच्यते। मुक्तत्याग इत्युच्यते। सर्वसुखसम्पत्तिसमन्वागत इत्युच्यते। सर्वाभिप्रायदातेत्युच्यते। सर्वलोकहितसुखानुपालक इत्युच्यते। इन्द्रसम इत्युच्यते। ज्ञानबलवज्रभा-

---

१ "मर्दितमारक्लेशकण्टकः" मर्दितक्लेशकण्टक इति वा पाठः।

२ इति कुत्रचित् पाठः।

रीत्युच्यते। समन्तनेत्र इत्युच्यते। सर्व्वधर्म्मानावरणज्ञानदर्शी-त्युच्यते। समन्तज्ञानविकुर्व्वाण इत्युच्यते। विपुलधर्म्मनाटकदर्शनप्रविष्ट (१) इत्युच्यते। चन्द्रसम इत्युच्यते। सर्व्वजगदवृप्तिदर्शन इत्युच्यते। समन्तविपुलविशुद्धप्रभ इत्युच्यते। प्रीतिप्रामोद्यकर इत्युच्यते। सर्व्वसत्त्वाभिमुखदर्शनावभास इत्युच्यते। सर्व्वजगच्चित्ताशयभाजनप्रतिभासप्राप्त इत्युच्यते। महाव्यूह इत्युच्यते। मैत्रामैत्रज्योतिर्गणपरिवार इत्युच्यते। आदित्यमण्डलसमतिक्रान्त इत्युच्यते। विधुतमोहान्धकार इत्युच्यते। महाकेतुराज इत्युच्यते। अप्रमाणानन्तरश्मिरित्युच्यते। महावभाससन्दर्शक इत्युच्यते। सर्व्वप्रश्नव्याकरणनिर्देशासम्मूढ इत्युच्यते। महाविद्यान्धकारविध्वंसनकर इत्युच्यते। महाज्ञानालोकविलोकितबुद्धिर्निर्व्विकल्प इत्युच्यते। महामैत्रीकरुणाकृपासर्व्वजगत्समरश्मिप्रयुक्तप्रमाणविषय इत्युच्यते। प्रज्ञापारमितागम्भीरदुरासददुर्निरीक्षमण्डल इत्युच्यते। ब्रह्मसम इत्युच्यते। प्रशान्तेर्य्यापथ इत्युच्यते। सर्व्वार्य्यपथचर्य्याविशेषसमन्वागत इत्युच्यते। परमरूपधारीत्युच्यते। असेचनकदर्शन इत्युच्यते। शान्तेन्द्रिय इत्युच्यते। शान्तमानस इत्युच्यते। शमथसम्भारपरिपूर्ण इत्युच्यते। उत्तमशमथप्राप्त इत्युच्यते। परमदमशमथप्राप्त इत्युच्यते। शमथविदर्शनापरिपूर्णसम्भार इत्युच्यते। गुप्तो जितेन्द्रियो नाग इव सुदान्तो ह्रद इवाच्छोऽनाविलो विप्रसन्न इत्युच्यते। सर्व्वक्लेशवासनावरणसुप्रहीण इत्युच्यते। द्वात्रिंशन्महापुरुषलक्षणसमन्वागत

१ "विपुलधर्म्मनाटकदर्शनप्रविष्टः" विपुलधर्म्मनाटकप्रविष्ट इति वा पाठः।

इत्युच्यते। परमपुरुष इत्युच्यते। अभीत्यनुच्छम्भनपरिवारविचिचरचितगात्र इत्युच्यते। पुरुषर्षभ इत्युच्यते। दशबलसमन्वागत इत्युच्यते। चतुर्वैशारद्यप्राप्तानुत्तरपुरुषदम्यसारथिरित्युच्यते। शास्तेत्युच्यते। अष्टादशावेणिकबुद्धधर्म्मपरिपूर्ण इत्युच्यते। अनिन्दितकायवाङ्मनःकर्म्मान्त इत्युच्यते। प्रतीत्यसमुत्पादसमताभिसंबोधादनिमित्तविहारी इत्युच्यते। सर्व्वाकारवरोपेतसुपरिशोधितज्ञानदर्शनमण्डलत्वात् शून्यताविहारीत्युच्यते। परमार्थसत्यनयप्रतिवेधादप्रणिहितविहारीत्युच्यते। सर्व्वप्रस्थानाखिन्नत्वादनभिसंस्कारगोचर इत्युच्यते। सर्व्वसंस्कारप्रतिप्रश्रब्धत्वाद्भूतवादीत्युच्यते। भूतकोट्यविकोपितज्ञानविषयत्वादवितथान्यथावादीत्युच्यते। तथताधर्म्मधात्वाकाशलक्षणज्ञानविषयत्वादरण्यधर्म्मसुप्रतिलब्ध इत्युच्यते। मायामरीचिस्वप्नोदकचन्द्रप्रतिश्रुत्काप्रतिभाससमतासर्व्वधर्म्मविहारित्वादमोघदर्शनश्रवण इत्युच्यते। परिनिर्व्वाणहेतुजनकत्वादमोघपदविक्रमीत्युच्यते। सत्यविनयपराक्रमविक्रान्तत्वादुत्क्षिप्तपरिखेद इत्युच्यते। अविद्याभवतृष्णासमुच्छिन्नत्वात् स्थापितसङ्क्रम इत्युच्यते। नैर्याणिकप्रतिपत्सुदेशिकत्वात् निर्जितमारक्लेशप्रत्यर्थिक इत्युच्यते। सर्व्वमारचर्याविषयानुलिप्तत्वादुत्तीर्णकामपङ्क इत्युच्यते। कामधातुसमतिक्रान्तत्वात् पातितमानध्वज इत्युच्यते। रूपधातुसमतिक्रान्तत्वादुत्थितप्रज्ञाध्वज इत्युच्यते। आरूप्यधातुसमतिक्रान्तत्वात् सर्व्वलोकविषयसमतिक्रान्त इत्युच्यते। धर्म्मकायज्ञानशरीरत्वात् महाद्रुम इत्युच्यते। अनन्तगुणरत्नज्ञानकुसु-

मित(१)विमुक्तिफलसंपन्नत्वादुदुम्बरपुष्पसदृश इत्युच्यते। दुर्लभ-
प्रादुर्भावदर्शनत्वाच्चिन्तामणिरत्नमणिराजसम इत्युच्यते। यथा-
शयनिर्वाणाभिप्रायसुप्रतिपूरकत्वात् सुप्रतिष्ठितपादप इत्युच्यते।
दीर्घरात्रं त्यागशीलतपोव्रतब्रह्मचर्य्यवृत्तसमादानाचलाप्रकम्प-
त्वाद् विचित्रस्वस्तिकनन्द्यावर्त्तसहस्रारचक्राङ्कितपादतल इत्यु-
च्यते। दीर्घरात्रं प्राणातिपातविरत्यन्यगुणवर्णनसम्प्रकाशनत्वान्
मृदुतरुणहस्तपाद इत्युच्यते। दीर्घरात्रं मातृपितृश्रमणब्राह्म-
णगुरुदक्षिणीयधार्म्मिकरक्षापरिपालनतया शरणागतानाञ्चाप-
रित्यागत्वादायतपार्ष्णिरित्युच्यते। दीर्घरात्रं प्राणातिपातोप-
रतत्वाद्दीर्घाङ्गुलीत्युच्यते (२)। दीर्घरात्रं प्राणातिपातविरत्यन्य-
परसमादानत्वादृजुगात्रेत्युच्यते। दीर्घरात्रं मातृपितृ-
श्रमणगुरुदक्षिणीयोपस्थानपरिचर्य्यास्नानानुलेपनसर्पिस्तैलाभ्य-
ङ्गस्वहस्तशरीरपरिकर्म्मपरिखेदत्वाज्जालाङ्गुलीहस्तपाद इत्यु-
च्यते। दीर्घरात्रं दानप्रियवचनार्थक्रियासमानार्थतासङ्ग्रह-
वस्तुजालेन सत्त्वसङ्ग्रहकौशल्यसुविचितत्वादुच्छङ्खपाद इत्युच्यते।
दीर्घरात्रमुत्तरोत्तरविशिष्टतरकुशलध्यानत्वादूर्ध्वाङ्गदक्षिणाव-
र्त्तरोमकूप इत्युच्यते। दीर्घरात्रं मातृपितृश्रमणब्राह्मणगुरुदक्षि-
णीयतथागतचैत्यप्रदक्षिणीकरणधर्म्मश्रवणचित्रीकाररोमहर्ष-
परसत्त्वसंहर्षणधर्म्मदेशनाप्रयोगत्वादैणेयजङ्घ इत्युच्यते। दीर्घरात्रं
सत्कृत्यधर्म्मश्रवणग्रहणधारणवाचनविज्ञापनार्थपदविनिश्चयनि-
र्घोषणकौशल्येन जराव्याधिमरणाभिमुखानाञ्च सत्त्वानां शर-

---

१ "उद्गुमित" वा पाठः।
२ "दीर्घाङ्गुलीत्युच्यते" दीर्घाङ्गुलीक इत्युच्यते। इति उचितम्।

पगमनानुप्रदानसत्कृत्यधर्मदेशनापरिभवबुद्धित्वात् कोशोपगतवस्तिगुह्य इत्युच्यते। दीर्घरात्रं श्रमणब्राह्मणानां तदन्येषाञ्च ब्रह्मचारिणां ब्रह्मचर्य्यानुगतसर्व्वपरिष्कारानुप्रदानम्रक्षणानुप्रदानपरदारागमनब्रह्मचर्य्यगुणवर्णसम्प्रकाशनापत्ताप्यानुपालनदृढसमादानत्वात् प्रलम्बबाहुरित्युच्यते। दीर्घरात्रं स्वकसंयमपादसंयतसत्त्वाविहेठनप्रयोगमैत्रकायकर्म्मवाक्कर्म्ममनस्कर्म्मसमन्वागतत्वात् न्यग्रोधपरिमण्डल इत्युच्यते। दीर्घरात्रं भोजनमात्रज्ञतात्पाहारतोदारसंयमग्लानभैषज्यानुप्रदानहीनजनापरिभवानाथाभवसन्दर्शन (१) तथागतचैत्यविशीर्णप्रतिसंस्कारणस्तूपप्रतिष्ठापनत्वात् भयार्दितेभ्यश्च सत्त्वेभ्योऽभयप्रदानत्वात् मृदुतरुणहस्तपादच्छविरित्युच्यते। दीर्घरात्रं मातृपितृश्रमणब्राह्मणगुरुदक्षिणीयानां स्नानानुलेपनसर्पिस्तैलाभ्यङ्गशीतलोष्णोदकानुष्णशीतोदकच्छायातपर्त्तुसुखपरिभोगानुप्रदानमृदुतरुणतूलसंस्पर्शसुकुमारवस्त्रास्तीर्णशयनासनानुप्रदानतथागतचैत्यगन्धतैलसेकपुष्पपट्टध्वजपताकागुणप्रदानत्वात् सुवर्णच्छविरित्युच्यते। दीर्घरात्रं सर्व्वसत्त्वाप्रतिघातमैत्रीभावनायोगवाङ्मैत्रारम्भपरसत्त्वसमादापनावैरव्यापादगुणवर्णसम्प्रकाशनतया तथागतचैत्यतथागतप्रतिमानां सुवर्णखचितसुवर्णपुष्पसुवर्णचूर्णाभिकिरणसुवर्णवर्णपट्टपताकाध्वजालङ्कारसुवर्णभाजनसुवर्णवस्त्रानुप्रदानत्वादेकैकनिचितरोमकूप इत्युच्यते। दीर्घरात्रं पण्डितोपसङ्क्रमणकिंकुशलाकुशलपरिपृच्छनसावद्यानवद्यसेव्यासेव्यधी-

---

१ "अनाथानथसन्दर्शन" अनाथावकाशदर्शन इति वा पाठः।

नमथ्यप्रणीतधर्म्मपरिपृच्छनार्थमीमांसनपरितुलनासम्मोहतथागतचैत्यकीटलूतालयाञ्जलिनिर्मार्जनागाढसर्करासमुद्धरणसम्प्रयोगत्वात् सप्तच्छद इत्युच्यते। दीर्घरात्रं मातृपितृज्येष्ठश्रेष्ठपूज्यश्रमणब्राह्मणकृपणवनीयकादिभ्य उपागतेभ्यः सत्कृत्य यथाभिप्रायमन्नपानासनवस्त्रोपाश्रयप्रदीपकल्पितजीवितपरिष्कारसम्प्रदानकूपपुष्करिणीशीतलजलपरिपूर्णमहाजनोपभोगानुप्रदानत्वात् सिंहपूर्व्वार्द्धकाय इत्युच्यते। दीर्घरात्रं मातृपितृश्रमणब्राह्मणगुरुदक्षिणीयावनमनप्रणमनाभिवादनाभयप्रदानदुर्बलापरिभवशरणागतापरित्यागदृढसमादानानुत्सृष्टत्वाद् चित्तान्तरांस इत्युच्यते। दीर्घरात्रं स्वदोषपरितुलनपरिस्खलितपरच्छिद्रदोषदर्शनविवादमूलपरभेदकरमन्त्रपरिवर्जनसुप्रतिनि:सर्गमन्त्रसारक्षितवाक्कर्म्मान्तत्वात् सुसंवृत्तस्कन्ध इत्युच्यते। दीर्घरात्रं मातृपितृश्रमणब्राह्मणगुरुदक्षिणीयानां प्रत्युत्थानप्रत्युद्गमनाभिवादनकामंनाश्च सर्व्वशास्त्रवैशारद्येन विवादकामसत्त्वनिग्रहस्वधर्म्मविनयानुलोमनसंहृष्टराजामात्यसम्यक्संहृष्टकुशलधर्म्मपथप्रतिष्ठापनप्रभावनतथागतशासनपरिग्रहसन्धारणसर्व्वकुशलचर्यासमादापनपूर्व्वङ्गमत्वात् सिंहहनुरित्युच्यते। दीर्घरात्रं सर्व्ववस्तुपरित्यागयथाभिप्राययाचनकक्रियाभिधानमुपसङ्क्रान्तानां याचमानानामजिह्मीकरणाविक्षेपं सर्व्वेषां यथाभिप्रायपरिपूरणदानपरित्यागदृढसमादानानुत्सृष्टत्वाच्चत्वारिंशत्समदन्त इत्युच्यते। दीर्घरात्रं पिशुनवचनपरिवर्जनभेदसन्धानग्रहणसन्धिसामग्रीगुणवर्णप्रकाशनप्रयोगत्वात्

शुक्लदन्त इत्युच्यते । दीर्घरात्रं कृष्णपक्षपरिवर्जनशुक्लपक्षकुशलोपचयकृष्णकर्मकृष्णविपाकपरिवर्जनशुक्लकर्मशुक्लविपाकसंवर्णनक्षीरभोजनशुक्लवस्त्रप्रदानतथागतचैत्येषु सुधाक्तक(१) क्षीरमिश्रसम्प्रदानसुमनावार्षिकीधातुष्कारिमाला (२) गुणपुष्पदामशुक्लवर्णकुसुमानुप्रदानत्वादविरलदन्त इत्युच्यते। दीर्घरात्रं शाठ्यविवर्जनानन्दकरणावागनुरक्षणानन्दकरणवागुदीरणपरिस्खलितापरच्छिद्रानुपरिमार्गणसर्व्वसत्त्वसमचित्तसमादापनसमप्रयोगसर्व्वधर्म्मदेशनदृढसमादानपरित्यागत्वाद्सागरवागित्युच्यते । दीर्घरात्रं सर्व्वसत्त्वाविहेठनाविहिंसनविविधव्याधिस्पृष्टोपस्थानग्लानभैषज्यानुप्रदानत्वात् सर्व्वरसार्थिकेभ्यश्च सर्व्वरसप्रदानापरिखेदत्वाद् रसरसाग्र इत्युच्यते । दीर्घरात्रममृतापहतकर्कशपराद्यपरकटुकपराभिष्वङ्गित्वप्रियपरमर्मघट्टनवाक्परिवर्जनमैत्रीकरुणाप्रयोगमुदिताप्रामोद्यकरणस्निग्धमधुरश्लक्ष्णहृदयङ्गमसर्व्वसत्त्वेन्द्रियप्रह्लादकरणमध्यवाक्यसम्प्रयोगत्वादभिनीलनेत्र इत्युच्यते । दीर्घरात्रं मातृपितृवत्सर्व्वसत्त्वाप्रतिहतचक्षुःप्रयोगैकपुत्रवधावनकमैत्रीकारुण्यपूर्व्वङ्गमसम्प्रेक्षणाजिह्मीकरणप्रसन्नेन्द्रियतथागतचैत्यानिमिषसम्प्रेक्षणपरसत्त्वतथागतदर्शनसमादापनदृढसमादानत्वाद् गोपक्ष्मनेत्र इत्युच्यते । दीर्घरात्रं(३)हीनचेतनावर्जनोदारविपुलाधिमुक्तिपरिपूरणानुत्तरधर्म्मच्छन्दसत्त्वसमादापनभ्रकुटीमुखपरिवर्जनस्मृतिमुखसर्व्वक-

---

१ "तथागतचैत्येषु सुधाक्तक" तथागतचैत्यसुधाक्त ।

२ "धातुष्कारिमाला" धातुपुष्पिकामाला ।

३ "हीनचेतना" हीनमति हीनचेतनमित्यपि पाठः ।

ल्याणमित्रोपसङ्क्रमणाभिमुखपूर्व्वङ्गमसर्व्वकुशलोपचयावैवर्त्तिक-
त्वात् प्रभूतजिह्व इत्युच्यते । दीर्घरात्रं सर्व्ववाग्दोषविवर्जनसर्व्व-
श्रावकप्रत्येकबुद्धधर्म्मभाणकाप्रमाणगुणवर्णसम्प्रकाशनतथागतस-
मान्तशिक्षणवाचनपठनविज्ञापनं तेषाञ्च धर्म्माणामर्थ(१)पदप्र-
भेदपरसत्त्वसम्प्रापणकौशल्यादुष्णीषशीर्षानवलोकितमूर्द्ध इत्यु-
च्यते । दीर्घरात्रं मातृपितृश्रमणब्राह्मणगुरुदक्षिणीयमूर्द्धच-
रणतलप्रणिपतितप्रव्रजितवन्दनाभिवादनकेशावरोपणसुगन्धतै-
लमूर्द्धपरिषिञ्चनं (२) सर्व्वयाचनकेभ्यश्चूर्णमाल्यगुणमूर्द्धाभरणा-
नुप्रदानत्वाद् भ्रूमध्यसुजातप्रदक्षिणावर्त्ताक्तप्रविशुद्धवर्णाभा-
सोर्ण इत्युच्यते। दीर्घरात्रं निरर्गलसर्व्वयज्ञयजनसमादापनस-
र्व्वकल्याणमित्रानुशासनानुद्धरधर्म्मभाणकानां दौत्यप्रेषणदिव्य
श्रवणागमनोपरिखेदनसर्व्वबुद्धबोधिसत्त्वप्रत्येकबुद्धार्य्यश्रावकधर्म्म-
भाणकमातृपितृगुरुदक्षिणीयतमोन्धकारविधमनतैलघृतदो-
ल्काप्रदीपननानागन्धतैलप्रदीपसर्व्वाकारवरोपेतप्रासादिकत-
थागतप्रतिमाकारणशरीरप्रतिभास्वरत्नोत्तीर्णकोशप्रतिमश्चपर-
सत्त्वबोधिचित्तामुखीकरणकुशलसम्भारविपचित्वात् महाव्याम-
प्रभ इत्युच्यते । महानारायणबलोपेतत्वान्महानारायण इत्यु-
च्यते। कोटिशतमारधर्षणबलोपेतत्वात् सर्व्वपरप्रमर्द्दक इत्युच्यते।
दशतथागतबलोपेतत्वाद्दशतथागतबलोपेत इत्युच्यते । सामा-
ध्यानध्यानकुशलहीनप्रदेशिकज्ञानविवर्जनमहायानमुखसमुदा-

---

१ "विज्ञापनं तेषाञ्च धर्म्माणामर्थं" विज्ञापनतद्धर्म्मार्थं।
२ "परिषिञ्चनं सर्व्वयाचनकेभ्यश्चूर्णं" परिषिञ्चनसर्व्वयाचकचूर्णं।

नयनबलोपेतचिवस्तप्रयोगत्वात् स्थानास्थानज्ञानबलोपेत इत्यु-च्यते। अतीतानागतप्रत्युत्पन्नसर्वकर्म्मसमादानहेतुविपाकज्ञानब-लोपेतत्वादतीतानागतप्रत्युत्पन्नसर्व्वकर्म्मसमादानहेतुविपाकज्ञा-नबलोपेत इत्युच्यते। सर्व्वसत्त्वेन्द्रियवीर्य्यविमात्रताज्ञानबलोपेतत्वात् सर्व्वसत्त्वेन्द्रियवीर्य्यविमात्रताज्ञानबलोपेत इत्युच्यते । अनेकलोक-धातुनानालोकधातुप्रवेशज्ञानबलोपेतत्वादनेकधातुनानालो-कधातुप्रवेशज्ञानबलोपेत इत्युच्यते। अनेकाधिमुक्तिनानाधिमुक्ति-सर्व्वनिरवशेषाधिमुक्तिविमुक्तिज्ञानबलोपेतत्वादनेकाधिमुक्तिना-नाधिमुक्तिसर्व्वनिरवशेषाधिमुक्तिज्ञानबलोपेत इत्युच्यते। सर्व्वत्र-गामिनीप्रतिपज्ज्ञानबलोपेतत्वात् सर्व्वत्रगामिनीप्रतिपज्ज्ञानब-लोपेत इत्युच्यते । सर्व्वध्यानविमोक्षसमाधिसमापत्तिसङ्क्लेशव्य-वदानव्यवस्थापनज्ञानबलोपेतत्वात् सर्व्वध्यानविमोक्षसमाधिस-मापत्तिसङ्क्लेशव्यवदानव्यवस्थापनज्ञानबलोपेत इत्युच्यते। अने-कविधपूर्व्वनिवासानुस्मृत्यसङ्गज्ञानबलोपेतत्वात् अनेकविधपूर्व्व-निवासानुस्मृत्यसङ्गज्ञानबलोपेत इत्युच्यते । निरवशेषसर्व्वरूपा-वरणदर्शनदिव्यचक्षुर्ज्ञानबलोपेतत्वान्निरवशेषसर्व्वरूपावरणद-र्शनदिव्यचक्षुर्ज्ञानबलोपेत इत्युच्यते। सर्व्ववासनानुसन्धिगतनिर-वशेषसर्व्वास्रवक्षयज्ञानबलोपेतत्वात् सर्व्ववासनानुसन्धिगतनिर-वशेषसर्व्वास्रवक्षयज्ञानबलोपेत इत्युच्यते । निरवशेषसर्व्वधर्म्माभि-सम्बुद्धप्रतिज्ञारोहणसदेवलोकानभिभूतप्रतिज्ञावैशारद्यप्राप्तत्वा-न्निरवशेषसर्व्वधर्म्माभिसम्बुद्धप्रतिज्ञारोहणसदेवलोकानभिभूत-प्रतिज्ञावैशारद्यप्राप्त इत्युच्यते। सर्व्वासाङ्क्लेशिकान्तरायिकध-

र्म्मान्तरायकरणनिर्व्वाणस्येति तत्प्रतिज्ञारोहणसदेवके लोकेऽना-
च्छेद्यप्रतिज्ञावैशारद्यप्राप्तत्वात् सर्व्वाशाङ्क्षोभिकान्तरायिकध-
र्म्मान्तरायकरणनिर्वाणस्येति तत्प्रतिज्ञारोहणसदेवके लोके-
ऽनाच्छेद्यप्रतिज्ञावैशारद्यप्राप्त इत्युच्यते। नैर्याणिकीप्रतिपदं प्र-
तिपद्यमानो निर्वाणमारागयिष्यतीति प्रतिज्ञारोहणसदेवके
लोकेऽप्रतिपाद्यप्रतिज्ञावैशारद्यप्राप्तत्वान्नैर्याणिकीं प्रतिपदं प्रति-
पद्यमानो निर्वाणमारागयिष्यतीति प्रतिज्ञारोहणसदेवके लोकेऽ-
प्रतिपाद्यप्रतिज्ञावैशारद्यप्राप्त इत्युच्यते। सर्व्वाश्रवक्षयक्षयज्ञानप्र-
त्याख्यानप्रतिज्ञारोहणसदेवके लोकेऽवैवर्त्त्यप्रतिज्ञावैशारद्यप्रा-
प्तत्वात् सर्व्वाश्रवक्षयक्षयज्ञान(१)प्रत्याख्यानप्रतिज्ञारोहणसदेवके
लोकेऽवैवर्त्त्यप्रतिज्ञावैशारद्यप्राप्त इत्युच्यते। अस्खलितपदधर्म्मदेश-
कत्वादस्खलितपदधर्म्मदेशक इत्युच्यते। यथतागभिलाप्यधर्म्मस्व-
भावानुबुद्धत्वाद्यथतागभिलाप्यधर्म्मस्वभावानुबुद्ध इत्युच्यते। अवि-
रतत्वादविरत इत्युच्यते। सर्व्वसत्त्वरुतप्रमाणबुद्धधर्म्मरुतनिर्घो-
षाधिष्ठानसमर्थत्वात् सर्व्वसत्त्वरुतप्रमाणबुद्धधर्म्मरुतनिर्घोषाधि-
ष्ठानसमर्थ इत्युच्यते। अमुषितस्मृतित्वादमुषितस्मृतिरित्युच्यते।
नानात्वसंज्ञाविगतत्वान्नानात्वसंज्ञाविगत इत्युच्यते। सर्व्वसत्त्व-
चित्तसमाहितसुसमाहितत्वात् सर्व्वसत्त्वचित्तसमाहितसुसमा-
हित इत्युच्यते। अप्रतिसंख्यासमुपेक्षकत्वादप्रतिसंख्यासमुपेक्षक
इत्युच्यते। छन्दसंस्कारसमाध्यपरिहीनत्वाच्छन्दसंस्कारसमाध्य-
परिहीन इत्युच्यते। वीर्य्यसंस्कारसमाध्यनाच्छेद्यापरिहीनवीर्य्य-

१ "क्षयक्षयज्ञान" क्षयज्ञानेति उभयत्र वा पाठः।

त्वाद्वीर्य्यसंस्कारसमाप्यपरिहीनवीर्य्य इत्युच्यते । स्मृत्यपरिहीनत्वादपरिहीनस्मृतिरित्युच्यते । अपरिहीनप्रज्ञत्वादपरिहीनप्रज्ञ इत्युच्यते । विमुक्त्यपरिहीनत्वादपरिहीनविमुक्तिरित्युच्यते । विमुक्तिज्ञानादर्शनप्रहीणत्वादपरिहीनविमुक्तिज्ञानदर्शन इत्युच्यते । सर्व्वकायकर्म्मवाक्कर्म्ममनस्कर्म्मज्ञानपूर्व्वङ्गमज्ञानानुपरिवर्त्तिसमन्वागतत्वात् सर्व्वकायवाङ्मनस्कर्म्मज्ञानपूर्व्वङ्गमज्ञानानुपरिवर्त्तिज्ञानसमन्वागत इत्युच्यते । अतीतानागतप्रत्युत्पन्नेषु अध्वासङ्गाप्रतिहतज्ञानदर्शनसमन्वागतत्वात् अध्वासङ्गाप्रतिहतज्ञानदर्शनसमन्वागत इत्युच्यते । अनावरणविमोक्षप्रतिलब्धत्वादनावरणविमोक्षप्राप्त इत्युच्यते । अधिष्ठितसर्व्वसत्त्वचरित्र (१) प्रवेशकौशल्यावस्थितत्वादधिष्ठितसर्व्वसत्त्वचरित्रप्रवेशकौशल्यावस्थित इत्युच्यते । यथा प्रत्यर्हं धर्म्मदेशनाकुशलत्वाद्यथा प्रत्यर्हं धर्म्मदेशनाकुशल इत्युच्यते । सर्व्वस्वराङ्गमण्डलपरमपारमिताप्राप्तत्वात् सर्व्वस्वराङ्गमण्डलपरमपारमिताप्राप्त इत्युच्यते । सर्व्वरुतप्रतिरुतनिश्चारणकौशल्यप्राप्तत्वाद्देवनागयक्षगन्धर्व्वासुरगरुडकिन्नरमहोरगरुत इत्युच्यते । ब्रह्मस्वररुतरवितनिर्घोष इत्युच्यते । कलविङ्करुतस्वर इत्युच्यते । दुन्दुभिसङ्गीतरुतस्वर इत्युच्यते । धरणीतलनिर्नादनिर्घोषस्वर इत्युच्यते । सागरनागेन्द्रमेघस्तनितगर्जितघोषस्वर इत्युच्यते । सिंहवृषभितनिर्गर्जितनिर्घोषस्वर इत्युच्यते । सर्व्वसत्त्वरुतरवितानुचरणसन्तोषणस्वर इत्युच्यते । असङ्गानावरणसर्व्वपर्षन्मण्डलाभिरोधन-

१ क्वचिदपि ग्रन्थे चरित्र शब्दो नास्ति ।

स्वर इत्युच्यते। एकरुतात्सर्व्वरुतसम्प्रापणस्वर इत्युच्यते। ब्रह्मेन्द्रपूजित इत्युच्यते। देवेन्द्रसंस्कृत इत्युच्यते। नागेन्द्रनमस्कृत इत्युच्यते। यक्षेन्द्रावलोकितमुखमण्डल इत्युच्यते। गन्धर्व्वेन्द्रोपगीत इत्युच्यते। राक्षसेन्द्रप्रसन्नेन्द्रियानिमिषनयनसम्प्रेक्षित इत्युच्यते। असुरेन्द्राभिप्रणत इत्युच्यते। गरुडेन्द्राविहिंसाप्रेक्षित इत्युच्यते। किन्नरेन्द्राभिष्टुत इत्युच्यते। महोरगेन्द्राभिलषितदर्शन इत्युच्यते। मनुजेन्द्राभिसम्पूजित इत्युच्यते। अर्हन्गणसमासेवित इत्युच्यते। सर्व्वबोधिसत्त्वसमादायकसमुत्तेजकसम्प्रहर्षक इत्युच्यते। निरामिषधर्म्मदेशक इत्युच्यते। अक्षुणपदव्यञ्जनावन्ध्यधर्म्मदेशक इत्युच्यते। कालानतिक्रमणधर्म्मदेशक इत्युच्यते। इति।

इदमेतेषु धर्म्मचक्रप्रवर्त्तनं तथागतगुणवर्णप्रदेशस्य यत्किञ्चिदवतारमात्रं सङ्क्षेपनिर्द्देशतो विस्तरेण पुनरेतेषु तथागतः कल्पं वा कल्पावशेषं वा निर्द्दिशेत्। न चास्य निर्द्दिश्यमानस्य पर्य्यन्तो भवेत्।

अथ खलु भगवांस्तस्यां वेलायामिमा गाथा अभाषत।

गम्भीरं दुर्दृशं सूक्ष्मं धर्म्मचक्रं प्रवर्त्तितम्।
यत्र मार्गे न गाहन्ते (१) सर्व्वे च परतीर्थिकाः॥
अनालयं निष्प्रपञ्चमनुत्पादमसम्भवम्।
विविक्तं प्रकृतिशून्यं धर्म्मचक्रं प्रवर्त्तितम्॥
अनायूहमनिर्य्यूहमनिमित्तमलक्षणम्।

---

१ "यत्र मार्गे न गाहन्ते" यत्र मारा न गाहन्ते इति वा पाठः।

समताधर्म्मनिर्द्देशं चक्रं बुद्धेन वर्णितम् ॥

मायामरीचि स्वप्नोदक चन्द्रप्रतिश्रुत्काः ।

यथैते तथ चक्रं लोकनाथेन वर्त्तितम् (१) ॥

प्रतीत्यधर्म्मश्रोतारमनुच्छेदमशाश्वतम् (२) ।

सर्व्वदृष्टिसमुच्छेदो धर्म्मचक्रमिति स्मृतम् ॥

आकाशेन सदा तुल्यं निर्विकल्पं प्रभास्वरम् ।

अनन्तमध्यनिर्द्देशं धर्म्मचक्रमिहोच्यते ॥

अस्तिनास्तिविनिर्मुक्तमात्मनैरात्म्यवर्जितम् ।

प्रकृत्या जातनिर्द्देशं धर्म्मचक्रमिहोच्यते ॥

भूतकोटिमकोटी च तथतायां तथत्वतः (३) ॥

अद्वयो धर्म्मनिर्द्देशो धर्म्मचक्रं निरुच्यते ॥

चक्षुः स्वभावः शून्यं च श्रोत्रं घ्राणं तथैव च ।

जिह्वा कायश्च चित्तश्च शून्यात्मा नो निरीहकः ॥

इदं तदीदृशं चक्रं धर्म्मचक्रं प्रवर्त्तितम् ।

बोधयत्यबुद्धसत्त्वांस्तेन बुद्धो निरुच्यते ॥

स्वयं मयानुबुद्धोऽयं स्वभावो धर्म्मलक्षणम् ।

ऋते परोपदेशेन स्वयम्भूस्तेन चक्षुमान् ॥

सर्व्वधर्म्मवशिप्राप्तो धर्म्मस्वामी निरुच्यते ।

नयानयज्ञो धर्म्मेषु नायकस्तेन चोच्यते ॥

---

१ "मायामरीचि स्वप्नोदक चन्द्रप्रतिश्रुत्काः" मयामरीचिः स्वप्नोदकं चन्द्रप्रतिबिम्बा इत्यर्थः । "तथ" तथा ।

२ "प्रतीत्यधर्मश्रोतारम्" प्रतीत्यधर्मावतारम् ।

३ "भूतकोटिमकोटी च" भूतकोट्या अकोट्यामित्यर्थः ।

यथा भवन्ति वैनेया विनयन्त्यमितां जनां।
विनेयपारमिप्राप्तस्तेन प्रोक्तो विनायकः (१)॥
नष्टमार्गा हि ये सत्त्वा मार्गं देशेमि उत्तमम्।
नयामि पारिमं तीरं तस्मादस्मि विनायकः (२)॥
सङ्ग्रहावस्तुज्ञानेन संगृह्य जनतामहम्।
संसाराटविनिस्तीर्णः सार्थवाहस्ततो ह्यहम् (३)॥
वशवर्त्ती सर्व्वधर्म्मेषु तेन धर्म्मेश्वरो जिनः।
धर्म्मचक्रं प्रवर्त्तित्वा धर्म्मराजो निरुच्यते (४)॥
धर्म्मदानपतिः शास्ता धर्म्मस्वामी निरुच्यते।
सुयष्टयज्ञः सिद्धार्थः पूर्णोऽसि सर्व्वमङ्गलः (५)॥
आश्वासकः क्षेमदर्शी शूरो महारणञ्जहः।
उत्तीर्णभवसङ्ग्रामो मुक्तो मोचयिता प्रजाः॥
आलोकभूतो लोकस्य प्रज्ञाज्ञानप्रभङ्करः।
अज्ञानतमसोहन्ता (६) उल्काधारी महाप्रभुः॥
महावैद्यो महाज्ञानी सर्व्वक्लेशचिकित्सकः।
सत्त्वानां क्लेशविद्धानां शल्यहर्त्ता निरुत्तरः॥

---

१ "वैनेया" विनययुक्ता इत्यर्थः। "विनयन्त्यमितां जनां" विनयन्त्यमिताञ्जनानित्यर्थः। "विनेयपारमिप्राप्तः" विनेयपारमिताम्प्राप्तः।

२ "पारिमं तीरं" पारमितातीरे परतीरे वा। "देशेमि" उपदिशामि।

३ "सङ्ग्रहावस्तुज्ञानेन" सङ्ग्रहवस्तुज्ञानेन। "संसाराटविनिस्तीर्णः" संसाराटवीनिस्तीर्णः।

४ "प्रवर्त्तित्वा" प्रवर्त्तयित्वा "निरुच्यते" निरुत्तरो वा पाठः।

५ "सर्वमङ्गलः" सिद्धमङ्गल इति वाम पाठः।

६ "अज्ञानतमसोहन्ता" अज्ञानतमसोहन्तेत्यचितम्।

सर्व्वलक्षणसम्पन्नः सर्व्वव्यञ्जनशोभितः।
समन्तभद्रकायेन हीनानां चानुवर्त्तकः॥
दशभिर्बलैः सुबलवान् वैशारद्यविशारदः।
आवेणिकैरष्टादशैरग्रयानी महामुनिः॥
एष सङ्क्षेपनिर्द्देशो धर्म्मचक्रं प्रवर्त्तते।
तथागतस्य गुणवर्णः परीत्तोयं (१) प्रकाशितः॥
बुद्धं ज्ञानमनन्तं हि आकाशविपुलं समम्।
क्षपयेत्कल्प भाषन्तो (२) न च बुद्धगुणक्षय इति॥

इति श्रीललितविस्तरे धर्म्मचक्रप्रवर्त्तनपरिवर्त्तो नाम षड्विंशतितमः॥ २६॥

सप्तविंशाध्यायप्रारम्भः ॥

अथ खलु देवपुत्रा येस्तथागतोऽधिष्ठितोऽभूदस्य धर्म्मपर्य्यायस्य सम्प्रकाशनतायै सह महेश्वरनन्दनसुनन्दनचन्दनमहितप्रशान्तविनीतेश्वरप्रमुखा अष्टादशशुद्धावासकायिका देवपुत्रशतसहस्राणि ये तथागतस्य धर्म्मचक्रप्रवर्त्तनेऽपि सन्निपतिता अभूवन्। तत्र भगवांस्तान्महेश्वरदेवपुत्रप्रमुखाञ्छुद्धावासकायिकान्देवपुत्रानामन्त्रयते स्म। अयं मार्षा ललितविस्तरो नाम धर्म्मपर्य्यायः सूत्रान्तो महावैपुल्यबोधिसत्त्वविक्रीडितः। बुद्धविषये ललितप्रवेश आत्मोपनायिकस्तथागतेन भाषितस्तं यू-

---

१ "परीत्तोयं" परित्तोयं।
२ "कल्प भाषन्तो" कल्पं भाषमाणः कश्चिदित्यर्थः।

यमुद्गृह्णीध्वं धारयत वाचयत चैवमियं धर्म्मनेत्री वैस्तारिकी भविष्यति। बोधिसत्त्वयानिकाश्च पुद्गला इमं धर्म्मपर्य्यायं श्रुत्वा दृढतरं वीर्य्यमारप्स्यन्ते। अनुत्तरायां सम्यक्सम्बोधावुदारा-धिमुक्तिकाश्च सत्त्वा महाधर्म्महर्षवेगं सञ्जनयिष्यन्ति। मार-पक्षश्च निर्गृहीतो भविष्यति। सर्व्वपरप्रवादिनश्चावतारं न लप्स्यन्ते। युष्माकं च तद्धर्म्मदेशनाध्येषणा कुशलमूलं महा-र्थिकं भविष्यति महाफलं महानुशंसा। यःकश्चिन्मार्षा अस्य ललितविस्तरस्य धर्म्मपर्य्यायस्याञ्जलिं सम्प्रगृहीतं करिष्यति सोऽष्टावुत्कृष्टान्धर्म्मान् प्रतिलप्स्यते। कतमान्यष्टौ तद्यथा। उ-त्कृष्टरूपं प्रतिलप्स्यते। उत्कृष्टबलं प्रतिलप्स्यते। उत्कृष्टपरि-वारं प्रतिलप्स्यते। उत्कृष्टप्रतिभानं प्रतिलप्स्यते। उत्कृष्टनैष्क्रम्यं प्रतिलप्स्यते। उत्कृष्टचित्तपरिशुद्धिं प्रतिलप्स्यते। उत्कृष्टसमा-धिपदं प्रतिलप्स्यते। उत्कृष्टप्रज्ञावभासं प्रतिलप्स्यते। इमा-न्यष्टावुत्कृष्टान्धर्म्मान् प्रतिलप्स्यते। यः कश्चिन्मार्षा इमं ललि-तविस्तरं धर्म्मपर्य्यायं भाषितुकामस्य धर्म्मभाणकस्य धर्म्मासनं प्रज्ञापयिष्यति। तस्याष्टावासनप्रतिलम्भाः प्रतिकाङ्क्षितव्याः सहप्रज्ञप्त आसने। कतमा अष्टौ। तद्यथा। श्रेष्ठासनप्रतिलम्भः। गृहपत्यासनप्रतिलम्भः। चक्रवर्त्त्यासनप्रतिलम्भः। लोकपाला-सनप्रतिलम्भः। शक्रासनप्रतिलम्भः। वशवर्त्त्यासनप्रतिलम्भः। ब्रह्मासनप्रतिलम्भः। बोधिमण्डवराग्रगतस्य बोधिसत्त्वभूतस्य प्रत्युदावर्त्त्यनिहतमारप्रत्यर्थिकसिंहासनप्रतिलम्भः। अनुत्तरां सम्यक्सम्बोधिमभिसम्बुद्धस्य अप्रतोनुत्तरधर्म्मचक्रप्रवर्त्तनासनप्रति-

लम्भाश्च प्रकाङ्क्षितव्याः । इत्यष्टावायतनप्रतिलम्भाः प्रतिकाङ्क्षितव्याः ॥

यः कश्चिन्मार्षा इमं ललितविस्तरं धर्म्मपर्य्यायं भाषमाणाय साधुकारं दास्यति। सोऽष्टौ वाक्परिशुद्धीः प्रतिलप्स्यते ॥ कतमा अष्टौ ॥ तद्यथा। यथावादितथाकारितां सत्यानुपरिवर्त्तिवाक्परिकर्म्मपरिशुद्ध्या। आदेयवचनतां पर्षदभिभवनतया । ग्राह्यवचनतामनुद्धरणतया । श्लक्ष्णमधुरवचनतामपारुष्यसत्यसङ्ग्रहणतया । कलविङ्करुतस्वरतां कायचित्तौद्बिल्यकरणतया। मधुरवचनतां अपारुष्यसत्त्वसङ्ग्रहणतया । ब्रह्मस्वरतां सर्व्वस्वराभिभवनतया। सिंहघोषाभिगर्जितस्वरतां सर्व्वपरप्रवादिभिरनभिभवनतया । बुद्धस्वरतां सर्व्वसत्त्वेन्द्रियपरितोषणतया(१)। इमा अष्टौ वाक्कर्म्मपरिशुद्धीः प्रतिलप्स्यते॥

यः कश्चिन्मार्षा इमं ललितविस्तरं धर्म्मपर्य्यायं पुस्तकलिखितं कृत्वा धारयिष्यति सत्करिष्यति गुरु करिष्यति मानयिष्यति पूजयिष्यति अमात्सर्य्यचित्ततया चतुर्दिशमस्य धर्म्मपर्य्यायस्य वर्णना भविष्यति वर्णञ्चोच्चारयिष्यति आगच्छतीमं धर्म्मपर्य्यायं लिखितं धारयति वाचयति चिन्तयति स्वाध्येति सोऽष्टौ महानिधानानि प्रतिलप्स्यते ॥ कतमान्यष्टौ महानिधानानि ॥ यदुत स्मृतिनिधानं सममतमोषणतया । मतिनिधानं बुद्धिप्रभेदनतया । गतिनिधानं सर्व्वसूत्रान्तार्थगत्यनुरागतया । धारणीनिधानं सर्व्वश्रुतधारणतया । प्रतिभाननिधानं प्रति-

१ अत्र परिगणितवाक्शुद्धौ एकाऽधिका।

लभते सर्व्वसत्त्वसुभाषितसम्भाषणतया। धर्म्मनिधानं प्रतिलभते सद्धर्म्मप्रतिलक्षणतया। बोधिचित्तनिधानं त्रिरत्नवंशानुपच्छेदतया। प्रतिपत्तिनिधानञ्चानुत्पत्तिकधर्म्मक्षान्तिप्रतिलम्भतया। इमान्यष्टौ निधानानि प्रतिलप्स्यते॥

यः कश्चिन्मार्षा इमं ललितविस्तरं धर्म्मपर्य्यायं सुप्रवर्त्तितं कृत्वा धारयिष्यति। सोऽष्टौ सम्भारान् परिपूरयिष्यति॥ कतमानष्टौ॥ यदुत दानसम्भारं परिपूरयिष्यति अमात्सर्य्यचित्ततायै। शीलसम्भारं परिपूरयिष्यति सर्व्वकल्याणाभिप्रायपरिपूरणतायै। श्रुतसम्भारं परिपूरयिष्यति असङ्गप्रज्ञासमुदानतायै। शमथसम्भारं परिपूरयिष्यति सर्व्वसमाधिसमापत्त्यामुखीकरणतायै। विदर्शनासम्भारं परिपूरयिष्यति त्रैविद्याविद्याप्रतिपूर्त्त्यै। पुण्यसम्भारं परिपूरयिष्यति लक्षणानुव्यञ्जनबुद्धक्षेत्रालङ्कारपरिशुद्ध्यै। ज्ञानसम्भारं परिपूरयिष्यति सर्व्वसत्त्वयथाधिमुक्तिसन्तोषणतायै। महाकरुणासम्भारं परिपूरयिष्यति सर्व्वसत्त्वपरिपाचनतायै। इमानष्टौ सम्भारान् परिपूरयिष्यति॥

यः कश्चिन्मार्षा इमं ललितविस्तरं धर्म्मपर्य्यायमपरेभ्यो विस्तरेण सम्प्रकाशयिष्यति एवञ्चित्तो यदुत कथममी सत्त्वा एषामेवंरूपाणां धर्म्माणां लाभिनो भवेयुरिति। स तेन कुशलमूलेनाष्टौ महापुण्यताः प्रतिलप्स्यते॥ कतमा अष्टौ॥ तद्यथा। राजा भवति चक्रवर्त्ती इयं प्रथमा महापुण्यता। चतुर्महाराजकायिकानां देवानामाधिपत्यं कारयिष्यतीयं द्वितीया

महापुण्यता। शक्रो भविष्यति देवेन्द्र इयं तृतीया महापुण्यता। सुयामो भविष्यति देवपुत्र इयं चतुर्थी महापुण्यता। सन्तुषितो भविष्यतीयं पञ्चमी महापुण्यता। सुनिर्मितो भविष्यतीयं षष्ठी महापुण्यता। वशवर्त्ती भविष्यति देवराज इयं सप्तमी महापुण्यता। ब्रह्मा च भविष्यति महाब्रह्मा इयं अष्टमी महापुण्यता। अन्तेच तथागतो भविष्यति। अर्हन् सम्यक्सम्बुद्धः सर्व्वाकुशलधर्म्मप्रहीणः सर्व्वकुशलधर्म्मसमन्वागतः। इमा अष्टौ महापुण्यताः प्रतिलप्स्यते॥

यः कश्चिन्मार्षा ललितविस्तरं धर्म्मपर्य्यायं भाष्यमाणमवहितः श्रोता श्रोष्यति। सोऽष्टौ चित्तनिर्म्मलतां प्रतिलप्स्यते। कतमा अष्टौ॥ यदुत मैत्रीं प्रतिलप्स्यते सर्व्वदोषनिर्घाताय। करुणां प्रतिलप्स्यते सर्व्वविहिंसोत्सर्गाय। मुदितां प्रतिलप्स्यते सर्व्वाकाराऽरत्यपकर्षणताये। उपेक्षाम्प्रतिलप्स्यते अनुनयप्रतिघोत्सर्गाय। चत्वारि ध्यानानि प्रतिलप्स्यते सर्व्वरूपधातुवशवर्त्तिताये। चतस्र आरूप्यसमापत्तीः प्रतिलप्स्यते चित्तवशवर्त्तिताये। पञ्चाभिज्ञाः प्रतिलप्स्यते अन्यबुद्धक्षेत्रगमनताये। सर्व्ववासनानुसन्धिसमुद्घाटं प्रतिलप्स्यते शूरङ्गमसमाधिप्रतिलम्भाय। इमा अष्टौ चित्तनिर्म्मलताः प्रतिलप्स्यते॥

यस्मिंश्च मार्षा ग्रामे वा नगरे वा निगमे वा जनपदे वा जनपदप्रदेशे वा चङ्क्रमे वा विहारे वा ललितविस्तरो धर्म्मपर्य्यायः प्रचरिष्यति। तत्राष्टौ भयानि न भविष्यन्ति स्थापयित्वा पूर्व्वकर्म्मविपाकम्॥ कतमान्यष्टौ॥ यदुत राज्यसङ्क्षोभ-

भयं न भविष्यति। चौरसङ्क्षोभभयं न भविष्यति। व्याड-सङ्क्षोभभयं न भविष्यति। दुर्भिक्षकान्तारसङ्क्षोभभयं न भविष्यति। अन्योन्यकलहविवादविग्रहसङ्क्षोभभयं न भविष्यति। देवसङ्क्षोभभयं न भविष्यति। नागयक्षसङ्क्षोभभयं न भविष्यति। सर्व्वोपद्रवसङ्क्षोभभयं न भविष्यति। इमानि मार्षास्तत्राष्टौ भयानि न भविष्यन्ति स्थापयित्वा पूर्वकर्म्मविपाकम्॥

सङ्क्षेपान्मार्षा यदि तथागतकल्पस्थितिकेनायुःप्रमाणेन रात्रिन्दिवसमधितिष्ठमानोऽस्य धर्म्मपर्य्यायस्य वर्णं (१) भाषेत नैवास्य धर्म्मपर्य्यायस्य वर्णपर्य्यन्तो भवेत्। न च तथागतप्रतिभानस्य क्षयो भवेत्। अपि तु खलु पुनर्मार्षा यथैव तथागतस्य शील समाधिप्रज्ञाविमुक्तिज्ञानदर्शनमप्रमाणपर्य्यन्तमेवमेव। य इमं मार्षा धर्म्मपर्य्यायमुद्ग्रहीष्यति धारयिष्यति वाचयिष्यति लिखिष्यति लेखयिष्यति पर्य्यवाप्स्यति प्रवर्त्तयिष्यति पर्षन्मध्ये च विस्तरेण सम्प्रकाशयिष्यति अनेन चित्तेन कथममी सत्त्वा एवमुदारस्य धर्म्मस्य लाभिनः स्युरिति। तेषामपि नास्ति पुण्यपर्य्यन्तः॥

ततः खलु भगवानायुष्मन्तं महाकाश्यपमामन्त्रयते स्म आयुष्मन्तञ्चानन्दं मैत्रेयञ्च बोधिसत्त्वम्। महासत्त्वा इमामहं मार्षा असङ्ख्येयकल्पकोटिनियुतशतसहस्रसमुदानीतामनुत्तरां सम्यक्सम्बोधिं युष्माकं हस्ते परिदाम्यनुपरिदामि (२) परमया प-

१ "वर्णं" वर्णानामित्यर्थः। अत्र वर्णशब्दो वर्णनाशब्दार्थे व्यवहृतः सर्वत्र।

२ "परिदाम्यनुपरिदामि" परिददाम्यनुपरिददामि।

रिन्दया स्वयञ्चैवमिमं धर्म्मपर्य्यायं धारयत परेभ्यश्च विस्तरेण सम्प्रकाशयत ।

अथ खलु भगवानस्यैव धर्म्मपर्य्यायस्य भूयस्या मात्रयाऽनुपरिन्दनार्थं तस्यां वेलायामिमा गाथा अभाषत ।

सत्त्वा दृष्टा ये मया बुद्धदृष्ट्या
तुल्यास्ते सन्तु शारिपुत्रेण सुख्याः ।
तांश्च कश्चित् पूजयेत् कल्पकोट्या-
स्तुल्यां गङ्गावालिकाभिर्यथैव (१) ॥

प्रत्येकबुद्धाय तु यश्च पूजां
कुर्य्यादहोरात्रमपि प्रहृष्टः ।
माल्यैः प्रकारैश्च तथाऽपरैश्च
तस्मादयं पुण्यकृतो विशिष्यते ॥

सत्त्वा यदि प्रत्ययैर्जिनानां
तान् पूजयेत् कश्चिदिहाप्रमत्तः ।
पुष्पैश्च गन्धैश्च विलेपनैश्च
कल्याणलोकाः सततं हि तत्परे ॥

एकस्य यश्चैव तथागतस्य
कुर्यात् प्रणाममपि चैक (२) सोऽपि ।
प्रसन्नचित्तोऽथ वदेन्नमोऽर्हते
तस्मादिदं श्रेष्ठतरञ्च पुण्यम् ॥

---

१ "कल्पकोट्यास्तुल्यां गङ्गावालिकाभिः" कल्पकोटिपर्य्यन्तं (पूजकानां) गङ्गावालुकाभिस्तुल्यं पुण्यफलं भवेदित्यर्थः ।
२ "चैक" चैकं ।

बुद्धा भवेयुर्यदि सर्व्वसत्त्वा-
स्तां पूजयेद्यश्च यथैव पूर्व्वम्।
दिव्यैश्च पुष्पैरथ मानुषैर्वरैः
कल्याणलोकां सततं हि तत्परः (१) ॥
यश्चैव सद्धर्म्मविलोपकाले
त्यक्त्वा स्वकायञ्च तथैव जीवितम्।
दद्यादहोरात्रमिदं हि सूत्रं
विशिष्यते पुण्यमिदं हि तस्मात् ॥
यस्येप्सितं पूजयितुं विनायकां
प्रत्येकबुद्धांश्च तथैव श्रावकां (२)।
दृढं समुत्पाद्य स बोधिचित्तं
इदं सदा सूत्रवरं ददातु ॥
राजा स्वयं सर्व्वसुभाषितानां
योऽभ्युद्गतः सर्व्वतथागतानाम्।
गृहे स्थितस्तस्य तथागतः सदा
तिष्ठेदिदं यत्र हि सूत्ररत्नम् ॥
प्रतिभासमाप्नोति शुभामनन्ता-
मेकं पदं वक्ष्यति कल्पकोट्याः (३)।
न व्यञ्जनाद्भ्रश्यति नापि चार्था-

---

१ "तां पूजयेत्" तान् पूजयेत। "कल्याणलोकां सततं हि तत्परः" कल्याणलोकाम् सततं हि तत्परे चाश्नुतीत्यर्थः।
२ "विनायकां" विनायकाम्। "श्रावकां" श्रावकाम्।
३ "शुभामनन्तां" शुभमनन्तं। "कल्पकोट्याः" कल्पकोटिपर्यन्तं।

ददाति यः सूत्रमिदं परेभ्यः॥

अनुत्तरोऽसौ नरनायकानां

सत्त्वो न कश्चित् सदृशोऽस्य विद्यते॥

भवेत् समुद्रेण समश्च सोऽव्ययः

श्रुत्वा हि यो धर्ममिमं प्रपद्यत इति॥

इदमवोचद्भगवानात्तमनाः॥ ते महेश्वरदेवपुत्रपूर्वङ्गमाः शुद्धावासकायिका देवपुत्रा मैत्रेयपूर्वङ्गमाश्च सर्वबोधिसत्त्वा महासत्त्वा महाकाश्यपपूर्वङ्गमाश्च सर्वे महाश्रावकाः सदेवमानुषासुरगन्धर्वगरुडाश्च लोका भगवतो भाषितमभ्यनन्दन्निति (१)॥

इति श्रीललितविस्तरे निगमपरिवर्त्तो नाम सप्तविंशतितमः॥ २७॥

श्रीसर्वबोधिसत्त्वचर्याप्रस्थानो ललितविस्तरो नाम महायानसूत्रं रत्नराजमिति समाप्तम्॥

ये धर्मा हेतुप्रभवा हेतुस्तेषां तथागतः।

ह्यवदत्तेषाञ्च यो निरोध एवंवादी महाश्रमणः॥

समाप्तोऽयं ग्रन्थः॥

---

१ भाषितमभ्यनन्दन् इत्यतः परं वक्ष्यमाणपद्यद्वयमन्यतमपुस्तकानां मध्ये पुस्तकद्वये एव वर्त्तते।

सपर्षदा पूज्यति धर्मराजमतुल्यरूपस्य गौरवेण।

ध्वजापताकासमलङ्कृतेन सम्रक्षमारोपणम्प्रकरादयः॥

जग्मुर्देवाः सुमेरौ। त्रिभुवनमहितं शाक्यसिंहं प्रणम्य

गन्धर्वमण्डलाद्ये चपरसुरगणाः स्वालयं सम्प्रहृष्टाः।

नानारत्नैर्विचित्रैः प्रवरसुरचितं यानश्रेष्ठं प्रश्रेष्ठ-

मारुह्य सम्प्रगम्य सकलसुरजना दिव्यलोकं प्रययम्॥